connecting with law

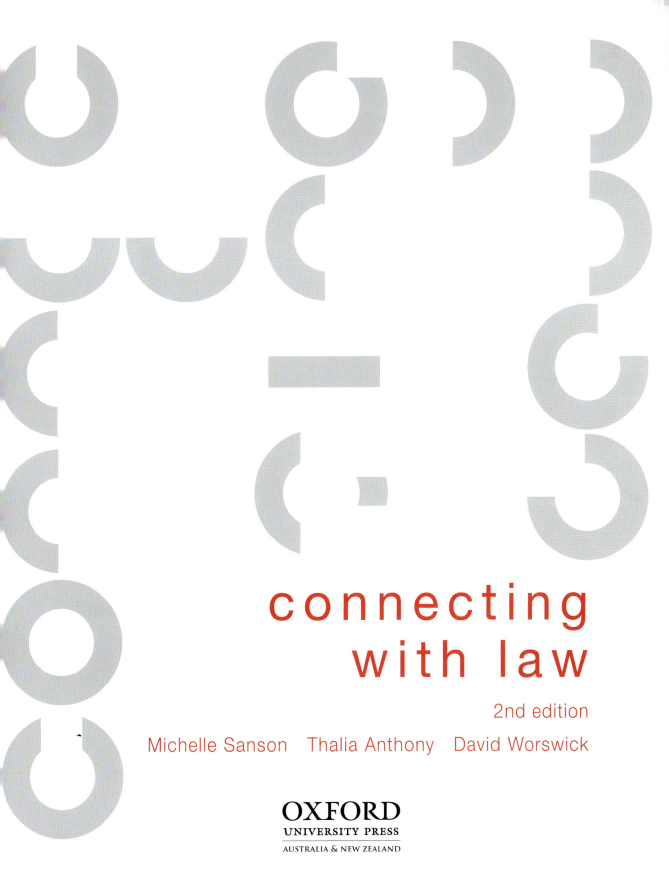

connecting with law

2nd edition

Michelle Sanson   Thalia Anthony   David Worswick

OXFORD
UNIVERSITY PRESS
AUSTRALIA & NEW ZEALAND

OXFORD
UNIVERSITY PRESS

Oxford University Press is a department of the University of Oxford.
It furthers the University's objective of excellence in research,
scholarship, and education by publishing worldwide. Oxford is a registered
trademark of Oxford University Press in the UK and in certain other
countries.

Published in Australia by
Oxford University Press
253 Normanby Road, South Melbourne, Victoria 3205, Australia

© Michelle Sanson, Thalia Anthony and David Worswick 2010

The moral rights of the authors have been asserted.

First edition published 2009
Second edition published 2010
Reprinted 2011 (twice)

All rights reserved. No part of this publication may be reproduced, stored in a retrieval system, or transmitted, in any form or by any means, without the prior permission in writing of Oxford University Press, or as expressly permitted by law, by licence, or under terms agreed with the reprographics rights organisation. Enquiries concerning reproduction outside the scope of the above should be sent to the Rights Department, Oxford University Press, at the address above.

You must not circulate this work in any other form and you must impose this same condition on any acquirer.

National Library of Australia Cataloguing-in-Publication data

Sanson, Michelle
Connecting with law / Michelle Sanson; Thalia Anthony; David Worswick
2nd edn
ISBN: 978 0 19 557240 7 (pbk)
Law—Australia
Justice, Administration of—Australia
Anthony, Thalia
Worswick, David

347.94

Reproduction and communication for educational purposes

The Australian *Copyright Act 1968* (the Act) allows a maximum of one chapter or 10% of the pages of this work, whichever is the greater, to be reproduced and/or communicated by any educational institution for its educational purposes provided that the educational institution (or the body that administers it) has given a remuneration notice to Copyright Agency Limited (CAL) under the Act.

For details of the CAL licence for educational institutions contact:

Copyright Agency Limited
Level 15, 233 Castlereagh Street
Sydney NSW 2000
Telephone: (02) 9394 7600
Facsimile: (02) 9394 7601
Email: info@copyright.com.au

Edited by Trischa Mann
Text design by Sardine
Typeset by Damage Design
Proofread by Puddingburn Publishing Services
Indexed by Puddingburn Publishing Services
Printed in China by Sheck Wah Tong Printing Press Ltd

Links to third party websites are provided by Oxford in good faith and for information only. Oxford disclaims any responsibility for the materials contained in any third party website referenced in this work.

brief contents

List of Figures	XVII
Table of Cases and Statutes	XIX
Preface	XXIV
Guided Tour	XXV
Acknowledgments	XXVII

1	Introduction: Overview of the Book	1
2	Learning Law: How Can I Develop a Legal Mind?	7
3	Sources: What Is the Law Itself?	41
4	Legal Institutions: How Is Law Made?	75
5	Classifying and Practising Law: How Are Cases Resolved?	111
6	Research: How Do I Find the Law?	137
7	Jurisprudence: What Is Law?	191
8	History: How Did Australian Law Develop?	228
9	Australia: Where Does Indigenous Law Fit In?	252
10	Precedent: How Do Judicial Decisions Become Law?	281
11	Statutory Interpretation: How Do Courts Interpret Legislation?	305
12	The Profession: What Do Lawyers Do?	353
13	Law in Society: What Are the Problems and Remedies For Accessing Justice?	387
14	My Law Career: How Can I Best Prepare for It?	414
	Glossary	436
	Index	442

extended contents

List of Figures	XVII
Table of Cases and Statutes	XIX
Preface	XXIV
Guided Tour	XXV
Acknowledgments	XXVII

1 Introduction: Overview of the Book — 1

1: Topics of study by chapter — 2
- Learning law: How can I develop a legal mind? — 2
- Sources: What is the law itself? — 2
- Legal institutions: How is law made? — 3
- Classifying and practising law: How are cases resolved? — 3
- Research: How do I find the law? — 3
- Jurisprudence: What is law? — 3
- History: How did Australian law develop? — 4
- Australia: Where does Indigenous law fit in? — 4
- Precedent: How do judicial decisions become law? — 4
- Statutory interpretation: How do courts interpret legislation? — 5
- The profession: What do lawyers do? — 5
- Law in society: What are the problems and remedies for accessing justice? — 5
- My law career: How can I best prepare for it? — 6

2: Online Resource Centre — 6

2 Learning Law: How Can I Develop a Legal Mind? — 7

Recommended approach to learning this topic — 8

1: Law as a discipline — 9
- How law is different from other disciplines — 9

2: Legal reasoning — 10
- Thinking like a lawyer — 10
- Inductive and deductive reasoning — 11
  - *Exercise: Inductive and deductive reasoning*

3: Graduate attributes — 13
- Development of attributes at different levels — 13
- Substantive legal knowledge — 13
  - *Exercise: Priestley 11 requirements*

Communication skills	15
Critical thinking	16
Exercise: Critical Thinking	17
Information literacy	18
Exercise: Assessing sources	
Lifelong learning	20
Self-management	20
In depth: A sample semester and week	
Understanding your personality	24
Ethical mindset	25
Diversity and social justice	26

4: Success in law school — 27

Being productive	27
Assessment: Legal writing	29
Assessment: Exam techniques	34
In depth: Plagiarism and its consequences	

3 Sources: What Is the Law Itself? — 41

Recommended approach to learning this topic — 42

1: Primary and secondary sources of law — 43

Primary sources of law	43
Secondary sources of law	43
Exercise: Sources practice	

2: Legislation — 44

Legislation-making authority	44
Legislation as a preferred source of law	44
Functions of legislation	45
Creating new legislation	45
Commencement of legislation	45
Delegated legislation	51
Amending legislation	53
Repealing legislation	54

3: Cases — 55

Anatomy of a case	55
Writing a case note	59
Exercise: Case summary 1	
Exercise: Case summary 2	

4: Secondary sources — 67
- Law reform commission reports — 67
  - *In depth:* ALRC inquiry on secrecy
- Academic commentary — 69
- International law — 70
  - *In depth:* Australia challenged internationally for measures on salmon
- Using secondary sources — 72

4 Legal Institutions: How Is Law Made? — 75

Recommended approach to learning this topic — 76

1: Government in Australia — 77
- Representative government — 78
- Responsible government — 78
- Separation of powers — 78
- Doctrine of parliamentary sovereignty — 79
- The rule of law — 79
  - *In depth:* History of the rule of law, and its contemporary importance

2: Constitutions of the Commonwealth and the states — 81
- State constitutions — 82
- The Commonwealth Constitution — 83
- Relationship between federal and state governments — 86
- Amending constitutions — 87
- Bill of rights? — 87

3: Parliament's role in creating law — 87
- How legislation is created — 88
- Application of federal and state legislation — 89

4: The executive's role in administering law — 91
- What is the executive? — 91
- Law making by the executive — 91
- The role of Attorney-General — 92

5: The judicature's role in interpreting law — 92
- The court system — 93
- Jurisdiction — 93
- Court hierarchy — 95
- Cross-vesting — 101
- Appeals — 101
- Judicial review — 102
  - *In depth:* Ultra vires

6: Alternatives to courts	**103**
The role of tribunals	103
Commonwealth tribunals	103
State and territory tribunals	104
Alternative dispute resolution (ADR)	104
In depth: Negotiating style	

5 Classifying and Practising Law: How Are Cases Resolved? — 111

Recommended approach to learning this topic	**112**
1: Major legal classifications	**114**
Common law distinguished from civil law	114
Common law distinguished from statute law	114
Common law distinguished from equity	115
Substantive law distinguished from procedural law	117
2: Branches of substantive law	**117**
Public law	118
Private law	122
3: Aspects of procedural law	**129**
Civil procedure	129
In depth: Case management	
Criminal procedure	132
The role of the jury in criminal and civil trials	134

6 Research: How Do I Find the Law? — 137

Recommended approach to learning this topic	**138**
1: The importance of legal research	**139**
2: Legal research methodology	**140**
Step 1: What am I trying to find?	140
Step 2: Decide on your research strategy	140
Step 3: Do the research and sort out the results	141
Step 4: Finalise your research outcomes	141
Exercise: Research strategy scenario	
Exercise: Ranking sources	
3: Using a library catalogue or search engine	**149**
Library catalogue searching	149
Using search engines	150
Boolean searching	151
Exercise	

4: Finding legislation — 153

- Finding legislation when you have the citation — 154
- Finding legislation by subject area — 156
- Finding delegated legislation — 158
- Finding bills — 158
- Finding out whether legislation has commenced — 159
- Finding legislation in force at a certain date — 159
- Updating legislation — 160
- Alerting services — 161

5: Finding cases — 161

- Finding a case from the citation — 162
- Finding a case from its common name — 164
- Finding an unreported judgment — 166
- Finding cases that interpret a statute — 167
- Finding cases that apply a particular case — 169
  - *Exercise: Using CaseBase and Firstpoint*
- Finding cases on a particular subject area — 171
- Finding a case that considers a particular word or phrase — 172
  - *Exercise: Searching phrases in CaseBase*

6: Finding and using secondary sources — 173

- Finding and using law books and dictionaries — 173
- Finding and using journal articles — 174
- Using legal encyclopedias — 177
- Finding and using law reform commission reports — 180
- Finding and using parliamentary debates on a bill — 182
- Finding and using explanatory memoranda — 182

7: Legal referencing — 184

- Referencing basics — 185
- Citing legislation — 186
- Citing cases — 187
- Referencing books — 188
- Referencing journal articles — 188
- Referencing reports and other documents — 188
- Referencing websites — 189

7 Jurisprudence: What Is Law? — 191

Recommended approach to learning this topic — 192

1: Introduction: What is jurisprudence? — 193

- Overview of different theoretical approaches to defining law — 195

2: Traditional theories	**195**
The birth of Western legal theory in Greek antiquity	196
Slow progress in the Middle Ages: Variations of natural law theory	198
Thomas Aquinas's religious conception of natural law	199
Renewed intellectual activity in the Renaissance: Legal positivism	199
The new industrial economy and liberal positivism	203
3: Modernism, Marxism and socio-legal theory	**205**
Marxism applied to law	207
4: Legal realism	**210**
5: Critical legal theories	**211**
Feminist legal theory	212
Critical race theory	214
Postmodern legal theory: Chaos and beyond	215
6: Dominant jurisprudence today	**217**
In depth: Applying jurisprudence to real cases	
Exercise: Applying jurisprudence	

8 History: How Did Australian Law Develop?   228

Recommended approach to learning this topic	**229**
1: Legal systems of Indigenous societies and their early exclusion from the common law	**231**
2: Displacement of Indigenous laws	**234**
3: Reception of British law	**237**
4: Military origins of the Australian legal system	**238**
5: Key concepts from English legal and constitutional history	**238**
In depth: The history and significance of Magna Carta	
In depth: The evolution of courts of equity and common law courts	
6: How English legal and constitutional history applies in Australia	**242**
The reception of English feudal land law	243
7: Adoption of British common law – from the frontier to the Australia Acts	**245**
Process of replacing Indigenous law with British law	245
Statutory adoption of British law	247
Development of an Australian legal system and popularly elected parliament	247
8: Federation and British remnants today	**249**

9 Australia: Where Does Indigenous Law Fit In? — 252

Recommended approach to learning this topic — 253

1: Historical developments in official policies relating to Indigenous people: Exclusion and inclusion — 254
Government policy — 254
Constitutional recognition — 256
In depth: The Northern Territory intervention – a new phase of Indigenous policy

2: Recognition of Indigenous rights to land — 259
Overturning *terra nullius* — 260
Native title rights — 263

3: Developments since *Mabo* — 264
Legislative response — 264
Wik and further legislative response — 264
Challenges for native title claimants — 266

4: Other forms of recognition of Indigenous land — 268
Land rights legislation — 268
Negotiated outcomes for Indigenous land rights — 270

5: Ongoing non-recognition of customary law — 272
Court reluctance to recognise Indigenous criminal law — 272

6: Alternative paths for incorporating customary law into the common law — 274
Law reform commission proposals on customary law — 274
Attempts to take customary law into account in criminal cases — 275
In depth: Indigenous sentencing scenarios
Government initiatives in 'customary' sentencing processes — 277

7: Filling the legal gap – treaty and sovereignty rights — 278

10 Precedent: How Do Judicial Decisions Become Law? — 281

Recommended approach to learning this topic — 282

1: Introduction to precedent — 283
What does 'precedent' mean? — 283
Where did the concept come from? — 283
Advantages of precedent — 284
Disadvantages of precedent — 284

2: Key concepts in the law of precedent — 285
Ratio decidendi: The main point of the case — 285
Obiter dicta: Judicial comments in passing — 285
Exercise: Finding ratio and obiter

3: Applying precedent — 286

- Where and how is precedent used? — 286
- When are precedents binding? — 288
- What about previous decisions of the same court? — 289
- What about precedents from appeal courts? — 289
- How are precedents avoided or distinguished? — 290

4: Judicial approaches to precedent — 291

- *Exercise: Judging Sophie*
- To make law or not to make law? — 292
- Legal correctness — 292
- Legal formalism — 293
- Legal realism — 293
- Judicial activism — 295

5: Problem solving using precedent — 298

- How can I solve a legal problem using precedent? — 298
- *Exercise: Which precedent takes precedence?*
- *In depth: Court use of precedents*
- *Exercise: Application of precedents*

11 Statutory Interpretation: How Do Courts Interpret Legislation? — 305

Recommended approach to learning this topic — 306

1: Introduction to statutory interpretation — 307

- What is statutory interpretation? — 307
- Why is statutory interpretation an important skill? — 307
- Why is statutory interpretation difficult? — 308
- How do courts interpret statutes? — 309

2: Modern statutory approach — 311

- Interpretation Acts — 311
- The main rule: Giving effect to the purpose of the legislation — 312
- How do courts find the purpose of the Act? — 313
- Using intrinsic materials — 313
- Using extrinsic materials — 315
- *Exercise: 'Make Poverty History'*
- Generic provisions — 317

3: Traditional common law approaches — 319

- Literal approach — 319
- The golden rule — 320
- The mischief rule — 320
- How are the common law approaches relevant today? — 321
- How does the modern statutory approach relate to the traditional common law approaches? — 322

4: Other tools of statutory interpretation	**323**
Presumptions for the interpretation of legislation	323
In depth: Wurridjal v The Commonwealth of Australia	
In depth: Do statutory presumptions constitute a common law bill of rights?	
Latin maxims	332
Exercise: Applying ejusdem generis	
Exercise: Latin maxims	
In depth: Relevance of Latin maxims today	
Other rules of statutory interpretation	337
5: Applying the rules of statutory interpretation	**338**
Statutory interpretation: Problem-solving method	338
Exercise: Jimbo and Baba visit Parliament House	
Exercise: No standing	
Exercise: Double jeopardy	
Exercise: Danny and his motorbike	

12 The Profession: What Do Lawyers Do? — 353

Recommended approach to learning this topic	**354**
1: Overview of Australian legal practice	**355**
Legal practitioners defined	355
Background to the legal profession	356
In depth: National Legal Profession Model Bill	
Specialist or generalist	358
Front end (drafting) and back end (disputes)	359
Value-adding services provided by lawyers	360
Professional indemnity insurance	360
2: Solicitors	**361**
The solicitor's role	362
Requirements in order to practise as a solicitor	362
Solicitors' duties	363
Exercise: Confidentiality and disclosure	
Law societies	370
Regulation of solicitors	370
3: Barristers	**373**
The barrister's role and work	373
Barristers' duties	374
Senior Counsel (Queen's Counsel)	375
Barristers' liability	376
Bar associations	377
Regulation of barristers	378

4: Judges	**378**
Federal judges	379
State and territory judges	380
5: Ethics	**380**
Exercise: Ethical decision making	
6: What kinds of work do lawyers do?	**383**
Trends for the profession	384

13 Law in Society: What Are the Problems and Remedies For Accessing Justice? — 387

Recommended approach to learning this topic	**388**
1: Access to justice – key issues	**389**
The cost of justice	389
Delay	390
Equality	391
2: Access to justice for specific groups	**392**
Women	392
Aboriginal and Torres Strait Islander peoples	392
People from a non-English speaking background	394
Children and young people	396
Sexuality: Gay, lesbian, bisexual and transgender	396
Self-represented litigants	397
People with disabilities	399
People with a mental illness	400
People in rural and regional communities	401
3: The role of legal aid	**401**
Legal aid explained	401
Legal aid schemes across Australia	402
Eligibility	402
Legal aid access issues	406
4: Other initiatives to promote access to justice	**407**
Community legal centres	407
Pro bono legal work	410
Law reform commissions	410

14 My Law Career: How Can I Best Prepare for It? — 414

Recommended approach to learning this topic — 415

1: Is law really for me? How do I know? — 416
- Interests — 416
  - *Exercise: Identifying your top interests*
- Skills — 417
  - *Exercise: Identifying your top skills*
- Values — 421
  - *Exercise: Identifying your top values*
- Personality — 422
  - *Exercise: Am I suited to becoming a lawyer?*

2: What kind of career can I expect as a lawyer? — 423
- Private practice — 425
- Public-sector and NGO lawyering — 425
- Academia — 426
- The judiciary — 426
- Other options — 428

3: What can I do as a student to become the lawyer I want to be? — 428
- Attitude — 428
- Systems — 429
- Extracurricular activities — 429
- Work experience — 429
- Mentoring — 430
- Use university resources and build social networks — 430

4: Important choices of subjects and course structures — 431
- Practical Legal Training (PLT) — 432

5: Preparing to maintain a decent work–life balance — 432

Glossary — 436
Index — 442

list of figures

Figure 2.1: Priority management tree	22
Figure 4.1: The three arms of government	79
Figure 4.2: The federal court hierarchy	96
Figure 4.3: The state court hierarchy	96
Figure 5.1: Substantive and procedural law	117
Figure 6.1: The Laws of Australia user interface	142
Figure 6.2: The search refined using quote marks	143
Figure 6.3: Exploring the results	143
Figure 6.4: A useful lead	144
Figure 6.5: The AustLII user interface	145
Figure 6.6: Index page of an Act	145
Figure 6.7: Homing in on particular sections	146
Figure 6.8: The content of section 57	146
Figure 6.9: Checking notations for extra information	147
Figure 6.10: The Noteup feature	147
Figure 6.11: The initial Google search result	150
Figure 6.12: Commonwealth legislation page at AustLII	153
Figure 6.13: Search options on ComLaw	155
Figure 6.14: Legislation on Lawlex	157
Figure 6.15: AustLII's Point-in-Time facility	160
Figure 6.16: AustLII High Court case search options	163
Figure 6.17: Cardiff Index example	164
Figure 6.18: CaseBase example	165
Figure 6.19: CaseBase results screen	165
Figure 6.20: CaseBase results screen	166
Figure 6.21: LexisNexis unreported judgments	167
Figure 6.22: CaseBase legislation judicially considered	168
Figure 6.23: AustLII Noteup function for legislation	168
Figure 6.24: The Firstpoint case citator entry screen	169
Figure 6.25: The Firstpoint case citator results screen	170
Figure 6.26: The CaseBase case citator results screen	170
Figure 6.27: The Firstpoint words and phrases entry screen	173
Figure 6.28: The Informit search screen	175

Figure 6.29: The Legal Online journals index	176
Figure 6.30: Journals on AustLII	176
Figure 6.31: Subject headings in *Halsbury* online at LexisNexis	178
Figure 6.32: Search facility in *Halsbury* online at LexisNexis	178
Figure 6.33: Laws of Australia at Legal Online	179
Figure 6.34: Checking currency of Laws of Australia information	179
Figure 6.35: ALRC download options	181
Figure 7.1: Jeremy Bentham	202
Figure 7.2: Karl Marx	206
Figure 7.3: Emile Durkheim	209
Figure 7.4: Relationships between schools of thought within critical legal theory	212
Figure 7.5: Michel Foucault	216
Figure 11.1 Depiction of case and statute development	311
Figure 11.2: An approach to statutory interpretation problems	339
Figure 12.1: Sources of fee income, other legal services	383
Figure 12.2: Sources of fee income, barristers	383
Figure 14.1: Some options after a law degree	424

table of cases and statutes

Commonwealth

Aboriginal and Torres Strait Islander Heritage Protection Act 1984   269
Aboriginal Land Rights (Northern Territory) Act 1976   91–2, 260, 268–9
   s 19   268
   s 67B   269
   s 70(2A)   270
   s 70(2BB)   270
   s 78   91
Aboriginal Land Rights (Northern Territory) Regulations 2007   92
Aboriginals Ordinance 1918   254
Acts Interpretation Act 1901   311
   s 5   45, 317
   s 7   54
   s 8   54
   s 13(1)   314
   s 13(2)   314
   s 13(3)   51, 314
   s 15AA   312, 322
   s 15AB(1)   315
   s 15AB(1)(a)   316
   s 15AB(1)(b)   316
   s 15AB(2)   315
   s 15AB(3)   316
   s 22(1)(c)   127
   s 23(a)   317
   s 33(2A)   318
   s 35   318
   s 36   317–18
Administrative Appeals Tribunal Act 1975   54, 103
Administrative Decisions (Judicial Review) Act 1977   120
Admiralty Act 1988
   s 19   336
Affirmative Action (Equal Employment Opportunity for Women) Act 1986   392
Age Discrimination Act 2004   55
Aged Care Act 1997
   s 2.1   314

Aged or Disabled Persons Care Act 1954   314
Australia Act 1986   84, 250
Australian Capital Territory (Self-Government) Act 1978   118
Australian Citizenship Act 1948   54–5
Australian Citizenship Act 2007   54
Australian Citizenship (Transitionals and Consequentials) Act 2007   53–4
   s 3   54
   Sch 1   54
Australian Federal Police Act 1979   49
Australian Law Reform Commission Act 1996   67
Biological Control Act 1984   46
Border Protection (Validation and Enforcement Powers) Act 2001   328
Broadcasting Services Act 1992   57
   s 11(d)   57
   s 16   57
Classification (Publications, Films and Computer Games) Act 1995   90
Communist Party Dissolution Act 1950   298
Constitution   76, 78–9, 86, 242, 249, 256, 391
   Ch I   84
   Ch II   84–5
   Ch III   85
   s 41   85
   s 51   85, 87, 89, 118
   s 51(ii)   86
   s 51(iii)   86
   s 51(xxvi)   257
   s 51(xxxi)   85, 330
   s 52   87, 88
   s 52(x)   91
   s 57   89
   s 62   85
   s 64   78
   s 71   96
   s 72   379
   s 80   85, 134

   s 90   88
   s 92   88
   s 109   44, 86
   s 114   88
   s 116   85
   s 117   85
   s 122   86, 331
   s 127   256
   s 128   87
Constitution Alteration (Retirement of Judges) Act 1977   379
Copyright Act 1968
   s 10(1)   57
   s 135AL   57
   Pt VAA   57
Corporate Law Reform Act 1992
   s 435A   326
   s 444D(1)   327
Corporations Act 2001
   Pt 5.3A   324–7
Crimes Act 1914   121
   s 4AA   318
Crimes (Torture) Act 1988   71, 121
Criminal Code Act 1995   121
   s 10.2(2)   303
   Div 104   297
Designs Act 2003
   s 149   52
Designs Regulations 2004   52
Families, Community Services and Indigenous Affairs and Other Legislation Amendment (Northern Territory National Emergency Response and Other Measures) Act 2007   330
Family Law Act 1975   97, 129
Federal Court of Australia Act 1976   95–6
   s 53A   105, 129
Federal Magistrates Act 1999   97
Freedom of Information Act 1982   119
Imperial Acts Application Act 1969   237
Judiciary Act 1903
   s 23   290

s 69(3) 404
Jurisdiction of Courts (Cross-vesting)
   Act 1987   101
Jury Exemption Act 1965   134
Legislative Instruments Act 2003
   s 12   53
   s 42   53
Marriage Act 1961   129, 186
   s 16   186
Migration Act 1958   104
Native Title Act 1993   53, 264, 267,
   271–2
Native Title Amendment Act 1998   265
Native Title Amendment Act 2007   53
Native Title Amendment Act 2009   268
Norfolk Island Act 1979   118
Northern Territory National
   Emergency Response Act 2007   258,
   265, 330
   s 90   276
   s 91   276
Northern Territory (Self-Government)
   Act 1978   83, 118
Offshore Minerals Act 1994   47
Ombudsman Act 1976   119
Racial Discrimination Act 1975   259,
   262–5
   s 8   259
Referendum and Subsequent
   Constitution Alteration (Aboriginals)
   Act 1967   257
Sex Discrimination Act 1984   392
Statute of Westminster Adoption
   Act 1942   84
Surveillance Devices Act 2004   48–9
Telecommunications Act 1997   154
War Crimes Act 1945   167–8

Australian Capital Territory

Civil Law (Wrongs) Act 2003   126
Classification (Publications, Films and
   Computer Games) (Enforcement)
   Act 1995   90
Crimes Act 1900   121
Freedom of Information Act 1989   119
Human Rights Act 2004   87
Juries Act 1967   134
Legal Profession Act 2006   356, 384
Legal Profession (Solicitors) Rules
   2006   365
Legislation Act 2001   311
   s 65   53
   s 73   46

s 73(2)   53
s 84   54
s 86   54
s 133   318
s 137   323
s 137(3)   329
s 139(1)   313
s 140   313
s 141(2)   316
s 142   315
s 145(a)   317
s 145(b)   317
s 146(1)   318
s 146(2)   318
s 150   318
s 151   318
s 151A   318
s 156   314
Limitation Act 1985   123
Magistrates Court Act 1930   100
Ombudsman Act 1989   119
Self-Government (Citation of Laws)
   Act 1989   83
Standard Time and Summer Time
   Act 1972
   s 7   317
Supreme Court Act 1933   98
Tenancy Tribunal Act 1994   336
Victims of Crime (Financial Assistance)
   Act 1983   121

New South Wales

Aboriginal Land Rights Act 1983   63,
   268–9
   s 36(5)   269
   s 36(9)   268
   s 36A   270
   s 40   268
Aborigines Protection Act 1909   254
Anti-Discrimination Act 1977   396–7
Civil Liability Act 2002   126, 144–8
   ss 55–7   146
   s 58   146–8
Civil Procedure Act 2005   128
   s 56   131
   s 59   131
Classification (Publications, Films and
   Computer Games) Enforcement
   Act 1995   90
Classification (Publications, Films and
   Computer Games) Enforcement
   Amendment (Uniform Classification)
   Act 2004   90

Community Protection Act 1994   80
Constitution Act 1855   82
Constitution Act 1902   82
Crimes Act 1900   121
   s 316(1)   369
   s 316(4)   369
Crimes (Appeal and Review)
   Act 2001   342
Crimes (Appeal and Review) Amendment
   (Double Jeopardy) Act 2006   342
Crimes (Criminal Organisations Control)
   Act 2009   344–50
Crimes (Sentencing Procedure) Act 1999
   s 17   318
Deer Act 2006
   s 36   329
District Court Act 1973   98
   s 164A   105, 129
Freedom of Information Act 1989   119
Internal Government Procurement and
   Contracting Act 2009   30
Interpretation Act 1987   311, 322, 324
   s 4   329
   s 6   314
   s 8(a)   317
   s 8(b)   317
   s 8(c)   317
   s 9(1)   318
   s 9(2)   318
   s 23   45
   s 28   54
   s 30   54
   s 33   312, 317, 337
   s 34   317
   s 34(1)   315
   s 34(2)   315
   s 35(1)   314
   s 35(2)   314
   s 36   317–18
   s 38   318
   s 39   53
   s 41   53
   Art 34
Jury Act 1977   134
Law Enforcement (Powers and
   Responsibilities) Act 2002   133
Law Reform (Miscellaneous Provisions)
   Act 1946
   s 6   326
Law Reform Commission Act 1967   68
Legal Profession Act 2004   356, 384
   Pt 7   357
   s 331   376

s 332A 376
Limitation Act 1969 123
Local Court Act 2007 99
National Parks and Wildlife
    Act 1974 269
Ombudsman Act 1974 119
Supreme Court Act 1970 97
    s 110K 105, 129
Uniform Civil Procedure Rules
    2005 128
    r 2.1 131
    r 2.2 132
    r 2.3 132
Victims Support and Rehabilitation
    Act 1996 121

Northern Territory
Aboriginal Ordinance 1911 254
Building Act 1993
    s 5 329
Classification of Publications, Films and
    Computer Games Act 90
Criminal Code Act 121, 276
    s 1 276
    s 126 276
    s 129(1) 276
Fisheries Act 1988
    s 53 275
Interpretation Act 1978 311
    s 3(2) 329
    s 6 46
    s 11 54
    s 12 54
    s 17 314
    s 24(1) 317
    s 24(2) 317
    s 27 318
    s 28(2) 318
    s 55(1) 314
    s 55(6) 314
    s 62A 312
    s 62B(1) 315
    s 62B(2) 315
    s 63 53
    s 63(9) 53
Juries Act 134
Justices Act 99
Legal Profession Act 356, 384
Limitation Act 1981 123
Local Court Act 99
Magistrates Act 99
Northern Territory Aboriginal Sacred Sites
    Act 1989 269

Ombudsman Act 1980 119
Penalty Units Act 1999
    s 3 318
Radiation Protection Act 154–5
Small Claims Act 99
Standard Time Act 2005
    ss 4–5 318
Supreme Court Act 98
Victims of
Crime Assistance Act 2006 121

Queensland
Aboriginal and Torres Strait Islander
    Affairs Act 1965 255
Aboriginal Land Act 1991 269
Aboriginal Protection Act and Restriction
    of the Sale of Opium Act 1897 254
Acts Interpretation Act 1954 311
    s 5 329
    s 13 329
    s 14 323
    s 14(1) 314
    s 14(7) 314
    s 14A(1) 313
    s 14B(1) 315
    s 14B(2) 316
    s 14B(3) 315
    s 15A 46
    s 19 54
    s 20 54
    s 32A 314
    s 32AA 314
    s 32B 317
    s 32C 317
    s 32CA(1) 318
    s 32CA(2) 318
    s 37 318
    s 38 318
Civil Liability Act 2003 126
Classification of Computer Games and
    Images Act 1995 90
Classification of Films Act 1991 90
Classification of Publications
    Act 1991 90
Community Services (Aborigines)
    Act 1984 255
Constitution Act 1867 82
Constitution Act Amendment
    Act 1922 82

Constitution of Queensland
    Act 2001 82
Criminal Code Act 1899 121
    s 31(1) 301
    s 31(1)(d) 299–301, 303
District Court of Queensland
    Act 1967 99
Fauna and Conservation Act 1974-
    79 275
Freedom of Information Act 1992 119
Jury Act 1995 134
Law Reform Commission Act 1968 68
Legal Profession Act 2007 356, 384
Limitation of Actions Act 1974 123
Magistrates Court Act 1921 99
Nature Conservation Act 1992 269
Parliament of Queensland Act 2001 82
Parliamentary Commissioner
    Act 1974 119
Penalties and Sentences Act 1992
    s 5 318
    s 9(2)(o) 278
Queensland Coast Islands Declaratory
    Act 1985 262
Queensland Heritage Act 1992 269
Statutory Instruments Act 1992
    s 32 53
    s 50 53
Supreme Court Act 1995 98
Supreme Court of Queensland Act 1991
    ss 101–2 105, 129
    s 126 105, 129
Torres Strait Islander Land
    Act 1991 269
Uniform Civil Procedure Rules
    1999 128
Victims of Crime Assistance
    Act 2009 121

South Australia
Aboriginal Heritage Act 1988 269
Aborigines Act 1911 254
Acts Interpretation Act 1915 311
    s 7 46
    s 10A 53
    s 14A(2)(d) 53
    s 16 54
    s 17 54
    s 19(1) 314
    s 20 329
    s 22(1) 313
    s 26(a) 317
    s 26(ab) 317

s 26(b) 317
s 26(c) 317
s 27 318
s 28 318
s 34 318
Civil Liability Act 1936 126
Classification (Publications, Films
 and Computer Games) Act 1995 90
Constitution Act 1855 82
Constitution Act 1934 82
Criminal Law Consolidation
 Act 1935 121
District Court Act 1991 99
Freedom of Information Act 1991 119
Juries Act 1927 134
Legal Practitioners Act 1981 356,
 371, 385
Limitation of Actions Act 1936 123
Magistrates Court Act 1991 100
Maralinga Tjarutja Land Rights
 Act 1984 269, 271
Offenders Probation Act 1913 334
Ombudsman Act 1972 119
Pitjantjatjara Land Rights
 Act 1981 269
Real Property Act 1857 249
Road Traffic Act 1961 334
Supreme Court Act 1935 98

Tasmania
Aboriginal Lands Act 1995 269
Aboriginal Relics Act 1975 269
Acts Interpretation Act 1931 53, 311
 s 5 53
 s 6(2) 314
 s 6(3) 314
 s 6(4) 314
 s 6(6) 329
 s 8A 312
 s 8B(1) 315
 s 8B(2) 316
 s 8B(3) 315
 s 9 45
 s 10A(1)(a) 319
 s 10A(1)(b) 319
 s 10A(1)(c) 318
 s 14 54
 s 16 54
 s 24(d) 317
 s 24A 317
 s 28 318
 s 29 318
Civil Liability Act 2002 126

Classification (Publications, Films and
 Computer Games) Enforcement
 Act 1995 90
Constitution Act 1855 82
Constitution Act 1934 82
Criminal Code Act 1924 121
Freedom of Information Act 1991 119
Juries Act 2003 134
Legal Profession Act 2007 356, 385
Limitation Act 1974 123
Magistrates Court Act 1987 100
Ombudsman Act 1978 119
Penalty Units and Other Penalties
 Act 1987
 s 4 318
Supreme Court Act 1856 98
Supreme Court Act 1887 98
Supreme Court Act 1959 98
Victims of Crime Assistance
 Act 1976 121

Victoria
Aboriginal Lands Act 1970 268
Archaeological and Aboriginal Relics
 Preservation Act 1972 269
Charter of Human Rights and
 Responsibilities Act 2006 87
 s 32 332
Classification (Publications, Films and
 Computer Games) (Enforcement)
 Act 1995 90
Constitution Act 1855 82
Constitution Act 1975 82
 s 1A 256
Constitution (Court of Appeal)
 Act 1994 98
County Court Act 1958 98
Crimes Act 1958 121, 406
 s 360A 406
 s 397 405
Fisheries Act 1928 331
Food Act 1984
 s 6 329
Freedom of Information Act 1982 119
Interpretation of Legislation
 Act 1984 311, 323
 s 5 329
 s 11 45
 s 14 54
 s 35 322
 s 35(a) 312
 s 35(b) 315
 s 36(1) 314

s 36(3) 314
s 37(a) 317
s 37(c) 317
s 37(d) 317
s 43 318
s 44 318
s 45(1) 318
s 45(2) 318
Juries Act 2000 134
Legal Profession Act 2004 356, 385
Limitation of Actions Act 1958 123
Magistrates' Court Act 1989 99
Magistrates' Court (Koori Court)
 Act 2002 277
Monetary Units Act 2004
 ss 5–7 318
Motor Car Traders Act 1986 47
Ombudsman Act 1973 119
Police Offences Act 1928
 s 5(10) 308–9
Subordinate Legislation Act 1994
 s 16 53
 s 23(2) 53
Summer Time Act 1972
 s 4 318
Supreme Court Act 1986 97
Supreme Court (General Civil Procedure)
 Rules 2005
 0.50.07 105, 129
Victims of Crime Assistance
 Act 1996 121
Victorian Law Reform Commission
 Act 2000 68
Wrongs Act 1958 126

Western Australia
Aboriginal Heritage Act 1972 269, 329
Aboriginal Protection Act 1886 254
Civil Liability Act 2002 126
Classification (Publications, Films and
 Computer Games) Enforcement
 Act 1996 90
Constitution Act 1889 82
Constitution Act 1890 82
Constitution Acts Amendment
 Act 1899 82
Criminal Code Compilation
 Act 1913 121
Criminal Injuries Compensation
 Act 2003 121
District Court of Western Australia
 Act 1969 99
Family Court Act 1997 97

Freedom of Information Act 1992   119
Interpretation Act 1984   311
   s 4   329
   s 10(a)   317
   s 10(c)   317
   s 18   312
   s 19(1)   315
   s 19(2)   315
   s 19(3)   316
   s 20   45
   s 31(2)   314
   s 32(1)   314
   s 32(2)   314
   s 34   54
   s 37   54
   s 41   53
   s 42(2)   53
   s 56(1)   318
   s 56(2)   318
   s 61   318
   s 65   318
Juries Act 1957   134
Land Administration Act 1997
   s 161   185
Law Reform Commission Act 1972   68
Legal Profession Act 2008   356, 385
   Pt 16   357
Limitation Act 2005   123
Magistrates Court Act 2004   100
Parliamentary Commissioner
   Act 1971   119
Police Act 1892
   s 84   320
Supreme Court Act 1935   98
Town Planning and Development
   Act 1928
   s 13   185

Imperial
Australia Courts Act 1828   115, 237–8, 245, 247
   s 24   237
Australian States Constitutions
   Act 1907   249
Colonial Laws Validity Act 1865   249
Commonwealth of Australia Constitution
   Act 1900   83, 249
Judicature Act 1873   116
Judicature Act 1875   116
New South Wales Act 1823   242
New South Wales Courts Act 1787   238

Statute of Westminster 1931   83
   s 4   250
Western Australia Act 1829   247

International
Agreement on Sanitary and Phytosanitary
   Measures   72
Agreement on Trade Related Aspects of
   Intellectual Property Rights   16
Declaration of Rights of Indigenous
   People
   Art 25–8   266
   Art 34   266
International Bill of Rights   87
International Covenant on Civil and
   Political Rights   87
   Art 14   391
   Art 14(3)   405
   Art 27   265
International Covenant on Economic,
   Social and Cultural Rights   87
   Art 1   265
International Convention on the
   Elimination of Racial Discrimination
   (CERD)
   Art 5   265
United Nations Declaration of Human
   Rights
   Art 17   265
Universal Declaration on Human
   Rights   87
   Art 7   391

United Kingdom
Australian Constitutions Act (No. 1)
   1842   247
Australian Constitutions Act (No. 2)
   1850   247–8
Increase of Rent and Mortgage Interest
   (Restrictions) Act 1920   334
Offences Against the Person Act 1861
   s 57   320
Official Secrets Act 1920
   s 3   320
Restriction of Offensive Weapons
   Act 1959   321
Street Offences Act 1959   321

preface

A fundamental and primary aim of this book is to provide a logical, easily understandable introduction to our law and legal system in Australia. Recognising that law students come from diverse backgrounds, this book does not assume that students studying law at an Australian university have a background in legal studies, or indeed any knowledge of Australia's history and system of law and government.

Our focus of this book is practical – for example we provide background on key events and developments in English legal and constitutional history only where those events and developments are instrumental in creating the system we have today in Australia; and we discuss theoretical underpinnings of law and judicial reasoning without taking the new law student into jurisprudential terrain that can only be understood with time and experience in law.

The book is structured according to the typical questions that a new law student may ask – What is law? Where did it come from? How is it made? How can I find it? What do lawyers do? How can I develop a legal mind? And when I am finished, what can I do with my law degree? It also creates an opportunity for students with particular interests – such as human rights law, Indigenous legal rights or commercial law – to begin to consider specialised content knowledge.

This book has been written and edited to maximise the learning outcomes for first year law students. Chapter design includes a recommended approach to learning the topic, key terms, tip boxes, discussion questions, and places to find further information. The chapters are backed up with an Online Resource Centre with teaching and learning resources, plus plenty of opportunities for students to practice applying what they have learned.

Each of the authors of this book has significant first-hand experience in teaching and mentoring first year law students, and the General Editor has both a Master of Education in Adult Education and a Graduate Certificate in Higher Education (Teaching and Learning).

Michelle Sanson, Thalia Anthony and David Worswick
Sydney, September 2010

guided tour

What we will cover in this chapter
Opens each chapter, and provides an overview of the subtopics covered.

Recommended approach to learning this topic
A guide for students on how to approach the topics in the chapter.

Key terms
A glossary of legal terms used in the chapter.

Tips
Margin notes explain aspects of the topic that students may find difficult or confusing.

In depth
These sections delve deeper into the topics discussed, providing real-life applications of the law.

xxv

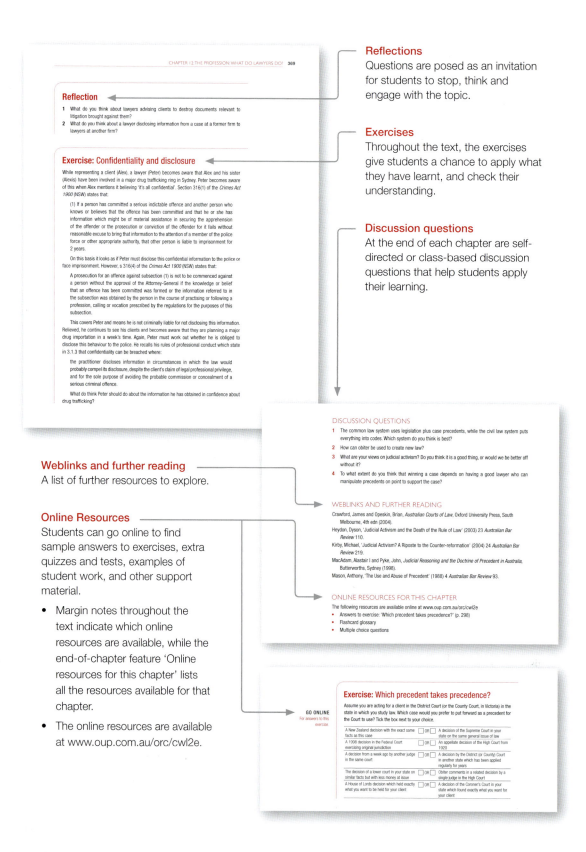

Reflections
Questions are posed as an invitation for students to stop, think and engage with the topic.

Exercises
Throughout the text, the exercises give students a chance to apply what they have learnt, and check their understanding.

Discussion questions
At the end of each chapter are self-directed or class-based discussion questions that help students apply their learning.

Weblinks and further reading
A list of further resources to explore.

Online Resources
Students can go online to find sample answers to exercises, extra quizzes and tests, examples of student work, and other support material.

- Margin notes throughout the text indicate which online resources are available, while the end-of-chapter feature 'Online resources for this chapter' lists all the resources available for that chapter.
- The online resources are available at www.oup.com.au/orc/cwl2e.

acknowledgments

The authors would like to express their personal appreciation to the following people: Amanda Porter for her outstanding research and compelling insights into Indigenous issues; Dorothea Anthony, Dr Michelle Burgis and Dr Scott Calnan for their critical reading of jurisprudence; Professor David Barker AM for his mentorship; Mark O'Donnell for his perpetual support; Colin Fong and David Sinfield for their input; the anonymous reviewers, who provided useful comments and suggestions; the copy editor Trischa Mann and all the people at Oxford University Press (particularly Karen Hildebrandt, Katie Ridsdale, Michelle Head and Tim Campbell) for their good work and patience, and for providing an attractive, modern layout and style and developing the online resources.

Thanks to all the academics who have had the confidence to set our text for their classes – we look forward to any comments you may have so that our third edition is even better! If you have scenarios or exemplars you feel would benefit first year students across the country you're welcome to send them to us, for the Online Resource Centre or body of the book, with appropriate acknowledgment given.

Finally, we are grateful to our families and friends who have supported us along the way.

The authors and the publisher wish to thank the following copyright holders for reproduction of their material: the Australasian Legal Information Institute for permission to reproduce the screenshots of the AustLII website; screenshots of the ComLaw website, copyright Commonwealth of Australia, reproduced with permission; permission to reproduce the Commonwealth Coat of Arms granted by the Department of the Prime Minister and Cabinet; the University of Cardiff for permission to reproduce the screenshot of the Cardiff Index to Legal Abbreviations; Corbis/Bettmann for the images on pp. 202, 206, 209, 216; RMIT Publishing for permission to reproduce the screenshot of the Informit website; LexisNexis Australia for permission to reproduce the screen shots from its website; extracts from legislation of the Parliament of the State of Victoria, Australia, are reproduced with permission of the Crown in right of the State of Victoria, Australia—the State of Victoria accepts no responsibility for the accuracy and completeness of any legislation contained in this publication; SAI Global for permission to reproduce the screenshot of its Lawlex Legislative Alert and Premium Research at http://my.lawlex.com.au; screenshots from Thomson Reuters—Legal Online (www.thomsonreuters.com.au) reproduced with permission of Thomson Reuters (Professional) Australia Limited; academics from The University of Sydney Law School, Ross Anderson, Jamie Glister, and Dr Belinda Smith, and students Stephanie Constand, Alexander Marechal-Ross and Alistair Oakes for loaning their questions, problems and solutions for use on the online resource centre; and academics Nikki Bromberger and Mary Wyburn.

Every effort has been made to trace the original source of copyright material in this book. The publisher will be pleased to hear from copyright holders to rectify any errors or omissions.

1

Introduction: Overview of the Book

Before you embark on reading this book from cover to cover, or by chapter as allocated throughout the teaching semester, it is useful to get an overall framework for learning and understanding.

Each chapter contains distinct pedagogical features:

- **What we will cover** – an overview of the subtopics covered, plus a table of contents style layout showing the breakdown of chapters into their parts and subparts
- **Recommended approach** – a handy guide for the newcomer on how the topic of the chapter may be tackled
- **Key terms** – a glossary of legal terms used in the chapter, as a ready reference
- **Tips** – usually picking up some aspect of the topic that students may find tricky or confusing
- **Reflections** – places where the material lends itself to reflection, as a means of allowing students to engage actively with it
- **Discussion questions** – useful for students to think about after reading the chapter, or better still, to discuss in their study groups, online or in class
- **Exercises** – giving students a chance to apply the material in practical situations and check their understanding
- **Weblinks and further reading**
- **Online Resource Centre** – to support the chapter with practice exercises and interesting further information relating to the subject. Online resources are indicated with 'Go online' margin notes.

Together these features aim to make the learning experience enjoyable and interesting for students, and to cater to different learning styles.

The following is a brief snapshot and overview of each chapter.

1: Topics of study by chapter

Learning law: How can I develop a legal mind?

The next chapter, Chapter 2, provides foundational guidance in how to study law. It considers the extent to which studying law is different from studying other disciplines, such as the arts or sciences. It also tackles the fundamental question, *What does it mean to have a legal mind?* Graduating from law school and being able to work as a lawyer is one thing, but successful law graduates possess many other attributes. These include an ethical mindset, having tools to respond effectively and independently when issues arise in practice, and having the capacity to update their legal knowledge and a broad understanding of culturally and socially diverse clients and their circumstances. As law graduates we should also have a concept of service – service to our clients, service to the legal profession, and service to the community.

Sources: What is the law itself?

It is important to identify the instruments in which the law can be found – cases and legislation. Chapter 3 explains how a case can create a new legal principle, or apply a narrow or broad interpretation of a piece of legislation. The chapter explains how cases and legislation interact with one another in practice, and looks at other sources which can contribute to the creation of new law, such as law reform commission reports, academic commentary, and international conventions and treaties.

Legal institutions: How is law made?

Chapter 4 covers the federal system of government in Australia and the main arms of government at federal and state levels, namely the legislature (parliament), the executive (government administration), and the judicature (the courts). It focuses on each of the arms of government, and gives examples of the way they operate, with parliament creating legislation, the executive bringing it into effect and administering its operation, and the courts interpreting it and resolving disputes under it. Chapter 4 also considers the practical reality that the separation of powers between these arms of government is often blurred. Finally, as courts are not the only place for resolving disputes, Chapter 4 also introduces tribunals and alternative methods of dispute resolution such as arbitration and mediation.

Classifying and practising law: How are cases resolved?

Chapter 5 examines the way cases are resolved in various areas of substantive law including criminal law, property law, and family law. It also considers the difference between substantive law and procedural law (the legal processes for applying the law in specific case situations). The two main areas of procedural law – civil and criminal procedure – are explained, as are fundamental legal principles such as due process (fair and equal procedures).

Research: How do I find the law?

It is a fundamental lawyer skill to be able to locate relevant law and establish, through legal research and analytical techniques, what the current state of law on any conceivable legal issue is. Chapter 6 explains how to go about legal research, and where to find legal information in libraries, electronic databases, and online. It also shows which resources carry greater weight and significance than others, and provides a technique for you to assess the hierarchy of authority between various sources. Finally, this chapter explains one of the most time-consuming but essential processes – preparing footnotes and a bibliography, so that others' ideas and publications are properly referenced and you can feel comfortable that you will avoid allegations of plagiarism while at law school and beyond.

Jurisprudence: What is law?

Chapter 7 considers law as a concept or 'thing' – what exactly is 'law', and what role does it play in society? Jurisprudence is the theory of law, and many of the ideas about law were developed from the earliest times in history. For many years it was thought that law was based in nature, and based on inherent human understandings of right and wrong or justice and injustice. This conception of law, known as *natural law* theory, was challenged by *legal positivists* who viewed law as something made by humans to serve their purposes; it could thus be changed and added to at will. *Legal positivism* is the dominant model of law in Western democracies, including Australia, today. It holds that a rule is not a law until and unless it is created by legislation or a court decision – a position that underpins the 'rule of law'. Chapter 7 also looks at the theoretical critiques of the uneven development and application of rules for marginalised groups in society, including non-English speaking groups, women and people from lower socio-economic backgrounds. It notes the way Marxist legal thinkers view the law as the domain of the upper class. In addition to these approaches, Chapter 7 addresses how postmodernists also have questioned the significance of rules in complex societies.

History: How did Australian law develop?

Chapter 8 considers the laws or legal systems that existed in Australia before English occupation and continue to operate in many Australian communities – Indigenous legal systems based upon customary laws. It discusses how English law and legal principles disregarded Indigenous law systems. The British colonisation of Australian territories led to the application of English laws. Chapter 8 shows how English cases and statutes played a role in the development of Australian law, and how Australia achieved legal independence in the 1980s, notwithstanding the continuation of a constitutional monarchy.

Australia: Where does Indigenous law fit in?

In Chapter 9 we ask the question, *If Indigenous laws and legal systems were disregarded or displaced upon British colonisation, where does Indigenous law fit in today?* Despite colonial attempts to segregate and assimilate Indigenous peoples, many Indigenous communities in Australia continue to practise their laws. There have recently been limited attempts to recognise these practices. Chapter 9 outlines how native title law allows for the recognition of ongoing Indigenous land systems where Indigenous claimants can meet legal requirements. By contrast, recognition of ongoing Indigenous 'criminal' laws and punishment has lagged. Chapter 9 addresses the arguments for constitutional recognition of Indigenous people and for a treaty between the Indigenous people and the Australian government, as occurred in New Zealand and some parts of Canada and the USA.

Precedent: How do judicial decisions become law?

Chapter 10 focuses on the common law, which is law created by judges. It shows how the main point of each case, the *ratio*, may be applied as a precedent in future cases which have similar facts and legal issues. It considers situations where a court may have to follow binding precedents, and where precedents that are not binding may still be highly persuasive. It shows that courts may conceivably take into account any previous decision of any court, but the decisions of certain courts, particularly appeal cases from superior courts, have greater precedent value. The different types of judgments of appeal courts are considered, including unanimous, majority and minority judgments, and there is a discussion of how judges view their role – some see themselves as applying the law as it is, and others see their role as doing justice between the parties. Chapter 10 considers whether it is possible for judges to strictly interpret precedent or whether judges' values and backgrounds invariably have a bearing on their law making or the adjudication process. A snapshot of how judges are selected is included to highlight the politicised nature of judicial appointment.

Statutory interpretation: How do courts interpret legislation?

Chapter 11 focuses on the role of courts in applying and interpreting legislation in the context of particular cases that come before them. It considers that the key task of courts is to give effect to parliament's legislative intention, which may be gleaned from an objects clause within the Act itself, or from materials outside the Act, such as the parliamentary debates that took place when the bill was in the process of becoming an Act. Chapter 11 presents statutory interpretation as a toolkit, in which the main tool is to interpret the legislation in accordance with the intention of parliament, but there are a number of secondary tools that courts may also use in interpreting legislation, such as guiding principles and presumptions. A process for solving legal problems that have issues of statutory interpretation is presented, and you will have the opportunity to apply your problem-solving skills to some statutory interpretation practice exercises.

The profession: What do lawyers do?

Chapter 12 considers the role lawyers play in the legal profession in assisting clients to resolve disputes and, where cases are litigated, in preparing the case so that the relevant facts and law can be convincingly presented before the court. The two main types of legal practitioners in Australia, solicitors and barristers, are considered, along with their main roles, in which solicitors tend to prepare cases in the lead-up to court, including filing of pleadings, and preparation of witness statements, while barristers, being expert in court procedures and oral advocacy techniques, typically run cases in court. The role of legal professional organisations such as law societies (for solicitors) and bar associations (for barristers) is discussed, as is the importance of a strong commitment to ethical and professional practice. The role of judges in each of the major courts in Australia is also covered.

Law in society: What are the problems and remedies for accessing justice?

Chapter 13 looks at the issues that certain individuals and groups in society face in accessing the court system. These issues include the cost of bringing legal proceedings, including paying for legal costs, and the system of legal aid that is in place, as well as the *pro bono* work that some committed legal practitioners offer, often through community law centres. Although, on the face of it, the rule of law means that the law applies equally to everyone, in some instances this can create injustice, particularly for minority and disadvantaged groups within the community such as the disabled, elderly, and mentally ill. Where most law studies involve looking at the law and the way it is applied, this chapter focuses on the broad impact that law has in society. Students are particularly encouraged to consider whether there is a connection between law and social justice.

My law career: How can I best prepare for it?

Chapter 14 enables law students to give some thought to what they might want to do with their law degree once they graduate, and what they can be doing in the meantime (apart from studying hard!) to ensure they are in a good position to obtain the position they seek. This includes part-time work in a legal-related field and participation in extracurricular activities such as mooting, law student societies, social justice programs, and the Australasian Law Students' Association (ALSA). Chapter 14 also provides practical guidance on the structure of a law degree in Australia, including compulsory subjects, and how to choose between a plethora of elective subjects as well as, in some universities, practical legal training. It includes an overview of some typical jobs that law graduates do, both in the private and public spheres – from becoming a legal aid lawyer, to working for the government in the Department of Foreign Affairs and Trade, to becoming a corporate counsel or working as a law lecturer. There are a great many different career paths open to law graduates, and this chapter will help new law students think about where they may, in the future, make best use of their legal studies in a way that they will find interesting, challenging and rewarding.

2: Online Resource Centre

To further develop and deepen your learning, this text is supported by an Online Resource Centre, which includes practice exercises and examples. We strongly encourage you to make use of the Online Resource Centre, particularly in areas you may find unclear, and in areas you find to be of special interest. You will notice throughout the book that we have indicated in the margin where there is relevant material in our Online Resource Centre. We welcome feedback as well as suggestions for useful future additions to the Online Resource Centre: www.oup.com.au/orc/cwl2e.

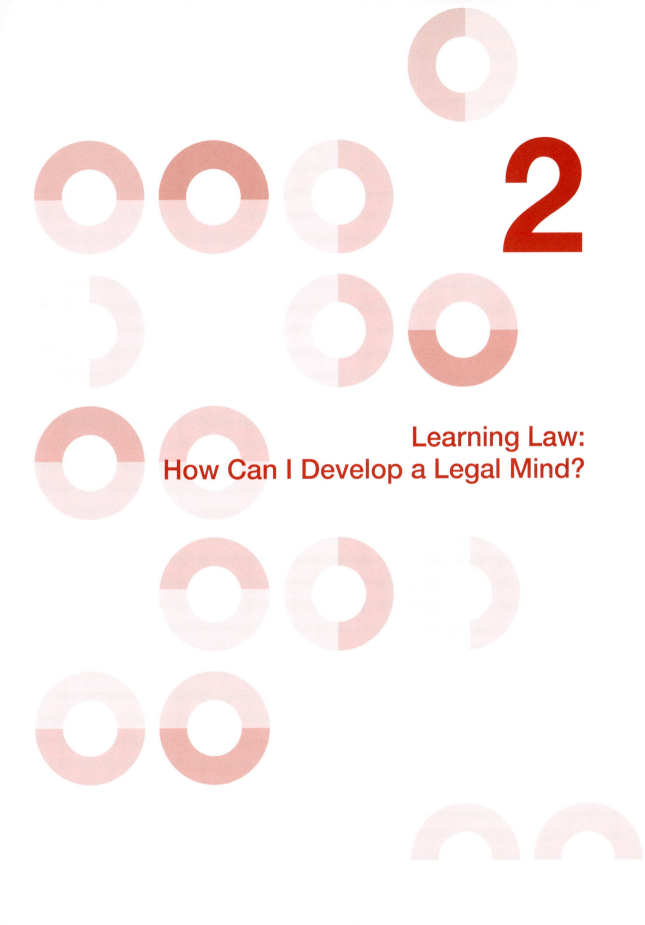

2

Learning Law: How Can I Develop a Legal Mind?

WHAT WE WILL COVER IN THIS CHAPTER:

- How learning law is different from other disciplines
- Inductive and deductive reasoning
- Learning to argue either side of any legal issue
- Key attributes of law graduates, and how to develop them
- How to succeed in law school
- How legal writing is different from other kinds of writing
- How to solve legal problems, and how to tackle exam questions

Recommended approach to learning this topic

This chapter gives you an overview of attributes that may take years to develop; you may still be developing them when you retire. Each area is both broad and deep, and you should treat this chapter as an introduction only. It may be all you need at this stage of your studies – to understand what the attributes are. You will develop them incrementally during your law course and across your professional career. We recommend you read through the material under headings 1 and 2, and then spend quite a bit of time reflecting on each attribute under heading 3. When you reach heading 4, you can start to try techniques for being productive in your studies straight away. Use what suits you best – there is no one 'right' way. You will have a chance to start developing legal writing and problem-solving skills, and you may have your first exams as well. We recommend that at the end of your first semester you come back to this chapter and give some further thought to what you could be doing outside the classroom to increase your development of these attributes.

KEY TERMS

Critical analysis = using powers of observation, reasoning, reflection and questioning to interpret information and make findings or form opinions based on it.

Deductive reasoning = using a general theory to test specific facts. For example 'All dogs bark. Rufus is a dog. Therefore, Rufus barks.'

Diversity = the coexistence of differences in gender, age, culture, capacity, and perspectives.

Ethics = a field of thinking about what is morally right, appropriate and acceptable.

Graduate attributes = generic skills, attitudes and values, plus specific content knowledge, expected of students who have completed a tertiary course of study.

Independent learning = students taking the primary responsibility and initiative for their own learning, including being able to recognise gaps in their learning and where to find the information to fill them.

Inductive reasoning = using specific examples to create generalisations. For example 'Apples rot. Pears rot. Bananas rot. Therefore, all fruit rots.'

Information literacy = knowing what information is available, when it is needed, how to find it and use it effectively, and recognising its inherent strengths and limitations.

Lifelong learning = a perspective that continuous learning is a fundamental part of one's personal and professional life.

Self-management = strategies and processes by which a person manages their time, their thoughts, feelings, goals and actions.

1: Law as a discipline

Law, in contemporary Western societies such as Australia, is formally an autonomous discipline. This means that, while it may be affected by morality, or politics, or religion, it is separate from them. We may have a law against murder but the basis for that is in cases and legislation, not the Bible or the Ten Commandments. This is different from religious systems of law, where the holy text is also the text of the law.

The consequence of law being an autonomous discipline is that legal reasoning often exists in a vacuum, and arguments can follow a path of mental gymnastics that generate an outcome that can appear illogical and unreasonable to a person not trained in legal reasoning. For example someone who has not studied law may conclude directly, as a matter of opinion, that a person who kills a child should be 'imprisoned' as 'punishment' for a 'crime'. A legal thinker resists reaching these direct conclusions, but instead addresses the question of whether the person had committed a crime, considering the relevant legislation and its interpretation, and then proceeds to consider whether a punishment of imprisonment was warranted and appropriate, and within the scope of penalties provided in legislation. Applying a process of legal reasoning may result in a child killer walking free, and this can be difficult for non-lawyers to comprehend.

TIP
Law is not completely apolitical. For example, Chapter 10 will consider the political process of judicial appointment and Chapter 7 will examine theoretical understandings of law as a political domain.

How law is different from other disciplines

Every discipline has its own style and way of thinking. Lawyers tend to throw around ideas in an abstract manner, without a great deal of thought for the consequences of the outcome of their reasoning on the lives and fortunes of others. Sociologists, on the other hand, adopt a holistic approach to reasoning, always bearing in mind predicted and potential, unpredicted consequences. Scientists seek an answer, and where people with a science background come to study law, they can often find it frustrating that there can be several 'correct' answers to a legal problem – it is all about the way you reason it, not just the outcome your reasoning produces. Journalists focus on the stories of cases and their significance and newsworthiness. A person with a background in journalism often writes a law essay like an article, usually with a top that is linked to the tail. A person with an arts background often throws in a quote from a poem or famous person at the beginning or end, and engages in a flowing discussion of its relevance to the topic at hand.

Law is different – it is a narrow, focused, succinct, judicious and frill-free process of thinking and writing. There is no flowery prose, there are no unsupportable presumptions. There is no one 'right' conclusion and there is merit in arguing both sides. At the same time, it is important to reach *clear* conclusions. It can be infuriating for others that lawyers think everything 'depends' – which, of course, it does. But despite the law being based on 'abstract principles', it is an *applied* discipline that requires careful consideration of how the facts of a case affect the legal outcome.

2: Legal reasoning

Thinking like a lawyer

Legal reasoning is so different from reasoning in other disciplines that the phrase 'thinking like a lawyer' has been coined. It was famously used in the Hollywood movie *The Paper Chase*,[1] where a law professor says to his students: 'You come here with minds full of mush, and leave thinking like a lawyer'. However, students rarely have minds of mush, and mostly have open minds that will take to thinking like a lawyer in a diligent and yet critical manner.

What exactly does it mean to 'think like a lawyer'? From a narrow perspective, it means being able to read cases and statutes and use them to develop legal arguments based on issues identified from a factual matrix. From a broad perspective, it is about precise, rational, dispassionate, analytical thinking. A critical perspective would see this approach as the legal profession's way of justifying its existence by making the law appear scientific and denying its human underpinnings. Other more cynical commentators would claim that lawyers make the most obvious and simple conclusion complicated, and twist and manipulate facts and words, and find loopholes, to achieve an outcome that furthers the client's interests.

In essence, we consider that there are six key aspects to thinking like a lawyer:

- **Non-assumptive thinking** – this involves resisting jumping to conclusions, or making assumptions. For example a lawyer would not consider whether their client is liable for breach of contract without first examining whether the contract was validly formed in the first place. Similarly, if a person was charged under crimes legislation, the lawyer would first look at the date the legislation entered into force, and the place where the law applied, before considering whether the provision applied or not.
- **Facts over emotions** – being able to detach from personal opinions, and personal notions of what is right and wrong. Instead, the facts are considered objectively, and the client's case assessed against the law. The focus is on the strategy and the outcome that is sought, rather than on feelings of justice or fair entitlements.
- **Tolerance of ambiguity** – being able to handle the fact that there is no black and white answer, that the answer depends on how you frame the question, and that the advice you give the client can never be given with absolute confidence, because everything depends on everything else, and laws can change at any time.

---

1   A dramatisation of John J Osborn's book, *The Paper Chase*, Cengage Learning (1971).

- **Ability to make connections between facts, documents and laws** – where the average person hits information that they cannot understand and therefore cannot fit into their current knowledge, they tend to switch off from it, and reject it. Lawyers instead are able to store surplus material somewhere in their brain, and in the future when the missing piece that links it to something they know already comes along, they are able to make the connection. This is essential, for example, in litigation, where the significance of communications or documents may not be apparent on their face, but later in the litigation process links may be made when more information comes to light or when a witness gives evidence.
- **Verbal mapping and ordering** – being able to structure thoughts and opinions, and express them orally in a manner that is more typical of written communication, for example 'I have three points to make. First …, Second …, and Third …'. Most people would not have three structured thoughts, but would instead have a stream of consciousness where they would raise thoughts as they had them. The mental process of verbal mapping and ordering is being able to create mental lists, or mental diagrams of relationships.
- **Automatic devil's advocacy** – no position is fixed, all are arguable. Thinking like a lawyer means having the intellectual flexibility to be able to convincingly reason one side of an argument, and in the next breath convincingly reason the completely opposite view. It also involves having a view, but being open to being challenged and changing the view when new information, or more convincing reasoning, is put. In litigation, we use automatic devil's advocacy to intellectually stand in the position of the opposing client, to see the case through their eyes, and thus prepare better for our client by pre-empting the arguments they are likely to make.

Inductive and deductive reasoning

Reasoning involves the application of logic to test a hypothesis. There are two broad approaches – inductive and deductive reasoning.

Inductive reasoning works from the specific to the general. We begin by examining specific observations, and from them we identify patterns and similarities, which enable us to create hypotheses to explore, and the outcomes are broad generalisations and theories. This can also be described as reasoning from a minor premise to a major premise. We use inductive reasoning when we perform case analysis – we consider several individual cases in order to describe broad rules of law.

Inductive arguments are always open to question because they are based on examination of only a limited portion of information to make assumptions and generalisations about the whole. For example a student may attend a Legal Research lecture and find it is boring. The student may then attend a Contracts lecture and find it boring, followed by a Torts lecture which is also boring. Using inductive reasoning, the student concludes that all law lectures are boring. This is open to question because the student is making the broad generalisation from a limited portion of all law lectures. The only way to prove the rule would be to attend every law lecture everywhere, which of course is impractical.

Deductive reasoning works from the general to the specific. We begin with a general theory which we use to create a hypothesis, and we test that hypothesis by specific observations in order to determine whether they confirm our original theory or not. This can also be described as reasoning from a major premise to a minor premise. We use deductive reasoning when we do a research essay on an area of law.

Syllogisms are commonplace in deductive reasoning. A syllogism is a logical argument where a conclusion is inferred from two premises, one major and one minor. The most famous syllogism is:

Major premise – All humans are mortal.
Minor premise – Socrates is human.
Conclusion – Socrates is mortal.

Deductive reasoning is less open than inductive reasoning, because we set out to confirm a specific hypothesis, whereas in inductive reasoning we explore specific instances to find unlimited potential conclusions. In practice we often use both forms of reasoning, and move between the two in the process of reasoning on an area of law. The legal profession treats the 'law' as deductive but in reality Australia's system of precedent is based on inductive reasoning (see Chapter 10).

Exercise: Inductive and deductive reasoning

Identify whether the following statements use inductive or deductive reasoning.

1. Taking a person's life is always wrong. Capital punishment involves taking a person's life. Therefore, capital punishment is always wrong.
2. The right to self-determination of minority peoples is a core part of international law. Therefore, if a majority of Aboriginal Australians vote for self-government, they must be allowed to do so.
3. Six in ten children who are allowed to drink at home with their parents become alcoholics later in life. Therefore, attitudes towards drinking are formed by others near to us.
4. Every human being has rights. John is a human being, therefore, John has rights.
5. Every time Mr Jones has taught Contract Law, students have achieved good results on the exam. This semester, Mr Jones is teaching Contract Law. Therefore, students will go well in the exam.
6. A's oral contract for sale of land was invalid in Case A. B's oral contract for sale of land was invalid in Case B. C's oral contract for sale of land was invalid in Case C. Therefore, all oral contracts for the sale of land are invalid.
7. Red cars go fast. Jenny's car is red. Therefore, Jenny's car goes fast.
8. We all have the right to equal treatment under the law. Therefore, Jane and Mary should be able to adopt a child, just as John and Mary are able to.

GO ONLINE
Go online for answers to 'Inductive and deductive reasoning' exercise.

3: Graduate attributes

Graduate attributes are the characteristics and qualities, skills and capabilities that students should possess by the time they complete their law degree. They show clearly that success in law is not simply about knowing the law and how to apply it. Lawyers need personal and professional skills such as superior communication and negotiation skills, time and priority management skills, and skills in critical analysis. They also need to appreciate cultural and gender diversity, understand how to function in an increasingly international legal environment, and know how to recognise and manage ethical issues when they arise in practice.

Development of attributes at different levels

It is useful to consider Biggs's SOLO taxonomy.[2] It is a good way to describe how a learner's performance grows in complexity when mastering many academic tasks:

- **Prestructural** – misses the point.
- **Unistructural** – identifies, does simple procedures.
- **Multistructural** – describes, lists, combines.
- **Relational** – discusses, compares, contrasts, applies, analyses.
- **Extended abstract** – reflects, theorises, hypothesises, generalises.

One of the difficulties students who have come directly from school may face is that their previous learning may be at the unistructural and multistructural levels – and for those with the marks to get into law, also partly at the relational level – but they do not realise that analysis is actually more than just comparing and contrasting. They hand in assignments that would earn them a high mark in high school and are deflated when they receive an average mark at university. They cannot see how their paper is in any way deficient, because they do not have advanced analytical or extended abstract capabilities. It is only when they are in their final year of law studies that they look back on papers handed in during first year, which they thought at the time were perfect, and cringe.

The attributes described below will be developed and understood at deeper levels as you progress in your law studies. The first step to learning involves knowing what you don't know, and that is the aim – to enable you to embark upon an investigation down paths you may not have realised existed.

Substantive legal knowledge

We refer to this first because it is what students think a law degree is about – learning the law, in substance. Learning, for example, the content of the law on murder, or defamation, or setting up companies. Having legal expertise means having a coherent and extensive knowledge of the law, usually with a specialty in a specific area, such as family law or maritime law.

---

2   J Biggs and K Collis, *Evaluating the Quality of Learning: The SOLO Taxonomy (Structure of the Observed Learning Outcome)*, Academic Press, New York (1982).

All law students must cover 11 key areas, known as the Priestley 11.[3] They are Constitutional Law, Criminal Law and Procedure, Contracts, Torts, Administrative Law, Corporate Law, Property Law, Equity and Trusts, Evidence, Civil Procedure and Professional Conduct. Some of these areas of law are considered in Chapter 4. Below is an exercise to see if you know what each of the 11 areas entails.

Exercise: Priestley 11 requirements

Draw a line from the description to the area of law. The answers can be found in the online resources.

Description	Area of law
Rights and responsibilities of company directors, employees, creditors and shareholders	Constitutional law
Legal rights in relation to ownership of land and dwellings on them	Administrative law
Negligence, trespass to the person, goods and land, nuisance, defamation, and allowable defences	Criminal law and procedure
Offences against the person and property, and how they are tried in a court of law	Torts
Legal mechanisms to make government officials who exercise broad discretionary powers accountable	Contracts
Legal requirements and standards for proving facts	Professional conduct
The law under which the Commonwealth and states operate, including the basis of their power	Real property law
Ethical responsibilities and legal accounting	Equity and trusts
Processes by which cases brought involving private individuals and companies are resolved in courts of law	Evidence
Legally binding promises and the issues that arise from breach of them	Corporate law
Injunctions, specific performance of obligations, and legal tools to separate legal and equitable ownership of property	Civil procedure

In addition to the compulsory units in a law degree, students have options to study specific topics of interest to them. Here are some of the electives that law schools commonly offer (noting that some law schools have decided to make some of these compulsory in their programs):

---

3   Prescribed by the Consultative Committee of State and Territorial Law Admitting Authorities, *Uniform Admission Requirements,* Discussion Paper and Recommendations (1992). The committee was chaired by the Honourable Justice Priestley.

- **Succession** – the law of wills (documents in which individuals provide for their assets to be dispersed upon their death). Succession covers what happens if someone dies without leaving a will, or leaves a will but cuts out one of the children, or was legally incapable at the time of making the will (due, for example, to illness such as dementia).
- **Labour Law** – also referred to as Workplace Law or Industrial Law, this subject focuses on the legal relationship between employers and employees, including industrial awards, trade unions, enterprise bargaining, industrial tribunals, and workers' compensation.
- **Family Law** – covers the recognition and regulation of relationships including marriage, de facto and other domestic relationships, and law regarding parenting rights and responsibilities. Often also covers topics such as domestic violence and children's rights.
- **Public International Law** – the main focus is on the legal relationship between states in the international system, and in their involvement in international organisations such as the United Nations. It encompasses the law of treaties, customary international law, the concept of state sovereignty, state responsibility, settlement of international disputes, and immunities and privileges for diplomatic and consular relations.
- **Private International Law** – although one would assume the focus of this subject to be the legal relationships between private individuals in international law, it is actually more narrowly focused on the question of which particular law applies between private individuals in international law. For that reason, this subject is sometimes called 'Conflict of Laws' instead.
- **International Trade Law** – covers private trade law (such as importing and exporting goods, carriage by sea or air, trade finance and dispute resolution) as well as public law aspects of trade involving commitments and legal obligations under the World Trade Organization, plus the established dispute settlement system.
- **Human Rights** – focuses on the principles behind, and implementation of, international agreements such as the Universal Declaration of Human Rights, the International Covenant on Civil and Political Rights, and the International Covenant on Economic and Social Rights. It may also address domestic legislation or constitutional provisions that incorporate human rights.
- **Jurisprudence** – the philosophy of law, which allows students to deepen their understanding of legal theory. The theories covered will usually depend on the areas of interest of the teaching staff, but may include feminism, race theory, postmodernism, or sociological legal theory.

Communication skills

Law graduates understand that the key way lawyers ply their trade is by communication. No amount of legal knowledge or analysis is of any use if it cannot be communicated effectively to clients, and to the court. Drafting skills used depend on the purpose of the written communication, be it drafting a letter of advice, a legal pleading, or a brief to counsel. Speaking skills also depend on the purpose of the communication

> **TIP**
> Discussions in class and in online forums facilitate expression of different views and perspectives. Some may 'push your buttons' emotionally, and you may be tempted to move from discussion to all-out argument. Remember to separate the 'person' from the 'problem' – attack what the other person *said*, not who they are. Also, sitting quietly and trying to understand the reasoning behind another student's view is a good way to develop your intellectual flexibility. You can always agree to disagree.

– to elicit information while taking instructions from a client or preparing a witness statement, or when manoeuvring a person into revealing information in the witness box while being cross-examined.

Legal communications can be informative, analytical, persuasive, and argumentative. At all times, lawyers remain cognisant of the outcome they seek to achieve, the point they seek to get across, and the optimal manner and method in which to communicate. They monitor the effect their communication is having, and adjust their style and content accordingly.

Within a law school context, students have various opportunities to develop oral communication skills – participation in class discussion, class presentations, client interviewing, mooting, and witness examination. Likewise, they have a variety of opportunities to develop writing skills – essays, problem questions, court reports, legal correspondence, case notes and draft court documents. Some of these are considered under heading 4 below.

Critical thinking

Critical thinkers do not take information for granted. They consider who prepared it, what motivations they may have, whether the process for obtaining the data was sound, and whether the conclusions reached from it are valid. They recognise where assumptions are made and have a view on the impact of assumptions on the validity of the outcomes. They are able to compare and contrast different sources of information, and apply reasoning to form a view on which is more reliable. They are able to develop and defend arguments, and to understand and reflect upon how they fit within a larger picture.

In law school, you will be expected to engage in critical thinking from the outset. The expectations on you will be lower in first year than in your final year, but even in first year you will not be able to achieve high grades if you merely describe, or regurgitate, what you have learned. Most law exams are 'open book', meaning you can take your texts in with you. That is because what is being tested is not the capacity to find the place in the text book and write it as an exam answer, but to think critically about the question and follow a logical process to analyse the relevant parts of the question.

> ## Example: Critical and non-critical thinking
>
> **A**
> Countries offer incentives to companies to engage in research and development by allowing them to register patents for their inventions (a patent gives the inventor a certain period of time in which they have sole power to exploit the invention). Patents are governed by domestic and international law (such as the *Agreement on Trade Related Aspects of Intellectual Property Rights*). There are some exceptions, for example with pharmaceutical patents, where a country is faced with a national emergency like avian flu or mad cow disease and can grant a compulsory license to produce products under the patent.

B

The shift towards compulsory licensing under the *Agreement on Trade Related Aspects of Intellectual Property Rights* has changed the power balance between poor countries and large pharmaceutical manufacturers. While patents typically protect an inventor from competition for a certain period through the grant of exclusive rights, compulsory licensing enables developing and least-developed countries to announce that they will authorise use of patented drugs in a national emergency, and the pharmaceutical company then has to decide whether the risk of having the patent in the hands of another company is greater than the cost of offering their products to the developing country at an affordable price. Here, a just outcome is achieved that would have been impossible without regulatory intervention.

Can you see that the first example, while competently written (and likely to achieve an excellent mark in high school, for example) is only descriptive? It only explains and describes, without looking at what the bigger picture context is, or what consequences flow from changes in the law, which the second one does.

TIP

Do not confuse critical thinking with criticising – critical thinking is not necessarily negative.

In our many combined years of experience in teaching first-year law, we have concluded that, after poor time management, failure to develop critical thinking skills is the second major reason students do not perform as well in their first semester as they would have liked. Students often have difficulty seeing that regurgitation of information is not the goal in law school – it is about thinking, analysing, reflecting, and developing persuasive arguments.

Exercise: Critical thinking

Here is an example of an actual question from a first-year examination paper:

> 'The rule of law prevents citizens being exposed to the uncontrolled decisions of others in conflict with them … Officers of the state are not permitted to imprison or otherwise deal forcibly with citizens or their property merely because they think it is their duty to do so'.
>
> Dyson Heydon, 'Judicial Activism and the Death of the Rule of Law' (2003) *Quadrant* 9, 10.

Discuss the application and development of the rule of law in Australia in light of the above quote and the materials you have examined this semester.

Think about how you would begin to answer that question under exam conditions. If the exam was open book, how might that change the way you would answer?

This is a very common way of asking essay questions – providing a quote followed by a question. If you respond to this question by stating what the rule of law means, refer to early theorists who spoke about the concept, and describe landmark events that developed the rule of law in England and Australia, you will be lucky to achieve a pass mark in law school, particularly if the exam is open book.

This comes as a bit of a shock to most first-year law students, who did exactly that in high school or in another degree and got marks over 90 per cent. Why? Because it is merely descriptive, regurgitating what is in the text and materials provided. The information is not wrong, it is just limited. It is enough to scrape through, but not enough to excel. To achieve a better mark in a law essay, you need to develop a line of argument and engage with the quote that is given and the question that is asked.

Here, look at where this quote came from – it is from 2003, which is relatively recent, and is by an incumbent High Court judge. We are told that it is from an article about judicial activism being the death of the rule of law, so it is important to consider that topic, and raise the relevant arguments. You may not know at this stage of the course what judicial activism is – we cover it in Chapter 10. But you will find that there are schools of thought, so it is worth referring to them, and forming an opinion of your own.

Do you think that the rule of law, which requires decisions to be made according to law, and law being applied the same to everyone, is compromised when judges, faced with an injustice or other situation that does not neatly fit within the law, go ahead and change the law, or make new law? Does that make it an 'uncontrolled decision' to use the words in the quote? Or do you think that judicial discretion is necessary and important, and does not compromise the rule of law? Can you give examples? *Mabo* comes to mind, which we cover in Chapter 9. Indigenous people, law and perspectives definitely come to mind when one reads the words 'deal forcibly with citizens and their property', so this is fertile ground for discussion in this essay. Indigenous people have been dealt with forcibly right from the start, in the eighteenth century, through to today – with policies of segregation, assimilation (leading to the stolen generation), the White Australia Policy, and the Northern Territory intervention. Perhaps as a point in your critique you might say that the rule of law is fine in theory, but if the law is itself discriminatory, then applying it will not achieve useful outcomes.

Can you see that a good answer to this question should go well beyond regurgitation of what the rule of law is and where it came from? If you see every essay question as an opportunity to develop a line of argument and engage in critical thinking and analysis, rather than merely as an opportunity to show that you have learned what you have been told in class and read in the book, you will find your marks in first-year law will be greatly improved.

Information literacy

Information literacy means being able to recognise when information is needed and to use appropriate research methods to locate and use relevant information. It encompasses understanding the relative value and authority of different sources, taking into account who created them, when, and for what purpose. A variety of resources can be used, including library resources in print and online: databases to locate cases, legislation, law journal articles, government reports, looseleaf commentary services, and so on.

Context: To wiki, or not to wiki, that is the question

Wikipedia, the online free encyclopedia, is increasingly popular. There is nothing wrong with using Wikipedia as a means to get started on a topic you know nothing about, but it is only a start. Anyone can create and update Wikipedia entries, and the information there may be misleading or incorrect. It is unacceptable to cite Wikipedia as a source in a legal essay. In any event, it will always be a secondary source, so you need to do a separate search for the primary documents and other sources referred to in the Wikipedia entry and decide for yourself whether they are relevant to your research or not.

Particularly important for the modern student is understanding that there is a hierarchy of authority in sources. For example a book by a leading expert commentator and published by a pre-eminent publisher will carry more weight than a blog on the topic that allows anyone to post their views. A report of a non-government organisation (NGO) may carry a lot of weight, depending on the circumstances. Government reports are highly respected, but may be challenged where they are written with a particular motivation, such as to justify a government approach or decision. A non-government organisation report may be less respected, unless the organisation itself is well regarded. For example a report of Amnesty International is likely to be more authoritative and reliable than a report of a small organisation called something like 'United Manhood Against Female Domination'. NGOs that are accredited with the United Nations will generally have more credibility than those that are not. Similarly, the official website of the Department of Foreign Affairs and Trade will be more reliable than a website created by an individual to express their views on Australia's foreign policy.

TIP
Wiki: A collaborative website which can be directly edited by anyone with access to it

Exercise: Assessing sources

Assume you are undertaking some research on access to justice for Indigenous Australians. Let's say you find the following:

- an Australian Law Reform Commission (ALRC) report which shows lower rates of legal representation and higher rates of incarceration of Indigenous Australians
- an appeal decision from the Supreme Court of Tasmania which overturned a conviction where it was shown that the Indigenous Australian defendant did not have access to an interpreter during the trial and did not speak fluent English
- an article in the *South Sydney Herald* quoting Indigenous Australians saying they get a raw deal and don't feel that they have an equal degree of respect from people in the law
- an amendment to the USA Constitution to the effect that every person has the right to a fair and proper trial, and the right to legal representation
- a webpage by the Aboriginal Legal Service, citing Australian Census data
- a World Vision report on the lower birth weight and educational opportunities for all rural Australians, particularly those in remote Indigenous communities

- an Australian High Court decision stating that everyone has a right to a fair trial but this does not extend to a right to legal representation.

How would you rank the authoritative value of these sources? Are any of them irrelevant? Do any of them refer to a secondary source, suggesting that you would be wise to access the original source and cite that instead? What do these research findings suggest? Do you have enough information to prepare a legal argument on the topic? If not, where else might you look for further information?

Lifelong learning

Lifelong learning is an attitude: one never stops learning. It is a commitment to continuously update legal knowledge, skills, and awareness. This is essential in the legal profession, because law is not a static body of rules and principles – new cases are decided and new legislation is enacted on a daily basis. Court procedures are amended and practice notes are issued by courts. Professional and personal development literature continues to grow, with new approaches and insights being made. Skills such as negotiation and advocacy can never be perfected – even the most famous mediators and barristers can find ways to improve.

A commitment to lifelong learning entails recognising when one's current knowledge and skills need updating. This may be through subscribing to email updates, law journals, or attending conferences, to name a few.

Example: Cultivating a habit of lifelong learning

We recommend that you practise setting a fortnightly time in your diary to check a legal source of some description. For example you could visit www.austlii.edu.au and look at the latest decisions. Or if you hear about a case in the news, search for the names of the parties and try to find the decision to read. This will help to get you in the habit of seeking out updated information, and habits once formed are easy to sustain.

Self-management

Self-management comprises a vast amount of territory – it includes the things we do to look after our physical selves, our emotional and mental wellbeing, our work–life balance, our emotions, our time, our goals and our career. It encompasses a degree of self-awareness – awareness of our own strengths and limitations, our opportunities and threats. It also encompasses our capacity to harness resources necessary to achieve outcomes.

Important areas of self-management include:

- **Direction** – having a clear sense of purpose and motivation in our professional lives. This comes from assessing where we want to go, and how we are going

to get there, and having a process to ensure we take regular small steps towards our goals. Having a sense of purpose and direction for the future makes us more focused and motivated in the present.
- **Growth** – being able to identify the areas in which we need to grow and develop professionally and personally. This requires a degree of self-reflection – identifying where we could have done better, where we have gaps or areas we feel lacking in confidence or understanding, and deciding on courses of action to grow and improve. For example we may have become demanding when someone did not do what we wanted them to do. On reflection, we may realise that our behaviour was aggressive when we wanted it to be assertive, and we might attend some assertiveness training, read a book on it, or just try our own techniques to remain assertive and not progress into being aggressive and demanding.
- **Priority management** – having a method of listing what needs to be done and to assess relative priorities. Lawyers in practice often run several matters for several clients at once, and steps need to be taken at various times. Lawyers need to have processes to make sure they do not miss court deadlines and appointments.
- **Work–life balance** – there is little point in working oneself into the ground, so that any time outside work is spent recovering from it. Work to live, don't live to work. You may, from time to time, need to work ridiculous hours on a case, just as you may in law school need to tip your balance in favour of studying in the lead-up to exams. The trick is to have breaks planned, and not stay out of balance for too long.
- **Emotional intelligence** – understanding, using and managing emotions in relation to ourselves and others. Having a high intelligence quotient (IQ) is no guarantee of success in a career in law. It must be coupled with a high emotional intelligence quotient (EQ). We must maintain professional composure and be *dispassionate* – capable of separating one's own emotions about a client's case, about the behaviour of others, about fairness and justice from the outcome we seek to achieve. We don't get mad, we get legal.
- **Awareness** – we need to inform ourselves about things that may have an impact on our personal performance. These may include stress, anxiety, and depression, for example. Being aware of the risk of depression, and the high levels at which depression is experienced in the legal profession, and knowing the signs, can ensure we take remedial steps at an early stage. Similarly, knowing what triggers stress and anxiety allows us to take measures to reduce the build-up, including activities that help to release stress.

GO ONLINE
Go online for worksheets and fact sheets on time management.

Example: Priority management technique

A tree diagram (Figure 2.1) is a useful way to manage priorities. The trunk represents the overall objective. The major branches are the major strategies. The smaller branches are the individual actions and steps to address the strategies. Here is an example:

Priority management technique

A tree diagram is a useful way to manage priorities. The trunk is the overall objective. The major branches are the major strategies. The smaller branches are the individual actions and steps to address the strategies. Here is an example:

FIGURE 2.1

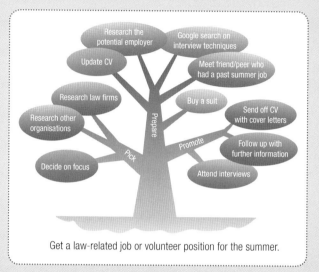

Get a law-related job or volunteer position for the summer.

In depth: A sample semester and week

Let's assume a full-time straight law student in their first semester is studying the following subjects, with the following assessment items.

- **Introduction to Law**: court report 25% due week 5, case note 25% due week 9, exam 50% during formal exam period
- **Criminal Law**: first problem-solving assignment 25% due week 4, second problem-solving assignment 25% due week 8, exam 50% during formal exam period
- **Contracts**: class presentation 10% week 3, essay 40% due week 10, exam 50% during formal exam period
- **Torts**: mid-semester exam 50% week 7, final exam 50% during formal exam period

Plotting these assessment items across the semester would look like this:

Wk 1	Wk 2	Wk 3	Wk 4	Wk 5	Wk 6	Wk 7
		Contracts Class Presentation	Criminal Law 1st Assignment	Intro Court Report		Torts Mid-Sem Exam

Wk 8	Wk 9	Wk 10	Wk 11	Wk 12	Wk 13	Wk 14	Stuvac/Exams
Criminal Law 2nd Assignment	Intro Case Note	Contracts Essay					Intro Criminal Contracts Torts

Most first-year students would get started on their Contracts Class Presentation, and would mostly leave their Criminal Law assignment until after the presentation was over.

But this means giving three weeks to an assessment item worth 10% and only one week to an assessment item worth 25%. It is better to prepare them both at the same time, as well as getting started on the Court Report and making summary notes for the Torts Mid-Semester exam.

A useful method is to break down each assignment into a set of tasks. For example:

- **Contracts Class Presentation**: read about the topic, plan what to say, prepare slides, practice, present
- **Criminal Law 1st Assignment**: identify the relevant issues in the problem, learn the elements of the relevant crime, apply the law to the facts, reach a conclusion, draft the answer, proofing, submission
- **Introduction to Law Court Report**: read the instructions, attend court, type up notes, reflect and think, drafting, references, proofing, submission
- **Torts Mid-Semester Exam**: prepare summaries of each topic, do reading on topics that do not make sense, do practice questions from a past exam, study the text and other readings, refine summaries, do exam

These tasks could then be scheduled into your diary for each week, through creating 'artificial deadlines'. Here might be an example of your diary for Week 2.

Monday	Tuesday	Wednesday	Thursday	Friday	Saturday	Sunday
10–11 Travelling to Uni – read Criminal text on train	9–11 Torts reading for this week	8–9 Travelling to Uni – review this week's Torts topic	Sleep in	9–5 Work part-time job	Sleep in	Day Off
11–1 Criminal Law Lecture	11–11.30 Morning tea	9–12 Torts Class	11–12 Prepare Torts summary notes from this week's topic	5–6 Practice Contracts presentation, changing some paragraphs to point form	Swim	
1–2 Lunch	11.30–1.30 Weekly Intro reading	12–1 Lunch	12–1 Travelling to Uni, reading over Contracts photocopies made in library on Wed	6–7 Criminal Law Reading for next week	Housework	
2–3 Criminal Law Tutorial	1.30–2.30 Lunch and walk, call friend for chat	1–3 Library Research: court process for Intro, Contracts topic for presentation			1–4 Work on Criminal Law Assignment – complete first full draft including references	
3–5 Introduction Seminar	2.30–4.30 Read on topic for Contracts class presentation, list unclear areas, watch YouTube video 'Giving Effective Class Presentations'	3–4 Introduction Workshop	1–3 Contracts Lecture	7–8.30 Prepare slides for presentation, rehearse presentation using slides, check timing and adjust, convert notes to points only	4–5 Torts reading for next week	
5–6 Travelling Home – more reading Criminal text on train	4.30–6 Gym	4–5 Meet with Intro study group	3–4 Contracts Tutorial		5–6 Email and chat on phone to friend	
6–8.30 Dinner and TV	6-8.30 Dinner	5–6 Meet with study group for Torts	4–5 Travelling home, listen to Ipod		6–6.30 Quick practice of presentation for Contracts	
8.30–11,00 Prepare summary notes for Criminal Law read over problem question	8.30–10.30 Read Court Report instructions and background articles	6–7 Travelling home – reading Contracts text	5–6 Prepare summary notes on Contracts	8.30 onwards: Going to party!	6.30 onwards: Getting ready and going out!	
		7–8.30 Dinner	6–8.30 Dinner			
		8.30 onwards: catching up with friend to see a movie	8.30–10.30 Plan Contracts presentation, type up, read out loud			

This diary allocates the expected amount of hours in total to University studies – 10 hours per subject per week. In this particular week, there have been more hours allocated to Contracts and Criminal Law, because of the assessment tasks soon to be due. It can be daunting to a new law student to see such a weekly schedule, and realise that the bulk of the work is done outside of class time. But it is important that you understand this early in your studies, as it can help you avoid seriously underestimating the amount of work needed to succeed in law school.

Self-management is not something you master – you will be a student of self-management for the rest of your life. There will always be things that throw us off balance, and it is just a matter of recognising when that has happened and taking steps to move back into balance. It can be useful to have people we know and respect who can identify when we are out of balance, in case we do not recognise it ourselves. For example law students can have a habit of being perfectionists – that is a positive trait, and is how you got to where you are today – but it can also be a negative trait if it means we fail to hand an assignment in on time because we are trying to make it perfect. Nothing is perfect – everything is a compromise. This is because we only have 24 hours in a day, and we all have several conflicting demands. We must make sure we produce quality work without being obsessive about it.

Understanding your personality

Psychologists have created a number of personality preference indicators that classify people according to their consistent patterns of thought, feeling and action. The most famous is the Myers Briggs Personality Type Indicator® (MBTI). It divides personalities into 16 types on four dimensions:

- **Extroverted or introverted** – whether we draw our energy from the external world, including people in groups, or internally, 'recharging our batteries' away from people.
- **Sensing or intuitive** – whether we live in the 'now' and take in information using our five senses, or whether we tend to make intuitive connections and see information with a more global, big-picture view of possibilities and dreams.
- **Thinking or feeling** – whether we make decisions based on what is logical in our head (rational thinking) or what feels right in our heart (values).
- **Judging or perceiving** – whether we make a final and snappy decision or whether we like to hold off on deciding so we can consider all the options.

Of course in practice all of us are a bit of all of those things – but most of us tend to be one or the other in each of those dimensions, most of the time. The 'TJ' combination is very common among lawyers (being logical and decisive).

Knowing the key personality dimensions can help us in our interaction with others. For example a client who is intuitive rather than sensing is likely to be impatient with step-by-step explanations. Once they have grasped the issue they feel they have the gist and do not like to have the point laboured. On the other hand, a person who weighs up evidence is more likely to appreciate a logically structured overview and an explanation that proceeds step by step. Some clients, particularly introverts, do not like being hit with sudden floods of information and then being asked to decide immediately. They may like to go away and read legal information, think about it, and make a time to meet to discuss it further. If we can detect preferences like these from clients' behaviour, we can tailor the way we provide information to them.

Knowing the key personality dimensions can also help us in managing ourselves. For example if we are strongly a thinking person, we can remind ourselves to think about how the client must be feeling, and have some empathy for their plight. If we are strongly intuitive, we can run our big-picture, novel legal arguments and law reform proposals past someone who is 'sensing', so they can help us to think through the practicalities and present hurdles that may arise.

Ethical mindset

Legal ethics is a fundamental and crucial part of being a lawyer. Acting ethically broadly means doing the right thing morally. Ethical legal professionals act honestly, are accountable, value personal, intellectual and professional integrity, and take responsibility for their actions and the impact they may have on others.

Ethical situations commonly arise in practice. For example we may come across confidential information about a company we hold shares in, and we may be tempted to use this information for our own benefit. We may have clients who ask us to lie, or to mislead the other party or the court as to certain facts or law. The challenge arises in the grey areas, where the legal practitioner is still technically within the letter of the law, but not its spirit.

Reflection

Imagine a lawyer is acting for a major Australian company that is sued by an individual who used their product and suffered loss. Is it ethical to use the knowledge that the individual has limited resources to drag out the litigation into a multitude of procedural steps so the individual eventually drops the case because they cannot afford to continue? Say the injury being complained of is a psychological one, where the person goes into a state where they cannot function if their stress levels become too great – if this knowledge was used in an aggressive manner to defend litigation brought by such a person, enforcing unreasonable requirements and timeframes, such that the person could not continue the case due to poor health – is that ethical? What about offering a small amount in settlement on the basis of immediate payment, even though you know if the individual could hold out until trial they would receive a great deal more in damages? And if the individual was not using a lawyer, and you exploited that by putting 'legalese' or jargon into your communications so they would have difficulty understanding it, would that be ethical? Where exactly should the watermark lie between what is ethical and unethical? Should there be some extent that you can, as a lawyer, negotiate in a way that achieves a tactical advantage?

No law school can guarantee that its graduates are ethical – the choice of how we act is in our own hands as lawyers. We can certainly approach colleagues or the relevant law society or institute to obtain confidential advice, but ultimately how we behave is our call, and different people may have different views on what legal ethics requires in a given situation. All law schools can do is ensure that you understand the importance of ethics, how to recognise an ethical problem when it arises, and how to deal appropriately with it. The aim is for you to have a mindset, or way of thinking, that is ethical – but ultimately the success in creating this outcome is in your hands. A student may answer an ethics test perfectly, but if they are applying purely academic reasoning without any engagement or commitment to ethics, it is unlikely that this intellectual strength will serve to identify ethical issues in practice.

A failure to act ethically in practice can have serious consequences – a finding of unsatisfactory professional conduct, which is conduct which falls below the standard expected of a lawyer, or professional misconduct, which is a more serious finding and can result in the suspension or revocation of one's ability to practise. See Chapter 12 for more information.

Diversity and social justice

People are many and varied – gender, race, religious beliefs, and cultural practices all vary across the world, and often a country's population comprises people from all over the world. The law is intended to be neutral and objective, such that everyone is equal in the eyes of the law. Often this is not achieved because of biases against marginalised groups. Therefore, it is incumbent on law professionals and law students to become conscious of biases or opinions about certain groups in society that underlie the law. and to make sure that those biases do not affect our practice of law. It means avoiding discrimination on the basis that someone has a disability, dresses differently, prays several times a day, eats restricted foods, or expresses opinions different from ours. Diversity should be cultivated at law school, including by recognising that your learning experience can be heightened by being open to discussion with people who have vastly different views from your own.

Reflection

To what extent do you believe the law caters to diversity in society? Do you believe the rule of law should apply equally to everyone? Affirmative action is an approach where the disadvantaged are given preferential treatment as a means of removing the disadvantage. For example an employer recruiting for a position where there are two equally good candidates may have a policy for hiring the female, on the basis that women are underrepresented in the relevant field. What do you think of that approach?

Appreciating diversity and supporting the rights of groups which are exposed to injustice are part of social justice. A lawyer who has a commitment to social justice believes that all individuals, in all their diversity, have equal rights, and where there is social disadvantage or inequity, lawyers should do something to address it. Social justice is about taking individual responsibility for our own actions and for our obligations towards others and society as a whole. Not all lawyers will be actively engaged on a full-time basis in public interest litigation, but they can nonetheless have a commitment to social justice. It may be as simple as recognising that a person needs legal help, and referring them to legal aid or a community law centre for advice. It may also involve recognising a litigant's language difficulties and need for interpreter assistance.

4: Success in law school

The pressure to succeed in law school can be great. Law school differentiates between students' capabilities to a much finer degree than does secondary education. Law students who have come to university directly from school are typically accustomed to being at the top of the class. At law school, everyone in the room was in the top of the class, and suddenly being 'average' can be a difficult thing to handle. This part of the chapter provides some tips and strategies for success in law school. But it's important to remember that 'success' is not always measured in marks. Involvement in extra-curricular activities, volunteer work, or even mooting can be just as important for mapping out your future.

Being productive

The competitive environment at law school means that law students can be the most over-extended group of students in any tertiary setting, and they need tools to maximise the output of their study in a limited time period. This is part of the self-management attribute discussed under heading 3 above. Here are some tips and strategies that can help you be productive.

- **Get organised** – make sure you keep a diary and a 'to do' list. At the start of semester, put important dates such as assignment due dates and exam periods in your diary. Have a folder for each subject, with notes from class, summaries from readings, and important cases under various tabs (usually by class topic). Keep your study area clean and avoid clutter – whatever is not needed you should throw out.
- **Plan and prioritise** – take a few minutes at the start of each day to plan what you will accomplish. Rank tasks according to how urgent and important they are, and do the most urgent and important first. Some things may not be of sufficient priority to do at all.
- **Speed read** – there are courses that teach a person to read quickly. The average person reads between five and seven words at a time, without realising it. Speed reading can enable a person to read several lines, or even a whole paragraph, at a time. The benefits of this in law school, where the volume of reading is enormous, are obvious. Even without a course in speed reading, you can get into the habit of skim-reading to identify important passages and slow down for them. These skills do not come overnight, and the more reading you can do, the better you become.

- **Find synergies** – when you are busy, finding synergies can mean getting several things done at once, or as the saying goes, 'killing two birds with one stone'. For example a person who walks their dog with a friend is getting not just the walk but also the social catch-up, and this is a synergy. A part-time law job that involves learning an area of law doubles up as a form of study, and that is also a synergy.
- **Block out time** – the most difficult things to get done are those with no fixed time allocation. It is easy to make sure you get to a lecture which is on between certain hours on a certain day, but what about reading a textbook? It can be useful to block out periods for things that otherwise have no specific time allocation – for example setting aside Wednesday evenings to do case summaries.
- **Snippets** – be set up to study in small snippets by having some reading material with you at all times. You will be amazed how much more you get done if you use a bus journey or the time waiting for the dentist or for a friend you are meeting somewhere. Getting five or ten minutes' worth of study done in each of these pockets can add to hours across the course of the week.
- **Study groups** – get together with other students in the same subject and divide the non-assessable work between you. If there are eight key cases that week, and you have four in your group, each of you could read and summarise two and then meet to brief each other on them, swapping written summaries of 1–2 pages.
- **Best time** – each of us has a 'most productive' time of day. Some are early risers, some like to work late at night. Everyone will remember times when they were 'in the zone' where they achieved great productivity and focus. These are our 'best times' and you can achieve a great deal of productivity if you time your study around your most efficient times. What might take you all day normally may take just a few hours when you work at your naturally most productive times.
- **Self-negotiation** – negotiate with yourself – do deals. For example you might say to yourself that you will read Chapter 5 and then go for a walk. Or you might proofread your essay and then you can watch your favourite TV show. This is a way of getting that bit extra out of yourself. Remove things that will tempt you to procrastinate, such as having your iPod on your desk, or a TV on close by. If you have blocked out time to study, try turning off your mobile phone, or if you cannot cope with that, tell callers you will ring back. The cost in terms of productivity from even a small distraction can be great, particularly when you are trying to decipher complex legal concepts.
- **Back up** – be manic about saving your work in more than one place. Three is a good number. For example you might save your draft essay on your computer, on a memory stick, and email it to yourself each time you have updated it. Many students cause themselves a lot of unnecessary work by failing to back up their work. Also, carrying all the notes for a particular subject at once is risky – what if you leave it somewhere or you have it stolen? You will have lost a great deal of work and will need to start from scratch. Why not get into the habit of typing up topic summaries?

Assessment: Legal writing

Legal writing style is distinctly different from creative writing, journalistic writing, and business reporting. The easiest way to learn about legal writing style is to read material written in it, for example in refereed law journals. The first thing you will notice is the highly structured and succinct nature of legal writing. You will also notice that the first person is rarely used in law. This means that, rather than writing 'I think that view is wrong because …' we write 'It is difficult to see how this view can be sustained in light of the fact that …'.

Colloquialisms and clichés are not used, and while occasionally legal writing may begin with a quote from a famous case, it rarely includes quotes from literature or poetry, as is common in the arts. Writing is not sensationalist – it is understated. For example we may describe something as being 'inadequate' or 'unreasonable' but we would not use the words 'ridiculous' or 'crazy', and exclamation marks are also extremely rare.

Typical forms of legal writing that you will use at this stage of law school are essays, reports, case notes and simple letters of advice. Later in your studies you will learn to draft court documents and submissions, as well as lengthy research papers and theses, but we will focus below on the forms of legal writing you are likely to use in your first year of legal studies.

Essays

Legal essays follow the standard structure of essays – 'introduction – body – conclusion', but almost always also have footnotes and often, a bibliography. Headings are also used.

There are many steps in essays before actual writing. The first thing you need to do is to read and think about the question. You may need to do some initial reading or research to make sure you understand what the question is asking. Then you will need to do in-depth research and reflect on the question further. It is only when you decide your position on the topic, or what issues you believe arise that you want to analyse, that you are ready to commence writing.

The important thing to remember is that an essay is not just a summary of information found in a text. It is not merely a description. It is a coherent argument on the topic or question provided, which is supported by evidence.

It is useful to do a skeleton, which will help you stay on track when you start writing, and enable you to make sure you spend an even amount of words on the various parts of the essay. For example if you were writing an essay on whether same-sex marriages should be legal, you may create a skeleton like this:

- introduction
- legal concept of marriage
- non-marriage relationships that are recognised (e.g. de facto relationships)
- issues around the legalisation of same sex marriages
- places where such laws are in force, their experience
- analysis
- conclusion
- bibliography.

GO ONLINE
To see an example student essay, and for essay practice on the topic of the High Court.

If the essay was 2500 words, and you allowed 300 for your introduction and conclusion, you could then divide the remaining words among the five other sections. You may end up with only 350 words to discuss the legal concept of marriage, and if you bear this in mind when you are writing it will save you from falling into the trap of writing 2000 words describing marriage as a legal concept and not having enough words (or time!) to balance it out.

When writing, you will often create abbreviations to save you writing the whole title of a case, piece of legislation, or organisation. The very first place in the essay that you use the term, you must write it in full, and put the abbreviation in brackets. For example 'the United Nations (UN)'; '*Jones v Ministry for Transport and Public Utilities & Others*' (2008) 34 ULR 23 ('*Jones's case*' or the *Jones* case')'; or '*Internal Government Procurement and Contracting Act 2009* (NSW) ('the Act')'. After you have done this you can freely use the abbreviation. For example 'The *Jones* case is not consistent with the Act, and may breach UN obligations'.

Throughout the research and writing process, return to the essay topic or question. What does it ask you? To 'discuss'? To 'analyse'? To 'describe'? Does it ask you to explain, or give examples? Does it ask you to compare something with something else? Does it ask you a normative question, such as whether something should or should not be legal? Does it ask you to propose where the law on the topic area should head in the future?

Always create for yourself an artificial deadline – a deadline before the real deadline. You might pretend the essay is due the week before it is really due; that gives you plenty of time to leave it, get a clear head, and return to it with fresh eyes to fine-tune your arguments and thoroughly proofread it. Typographical errors and oversights such as leaving a stray heading on the last line of a page are unacceptable, and can distract the marker. A high distinction paper is excellent in its content and its presentation.

> **TIP**
> Creating your table of contents manually is messy and time-consuming, and usually inaccurate. Use Word to classify your headings as 'Heading 1' for main headings, 'Heading 2' for subheadings, etc. Then put the cursor where you want the Table of Contents, click on 'References' then 'Index and Tables' then 'Table of Contents' and then 'OK', and the table of contents will be automatically generated. To update, just right-click anywhere in the table.

Reports

Reports are similar to essays in that they have similar written expression, they have an introduction, body and a conclusion, they can raise and support arguments, and they have footnotes and a bibliography. But a report tends to have a summary at the beginning, often called an abstract or synopsis (similar to an executive summary in a business report), and it tends to have a table of contents, as well as numbered headings and subheadings, tables, graphs, and annexes or appendices. A common report required of first-year law students is an experiential court report. This involves students reading preparatory articles, attending court, then writing a report discussing their experiences and analysing their experience against the experiences described in the preparatory material.

Case notes

A case note is a short analytical commentary about a judicial decision. Case notes are often found in law journals, which cover cases that contribute to the development of law in a particular area. They are also routinely used in law school by students who wish to save themselves the work of reading cases twice. When they read the case, they prepare a case note. Then when they wish to refresh their understanding of the case, all they need to do is read their case note. Students also form study groups and divide the labour of preparing case notes among themselves. Case notes may also be set as an assessment task – in which case it is not appropriate to collaborate with the study group because problems of plagiarism may arise. The technique for preparing a case note, including the typical structure used, is covered in Chapter 3, because it uses concepts that we have not yet covered.

Problem questions

Solving legal problems is what lawyers do in practice (although they do tend to find a solution that best serves the interests of their client at the time). Legal problem solving in law school involves the student acting like a judge, in the sense of being neutral towards the plight of the parties. In essence, a scenario is given, and the student must identify the relevant facts, identify the relevant law, apply the law to the facts and reach a conclusion. This is known as the IRAC method because it involves:

I – Identify the **I**ssues
R – Identify the applicable legal **R**ules
A – **A**pply the law to the facts
C – Reach a **C**onclusion

If you have just one issue, you can simply go through I-R-A-C. But if you have a scenario with several issues, it is best to identify them all as the first step, then for each issue do R-A-C, and then finish up with an overall conclusion.

TIP

If you are given a problem question as an assessment during the semester, it will usually raise legal issues drawn from the law you have covered so far in the subject.

Example: IRAC in action

Let's say for example you are given the following problem question for criminal law:

> Ivan was walking home from Uni when four males approached him. He tried to keep his head down and keep walking, but one of them grabbed his bag. Another one said, 'What's the rush, buddy?' Before he knew it he was on the ground being beaten. Through the pain and fear he heard one of them say 'We'll have to finish him off, he's seen us', and another, 'Yeah, right'. As he passed out of consciousness he heard another say, 'C'mon that's a bit over the top, we're just roughing him up a bit', and another saying 'We'll do it anyway'. When Ivan awoke in hospital with broken ribs, he was told that campus security guards had spotted what was happening and came to assist him. As there were four of them and they'd run in separate directions, security managed to catch only two of them, Dale and Michael. What offences can they be charged with, and do you think they are likely to be made out?

Using the knowledge you have gained from your study of criminal law, brainstorm the issues. Here, Ivan was beaten, so that makes us think of assault.[4] He ended up with broken ribs, so it was assault that occasioned some harm to him. The intention of the attackers seemed to differ between them – three seemed content to kill him, but one seemed just to want to beat him. It is unclear which of these was Dale and which was Michael, but certainly one of them wanted to kill Ivan. There seems to be an issue of a joint criminal enterprise here. Therefore the outcome of your brainstorming is that you think the issues are assault occasioning actual bodily harm, attempted murder, and liability in a joint criminal enterprise, which you think is mainly relevant to the second issue.

You turn first to assault occasioning actual bodily harm, putting a heading to make it clear. You have the issue (I) and now you are going to do the R-A-C. You state the relevant provision of the legislation in your state or territory, and the elements of the offence. Then you need to apply each element to the factual scenario. You might reason that yes, there was an act that involved direct physical contact, because Ivan was knocked down and beaten. You may reason that it did cause actual bodily harm, because his leg was broken. You reason that there is no applicable defence, as Ivan did nothing to threaten Dale or Michael that could cause them to claim they were acting in self-defence. Now you need to state your conclusion, and based on your reasoning you would say it would be likely the charge would be made out.

Now you return to the second issue, which you give a heading and start with a sentence about attempted murder. You identify the applicable section of the applicable legislation in your state or territory, and you name the elements. You then apply these to the facts. Yes, there was enough to go beyond mere preparation – they had assaulted him, he was injured and lying on the ground, and they had the capacity to carry out the offence. At least one, if not both, of Dale or Michael had the intention to murder Ivan, as we know three of them expressed 'We'll have to finish him off, he's seen us', 'Yeah, right', and 'We'll do it anyway'. Only one said 'C'mon that's a bit over the top, we're just rustling him up a bit', which suggests he did not have the requisite intent. You are therefore only able to reach a tentative conclusion here, because you need to consider the third issue.

You create a heading to show you are moving on to discuss joint criminal enterprise. You identify the applicable section of the applicable legislation in your state or territory. You apply it to the facts, saying that clearly the four men were intending, at the outset, to approach Ivan and beat him up. This is a crime, and therefore they were in a joint criminal enterprise. You may refer here to some applicable precedents, such as cases where people go in with guns to rob a bank, and one of the robbers shoots someone, even though they had agreed nobody would get hurt. You reach a conclusion that they are all responsible for each other's actions, and you tie this back to the issue of attempted murder and consider it likely the charge would be made out with respect of both Dale and Michael.

As you have been down the branches of a few issues, now is the time to wrap it all up with a concluding sentence that answers the question. You might phrase it as, 'Therefore, the offences Dale and Michael can be charged with are attempted murder and it is likely that attempted murder would be made out'.

---

4   The terminology used for specific assault-based offences varies in the different states and territories.

Letters of advice

A letter of advice is usually used to test the ability of students to take the conclusions they have reached in a problem-solving scenario and convert them into advice to the client. Typically students are expected to write in plain English, and avoid reciting sections from legislation or passages from court judgments. It is best to think about what the client would want to know, and draft the letter accordingly. Most clients want to know where they stand legally, what their options are, and the pros and cons of each option, plus a recommended path of action. Clients might also want you to give them other kinds of advice, but you need to remember that you are pretending to be a lawyer – not a priest offering spiritual guidance, or a psychologist, or a financial planner. If you feel the client needs more than legal advice, you can put a recommendation to that effect in your letter of advice.

Letters of advice tend to have a standard structure; below is a typical example.

Joe Legal Solicitors

24 Jones Street
SOUTH YARRA VIC 3141
T (03) 9876 5432
F (03) 9876 4321

23 May 2010
Ref: AB/TH/1079845

Ms Mary Kay
13 Polite Street
CAMBERWELL VIC 3124

Re: Your Contract Dispute with Petcar Carpets Pty Ltd

Dear Ms Kay

We refer to our meeting on 20 May 2010, at which you sought our advice in relation to a contractual dispute you have with Petcar Carpets Pty Ltd. You instructed us that you ordered a handmade carpet to be made, and paid a sum of $10,000 for it. You were told it would be produced in India and shipped to your home. It has been six months and the carpet has not arrived, and you made enquiries with Petcar, who say the carpet is not yet finished. You say you are tired of waiting and want your money back.

Generally speaking, when parties enter into a contract, they are free to agree on the terms and conditions, including the price, the quantity and quality, and time for delivery. In your case, only a receipt was issued, and it did not refer to any standard terms and conditions being applicable. In the absence of a specific agreement as to delivery time, the courts will usually infer a reasonable period of time. In this case, you ordered a handmade carpet to be made in a foreign country. The court will take into consideration that handmade carpets can take up to a year for a whole family to make, and time is also needed for shipping the finished carpet. Unfortunately it is unlikely the court will conclude that the delay in providing you the carpet amounts to a breach of contract on the part of Petcar at this stage. However, if another six months passes and you are still unable to get confirmation that the carpet is complete, please contact us further and we will make representations on your behalf.

We also raise another issue that we suggest you consider. As no specific delivery terms were agreed between you and Petcar, we are concerned that if the carpet were to go astray or be damaged during the shipping process, Petcar may refuse to accept liability. We therefore recommend that you make enquiries as to insurance, in case such a situation arises.

If you would like to discuss this matter further please do not hesitate to contact me on (03) 9876 5433.

Yours sincerely

Joe Legal

Joe Legal
Partner

Assessment: Exam techniques

Law exams rarely count for 100 per cent of the assessment in a subject, but they are still very important. There are four types of exams – open book, restricted open book, closed book, and take home.

An 'open book' exam is one where students can take in as much material as they want to, be it text books, summaries, dictionaries, law reports, anything. The reason for having an open book exam is that law school typically does not test memory, but tests understanding. It is artificial to expect students to memorise legislation when in legal practice they will have legislation and reference books to refer to. But having an open book exam does not mean there is no need to study. Few marks will be earned by simply looking up the topic of each question in the text book and copying what is written in the text (indeed it may result in issues of plagiarism). The most common pitfall in an open book exam is taking in too much material. The student then wastes time looking up and reading on the topic, instead of analysing and answering the questions. Any material taken in should have post-it notes and be in folders with dividers for each topic. It is useful to think before the exam of examples from case law and contemporary life where certain key principles are applied, and make a note of them.

A 'restricted open book' exam is used to prevent students from making the error of taking too many materials into the exam. Students are allowed to take notes, which may be limited in the number of pages and may or may not allow photocopies from texts. Students may be able to take their subject materials and text books into

> **TIP**
> Check with your lecturer about the requirements for referencing in exams. Usually footnotes are not required, but it is still necessary to refer to the source of your ideas, for example by referring to the case name.

the exam. Essentially the restrictions are decided by the examiner and communicated to students ahead of time, usually in the subject outline or brief. The key to restricted open book exams is knowing your way around the notes that you take in. A good way to test their value is sitting down to a past exam and doing it under exam conditions, using only what you intend to take into the exam.

A 'closed book' exam is one where students are not allowed to take anything into the exam. These are uncommon in law. Students should condense their notes down to the very key points, and memorise those. They should also make a list of the key cases and memorise what point of law they stand for. Mnemonics are useful – these are methods to help remember things. For example if *White's* case was about a drug dealer who tried to get a court to award him damages against a client who failed to pay for his drugs, and the court held that it would not rule on an illegal contract, a way to remember what the case stood for might be to think about white being the powder of the drug or white being innocence – clean hands, an unblemished record. It is worth having a friend or family member test you on the case list before the exam, with the helper calling out the name of the case and you stating what it was about and its legal principle.

A 'take home' exam is one where the exam paper is handed out and students are given a certain amount of time (usually a few days) to complete it and hand it in. It is by definition an open book exam, because lecturers cannot control what information students access in preparing their answers. In a way, a take home exam is in between an assignment and an exam, as there is sufficient time to do research on the exact questions. The plus side is that students have time to think about their answers and edit them, and the down side is that the level of work expected by the examiner is higher than for a regular exam, and may include referencing. Even though you have time to do the exam at home, it is worth doing preliminary study and research on the expected topics. It is also important to communicate in advance to the people you live with that you are not available for that period of time, and to switch off your mobile phone while you are doing the exam. Check also that there are no scheduled distractions near the place you will sit down and do the exam, such as construction and roadworks, or loud parties.

The types of questions included in law exams tend to be essay questions, problem questions, short answer questions, and multiple choice questions.

If you get an essay question, read it carefully, then prepare a skeleton. Work out how many parts there are to the question, and divide your time for writing between them. For example if you had an essay question, 'To what extent did *Reynolds'* case change the face of intellectual property law? Discuss.' you would want to say what the state of intellectual property law was before *Reynolds'* case; what *Reynolds'* case was about; and what change it brought about. This is three sections, and if you have half an hour to answer it, allowing a few minutes to think and plan the answer, and a few minutes each for the introduction and conclusion, you have about seven minutes for each part. Being methodical like this will save you from spending 20 minutes discussing the first part and never getting to answer the question. When you have finished the answer, go back and read the question to make sure you have actually answered it fully.

TIP

Poor time management is the number one cause of failure in first-year law exams. The most perfect answers to the first half of the exam paper will mean nothing if you don't write anything for the second half. It is best to allocate time and stick to it.

> **Example: Pacing yourself in exams**
>
> Say you have a three-hour exam with three parts of equal value. That is one hour per part. If each part has two questions, that is half an hour per question. If the first question is an essay question with two parts, then, allowing for 10 of the 30 minutes for that question to be used up with reading, thinking, planning, and writing the introduction and the conclusion, you have 10 minutes per part. This may sound excessive, but if you can divide your attention according to the weight of the exam questions, you will maximise your marks in the exam overall. This takes practice, and doing past exams for practice, using this method, is the best way to prepare.

Problem questions require you to read carefully and identify important words, perhaps by underlining, highlighting, or numbering them on the exam paper. Identify the issues and answer following a standard structure, referred to in Chapters 9 and 10, and also under 'Problem questions' in this chapter.

Short-answer questions require about a paragraph-length answer; usually less than a page. They are usually presented as numbered subquestions within a part of the exam; if so, you should count them and divide your time for that part of the exam between them. Read them all before you start answering them. Write in full sentences, as if you were writing an essay, but without the introduction and conclusion. Write as succinctly as possible and try to give examples or authorities for everything you say. Don't make your short answer so short that you have not given an explanation! For example if the questions were all about whether evidence was admissible or not, and the scenario you have to comment on is 'Clive says that Ron's wife told him Todd had confessed to her that he had murdered Bob', then writing 'Inadmissible – hearsay' is not enough information. A better answer would be 'The reason this evidence would not be admissible is that it is hearsay. As stated in s 59 of the *Evidence Act*, "Evidence of a previous representation made by a person is not admissible to prove the existence of a fact that the person intended to assert by the representation". This reflects the previous common law position as set out in *Subramaniam*. There are exceptions to inadmissibility, such as incapacity or death of the person who can give first-hand evidence.'

Multiple-choice questions are uncommon, but are sometimes used as a mid-semester assessment. Read the question carefully to make sure you understand what it is asking. Sometimes multiple-choice questions are framed in the negative (such as 'Which of the following is not allowed under the *Corporations Act*?') so you should look for the 'not'. Usually with multiple-choice questions one of the options, and possibly two, are obviously wrong. This narrows the choice. If you are unsure and you are taking too much time with an answer, take a guess and move on. On the question sheet, mark an asterisk beside the ones you guessed so that if you have time you can come back to them at the end of the exam and give them more thought.

In depth: Plagiarism and its consequences

Plagiarism occurs when a person presents someone else's work as if it were their own. Plagiarism can be deliberate or inadvertent. Deliberate plagiarism includes handing in someone else's assignment as if it were your own, or getting someone else to write your assignment. Inadvertent plagiarism includes the situation where you take notes from a book early in the semester, and put them with your notes for the assignment, and when it comes to assignment time you see the notes and think they were your own. Situations where the plagiarism could be due to sloppy work or a lack of understanding of referencing requirements include where the person uses another person's exact words without using quotation marks and a footnote saying where they got the words from; where the person paraphrases someone else's words but does not footnote the source; or where a person has discussed the matter with someone in the profession or in their study group and includes that person's idea as if it were their own.

Learning proper referencing in first-year law is critical. It can protect you from committing plagiarism and thereby having your reputation and integrity called into question. Let's use an article on the consequences of plagiarism to learn more about it. It is Mary Wyburn, 'Disclosure of prior student academic misconduct in admission to legal practice: lessons for universities and the courts' (2008) 8(2) *QUTLJJ* 314. Say we reproduce part of the article, like this:

> There are various definitions of plagiarism but it is generally understood to mean the appropriation of the work (the words or ideas) of another without attribution. It is a breach of ethical principles rather than legal rules. There appears to be genuine widespread confusion about the precise parameters of the term. The definition of plagiarism adopted in university rules therefore tends to be detailed; for instance it may distinguish between intentional acts (e.g. dishonest plagiarism) and those acts done carelessly or recklessly (e.g. negligent plagiarism). The failure to clearly define plagiarism, in particular whether it requires intent, can create confusion.
>
> While the universities ensure there are detailed rules in place, the question is whether adequate time is taken in the curriculum to explain the reasons behind the rules and explore their practical application across the variety of assessment tasks students will meet in their studies.

This is plagiarism because it has taken two paragraphs from a published article and put them into a piece of work without any attribution at all (including the footnotes that were in the original article). So, what about a rewording? We could alter the text like this:

> There are several definitions of plagiarism. It is usually used to refer to the appropriation of the work of another without attribution. Arguably, it breaches ethical principles more so than legal rules. Across universities there seems to be genuine confusion about the true meaning of the term. University definitions of plagiarism tends to be detailed, and distinguish between intentional and reckless acts of plagiarism. It is argued that the failure to clearly define plagiarism has caused a great deal of confusion.

> Even though universities ensure they have detailed rules, the real issue is whether they have taken the time to explain the rules properly to the students and the reasons behind them.

This is also plagiarism because although it has moved around the sentences and paraphrased to some extent, the ideas are still not being attributed to the original author and there is no note to say footnotes have been omitted. Something more is needed:

> Mary Wyburn has identified that plagiarism is defined in various ways, differentiating for example between intentional and reckless acts that result in the use of another's words and ideas without attribution.[5] She has challenged the value of having detailed university rules on plagiarism unless 'adequate time is taken in the curriculum to explain the reasons behind the rules and explore their practical application across the variety of assessment tasks students will meet in their studies'.[6] This is particularly important in first-year law, where students already face a massive learning curve in managing their own timetable, making friends, and learning how to use University resources – all time-consuming activities.

---

5   Mary Wyburn, 'Disclosure of prior student academic misconduct in admission to legal practice: lessons for universities and the courts' (2008) 8(2) *QUT Law and Justice Journal* 314, 316.

6   Ibid, 317 (citing Terri LeClerq).

This is not plagiarism, because where there has been use of Wyburn's ideas, they have been attributed. You will notice that the first sentence, which uses her ideas but not the actual words, has been referenced at the end of the sentence. The second sentence includes actual words from Wyburn's articles in quotation marks with a reference. The final sentence brings the reader back to the argument the person is using Wyburn's article to make about first year law.

The Wyburn article also provides some useful case studies on the consequences of law student plagiarism. We encourage students to read the article in full (you can do a journal search online) or in digested form (on the Online Resource Centre), but here is a brief overview of some of the cases discussed.

1   *Re AJG*. When undertaking practical legal training, the law student copied the work of another student and, when disclosing this to the Solicitors' Board in Queensland, he said it was an isolated incident occurring during a time of stress. The Queensland Court of Appeal took into account the fact that the plagiarism took place so late in the degree, and did not consider stress to be an excusing factor for such behaviour, concluding that the student was not a fit to be a legal practitioner.

2   *Re Liveri*. A commerce law student was found by her University to have handed in a published article, with only minor amendments, as her own work for an assignment. Her previous law assignments were reviewed and two other incidents of plagiarism discovered, including another instance of using an academic's commentary as her own, and using words from a government publication without giving the source. She disclosed the findings when she sought to be admitted in New South Wales and was rejected. She then applied for admission in Queensland and was unsuccessful. Two

years later she reapplied, admitting her conduct and taking full responsibility, but she was again refused admission.

3   *In the Matter of OG, a Lawyer*. The assignments of two business law students were found to be significantly similar, and both students received a zero mark. When it came time for them to apply for admission, one of them decided to disclose the matter and was refused admission. The other initially did not disclose the matter fully, describing it as a 'misunderstanding' and saying it was minor and was not found to be plagiarism. He was consequently admitted to practice. However, he was found by the Supreme Court of Victoria to have misrepresented the true circumstances; the Court ordered that he be struck off the roll of legal practitioners.

These cases demonstrate the importance of the utmost integrity, honesty and good referencing in law school – the consequences of plagiarism being found, and receiving a finding of academic misconduct as a result, are significant.

DISCUSSION QUESTIONS

1   There can often be an imbalance of power between parties to litigation. Do you think lawyers have greater ethical obligations where their client is more powerful than the opposing lawyers' client? Why, or why not?

2   Why is lifelong learning important? Do you think it is becoming more, or less important? Why?

3   Obtain a copy of the graduate attributes statement at your place of study. What additional attributes are listed there? How do you think you can best develop those attributes across your course of study? Will you be doing anything beyond formal instruction by your lecturers?

4   Find the latest edition of the *Australian Law Journal* and read an article that interests you. Pay particular attention to the way the article is written. What do you notice about the style of writing, the structure, and other aspects?

WEBLINKS AND FURTHER READING

Behrendt, Larissa, *Achieving Social Justice: Indigenous Rights and Australia's Future*, Federation Press, Sydney (2003).

Brogan, Michael and Spencer, David, *Surviving Law School*, Oxford University Press, South Melbourne, 2nd edn (2008).

Cranston, Ross (ed), *Legal Ethics and Professional Responsibility*, Clarendon Press, Oxford (1995).

Diestler, Sherry, *Becoming a Critical Thinker: A User-Friendly Manual*, Macmillan, New York (1994).

Evans, Adrian and Palermo, Josephine, 'Australian Law Students' Values: How They Impact On Ethical Behaviour' (2005) 15 *Legal Education Review* 1.

Goleman, Daniel, *Emotional Intelligence: Why It Can Matter More Than IQ*, Bloomsbury, London (1996).

Hutchinson, Allan C, *Legal Ethics and Professional Responsibility*, Irwin Law, Toronto (1999).
Hutchinson, Ian, *52 Strategies to Work Life Balance*, Pearson Education, Melbourne (2003).
Jarvis, Peter, *Adult Education and Lifelong Learning: Theory and Practice*, Routledge, London, 3rd edn (2004).
Keyzer, Patrick, *Legal Problem Solving: A Guide For Law Students*, Butterworths, Sydney, 2nd edn (2003).
Krever, Richard, *Mastering Law Studies and Law Exam Techniques*, LexisNexis Butterworths, Sydney, 6th edn (2006).
Macken, Claire, *The Law Students' Survival Guide: 9 Steps to Law Study Success*, Lawbook Co, Sydney, 2nd edn (2009).
Melbourne University Law Review Association Inc, *Australian Guide to Legal Citation* – Electronic Edition, 3rd edn (2010), www.mulr.law.unimelb.edu.au/go/AGLC3
Roach, Steven C, *Cultural Autonomy, Minority Rights, and Globalization*, Ashgate, Aldershot, Hampshire (2005).
Statsky, William P, *Case Analysis and Fundamentals of Legal Writing*, West Publishing Co, St Paul, Minn, 4th edn (1995).
Theophanous, Andrew C, *Understanding Social Justice: An Australian Perspective*, Elikia Books, Melbourne, 2nd edn (1994).
Tierney, Stephen (ed), *Accommodating Cultural Diversity*, Ashgate, Aldershot, Hampshire (2007).
University of Technology Sydney: Law (2010), *Test your skills*, www.law.uts.edu.au/ga/exercises.html.
Watt, Robert, and Johns, Francis, *Concise Legal Research*, Federation Press, Sydney, 6th edn (2009).

ONLINE RESOURCES FOR THIS CHAPTER

The following resources are available online at www.oup.com.au/orc/cwl2e
- Activity sheet: Achieving goals
- Activity sheet: Finding motivation
- Activity sheet: Time management
- Fact sheet: Anxiety
- Fact sheet: Assertiveness
- Fact sheet: Depression
- Fact sheet: Goal setting
- Fact sheet: Motivation
- Fact sheet: Perfectionism
- Fact sheet: Stress
- Fact sheet: Work–life balance
- Answers to Inductive and deductive reasoning exercise (p.12)
- Flashcard glossary
- AGLC citation quiz
- Example of student essay
- Essay practice on the topic 'the best court is the High Court'

3

Sources:
What Is the Law Itself?

WHAT WE WILL COVER IN THIS CHAPTER:

- Key sources of law – cases and legislation
- Primary and secondary sources
- How legislation is made, amended and repealed
- The anatomy of a statute and a case
- How to write a case note
- Academic commentary as sources of law
- International conventions and treaties as sources of law

Recommended approach to learning this topic

This is a fairly straightforward chapter (except for the case note practice). Once you have read it a first time, we recommend that you explore other primary and secondary materials (discussed below). You will enjoy learning by reading on topics that interest you, so perhaps a simple web search will set you in the right direction. For example if human trafficking concerns you, you may find the Trafficking Protocol, the legislation that implements it, and cases brought against trafficking offenders, or brought by trafficking victims seeking humanitarian protection visas. Or if car racing interests you, you might want to do a search to find cases and legislation relevant to spectator safety, or to the periodic conversion of Albert Park in Melbourne into a race track. If you find the case note practice exercises difficult, it may be worth reading about ratio and obiter in Chapter 10, or even the whole of that chapter, and then coming back to the case note practice.

KEY TERMS

Assent = approval of a bill by the relevant Governor or Governor-General.

Bill = a draft piece of legislation which is proposed through parliament.

Commentary = views on law and policy expressed by persons with expertise, such as current and former judges, academics, and practitioners. Can also be official commentary, which is created by the same organisation or parliament that created the treaty or legislation.

Delegated legislation = legislation made by a non-parliamentary body or minister under power given by parliament. Includes regulations, rules, ordinances, and by-laws.

Primary legislation = an Act or statute created by parliament.

Repealed = legislation which parliament cancelled.

Royal Assent = as for 'assent' above. In some jurisdictions the term 'royal assent', to denote that assent is being made on behalf of the Queen, is still used.

Treaty = convention = a legal agreement between/among states.

1: Primary and secondary sources of law

There is a distinction between primary sources of law and secondary sources of law.[1] A *primary* source of law is a document in which you can find the law itself, such as in a case or statute. A *secondary* source of law is something that could be used, or taken into account, by those who make statutes or decide cases. These include law reform commission reports, academic commentary in law journals, and the interpretation of international treaties to which Australia is party.

Primary sources of law

There are effectively three primary sources of law:

- legislation (statutes, Acts of parliament)
- delegated legislation (rules, regulations, orders and by-laws of bodies to whom parliament has delegated authority)
- court judgments.

These sources are considered in some detail below. As delegated legislation is a type of legislation it is covered under heading 2, 'Legislation'.

Secondary sources of law

The number of secondary sources of law is not fixed, because courts and parliaments can effectively take anything into account in making law. However, the following are three common types of secondary sources:

- international law, especially treaties ratified by Australia
- law reform commission reports
- academic commentary – journal articles, books and conference papers.

Secondary sources are not 'sources' in the same sense as primary sources of law – a case or a statute *is* the law itself, but a journal article or a law reform commission report is better described as a resource for law makers than a source itself.

International law is a little more complicated. It is a primary source of law internationally, but in the domestic system the international treaty itself is a secondary source, while the domestic legislation that gives effect to the international treaty in Australia is the primary source. This will be explained further below.

Exercise: Sources practice

This exercise gives you a list of documents and asks you to identify whether each is a primary or secondary source of law in Australia.

GO ONLINE

Go online to complete the 'Sources practice' exercise.

---

1   Note that, as Chapter 9 covers Indigenous sources of law, this chapter focuses on sources of law that were received from England.

2: Legislation

GO ONLINE
For links to Acts and legislation.

Legislation, in the form of a statute, also referred to as an Act of parliament, is a primary source of law.

Legislation-making authority

Each of the nine parliaments in Australia (Commonwealth, the Australian Capital Territory, New South Wales, Northern Territory, Queensland, South Australia, Tasmania, Victoria, Western Australia) has the authority to pass legislation, and that power comes from the Australian Constitution (in the case of Federal parliament), the state constitutions (in the case of the state parliaments) and self-governing legislation (in the case of the territories). These documents are discussed in Chapter 4.

The legislation of each of the nine parliaments in Australia is an authoritative source of law. Additionally, there remain certain English statutes that were received as law in Australia and have not yet been repealed. Unless specified otherwise, a statute does not have an automatic expiry date: those statutes remain authoritative sources of law until such time as they are repealed.

One consequence of having a federation is that each individual is covered simultaneously by state or territory and federal legislation. In situations where the applicable state legislation is inconsistent with the applicable federal legislation, the federal legislation will prevail, and the state law will be invalid to the extent of the inconsistency. Commonwealth legislative supremacy is guaranteed by s 109 of the *Commonwealth Constitution*. Commonwealth Acts can, however, be invalidated where the parliament did not have the legislative power (under the Constitution) to enact the legislation. In that case, the High Court of Australia may deem the federal legislation to be invalid, which means the state legislation will apply.

Legislation as a preferred source of law

Historically there were few statutes – most law was created in England through common law courts. However, over the past two centuries the popularity of legislation as a form of law has grown, and legislation is now the dominant source of law. There has been a proliferation of legislation. Indeed, there is so much legislation that parliaments cannot cope with the workload and must delegate the power to legislate to other bodies with expertise in each particular area. Also, parliament does not have the capacity to review and update each piece of legislation every year, and legislative efforts tend to focus, particularly around election time, on topics that are of current interest to the electorate, or which will provide parliamentarians with political mileage.

Legislation has now become the preferred form of regulation in our legal system. There are several possible explanations. First, unlike courts, which have to wait for a dispute which raises particular issues of law, parliament is a self-starting agent for legal change – it can pass new legislation, or amend or repeal existing legislation, at any time. It can be proactive, where courts can only be reactive. Second, courts are retrospective, in that they are limited to resolving disputes arising from past conduct, while parliaments can make new law that has a future, or prospective, effect. Third, if there is an inconsistency between statute and common law, the statute will prevail. This is in keeping with the doctrine of parliamentary sovereignty – as parliament's key role is to make law, it prevails over law-making efforts by the courts and the executive. This is discussed further in Chapter 4.

Functions of legislation

Legislation may be used to make new law, repeal old law, or codify existing law.

Making new law may be done to override what parliament considers to be unsatisfactory common law, or to cover an emerging area which has not yet been subject to law – this happens with new technologies such as DNA testing and e-commerce, and where new issues such as cloning and space tourism arise.

Repealing old law means removing laws which are no longer necessary. These can be old statutes, or principles in old cases which are now obsolete. Parliaments can repeal whole statutes, or particular sections or parts of a statute.

Codifying existing law means bringing together the law in a particular area, which may presently be spread throughout a number of cases and statutes, into the one statute. This makes it easier for interested persons to find the law on that particular area, and it gives parliament the chance to streamline and improve the structure and operation of the law.

Creating new legislation

The process by which a bill becomes an Act of parliament is covered in Chapter 4. It essentially involves a bill being passed through both houses of parliament, except in the Australian Capital Territory, the Northern Territory and Queensland, where parliament is unicameral (one house) instead of bicameral (two houses) as in the remainder of the states and at federal level. Once it has passed through parliament, the Act goes to the Governor (or Governor-General for Commonwealth or Administrator for the Northern Territory) for assent (or, in the case of the Australian Capital Territory, by notification in the Australian Capital Territory *Gazette*).

Commencement of legislation

The general rule – for the Commonwealth, New South Wales, Victoria and Western Australia – is that legislation comes into force 28 days from the date of assent unless the legislation itself says otherwise.[2] In Tasmania, legislation comes into force 14 days from the date of assent;[3] and in Queensland, South Australia and the Northern Territory, legislation comes into force on the actual day of assent, unless

TIP
Don't confuse codifying (consolidating) legislation and creating codes. Consolidating legislation, where it results in the one Act that draws together in one place all relevant law, is a type of spring-cleaning exercise – it will soon be cluttered again by further cases that interpret the Act, and further amending Acts. *Codification* results in a code, as in criminal law in Queensland. The code encapsulates the entire law in that area definitively.

---

2   See s 5 of the *Acts Interpretation Act 1901* (Cth); s 23 of the *Interpretation Act 1987* (NSW); s 11 of the *Interpretation of Legislation Act 1984* (Vic); and s 20 of the *Interpretation Act 1984* (WA).

3   Section 9 of the *Acts Interpretation Act 1931* (Tas).

the legislation itself says otherwise.[4] In the Australian Capital Territory, legislation commences on the day after notification in the *Gazette*.[5]

This means that to determine when an Act comes into force, you usually need to check the actual wording of the statute. If it does not have a commencement provision, you need to check the date of assent, which should be stated in the Act itself, and apply the relevant rule set out above, depending on which parliament has enacted the legislation. If the statute does have a commencement provision, it will either specify an actual date upon which the legislation comes into force, or it will say that it commences on a date to be proclaimed. If the latter, you will need to check the Government *Gazette* to find out the date of proclamation.

Below are some examples of actual legislation.

Example: Unspecified commencement

Biological Control Act 1984 (Cth)

TABLE OF PROVISIONS (long title)
PART I—PRELIMINARY
1   Short title [see Note 1]
2   Interpretation
3   Biological control
4   Extension of Act to external territories
5   Saving of other laws
6   Act to bind Crown
6A Application of the Criminal Code
7   Act not limited to agricultural pests
8   Commonwealth Biological Control Authority
9   Relevant state laws
10 Delegation

As there is no specific commencement provision, this Commonwealth Act commenced 28 days from the date of assent.

---

4   *Acts Interpretation Act 1915* (SA) s 7; *Acts Interpretation Act 1965* (Qld) s 15A and *Interpretation Act 1978* (NT) s 6.

5   *Legislation Act 2001* (ACT) s 73. For further discussion on commencement of legislation see Chapter 11.

Example: Specified commencement

Offshore Minerals Act 1994 (Cth)

2   Commencement
This Act commences on the day on which it receives the Royal Assent.

As there is a specific commencement provision, we know that this Act commenced on the day specified in that provision (i.e. the same day as the date of assent).

Example: Conditional commencement

Motor Car Traders Amendment Bill 2007 (Vic)

2   Commencement
  (1) Subject to subsection (2), this Act comes into operation on a day or days to be proclaimed.
  (2) If a provision of this Act does not come into operation before 1 December 2008, it comes into operation on that day.

This means the Motor Car Traders Amendment Bill 2007 (Vic) was passed and received assent on 4 March 2008. No proclamation took place in the following eight months and so the amendments took effect on 1 December 2008, and are now incorporated into the *Motor Car Traders Act 1986* (Vic).

You can find this legislation – visit www.austlii.edu.au and click on 'Victoria' in the left column, then 'Victorian Consolidated Acts 1996-' then the letter 'M' and scroll down to 'MOTOR CAR TRADERS ACT 1986'. The Act will come up and you will see a note saying 'Version incorporating amendments as at 1 December 2008'.

TIP
Some Acts provide for different commencement dates for different parts of the Act. This may occur where the parliament wants to phase in legislation. An example was the Goods and Services Tax (GST) legislation – parliament wanted people to have time to adjust critical business systems to cope with the new structures.

Example: Anatomy of an Act

We will use the following piece of legislation as an example to show the operative parts of an Act.

Surveillance Devices Act 2004

Act No. 152 of 2004

Contents

Part 1—Preliminary
1 Short title
2 Commencement
3 Purposes
4 Relationship to other laws and matters
5 Schedule(s)
6 Definitions
7 State offence that has a federal aspect
8 External territories
9 Binding the Crown

Part 2—Warrants
Division 1—Introduction
10 Types of warrant
11 Who may issue warrants?
12 Eligible Judges
13 Nominated AAT members.

Division 2—Surveillance device warrants
14 Application for surveillance device warrant
15 Remote application

…

Schedule 1—Amendment of other legislation and transitional and saving provisions
An Act to set out the powers of Commonwealth law enforcement agencies with respect to surveillance devices, and for related purposes
[Assented to on 15 December 2004]

Part 1—Preliminary
1 Short title
   This Act may be cited as the *Surveillance Devices Act 2004*.
2 Commencement
   This Act commences on the day on which it receives the Royal Assent.
3 Purposes
   The main purposes of this Act are:
   (a) to establish procedures for law enforcement officers to obtain warrants, emergency authorisations and tracking device authorisations for the installation and use of surveillance devices in relation to criminal investigations and the location and safe recovery of children to whom recovery orders relate; and

(b) to restrict the use, communication and publication of information that is obtained through the use of surveillance devices or that is otherwise connected with surveillance device operations; and

(c) to impose requirements for the secure storage and destruction of records, and the making of reports, in connection with surveillance device operations.

…

6 Definitions

(1) In this Act:

AFP employee has the same meaning as in the *Australian Federal Police Act 1979*.

applicant for a warrant means the law enforcement officer who applies, or on whose behalf an application is made, for the warrant.

…

computer means any electronic device for storing or processing information.

…

surveillance device means:

(a) a data surveillance device, a listening device, an optical surveillance device or a tracking device; or

(b) a device that is a combination of any 2 or more of the devices referred to in paragraph (a); or

(c) a device of a kind prescribed by the regulations.

…

Part 2—Warrants

Division 1—Introduction

10 Types of warrant

(1) The following types of warrant may be issued under this Part:
(a) a surveillance device warrant;
(b) a retrieval warrant.

(2) A warrant may be issued:
(a) in respect of more than one kind of surveillance device; and
(b) in respect of more than one surveillance device of any particular kind.

11 Who may issue warrants?

Any warrant under this Part may be issued by an eligible Judge or by a nominated AAT member.

Number

Typically each Act has a number that includes the year. The example above is Act 152 of 2004. We as lawyers rarely use this information, as we tend to use the title and year of the Act, and the parliament that enacted it, for example *Surveillance Devices Act 2004* (Cth).

Date

The date the Act was assented to is usually given in square brackets, and this information is useful to check whether the Act was in force at the time of the relevant conduct or event. The above Act was assented to on 15 December 2004.

Long title

The long title states the purpose of the Act, and can be useful when interpreting the statute (discussed in Chapter 11). The long title usually begins with 'An Act to …' or 'An Act for …'. The long title of the above Act is 'An Act to set out the powers of Commonwealth law enforcement agencies with respect to surveillance devices, and for related purposes'.

Short title

The short title is usually contained in the first section of the Act, saying 'This Act may be cited as …'. See s 1 of the above Act for the short title.

Preamble

Traditionally preambles were used in international conventions, to set out the rationale and reason for developing a convention on the relevant subject matter. As the purpose of an Act is now important to interpretation, it is becoming more common to have a preamble that explains why the parliament has decided to enact legislation on the relevant topic. The above Act does not have a preamble.

Parts and divisions

In longer Acts sections may be grouped into logical parts or divisions to make it easier for the reader to follow. You can see from the contents table of the above Act that it is divided into Parts 1 and 2, and Part 2 is in turn divided into Divisions 1 and 2.

Objects or purpose section

Although many Acts have a long title which states the purpose, most new Acts have a specific objects or purpose section. These are used, for example, where an Act has several purposes, or it is not convenient to sum up the overall purpose in one sentence. See s 3 of the above Act.

Interpretation section

Most Acts, particularly long Acts, have an interpretation section, which is like a glossary in a book, or the 'key terms' section at the start of each chapter of this book. The interpretation section sets out the meaning of words used in the Act, or if it is at the beginning of a part or division of the Act, it is the meaning of words used in that part or division. See s 6 of the above Act. Occasionally the interpretation section is put at the back of the Act, in a specific schedule.

Footnotes, endnotes, and margin notes

Footnotes, endnotes and margin notes are used for the sake of explanation or to make the Act more user friendly. They are typically not a formal part of the Act,[6] but can be if the Act specifically incorporates them.

Schedules

These follow the main sections of the Act, and are usually used for detailed information in table form, or long lists. They serve a similar purpose to an appendix to a book, or an annexure to a report. The schedule to the above Act lists four other Acts that are amended by this Act, and gives the text of the newly amended sections of those Acts.

Explanatory memoranda

Another trend of parliament in an age where statutes are interpreted in the light of their purpose, and where statutes aim to be drafted in plain English language to make them comprehensible to non-lawyers, is to use explanatory memoranda. These can sometimes be as lengthy as the Act itself, and may go through, section by section, stating what is intended to be covered and giving examples. Like notes, the explanatory memorandum is not a formal part of the Act – but it may be useful as an external document (or 'extrinsic' material) to interpret its provisions.

Delegated legislation

With the power to pass primary legislation comes the power to delegate the authority to make law, and parliaments often do this where the main Act covers the law, and they want the relevant government ministry to devise suitable regulations that give effect to the Act. This is known as delegated legislation, or sometimes subordinate legislation or secondary legislation. Typical entities to which parliament delegates law-making power are the Governor-General or Governor and ministers. In practice it is the relevant government department, consulting with the Office of Parliamentary Counsel, that develops the delegated legislation and advises the Minister on its acceptance and implementation. Take for example legislation with respect to road safety. Parliament may create a statutory body such as a roads and transport authority, and may give it the power to make laws necessary or convenient to give effective application to the Act. The legislation itself may contain a section stating that no person shall operate a motor vehicle without a driver's licence, and the regulations created by the statutory body will give effect to this by creating a requirement that a certain application be made, fee be paid, and test be passed before a driver's licence is issued.

---

6   *Acts Interpretation Act 1901* (Cth) s 13(3).

> **Example: Statute and regulations**
>
> ### Designs Act 2003 (Cth)
>
> s 149 Regulations
> (1) The Governor-General may make regulations prescribing matters:
>   (a) required or permitted to be prescribed; and
>   (b) necessary or convenient to be prescribed for carrying out or giving effect to this Act; and
>   (c) necessary or convenient for the conduct of any business relating to the Designs Office.
>
> ### Designs Regulations 2004 (Cth)
>
> Made under the *Designs Act 2003*
>
> **TABLE OF PROVISIONS**
> CHAPTER 1—Introductory
>
> 1.01 Name of Regulations
> 1.02 Commencement

As you can see in the above example, the main Act at the top contains the delegation (known as an enabling provision, because they enable another entity besides parliament to make law). The resulting delegated legislation is directly below, and specifies where the power came from ('Made under the *Designs Act 2003*'). In most instances, delegated legislation is structured in a similar way to legislation.

The benefits of delegated legislation are:

- It is quicker and cheaper than going through the formal parliamentary processes.
- It reduces pressure on parliament.
- It enables more complex pieces of legislation to be created by those with specific expertise.

The criticisms of delegated legislation are:

- It is not subject to the same level of public and parliamentary scrutiny as a bill.
- It is often passed in secret and the public may not know it has been passed.
- It offends the doctrine of separation of powers because it involves government ministers (the executive) making law.
- It has traditionally been more difficult to locate than primary legislation (this is becoming easier with the Internet).
- Parliament has some oversight of delegated legislation. Typically there is a committee of members which scrutinises delegated legislation, and if in its opinion the delegated legislation is problematic – perhaps because it breaches some fundamental principle – the committee can recommend it be disallowed or

redrafted. Parliament usually has a limited time in which to disallow delegated legislation after it has been tabled in parliament. At the federal level and in New South Wales and Western Australia it is 15 days.[7]

In New South Wales, Victoria, and South Australia delegated legislation commences on the day it is made unless the delegated legislation itself provides otherwise.[8] However, federal and Australian Capital Territory delegated legislation commences on the day after registration of the legislative instrument in the legislative instruments register, unless another day is specified.[9] In Western Australia and the Northern Territory it commences on the date of publication in the *Gazette* unless the subsidiary legislation says otherwise.[10] In Queensland the instrument commences on the date on which it is made, or published in the *Gazette*, or other date specified.[11] In Tasmania the same commencement provisions apply to delegated legislation as to primary legislation.[12]

Parliament is able, at any time, to repeal delegated legislation. Also, if there is any inconsistency between a piece of delegated legislation and primary legislation, that is, between a regulation and an Act of parliament, the Act will prevail.

Amending legislation

Legislation is amended by passing a new piece of legislation that contains amendments to the older Act. Typically the title of such legislation is the same short title plus the word 'Amendment'. For example the *Native Title Act 1993* (Cth) is amended by the *Native Title Amendment Act 2007* (Cth).

There can also be 'omnibus' amending legislation, which is one Act that amends a number of different Acts. See the example below of the *Australian Citizenship (Transitionals and Consequentials) Act 2007* (Cth).

---

7 *Legislative Instruments Act 2003* (Cth) s 42; *Interpretation Act 1984* (NSW) s 41; *Interpretation Act 1984* (WA) s 42(2). In Victoria it is 18 days (*Subordinate Legislation Act 1994* (Vic) s 23(2)); in Queensland it is 14 days (*Statutory Instruments Act 1992* (Qld) s 50); in the Northern Territory it is 12 days (*Interpretation Act* (NT) s 63(9)); and in the Australian Capital Territory it is 6 days (*Legislation Act 2001* (ACT) s 65). In South Australia there is no specific time provided for disallowance, but *Acts Interpretation Act 1915* (SA) s 14A(2)(d) provides generally that the provisions in s 16 which relate to repeal of an Act also apply to the disallowance of a statutory instrument. In Tasmania there is also no specific provision in the *Acts Interpretation Act 1931* (Tas) for disallowance of legislative instruments.

8 *Interpretation Act 1984* (NSW) s 39; *Subordinate Legislation Act 1994* (Vic) s 16; *Acts Interpretation Act 1915* (SA) s 10A.

9 *Legislative Instruments Act 2003* (Cth) s 12; *Legislation Act 2001* (ACT) s 73(2).

10 *Interpretation Act 1984* (WA) s 41; *Interpretation Act* (NT) s 63.

11 *Statutory Instruments Act 1992* (Qld) s 32.

12 *Acts Interpretation Act 1931* (Tas) s 5. The relevant provision is s 9, which provides for commencement 14 days after Royal Assent unless the instrument specifies a day, in which case it commences on that day.

Repealing legislation

Some legislation is automatically repealed as a result of a 'sunset clause' in the legislation – a clause which says that the Act has force for a definite period, or until a certain date. Other legislation is repealed by a newer piece of legislation that names a certain Act or Acts and states that they are hereby repealed. An Act may also be impliedly repealed if a new piece of legislation is enacted which is inconsistent with it, such that it would be impossible for both Acts to apply. This is less common today, as parliaments attempt to avoid confusion by expressly stating if an Act is to be repealed or not.

The effect of repealing legislation is that the repealed Act no longer has force. This does not mean, however, that it is repealed from the beginning – it still was valid law for the time it was in force. This means that rights and liabilities accrued under the legislation while it was in force may still be the subject of litigation before the courts.[13] But if the legislation that repealed the former legislation is itself repealed, this does not revive the former legislation.[14]

Australian Citizenship (Transitionals and Consequentials) Act 2007 (Cth)

s 3 Schedule(s)

Each Act that is specified in a Schedule to this Act is amended or repealed as set out in the applicable items in the Schedule concerned, and any other item in a Schedule to this Act has effect according to its terms.

Schedule 1—Consequential amendments
Part 1—Amendments
Administrative Appeals Tribunal Act 1975
1   Paragraph 21AA(5)(c)
    Omit '*Australian Citizenship Act 1948*', substitute '*Australian Citizenship Act 2007*'.

---

13   See s 8 of the *Acts Interpretation Act* (Cth); s 30 of the *Interpretation Act 1987* (NSW); s 14 of the *Interpretation of Legislation Act 1984* (Vic); s 20 of the *Acts Interpretation Act 1954* (Qld); s 16 of the *Acts Interpretation Act 1985* (SA); s 37 of the *Interpretation Act 1984* (WA); s 84 of the *Legislation Act 2001* (ACT); s 16 of the *Acts Interpretation Act 1931* (Tas); and s 12 of the *Interpretation Act* (NT).

14   See s 7 of the *Acts Interpretation Act* (Cth); s 28 of the *Interpretation Act 1987* (NSW); s 14 of the *Interpretation of Legislation Act 1984* (Vic); s 19 of the *Acts Interpretation Act 1954* (Qld); s 17 of the *Acts Interpretation Act 1985* (SA); s 34 of the *Interpretation Act 1984* (WA); s 86 of the *Legislation Act 2001* (ACT); s 14 of the *Acts Interpretation Act 1931* (Tas); and s 11 of the *Interpretation Act* (NT).

> *Age Discrimination Act 2004*
> 2   Paragraph 43(2)(a)
>   Repeal the paragraph, substitute:
>   (a) the Australian Citizenship Act 2007; or
> …
> Part 2—Repeal
> *Australian Citizenship Act 1948*
> 42 The whole of the Act
>   Repeal the Act.

3: Cases

Judicial decisions – or cases, or precedents – are a source of law in our common law system. They may be common law cases (cases in which the legal principles themselves have developed across a number of decisions in an area where there was no relevant legislation on point) or they may be case law, in which courts interpret legislation. The process by which courts use previous decisions as law in a current case are discussed in Chapter 10. This chapter focuses on reading and understanding cases, which is necessary groundwork for tackling the law of precedent.

Anatomy of a case

A case (judgment) contains the following main parts:

- **Citation –** this is akin to a street address for a physical location, or a URL for a website – it is a unique identifier that should enable the holder to reach the exact case. To explain, let's use the hypothetical case of *Smith v Jones* (2009) 215 QLR 56. The parts of this citation are:
    - *Title* – this is the names of the parties. The 'v' in the title is pronounced as 'and' or 'against' not 'versus' – that is, 'Smith and Jones' (common in civil cases) or 'Crown against Jones' (common in criminal cases), not 'Smith versus Jones' like a football match. The party initiating the action is named first, and the responding party (or parties) is named second. This sounds straightforward but it can be extremely confusing. For example let's say Smith is the Plaintiff and Jones is the Defendant. If Jones then appeals the decision, the title will be *Jones v Smith*. This is because the party initiating the action is named first, and Jones initiated the appeal. If Smith again appeals from that decision, the title will become *Smith v Jones* again.
    - *Year* – this is the year the decision was reported, which is usually the same year of judgment. If the year is written in square brackets, it means the law reports it is reported in are bound by the year, so there will be a 2009 volume that you can locate. If the year is written in round brackets, it means the law reports are bound by volume, from one upwards, and there may be more than one volume in each particular year.
    - *Law Report* – this will include the name of the law reports, the volume, and the page reference. In our case, it is volume 215 of the Queensland Law Reports (QLR), at page 56.

TIP

The word 'case' can be used in different ways. When a dispute is taken to court, we call it a case, as in 'he's still wound up in that court case'. When we refer to the written judgment of a court, we often also call it a case, as in 'this principle is seen in the case of *Donoghue v Stevenson*'. Plus there are the general uses of case, such as 'in that case', and 'just in case', and 'it is a bad case of prejudgement'.

- **Court** – this includes not only the name of the relevant court, but the judge(s) who sat to hear the case. For example our case would say 'Supreme Court of Queensland' and 'Williams J', which means it was being heard before a single judge (if three judges had been listed then we would say it was being heard before a Full Court).
- **Date** – this is the date on which judgment in the case was handed down.
- **Headnote** – legal publishers arrange with lawyers (generally barristers) to write a brief note summarising the case. Usually the headnote will give a short summary of the facts, and the court's decision in the case. This is not officially part of the case itself, but is used by those who want a quick overview to see if the case is relevant, in which case they will read the whole case. It is risky to rely on the headnote alone, without satisfying yourself that the case really covers the legal point you think it does.
- **Legal representatives** – it is also common for judgments to list the main solicitor and barrister(s) who ran the case on behalf of each party. This does not usually appear in the reported judgment.
- **Judgment** – if there is only one judge, there will be only one judgment, which will start with the judge's name, for example 'Williams J: …'. If there are three judges, there may still be only one joint judgment, in which case it will begin with all of their names, for example 'Williams, Brown and Adams JJ: …'. Judgments are usually written in a logical order, with the facts, then the legal issues, the analysis and then the order that the court has made, but they tend to have few headings, and do not have an 'executive summary' or 'synopsis' at the beginning. Lengthy judgments, usually by superior courts, are increasingly written with headings, to the relief of many a lawyer and law student. Reported judgments also often have footnotes with details of sources used and cases cited. (In electronically available judgments, endnotes are used.)

Example: Anatomy of a case

Locate the main parts of the following case – citation, court, date, headnote, legal representatives and the judgment.

IN THE FEDERAL COURT OF AUSTRALIA
WESTERN AUSTRALIA DISTRICT REGISTRY   WAD 74 OF 2007
ON APPEAL FROM A SINGLE JUDGE OF THE FEDERAL COURT OF AUSTRALIA
BETWEEN: FOUAD HADDAD (ALSO KNOWN AS PHILLIP HADDAD)
           Appellant
AND: FOXTEL MANAGEMENT PTY LTD
       First Respondent
       FOXTEL CABLE TELEVISION PTY LTD
       Second Respondent
JUDGES: HEEREY, SACKVILLE and MCKERRACHER JJ
DATE OF ORDER: 22 FEBRUARY 2008
WHERE MADE: PERTH

Counsel for the Appellant: R Nash
Solicitor for the Appellant: Appellant in person
Counsel for the Respondent: R Cobden SC
Solicitors for the Respondent: Gilbert & Tobin
Date of Hearing: 15 February 2008
Date of Judgment: 22 February 2008

Haddad v Foxtel Management Pty Ltd

[2008] FCAFC 11

THE COURT ORDERS THAT:

1   The appeal is dismissed with costs.

REASONS FOR JUDGMENT

HEEREY and MCKERRACHER JJ:

1   The appellant, along with others, was found to have been involved in the commission of flagrant breaches of Pt VAA of the *Copyright Act 1968* (Cth) by unauthorised use of Foxtel smartcards: *Foxtel Management Pty Limited v The Mod Shop Pty Limited* [2007] FCA 463.

2   The sole ground of appeal is the argument that Foxtel did not make an 'encoded broadcast' within the meaning of s 135AL of the *Copyright Act*. Relevantly for present purposes that definition refers to a broadcast

> ... that is made available only to persons who have the prior authorisation of the broadcaster and *only on payment by such persons of subscription fees* (whether periodically or otherwise). (emphasis added)

3   The evidence was that Foxtel made its broadcasts available without charge to certain of its employees and contractors, to certain 'complimentary account holders', being (i) persons with senior roles within Foxtel's shareholder corporations and persons with a commercial connection to Foxtel's business, and (ii) 'opinion leaders', persons whose office or position in the community was of significance to Foxtel's business. In addition, broadcasts were made available without charge to a number of unidentified charitable organizations and children's hospitals ...

6   The short answer of Foxtel, with which we agree, is that to have an 'encoded broadcast' there must first be a 'broadcast'. The latter term is defined in s 10(1) to mean

> ... a communication *to the public* delivered by a *broadcasting service* within the meaning of the *Broadcasting Services Act 1992*. (emphasis added)

7   In the *Broadcasting Services Act* 'broadcasting service' is defined to mean ...

8   Section 11 sets out specified categories of broadcasting services, including:
    (d) subscription broadcasting services

9   'Subscription broadcasting services' are defined in s 16 as broadcasting services that:
    (a) provide programs that, when considered in the context of the service being provided, appear to be intended to appeal to the *general public*; and
    (b) are made available to the *general public* but only on payment of subscription fees (whether periodical or otherwise); and

(c) comply with any determinations or clarifications under s 19 in relation to subscription broadcasting services. (emphasis added) …

13 In the present case, the complimentary account holders and the charitable institutions and hospitals had a rational connection or relationship with Foxtel. They were not members of the public, like, for example, all residents of a particular town. Still less were they 'the general public'. They were few in number compared with ordinary paid subscribers.

14 Parliament is not to be taken as having intended a provider of subscription broadcasting services to lose that character because it engaged in the common kind of promotional and philanthropic activities as occurred in the present case. Counsel for the appellant suggested that the hardship that would arise from his construction where Foxtel wished to provide broadcasts to children's hospitals could be overcome by charging one dollar for, say, ten years subscription. In our view, the need to resort to such an artificial device points in favour of a construction that would simply treat such bodies selected by Foxtel as not 'the public'.

15 The appeal should be dismissed with costs.

SACKVILLE J

…

27 In my opinion, the provision of the Foxtel broadcasting service to a small number of individuals selected by Foxtel on the basis of commercial or philanthropic considerations, also cannot be said to be a communication to the public for the purposes of the definition of '*encoded broadcast*' …

28 Mr Nash argued that this construction would deprive the latter part of par (a) of the definition of '*encoded broadcast*' of any meaning. In my view, that is not so. If, for example, Foxtel allowed all residents of a particular area to subscribe to its programming without charge, that would take Foxtel's programming outside the definition of '*encoded broadcast*'. The recipients of such an offer would not be selected by reason of a prior association with the broadcaster or by reason of particular characteristics that each recipient possesses individually. Rather they would be offered the service in their capacity as members of the general public. Such a conclusion would be consistent with the legislative purpose of distinguishing between the services provided by free-to-air broadcasters and subscription broadcasters.

…

30 I agree that the appeal should be dismissed, with costs.

The neutral citation is *Haddad v Foxtel Management Pty Ltd* [2008] FCAFC 11. It is a decision of the Full Court of the Federal Court, made on 22 February 2008. There is no headnote given in this version (to see a headnote you need to look up the bound law reports). There is no legal representative for the appellant as the appellant is acting as solicitor in the case himself, with Mr Nash as the barrister, and for the Respondent is Gilbert & Tobin as the solicitors and Mr Cobden (Senior Counsel) as the barrister. All judges agreed the appeal should be dismissed, but Sackville J decided to write a separate judgment showing that his reasoning was different from Heerey and McKerracher JJ.

Writing a case note

A case note has two parts – a case summary and a case analysis.

- **Case summary** – this sets out the formal details of the case, including the citation, the court, and the procedural history, along with the facts, the issues, and an outline of the court's reasoning and orders made.
- **Case analysis** – this contains comments on the case, critiquing the judgments made in the case in the context of other cases in this area, considering whether the case is likely to open up the law or narrow it, and the significance of the case when looked at from various perspectives (e.g. social, political, ethical, moral).

Tackling the task

The way you, as a student, prepare a case note will depend on your purpose in writing. If you are writing a case note for an assignment, then it should be written in an essay style, with the first part (the case summary) set out separately and the second part (the case analysis) following. If you are writing a case note for yourself, when you are reading a case for the purpose of studying for a problem question or exam, you will focus on the case summary aspect, and write your analysis in point form rather than essay style.

It is worth doing at least the case summary aspect of a case note after each and every case you read. If you do that, you will save yourself a lot of time later on, because even though the case may be clear to you when you have just finished reading it, trust us, when you have read a multitude of cases you will find they tend to blur into one another.

Even better, if you take the time to add the analysis, you will have a full case note. A good case note should mean that, 95 per cent of the time, you will not need to go back and read the case itself ever again.

The case summary

A good case summary should contain the following:

- **Citation** – this has been described above.
- **Court** – this should state the name of the court, and the judge(s) that heard the case. For example you may write 'Federal Court of Australia – Justice Tamberlin' or you may write 'High Court – full court', or 'High Court – French CJ, Gummow, Kirby, Crennan, Hayne, Heydon and Kiefel JJ'.

GO ONLINE

Go online for an annotated case note prepared by a first-year student. Before you refer to it, please read the actual decision in *Minister for Immigration* and *Citizenship v SZJXO* (2009) 238 CLR 642. Have a go at preparing your own case note, then compare yours against the one in the Online Resource Centre, taking into account the annotations by the marker.

- **Procedural history** – this will give you a snapshot of where the case has come from. For example you may write 'District court – first instance decision. Supreme Court – appeal. Supreme Court, Court of Appeal – present case'.
- **Facts** – the aim is not to include *all* the facts, only the material facts. Therefore, if a date (say, 12 April 2009) is critical to the case, include it, but otherwise just put 'in April 2009' or even 'in 2009'. It is useful to ask yourself which facts are those that ground the legal issues (why did these parties end up in court?). An example may be 'Defendant assaulted young girl. Girl refused blood transfusion on the basis she was a Jehovah's Witness. Girl would have lived if she had had a blood transfusion'.
- **Issues** – here is where you identify each of the legal issues raised in the case. It is useful to number them. For example:
  1 Did the pub owe a duty of care to ensure that noise from the premises did not disturb local residents?
  2 Did the pub's actions fall below the standard of care that could be expected in the circumstances?
  3 Should the pub be liable in damages, and if so, what for, and how much?
- **Reasoning/decision** – this is a summary of the court's reasoning in answering each of the issues identified. If there is more than one issue in the case, and you have numbered the issues, then it is useful to number the court's analysis on each of those issues. This way, if you are returning to the case note to only look at one issue, it will be easy to locate that issue and the court's analysis of it. For example:
  1 The court referred to the good neighbour principle, and the fact that pubs, if not managed effectively, can cause a great deal of nuisance and interference in residential amenity. The court held that the pub did owe a duty of care to its neighbours.
  2 The court referred to the lack of a security management program, the lack of soundproofing in the roof of the pub, and the lack of response to complaints from local residents over a two-year period, and held that these factors demonstrated that the pub's actions fell below the standard of care that was expected.
  3 The court held that, as the pain and suffering from sleep deprivation suffered by the plaintiff, a local resident, was difficult to quantify, no damages would be awarded.
- **Ratio** – the ratio of the case is the answer to the main issue in the case, and so in most instances the section above on analysis/decision will contain a statement of the ratio. However, it can be useful to restate it in as short and clear a sentence as you can, as this will help when you refer back to the case note. For example 'You take the victim as you find them, including not only physical susceptibilities but also religious convictions'.
- **Obiter** – if there was some useful discussion in passing by the court, it may be useful to refer to it here, and put in brackets the place in the judgment where the discussion can be found, in case you want to refer back to it. For example 'The majority stated that although the defendant is liable to the plaintiff to fix the damage to the plaintiff's trees as a result of mixing up which property the

defendant was booked to do gardening for, if the defendant had done a good job on the garden then he could have claimed for the cost of his services'.
- **Order** – this will simply state what was held. For example 'The appeal was dismissed, and the appellant was ordered to pay the respondent's costs'.

GO ONLINE
Go online to compare your case summary with the authors' sample.

Exercise: Case summary 1

Write a case summary on the following hypothetical case. (Focus on the summary part of a case note, rather than attempting a wider analysis at this stage.)

Lottie v Lottie

[2011] HCA 17

10 March 2011

WANG J:

This is a dispute between Mr and Mrs Lottie, arising from an alleged breach of marriage vows. The matter was brought by Mrs Lottie and was heard at first instance in the District Court at Parramatta, where Mrs Lottie was successful. Mr Lottie appealed to the Supreme Court of New South Wales against the decision, arguing that no such cause of action existed at law, people have been breaching marriage vows without consequence since time immemorial. The Supreme Court allowed the appeal. Mrs Lottie is now appealing to this court. Her application for special leave to appeal was allowed because if this cause of action is found to exist, it is likely to have a significant impact on the volume of matters being heard by the lower courts.

The facts of the matter are as follows. On 25 April 2010 Mrs Lottie awoke feeling unwell. She believed that she had food poisoning from some suspicious tasting prawns she had eaten the previous day. Symptoms included nausea, vomiting, dizziness, headache, and Mrs Lottie was running a high temperature. Mrs Lottie gave evidence before the District Court that she was 'feeling weak and ill, and in need of my husband's support'. Instead, Mr Lottie left the marital home and went to The Oaks pub to play 'two-up' with his mates.

Mr and Mrs Lottie were married on 2 March 2002, in St Anne's Church at Top Ryde. Both signed a marriage agreement, and vowed before 120 witnesses that they would love and cherish one another 'in sickness and in health'. Mrs Lottie alleged that Mr Lottie, in going to the pub with his mates on Anzac Day in 2010, had breached the agreement he had entered into on 2 March 2002, and claimed damages for that breach in the sum of $100 000. She also pleaded, in the alternative, that her husband owed her a duty of care, and was negligent in leaving her to suffer at home alone that day.

Therefore the claim was made out in contract and tort (negligence). The grounds for appeal to this court do not specify any tortious grounds, and therefore I shall only examine contractual ones.

The marriage contract, signed by both parties on 2 March 2002, was in simple wording, mainly in the form of a certificate. This court cannot rewrite the contract for the parties, it can only discover the terms initially agreed, by necessary implication from the circumstances taken as a whole.

Each party commenced their vows in the following manner: 'I [name] take you [name] to be my lawfully wedded [husband/wife] …' This is a verbal declaration of the agreement between them, and the fact that they state that they are lawfully wedded means that they intended their agreement to have the force of law. Therefore I conclude that the marriage contract included the verbally agreed vows, including, relevantly, for the parties to love and cherish one another in sickness and in health. If the parties had not used the term 'lawfully wedded' such an intention could not be found.

The next issue to decide is whether there has been a breach of that contract. Mr Lottie has given evidence that he has been working overtime for the past two months, and that the public holiday of 25 April 2010 was the first day he had had off work for this period of time. Evidence showed that his employer, the Returned Servicemen's League (RSL), is very particular about this day being a non-working day, in memory and respect for those who lost their lives in fighting for this country at war. Mr Lottie says that looking after his wife would have been a form of work, and he was mindful not to upset his employer by working on Anzac Day because he and his wife were living off one income. He says that going to the pub that day was in effect a way of cherishing his wife, and that if he had lost his job instead he would have been unable to provide for his wife's needs, for food, clothing and shelter, which in his opinion took priority to his wife's needs for emotional support. I find that Mr Lottie did breach the marriage agreement, in choosing to avoid a remote potential loss (of employment) over a proximate, real loss (of his wife's wellbeing). Of course, if his employment contract had specifically stated that 'work' included helping family members, and any such 'work' had to be declared to the employer and would result in immediate dismissal, it is unlikely a breach would have been found.

I now turn to the issue of damages. What damages flow from Mr Lottie's breach? Mrs Lottie gave evidence at the District Court that since Anzac Day 2010, she has had a strong aversion to performing her usual duties in the marriage. Her treating doctor has diagnosed her with having Aversive Non-compliant Grandiose Reactive Yunction (ANGRY). Sufferers of this syndrome tend to exhibit symptoms such as those Mrs Lottie had been experiencing, including the inability to cook, clean, or be civil towards the causing party. As a consequence, Mrs Lottie has been spending a great deal of time relieving her symptoms, including visitations to health spas, restaurants with friends, the cinema, and miscellaneous other efforts within the general heading of 'retail therapy'. She has charged her expenditures to credit cards, and has accumulated a debt of $37 000, which her counsel has pleaded is a direct loss caused by her husband's breach. Consequential losses claimed, in the sum of $63 000, are for surgery Mrs Lottie claims is necessary to restore her figure to her pre-Anzac Day 2010 state. Surgery includes liposuction, a facelift, and breast augmentation. I find that Mr Lottie's actions caused Mrs Lottie to get ANGRY, and therefore he is responsible for direct consequences in the sum of $37 000. However, I discount the claim for consequential losses to $3000, on the basis that Mrs Lottie would have experienced normal wear and tear on her body during this period anyway, and she is young enough to regain her figure with the assistance of a personal trainer rather than surgery. The figure is based on the cost of a personal trainer for a period of one year.

Accordingly I allow the appeal, and order that the Respondent pay damages in the sum of $40 000 plus costs.

GO ONLINE

Go online to compare your case summary with the authors' sample.

Exercise: Case summary 2

Write a case summary on the following real case, which has been extracted. It has since been reported in Volume 233 of the Commonwealth Law Reports at page 115.

HIGH COURT OF AUSTRALIA
GLEESON CJ
GUMMOW, KIRBY, HEYDON and CRENNAN JJ

Koompahtoo Local Aboriginal Land Council v Sanpine Pty Limited

[2007] HCA 61
13 December 2007
S221/2007

GLEESON CJ, GUMMOW, HEYDON and CRENNAN JJ

This litigation arises from the termination, or purported termination, of a joint venture agreement for the commercial development of land. On 14 July 1997, the first appellant, Koompahtoo Local Aboriginal Land Council ('Koompahtoo'), and the first respondent, Sanpine Pty Limited ('Sanpine'), entered into a joint venture agreement ('the Agreement') for the development and sale of a large area of land near Morisset, north of Sydney. The land had become vested in Koompahtoo as a result of claims made under the *Aboriginal Land Rights Act 1983* (NSW). Koompahtoo contributed the land. Sanpine, which had no other business, was the manager of the project.

Although attempts were made to obtain the approval of the relevant authorities, including necessary rezoning of the land, and although liabilities in excess of $2 million were incurred on the security of mortgages over the land, the project, which was controversial within the Koompahtoo community, which involved sensitive environmental issues, and which evidently was unattractive to financiers, never proceeded even to the initial stage of obtaining rezoning of the land. On 25 February 2003, the second appellant, Mr Lawler, was appointed as administrator of Koompahtoo. On 12 December 2003, the administrator, on behalf of Koompahtoo, terminated the Agreement. Sanpine commenced proceedings in the Supreme Court of New South Wales, seeking a declaration that the termination was invalid and that the Agreement was still on foot.

Campbell J, at first instance, formulated a preliminary question as follows:

'Whether, on the proper construction of the agreement ... the Agreement was validly terminated by [Koompahtoo] by its letter to [Sanpine] dated 12 December 2003.'

Campbell J answered that question in the affirmative and dismissed Sanpine's proceedings. The basis of Campbell J's decision was that there had been 'gross and repeated' departures by Sanpine from its obligations under the Agreement, including a 'total failure to adhere to the accounting obligations', and that, having regard to the nature of the Agreement and the consequences of the breaches, the breaches were 'sufficiently serious' to give Koompahtoo a right to terminate. The Court of Appeal of the Supreme Court of New South Wales, by majority (Giles and Tobias JJA, Bryson JA dissenting), allowed an appeal by Sanpine. For the reasons that follow, the conclusion of Campbell J was correct.

In its letter of termination, Koompahtoo claimed that the conduct of Sanpine amounted to repudiatory breach of contract. The term repudiation is used in different senses. First, it may refer to conduct which evinces an unwillingness or an inability to render substantial performance of the contract. The test is whether the conduct of one party is such as to convey to a reasonable person, in the situation of the other party, renunciation either of the contract as a whole or of a fundamental obligation under it. Secondly, it may refer to any breach of contract which justifies termination by the other party. There may be cases where a failure to perform, even if not a breach of an essential term, manifests unwillingness or inability to perform in such circumstances that the other party is entitled to conclude that the contract will not be performed substantially according to its requirements. In contractual renunciation, actions may speak louder than words.

For present purposes, there are two relevant circumstances in which a breach of contract by one party may entitle the other to terminate. The first is where the obligation with which there has been failure to comply has been agreed by the contracting parties to be essential. Such an obligation is sometimes described as a condition. In Australian law, a well-known exposition was that of Jordan CJ in *Tramways Advertising Pty Ltd v Luna Park (NSW) Ltd*. It is the common intention of the parties, expressed in the language of their contract, understood in the context of the relationship established by that contract and the commercial purpose it served, that determines whether a term is 'essential', so that any breach will justify termination.

The second relevant circumstance is where there has been a sufficiently serious breach of a non-essential term. As it is put in the eleventh edition of Treitel [*The Law of Contract*, 11th edn (2003) at 797]:

> '[T]he policy of leaning in favour of classifying stipulations as intermediate terms can be said to promote the interests of justice by preventing the injured party from rescinding on grounds that are technical or unmeritorious.'

We add that recognition that, at the time a contract is entered into, it may not be possible to say that any breach of a particular term will entitle the other party to terminate, but that some breaches of the term may be serious enough to have that consequence.

The approach of Campbell J was correct. The focus of attention should be the contract, and the nature and seriousness of the breaches. Sanpine's obligations as to dealing with joint venture funds (which were borrowed on the security of Koompahtoo's land) and maintaining proper books and accounts were of importance. On its true construction, it required Sanpine to ensure that it kept such books and accounts as would permit the affairs of the joint venture to be assessed with reasonable facility and within a reasonable time. It is difficult to resist a conclusion that such an obligation was essential. The clearest evidence of breach of that obligation was what occurred when Mr Lawler was appointed administrator. Plainly, Sanpine was unable to provide him with proper joint venture books and accounts that would permit such assessment.

The appeal should be allowed with costs. The orders of the Court of Appeal made on 2 November 2006 should be set aside and, in their place, it should be ordered that the appeal to that Court be dismissed with costs.

KIRBY J

The principle that parties should ordinarily fulfil their contractual obligations not only underpins the law of contract, but comprises a basic assumption on which our society and its economy and well-being depend. It is for that reason that strong grounds are needed to support unilateral termination of a contract.

I agree with the other members of this Court that the appeal must be allowed. In part, I agree in the reasons of Gleeson CJ, Gummow, Heydon and Crennan JJ. Nevertheless, it is important to elucidate the governing principles of the common law that are relevant to this decision. Respectfully, I prefer a statement of the common law rules different from that adopted in the joint reasons. However, the difference has no ultimate consequence for the outcome of the appeal. The appeal must be allowed. The orders of Campbell J should be restored.

The case analysis

The above case summaries are very useful when you are reading cases in a case list provided for a particular subject. You can eventually have a one- or two-page summary for each case in the list, which will be useful in revising for exams, particularly if you have added your analysis in point form.

However, if you are given a case note as an assignment, you will need to write the case summary and the case analysis in essay style. Recall that your case summary will become Part I of the case note.

Part II is the case analysis. Let's use the above hypothetical case of *Lottie v Lottie* [2011] HCA 17 (Unreported, Wang J, 10 March 2011) as an example.

Example

Writing Part II of a case note in essay form: Analysis of *Lottie v Lottie*

First, we might ask ourselves the significance of the decision. Here, it is that marriage vows are legally enforceable. To date, that has not been the case, unless the breach complained of is already proscribed in law – such as domestic violence or incest. So having a High Court decision providing damages for breach of a marriage vow, which is then binding on all courts in Australia, is very significant. You might therefore consider the impacts of the decision on the volume of cases to come before the court, on the way married couples interact, on whether the law is now quite different for domestic relationships outside of marriage (de facto or same-sex relationships) because they have not taken the legal vow, etc.

It is useful to approach the decision from various perspectives, including social, economic, political, ethical, and moral. Also look to the future – are couples more likely to edit their vows to avoid having them held contractually binding in law? Does it make it more likely that other forms of social agreement, such as regularly giving someone a lift to work, will be recognised in law? The decision does suggest that marriage partners may face situations where they cannot simultaneously comply with their various vows – here, the husband decided to avoid a (remote, potential) loss of employment over a (proximate, real) loss of his wife's wellbeing. How are married partners expected to weigh up their various obligations, and will a hierarchy of obligations be developed by the courts in future cases? Looking more broadly, does this decision represent a major break away for Australia from the approach to marriage across common law countries? Is it likely that others will follow suit in the future?

From the above reasoning, you can see that, while the case *summary* looks at the case itself, the case *analysis* looks at the decision in the light of other decisions, in the light of various perspectives and other laws and jurisdictions, and generally considers the impact and likely longer term significance of the decision.

For further practice, you could write a case note on the case example given under 'Anatomy of a case' (above). Also it is useful to search on www.austlii.edu.au for a case that you find interesting, read it and write a case note on it. The more case notes you do, the easier it becomes. You may be able to improve your results in other subjects if you read cases mentioned in class and write case notes on those as well.

4: Secondary sources

Secondary sources are documents courts may use to guide their decisions, and parliament may take into account in drafting legislation. That is, secondary sources are resources that courts and parliaments use to create *primary* sources of law. The main secondary sources are discussed below.

Law reform commission reports

Each legislature in Australia has a law reform commission or other body serving a similar commentary role. The aim is to have an expert body dedicated to considering reform of existing laws. This is particularly important where parliament is busy creating new law, and areas of law reform may need input from those with technical expertise and free from the vicissitudes of party politics.

At the federal level, the Australian Law Reform Commission (ALRC), which was established in 1975, is regulated by the *Australian Law Reform Commission Act 1996* (Cth).[15] It is an independent statutory corporation which conducts 'references' (inquiries) into areas of potential law reform at the request of the Attorney-General. It undertakes research and receives submissions, and ultimately provides a report to the Attorney-General containing recommendations for reform.

The typical process for an ALRC reference encompasses:

- Terms of reference from the Attorney-General setting out the nature and scope of the inquiry.
- Background research.
- Establishment of an expert Advisory Committee.
- Issues paper – identifies background and issues that need to be addressed.
- Consultation with and submissions from individuals and organisations.
- Discussion paper – initial findings and options for law reform.
- Consultation with and submissions from individuals and organisations.
- Final report – to the Attorney-General.

Final reports are tabled in parliament. To date the ALRC has produced 112 final reports, several of which include proposed draft legislation. The large majority of recommendations are made into law by the Federal Parliament. Although many of the topics of law reform are federal laws, the ALRC also considers areas for harmonisation of state and territory laws, to promote a national approach. Topics

---

15 Other federal law reform or review bodies, whose reports may also be used as a secondary source, include the Administrative Review Council, Australian Competition and Consumer Commission, Australian Institute of Judicial Administration, Australian Family Law Council, Australian Drug Law Reform Foundation, Copyright Law Review Committee, Council of Australian and New Zealand Law Reform Agencies, and the Judicial Conference of Australia.

that have been addressed include privacy, consumer protection, evidence, human rights and women.

Most of the states and territories have law reform bodies which follow roughly similar processes to the ALRC. In New South Wales, the New South Wales Law Reform Commission (NSWLRC) is regulated by the *Law Reform Commission Act 1967* (NSW).[16] There have been 123 reports to date, on topics such as juries, surveillance, sentencing, and the right to silence.

The Victorian Law Reform Commission (VLRC) is regulated by the *Victorian Law Reform Commission Act 2000* (Vic).[17] It has completed 12 projects to date, with reports on topics such as family violence, evidence, disputes between co-owners, assisted reproductive technology and abortion.

In Queensland, the Law Reform Commission (QLRC) was formed in 1969 and is regulated by the *Law Reform Commission Act 1968* (Qld).[18] There have been 65 reports to date, on topics such as the right against self-incrimination, de facto relationships, civil liability, and rape.

The Law Reform Commission of Western Australia (WALRC) is regulated by the *Law Reform Commission Act 1972* (WA). It has produced 99 reports to date, on topics such as homicide, sale of goods, Aboriginal customary laws, wills, and medical treatment for the dying.

In the Australian Capital Territory, the Law Reform Commission (now disbanded) was formed in 1990 with its own constitution. It made 20 reports on topics such as negligence, victims of crime, domestic violence, and peaceful assemblies. The contact point for law reform in the Australian Capital Territory is now the Safety, Policy and Regulatory Division of the Department of Justice and Community.

The Northern Territory Law Reform Committee is a non-statutory committee that advises the Attorney-General on law reform for the territory. It has produced 14 reports to date, on topics such as whistleblowers, Aboriginal customary law, sexual assault, self-defence and provocation.

In Tasmania, in 2001 the Tasmania Law Reform Institute was established by an agreement between the Tasmanian government, the University of Tasmania and the Law Society of Tasmania. There have been 11 reports to date, on topics such as bail, adoption by same sex couples, intoxication and a charter of rights for Tasmania.

---

16 Other bodies in New South Wales engaged in law reform activities, whose reports may be used as a secondary source, include the Judicial Commission of New South Wales, Justice Research Centre Law Foundation of New South Wales, Law Foundation of New South Wales and the New South Wales Privacy Committee.

17 Other bodies in Victoria engaged in law reform activities include the Office of Regulation Reform Victoria, Tax Law Improvement Project Victoria, Victorian Attorney-General's Law Advisory Council, Victorian Parliamentary Law Reform Committee, and the Victorian Scrutiny of Acts and Regulations Committee.

18 Other bodies in Queensland engaged in law reform activities include the Crime and Misconduct Commission Queensland, Queensland Criminal Justice Commission, Queensland Legal, Constitutional & Administrative Review Committee, Queensland Parliamentary Research Papers, and the Queensland Scrutiny of Legislation Committee.

South Australia's Law Reform Committee existed between 1968 and 1987, during which time it issued 84 reports on topics such as criminal records, tenancy agreements, group defamation and prisoners' rights. There is currently no law reform body in South Australia, although the Legislation and Legal Policy arm of the Attorney-General's Department does receive submissions on matters relating to law reform.

In depth: ALRC inquiry on secrecy

In 2008 the Attorney-General of Australia referred to the ALRC the issue of protection of Commonwealth information, including state secrets. It had been recognised that there were a variety of provisions providing for certain information to be kept confidential by public servants, with serious criminal penalties for unauthorised disclosure of information. The aim is to achieve a consistent approach across the federal government, striking an appropriate balance between openness and accountability, with the legitimate need for confidentiality to be maintained over some information. The current reference flows from a 2004 report of the ALRC 'Keeping Secrets: The Protection of Classified and Security Sensitive Information' (ALRC 98) and a 2008 report 'For Your Information: Australian Privacy Law and Practice' (ALRC 108).

In December 2008 an Issues Paper titled 'Review of Secrecy Laws' (Issues Paper 34) was released. In early 2009, the ALRC invited submissions from the community on the topic, including a 'National Secrecy Phone-In'. In June 2009 a Discussion Paper titled 'Review of Secrecy Laws' (Discussion Paper 74) was released containing preliminary proposals for reform. Submissions on the proposed reforms were open for a two month period, following which the ALRC drafted a final report for the Attorney-General. At the time of writing it had yet to be released.

The Discussion Paper can be downloaded from www.austlii.edu.au/au/other/alrc/publications/dp/74/. It includes 65 proposals for reform. It identifies more than 350 secrecy offences scattered across 175 pieces of legislation, and seeks to consolidate these into a single, general secrecy offence with a common set of principles to be applied. The aim is to stimulate a more open and 'pro-disclosure' culture through limiting criminal prosecution for disclosure of information to situations where harm has or is likely to be caused to a compelling public interest such as national security, defence and international relations. The intention of the person making the disclosure would be taken into account in determining the severity of the offence, and there is provision for disclosure in the public interest.

Academic commentary

Academic writings can influence the development of law – courts and parliament may refer to textbooks, journal articles and conference papers when preparing judgments or drafting legislation. Specifically, a law may have been the subject of much academic criticism, or an academic may have made specific proposals for how the law can best develop in a particular area. Academic empirical research may also be valuable in assessing the effectiveness of the law. The academic writing is not law in itself, but influences those who make law.

The three main types of academic commentary are textbooks, journal articles and conference papers:

- **Textbooks** – these are useful because, in writing them, academics attempt to bring together the relevant law on a particular topic in a succinct way. In doing so, they may label the main schools of thought, or the key principles that are applied, and they may also identify gaps and inconsistencies in the law.
- **Journal articles** – these are usually refereed articles in respectable law journals. The refereeing process involves peer review by other academics and practitioners (usually two). Review means reading and commenting on an article proposed for publication to ensure it is logically and precisely argued, has intellectual rigour in terms of the literature and theory, and makes a sound contribution to knowledge.
- **Conference papers** – academics regularly attend and speak at conferences on topics they have been researching and teaching. Usually conference papers will be given on topics of contemporary legal interest, or unsettled areas of law. They are often published, either in hard copy or online.

Example of use of academic commentary

In *Koompahtoo Local Aboriginal Land Council v Sanpine Pty Limited* [2007] HCA 61, extracted above, the majority of the High Court used a textbook on contract law to support their reasoning:

As it is put in the eleventh edition of Treitel, *The Law of Contract*, 11th edn (2003) at 797:

> '[T]he policy of leaning in favour of classifying stipulations as intermediate terms can be said to promote the interests of justice by preventing the injured party from rescinding on grounds that are technical or unmeritorious.'

International law

International law is becoming increasingly important as a source of law in a globalised world. Once the Australian government signs a treaty, or convention,[19] the next step it may take is to enact it as domestic legislation. It may do this directly, by creating an Act which names the convention, and says it has the force of law, or it may do this indirectly, by amending existing Acts to ensure they comply with the substance of the obligations in the treaty or convention. In the following example the convention has been included as a schedule to the Australian legislation.

---

19 In addition to treaties as sources of international law there is customary international law and general principles of law, but you will learn more about those if you study subjects such as public international law.

> # Example: Australia's Implementation of the Torture Convention
>
> *Crimes (Torture) Act 1988*
> Act No. 148 of 1988
>
> **Contents**
> 1 Short title
> 2 Commencement
> 3 Interpretation
> 4 Application
> 5 Effect of this Act on other laws
> 5A Application of the Criminal Code
> 6 Offence of torture
> 7 Only Australian citizens or persons present in Australia may be prosecuted
> 8 Prosecutions
> 9 Jurisdiction of courts and choice of law
> 10 Alternative verdicts
> 11 No defence of exceptional circumstances or superior orders
> 12 Section 38 of the *Judiciary Act*
> 13 Assistance under article 6 of Convention
>
> Schedule—Convention Against Torture and Other Cruel, Inhuman or Degrading Treatment or Punishment
> Notes

Internationally, as between national governments, international law is a primary source of law. Australia as a member of the United Nations and the World Trade Organisation (WTO) has made international legal commitments. This means that the Australian government may, for example, have an action brought against it by another state before the International Court of Justice of the United Nations, or the WTO Dispute Settlement Body for an alleged failure to comply with a term in an international treaty.

Domestically, international law is a secondary source of law. The primary law is the legislation that gives domestic effect to the treaty or convention. The text of the treaty itself, as well as any explanatory memoranda and international cases that apply and interpret the convention, are secondary sources which the courts may use in their own interpretation of the legislation that gives effect to the international treaty or convention.

In depth: Australia challenged internationally for measures on salmon

The World Trade Organization is a global organisation formed in 1995 for the regulation of international trade. It includes a number of agreements relating to trade in goods and services, and protection for trade-related intellectual property rights. It also includes a dispute settlement mechanism which applies to disputes between states relating to any WTO agreement. One of the agreements is the Agreement on Sanitary and Phytosanitary Measures (SPS Agreement). It recognises that some requirements for packaging and storage of goods are necessary to ensure the goods are safe for human consumption, but also recognises that some restrictions could be used as a disguised way of protecting domestic industries from foreign competition.

In *Australia – Measures Affecting the Importation of Salmon*, Canada complained about Australia's import prohibition on salmon from Canada, based on a quarantine regulation which required that fresh, chilled or frozen salmon products be 'consumer ready' (gutted, with heads removed). Australia argued their restriction was necessary to address the risk of imported salmon containing salmonella bacteria, which could be harmful to human health. However, it was held that Australia was in breach of the SPS Agreement because the measure was not based on a risk assessment. It created 'arbitrary or unjustifiable' levels of protection and resulted in 'discrimination or a disguised restriction' on trade, because these strict measures that applied to salmon were not applied to other fish products such as herring and finfish which could be equally susceptible to salmonella bacteria.

In response to this adverse decision, Australia undertook a full risk assessment on salmon, and modified quarantine legislation to provide a system for issuing permits for the import of consumer-ready salmon, herring, and finfish. This was again found to be in breach of the SPS Agreement because the requirement that salmon be 'consumer-ready' was unnecessary – there were technical and economically feasible alternative measures that were less trade restrictive but would still provide the appropriate level of protection (for example, 'special packaging'). To read more about the decision visit http://www.wto.org/english/tratop_e/dispu_e/cases_e/ds18_e.htm.

Using secondary sources

Secondary sources can be useful to you as a law student, when researching for an essay or preparing for an exam. But it is important to understand that, wherever you have the choice of citing a primary or a secondary source, you should use the primary source. Let's say for example you want to write 'In *Walton Stores (Interstate) v Maher* (1988) 164 CLR 387, the High Court held that promissory and proprietary estoppel were part of a larger principle of equitable estoppel'. This is something you can get from the case itself, and so you should read and cite the case, not some secondary source, be it the speech of a judge, a journal article, or law reform commission report. However, if you want to write what you read in your textbook, that 'The decision of *Walton Stores (Interstate) v Maher* (1988) 164 CLR 387 represents a significant moment in judicial law making in Australian legal history' then you should cite the textbook. Similarly, if you want to say what s 8 of a certain Act provides, then cite the Act, not someone else who has cited s 8, unless that person has made some comment or given some opinion on the operation of s 8.

DISCUSSION QUESTIONS

1. What do you think about the way judgments are written? For example do you think that there should be a standard format for judgments, with standard headings? Should judges have to make a summary of their decision? Should there be a limit on the length of judgments, to help reduce complexity in the law?
2. What role do law reform commission reports play in our law, and our society? Do you know of anyone who has taken the opportunity to contribute to a law reform commission report by making a submission on an issues or discussion paper?
3. What is the difference between primary and secondary sources of law?
4. Do you think international conventions to which Australia is a signatory should be capable of being applied directly in court cases, without having first to be specifically incorporated into Australian legislation? What challenges and issues would arise if this were the case?

WEBLINKS AND FURTHER READING

Charlesworth, Hilary, Chiam, Madelaine, Hovell, Devika and Williams, George, 'Deep Anxieties: Australia and the International Legal Order', (2003) 25 *Sydney Law Review* 423.

Department of the Prime Minister and Cabinet, *Legislation Handbook*, Australian Government Printing Service, (1999) current version available at www.dpmc.gov.au/guidelines/docs/legislation_handbook.rtf.

Gifford, Donald J and Gifford, Kenneth H, *How to Understand an Act of Parliament*, Lawbook Co, Sydney, 8th edn (1994).

Pearce, Dennis and Argument, Stephen, *Delegated Legislation in Australia*, LexisNexis Butterworths, Sydney, 3rd edn (2005).

ONLINE RESOURCES FOR THIS CHAPTER

The following resources are available online at www.oup.com.au/orc/cwl2e
- Answers to sources exercise (p. 43)
- Annotated sample answer to case note exercise: *Minister for Immigration and Citizenship v SZJXO* (p. 59)
- Additional sample case note, with and without annotation
- Sample answer to Case summary exercise 1: *Lottie v Lottie* (p. 61)
- Sample answer to Case summary exercise 2: *Koompahtoo Local Aboriginal Land Council v Sanpine Pty Limited* (p. 63)
- Examples of student work: case analysis and commentary
- Flashcard glossary
- Links to Acts and legislation
- Multiple choice questions

4

Legal Institutions: How Is Law Made?

WHAT WE WILL COVER IN THIS CHAPTER:

- The basic principles and structure of government in Australia
- The role that the Commonwealth and state constitutions play
- What it means to have a federal system of government
- The main arms of government responsible for making, administering and interpreting law
- How parliament makes law
- How the executive administers the law
- How the judicature interprets the law
- The role of tribunals in Australian law
- Alternatives to court: the role of negotiation, mediation and arbitration

Recommended approach to learning this topic

It may be useful preparation to do some internet surfing on the key terms on the next page. Give some thought to how those terms are used, and what you understand to be the institutions of government. Read through the chapter once, then go back and read slowly, with the documents referred to at hand for cross-reference – for a start, the *Commonwealth Constitution*, and the constitution of the state in which you are studying. If you were raised in a place with a system of government different from that in Australia, it may be worth giving some thought to the pros and cons of each system. This is because we learn more deeply when our brain is able to connect new information with existing information.

KEY TERMS

Alternative Dispute Resolution = processes, other than judicial determination, in which an impartial person assists those in dispute to resolve the issues between them (as defined by the National Alternative Dispute Resolution Advisory Council). It can also encompass informal dispute resolution such as party-to-party negotiations.

Arbitration = an adversarial process where an independent third party chosen by the parties receives the parties' submissions, and then makes a written, binding determination.

Cabinet = the decision-making group of the parliament that comprises the senior ministers of government.

Commonwealth = federal government, created by the Australian Constitution.

Constitution = a foundational document of the state and Commonwealth system of government in Australia, containing rules by which the state or federal governments must operate.

Cross-vesting = the granting, or vesting, of power in a state court to exercise Commonwealth judicial power.

Delegated legislation = law made by a body to whom parliament has delegated authority. Common forms of delegated legislation include regulations, rules, ordinances, and by-laws.

Doctrine of parliamentary supremacy = the notion that, of the three arms of government (legislature, executive and judiciary), the legislature is supreme.

Executive = the body that administers the law, ranging from government ministers and the Governor-General to public servants and police officers.

Federation = a system of government in which a national federal government rules in combination with state governments.

Judicial review = review of an executive decision by a court, to determine whether the government official had the power to make the decision or applied procedural fairness in making the decision.

Judiciary = the body of judges within a court system, also referred to as the judicature.

Jurisdiction = the power of a court to hear a particular matter.

Legislature = the law-making body, also referred to as parliament.

Mediation = a voluntary process that involves a neutral third party facilitating negotiations between disputing parties with a view to discussing, clarifying and settling disputes. Also referred to as conciliation.

Minister = responsible for a parliamentary portfolio, such as health, education and defence.

Primary legislation = statute law made by the passage of a bill through parliament.

Representative government = the government is chosen by, and represents, the people.

Responsible government = the parliament is independent and responsible to the people.

Rule of law = law is supreme and applies universally, equally and fairly.

Separation of powers = the three arms of government carry out their functions independently: parliament legislates, the executive administers the law and the judiciary interprets the law.

1: Government in Australia

The 'Commonwealth', or 'Federal', or 'Australian' government is a federal democratic constitutional monarchy – 'federal' because the states have formed a federal government with certain powers; 'democratic' because the people vote for their political representatives; 'constitutional' because the fundamental document by which government is given power is a constitution; and 'monarchy' because we have a Queen, also referred to as the Crown, as the head of state.

Several broad principles underpin the Australian government. These include the principles of representative government, responsible government, separation of powers, and the doctrines of parliamentary sovereignty and the rule of law. These are considered below.

Representative government

The origins of representative government are discussed in Chapter 8. Representative government is the notion that those people who govern are chosen by the people, and act as representatives of the people. Representative government may be contrasted with other forms of government, such as direct democracy and military dictatorship.

Responsible government

The principle of responsible government was inherited from England. It means that the Crown (the Queen) who is represented in Australia by the Governor-General, acts upon the advice of the Crown's ministers, who are in turn members of, and responsible to, parliament.

There do remain some powers which the Governor-General may exercise without being beholden to the ministers. These are known as 'reserve powers'. They include the power to appoint or dismiss a prime minister, the power to force a dissolution of the parliament, and the power to refuse to dissolve the parliament. However, in exercising a reserve power, the Governor-General ordinarily acts in accordance with conventions – established and politically accepted rules of practice. For example when appointing a prime minister under s 64 of the *Constitution*, the Governor-General must, by convention, appoint the parliamentary leader of the party or coalition of parties which has a majority of seats in the House of Representatives.

There can be circumstances, however, where there is no generally agreed convention to control the exercise of the Governor-General's reserve powers. Such a situation arose in 1975 when the Senate, which was not controlled by Prime Minister Gough Whitlam's government in the House of Representatives, blocked the passage of a Supply Bill. This effectively meant that the government would have no money to govern effectively. The Governor-General at the time was Sir John Kerr. He stepped in and dismissed Prime Minister Whitlam. Some people argue that Kerr acted properly in dismissing Whitlam, as that was consistent with a convention that a prime minister who cannot obtain supply should either seek a general election or be dismissed. Others contend that the dismissal of Whitlam breached the convention that a person who retains majority support of the House of Representatives, as Whitlam did, is entitled to remain prime minister.

Separation of powers

The principle of separation of powers is that the various powers of government should be divided between distinct arms of government, creating a balance of power so that no one arm of government holds all the power. The rationale is that humans have a tendency to abuse power, and where the power to make laws is separated from those who give effect to them and interpret them, each arm of government can act as a check on the actions of the other.

There are three main arms of government, which exercise the power to *make*, *administer* and *interpret* law. They are, respectively, the *legislature, executive,* and *judicature* (Figure 4.1). The legislature is parliament – it has the power to legislate, to make law. The executive includes ministers, the Attorney-General, the Governor-

General and public servants who develop policy and administer the law. In effect, the ministers are responsible for the decisions of the public servants administering their portfolio. The judicature is the court system, embodied in the judiciary, which interprets law in order to resolve disputes and, in the case of the High Court, to check that parliament is acting in accordance with the powers given to it in the *Constitution*.

FIGURE 4.1: THE THREE ARMS OF GOVERNMENT

Certain practices aim to ensure a separation of powers. For example members of the judiciary have security of tenure and fixed salaries. This prevents the executive or parliament from removing judges from office if they make decisions considered unfavourable, or otherwise exercising undue influence over judges by controlling their salaries. However, in practice we do not have a strict separation of powers. For example the executive appoints judges; government ministers are both part of the executive and in the parliament; parliament delegates the law-making role to the executive and the executive (and specifically the Cabinet) drafts most bills.

Doctrine of parliamentary sovereignty

Because the role of parliament is primarily to make law, parliament is supreme or sovereign over the executive and the courts in the *law-making* role, despite the separation of powers. This means that if parliament does not like the law the courts are making, or the way they are interpreting the legislation, the parliament may make new law, and this new law will override the legal principles propounded by the courts. It also means that, if the executive makes law under authority delegated by parliament, and parliament does not agree with the regulations made, parliament may override them with new legislation.

There is, however, an exception to the doctrine of parliamentary sovereignty. The High Court is given, by virtue of the *Australian Constitution*, the power to interpret the *Constitution* and to rule on whether the laws created by the Federal Parliament are within power (*intra vires*) or are outside the powers granted to the Federal Parliament in the *Constitution* (*ultra vires*). Where the High Court rules that a piece of federal legislation is invalid, Parliament cannot in turn override that decision by issuing further legislation on the point. In this matter, the High Court is supreme over the Parliament.

The rule of law

A fundamental principle of law and government is the rule of law. The nation is governed by laws, not by brute force, thuggery, or nepotism. All people are bound by the law – including the prime minister and the government. No person is above the law; it applies equally to everyone at all times.

Kable v Director of Public Prosecutions (NSW)

(1996) 189 CLR 51

Kable stabbed his wife to death and pleaded guilty to manslaughter with diminished responsibility, based on acute depression arising from a bitter custody dispute. He was sentenced to prison, and during his sentence wrote threatening letters to the carers of his two young children. As his sentence neared an end, fears grew about what he might do if released. According to longstanding legal principle, once a person has served their sentence they must be released from prison. But the New South Wales government enacted the *Community Protection Act 1994* (NSW), which stated 'The object of this Act is to protect the community by providing for the preventive detention (by order of the Supreme Court made on the application of the Director of Public Prosecutions) of Gregory Wayne Kable'. Here was the whole force of the state's law-making power being directed at one person, and it was created retrospectively, in the sense that he had already served his custody in accordance with the law in force at the time of his crime.[1] The High Court struck down the legislation for (among other things) breaching the separation of powers, namely the parliament usurping the role of the judiciary.

In depth: History of the rule of law, and its contemporary importance

The rule of law is a principle with a history dating as far back as Ancient Greece and China. In 350 BCE Socrates told a story about the consequences of disobeying law, not just for the individual but for society, inferring that one should consent to laws even if one does not personally agree with them because otherwise the rule of law is itself rendered vulnerable. His student, Plato, wrote about it being more proper that law should govern than any one individual, but if individuals are given the supreme power of law, they should only be 'guardians' and 'servants' of it. In other words, the law should apply to those who make the law as equally as those to whom it is addressed. Plato's student, Aristotle, likewise wrote about those in power being the servants of the laws. Similarly in China around the same time, Han Fei Zi and Li Si wrote that it is laws and not rulers that run the state; the law must be clearly written and made public; all people are equal before the law; laws should reward those who obey them and punish those who break them, in order to guarantee predictability of action. This way, even a weak ruler can be made strong. In England, the defining moment for the rule of law came in 1215 with the signing of the Magna Carta (see Chapter 8 for discussion).

---

1   See discussion in PA Fairall, Imprisonment Without Conviction in New South Wales: *Kable v Director of Public Prosecutions* (1995) *Sydney Law Review* 17(4) 573–80.

The rule of law was further theorised about by Samuel Rutherford in *Lex Rex* (1644), by John Locke in *Second Treatise of Government* (1690) and by the Enlightenment philosopher Montesquieu in *The Spirit of the Laws* (1748). Montesquieu based his reasoning in the fallibility of human beings, which he described as being subject to 'ignorance and error ... hurried away by a thousand impetuous passions'. Law is an avenue through which law-abiding citizens can live their lives more or less free in a stable, non-despotic government. Two centuries later A.V. Dicey, in writing on constitutional law, stated that the rule of law has three meanings: first, that the law predominates, not arbitrary power; second, that the law applies to everyone, including government officials; and third, that the law of the constitution is created by the will of the people. Have these three meanings been upheld in practice? Consider the discretionary powers the government has – does this mean we are ruled by arbitrary power not law, or is it acceptable that a law can itself confer a discretion? If a rule that applies the same to everyone, but has different levels of impact and consequence to some people, does that affect the rule of law? If our High Court takes an organic approach to interpreting the constitution, is it enough that seven people can gauge the ongoing will of the people?

Some countries are still struggling today to implement the rule of law. Take for example the post-conflict society of Sierra Leone, a West African country which experienced a brutal civil war in the late 1990s. From the time of peace in 2002 until today, efforts are being made to replace the rule of those in power with the rule of law. A challenge exists in the fact that people are accustomed that those with power will abuse it, because they can. It is also apparent that, as Han Fei Zi wrote over 2000 years ago, the laws must be clearly written and made public – in Sierra Leone the law is not readily located (existing in a combination of 19th century English statutes, Sierra Leonean statutes, and decisions from English and Sierra Leonean courts, many of which are not in the possession of the lawyers and the courts let alone the public arena). Therefore, for the rule of law to be properly applied, laws need to be readily available and understood, there needs to be a reliable mechanism for identifying and punishing breaches, and those who create, administer and enforce the law must also be seen to be bound by it.

2: Constitutions of the Commonwealth and the states

A constitution is a founding document which creates an entity and gives it certain powers. From the time of settlement in 1788 until federation in 1901 there was no Commonwealth, and no Commonwealth Constitution. There were only the Australian colonies, with their own constitutions. After federation two additional territories, the Australian Capital Territory and the Northern Territory, were created, as was the Commonwealth.[2]

---

2   See Chapter 8 for a discussion on the development of colonies as governmental states.

State constitutions

New South Wales

The *Constitution Act 1855* (NSW) established a constitution for the colony of New South Wales and a parliament comprising a Legislative Council and a Legislative Assembly. It also allowed for the Crown to separate part of the northern region of the colony to create a separate, new colony. The *Constitution Act 1902* (NSW) sets out the powers of the legislature and executive, including continuation of having a Governor of New South Wales, an Executive Council to advise the Governor and the Chief Justice of the Supreme Court.

Queensland

Letters patent in 1859 established the colony of Queensland on land which was formerly part of the colony of New South Wales. The *Constitution Act 1867* (Qld) clarified the role of the Governor of Queensland, the Legislative Council and the Legislative Assembly and in the ensuing century a number of further Acts and amendments led to the *Constitution of Queensland Act 2001* and the *Parliament of Queensland Act 2001* (Qld). One of those Acts, the *Constitution Act Amendment Act 1922* (Qld), had abolished the Legislative Council, and Queensland remains today with a unicameral system (having only one house, the Legislative Assembly).

South Australia

The *Constitution Act 1855* (SA) established a parliament comprising a Legislative Council and a House of Assembly. The *Constitution Act 1934* (SA) sets out the powers of the legislature and executive.

Tasmania

The *Constitution Act 1855* (Tas) established a parliament in what was then Van Diemen's Land, comprising a Legislative Council and a House of Assembly. The name of the colony was changed to Tasmania by an Order in Council of the British government the same year. The *Constitution Act 1934* (Tas) provides for a Governor as well as the Legislative Council and the House of Assembly.

Victoria

The *Constitution Act 1855* (Vic) established a parliament comprising a Legislative Council and a Legislative Assembly. The *Constitution Act 1975* (Vic) sets out the parliament as comprising the Queen, the Council and the Assembly, and the composition of the executive government.

Western Australia

The *Constitution Act 1890* (WA) and letters patent of the same year established a constitution for Western Australia. The *Constitution Act 1889* (WA) provides for a parliament comprising the Queen, the Legislative Council and the Legislative Assembly, and the *Constitution Acts Amendment Act 1899* (WA) sets out the powers of the executive government. Letters patent are discussed on the next page.

The territories

As federal territories, they were for many years under the control of the federal minister for federal territories.

The Australian Capital Territory

The Federal Capital Territory was created in 1911, within the territory of New South Wales, to be the site of the new federal government that had been created in 1901. The name was changed to Australian Capital Territory in 1938. The Australian Capital Territory achieved self-government in 1989, with the *Self-Government (Citation of Laws) Act 1989*. It has a unicameral system of parliament (that is, only a Legislative Assembly).

The Northern Territory

The Northern Territory achieved self-government in 1978 with the passage of the *Northern Territory (Self-Government) Act 1978* (Cth). South Australia had administered the Northern Territory until 1911, and the Commonwealth between then and 1978, during which time it was governed by ordinance.

The territory has a unicameral system of parliament, comprising a Legislative Assembly with a Chief Minister, an Executive Council and an Administrator.

The Commonwealth Constitution

The Australian Constitution was passed as part of an Act of the British Parliament in 1900, the *Commonwealth of Australia Constitution Act 1900* (Imp). The Constitution itself is contained in clause 9 of the British Act. A British Act was necessary because, before 1900, Australia was merely a collection of six self-governing British colonies and ultimate power over those colonies rested with Great Britain. The Act came into force on 1 January 1901, and at that time the Commonwealth came into being; the six colonies became the six states of Australia. Because it created a federal level of government above the states, this event is also known as federation. The Australian Constitution provides the basic rules for the government of Australia, and binds not only the Commonwealth Parliament but also the parliament of each state, and everyone living in Australia.

In addition to the Australian Constitution itself, there are other important constitutional documents:

- **Letters patent** – these are a type of legal instrument in the form of an open letter issued by the Crown on advice of the government ministers, granting an office, right, monopoly, title, or status to a person or to some entity such as a corporation. They are a rare form of legislation that can be made by the monarch without the consent of parliament, and they form part of our Constitution. For example in October 1900 Queen Victoria issued letters patent to create the office of Governor-General as her representative in Australia.
- **Statute of Westminster** – the *Statute of Westminster* 1931 (Imp) provided that new British legislation did not extend to British colonies unless they expressly consented to it. The Act also provided that it would not apply to the

Commonwealth of Australia unless it was formally adopted. This took place with the *Statute of Westminster Adoption Act 1942* (Cth). The states, preferring a potential counterbalance to Commonwealth power, did not adopt the Statute of Westminster, and so they remained for a time subject to British laws.

- **Australia Acts** – the *Australia Act 1986* was passed in equivalent forms by the Commonwealth, the states, and the United Kingdom parliament. It removed any residual power of the British parliament to pass laws with respect to Australia, as well as any right to appeal to British courts (the Privy Council). It effectively made Australia legally and constitutionally independent from Britain. Of course, the Queen retains a role, but that is as the head of state in Australia and not by virtue of being the Queen in the United Kingdom.

The first three chapters of the Commonwealth Constitution create the institutions of government – parliament, the executive, and the judicature.

Parliament

Chapter I of the Constitution creates and gives the legislative power of the Commonwealth to the Commonwealth Parliament. The Parliament comprises the Queen and the two houses of parliament – the Senate and the House of Representatives. The Senate is the upper house of Parliament, and is directly elected. There are 76 senators in total, comprising 12 senators elected from each state plus two each from the Northern Territory and the Australian Capital Territory. Senators have a six-year term. The House of Representatives is the lower house of Parliament, and is also directly elected. It has approximately twice as many members as the Senate (currently 150 members), and the number of seats held by each state depends on the state's population, although each state is guaranteed five seats. Members of Parliament have a three-year term.

Executive government

Chapter II of the Constitution vests the executive power of the Commonwealth in the Queen, to be exercised by the Governor-General as her representative. The Governor-General is also the commander in chief of the defence forces. 'Executive power' is the power to administer laws and carry out the business of government through such bodies as government departments, statutory authorities and the defence forces, and that power belongs to the executive.

Another source of executive power is the prerogative of the Crown. The Royal Prerogative is a body of customary authority, privilege, and immunity for the Crown that is recognised in common law jurisdictions that have a monarchy. Traditionally they were powers exercised by the monarch, or in Australia by the Governor-General, without parliamentary consent. But the practice is that they are now always exercised on the advice of the prime minister or the Cabinet, who is then accountable to parliament for the decision. In an emergency the Royal Prerogative could be exercised without the advice of the prime minister and the Cabinet, but this would create a constitutional crisis. Therefore, although a literal reading of the Constitution would suggest the Governor-General has extensive powers, in practice the position does not carry that weight.

Section 64 of the Constitution provides for the appointment of government ministers and departments of state to administer the government, and it also provides that government ministers must also be members of parliament. In practice they are members of the parliamentary party or coalition which holds a majority of seats in the lower house, and may themselves sit in the Senate or the House of Representatives.

Although not expressly referred to in the Constitution, the prime minister is the head of the government and a member of the House of Representatives. Also not mentioned is the principal decision-making body in the government, the Cabinet, which is composed of senior government ministers. What *is* mentioned, in s 62, is the Federal Executive Council, which is to advise the Governor-General. It is often referred to as the 'Governor-General in Council', and technically includes all past and current ministers. In practice only a small number of current ministers advise the Governor-General and get him or her to sign formal documents such as regulations and statutory appointments.

Commonwealth Judicature

Chapter III of the Commonwealth Constitution creates the Commonwealth Judicature. It vests the judicial power of the Commonwealth in the High Court of Australia, and other courts it vests with federal jurisdiction, namely the Federal Court and the Family Court.

The High Court has an appellate jurisdiction, which means it may hear appeals from all other courts, be they federal or state. The High Court also has original jurisdiction in constitutional matters. This means that cases that involve constitutional issues, requiring interpretation of the Constitution, may be brought directly before the High Court. The High Court has the power to determine whether legislation passed by the Commonwealth Parliament validly comes within one of its heads of power in s 51; if not, the High Court may declare the legislation invalid. However, the High Court's power to declare legislation invalid is limited to disputes in which such legislation is raised. The High Court does not have a general supervisory or advisory role in this regard.

There are seven High Court justices, and they are appointed by the Governor-General on the advice of the government. They serve until 70 years of age.

Rights

There is little mention of individual rights in the Commonwealth Constitution, except for a right to vote (s 41), a right to trial by jury (s 80), freedom of religion (s 116), reasonable compensation where the Crown acquires a person's property (s 51xxxi), and the right of citizens not to be discriminated against by governments in other states (s 117). There have also been some rights implied in the Constitution (these are discussed below). The very limited rights set out in the Australian Constitution, as opposed to constitutions of countries such as the USA, have led to calls for a Bill of Rights – see below.

TIP
Don't be confused when you read in different places 'federal government', 'the Australian government' and 'the Commonwealth'. They are all the same thing, as are the terms '*Federal Constitution*', '*Australian Constitution*' and '*Commonwealth Constitution*'.

Conventions and implications

There are certain conventions as to how constitutional powers are to be exercised. Conventions are usages and customs that have evolved over the decades and define the way various constitutional mechanisms operate in practice. For example although there is no mention in the Constitution of a prime minister, the convention is that the prime minister is the head of Cabinet, and the head of government. Conversely, the Governor-General has extensive powers given by the Constitution, but the convention is that he or she acts on the advice of the prime minister.

Additionally, certain implications are made – the High Court has implied certain terms into the Constitution. They are not expressly contained in the Constitution, but the High Court has ruled that they must apply by necessary implication. For example in *Dietrich v R*[3] the High Court held that, because the judiciary was created by the Constitution, it could be implied that courts should act according to the traditional role and values of courts generally, and therefore it is implied that there is a right to a fair trial (also known as the right to 'due process'). In *Australian Capital Television Pty Ltd v Commonwealth*[4] the High Court held that, because the Constitution created a representative form of government, there was an implied right to freedom of political communication, so that people could understand the issues and make an informed decision when it came time to vote.

As a consequence of constitutional conventions, along with implied rights found by the High Court, the *Australian Constitution* is subject to dynamic interpretation. It is by no means a static document.

Relationship between federal and state governments

The basic relationship between the federal and state governments is clear – states are free to govern within their territory in the manner they choose, and legislate on any topic they choose, subject to the terms of the Commonwealth Constitution. However, where an area of law comes under a head of power enumerated in the Constitution, the federal government has power to pass laws with respect to it, and, under s 109 of the Australian Constitution, any state law that is inconsistent is invalid to the extent of the inconsistency. This means that Commonwealth laws prevail over state laws.

With respect to states, the power of the Commonwealth Parliament is controlled so that no one state can be favoured over the others. For example the Commonwealth cannot tax residents in one state at a higher rate than residents in another state (s 51ii), or tax products from one state higher than products from another state (s 51iii).

The Commonwealth Parliament also has power, under s 122 of the Constitution, to make laws with respect to Australian territories.[5] In practice the Commonwealth Parliament has conferred self-government on the Australian Capital Territory and the Northern Territory and also, to a large extent, Norfolk Island.

---

3   (1993) 177 CLR 292.

4   (1992) 177 CLR 106.

5   There are currently ten territories: the Australian-Antarctic Territory, the Australian Capital Territory, the Northern Territory, Norfolk Island, Christmas Island, Cocos (Keeling) Islands, Jervis Bay, Ashmore and Cartier Islands, Coral Sea Islands, Heard and McDonald Islands.

Amending constitutions

Although the Australian Constitution began as part of a British Act of parliament, the Parliament of the United Kingdom has no power to change the Constitution. Section 128 provides that any change to the Constitution can only be approved by the people of Australia. The mechanism through which the people of Australia approve a change to the Constitution is by referendum. Once a proposed amendment has passed by majority in both houses of parliament, the people of Australia are asked to vote 'yes' or 'no' to the amendment. If the referendum achieves the approval of the majority of all voters, plus a majority in at least four of the six states, then the Constitution will be changed.

Constitutional change has proved difficult in practice – of 44 referenda held since 1901, only eight have passed. One of the challenges is that a referendum must be worded as a question with a 'yes' or 'no' answer. The 1999 referendum, for example, proposed that Australia change from a constitutional monarchy to a republic in a particular form favoured by the government. Some of those who voted against the change may not actually have been in favour of retaining a constitutional monarchy – perhaps they just did not agree with the particular model of republic that was put forward in the 'yes' or 'no' question that was posed.

Bill of rights?

Most modern systems of government have a bill, or charter of rights, as a fundamental document that sets out the protections individuals are entitled to and prohibits laws that infringe on basic freedoms and rights. Australia is the only common law country that does not have a bill of rights. As discussed above, there are limited express and implied rights. Therefore, individual rights in Australia are left in the hands of parliament and the judiciary.

There have been increasing demands for a bill of rights, especially in the aftermath of the 2020 Summit in which hundreds of Australians discussed a long-term agenda for national change in 2008. Many believe that this would secure rights, frame the parliament's drafting of bills, inform executive powers and give the courts power to infer human rights in statutory interpretation. A bill of rights is consistent with Australia's international obligations. Australia is a signatory to the *International Bill of Rights*, which includes the *Universal Declaration on Human Rights*, the *International Covenant on Civil and Political Rights*, and the *International Covenant on Economic, Social and Cultural Rights*.

In recent years some states and territories have enacted their own bills of rights – see the *Human Rights Act 2004* (ACT) and the *Charter of Human Rights and Responsibilities Act 2006* (Vic). At the federal level, a bill of rights is still a matter of debate and there are many unresolved issues, such as whether it would be legislated or proposed in a referendum, and what impact it would have on law-making.

3: Parliament's role in creating law

The law-making powers of the Federal Parliament are in sections 51 and 52 of the Constitution. Section 51 is a famous provision because it enumerates the heads of power under which the Parliament may make law. All residual power to make law remains with the states.[6] The enumerated heads of power include taxation, defence, external affairs, interstate and international trade, corporations, bankruptcy, marriage and divorce, and immigration. Although technically this means the Federal Parliament does not have power to make laws with respect to education, for example, it can exercise a degree of control by establishing requirements for universities to obtain funding. Similarly, although the Parliament has no power to make laws with respect to the environment, it can use the external affairs power to give effect to an international treaty on the environment. This was seen in operation in the *Franklin Dam* case,[7] where the Federal Parliament was able to prohibit the construction of a dam on the Franklin River in Tasmania.

How legislation is created

A proposed law, in draft form, is referred to as a bill. Typically bills are proposed by the government in power, that is, the parliamentary party or coalition of parties that holds a majority of seats in the House of Representatives. Before a bill becomes an Act of parliament, it must be passed by parliament – in bicameral legislatures, that means both the lower and the upper houses of parliament. Once the bill has been passed it typically is presented to the Governor-General (in the case of federal legislation) or the relevant Governor (in the case of state legislation), for assent. Once a bill receives assent, it becomes an Act of that parliament.

Using the federal system as an example, a bill will first be presented in the House of Representatives (also known as the Legislative Assembly), where it is read a first time. The member of parliament who proposes the bill, usually the minister responsible for a particular area of government such as health or defence, says 'I move that the bill be read a first time', and the long title of the legislation is read. This is, in most cases, a formality, and little real debate takes place on the bill at this time. Most of the debate takes place during the second reading speech. The second reading speech is where the responsible Minister outlines the rationale for the legislative changes contained in the bill, frequently highlighting key changes. The transcripts of the second reading speech debates are published in *Hansard*, and can be useful to courts in interpreting the legislation once is it passed. The bill can also go through committee stages where detailed amendments are discussed and voted upon. The third reading speech is rarely the topic of substantive debate – typically by this stage debate is on the detail of the proposed legislation as opposed to its larger purpose. The bill is voted upon, and if passed by a majority in the House of Representatives, it then goes before the Senate (known as the Legislative Council in the USA), where the process of reading speeches that took place in the House of Representatives, is repeated. If passed by a majority in the Senate, the bill is sent for assent by the Queen's representative, the Governor-General.

---

6   There are some exceptions to this, such as states being unable to impose customs duties on trade (ss 90, 92) – they cannot make laws in places where the Commonwealth is operating (s 52) and they cannot raise defence forces without Commonwealth consent (s 114).

7   *The Commonwealth v Tasmania* (1983) 158 CLR 1.

Difficulty is created where the government of the day, which holds a majority in the House of Representatives, does not hold a majority of seats in the Senate. This can create conflict between the houses as to whether or not a bill should be passed. The procedure set out in s 57 of the Constitution, for resolving irreconcilable disagreement between the two houses, involves the dissolution of both houses of parliament by the Governor-General, in what is known as a 'double dissolution'. An election is then held for both the House of Representatives and the Senate, and once constituted, a joint sitting of the two houses may be convened in order to determine whether the proposed law which led to the double dissolution should be passed.

> **Context:** The 1975 dismissal
>
> The most dramatic moment in Australian politics took place in 1975, when the Labor government of the day did not hold a majority of seats in the Senate. The Senate blocked the government's budget bills (known as 'supply' bills). The Governor-General Sir John Kerr dismissed the Labor government and the Prime Minister Gough Whitlam, and appointed a caretaker prime minister, Malcolm Fraser. Gough Whitlam was unaware that Malcolm Fraser had already been sworn in as a caretaker prime minister, and drafted a notice of motion that the House of Representatives would have confidence in him as prime minister but not Malcolm Fraser. He never had the chance to read the note to the parliament.[8] Some weeks later the double dissolution election was held and the Labor government was defeated. The dismissal was highly controversial and the Governor-General was admired by some and criticised by others for taking the action of dismissing the government.[9]

Application of federal and state legislation

Individuals living in Australia are governed simultaneously by federal and state legislation. Valid federal legislation will prevail over state legislation to the extent of any inconsistency between them, and generally such conflicts are resolved without a great deal of controversy.[10] Where a state challenges the validity of a piece of federal legislation, action is brought in the High Court.

As indicated above, the Federal Parliament only has power to make law with respect to those matters stated in s 51 of the Commonwealth Constitution. Some areas of law that are principally under state jurisdiction, such as criminal law and legal professional regulation, might be better served by a uniform national approach.

---

8   The National Archives of Australia story, 'The motion that might have saved the Whitlam government' is at www.naa.gov.au/whats-on/online/feature-exhibits/dismissal/index.aspx.

9   A transcript of a related Radio National PM program by Sabra Lane is available here: www.abc.net.au/pm/content/2008/s2270546.htm.

10 Indeed, parliamentary drafters are very careful not to create such inconsistencies. See points 113 and 114 in www.opc.gov.au/about/docs/drafting_manual.pdf.

It does not, for example, make a lot of sense that a person who has been acquitted on a murder charge in New South Wales may be retried where compelling DNA evidence later comes to light, but if that same person had been tried before a Victorian court they would be protected from retrial by the principle of double jeopardy. In these areas, and in other areas when politically convenient, there is collaboration between the federal and the state attorneys-general in an effort to create a national scheme legislation. This involves agreement on the wording of particular legislation, which is then enacted by each of the nine parliaments, with the effect that s 16 of the Tasmanian Act is the same as s 16 of the Western Australian Act, and of the Commonwealth Act, and so on.

Example: Classification of films, computer games and magazines

An example of national scheme legislation in Australia relates to the classification of publications, films and computer games through a cooperative arrangement between the states and territories known as the Commonwealth National Classification Scheme. Government ministers responsible for censorship meet to discuss the operation of the scheme and the legislation it operates under. The Office of Film and Literature Classification is the Australian government agency that administers the National Classification Scheme for all films, computer games and submittable publications that are exhibited, sold or hired in Australia. For example in relation to films, there may be classifications such as G (general viewing), M (mature audience) and R (restricted to adult viewing). If someone purchases a DVD classified as MA15+ (mature audience, fifteen years of age and over) and shows it to their family including children under fifteen, this does not make them liable to a penalty. The scheme is designed to help parents make informed decisions about what their children watch, and play, and read, and while it restricts those who sell the publications from selling them to children under the age of the relevant classification, the actual parent is not in breach of the law for not following them.

The *Classification (Publications, Films and Computer Games) Act 1995* (Cth) establishes the Classification Board and the procedures it follows to make classification decisions. A Classification Review Board is also created by the Act. The states and territories each have their own classification legislation which mirrors the Commonwealth Act and also provides for enforcement action.[11]

---

11 *Classification (Publications, Films and Computer Games) (Enforcement) Act 1995* (ACT); *Classification (Publications, Films and Computer Games) Enforcement Act 1995* (NSW); *Classification (Publications, Films and Computer Games) Enforcement Amendment (Uniform Classification) Act 2004* (NSW) (with amendments); *Classification Of Publications, Films and Computer Games Act* (NT); *Classification Of Computer Games and Images Act 1995* (Qld); *Classification Of Films Act 1991* (Qld); *Classification Of Publications Act 1991* (Qld); *Classification (Publications, Films and Computer Games) Act 1995* (SA); *Classification (Publications, Films and Computer Games) Enforcement Act 1995* (Tas); *Classification (Publications, Films and Computer Games) (Enforcement) Act 1995* (Vic); and *Classification (Publications, Films and Computer Games) Enforcement Act 1996* (WA).

4: The executive's role in administering law

What is the executive?

The executive is the arm of government that is responsible for administering laws and carrying out the business of government. Government ministers and their departments administer laws in respect of different portfolios such as health, education, aged care, and transport. Public servants – people who are employed by the government – are also part of the executive, and this includes not only bureaucrats in Canberra but also the Federal Police and armed forces.

As many students find the concept of the executive confusing, it is worth giving an example. If parliament creates a law with respect to fishing, the executive will administer that law, including creating a fisheries department, licensing fishing operators, and employing fisheries personnel to do spot inspections of individual boats to ensure they are complying with the legislation. If a person breaks the law, the executive may make an administrative decision to issue a fine, or if the matter is very serious, the police may arrest the person and bring them before the courts.

TIP
Judges 'serve the public' but it is incorrect to call them public servants. They belong to the judicial branch of government, and are not employed by the executive.

Law making by the executive

Technically, under the separation of powers doctrine, the executive does not make law. However, in practice, with the amount of legislation in existence, parliament delegates authority to the executive to make delegated legislation. In the above example, Federal Parliament may create an Act with respect to fishing,[12] and in that Act it may state that the Minister of Fisheries may make regulations necessary and convenient to give effect to the Act.

> ## Example: Aboriginal land rights legislation
>
> ### *Aboriginal Land Rights (Northern Territory) Act 1976* (Cth)
>
> 78. Regulations
> The Governor-General may make regulations, not inconsistent with this Act, prescribing all matters required or permitted by this Act to be prescribed, or necessary or convenient to be prescribed for carrying out or giving effect to this Act and, in particular, prescribing penalties, not exceeding a fine of 6 penalty units, for offences against the regulations.

---

12 Note that this is only in Australian waters beyond territorial limits, under s 52(x) of the Constitution.

> **Aboriginal Land Rights (Northern Territory) Regulations 2007 (Cth)**
>
> Select Legislative Instrument 2007 No. 184 as amended made under the *Aboriginal Land Rights (Northern Territory) Act 1976*. Prepared by the Office of Legislative Drafting and Publishing, Attorney-General's Department, Canberra.

In practice, the executive, namely the Cabinet, drafts bills. Indeed the Cabinet typically delegates the drafting to the offices of parliamentary counsel. Very rarely is a private member's bill put, and even more rarely is it passed. Legislation is endorsed by the executive and moved by the responsible minister.

The role of Attorney-General

The Commonwealth, and each of the states and territories, has an Attorney-General – a politician (usually a member of Cabinet) appointed as principal law officer. Historically the position arose because a sovereign could not appear personally in his or her own courts to plead any case affecting state interests, so it was necessary to have an attorney to plead the sovereign's case. The modern role of the Attorney-General is to give legal advice to the government, to bring and defend legal actions in the name of the Crown, to make recommendations on judicial appointments, budgetary requirements, law reform, and more generally to safeguard the administration of justice and the independence of the judiciary.

Part of the role of the Attorney-General is to maintain public confidence in justice and the rule of law. Traditionally, because judges are unable to defend themselves publicly, the Attorney-General has publicly defended the judiciary. This is typically a public relations role. For example if there is media uproar over a particular judicial decision, the Attorney-General may issue press releases or give interviews that help explain the legal basis and rationale behind the decision, or to otherwise correct inaccurate reporting of the case. There has in recent years, however, been some debate about whether it is indeed part of the Attorney-General's role to defend the judiciary. This arose as a result of the silence of former Commonwealth Attorney-General, Daryl Williams, in the face of significant attacks on the High Court. In his opinion, the role was primarily a political one, and defending the judiciary conflicted with that role. The true position remains unclear.

5: The judiciary's role in interpreting law

The judicature is the system of judges (the judiciary) and courts. The judiciary's role is to resolve disputes according to law. For the judicature to be effective, people have to consider its judgments to be relatively fair – not every judgment, but court decisions as a whole. They have to be confident that people are dealt with by the courts according to law, and not according to some ad hoc discretion. There has to be some degree of consistency between cases, so decisions in civil matters can be explained according to legal principle, and the penalty for particular criminal conduct will be approximately the same, regardless of the perpetrator's identity or the court deciding the case.

The court system

The key thing that distinguishes a court is that it has been vested by statute with judicial power – that is, the power to adjudicate disputes according to law. If there is a dispute over whether a particular body or tribunal is a court (no matter what the body calls itself), the court deciding the issue will look at whether that body has been vested with judicial power. The court in the sense used here is not the courthouse (the building). We may say we are 'going to the Supreme Court' and mean going to the courthouse, but that is the least important meaning of the word 'court'.

The court is actually the judges – individually and collectively – who embody judicial power. Collectively, the numerous individual judges who have been vested with that power are called the judiciary (also, less formally, the Bench). The judges of a particular court together constitute that particular court (its Bench). For example at the state level, the judges of the most senior court together make up the Supreme Court.

One cannot, for example, expect the court registry office to issue decisions – it is only the judges of a court who constitute that court. This is why, when lawyers address a judge in court, they say 'May it please the Court' rather than 'Thank you judge'. The judge is the embodiment of the court.

The basic function of a judge is to exercise the power of the court to adjudicate disputes that arise under law, and in doing so, interpret and declare the legal principles that underlie the rationale for the decision.

Courts administer justice, resolve disputes, interpret, create and enforce the law. In relation to each particular case, the judge or judges who constitute the court ascertain the relevant facts, the applicable law, and apply the law to the facts to reach a decision, which they issue in the form of a judgment. If necessary, the court may also order enforcement of the decision by ordering seizure of property or deductions from a person's wages. Lawyers assist the court in performing these functions by preparing documents and presenting arguments before the court detailing what they consider to be the relevant facts and the applicable law, and how they say the court should apply the law to the facts.

Jurisdiction

Jurisdiction means the power to hear a certain matter, or type of matter. Different courts have different levels of power to determine disputes. A court that has the power to resolve a particular dispute is said to have jurisdiction over it. Each court's jurisdiction is determined by the Act of parliament (or Constitution) that created the court.

There are several ways in which a court's jurisdiction may be limited:

- Sum of money in dispute – local courts have the power to hear disputes where the sum of money in dispute is less than a certain amount (e.g. $40 000 for general claims, or $80 000 for motor vehicle accidents, in the Magistrates Court of South Australia).
- Place where the property in dispute is located.
- Place of residence of the parties.
- Age of the parties – disputes involving minors may be heard, for example, in a children's court.
- Place where the offence occurred.
- The nature or type of the offence or dispute – driving offences are often heard at the local or magistrates court level, and motor vehicle accidents are often heard at the district or county court level.

The concept of jurisdiction may be expressed in various ways:

- **Original jurisdiction** – the power to hear a case when it first comes to court, at first instance. The court determines the facts and the law, and makes a decision. Most lower courts, at the local or magistrates court level, have original jurisdiction only.
- **Appellate jurisdiction** – the power to hear a case on appeal from the first instance decision, or even an appeal from an appeal in a lower court. The appeal court typically only considers issues of law – it does not reopen facts by hearing the witnesses again. Most superior courts, such as supreme courts, have both original and appellate jurisdiction.
- **Civil jurisdiction** – power to hear cases between private parties, such as contract disputes, and property disputes.
- **Criminal jurisdiction** – power to hear cases between the Crown and an accused. The extent of a court's criminal jurisdiction usually varies according to the severity of offences.
- **State jurisdiction** – a case that is brought under state law may be heard by state courts. State courts sometimes also exercise federal jurisdiction – see 'cross-vesting' below.
- **Federal jurisdiction** – a case that is brought under federal law may be heard by state courts.

The concept of jurisdiction is closely tied to the judicial hierarchy of courts, which is discussed below. Generally speaking, superior courts such as the supreme courts have more power, or broader jurisdiction, and inferior courts such as the local or magistrates courts, and district or county courts, have more limited jurisdiction, or less power. This is because traditionally an inferior court was not a court of record, meaning its decisions were not recorded and so it was difficult to locate these decisions to use as precedent, and thus only the decisions of superior courts were used. This position may be changing somewhat given that we now have the Internet and free access to decisions on AustLII, even though a website is not technically a law report. However, the decisions of magistrates remain difficult to locate.

Example: Jurisdiction of New South Wales courts

The local courts in New South Wales have jurisdiction to resolve disputes involving monetary amounts up to $60 000. They also have original jurisdiction for most minor criminal offences (referred to as 'summary offences'). The district courts in New South Wales have jurisdiction to resolve disputes involving amounts up to $750 000 and unlimited jurisdiction in motor vehicle accident claims. They can also hear more serious criminal matters (referred to as 'indictable offences'). The Supreme Court has unlimited jurisdiction in terms of the money in dispute between the parties, and handles the most serious criminal matters. It also undertakes review of administrative decisions (by the New South Wales executive).

It is not always easy to determine the exact jurisdiction of each particular court. A useful place to start is the Act of parliament that created the court, such as the *Local Court Act* or the *Federal Court of Australia Act*. But other Acts may also confer jurisdiction on a particular court to determine disputes arising under that Act. For example the Federal Court has jurisdiction conferred on it by more than 120 different statutes.

There is also some flexibility about which court exercises jurisdiction in a particular case. For example even though a case concerning a monetary sum of $30 000 will most likely be dealt with by a local or magistrates court, there is nothing to stop the plaintiff from bringing the action in the intermediate (district or county) court or even the relevant Supreme Court. However, if the fact that a case is brought before the Supreme Court means that the opposing party is subjected to higher costs of litigation, the plaintiff may be subject to an adverse order of costs (only being permitted to recover costs at the level applicable to the lower court if they win the case). Also, the Supreme Court of each state has power to remit matters to a lower state court. Conversely, if a plaintiff commences a proceeding in, for example, the District Court, and the other party believes it is better handled by another court, for example the Supreme Court, that party may make an application to the Supreme Court to have the matter transferred.

Court hierarchy

There are nine court hierarchies in Australia. Figure 4.2 shows the federal court hierarchy, and, as the state court hierarchies are similar, a single diagram (Figure 4.3) is used to show the eight hierarchies in the states and territories. The diagrams do not include tribunals or specialist courts, which will be discussed below.

Each of these courts is considered below.[13]

---

13 If you would like to read more about any of the courts discussed, see www.aija.org.au for links to each court.

FIGURE 4.2: THE FEDERAL COURT HIERARCHY

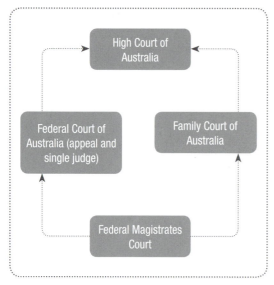

FIGURE 4.3: THE STATE COURT HIERARCHY

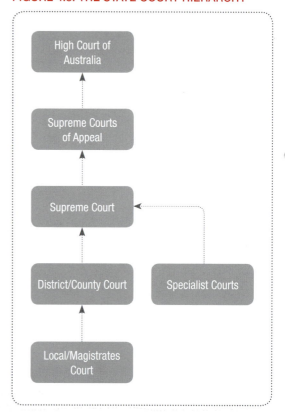

High Court of Australia

GO ONLINE
Go online for essay practice on the powers of the High Court.

The High Court sits at the apex of both the federal and the state court hierarchies. This is because it is the highest court in the country, and it may receive appeals from both state and federal courts. The High Court was created by s 71 of the Commonwealth Constitution. It has an original jurisdiction in relation to constitutional matters, and an appellate jurisdiction in federal and state matters. There are seven judges on the Court: Chief Justice French, and Justices Gummow, Hayne, Heydon, Crennan, Kiefel and Bell. Three of these judges (Crennan, Kiefel and Bell) are women. Typically a single judge will hear matters of original jurisdiction, and three or five judges will hear appeals. However, all seven judges may hear significant constitutional cases and appeals. To have an appeal heard in the High Court requires a successful application for special leave. This is heard by between one and three judges. (See 'Appeals' later in this chapter.)

Federal Court of Australia

The Federal Court of Australia was created by the *Federal Court of Australia Act 1976* (Cth). Judges are appointed to the Federal Court by the Governor-General. There is a Chief Justice and 47 judges. The Federal Court has original jurisdiction in cases concerning bankruptcy, trade practices, administrative law, corporations law and industrial law. It also has appellate jurisdiction, with the Full Court hearing appeals from single judges of the same court, and from the Federal Magistrates Court. Cases are heard before a single judge or the Full Court, consisting of at least three judges. As a court, the Federal Court may only exercise judicial power, not administrative power.[14] This means that, for example, in industrial cases the court has no power to make industrial awards (but it can enforce them).

The Family Court

The Family Court is a Federal Court created by the *Family Law Act 1975* (Cth). The Family Court was created with the aim of being less adversarial, emphasising conciliation as a means of resolving disputes, so that the parties could, for example, be assisted in coming to an agreement on shared custody of children rather than having a decision imposed upon them. It was also designed to be family friendly, with child-minding facilities and so on. Just because we have a specialist Family Court does not mean that other courts have no jurisdiction in family matters – some family matters are dealt with by state courts. The Family Court comprises a Chief Justice, Deputy Chief Justice, 33 regular judges and nine judges of the Appeal Division. There are also two Judicial Registrars who exercise delegated judicial powers in routine matters.

TIP

Western Australia has its own court, the Family Court of Western Australia, established under the *Family Court Act 1997* (WA).

The Federal Magistrates Court

The *Federal Magistrates Act 1999* (Cth) established the Federal Magistrates Court of Australia. The aim was to reduce the workload of the Federal Court, particularly in straightforward matters, and to provide a cheaper, quicker, simpler option for litigants in federal matters, to be heard without undue formality. There is a Chief Federal Magistrate and 60 magistrates across Australia.

The Federal Magistrates Court has jurisdiction in areas of administrative law, bankruptcy, consumer protection, copyright, privacy, migration, trade practices, admiralty and human rights and equal opportunity. The jurisdiction of the Federal Magistrates Court is concurrent with that of the Family Court and the Federal Court. This means that there are not any areas of jurisdiction that belong solely to Federal Magistrates Court – instead, it takes cases that would otherwise have gone before the other federal courts, but which the parties have opted to bring before it instead. Court filing fees in the Federal Magistrates Court are approximately half the cost of fees in the Federal and Family Courts, and this offers an incentive to parties.

State Supreme Courts

The Supreme Court of New South Wales was created by Letters Patent sealed in 1823 and proclaimed in 1824. Now regulated under the *Supreme Court Act 1970* (NSW), the Court has 49 Supreme Court judges plus four Associate Judges who handle less complex cases. There are two divisions – the Common Law Division and the Equity Division, each with its own Chief Judge. There is also a Court of Appeal and a Court of Criminal Appeal, which comprises the Chief Justice, a President, and 10 judges.

---

14 *Attorney-General (Cth) v R* (Boilermakers' Case) (1957) 95 CLR 529.

The Supreme Court of Victoria, established in 1852, is regulated by the *Supreme Court Act 1986* (Vic). It is divided into a Trial Division and a Court of Appeal. The Trial Division consists of the Chief Justice and 25 other judges, plus Associate Judges. It is divided into the Commercial and Equity Division (which includes a separate Commercial Court), the Common Law Division, and the Criminal Division. The Court of Appeal was created under the *Constitution (Court of Appeal) Act 1994* (Vic) and comprises the Chief Justice, the President of the Court of Appeal, and nine Judges of Appeal.

The Supreme Court of Queensland is regulated by the *Supreme Court Act 1995* (Qld). The Trial Division hears the most serious criminal cases before a jury. In civil matters involving sums in dispute over $250 000, juries are sometimes used. Appeal cases are heard before a panel of three or five judges in the Court of Appeal. There are presently 17 judges of the Trial Division, a Chief Justice, five Court of Appeal judges, a President of the Court of Appeal and a Senior Judge Administrator.

The Northern Territory Supreme Court is regulated by the *Supreme Court Act* (NT). It consists of the Chief Justice, five judges, two additional judges, two acting judges, and one Master. The Supreme Court has a Court of Appeal and a Court of Criminal Appeal, although in practice the Court does not have formal divisions, and the work of the judges is shared between them as the Chief Justice directs. The jurisdiction of the Master is governed by Rules of Court. The Court has jurisdiction in all matters, civil and criminal, which are not expressly excluded by statute.

The Supreme Court of Western Australia is regulated by the *Supreme Court Act 1935* (WA). It is comprised of a Chief Justice, 20 judges, a Master and nine registrars. It also has a Court of Appeal. Like other Supreme Courts, the Supreme Court of Western Australia has unlimited jurisdiction in civil matters, and deals with serious criminal offences.

The Supreme Court of South Australia is regulated by the *Supreme Court Act 1935* (SA). It has a Chief Justice, 12 judges and two Masters. In addition to civil and criminal divisions, there is a division for Probate (wills and estates) and Land and Valuation (planning and development).

The Australian Capital Territory Supreme Court was created under the *Supreme Court Act 1933* (ACT) and since 2001 there has also been a Court of Appeal. There is presently a Chief Justice, President of the Court of Appeal, two resident judges (usually four), 18 additional judges (whose main role is to be judge in the Federal Court of Australia), and a Master.

The Tasmanian Supreme Court is regulated by the *Supreme Court Acts 1856, 1887* and *1959* (Tas). It has unlimited jurisdiction in civil matters, and exclusive jurisdiction in criminal matters. There are currently six judges, an acting judge, a Chief Justice and a Master.

District or County Courts

District Courts in New South Wales are regulated by the *District Court Act 1973* (NSW). It is a trial court which also hears appeals de novo (from the start) from the Local Court. It consists of a Chief Judge and 73 judges.

The Victorian County Court is regulated by the *County Court Act 1958* (Vic). Since 2006 its jurisdiction has not been subject to a monetary limit, and the County

Court has jurisdiction for all personal injury claims and public liability claims brought against municipal councils. It also has jurisdiction conferred upon it by a number of Victorian Acts, including strata titles and adoption. Its criminal jurisdiction covers all indictable offences except treason and murder.

District Courts in Queensland are regulated by the *District Court of Queensland Act 1967* (Qld). They have civil jurisdiction over disputes involving amounts of between $50 000 and $250 000, and deal with serious criminal offences including sexual assault, armed robbery and fraud. Criminal matters, and some civil matters, are heard before a jury. There are presently 37 District Court judges in Queensland, including the Chief Judge.

District Courts in Western Australia are regulated by the *District Court of Western Australia Act 1969* (WA). They have jurisdiction in criminal matters carrying a maximum sentence of 20 years or less, and civil matters to a limit of $500 000. They have unlimited jurisdiction for damages relating to personal injuries. The District Court hears appeals from magistrates in civil actions. Appeals from the District Court are typically to the Court of Appeal of the Supreme Court.

District Courts in South Australia are regulated by the *District Court Act 1991* (SA). They have four divisions – Civil Division, Criminal Division, Criminal Injuries Division, and Administrative and Disciplinary Division. South Australia is the only state with an administrative appeal court at the intermediate level of the judicial hierarchy.

There is no intermediate court between the magistrates and supreme court levels in Tasmania, the Northern Territory or the Australian Capital Territory.

Local or Magistrates Courts

Local Courts in New South Wales are regulated by the *Local Court Act 2007* (NSW) and hear most civil and criminal cases in New South Wales. There are 159 Local Courts in New South Wales. Parties may appeal from the Local Court to the District Court, or directly to the Supreme Court.

The Magistrates' Court in Victoria is regulated by the *Magistrates' Court Act 1989* (Vic). Parties typically appeal from the Victorian Magistrates' Court to the County Court, but may also appeal directly to the Supreme Court.

The Queensland Magistrates Court is regulated by the *Magistrates Courts Act 1921* (Qld). The Magistrates Court can deal with less serious criminal offences (summary offences) and civil cases where the amount in dispute is less than $50 000. There are presently 86 magistrates plus a Chief Magistrate and Deputy Chief Magistrate.

The Northern Territory Magistrates Court is regulated by the *Magistrates Act* (NT). There is a Magistrates Court, Local Court (which handles civil cases with up to $100 000 in dispute and is governed by the *Local Court Act* (NT)), a Small Claims Division (regulated by the *Small Claims Act* (NT) and with jurisdiction to hear civil matters with up to $10 000 in dispute) and a Court of Summary Jurisdiction (constituted under the *Justices Act* (NT) and which handles less serious criminal cases that are often heard before Justices of the Peace instead of Magistrates). There are presently 12 magistrates in the Northern Territory, including Chief Magistrate. Appeals go directly to the Supreme Court, as there is no intermediate court.

TIP
In most states there is no apostrophe in Magistrates Court. However, in Victoria it is the Magistrates' Court.

TIP
Most legislation is cited with a date. However, in the Northern Territory the year of enactment is used only until an Act is first amended. After that, the date is dropped from the title. The *Magistrates Act* (NT) has no year because it has been amended at some stage.

The Magistrates Court of Western Australia is regulated by the *Magistrates Court Act 2004* (WA). It deals with civil matters involving claims up to $50 000. For minor cases the jurisdictional limit is $7500. Parties in civil matters may appeal from the Magistrates Court to the District Court, and in criminal matters appeals lie to the Supreme Court. There are presently 28 magistrates courts in Western Australia.

The Tasmanian Magistrates Court is regulated by the *Magistrates Court Act 1987* (Tas). It handles civil law cases involving amounts of up to $50 000, summary offences, and committal hearings in criminal cases. There is also an Administrative Appeals Division, which reviews administrative decisions. There are presently four magistrates courts in Tasmania, with a total of 13 magistrates.

The Magistrates Court of South Australia is regulated by the *Magistrates Court Act 1991* (SA). It handles summary criminal offences, and civil matters involving amounts of up to $40 000, and up to $80 000 for motor vehicle accidents damages claims. There are currently 36 magistrates in South Australia, including the Chief Magistrate.

The Australian Capital Territory Magistrates Court is regulated by the *Magistrates Court Act 1930* (ACT). It handles civil claims involving amounts up to $50 000, and the Small Claims Court handles claims up to $10 000. As with other Magistrates Courts, the Australian Capital Territory Magistrates Court also handles summary criminal offences.

> **TIP**
> All judicial officers, including magistrates, are now referred to as Your Honour. In the past, magistrates were referred to as Your Worship but it became too confusing for unrepresented litigants, who addressed the Court with everything from 'Your Lordship' to 'Your Highness'.

Specialist courts

In most states and territories there are specialist courts which make decisions on particular areas and are usually subject to appeal to the Supreme Court.

- In New South Wales, there is a Land and Environment Court, Drug Court, Children's Court, Compensation Court, and Coroner's Court.
- In Victoria there is a Children's Court of Victoria, Drug Court, Koori Court and Coroner's Court.
- In Queensland there is an Environment Court and Office of the State Coroner.
- In Western Australia there is a Family Court of Western Australia (a significant court of its own, with five judges and eight magistrates), Children's Court (offences by children 10–17 years of age, and care and protection matters), Coroner's Court, Industrial Relations Commission (disputes between employers and employees) and Drug Court (treatment programs for drug-related offenders).
- In South Australia there is an Environment and Resources Court, Youth Court, Coroner's Court and Industrial Relations Court.
- In the Australian Capital Territory there is a Children's Court, and a Coroner's Court.
- In the Northern Territory there is a Youth Justice Court, Community Court, Family Matters Court, Work Health Court, Small Claims Court, and Coroner's Coronial Court.

> **Context: common law jurisdictions**
>
> If there are numerous courts in nine different court hierarchies in Australia issuing judicial decisions which form part of our common law, does this mean there are nine different common laws in Australia? No, it does not. The High Court sits at the top of all the court hierarchies, and that Court's decisions on the common law are binding on all federal, state, and territory courts. See *Lipohar v R* (1999) 200 CLR 485, 505 (Gleeson CJ).

Cross-vesting

Cross-vesting is the granting, or vesting, of power in a state court to exercise Commonwealth judicial power. In 1987 legislation was introduced to allow federal courts to hear state matters, and state courts to hear federal matters.[15] This enabled cases that raised issues under both state and federal jurisdiction to avoid having to commence two separate proceedings, one before a court with state jurisdiction and one before a court with federal jurisdiction. Instead parties could simply commence the action in the most convenient court, and that court would decide matters under both state and federal jurisdiction.

In 1999 the validity of this legislation was challenged in *Re Wakim* (1999) 198 CLR 511. The High Court held that federal courts had no power under Chapter III of the Commonwealth Constitution to exercise the power of state courts. Chapter III only allowed federal courts to exercise federal jurisdiction. Therefore the legislation was held to be invalid, and it was necessary for parliament to pass legislation to retrospectively validate the decisions that had been made over the 12 years the legislation had been in place. Since 1999 federal courts have not been able to exercise state jurisdiction, but state courts remain able to exercise both state and federal jurisdiction, because the state courts are established under the state constitutions and they allow the exercise of the federal jurisdiction.

Appeals

Where a party to a civil or criminal case is not satisfied with the outcome, they may appeal to a higher court that has appellate jurisdiction. For the matter to have been appealed, there must be some level of ambiguity in the law as it stands, or perhaps some contradiction between two bodies of legal principle as they apply to the present case. The appeal court is therefore likely to consider matters of principle and policy, in shaping the area of law under question. Appeals are generally limited to questions of law, which means a legal error in the decision (as opposed to an error in fact, such as believing one witness over another). However you can have a full rehearing if a matter goes on appeal from a local or magistrates court to a district or county court. This is described as a hearing *de novo*.

TIP
A rehearing *de novo* is a 'hearing on the merits' of the whole case. An appeal is made on one on more specific points.

---

15 See *Jurisdiction of Courts (Cross-vesting) Act 1987* (Cth) and mirror state legislation.

There is a right of appeal from a lower court to a higher court except in the case of the High Court, which has limited capacity to hear cases, as it has only seven judges. Applications for special leave to appeal are made, and each party has 20 minutes to address the Court (usually two of the judges) on the application for special leave, saying why leave should be granted; the applicant gets a five minute right of reply. Typically these applications take place by video link to save the parties and their lawyers travelling to Canberra. The High Court will consider, for each case, how great the potential injustice is and how relevant and important the legal issues are. There may be particular areas of law which are unclear and the High Court may welcome a case that enables it to pronounce the applicable law in that area. This means that cases where the principle at issue is likely to be of general application, and those where there is demonstrated a difference of opinion in the lower courts, are more likely to be accepted. Proportionately few special leave applications are granted. For example in the months of November and December 2009, of the 63 applications for special leave to appeal that were made to the High Court, all were refused. This means that, for all those litigants, the last court of appeal is the Federal Court or the relevant state Supreme Court.

Judicial review

Superior courts not only have jurisdiction to hear appeals, they also have jurisdiction to undertake a judicial review of an administrative decision. What is the difference between appeal and judicial review? An *appeal* is made on the basis that some matter of law that was decided incorrectly at the first instance – for example that the judge failed to take into account a leading precedent on point, whereas *judicial review* is where a judge reviews an administrative decision to check that it was made in accordance with the power of the administrative officer and whether the administrative officer has afforded the affected individual procedural fairness. The court can review decisions of government officials to ensure that they are made within the power given to them in the relevant delegated legislation.

In depth: *Ultra vires*

If an administrative decision is to be valid, it must be within power – that is, the administrative officer must not go beyond the scope of the power granted to his or her position or role via statute by the relevant parliament. If the decision is not authorised under law, or is outside the power given by the law, then it is '*ultra vires*' (beyond power) and therefore invalid. When courts undertake judicial review, they can consider whether the administrative decision was *ultra vires* or not. If the decision was one that involved discretion, the courts will apply a test of reasonableness – that is, was the decision one that could reasonably fit within the discretionary power delegated to the relevant administrative official? This means that the granting of a discretion always has an implied limitation that the discretion be exercised reasonably.

Reflection

To what extent, if any, is judicial review a manifestation of the rule of law?

6: Alternatives to courts

Although the power to resolve disputes is vested in the court system, as discussed in Part 3 above, this is not exclusive. In practice, not all cases are adjudicated through the court system. The tribunal system in Australia (Commonwealth and state) is well developed and offers many options for resolving disputes, as do alternative methods of dispute resolution such as negotiation, mediation and arbitration. These alternatives are explained below.

The role of tribunals

Tribunals are publicly created administrative alternatives to court. This means that they are created by an Act of parliament which gives them the power to hear and decide upon certain matters. They are administrative alternatives to court, not judicial alternatives. This means that the power of a tribunal is limited to applying the relevant rules – they have no power to declare the rules themselves to be invalid. Only a court can do this, because it is an exercise of judicial power.

Tribunals were designed to provide a cheaper, less formal, more efficient, and more specialised alternative to courts. The original intention was that parties would appear before tribunals without lawyers, but in practice lawyers are often involved in tribunal cases.

There are both Commonwealth and state tribunals. Each derives its power from a Commonwealth or state piece of legislation. For example the Administrative Appeals Tribunal derives its powers from the *Administrative Appeals Tribunal Act 1975* (Cth). Additionally, various pieces of legislation include provisions stating that disputes arising under them are to be referred to the AAT.

Commonwealth tribunals

The most important tribunal system is the Commonwealth's administrative law tribunals. It includes the following tribunals:

- **Administrative Appeals Tribunal (AAT)** – offers a speedy, independent process that can review a wide range of administrative decisions by Commonwealth government Ministers, their delegates, other officials and the decisions of other tribunals. The AAT will usually only review decisions where the applicant has exhausted other pathways, such as lodging a complaint to the Ombudsman.[16]
- **Social Security Appeals Tribunal (SSAT)** – enables those who believe a wrong decision has been made in relation to their social security, education or training payment or a child support allowance to appeal. For example the SSAT has the

---

16 For more information about the AAT see its website at www.aat.gov.au/.

power to vary Centrelink decisions (the agency that delivers social security and student assistance services).[17]
- **Veterans Review Board (VRB)** – provides for review of decisions by the Repatriation Commission and the Department of Veterans' Affairs about war widows' and orphans' pensions.[18]
- **Migration Review Tribunal (MRT)/Refugee Review Tribunal (RRT)** – Established under the *Migration Act 1958* (Cth), these tribunals provide an independent and final merits review of decisions made in relation to visas to travel to, enter or stay in Australia. The MRT reviews decisions made in respect of general visas (e.g. visitor, student, partner, family, business, skilled visas) and the RRT deals with decisions made in respect of protection (refugee) visas.[19]
- **National Native Title Tribunal** – mediates and arbitrates disputes between land title claimants and titleholders. It does not decide whether native title exists or not, but where a settlement is reached between the parties, the Tribunal registers the agreement.[20]

State and territory tribunals

There is a wide variety of tribunals in the states and territories. Most are listed in the weblinks at the end of this chapter but the basic groupings of tribunals that exist in states and territories are:

- Residential tenancies tribunals (these resolve disputes and establish a framework for relations between landlords and tenants)
- Administrative tribunals (these resolve disputes people have with state government agencies)
- Credit tribunals (these resolve disputes about credit contracts)
- Guardianship tribunals (these resolve issues for people with disabilities who lack capacity to make certain decisions)
- Anti-discrimination tribunals.

Numerous other tribunals have been created. Some, like the Dust Diseases Tribunal of New South Wales, are unique.

Alternative dispute resolution (ADR)

While tribunals are alternatives to courts that are created by parliament, there are also alternative methods of resolving disputes that are created by the parties. They are voluntary, and often less adversarial than litigation through courts and tribunals.

Negotiation does not always have to be a matter of one party winning and the other party losing – there can be a win–win outcome, and there can be solutions that a court could not provide. For example a commercial party claiming for delay in

---

17 More information can be found at www.ssat.gov.au/.

18 More information can be found at www.vrb.gov.au.

19 For more information see www.mrt-rrt.gov.au.

20 More information can be obtained at www.nntt.gov.au/.

receiving goods purchased under contract can only get an award of damages from a court. It may prefer to negotiate a special discount applied to all purchase orders for the next two years. This also makes good business sense for the responding party, because they avoid having to pay a sum of money and are instead guaranteed orders from the other party for a two year period. The outcome preserves their ongoing business relationship and is a win–win situation. It is also a lot faster and cheaper than resolving the matter through court.

Common methods of alternative dispute resolution include:

- **Negotiation** – this is the most common form of dispute resolution. It involves the parties discussing the matter in order to reach a mutually acceptable outcome.
- **Mediation** – this involves getting a neutral, independent third party to assist in negotiations. The mediator facilitates the discussion and helps the parties move towards a resolution of their dispute. The mediator has no power to force an outcome, but can assist by helping to flesh out the issues, explore solutions, and draft what the parties agree on into a settlement agreement.
- **Arbitration** – this involves deferring to the neutral, independent third party to decide the dispute. The arbitrator acts like a judge, hearing the submissions of the parties and reviewing the documents, and makes a final and binding decision from which there is typically no right of appeal (except of course in cases where the arbitrator was biased or there was fraud involved). The benefit of arbitration over litigation is that the parties can choose the arbitrator, and they can keep the matter confidential, and maintain control over the process.

Parties to litigation can sometimes be referred by the court to mediation or arbitration.[21] Where this occurs, it is described as 'court-annexed' mediation or arbitration. Typically the courts maintain a list of accredited mediators and arbitrators for use in these circumstances.

In depth: Negotiating style

Each of us has a natural negotiating style, which we developed as we grew up. Some of us are more focused on outcomes, even where it may wreck a relationship or two along the way. Others are more focused on getting along with people, even if it means we don't always achieve the best outcome. The best negotiators are people who are aware of their natural, inherent negotiation style, and are able to flex their style to accommodate each particular negotiation.

In their international best seller, *Getting to Yes*,[22] Ury and Fisher set out the results of the Harvard Negotiating Project, which focused on an alternative negotiation technique to the traditional, competitive style in which the parties act like adversaries, and each one

---

21 See *Supreme Court Act 1970* (NSW) s 110K; *District Court Act 1973* (NSW) s 164A; *Supreme Court of Queensland Act 1991* (Qld) ss 101, 102, 126; *Supreme Court (General Civil Procedure) Rules 2005* (Vic) O.50.07; *Federal Court Act* (Cth) s 53A.

22 Roger Fisher, William Ury and Bruce Patton, *Getting to Yes*, Penguin Books, 2nd edn (1981).

aims to win. The approach that is described is known as principled negotiation, cooperative negotiation, or negotiation on the merits. The idea is to avoid gamesmanship and competitiveness, and instead have the parties working side by side to achieve a solution to the problem that is both efficient and amicable. There are four key aspects of this approach.

People: Separate the people from the problem

This means attacking the *problem* and keeping people issues separate. Parties to the negotiation refrain from criticising the other side, and instead focus on the offer or the argument the other side is making. This can be difficult to do in practice, particularly when emotions are involved. Try to avoid making internal judgements about the other side, based on the inferences you draw from their words and actions, their appearance and body language, which could lead you to communicate your opinion of them in the negotiation. If the other side become emotional, allow them to vent, listen carefully to what they are saying, show them you are really listening, and then paraphrase what they have essentially said, in a sentence such as 'So what I'm hearing is that it is really important for you that …'

Interests: Focus on interests, not positions

Typically when you enter a negotiation, you have a position – what you think the other side should do, and what you are willing to do. That position will have some basis – it will be what you see as a way to achieve your interests. But for every interest, there are likely to be several outcomes which can address it, not just the position you take. So instead of running the negotiation from the *positions* of the parties, focus instead on the *interests* of the parties. This might be to secure cash flow, or to avoid harmful publicity, or to maintain an ongoing business relationship, or to establish a presence in a new market, or whatever. As well as looking at the interests of each of the parties, look at *shared* interests (things that both parties would like to occur or would prefer to avoid).

Options: Generate many possibilities before deciding what to do

The benefit of generating as many options as possible, in a brainstorming process, without either party being bound by any option they may suggest, is to fully explore the possibilities before moving into the phase of making settlement offers. This can often bring up options that will 'expand the pie' in the sense of creating something of value for both parties in the settlement. This usually occurs where something that is cheap for one party is of great value to the other. This is often the case. Let's say for example you have a software system set up for your business. You have been using it for a few years and it works well. If another business does not have such a system, it would cost them a lot of money to have it developed especially for them, but it costs you nothing to give them a copy of it. Similarly, if one party regularly ships goods overseas and the other does not, it is likely the first party can negotiate better rates for carriage than the second party, and that also creates value in the settlement. Another example may be a business that is happy to write off a loss from a contractual dispute if the other party is willing to commit to supply the products for the next five years at the fixed price from this year.

Criteria: Insist that the result be based on some objective standard

It helps when you formulate a proposal to make it clearly legitimate by making it seem the right thing to do – fair, legal, honourable, in accordance with some objective standard which is independent of the naked will of either side. For example if the dispute was over a car accident, an objective criterion might be the replacement value of the car, or the market value. If the argument is between parties on a construction site and the contract failed to specify the thickness of glass that should be used in the windows, it is useful to refer to the Australian Standards and settle upon that specification. It means that, if the other party makes an offer, you find out how they arrived at that figure – what criterion did they use? Is it a valid one? Of course, there may at times be two criteria that are equally legitimate and come out with different outcomes, so it might be a matter of meeting half way.

Fisher and Ury also talk about parties having a BATNA and a WATNA. A BATNA is the best alternative to a negotiated agreement. It is a reminder of your options if the agreement does not go ahead. If it is a negotiation to purchase a house, the alternative is to buy another house, for example. If the negotiation is of a dispute, the alternative is to go to court or arbitration. Bearing in mind your BATNA means that if you are getting something less, you should walk away from the negotiation. With the WATNA, which is your worst alternative to a negotiated agreement, this is useful to bear in mind in case you feel like walking away from the negotiation, but what you are being offered is actually better than the worst alternative. An example might be a dispute negotiation where, if you cannot reach a conclusion and get some money from the other party in the next week, your company may become insolvent. Or it might be a contract negotiation where, if you cannot reach agreement, you may not be able to sell the goods at all before they rot, go out of fashion, or become technically obsolete.

DISCUSSION QUESTIONS

1 A federal system involves balancing power between the state and federal levels. How does the Commonwealth Constitution strike that balance, and how does it resolve any conflicts over law-making power between the state and federal governments?

2 Most parliaments in Australia have a bicameral system, meaning two houses of parliament. How is irresolvable conflict between the houses of parliament overcome?

3 What are the arguments for and against having a bill of rights for Australia?

4 What are the arguments for and against Australia becoming a republic?

5 Does alternative dispute resolution undermine one's right to a trial and procedural fairness or further access to justice?

WEBLINKS AND FURTHER READING

Australia, Constitution: www.aph.gov.au/senate/general/constitution
Australian Law Reform Commission, *Managing Justice: A Review of the Federal Civil Justice System*, Report 89 (2000).
Bar Associations: www.austbar.asn.au/ then left menu item 'Links', then 'Australian barrister sites'
Bennett, David, 'The Roles and Functions of the Attorney-General of the Commonwealth', (2002) 23 *Australian Bar Review* 61.
Coper, Michael and Williams, George (eds), *Power, Parliament and the People*, Federation Press, Sydney (1997).
Coper, Michael, *Encounters with the Australian Constitution*, CCH Australia, Sydney (1988)
Crawford, James and Opeskin, Brian, *Australian Courts of Law*, Oxford University Press, South Melbourne, 4th edn (2004).
Kinley, David, 'Constitutional Brokerage in Australia: Constitutions and the Doctrines of Parliamentary Sovereignty and the Rule of Law' (1994) 22 *Federal Law Review* 194.
Kirby, Michael, 'The Constitutional Centenary and the Counting of Blessings', Fifth Sir Ninian Stephen Lecture, University of Newcastle, 20 March 1997.
McCarthy, Alana, 'The Evolution of the Role of the Attorney-General', Paper presented at the 23rd Annual Australia and New Zealand Law and History Society Conference, Murdoch University, Western Australia, 2–4 July 2004.
National Alternative Dispute Resolution Advisory Council: www.nadrac.gov.au
Parkinson, Patrick, *Tradition and Change in Australian Law*, LBC, Sydney, 4th edn (2009).
Parliament of Australia, Information Sheets: www.aph.gov.au/house/info/infosheets/index.htm

Web Resources on law societies

ACT: www.actlawsociety.asn.au/; NSW: www.lawsociety.com.au/; NT: www.ntba.asn.au/; Qld: www.qls.com.au/; SA: www.lawsocietysa.asn.au/; Tas: www.taslawsociety.asn.au/; Vic (Law Institute): www.liv.asn.au/; WA: www.lawsocietywa.asn.au/links.htm

Web Resources on courts

Family Court: www.familycourt.gov.au/
High Court of Australia: www.hcourt.gov.au/
Federal Court of Australia: www.fedcourt.gov.au/
State courts: www.lawlink.nsw.gov.au/ then left menu item 'Courts & Tribunals'

Web resources on tribunals

Australian Capital Territory

Administrative Appeals Tribunal: www.courts.act.gov.au/magistrates/tribunals/aat/aat.html
Credit Tribunal: www.courts.act.gov.au/magistrates/tribunals/CT/CT_home.html
Discrimination Tribunal: www.courts.act.gov.au/magistrates/tribunals/dt/dt.html
Guardianship and Management of Property Tribunal: www.courts.act.gov.au/magistrates/tribunals/gmpt/GMPT_home.html
Health Professions Tribunal: www.courts.act.gov.au/magistrates/tribunals/hpt/hpt.html
Mental Health Tribunal: www.courts.act.gov.au/magistrates/tribunals/mht/mhthome.htm
Residential Tenancies Tribunal: www.courts.act.gov.au/magistrates/tribunals/rtt/rtt.html
Tenancy Tribunal: www.courts.act.gov.au/magistrates/tribunals/tt/tt.html

New South Wales

Administrative Decisions Tribunal: www.lawlink.nsw.gov.au/adt
Consumer, Trader and Tenancy Tribunal: www.fairtrading.nsw.gov.au/corporate/cttt.html
Dust Diseases Tribunal: www.lawlink.nsw.gov.au/lawlink/ddt/ll_ddt.nsf/pages/DDT_index
Government and Related Employees Tribunal: www.industrialrelations.nsw.gov.au/great/index.html
Guardianship Tribunal: www.gt.nsw.gov.au
Local Government Pecuniary Interest Tribunal: www.dlg.nsw.gov.au/dlg/dlghome/dlg_CommissionTribunalIndex.asp?areaindex=PIT&index=3&mi=4&ml=1
Mental Health Review Tribunal: www.mhrt.nsw.gov.au
Victims Compensation Tribunal: www.lawlink.nsw.gov.au/lawlink/victimsservices/ll_vs.nsf/pages/VS_aboutus vct

Victoria

Victims of Crime Assistance Tribunal: www.vocat.vic.gov.au
Victorian Civil and Administrative Tribunal (VCAT). VCAT deals with disputes about consumer matters, credit, discrimination, domestic building works, guardianship and administration, residential tenancies, and retail tenancies. VCAT also deals with disputes between people and government about land valuation, licences to carry on businesses including travel agents, motor car traders and others, planning, state taxation and many other government decisions such as Transport Accident Commission decisions and freedom of information issues. Comprehensive information as well as legislation and VCAT decisions are available at its website www.vcat.vic.gov.au.

Northern Territory

The Lands, Planning and Mining Tribunal: www.nt.gov.au/justice/courtsupp/landplantrib
The Mental Health Review Tribunal: www.nt.gov.au/justice/courtsupp/mentalhealth
Northern Territory Remuneration Tribunal: www.dcm.nt.gov.au/strong_service_delivery/supporting_government/remuneration_tribunal

Queensland

Queensland Civil and Administrative Tribunal (QCAT): www.qcat.qld.gov.au/index.htm
From 1 December 2009, the QCAT administers anti-discrimination matters, children services, small claims, commercial and consumer matters, fisheries, guardianship and administrative matters, health practitioner matters, misconduct, retail shop leases, teachers disciplinary proceedings, veterinary matters and racing appeals.

South Australia

Equal Opportunity Tribunal: www.courts.sa.gov.au/courts/district/equal_opportunity_tribunal.htm
Remuneration Tribunal: www.remtribunal.sa.gov.au
Residential Tenancies Tribunal: www.ocba.sa.gov.au/tenancies/res/tentribunal/index.html
Workers Compensation Tribunal: www.industrialcourt.sa.gov.au

Tasmania

Anti-Discrimination Tribunal: www.magistratescourt.tas.gov.au/divisions/Anti-Discrimination_Tribunal
Mental health Tribunal: www.mentalhealthtribunal.tas.gov.au
Mining Tribunal: www.magistratescourt.tas.gov.au/divisions/mining_tribunal
Motor Accidents Compensation Tribunal: www.magistratescourt.tas.gov.au/divisions/motor_accidents_compensation_tribunal
Workers Rehabilitation and Compensation Tribunal: www.workerscomp.tas.gov.au

Western Australia

State Administrative Tribunal (SAT). SAT deals with a broad range of administrative, commercial and personal matters. These matters span human rights, vocational regulation, commercial and civil disputes, and development and resources issues. The Tribunal is the primary place for the review of decisions made by government agencies, public officials and local governments. It also makes a wide variety of original decisions. See www.sat.justice.wa.gov.au
Building Disputes Tribunal: www.buildingdisputes.wa.gov.au
Equal Opportunity Commission of Western Australia: www.equalopportunity.wa.gov.au/index.html
Racing Penalties Appeal Tribunal of Western Australia: www.rgl.wa.gov.au/Default.aspx?NodeId=72&DocId=139
Salaries and Allowances Tribunal: www.sat.wa.gov.au

ONLINE RESOURCES FOR THIS CHAPTER

The following resources are available online at www.oup.com.au/orc/cwl2e
- Essay practice on the topic 'the best court is the High Court'
- Flashcard glossary
- Multiple choice questions

5

Classifying and Practising Law: How Are Cases Resolved?

WHAT WE WILL COVER IN THIS CHAPTER:

- Major common law classifications
- The difference between substantive and procedural law
- The basic framework of major fields of substantive law
- An overview of procedural law: civil and criminal procedure
- The basic law and procedure governing the use of juries

Recommended approach to learning this topic

In studying this chapter, be mindful of the distinct legal use of words. Some words have meanings that are different from their colloquial use. Other terms, such as 'common law' have several legal meanings, depending on the context. Moreover, it is worth treating this chapter as a taste of what is to come in your law degree. Remember that this chapter is introducing you to some areas of law that you will soon study for a whole semester or year! You will also find more information on the Online Resource Centre. The chapter will sketch some of the delineations of the key branches of law – between substantive and procedural law, as well as the various types of substantive laws. The branches of law discussed in this chapter (with the exception of Professional Conduct, discussed in Chapter 12), make up the compulsory subjects of a law degree: Criminal Law and Procedure, Torts, Contracts, Property, Equity, Company Law, Administrative Law, Federal and State Constitutional Law, Civil Procedure and Evidence. Collectively, these are known as the Priestley 11, and they are mandatory for anyone wanting to qualify as a legal practitioner in Australia.

Also read this chapter with a view to extending your practical knowledge of litigation and dispute resolution. It will give you a feel for the work of a lawyer and the processes required in litigation. It is important to remember that although this chapter focuses on practice in the areas of civil and criminal procedure in the courts, Alternative Dispute Resolution (ADR) is just as central to a lawyer's job. ADR (discussed in Chapter 4) is becoming more common as courts attempt to resolve cases more quickly. It is part of what is known as 'case management'. Cases may be diverted from the courts into ADR in order to address the backlog and ensure faster outcomes for the parties. Most cases will never get to a court as they will be settled before litigation is necessary. As you read this chapter, think about how case management may limit the principle of a fair trial (which will be discussed further in Chapter 13).

KEY TERMS

Administrative law = a body of law enabling individuals to challenge government decisions that relate to them.

Adversarial system = a system of resolving legal disputes in which the parties present their arguments before an independent fact finder who assesses the facts, evidence and applicable law and makes a binding ruling based upon them.

Case management = courts managing the progress of each case by directing parties to fulfil obligations (such as negotiating to reach an outcome) and meet timelines in order to ensure quicker and more efficient outcomes.

Civil law = has two meanings. First it is a legal system that relies heavily on consolidating as much law as possible into statutory codes. Second, it is a classification of law within common law systems which refers to law that applies between private individuals.

Common law = has three meanings. First it is a system of law that originated in England. Second it is a body of law made by judges, as opposed to statute law made by parliament. Third, it is a term used to refer to the application of black letter law without reference to general principles of fairness (equity).

Constitution = an Act of parliament which sets out fundamental rules of government.

Contract law = the law governing agreements involving individuals, organisations or corporations.

Damage = injury or loss.

Damages = compensation awarded for loss, injury and suffering that is designed to place the injured party in the position they were in prior to the injury or damage.

Defendant = a legal entity (individual, company, association, the state) against whom legal proceedings are brought. The defendant answers the plaintiff's allegations (in civil matters) or the prosecution's allegations (in criminal matters).

Equity = a body of law that arose to correct and modify the harshness and inflexibility of the common law.

Federal system = a political system that involves the sharing of government power between a central government (here the Commonwealth or Federal government) and regional governments (here, the states and territories). This is contrasted with countries with a unitary (i.e. central) government like the United Kingdom and New Zealand.

Plaintiff = a legal person (individual, association, company, the state) who seeks legal relief against another legal person through court proceedings.

Pleadings = written statements by parties to a legal dispute that set out the relevant facts about the dispute and an outline of the case that each party relies upon.

Tort law (Torts) = a classification of law that involves particular civil wrongs. Tort law protects people's bodily autonomy and integrity (physical and psychological), their property, their reputation, and their financial interests.

1: Major legal classifications

Common law distinguished from civil law

'Common law' is used as an adjective to distinguish between common law legal systems and civil law legal systems. This is a worldwide distinction that separates countries with legal systems that rely predominantly on the common law tradition (supplemented by statutes that frequently contain modified common law principles) from countries that have chosen to have a legal system that relies to varying degrees on codifying the law (i.e. placing it all in statutes or codes). This latter type of legal system is known as a civil law system.

Common law legal systems predominate in the United Kingdom and Commonwealth countries colonised by Britain (such as Australia, New Zealand, and India). Civil law legal systems predominate in Europe (in countries such as France, Germany, Italy and Switzerland), some Asian countries (such as Japan, South Korea and Taiwan), Latin and South America, and some African countries. Civil law systems are based on Roman law, particularly the *Corpus Juris Civilis* (Body of Civil Law) which was a consolidation of Roman law ordered by Emperor Justinian and carried out between 529 and 534 CE.

The major differences between common law legal systems and civil law legal systems include the following:

- Common law was largely derived from customary law that evolved and was eventually written down. Civil law is based on Roman law, which had always been written down and was consolidated in 534 CE.
- Common law lawyers argue that there are many sources of law: common law, statute law, customary law and international law. Civil lawyers tend to treat civil Codes as *the* primary source of their law.
- Common law countries focus on the notion of binding precedent and focus on parts of key legal judgments. Courts in civil law countries may refer to past decisions but are not bound by them.
- Civil law countries have an inquisitorial system of justice, in which judges can conduct their own investigations, examine and cross-examine witnesses. In contrast, common law countries have an adversarial system of justice, where the judge and jury cannot seek additional information outside what the parties present.
- Judges in civil law systems train specifically to become a judge, whereas judges in common law countries tend to be drawn from the ranks of senior lawyers and have no formal judicial training.

Common law distinguished from statute law

The term 'common law' is also used as a noun, to refer to the body of law derived from English legal customs and practices. It continues today in the binding rulings made by judges. The common law is not static; it is constantly evolving as new cases come before the courts. The early Australian colonies inherited English common law in its entirety. The British Imperial Parliament enacted the *Australian Courts Act* (UK) in 1828 to provide that all legislation in force in England on 25 July 1828 would operate in Australia's colonies, if those laws were applicable to local Australian conditions. Since then Australian law, while heavily informed by English legal principles, has evolved into a distinctly Australian common law.

As a classification of law, the common law is somewhat elusive. This is because there is no one single repository of this 'common law'. One has to search through legal judgments looking for the judicial principles that constitute binding precedents, which are then reapplied, approved, or sometimes rejected by other judges – thus forming more common law. Unlike statutes, common law is not consolidated in a document as a system of rules.

Statute law is frequently contrasted with common law. Statute law is a body of Acts, Regulations and Rules created by parliaments, while common law is a body of law made by judges. Common law applies broadly throughout Australia, except where it is modified by statute.

Statute law is distinguished from the common law in three key ways:

- Statutes are created in a process that originates with people, politicians or parliaments. More widespread social thinking goes into statutes, as legislators frequently seek the views of community. This is in stark contrast to common law, where the judge seeks submissions from the two parties only, and can only decide cases based on the material submitted, however limited that may be.
- Statutes are designed to be self-contained. That is, the law is largely stated in the legislation, not found by searching through numerous law reports as is the case with common law.
- Common law can be changed by judges, but requires a case to arise to accomplish this. Statute law can be changed at any time, but requires parliament to do so. In other words, courts are reactive while parliament can be proactive.

TIP
Common law can be difficult to locate because it is frequently scattered in different cases, so you'll need to find the most authoritative judgments at the relevant point in time, and analyse how you think a court or judge would go about applying those principles to your case scenario. See Chapter 10 for a discussion on how to use court judgments as precedents.

Common law distinguished from equity

A third way the term 'common law' is used is to refer to applying the law on its face, 'black-letter law', as opposed to applying the principles of equity. Equity is a branch of law that has been developed by the courts to provide remedies where a strict application of common law rules would result in some injustice. Equity usually focuses upon whether the parties have acted in good conscience or good faith.

An example where the High Court used equity is *Garcia v National Australia Bank*.[1] Mr Garcia took out a business loan, using the family home as collateral (security), and had his wife countersign the mortgage with the bank. The business failed, the mortgage payments were not made, and eventually the bank sought to repossess the house to pay off the loan. Applying the common law, the bank had the right under contract to seize the home. However, using the principles of equity, the failure by the bank to ensure that Mrs Garcia understood the consequences of signing it meant that in equity the bank could not take the house.

---

1 *Garcia v National Australia Bank Ltd* (1998) 194 CLR 395.

Equity is a unique feature in common law legal systems, arising from English legal history. In the late thirteenth century three common law courts were created by King Edward: the Court of Common Pleas, the King's Bench, and the Exchequer. These courts had considerable discretion to grant remedies on the basis of customary law, and so the common law was relatively flexible to meet the particular justice needs of each case. But over the next century, a concern for consistency became paramount, and the common law became increasingly inflexible and procedurally complex. This led to unjust results. Increasingly, dissatisfied litigants petitioned the King directly for a pardon. When the demand for pardons became too great the King delegated the role to his key legal officer, the Lord Chancellor. This arrangement was formalised with the creation of the Court of Chancery in the fifteenth century. The chancellors in the Court of Chancery were drawn from the Church, and they infused their decision making with principles based on their conscience. This was explained in the *Earl of Oxford's Case*:[2]

> The Office of the Chancellor is to correct Men's consciences for Frauds, Breach of Trusts, Wrongs and oppressions, of what Nature soever they be, and to soften and mollify the Extremity of the Law … [W]hen a Judgment is obtained by Oppression, Wrong and a hard Conscience, the Chancellor will frustrate and set it aside, not for any error or Defect in the Judgment, but for the hard Conscience of the Party.

Over time, the principles based on the exercise of the Chancellors' conscience crystallised into equitable principles and remedies. An example of an equitable principle is 'he who comes to equity must have clean hands' – meaning that you cannot seek equity if you have done something unfair yourself.

For more than three centuries there were separate courts of common law and equity, which meant that if someone was dissatisfied with the application of the common law, they had to start a new action in a court of equity. The English *Judicature Acts* of 1873 and 1875 removed this division, allowing courts to apply both principles of common law and equity at the same time.

Australia had, at that time, already received the English traditions of common law and equity, and had likewise adopted separate courts for common law and equity. Australian courts followed the removal of separation between the common law and equity jurisdictions: Queensland in 1876, South Australia in 1878, Western Australia in 1880, Victoria in 1883, Tasmania in 1932, and New South Wales as late as 1970.

The principles of common law and equity remain different, but the application and administration of these principles by the courts is now fused.[3] Equity is therefore a body of legal principles in its own right, and students study it as a subject (see 'Private law' below).

---

2   *Earl of Oxford's Case* (1615) 21 ER 485, 486–7.

3   See *O'Rourke v Hoeven* [1974] 1 NSWLR 622, 626.

Substantive law distinguished from procedural law

The above discussion about the fusion of common law and equity highlighted the difference between the legal principles themselves, and the way courts apply them. This distinction exists throughout the law, and is known as the distinction between 'substantive law' and 'procedural law'.

Substantive law defines legal rights and duties – it defines the elements of each particular law. Procedural law, on the other hand, regulates the process, method, and rules by which the substantive law is administered. For example the substantive law defines 'murder' or 'homicide' as the act of killing another person with an intention to kill, to inflict grievous bodily harm, or to be recklessly indifferent to human life. The procedural law states that when someone is arrested for murder they have to be read their rights, to be charged, to have a bail hearing, to plead guilty or not guilty, and to have a trial and potentially a sentencing hearing.

The next two sections in this chapter look more closely at substantive law (heading 2) and procedural law (heading 3). Figure 5.1 shows how they relate to one another.

FIGURE 5.1: SUBSTANTIVE AND PROCEDURAL LAW

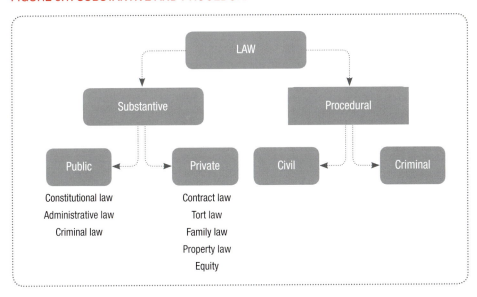

2: Branches of substantive law

Each substantive law is classified as a particular branch or doctrine of law – for example contract, constitutional, property and criminal law. Within each doctrine there are substantive elements of the law. For example the elements of a contract include someone making an offer, another person accepting it, and an exchange of something of value between them. This is the substantive law of contracts.

The branches of law are also broadly divided into public law and private law. Public law governs the legal relationships between governments, and between a government and individuals or organisations. Private law regulates relationships between individuals or organisations. It can also cover governments when they act like a private organisation – for example in purchasing office stationery.

Public law

The three main areas of public law in a domestic context are constitutional law, administrative law, and criminal law.

Constitutional law

You will recall from Chapter 4 that Australia is a federal system of government with seven constitutions – one for the Commonwealth government, and one for each of the six states. Australian territories come under the power of the federal government,[4] although some of them (the Australian Capital Territory, the Northern Territory and Norfolk Island) have been given self-government powers by federal legislation, which is in practice very similar to a constitution.[5]

Principles of law have developed to interpret the constitutions, and their relationship with one another. The constitutions and the cases that interpret them are referred to as 'constitutional law'. Constitutional law controls the most fundamental rules about how Australia is governed.

Constitutional interpretation is primarily conducted by the High Court of Australia, which has the power to decide whether the Commonwealth government had the power to make the relevant piece of legislation before the court. We saw, in Chapter 4, that the power of the Commonwealth government is set out in s 51 of the Commonwealth Constitution. Important powers found in that section include trade and commerce, taxation and external affairs.

> **TIP**
> Constitution is an Act of parliament which sets out fundamental rules of government. We covered this topic in Chapter 4, 'Legal Institutions: How is law made?'

Administrative law

Just as constitutional law limits the powers of parliament, the powers of the executive in administering and applying law are limited by administrative law. This branch of law governs the way people can challenge decisions of government departments and bodies. It is a key accountability mechanism over the powers of governors, ministers, local councils, boards, government business enterprises and public servants. It is particularly important given the extensive nature of government decision making.

If you wish to challenge a government decision that affects you, such as refusal of an application for permanent residency, here are some options for action, using the Commonwealth system as an example:

> **TIP**
> Students often get confused about the executive (the administrative arm of government that implements parliament's decisions). The executive is the embodiment of the monarch, the Queen. It includes the Governor-General and all public servants, including the police force.

---

4   Australia has three mainland territories (Australian Capital Territory, Northern Territory and Jervis Bay) and seven external territories (Ashmore and Cartier Islands, Australian Antarctic Territory, Norfolk Island, Christmas Island, Cocos (Keeling) Islands, Coral Sea Islands Territory, and the Heard and McDonald Islands.

5   *Australian Capital Territory (Self-Government) Act 1988* (Cth), *Northern Territory (Self-Government) Act 1978* (Cth), *Norfolk Island Act 1979* (Cth).

- **Freedom of information** – you can apply for access to government documents under the *Freedom of Information Act 1982* (Cth) and the equivalent state and territory freedom of information (FOI) Acts.[6] The FOI Acts provide that access should be granted to documents in the possession of government that contain personal information relating to a member of the public. Some types of government documents are excluded, such as Cabinet papers and documents that affect national security, law enforcement, privacy, and trade secrets.[7]
- **Ombudsman** – you can complain to an ombudsman – a neutral, respected person appointed to investigate complaints by individuals, corporations or parliament, or act on their own initiative. The ombudsman will look for breaches of law, unreasonableness, injustice, oppressiveness, impropriety and discrimination in government decision making. If maladministration is detected, the ombudsman can make recommendations as to corrective action, but cannot actually overrule or modify the decision. Ombudsman's offices exist in all Australian jurisdictions, although in Western Australia the office is called the Parliamentary Commissioner for Administrative Investigations.[8] They are publicly funded and provide free services.[9]
- **Merits review** – you can seek a review of a government decision 'on the merits'. A tribunal will then place itself in the shoes of the decision maker, review all the facts, law and information available to that decision maker, and decide whether the decision in question was the correct or preferable one. If not, the tribunal has the power to substitute its own correct and preferable decision. The peak Commonwealth merits review agency is the Administrative Appeals Tribunal (AAT), which is discussed under heading 4 below.
- **Judicial review** – you can also seek a review of an administrative decision by the courts (that is, a decision by a member of the executive, such as someone working for Centrelink). The courts will not review the matter 'on the merits', because the judicature has no power to make decisions, that is the role of the executive. Instead, the role of the courts is to interpret law. Judicial review, therefore, focuses on the *way* a decision has been made: whether lawful processes have been followed, and whether the decision is within the powers given to the decision maker.

TIP
Each state and territory also has its own legislation, tribunal system and appeal processes.

---

6 *Freedom of Information Act 1982* (Cth); *Freedom of Information Act 1989* (ACT); *Freedom of Information Act 1989* (NSW); *Freedom of Information Act 1992* (Qld); *Freedom of Information Act 1991* (SA); *Freedom of Information Act 1991* (Tas); *Freedom of Information Act 1982* (Vic); *Freedom of Information Act 1992* (WA).

7 The Commonwealth's FOI legislation is now administered by the Privacy & FOI Policy Branch of the Department of the Prime Minister and Cabinet. Prior to December 2007 this legislation was administered by the Information Law Branch of the Attorney-General's Department. For more information see www.pmc.gov.au/foi/index.cfm.

8 *Ombudsman Act 1976* (Cth); *Ombudsman Act 1989* (ACT); *Ombudsman Act 1974* (NSW); *Ombudsman Act 1980* (NT); *Ombudsman Act 1972* (SA); *Ombudsman Act 1978* (Tas); *Ombudsman Act 1973* (Vic); *Parliamentary Commissioner Act 1974* (Qld); *Parliamentary Commissioner Act 1971* (WA).

9 For more information see www.ombudsman.gov.au.

The statutory basis for judicial review at the Commonwealth level is the *Administrative Decisions (Judicial Review) Act 1977* (Cth). The states have rules under common law. You will learn all about these when you study administrative law as a full subject.

Before judicial review can take place, a court must address the following threshold issues to determine whether judicial review is possible and appropriate:

- Which government made the decision – a state, territory, or the Commonwealth?
- Is the subject matter of the decision 'justiciable' (one that can be reviewed)? Some examples of decisions that are not justiciable are decisions of Cabinet, the Governor-General, and security services.
- Has a legal decision been made? If it is only advice or the provision of information, instead of a decision, it will not be suitable for review.
- Does the applicant have standing to raise a complaint, by virtue of a legal interest that is affected by the decision?

Once these threshold issues have been satisfied, the court will exercise judicial review on certain grounds. The court will ask whether the decision maker:

- Exercised a power it did not have?
- Exercised a power in an unreasonable manner?
- Failed to apply the proper law?
- Failed to follow the proper procedures?
- Made a decision with little or no information?
- Took into account an irrelevant consideration?
- Failed to take into account a relevant consideration?
- Acted in a biased or fraudulent manner?

If the court finds the answer to any of those questions is 'yes', the court can make orders to:

- Set aside or quash the decision
- Refer the matter back to the decision maker for reconsideration
- Declare the rights of the parties
- Direct the parties to refrain from doing certain acts

Example: Dr Haneef

In June 2007 Dr Haneef, a doctor from India practising in Queensland, was accused of being implicated in bombing incidents in London and Glasgow. The alleged bombers were his second cousins, and one of them used Dr Haneef's mobile phone SIM card in the bombings. Dr Haneef was arrested by the Australian Federal Police, detained and questioned for two weeks about his association with the London bombings. He was released on bail by a magistrate, at which point the Minister for Immigration cancelled his migration visa on the ground that he was not of good character. Two

> weeks later all charges against Dr Haneef were dropped and he returned to India. Litigation resulted that required administrative law remedies to quash the Minister's order to cancel this visa. This judgment was unsuccessfully appealed by the Minister.[10]

Criminal law

Criminal law is considered public law for historical reasons. In feudal England the King had an obligation to maintain the peace. Criminal behaviour by individuals – such as robbery and rape – disturbed the peace. It was therefore an offence against the King's peace – against the state. For this reason, criminal cases are brought by the state against the offender,[11] rather than being brought by the victim against the offender. This is why reports of criminal cases are written '*R v Smith*'. The 'R' stands for Regina or Rex, depending on whether we have a reigning Queen or King.

Criminal law is largely regulated by the states and territories. Some states rely on a combination of statute and common law – these include the Australian Capital Territory, New South Wales, South Australia and Victoria.[12] Other states have 'codified' (brought together in one place) crimes into Codes – these include Queensland, Tasmania, Western Australia and the Northern Territory.[13] The Commonwealth has enacted the *Criminal Code Act 1995* (Cth), which codifies some criminal principles but is not comprehensive.[14] Therefore, several other Commonwealth crimes are regulated by other legislation (e.g. *Crimes Act 1914* and *Crimes Torture Act 1988*) and the common law.

A crime is behaviour that is prohibited at law and punishable by a court. If an act is not covered by statute or common law, no matter how unsavoury, offensive, immoral, unethical or rude it is, it will not be a crime. Typical crimes that you are likely to study include assault, sexual assault, manslaughter, murder, larceny (theft), and drug offences.

TIP
Where we refer to 'state' in this paragraph we mean government generally (as opposed to a state of Australia, like New South Wales or Victoria).

---

10 See *Haneef v Minister for Immigration and Citizenship* [2007] FCA 1273 and *Minister for Immigration and Citizenship v Haneef* [2007] FCAFC 203.

11 However, the victim may bring an ancillary claim for damages in civil law. More commonly, damages are sought through victim's compensation tribunals and financial assistance schemes of the state and territory governments, see: *Victims Support and Rehabilitation Act 1996* (NSW), *Criminal Injuries Compensation Act 2003* (WA), *Victims of Crime Assistance Act 2009* (Qld), *Victims of Crime Assistance Act 1996* (Vic), *Victims of Crime Assistance Act 1976* (Tas), *Victims of Crime (Financial Assistance) Act 1983* (ACT), *Victims of Crime Assistance Act 2006* (NT).

12 See *Crimes Act 1900* (ACT); *Crimes Act 1900* (NSW); *Criminal Law Consolidation Act 1935* (SA) and *Crimes Act 1958* (Vic).

13 See *Criminal Code Act 1899* (Qld), *Criminal Code Act* (NT), *Criminal Code Act 1924* (Tas), and *Criminal Code Compilation Act 1913* (WA).

14 However, Chapter 2 of the Model Criminal Code has applied to all Commonwealth offences since 2001. The Model Code site is at the Attorney-General's Department website www.ag.gov.au/ (select menu items 'Crime prevention and enforcement' then Model criminal code).

All crimes have set elements which must be proved. In common law criminal systems, the elements fall into two categories:

- The act itself – referred to as the *actus reus*, this is the voluntary physical act or omission (failure to act), and
- The intention – referred to as the *mens rea*, this is the mental element or fault required. It may be an intention to do the act or cause the outcome from the act, or it may be recklessness as to whether one's actions caused harm to others.

There is also a requirement that the act must have caused the outcome. It does not need to be the only cause, but there must be at least a 'causal connection' between the act and the outcome. Let's take homicide as an example. There must be an act or omission (*actus reus*) that causes (*causation*) death, done with either an intention to kill, an intention to inflict grievous bodily harm, or a reckless indifference to human life (*mens rea*). Different terminology is used in states with criminal codes. You will learn about these differences when you study criminal law as a full subject.

Not all crimes have a *mens rea*, or fault, requirement. Some only require the act that caused the outcome. These are known as *strict liability offences*. An example would be 'It is an offence to drive at a speed exceeding 40 kms per hour'. It doesn't matter if you didn't realise you were speeding, or weren't intending to speed. But a defendant may in some jurisdictions still raise a defence of honest and reasonable mistake of fact to a strict liability offence. For example, a faulty speedometer on a motorbike incorrectly displayed the speed such that the rider honestly and reasonably believed the motorbike was within 40 kms per hour. However, some offences do not even allow the defence of reasonable mistake of fact, and they are called *absolute liability offences*. An example of an absolute liability offence is the sale of contaminated food. It would not matter if you didn't know the supplier's food was contaminated, or that you made an honest mistake in serving it – you are absolutely liable.

Because of the serious consequences that a finding of guilt can have on a person, crimes must be proven 'beyond reasonable doubt'. This is referred to as the *standard of proof*. The prosecution is required to prove the case, and the defence has to prove any defence it raises. The prosecutor's obligation to prove the case is called the *burden of proof*.

Virtually every crime has available defences, which act to negate or excuse otherwise criminal conduct. Consent will often rule out criminality. For example it is generally an offence to cut somebody with a knife. However, where a person gives consent for a person to perform surgery on them, no offence has been committed.

Typical criminal defences include *self-defence* – 'I had to save myself from her imminent violence'; *provocation* – 'He said something highly offensive and I just saw red'; *mistake* – 'I thought she was about to jump under the train'; and *insanity* – 'I suffered a serious defect of mind'.

TIP
It is easy to get confused between burden of proof and standard of proof. Think of it like a high jump competition. The question of 'who must jump?' is the burden of proof, and the question of 'how high?' is the standard of proof. In criminal matters, the prosecution must 'jump', and the threshold to get over is 'beyond reasonable doubt'.

Private law

Private law regulates legal relationships between individuals or organisations. At times, a government can be a party to a private law dispute, but that dispute is usually unrelated to the functioning of government. For example if a government employee crashes a government car, the dispute is private, as it is not one at the heart of the core functioning of government. In such cases the government is treated in the same way as an individual or company would be.

In private law disputes the person or organisation suffering a loss or damage brings the action against the person or organisation they believe to be responsible. The person bringing the action is called the plaintiff (or applicant), and the party defending the action is the defendant. The plaintiff has to prove the elements of the law on the balance of probabilities – the court has to be satisfied that it is more likely than not that the facts they are asserting are true (compare this to the higher standard that applies under criminal law, where the prosecution has to prove the facts beyond reasonable doubt). Typically, private court cases have to be commenced within three or six years of the loss being suffered. This is described as the 'limitation period'. It is prescribed in law by statute.[15] If the action is not brought within the limitation period it is 'statute barred' – unable to be brought before the court.

The categories of law that traditionally fall under the umbrella of private law include contract law, tort law, equity, land law, and family law. These are considered below. The procedures by which civil actions are brought before the courts are discussed under heading 3, 'Procedural law'.

Contract law

Contract law governs legally binding agreements made by individuals, organisations or corporations. Contract law has evolved over many hundreds of years, and is largely derived from English common law. This means that many principles of contract law are found in cases rather than statutes.

A legally binding contract is formed where the following elements are satisfied:

- **Offer** – typically one party (the 'offeror') offers to buy or sell something, do or refrain from doing something (the offer must be clear, definite and clearly addressed to a person or group of people).
- **Acceptance** – the other party (the 'offeree') communicates that they agree to the offer (it must be unqualified – if the terms of the acceptance are different from the terms of the offer then it is actually a counter-offer).
- **Consideration** – something of value is exchanged between the parties pursuant to the offer, such as money, a physical thing, or a service.
- **Capacity** – both parties are legally capable to enter into a contract (people who lack legal capacity include children, persons overwhelmed by drugs or alcohol, and people who are not of sound mind or otherwise lacking in the capacity to understand what they are doing).
- **Legality** – the contract is not contrary to law or public policy (such as a contract for dealing drugs or to kill someone).
- **Validity** – the contract is not otherwise made invalid. Examples include where a party agreed to the contract under pressure ('duress' or 'undue influence'), or

---

15 *Limitation Act 1985* (ACT); *Limitation Act 1969* (NSW); *Limitation Act 1981* (NT); *Limitation of Actions Act 1974* (Qld); *Limitation of Actions Act 1936* (SA); *Limitation Act 1974* (Tas); *Limitation of Actions Act 1958* (Vic); *Limitation Act 2005* (WA).

because of a lie ('misrepresentation'), or mistake as to something fundamental in the contract.

There is nothing to stop a person withdrawing an offer at any time, unless the offer was specified as being available for a certain time period or until a certain date. Even then, withdrawal of the offer will usually be valid if it is properly communicated, unless some consideration was paid (such as a deposit) in order to keep the offer open.

Contracts do not typically have to be in writing to be legally valid – an exception is a contract for sale of land. If the contract is in writing, though, it is usually easier to prove that a contract existed, and what its terms were. The best approach is to set out all relevant terms and conditions in a written contract that is signed by both parties, and which includes an agreed procedure that they will follow should a dispute arise between them.

Where there are problems that commonly arise in a particular kind of contract, it is useful to agree in advance on the way they will be resolved. For example if someone arranges an open-air event which depends upon fine weather, it is useful to spell out in the contract what will happen if it rains on the intended date – will the event be rescheduled, or cancelled, and if so, will any cancellation fee apply?

We call these terms, which have been clearly thought about and included (expressed) in a contract, 'express terms'. On occasion a court may also imply terms into a contract. Take for example a contract to lease a two-bedroom apartment – but when the tenant moves in they find the landlord living there. In such case, the court would follow statute law on residential tenancies, or general property law principles, and imply a term into the contract that the property would be vacant and ready for the tenant to use. Another example is where a court implies into a consumer transaction the consumer protection laws that are there to protect the public and cannot be excluded.

GO ONLINE

Go online for a contract exercise. A scenario is posed and you are asked to work out whether a valid contract exists.

Tort law

A tort is a civil wrong. The aims of tort law are: to deter certain behaviour; to compensate for loss caused by others' wrongful behaviour; to return the injured party to the position before the loss; to appease the victim; and to provide justice between the parties.[16]

Key torts include trespass (entering someone's property without permission), defamation (spreading offensive information about someone), nuisance, and negligence.

Negligence is the most far-reaching tort and a relatively recent branch of the law. The modern law of negligence is frequently traced to the landmark case of *Donoghue v Stevenson*.[17] Mrs Donoghue drank a bottle of ginger beer which contained the decomposing remains of a snail. She sued the company that produced the ginger beer, seeking damages for the shock and gastroenteritis she suffered

TIP

Most non-lawyers don't use the word 'tort' in normal conversation, and so this area may seem unfamiliar. But in fact we tend to use the name of particular torts quite regularly, such as negligence or trespass, and so if you just remember that 'torts' is the umbrella term to cover all these sorts of action, you will feel more comfortable with this area of the law.

---

16 Glanville Williams 'The Aims of the Law of Tort' [1951] 4 *CLP* 137.

17 *Donoghue v Stevenson* [1932] AC 562.

as a result. The problem was that there was no contract between Mrs Donoghue and the manufacturer – she had bought the drink in a shop. In order to avoid the manufacturer from escaping liability, the court held that manufacturers owed a duty of care to all potential consumers of their product, because there was a relationship of 'proximity'. In failing to properly wash and inspect the bottles before filling them, the manufacturer had breached its duty of care, and the manufacturer was held liable for the damage that flowed from that failure.

Negligence has been refined, expanded and developed since that case. Generally speaking, the elements of negligence that must be established are:

- **Duty of care** – the court must be satisfied that the defendant owed the plaintiff a duty to take care. This can be established by the relationship between the parties – doctor and patient, producer and purchaser, council and local resident. The court will look at how foreseeable it is that people in the position of the plaintiff could suffer harm from the actions of the defendant, and whether there are good policy reasons for imposing a duty of care on the defendant.
- **Breach** – the defendant's conduct must fall below the appropriate standard of care, which is determined by assessing what a reasonable person in the shoes of the defendant would have foreseen in terms of potential injury, and what response to that perception of risk would be appropriate, taking account of the probability of the event occurring, how serious the potential risk could be, and the cost of rectifying any damage.
- **Loss** – the plaintiff must have suffered some harm, injury, loss or damage. The kind of harm suffered by the plaintiff must be one recognised by law. For example a person may suffer inconvenience or embarrassment, but the law does not typically consider inconvenience or embarrassment to be a kind of harm recognised by law. Typical heads of damage include physical injuries (broken bones, cuts), mental or psychiatric injuries (such as post traumatic stress disorder), and economic loss (such as loss of income).
- **Causation** – the breach of the duty of care *caused* the plaintiff's loss. The court has particular legal tests to establish whether the breach caused the plaintiff's injury, loss or damage, which you will learn about when you study torts as a subject.

If a plaintiff can prove these elements then there is a prima facie case of negligence. (Prima facie means 'on the face of it'.) The burden then shifts to the defendant to raise a valid defence. These include:

- **Voluntary assumption of risk** – the defendant may argue that the plaintiff assumed the risk of the injury they suffered. For example a person who decides to go in the car with a drunk racing car driver can be seen to have voluntarily assumed the risk of injury.
- **Contributory negligence** – the defendant may argue that the actions of the plaintiff to some degree caused the loss, and therefore the plaintiff is to some extent responsible for their own injury. For example if the passenger in the car with the drunk racing car driver chooses not to wear a seatbelt, they could be

TIP
The parties to a private dispute are generally the plaintiff, who brings the action, and the defendant, against whom the action is made.

TIP
'Damage' means the injury suffered, 'damages' means the award of compensation for the damage.

considered to be contributorily negligent, as their behaviour contributed to the harm suffered.

Contributory negligence may operate as a full or partial defence. If a full defence, the defendant is held to not be liable at all for the loss. If a partial defence, the court will calculate a percentage of the plaintiff's contribution to his or her loss, and reduce the damages awarded by that percentage. This is known as 'apportionment'.

Tort law is primarily common law, meaning the principles are found in cases. But there has been growth in tort legislation, some of which attempts to stop some torts, such as negligence, from expanding and causing insurance companies to pay more claims.[18] These laws were introduced by each state and territory as a result of Justice Ipp's 2002 report on tort law reform.[19] The changes included caps (ceilings) of the amount of damages that can be claimed for certain types of damage, and new threshold requirements that must be met before one can be classified as injured. Evidence so far indicates that the legislative amendments to tort law have had a beneficial impact on the profits of the insurance companies and a detrimental impact on financial assistance to injured parties.[20]

Equity

As discussed earlier in this chapter, equity is a branch of law designed to soften, or ameliorate, the effect of the common law. Equity law is found at common law, which means the principles are in cases rather than in statutes. While there are many equitable principles, or maxims, the key ones include:

- **One who seeks equity must do equity** – in order to receive some equitable relief, the party must be willing to complete all of their own obligations as well. The applicant to a court of equity is as subject to the power of that court as the defendant. This may also overlap with the clean hands maxim.
- **Clean hands** – a person who seeks equity must have 'clean hands', meaning that nothing in their own behaviour contributed to the situation.
- **Equity aids the vigilant** – this principle is that once a party has suffered damage or has been legally wronged, the wronged party should not delay in bringing this claim to the court.
- **Equity follows the law** – equity will not allow a remedy that is contrary to the existing common law.

Over time courts of equity developed the following equitable remedies in keeping with their maxims:

---

18   See *Wrongs Act 1958* (Vic); *Civil Liability Act 2002* (NSW); *Civil Liability Act 2003* (Qld); *Civil Liability Act 1936* (SA); *Civil Liability Act 2002* (WA); *Civil Liability Act 2002* (Tas); and *Civil Law (Wrongs) Act 2003* (ACT).

19   Justice Ipp, *Review of the Law of Negligence* (Final Report 2002) at http://revofneg.treasury.gov.au/content/review2.asp

20   Queensland Parliament, *Hansard*, 13 March 2007, p 914; Richard Cumpston, 'High insurer profits allow better benefits to the injured?' Consulting Actuaries, Melbourne (2005) at www.lawcouncil.asn.au/ (then search using key word 'Cumpston').

- **Specific performance** – the court orders a party to do something they failed to do under a contract. This may be useful where monetary damages may not be suitable, for example where a person has contracted to buy a famous painting.
- **Injunction** – the court orders that the party must stop or refrain from doing something. For example an injunction may stop the person with the famous painting from selling it to someone else.
- **Declaration** – the court may declare a contract void, for example where it was entered as a result of undue influence or fraud.
- **Estoppel** – the court may declare a person who has relied on their representations to be stopped (we use the term 'estopped') from denying them just because they were not in the contract. For example if a person says they will go ahead and lease a shop, and asks the landlord to make certain changes to it, such as new shelving and flooring, it would be inequitable for them to simply change their mind after the landlord had spent a lot of money fitting the shop out how they want it.[21]

Example: Multiple possibilities under private law

In practice, a plaintiff may raise several different areas of private law in the one dispute. Let's say for example that a person ordered a cargo of apples, and they arrived in a putrid and decaying state. The purchaser may bring an action in a state Supreme Court claiming: a breach of a term in the *contract*; the *tort* of negligence in the failure to exercise care in storing and handling the apples; and estoppel in *equity*, because the carrier represented that it could carry the apples at below 10 degrees Celsius, and this was relied on, even though the contract did not specifically include this as a term.

Land law

Land law (or real property law) is that body of law that regulates the ownership, creation, acquisition and disposal of interests in land. Modern Australian real property law is largely state-based. Its historical origins lie in English property law.

What is land? Section 22(1)(c) of the *Acts Interpretation Act 1901* (Cth) defines land as the surface of the Earth and all things growing on it or built on it, the airspace immediately above the property and the soil and rock beneath that geographic area.

In Australia the Crown technically owns all land. This is a result of feudalism in English legal history, under which the King owned all the land and granted use of it to individuals in return for the provision of knights to fight in war. A system of title called 'Old System title' developed from this. Under this system land was granted by deed. A person may have a deed from the Crown, and may execute a deed of sale with a third person, who may in turn exercise a deed with a fourth person. To

TIP
Land law is part of property law, which covers both 'real property' (immovable assets, that is, land) and 'personal property' (movable assets, such as goods and chattels, and also some rights, such as copyright). Chattels include most things, from cars to televisions to clothes and jewellery. Just think of chattels as any physical thing of value besides land.

---

21 *Waltons Stores (Interstate) Ltd v Maher* (1988) 164 CLR 387.

establish title, the deed a person holds must be tracked back to each of the people who have had a deed of title in the land since the original grant by the Crown. This system was extremely complicated because there may be several people claiming to have title over the same piece of land.

Since 1858 a system of land registration called 'Torrens title'[22] has applied in parts of Australia. The system provides that only one person can be listed on the public register as having title to each parcel of land, and they can prove that title using a certificate of title, which is issued by the government office that oversees the operation of the register. Whenever someone buys that land, they must register the passing of title from the vendor (seller) to the purchaser. Provided there was no fraud involved in becoming listed on the register as the owner, the person (or persons) who is registered as having title in the land has the exclusive ('indefeasible') right to lease it, sell it, give it away, or occupy it – a right they have against all other people besides the Crown. The Crown, the modern embodiment of the King from feudal times, retains the right to take back the land, provided reasonable compensation is paid. This is how governments are able to put highways through land that has houses on it – they 'compulsorily acquire' the land from those who currently have title to it (paying reasonable compensation to the owner).

> **TIP**
> Most of the Australian land mass continues to be Crown land held under pastoral leases. Land is therefore possessed (rather than owned outright), with rents and obligations owed to the government (obligations such as stocking and fencing the land). The leasehold system resonates with feudal obligations to a superior lord (see Chapter 8).

Apart from the large areas of Crown land which are leased or held under licence for specific purposes such as grazing, or land held as native title (see Chapter 9), the typical type of commercial or residential land ownership is 'freehold title' – the closest thing to full private ownership.[23] Where freehold land is owned by more than one person, the relationship between those people can be one of two kinds – joint tenancy, or tenancy in common. Under *joint tenancy* the owners own the land 'jointly and severally', which means that if three people own the land and one dies, the remaining two then own half each. Under *tenancy in common* the owners own a certain portion of the land, which means that if three people own the land in equal shares and one dies, that person's one-third share goes into their estate to be left as provided in their last will and testament. Tenancy here just means 'type of holding'; it should not be confused with being a tenant for rent.

Freehold land can also be the subject of a lease to someone else (a tenant, or 'lessee', for rent). For example a person may have the freehold title in a shopfront, which means they own the land and the buildings on it, whereas another person (say a pharmacist) may lease (rent) the property to run a pharmacy there. The person who owns the pharmacy business will have a leasehold title in the property, which means they are able to occupy the land and run the pharmacy for the term of the lease, as long as they pay rent. The lease can be for a fixed period, a yearly tenancy or a tenancy at will (tenancy can be terminated at any time by notice). Some

---

22 This system of title was devised by Sir Robert Torrens, the Registrar-General of South Australia.

23 The Australian Capital Territory is a notable exception: land is held on long leases from the Crown rather than being freehold. For a discussion of the history see www.prosper.org.au/2008/01/16/canberra/; www.aph.gov.au/library/Pubs/BD/1997-98/98bd135.htm. See for example the *Uniform Civil Procedure Rules* in New South Wales in the *Civil Procedure Act 2005* (NSW) and the *Uniform Civil Procedure Rules* 1999 (Qld).

tenancies operate according to the common law, but other tenancies are regulated by state legislation. These include retail tenancies (for shops of a certain size) and residential tenancies (rental of flats and houses). Specialist tribunals operate in these areas and the form of leases and other obligations of both landlords (lessors) and tenants (lessees) may be clearly set out in the legislation.

Family law

Family law regulates marriage and marriage-like relationships, such as de facto relationships. It also regulates parenting, including paternity, child welfare, child support, child protection and representation of children. Family law also covers aspects of property law: where marriages are dissolved a property settlement is usually made. A combination of common law and statute law applies.

The *Marriage Act 1961* (Cth) covers all aspects of marriage: who can marry, at what age, where marriages can be solemnised, which ceremonies are appropriate, licensing of marriage celebrants, the offence of bigamy, prohibitions against marrying near relations, and recognition of foreign marriages. The *Family Law Act 1975* (Cth) covers divorce and property settlements, and provides for arrangements that ensure the welfare of children – which is stated by the Act to be paramount in any family law proceeding.

3: Aspects of procedural law

Procedural rules are the rules that determine how a particular law is applied in specific factual situations. For example if a person wants to sue for breach of contract, or is being charged with murder, what is the process by which the action is brought, and the decision made? Procedural law is divided into civil and criminal procedure. You will study these courses as part of your law degree.

Civil procedure

Civil procedure covers all cases besides criminal cases and includes disputes relating to contract, tort, employment, equity or corporate law. Civil actions are brought by the person or organisation affected (the plaintiff) against the person or organisation they hold responsible (the defendant). Civil procedure in state and federal courts is different, according to the rules and regulations laid down by parliament, and the practice directions issued by the relevant court. Some states have different rules in each of their courts, while others have uniform civil procedure rules for all state courts.[24]

Here are the typical steps that are involved in civil litigation:

- **Advice** – typically the first step involves a person seeking legal advice. The lawyer advises on applicable laws that may have been breached, and relevant procedures that need to be followed to establish a breach.

---

24 See *Supreme Court Act 1970* (NSW) s 110K; *District Court Act 1973* (NSW) s 164A; *Supreme Court of Queensland Act 1991* (Qld) ss 101, 102, 126; *Supreme Court (General Civil Procedure) Rules 2005* (Vic) O.50.07; *Federal Court of Australia Act 1976* (Cth) s 53A.

> **TIP**
> As a practitioner, don't expect all your cases to go to court. More than 90% of legal proceedings settle before trial. Many more disputes are settled before the parties even retain lawyers; in fact 'lawyers and courts play only a marginal role in resolving disputes'.[25]

> **TIP**
> In legal proceedings documents are 'filed with' the court for its records or 'issued by' the court under its seal, and 'served on' the other side (formally given to the other party).

- **Negotiation** - at the initial stage, the lawyer will send a letter of demand to the other party and attempt to negotiate and resolve the matter through non-court processes (known as Alternative Dispute Resolution (ADR), discussed in Chapter 4). If negotiations are unsuccessful, court processes will be pursued. An action proceeds in the following steps. Nonetheless, throughout court proceedings, parties typically negotiate on a 'without prejudice' basis, which means that any offers they make privately cannot be mentioned to the judge in court.
- **Jurisdiction** – this involves deciding which court has jurisdiction (power) to hear the case. It may be a federal court (Family Court, Federal Court, Federal Magistrates Court) or a state court (typically there are local/magistrates, district/county, and supreme courts). In civil matters it usually depends on the amount of money in dispute (the more money, the higher court) or the type of dispute (for example, motor vehicle accidents are generally handled at the district court level).
- **Initiation of action** – the matter will usually be initiated by a summons or writ drafted by the plaintiff's lawyer and lodged with the appropriate court, and then a stamped copy is served on the defendant. The summons states the nature of the claim against the defendant, and will include a 'statement of claim' setting out the facts that go towards showing each of the elements of the relevant law. The statement of claim is the first of a set of documents exchanged by the parties known as *pleadings*.
- **Defence** – once the statement of claim is delivered to the court and forwarded to the defendant, the defendant must draft a 'statement of defence' (or risk losing the case). The defence responds to each of the paragraphs in the statement of claim, with either 'admitted', 'denied', or 'does not admit' the allegation. The defendant also raises new paragraphs with defences it is relying upon. The defendant may also raise a counterclaim, which is an allegation against the plaintiff. Often the defendant will need more information before completing a statement of defence.
- **Reply** – the plaintiff will reply to the defence with a response to any issues raised by the defendant.
- **Directions hearing** – the court directs the parties on what they have to do according to a set timetable. Such directions are part of the process of case management by the courts, which attempts to make the process more efficient and less drawn-out. The court will then periodically meet with the parties to find out what stage the litigation is at and set further directions. At each hearing, the last direction is always when the parties should next appear before court having done what has been ordered by the court.
- **Seeking information** – each party may need to rely on documents or information that is in the possession of the other party. A party may serve on the other party a 'Request for Further and Better Particulars' or interrogatories, which is a series of questions about the facts of the case. There may also be an order from the court for 'discovery' under which each side files a list of documents in their possession that are relevant to the matters at issue between the parties. The court may set dates for this information to be provided at its directions hearing.

---

25   Hilary Astor and Christine Chinkin, *Dispute Resolution in Australia,* LexisNexis Butterworths, Sydney (1992), 29.

- **Witness evidence** – once all the documentary evidence has been reviewed by all parties, the parties exchange witness statements (sometimes in the official form of a sworn affidavit) which contains the information that relevant witnesses intend to say, should the matter proceed to trial. There are two common types of witness evidence: lay evidence and expert evidence. Lay witnesses are those who were involved in the dispute (i.e. they saw the tort result in an injury). Expert witnesses often give evidence in relation to medical, psychological/psychiatric and accounting expertise.
- **Pre-trial procedures** – the matter is listed for trial, and efforts are made to settle the case to save going to trial. Written submissions to the court are prepared and a court book containing all the documents that will be referred to in the trial is collated.
- **Trial** – the parties argue their case before the court, with the plaintiff having to prove the allegations made on the balance of probabilities. Witnesses who have been ordered by the court ('subpoenaed' or 'summonsed') to appear before the court are examined by the party who called the witness and cross-examined by the opposing party.
- **Judgment** – the court issues a judgment with its findings. A successful claim will typically result in an award of monetary damages as well as interest and legal costs (usually the losing party is ordered to pay some legal costs of the winning party).
- **Enforcement** – should a party fail to comply with an order of the court, the court can make an enforcement order. Typically this will involve ordering the sheriff to seize and sell the defendant's assets, or garnishee (deduct instalments from) their wages.

In depth: Case management

Courts are increasingly attempting to manage cases in order to speed up the justice process. In New South Wales, the *Civil Procedure Act 2005* endeavours to 'facilitate the just, quick and cheap resolution of the real issues in the proceedings' (s56). Section 59 states, 'In any proceedings, the practice and procedure of the court should be implemented with the object of eliminating any lapse of time between the commencement of the proceedings and their final determination beyond that reasonably required for the interlocutory activities necessary for the fair and just determination of the issues in dispute between the parties and the preparation of the case for trial'. A similar objective has been incorporated into civil procedure regulations in a number of jurisdictions across Australia. For example, the *Uniform Civil Procedure Rules* 2005 (NSW) stipulate:

> 2.1 Directions and orders
> The court may, at any time and from time to time, give such directions and make such orders for the conduct of any proceedings as appear convenient (whether or not inconsistent with these rules or any other rules of court) for the just, quick and cheap disposal of the proceedings.

2.2 Appointment for hearing
The court may, at any time and from time to time, of its own motion, appoint a date for a hearing at which it may give or make the directions or orders referred to in rule 2.1.

2.3 Case management by the court
Without limiting the generality of rule 2.1, directions and orders may relate to any of the following:
(a) the filing of pleadings,
(b) the defining of issues, including requiring the parties, or their legal practitioners, to exchange memoranda in order to clarify questions,
(c) the provision of any essential particulars … [etc]

Reflection

Is there a conflict between case management and speedy resolution on the one hand, and individual justice on the other hand? Could case management compromise a fair trial or is 'justice delayed justice denied'?[26]

Criminal procedure

Criminal procedure covers all cases involving criminal law. Proceedings are brought by the Crown (the prosecution) against the person who has allegedly committed a crime (the defendant or accused). In practice the prosecution case is brought by lawyers who assist the Director of Public Prosecutions (DPP). Most criminal law is state-based, and each state has its own rules and regulations on how criminal matters are handled, and by which courts. In all cases, there is a presumption of innocence in favour of the defendant.

Here are the typical steps that are involved in criminal procedure:

- **Arrest** – police take the accused person into custody for questioning. This is usually where the alleged crime is quite serious. Lesser crimes, such as minor assaults, or regulatory offences such as breaches of motor vehicle laws, may not involve the person being arrested.
- **Application for bail** – this may be granted by the officer in charge at the relevant police station, or the court after a hearing. The notion of bail is that the accused person is released from custody on the basis that he or she will return to stand trial. Typically conditions are imposed, such as surrender of passport and bond,

> **TIP**
> Criminal procedures are outlined in various legislation in states and territories and guidelines such as the NSW Police Force Code of Practice for Custody, Rights, Investigation, Management and Evidence (CRIME).

[26] If you are interested in exploring case management issues further, you might like to refer to Chapters 9 and 10 of ALRC Discussion Paper 62, Review of the Federal Civil Justice System (1999), available at the ALRC website, www.alrc.gov.au/ (choose 'Publications' then 'Consultation papers' then 'Discussion papers').

where someone agrees to pay a sum of money if the accused does not appear at their hearing. A defendant who is not granted bail will remain in custody until the trial or sentencing (which may be for a number of months or years).[27]
- **Charge** – the particular offence that the defendant will be tried or sentenced for. The police prosecutors can negotiate with the accused about the charges, and may get them to agree to plead guilty to a lesser charge or provide information that incriminates others or helps solve a crime. At times there may be a plea bargain, where the accused agrees to plead guilty in return for a lesser charge.
- **Pre-trial processes** – these are similar to civil pleadings, including requests for further and better particulars and discovery of evidence.
- **Type of trial** – the type of trial that takes place will depend on the type of criminal offence that is alleged. There are two broad categories – summary and indictable offences. *Summary offences* are less serious, and are heard by a magistrate alone in a local or magistrates court. These include property offences of little value, offensive behaviour, trespass and assault. *Indictable offences* are more serious crimes, including homicide, kidnapping, armed robbery and sexual offences. They are generally tried before a judge and jury (although in some jurisdictions defendants may opt for some matters to be heard summarily instead). Generally, more serious offences are dealt with in a district court, although murder trials are heard in the Supreme Court.
- **Committal hearing** – a preliminary hearing for indictable offences in a local or magistrates court, to look at the strength of the prosecution case. If the court considers that the evidence could not sustain the charge, it will be dismissed and the accused released. Otherwise, the case will proceed to trial in a higher court.[28]
- **Trial** – usually involves a plea being entered by the defendant. If the plea is 'guilty', the matter can go straight to sentencing. If 'not guilty', the prosecution must prove beyond a reasonable doubt that the defendant did what was alleged. The trial will involve opening addresses, witnesses, and then closing addresses. In a jury trial, the jury reaches the verdict of guilty or not guilty, and the judge determines the penalty. If there is no jury, the judge will decide both the verdict and the sentence. Sentences may include a period of detention, release on a period of probation, release on a good behaviour bond, a fine, a community service order, or confiscation of property.

TIP
Arrest should only occur as a last resort. For example, the *Law Enforcement (Powers and Responsibilities) Act 2002* (NSW) makes it clear that an arrest should only be enforced to ensure a court appearance, prevent further offending, prevent the destruction of evidence, prevent harassment of witnesses or preserve the safety of the defendant (s 99(3)).

TIP
Fines are the most common type of penalty.

---

27 About 15% of defendants who have been refused bail will not even reach the sentencing stage: NSW Bureau of Crime Statistics and Research, *New South Wales Criminal Courts Statistics 2008*, Department of Attorney-General, Sydney (2009), 102 www.bocsar.nsw.gov.au/lawlink/bocsar/ll_bocsar.nsf/vwFiles/CCS08.pdf/$file/CCS08.pdf

28 Of the cases heard at the committal, almost 8% are discharged by the magistrate and a further 4% are withdrawn by the prosecution: Pia Salmelainen, 'Understanding Committal Hearings' *Crime and Justice Bulletin, Contemporary Issues in Crime and Justice*, NSW Bureau of Crime Statistics and Research, No. 18 (1992) 2, Figure 1: Outcome of committal hearings in NSW Local Courts, available at www.bocsar.nsw.gov.au/lawlink/.

The role of the jury in criminal and civil trials

The law on juries is largely statute based, except in relation to Commonwealth offences which are also governed by s 80 of the Constitution.[29] Most criminal cases, and virtually all civil cases, are decided by a judge without a jury. In 2005, for example, less than one per cent of criminal cases in New South Wales had a jury.[30] South Australia has abolished the use of juries in all civil cases and other states have placed severe restrictions upon their use. For example in New South Wales civil juries are largely limited to defamation cases.

Where a jury is used, the jury will be responsible for hearing all the evidence, including directions from the court, and deciding in secret whether the facts have been proved beyond a reasonable doubt. In some jurisdictions, such as Queensland, unanimous verdicts are required. This means that all jury members must agree on the outcome. If they cannot agree, the trial must begin again with a new jury. In some jurisdictions, such as New South Wales, Victoria, South Australia, Western Australia, the Northern Territory and Tasmania, majority verdicts are allowed (usually 10 or 11 out of 12 have to agree on the outcome).

Jury members are adult members of the community selected at random from the electoral roll. Some people are ineligible to serve on a jury – including lawyers, judges, police officers, prison officers, and government ministers.[31] Persons summoned for jury duty must attend court at the relevant date and time. Some may be challenged by the prosecution and defence, and may as a result be excused from jury duty. At the end 12 people are needed for a criminal jury, and in most states and territories there are varying numbers for civil cases: 12 in New South Wales; four in Queensland, the Northern Territory and the Australian Capital Territory; six in Victoria and Western Australia; and seven in Tasmania.

Juries have decided cases since the eleventh century under their historical name the assizes. Itinerant justices would travel around England, dispensing justice according to the customs of each village. Juries were initially used to inform the justices of the applicable customs and the facts of the case. The right to trial by jury appears to have originated in the Magna Carta in 1215, and the modern right to a trial by jury for any Commonwealth indictable offence exists in s 80 of the Constitution.[32] Unlike state trials, an accused may not waive their right to a jury in Commonwealth indictable offences (such as drug trafficking).

TIP
If you are summoned for jury duty while studying law, and it is not right in the middle of semester or exams, we strongly recommend that you do it. It is a valuable experience and one you cannot have once you are a lawyer.

---

29 See *Juries Act 1967* (ACT); *Jury Act 1977* (NSW); *Juries Act* (NT); *Jury Act 1995* (Qld); *Juries Act 1927* (SA), *Juries Act 2003* (Tas); *Juries Act 2000* (Vic); *Juries Act 1957* (WA). Also see *Jury Exemption Act 1965* (Cth).

30 New South Wales Law Reform Commission, Jury Service, (Issues Paper 28, 2006) at [1.6]. Available at www.lawlink.nsw.gov.au/lawlink/lrc/ll_lrc.nsf/pages/LRC_ip28toc

31 The New South Wales Law Reform Commission has recommended that lawyers be allowed to serve on juries: Jury Selection, (NSW LRC Report 117, 2007). In 2010 the NSW Attorney-General endorsed the recommendation.

32 This right was confirmed by the High Court in *Cheatle v R* (1993) 177 CLR 541, 562.

Reflection

Trial by jury is considered one of the cornerstones of a democratic system of justice, and jury service is seen as an important civic duty. Juries bring community values into the judicial process by allowing for public involvement in the administration of justice. However, juries are often criticised because they are expensive to run; they are not representative of the community, because many groups are excluded and often working adults get themselves excused from jury duty; cases are complex and jurors may not be equipped to assess the evidence; jury duty can be enormously stressful and, in violent crimes, distressing for jurors who are not used to seeing the darker side of the human psyche; and jury room deliberations are held in secret, so jurors with dominant personalities may impose their views on other jurors. Consider the pros and cons of a jury. When might a judge-only trial be preferable to a jury trial?

DISCUSSION QUESTIONS

1. Does our common law legal system put undue weight on resolving disputes in an adversarial manner?
2. Do you think that the growth of tribunals over the past 30 years shows that the courts are perhaps not the appropriate place to resolve certain issues – or is it merely evidence that the courts are too busy or lacking sufficient resources to resolve such disputes?
3. Which kinds of disputes are best suited to tribunals, and which are still best resolved by courts?

WEBLINKS AND FURTHER READING

Cairns, B *Australian Civil Procedure*, 7th edn, Lawbook Co, Sydney (2007).
Fitzroy Legal Service, The Law Handbook: your practical guide to the law in Victoria, www.lawhandbook.org.au/handbook.php
Legal Services Commission of South Australia, The Law Handbook Online, www.lawhandbook.sa.gov.au/
New South Wales Law Handbook Online, 10th edn, www2.lawhandbookonline.com.au/content/LHB-title.1.1.html
Sussex Street Community Law Service, The WA Law Handbook www.sscls.asn.au/law%20handbook/handbook.htm

Web resources on tribunals

Commonwealth AAT: www.aat.gov.au.

Veterans' Review Board: www.vrb.gov.au

Migration Review Tribunal: www.mrt-rrt.gov.au

National Native Title Tribunal: www.nntt.gov.au

State and territory tribunals – ACT: www.courts.act.gov.au/magistrates/; NSW: www.lawlink.nsw.gov.au/ then left menu Courts and tribunals; NT: www.nt.gov.au/justice/ntmc/; Qld: www.qcat.qld.gov.au/; SA: www.ssat.gov.au; Vic: www.vcat.vic.gov.au/; WA: www.sat.justice.wa.gov.au/

ONLINE RESOURCES FOR THIS CHAPTER

The following resources are available online at www.oup.com.au/orc/cwl2e
- Flashcard glossary
- Multiple choice questions
- Contract exercise
- Example of student work: torts problem question

6

Research: How Do I Find the Law?

WHAT WE WILL COVER IN THIS CHAPTER:

- Why legal research is important
- Where legal sources can be found
- Strategies and methodology for conducting legal research
- How to use a library catalogue
- How to find cases, legislation and secondary materials
- How to select the best research tool
- The need to keep your research updated
- How to cite cases and reference sources

Recommended approach to learning this topic

This chapter has been structured around examples, and we strongly recommend that you go through it while in the library and connected to the internet, so you can find the relevant sources on the shelves or online. Learning by doing is the best way to learn, so don't be lazy and just read how to do it – try doing it yourself! Like everything new, it can be a little confusing and even overwhelming at first – there are so many different research products and places to find information, and there are so many pitfalls to avoid. But the more you practise, the more comfortable and proficient you become. Putting in the time and energy now to become an effective legal researcher will repay itself in every single subject you study, from here until you graduate – and beyond. Trust us!

KEY TERMS

Annotations = notes added to a text to provide explanation, evaluation, or references to further information

Boolean searching = a method of using the operators AND, OR, and NOT between search terms in order to increase or limit the information retrieved when searching a database

Browsing = looking for information from a particular resource by a general or casual process, usually moving around the resource using main headings as a guide

Case citator = a research aid used to identify case names, the places where cases have been reported, the cases mentioned within a case, the articles which have been published discussing a case, and any later cases which refer to the case

Electronic resources = places to locate information on electronic devices, including CD-Rom, bibliographic databases, e-books, e-journals, websites and search engines

Encyclopedia = a comprehensive, concise compilation of information, divided into articles, and arranged systematically (e.g. alphabetically or by subject area)

Gazette = an official report, legal notice or public announcement published by government

Index = an alphabetised list of topics such as cases, legislation, or subjects with a link to or indication of where related material can be found in a resource

Law journal / Law review = a publication containing a series of articles on particular topics, issued periodically in print or online. A refereed journal is one that has been reviewed by two 'blind' referees (they do not know who the author is) with knowledge of the relevant field. Law journals are typically published by law schools, with editorial boards and committees that sometimes include law students

Law reports = the official publication, usually in print, of decisions from a specific court which raise significant points of law

Looseleaf service = a legal encyclopedia published in unbound sheets of paper, held in ring binders arranged alphabetically by subject area. Publishers regularly send subscribers replacement pages on topics where the law has changed, with instructions for which pages to discard and replace (often available online as a commentary service)

Medium-neutral citation = a form of reference for a case which allows a case to be cited the same way, whether it is in print or electronic format

Primary sources = the law itself, namely cases and legislation (statutes and regulations)

Print-based resources = places to locate information in printed (hard copy, paper) format, including dictionaries, text books, encyclopedias, law journals, law reports

Research methodology = the process adopted when conducting legal research, including deciding what needs researching, where to look, what search terms to use, and what to do with the results

Secondary sources = materials that help us understand the law, such as legal dictionaries, text books, law journals, and transcripts of parliamentary debates

Unreported judgments = court decisions which do not raise significant points of law, or which are so recent that they have not yet been officially published in a law report (typically law reports are published in volumes once a year)

> **TIP**
> There is a difference between reporting a judgment in a law report series and merely making it available online (where it is published but may still be unreported).

1: The importance of legal research

Students often completely underestimate the importance of legal research, seeing it as a skill they learn in first-year law and nothing more. In fact, legal research is one of the most important tools in a lawyer's toolkit. It is the key to finding out what the law is.

Every time you see a scene on a legal drama where the lawyer is demolishing the opponent's case, you are seeing the outcome of extensive, meticulous legal research. Imagine finding a case that supports your client's position, and advising them that they are sure to win. Then you go to court and it turns out that the case has been overruled, or recent legislation has been enacted that completely changes the law. Aside from having an angry client, you will feel silly!

Even if you study a particular area of law while at university, you are not likely to go into such fine detail as to be able to fully advise a client based on what you have learned. You will need to search for cases that are similar to the particular facts of the client's case.

Also, law is constantly changing and evolving, and lawyers need to use legal research to find out what the law currently is, or what the law was at a certain point in time that may be relevant for the client (for example when the alleged offence took place, or when a contract was concluded).

You can't assume that the answers will always be available online – what if you get a job in a country with few legal internet resources, or sporadic internet access? What if you get a job in a small firm with a very small library? The best lawyers are able to flexibly use whatever legal research resources are at their disposal, be they electronic or print-based.

There is no one place where every law and case is set out clearly and in a way that tells you it is up to date. For this reason, you need to have a research strategy that involves using different research tools and resources. Yes, that's right – you look for the same answer using various different sources, and you work out which answers are the most relevant and reliable. It is all about having a strategy which will allow you to check and cross-check your research, which will reduce the likelihood of missing anything important.

It seems a daunting task, but this chapter will help you learn the fundamental legal research skills and methodologies that will serve you throughout your law degree and your career ahead. As you go along, you will build upon these skills, learn new resources that technology makes available, and become increasingly more efficient and effective as a legal researcher.

2: Legal research methodology

In academia, research methodology is often used to refer to decisions about methods for conducting primary research – such as doing a survey or holding focus group interviews.[1] But in undergraduate law, it is uncommon for students to be given an assignment that requires them to conduct research involving human subjects. Usually the research involves locating particular law and analysing the issues that arise, or using it to solve a particular problem or draft a legal advice. Here's a simple methodology for approaching legal research tasks in law school.

Step 1: What am I trying to find?

Take a moment before you start researching, to think about what you are trying to find. Are you researching for a research essay, a problem question, or something else? Are you trying to find cases, legislation, secondary sources, or all of these? Are you trying to find the one right answer to a specific question, such as whether euthanasia is legal in your state or territory, or are you trying to find general information on a topic, such as children's rights?

Step 2: Decide on your research strategy

Decide how you are going to tackle the research. It is useful to look at what information you have already, to see whether it contains some useful pointers. If you only have a general area or scenario, you may need to brainstorm some key words that you might use to start researching, or give some thought to what area of law you think the topic relates to. Are there some obvious legal issues that need to be researched?

---

1 For detailed legal research methodology, see Terry Hutchinson, *Researching and Writing in Law*, Pyrmont, NSW, Lawbook Co (2006).

Don't just open up Google and type in some words – before you start researching, choose your research tools. The resources you use will depend on the information you are seeking. In this chapter we will cover the main research tools, and describe their use in finding different types of information. The better researchers use several different research tools to answer the one question – they may consult an index, a text book, an encyclopedia, some statutes and some cases.

Step 3: Do the research and sort out the results

As you undertake your searches, keep a note of where you have looked and what search terms you have used. This will save you repeating the same searches. You will soon find you have a mass of information. Keeping in mind the purpose of your research, you can sort through the research results to get rid of anything irrelevant and hone in on the most important results, which will themselves often lead you to further research. If you find conflicting results, check back to the currency of the source – one of them may be out of date. You should keep all relevant results, be they for or against your 'client'.

Step 4: Finalise your research outcomes

Now that you have the results – what have you found? Have you reached a conclusion on a particular question? Have you uncovered some anomaly in the law that needs to be addressed? Have you discovered that the relevant area of law is one that has changed little for years, or one that is in a constant state of flux? Most importantly, has the research you have undertaken and results you have found addressed your initial purpose for undertaking the research? If so, well done! You can now write it up in an essay or whatever format has been set for your assignment.

Exercise: research strategy scenario

Jenny has just completed her first aid course through St John Ambulance. She did the course because she has some young children and would hate for a situation to arise and not know what to do – for example if her child was burnt or bitten by something, or had an allergic reaction. But if she was at the scene of a car accident or she saw someone collapse in the street or in the office, she would most likely want to use her first aid to render assistance until an ambulance arrived. It has got her wondering – what would be her position in law if she helped a stranger or co-worker in that way? What if, despite her best efforts, the person died? What if, when giving CPR, she broke the person's ribs, which she has heard is common to do? Can she be sued? What if she catches something from the person – can she claim for that? She has heard that you have started studying law, and has approached you for the answer.

To start with, you would explain that you are not a lawyer and can't give her legal advice, but that as you are learning legal research you will use her scenario to see what information you can find – all care and no responsibility!

Let's use a stepped process to work our way through the problem.

Step 1: What am I trying to find?

You decide that what you're trying to find is the law that covers the legal rights and responsibilities of helpers. As you're not going to use the research results for an assignment or problem question, you won't need to keep such meticulous notes as you would if you were going to be referencing your research.

Step 2: Decide on your research strategy

At this stage you're not sure if this will be in a piece of legislation or some cases, so you decide it is best to brainstorm some useful search terms to start. Here are some ideas you have jotted down:

- first aid
- assistance
- causing harm
- liability
- emergency.

You decide to start off with a few legal encyclopedias to search for some of these terms, thinking that the results will give you some general reading which may lead you to some useful cases and pieces of legislation. You can then search for those primary sources and see if they contain the answer.

Step 3: Do the research and sort out the results

Let's start with *Laws of Australia*. It is available in the university library or via Legal Online. Why not open it up and do the search right now? Figure 6.1 shows what the starting page looks like.

FIGURE 6.1: THE LAWS OF AUSTRALIA USER INTERFACE

Let's see what happens if we just put in 'first aid' in the free text search and click 'search'. It gives us 113 hits! As we scroll through the results, we can see that the program has searched for 'first' and 'aid' instead of 'first aid', so we run the search again with double quotation marks ("first aid") and it comes back with 16 hits (Figure 6.2).

FIGURE 6.2: THE SEARCH REFINED USING QUOTE MARKS

That's a more manageable number of results. We click on some of them to see what we can find. If we click on the first hit, we get the result in Figure 6.3.

FIGURE 6.3: EXPLORING THE RESULTS

That is a start – there is no general duty to render first aid, except in Northern Territory where the failure to act must be 'callous'. So we can tell Jenny she doesn't *have* to render first aid.

As we go back to our list of 16 hits we find some unhelpful information. But as we get close to the bottom we see something relevant – 'Medical professionals and other good samaritans who provide aid in emergency situations are statutorily protected from liability in some jurisdictions'. We click on that (Figure 6.4).

FIGURE 6.4: A USEFUL LEAD

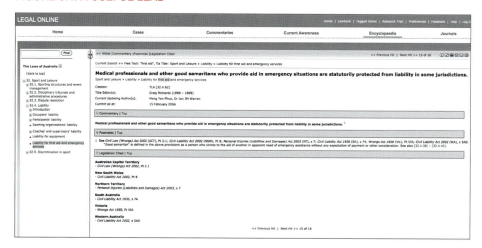

What is useful about the above finding is that it gives us the definition of a good samaritan as being someone who aids in an emergency situation without expectation of payment, and it gives us a reference to more information (which we look at but find it is more about sporting volunteers), plus some useful pieces of legislation. However, note the currency information at the top 'Current as at: 15 February 2006'. This is not very current! We'll need to look at the relevant legislation and check it is still in force.

Let's assume Jenny is in New South Wales. So we want to find the *Civil Liability Act 2002* (NSW). Let's use a free search engine, AustLII, to find it. Figure 6.5 shows us what the home page looks like.

FIGURE 6.5: THE AUSTLII USER INTERFACE

About AustLII | Media Releases | Contact | Translate | Privacy | Disclaimers | Feedback | H
Australasian Legal Information Institute
A joint facility of UTS and UNSW Faculties of Law
Search
[Advanced Search] [LawCite] [Help]
401 databases from all Australasian jurisdictions
Last updated 10 May 2010
News & Database Additions
Cases & Legislation
>> Australia
All Databases
Commonwealth
ACT
New South Wales
Northern Territory
Queensland
South Australia
Tasmania
Victoria
Western Australia
>> New Zealand (NZLII)
Libraries
Law Journals
Law Reform
Legal Scholarship
Treaties
Indigenous Law
Intellectual Property Law
Military Law
Employment Opportunities at AustLII for 2010 - Expressions of interest sought
AustLII requests new and renewed funding for 2010 - Contribution Form
High Court of Australia Bulletin [2010] HCAB 4 (4 May 2010)
Supreme Court of Tasmania - Full Court (TASFC) 2010-
Australian Construction Law Newsletter (AUConstrLawNlr) 1988-
Australian Capital Territory Numbered Regulations Explanatory Statements 1989-
Monash Business Review (MonashBusRw) 2005-
Fair Work Australia Decisions (FWA) 2009-
Victorian Scrutiny of Acts and Regulations Committee - Alert Digests 2009-
New South Wales Acts As Made
New South Wales Regulations As Made
New South Wales EPIs As Made
The Newcastle Law Review (NewcLawRw) 1995-
ATO Wine Equalisation Tax Determinations 2010-
Past announcements...
Latest Australasian Catalog Additions
Thorpe v Commonwealth of Australia [No 3] [1997] HCA 21 (12 June 1997)
Link added: >> Aboriginals & Torres Strait Islanders >> Case-law
Update Status
Update Status for Case Law
Update Status for Journals
Update Status for Legislation
AustLII Contributors
AustLII Annual Report 2008 (PDF)
Law Council encourages contributions (PDF)
Contribute $$$
All Contributors
By Jurisdiction
Legal Education
Business & Industry
Community
Competitive Grant Providers
Courts, Tribunals & Regulators
Government Agencies
Law Societies & Bar Associations

We need to click on the left side – on 'New South Wales' – and then, when the next page comes up, on 'New South Wales Consolidated Acts'. That brings up a handy list of letters and we click on 'C' and then scroll down to *Civil Liability Act* (Figure 6.6).

FIGURE 6.6: INDEX PAGE OF AN ACT

New South Wales Consolidated Ac...
CHILDREN LEGISLATION AMENDMENT (WOOD INQUIRY RECOMMENDATIONS) ACT 2009
CHILDREN'S COURT ACT 1987
CHIPPING NORTON LAKE AUTHORITY ACT 1977
CHIROPRACTORS ACT 2001
CHOICE OF LAW (LIMITATION PERIODS) ACT 1993
CHRIST CHURCH CATHEDRAL, NEWCASTLE, CEMETERY ACT 1966
CHRISTIAN ISRAELITE CHURCH PROPERTY TRUST ACT 2007
CHURCH OF ENGLAND (NORFOLK ISLAND) ACT 1981
CHURCHES OF CHRIST IN NEW SOUTH WALES INCORPORATION ACT 1947
CHURCHES OF CHRIST, SCIENTIST, INCORPORATION ACT 1962
CITY OF SYDNEY ACT 1988
CITY TATTERSALL'S CLUB ACT AMENDMENT ACT 1936
CITY TATTERSALL'S CLUB ACT OF 1912
CIVIL AVIATION (CARRIERS' LIABILITY) ACT 1967
CIVIL LIABILITY ACT 2002
CIVIL PROCEDURE ACT 2005
CLASSIFICATION (PUBLICATIONS, FILMS AND COMPUTER GAMES) ENFORCEMENT ACT 1995
CLASSIFICATION (PUBLICATIONS, FILMS AND COMPUTER GAMES) ENFORCEMENT AMENDMENT (UNIFORM CLASSIFICATION) ACT 2004
CLASSIFICATION (PUBLICATIONS, FILMS AND COMPUTER GAMES) ENFORCEMENT AMENDMENT ACT 2001
CLEAN COAL ADMINISTRATION ACT 2008
CLYDE WASTE TRANSFER TERMINAL (SPECIAL PROVISIONS) ACT 2003
CO-OPERATIVE HOUSING AND STARR-BOWKETT SOCIETIES ACT 1998
CO-OPERATIVE SCHEMES (ADMINISTRATIVE ACTIONS) ACT 2001
CO-OPERATIVES ACT 1992
CO-OPERATIVES AMENDMENT ACT 1997
COAL ACQUISITION ACT 1981
COAL ACQUISITION LEGISLATION REPEAL ACT 2007
COAL AND OIL SHALE MINE WORKERS (SUPERANNUATION) ACT 1941
COAL INDUSTRY (INDUSTRIAL MATTERS) ACT 1946
COAL INDUSTRY ACT 2001
COAL MINE HEALTH AND SAFETY ACT 2002
COAL MINING INDUSTRY LONG SERVICE LEAVE (REPEAL) ACT 1992
COAL OWNERSHIP (RESTITUTION) ACT 1990
COASTAL PROTECTION ACT 1979
COLLARENEBRI WATER SUPPLY ACT 1968

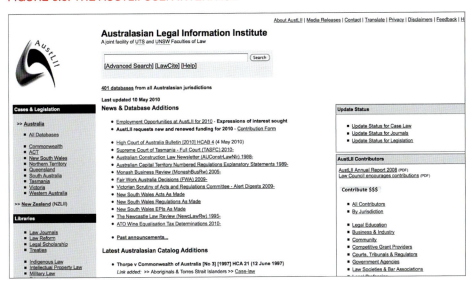

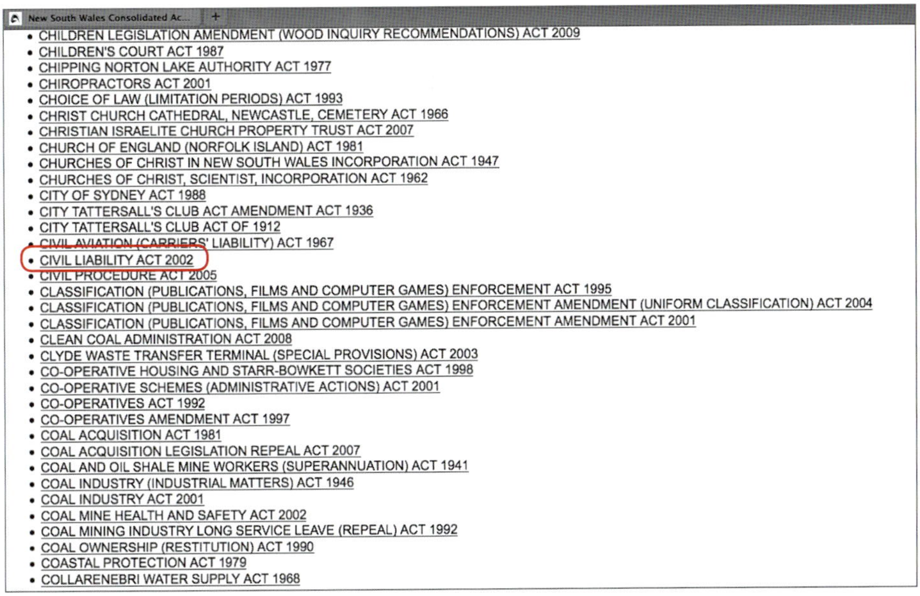

We were told in the *Laws of Australia* database that we need to look at Part 8 of the Act. So we scroll down the index until we see the relevant link (Figure 6.7).

FIGURE 6.7: HOMING IN ON PARTICULAR SECTIONS

```
CIVIL LIABILITY ACT 2002

54B.    Definitions
54C.    Application of Division
54D.    Damages supervision orders
54E.    Additional matters relating to damages supervision orders
54F.    Estates under supervision of Protective Commissioner
54G.    Hindering or obstructing NSW Trustee and Guardian
54H.    Evidence of NSW Trustee and Guardian's right to act

PART 8 - GOOD SAMARITANS

55.     Application of Part
56.     Who is a good samaritan
57.     Protection of good samaritans
58.     Exclusion from protection

PART 8A - FOOD DONORS

58A.    Interpretation
58B.    Application of Part
58C.    Protection of food donors

PART 9 - VOLUNTEERS

59.     Application of Part
60.     Definitions
61.     Protection of volunteers
62.     Liability not excluded for criminal acts
63.     Liability of intoxicated volunteer not excluded
64.     Liability of volunteer not excluded if acting outside scope of activities or contrary to instructions
65.     Liability not excluded if insurance required
66.     Liability not excluded for motor accidents
```

This tells us that there are four sections that are relevant. We might as well read them all, so we click on the hyperlink to 55, and from there, just click 'Next'. Section 57 (Figure 6.8) seems the most relevant to Jenny.

FIGURE 6.8: THE CONTENT OF SECTION 57

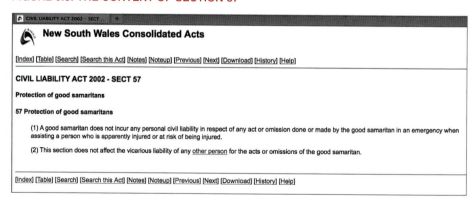

So a good samaritan will not incur personal civil liability for acts or omissions in an emergency. But we also check s 58, and it says that the protection from personal liability does not apply if it is an intentional or negligent act or omission by the good samaritan that caused the injury in the first place. It also does not apply if the good samaritan was under the influence of alcohol or drugs, and the good samaritan failed to exercise reasonable care and skill. It also does not apply if the good samaritan falsely represents having certain skills or expertise.

But before we run back to Jenny to give her this information, we had better check how up to date it is. We click on 'Notes' and we see the information in Figure 6.9.

FIGURE 6.9: CHECKING NOTATIONS FOR EXTRA INFORMATION

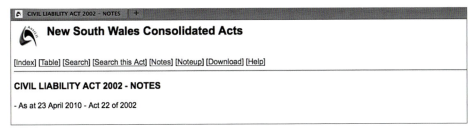

We think this is pretty up to date, but we feel we should warn Jenny that we're not sure whether anything else has happened since then, and when we learn how to find out ourselves, we'll let her know.

Because we are a budding legal researcher, we are curious whether anyone has been charged under s 58. We go back to s 58 and click on 'Noteup'. Figure 6.10 shows what we get.

FIGURE 6.10: THE NOTEUP FEATURE

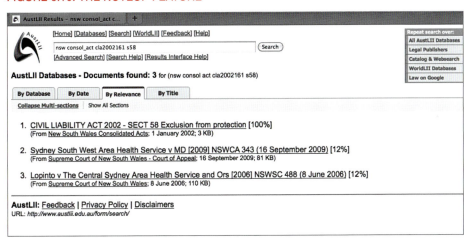

The first one is the section itself, which we have already seen. We click on the second document, which is a 2009 decision of the New South Wales Court of Appeal. Disappointingly, when we scroll down we find there is reference to the *Civil Liability Act*, and reference to a s 58, but of a different Act. So it is no use. We go back and click on the third document, which is a 2006 decision of the New South Wales Court of Appeal. Sadly it also refers to a s 58 of a different Act, and a different provision of the *Civil Liability Act*.

Step 4: Finalise your research outcomes

Let's go back to our original purpose, and check whether we found what we were looking for. We are pretty satisfied that if Jenny, armed with her first aid qualification, were to provide emergency assistance to a stranger at a car accident scene, she would be considered a good samaritan. If she rendered aid, and was not drunk or drugged or otherwise acting outside the scope of the first aid training she had completed, she should be protected from liability, even if the person died. This would include reasonable injury caused during rendering life-saving aid such as CPR. If she was sued she could use s 58 of the *Civil Liability Act 2002* (NSW) to protect her.

We feel pretty happy. But we need to think about what we might have missed. First of all, we have only really covered the NSW position. What would happen if she was on holidays interstate or overseas and she rendered aid? What about in the workplace – do different rules apply there, for example if she was a first aid warden or something? And we still haven't answered Jenny's question about whether she can claim against the person if she caught something from them while rendering first aid to them. So we are going to have to go back and do some further research before we can confidently report back to Jenny. How about using the above tools to do some further research on this topic and see what you come up with?

You can see that, with the above methodology, we used an encyclopedia and a free online search engine. Those are just two of the available research tools. In the next three sections, we will consider which tools are most effective to use for finding primary sources (cases and legislation) and information via secondary sources (such as indexes and legal encyclopedias). Bear in mind, though, that primary sources are the law itself, and that secondary sources are just writings about the law, and are not as authoritative as primary sources. For further information see Chapter 3.

IMPORTANT: Not all sources are of the same value!

It is extremely important that you are discriminating about the value of your research findings. A primary source (case reference or a reference to a section in a piece of legislation) is the most valuable authority you can get, because it is the actual law itself. A High Court decision will be more persuasive than the decision of an inferior court, or a tribunal. Below that are useful secondary sources, such as refereed law journal articles, or books that have been published analysing a particular area of law, by experts in that field. The words of a judge, expressed in a speech at a conference or other event, may also be useful. Below that are sources that may be unreliable, or published by persons with little legal expertise, such as newspaper articles, some websites (often found via a Google search), and Wikipedia (which anyone can change, even people who have never studied a day at law school!). First-year law students often have difficulty distinguishing between different sources, treating for example a newspaper report with as much authority as a High Court decision, or only citing from text books and websites. If you remember that there is a hierarchy of sources, you will remember to always cite the superior source. See 'Using secondary sources' in Chapter 3 for an example on this.

Exercise: Ranking sources

Put these sources in order of importance, from most authoritative to least authoritative, for the *Sons of Gwalia* decision.

Importance (1–10)	Source
	'Government to overturn Sons of Gwalia ruling', *Sydney Morning Herald* 19 January 2010
	Cary Di Lernia, 'Implications of the Sons of Gwalia decision' (2008) 7(1) *Journal of Law and Financial Management* 8
	Sons of Gwalia Ltd v Margaretic (2007) 231 CLR 160
	Cited in *White v Designated Manager of IP Australia (No. 2)* [2008] FCA 816 (3 June 2008)
	Australian Law Reform Commission, *Annual Report 2006–7*, Report 106, Appendix H
	deListed website, www.delisted.com.au, reference to *Sons of Gwalia* (ID 7589)
	'Sons of Gwalia', Wikipedia entry
	Sons of Gwalia Limited (Subject to Deed of Company Arrangement) v Margaretic [2006] FCAFC 92 (Unreported, Federal Court of Australia, Finkelstein, Gyles and Jacobsen JJ, 15 June 2006)
	Yahoo News, http://au.news.yahoo.com/thewest/a/-/breaking/5912273/e-y-agrees-to-125m-sons-of-gwalia-settlement/ – reference to Kate Emery, 'Ernst & Young agrees to $125m Sons of Gwalia settlement', *The West Australian*, 4 September 2009, 10.22am
	Australian Government Corporations and Markets Advisory Committee, 'Shareholder claims against insolvent companies: Implications of the Sons of Gwalia decision', Report, December 2008.

GO ONLINE
Go online for answers.

3: Using a library catalogue or search engine

Library catalogue searching

We use the library catalogue to find where in the library we can physically locate a particular book, journal, law report, video, or DVD, and how we can electronically connect to databases the university has access to via subscriptions.

Although every library has its own Online Public Access Catalogue (OPAC), the basic structure of most library catalogues is the same. We strongly recommend that you visit your university's library website and practise using the catalogue.

Catalogues usually allow you to search by the author, the title of a book or law journal, or the general topic area. Libraries classify topics under defined subject headings, so you should think carefully about what subject you should enter. If you are doing a subject on a particular area of law, then you could simply type that in – for example, 'criminal law', or 'contract law'. You may also find that you can search by the subject number and find resources that the lecturers in that subject recommend to students.

Usually you can access online versions of subscription-based legal databases via the library catalogue. You could, for example, do a title search for 'Casebase', and find the results include a hyperlink from the library catalogue to the subscription database.

Using search engines

Search engines accompany not only library catalogues but databases of legislation, cases, and journals, and also appear on most websites. For the majority of commencing university students, the most familiar search engine is Google. Although this is frowned upon as a method for conducting legal research – and a student should never put Google as a reference in a law assignment – Google may be useful when you are first starting out on an unfamiliar research topic, to draw your attention to the existence of a particular body or organisation that is involved in the relevant area of law.

However, Google will also link to a lot of 'junk' sites – junk because they are unofficial sites, containing information posted by individuals containing errors or unfounded opinions. Therefore you need to be vigilant when considering search results, asking yourself:

1. Is this a reliable source?
2. Is this information applicable in my jurisdiction?
3. How long ago was this information posted?
4. How relevant is the information to my needs?

Let's say for example that we were interested in using Google to help find out what law applies in outer space. We enter 'space law' in the search criteria and click 'the web' rather than 'pages from Australia' because it is likely to be an international form of law. The results shown in Figure 6.11 come up.

FIGURE 6.11: THE INITIAL GOOGLE SEARCH RESULT

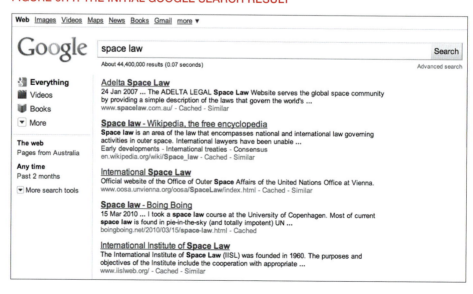

Of course thousands of results come up from such a general search, but let's just consider these first seven results.

The first is Adelta Space Law. We click on the link and find that the site is hosted by Adelta Legal, described as 'an Australian legal firm with a specialist practice in space and technology law'. The 'contact us' link takes us to Michael Davis, an Adelaide lawyer. It says he has a law degree from University of Adelaide and a Masters from the International Space University. He is also the Secretary of the Australian Space Industry Chamber of Commerce, and represented Australia at a UN space meeting in 1999. We look at his list of publications and find mainly presentations and lectures, as opposed to books and refereed journal articles. We conclude that he is likely to be a useful source for practical information and summaries on law but will not provide us with primary research data to use. So we decide to use the information on the website to provide background information about the main treaties on space law.

The second result is from Wikipedia. We know that anyone can contribute to Wikipedia, and read the information for general background and for the links and references contained. The third result takes us directly to the website of the United Nations Office of Outer Space Affairs. This is the most authoritative result so far, and contains an enormous amount of information.

The fourth result is a student blog, which we opt not to read, and the fifth result is the International Institute of Space Law. We know to be wary of the use of the word 'institute' because they are not necessarily official or authoritative (see for example the International Beauty Institute, which turns out to be a small college in Orange in New South Wales). We immediately go to the 'about us' link and find the International Institute of Space Law was created in 1960, is registered in the Netherlands, holds annual colloquia, and we conclude it may be useful from the point of view of its expert membership.

The sixth result takes us to the Institute of Air and Space Law at McGill University, whose mission is to provide graduate legal education on the topic. The seventh result is a Google book on 'Space Law: Basic Legal Documents', published in the Netherlands in 2005.

Therefore, our Google search has taken us to some reasonably useful documents, and has served as a useful primer for conducting research by bringing to our attention some useful bodies and organisations involved in space law. The Google search has been useful because of the discerning approach we have taken to the results, considering not only what information is provided, but also who is providing it, when it was posted, and what value we believe the information will have for us.

Boolean searching

The above search for 'space law' using a free online search engine returned 125 million hits, and we only looked at the first seven of them. It is impossible, unless you intend to spend the rest of your life researching space law, to go through that many hits. Clearly we need to have a method for refining our search so that we can find fewer results, which are more relevant. This can save us a lot of work. Boolean searching facilitates this, by using operators 'AND', 'OR' and 'NOT' (Table 6.1).

TIP
The name 'boolean' searching came from George Boole, a nineteenth-century mathematician who used algebra to create logical connectors between search terms.

TABLE 6.1: BOOLEAN OPERATORS

Operator	Purpose	Example
AND	Useful to reduce the number of results, by asking the search engine to only provide results which have both or all of the terms you have specified	Space and Treaty
OR	Useful where there may be two different terms which are used for the same topic, and you want to search for both of them	Treaty or convention
NOT	Useful to reduce the number of results, by asking the search engine to ignore some terms you don't want	Space not aviation

Databases usually put an 'or' automatically between two words, if you have not included a Boolean operator.[2] This means that a search for 'space law' will return 'space' or 'law'. If you want space law, you can use inverted commas. Doing this for the above Google search, which returned 125 million hits for space law without inverted commas, gives 234 000 hits. Inverted commas can be used for any title or phrase you want to search on, for example 'Office of Outer Space Affairs', 'Manual on Space Law' or 'common heritage of mankind'.

Other useful operators and symbols in conducting legal research are shown in Table 6.2.

TABLE 6.2: OTHER USEFUL OPERATORS

Operator	Purpose	Example
w/5	This is a proximity operator, which allows you to find a word that is within five words of another word (you can also use other numbers w/10 or w/20 words, and some databases use 'near' instead, defined as within 10 words)	Damage w/5 'space objects' (will find phrases such as 'damage caused by space objects' and 'space objects result in damage')
* or !	These are truncation symbols, which allow you to search for all versions of a root word	Launch* (will search for launch, launched, launching etc)
?	This is a wildcard character, which allows the replacement of any single character in a word. It is useful where a word may have more than one spelling	Organi?ation (will return both organisation and organization)
( )	Helps to show relationships between groups of words, just as you would use them in a mathematical calculation which used plus and multiply (e.g. 5 + 4 + (7 x 8))	space and law and (Australia or New Zealand) (will search for space law relating to Australia and/or New Zealand)

---

2   Note that different databases may have different default settings. For example even though Google defaults to 'and', LexisNexis AU defaults to reading words in a string as a phrase, so you need to manually add 'and' or 'or' if you want results that contain either both or either of your search terms.

You will need to find out which operators a particular database uses, and there will usually be a link from the home page, or a 'help' button.[3] For example, with truncation symbols, three legal databases use the * symbol (AGIS, Legal Online and CCH Online) while one uses the ! symbol (LexisNexis AU).

Exercise: Boolean searching

What would you enter into a search field if you wanted to find information about murder (which you understand is also referred to as homicide) but you don't want to get information on the murder of children, (which you understand is called infanticide)?

4: Finding legislation

Before you proceed to search for legislation, you should think about whether you are looking for a draft piece of legislation (bill) or one that has been enacted (Act or regulation). You should also think about which parliament made it – which is the same as asking which jurisdiction it is from. This is because there tend to be separate databases for legislation from each of the nine parliaments in Australia as well as separate databases for Acts, regulations and bills. See for example AustLII's interface for Commonwealth legislation (Figure 6.12).

FIGURE 6.12: COMMONWEALTH LEGISLATION PAGE AT AUSTLII

---

3   See for example www.austlii.edu.au/austlii/help/search.html (for AustLII searching) and www.google.com/help/refinesearch.html (for Google searching).

The contents in each of the nine links are as follows:

- **Commonwealth Consolidated Acts**[4] – the current version of each piece of legislation that is in force, including any amendments that have come into effect since it was enacted
- **Commonwealth Consolidated Regulations** – the current version of each regulation that is currently in force, including any amendments that have come into effect since it was enacted
- **Commonwealth Numbered Acts** – the Acts as they were passed by parliament, arranged alphabetically and by year (for example if an Act has been amended by a later Act, the original Act plus the amending Act will be in this database)
- **Commonwealth Numbered Regulations** – the regulations as they were passed by parliament, arranged alphabetically and by year
- **Commonwealth Bills** – draft legislation which has not yet passed through Federal Parliament
- **Commonwealth Repealed Acts** – these are Acts which used to be in force but have since been repealed
- **Commonwealth Bills Explanatory Memoranda** – documents produced by the parliamentary drafters to explain the bill and its intended effect
- **Commonwealth Numbered Regulations Explanatory Statements** – documents produced by whichever entity drafted the regulation, to explain the regulation and its intended operation
- **Commonwealth Legislation Tables** – lists legislation passed in each particular year, including new Acts and existing Acts that have been amended in that year

Finding legislation when you have the citation

You will use this approach where, for example, you have *Radiation Protection Act* (NT) or *Telecommunications Act 1997* (Cth). The first step is to ascertain which jurisdiction the legislation is from – Commonwealth, the Australian Capital Territory, New South Wales, the Northern Territory, Queensland, South Australia, Tasmania, Victoria, or Western Australia? This is because, for each of the nine parliaments, there is a website containing legislation enacted by it:

- Commonwealth: legislation passed by Federal parliament is available on ComLaw, www.comlaw.gov.au, which is a website hosted by the Commonwealth Attorney-General's Department (Figure 6.13). There is a 'Quick Search' (see the middle of the screen shot) or an option to 'Browse' (see the menu on the left side).

---

[4] Technically these are compilations, rather than consolidations. A consolidated Act is where parliament passes an Act that covers everything in the original Act plus all amendments that have been entered since. Here, AustLII is compiling the original Act plus the amendments set out in Amendment Acts, so that users always have the complete, current version. But as the complete, current version has not actually been passed by parliament in that form, it is a compilation and not a consolidated Act.

FIGURE 6.13: SEARCH OPTIONS ON COMLAW

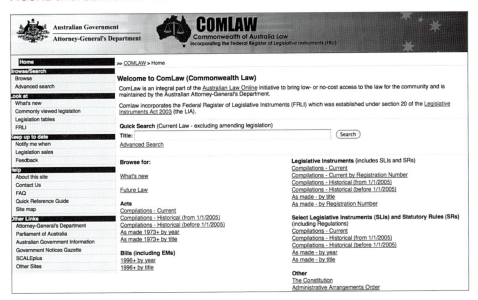

- Australian Capital Territory: www.legislation.act.gov.au
- New South Wales: www.legislation.nsw.gov.au
- Northern Territory: www.nt.gov.au/dcm/legislation/
- Queensland: www.legislation.qld.gov.au/
- South Australia: www.legislation.sa.gov.au
- Tasmania: www.thelaw.tas.gov.au/index.w3p
- Victoria: www.legislation.vic.gov.au
- Western Australia: www.slp.wa.gov.au/ then click through on the bar to reach the legislation database

As an alternative to using the separate websites provided for the legislation from each parliament, AustLII contains the legislation for all jurisdictions on the one site, at www.austlii.edu.au.

Let's say we have the *Radiation Protection Act* (NT).[5] We know this is a Northern Territory Act, so we go to the relevant link from the above list, and we click on 'View legislation alphabetically'. We then scroll down to R, which expands the list for all legislation commencing with R, and click on the *Radiation Protection Act*. It comes up with the HTML version, and a link to a Word and a PDF version.

Most law libraries also hold printed copies of legislation, at least from the state or territory in which the library is located, together with Commonwealth legislation (some also have legislation from other states and territories, and overseas jurisdictions such as England). The library catalogue will lead you to the relevant shelves, and you will find the statutes in bound volumes arranged by the year in which they were passed. Indexes listing legislation by title, number (e.g. 9/2009), and subject matter

TIP
Some jurisdictions continue to treat only the officially printed legislation as the authorised version in court, but in practice this is only of use in the unlikely event that there is some discrepancy between the officially printed version and the online version.

TIP
AustLII, which is short for Australian Legal Information Institute, is part of WorldLII, a global portal for legislation, case law and other legal resources from countries around the world. This initiative began in Australia in the 1990s and has since spread to the world. There are many LII's now, all of which come under the umbrella of WorldLII. See for example BAILII (British and Irish) CanLII (Canadian), PacLII (20 Pacific countries) and SAFLII (16 southern African countries).

---

5   It is customary for Northern Territory legislation not to state the year of enactment once it has been amended for the first time .

are also usually available. There is also a separate series of consolidated legislation which is the printed version of all statutes alphabetically organised by volume and with all amendments 'consolidated' into that legislation up to a point in time. You may find it necessary to use the print resources if the electronic resources are down and you are in a rush, or if you are looking for historical legislation which is not available online.

Finding legislation by subject area

You may need to find state or Commonwealth legislation that deals with a particular subject area, or topic that arises in the context of a legal problem scenario you have been given. There are various resources you can use here:

- **Legislative subject index** – a subject index lists legislation alphabetically by subject, with sub-headings under each subject. For each sub-heading, relevant legislation is listed, as well as 'see also' for other related subject headings that may be useful. Here is an example:[6]

    > Spouses
    > See also **De facto relationships**
    > **Domestic partners**
    > **Married women**
    > *Adoption Act 1984*
    > *Crimes Act 1958*
    > *Evidence Act 1958*
    > *Infertility Treatment Act 1995*
    > *Marriage Act 1958*
    > *Property Law Act 1958*

- Subject indexes exist for legislation from different jurisdictions – see: Commonwealth: Wicks Subject Index to Commonwealth Legislation
- New South Wales: Subject Index to the Acts and Regulations of New South Wales, New South Wales Statutes Annotations and References (Thomsons); New South Wales Statutes Annotations (LexisNexis)
- Queensland: Queensland Statutes Annotations (LexisNexis)
- South Australia: Subject Index to South Australian Legislation[7]
- Tasmania: Indexes to the Legislation of Tasmania, Part 2
- Victoria: Index to Subject Matter of Victorian Legislation, 9th edn (2008)
- Western Australia: Statutes of Western Australia, Vol 3, Index
- Note that the ACT and NT currently do not have general indexes.

---

[6] Taken from www.ocpc.vic.gov.au/CA2572B3001B894B/WebObj/subjectindexsamplepage/$File/subjectindexsamplepage.pdf.

[7] Available at www.alla.asn.au/sa/sisal/sisal.html.

- **Lawlex** – a product of SAI Global, available at www.lawlex.com.au has a subject index for legislation across all jurisdictions which you can browse, see the example in Figure 6.14, where we have expanded 'Family Law and Relationships' to give subjects such as adoption, children and young persons, and then expanded 'Marriage and De Facto Relationships' to give a list of relevant legislation around Australia for that subject.

FIGURE 6.14: LEGISLATION ON LAWLEX

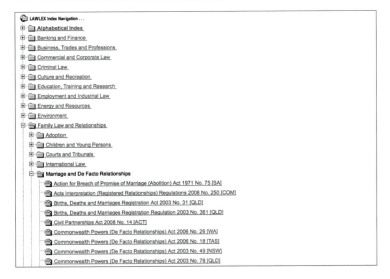

Other products with similar features are LawNow Legislation, a subscription-based product of LexisNexis, and LawOne, a subscription-based product of an Australian e-publisher, TimeBase.

- **AustLII** – at www.austlii.edu.au, you can do an 'Advanced Search' to search across a specific database (such as Victorian legislation) or across 'All legislation databases'.
- **Textbooks** – if you find a textbook on a particular area of law, you can use the index to find the chapter on the relevant subject matter, and usually the relevant legislation will be mentioned. This is useful for two reasons – first, because you get the citation and you know from above how to find legislation when you have the title, and second, because the textbook is likely to include some discussion on the legislation.
- **Legal encyclopedias** – the main two are *Laws of Australia* and *Halsbury's Laws of Australia*, but there are also specialised encyclopedias on topics such as industrial law or the goods and services tax (GST).

TIP
Always remember to check currency information when using any database product: this will show you how up to date it is.

Finding delegated legislation

Delegated legislation (also referred to as subordinate or subsidiary legislation), is law created by bodies under delegation from parliament, and includes regulations, rules, legislative instruments etc. The most common is regulations, and these are easy to locate on AustLII – where you find the link to legislation for each particular jurisdiction, you will also find the link to regulations. There are also specific sites for each jurisdiction:

- **Commonwealth** – www.comlaw.gov.au has a link from the homepage to legislative instruments, including current and historical compilations
- **Australian Capital Territory** – www.legislation.act.gov.au provides all subordinate laws, disallowable instruments, approved forms, notifiable instruments and commencement notices, both currently in force and repealed
- **New South Wales** – www.legislation.nsw.gov.au allows searching of regulations and environmental planning instruments
- **Northern Territory** – www.nt.gov.au/dcm/legislation/current.html includes a link to viewing legislation by type, which includes separate alphabetical lists of regulations, rules, by-laws, and fishery management plans
- **Queensland** – www.legislation.qld.gov.au/OQPChome.htm allows searching of current subordinate legislation in force, or by year in which the subordinate legislation was made
- **South Australia** – www.legislation.sa.gov.au/ includes current and historical regulations
- **Tasmania** – www.thelaw.tas.gov.au/index.w3p includes statutory rules, including a drop down menu for recent rules and a list of rules that have not yet commenced
- **Victoria** – www.legislation.vic.gov.au/ links to statutory rules, listed by title and number with a search facility also included
- **Western Australia** – www.slp.wa.gov.au/legislation/statutes.nsf/default.html includes subsidiary legislation in force and ceased, including rules, regulations and some legislative instruments

Finding bills

As with finding legislation, you have the choice of using one of the specific websites for each jurisdiction, or AustLII. Here are the links:

- **Commonwealth** – ComLaw, www.comlaw.gov.au contains links from the home page to bills since 1996, arranged by year and alphabetically by title
- **Australian Capital Territory** – www.legislation.act.gov.au/b/default.asp lists current bills alphabetically, and by year, by assembly, by those that are passed and awaiting notification, and a list by year of bills that have been discharged, negatived, withdrawn or have lapsed
- **New South Wales** – www.parliament.nsw.gov.au/prod/parlment/nswbills.nsf/V3BillsHome lists bills since 1989 alphabetically, including separate lists for bills introduced by private members, bills in the Legislative Assembly, and in the Legislative Council

- **Northern Territory** – www.dcm.nt.gov.au/strong_service_delivery/supporting_government/register_of_legislation lists bills since 1995 by parliamentary session, year, sponsor and bills currently before the Legislative Assembly
- **Queensland** – www.legislation.qld.gov.au/Bill_Pages/bills_home.htm includes bills since 1992 by year, date and parliamentary sitting
- **South Australia** – www.legislation.sa.gov.au/browseBills.aspx lists current bills and bills introduced to parliament since 2005
- **Tasmania** – www.thelaw.tas.gov.au/index.w3p includes bills since 2002
- **Victoria** – www.legislation.vic.gov.au/ lists current bills. Click on 'Parliamentary Documents' then 'Bills'
- **Western Australia** – www.slp.wa.gov.au/legislation/statutes.nsf/default.html includes bills since 1997

Remember, however, that a bill is a draft piece of legislation that has not yet passed through parliament or commenced, and is therefore not yet law.

Finding out whether legislation has commenced

As discussed in Chapter 3, there is a general rule that legislation comes into force on the date of assent, a specific number of days thereafter (14 or 28 days), or on a date to be proclaimed. If notification or proclamation is required, it is necessary to check the relevant government *Gazette*, which is the place of publication of such official announcements. These are available in print in libraries, although the more up-to-date version is online:

- **Commonwealth** – www.ag.gov.au/govgazette
- **Australian Capital Territory** – www.gazettes.act.gov.au
- **New South Wales** – http://more.nsw.gov.au/gazette
- **Northern Territory** – www.nt.gov.au/ntg/gazette.shtml
- **Queensland** – https://www.bookshop.qld.gov.au (choose menu items Browse Catalogue –> Law and safety –> You and the law –> Government gazettes)
- **South Australia** – www.governmentgazette.sa.gov.au
- **Tasmania** – www.publicinfo.tas.gov.au/
- **Victoria** – www.gazette.vic.gov.au/
- **Western Australia** – www.slp.wa.gov.au/gazette/gazette.nsf

TIP

Just because an Act says that it comes into force on a date to be proclaimed does not mean it is not now in force – you need to check whether it has since been proclaimed, by checking the *Gazette*.

Finding legislation in force at a certain date

To date we have assumed that you have been looking for the current legislation in force. But there may be times, such as when you are acting for a client in relation to an incident that occurred at a certain date, when you will want to find out the law that applied as at that date. You might, alternatively, be doing research into legislative developments in a particular area and want to see the legislation at the time of each particular amendment over the past century. Either way, you need to have tools which will enable you to establish what legislation was in force at a particular point in time.

The easiest tool is AustLII, which has a Point-in-Time Legislation Project, see http://portsea.austlii.edu.au/pit/. So far it has databases for New South Wales, Queensland and South Australian legislation. You simply open the database, locate the Act from the alphabetical list, and select a date. Figure 6.15 shows an example.

FIGURE 6.15: AUSTLII'S POINT-IN-TIME FACILITY

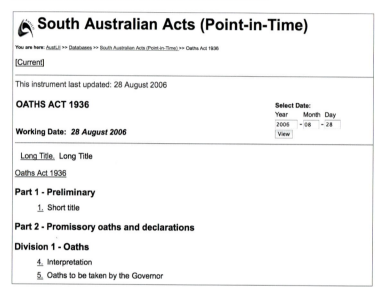

If the relevant Act and/or jurisdiction is not yet available, you can still use the note-up feature in AustLII, which allows you to see the table of amending Acts and which provisions they amended. If the relevant section of the relevant Act you are looking for has been amended, you can use the 'Numbered Acts' link to find the amending Act and see what it changed.

Updating legislation

Each year the major publishers issue an updated list of statutes, known as statute annotations. They list amendments subsequent to the last reprint or, if it is a new Act, since the date of assent. Generally you look up the name of the Act in the alphabetical list and note the latest reprint, check the amending Acts which are listed by number and year, and note which sections have been amended.

- **Commonwealth** – Commonwealth Statutes Annotated (Lawbook Co) and Federal Statutes Annotated (LexisNexis Butterworths)
- **Australian Capital Territory** – 'Table of ACT Laws' in the first annual bound volume of Acts includes amendments to principal Acts in that year
- **New South Wales** – New South Wales Statutes Annotations
- **Northern Territory** – Northern Territory of Australia Index to Legislation
- **Queensland** – Queensland Legislation Annotations
- **South Australia** – Index of South Australian Legislation

- **Tasmania** – no individual annotations available
- **Victoria** – Victorian Statutes Annotations
- **Western Australia** – Index to Legislation of Western Australia

During the year between the publications of the statute annotations, you can see if they have an updating supplement (e.g. the *Federal Statutes Annotated* and NSW/Victorian equivalents have a six monthly supplement). If not, use the *Australian Legal Monthly Digest* which has a choice of chronological and alphabetical tables of statutes in its 'Legislation Tables', and if need be the fortnightly updates provided by the *ALMD Advance*. Alternatively you could use *Australian Current Law, Legislation* which is published monthly and provides tables for amended and reprinted Acts.

Alerting services

If you are working in a particular area of law, it is possible to register for alerting services, which notify you if legislation in a particular area changes. Unless you check each day, or hear something in the news, you are not likely otherwise to find out if a change has been made.

Many alerting services are free and you can sign up for their alerts. Two such services are provided by LexisNexis Legal Express and CCH. Increasingly, websites and databases will also offer RSS (really simple syndication) feeds of their updates. Reading the legal journals, bulletins, newspapers or receiving information from the media in other formats will also inform you of proposed legal changes, issues and developments. It is important to be in these loops of information to keep your knowledge and skills current.

5: Finding cases

Cases, or legal judgments, are the decisions rendered in court. In a common law system, cases may create the law itself, and/or may contain interpretation of a particular piece of legislation. Either way, they are a primary source of law, and so are very important.

When cases are handed down, they are shortly afterwards made available online on court websites or via services such as AustLII. Although this is a form of publication of the statute, such decisions are still unreported, because they have not been proofed, had a head note drafted, and published in a law report series. Not all decisions end up being officially reported – only those that are considered to be important.

There are many reasons why a case may be important:

- because of the court (e.g. High Court cases are regularly reported in the Commonwealth Law Reports)
- because the case is in the media or is politically or socially important
- because the judgment made an important change to the law
- because this case applied existing law to a new and different set of facts
- because the analysis by the judges provides a new level of detail in this area of law.

TIP
Cases are given a 'medium neutral citation' when they are posted online, and it is quite acceptable to use this, but if an authorised reported version is available, it is better to cite it.

If, however, a case is in a lower court and simply applies accepted law, it will most likely not be reported.

When you are looking for a case, the material you have to work from will vary. You may have a:

- full citation
- popular or common name for a case
- statute and want to find cases that apply it
- case and want to find if it has been used as a precedent in other cases
- general subject area.

We will now look at each of these in turn, because our research strategy will vary depending on the information we have, and the information we need to find.

Finding a case from the citation

Let's begin by finding a case when you have been given the citation. This commonly occurs where, for example, you are doing your weekly readings for a particular law subject, and the textbook refers to a relevant case. You decide you want to find the case and read it.

We already know from Chapter 3 that the citation is the unique identifier for a case, and includes the names of the parties, the year in which the decision was handed down, and the jurisdiction in which the decision was reported (or information on the court, judge(s) and date if it is an unreported decision).

Let's assume we have been given the following citation: *Onus v Alcoa* (1981) 149 CLR 27.

We use what we know already to conclude that the parties are Onus and Alcoa, the decision is from 1981, and it can be found in volume 149 of the Commonwealth Law Reports at page 27. We can simply go into the library, find the shelves where the law reports are stored, find the Commonwealth Law Reports, select volume 149 and open it up at page 27. Or we could use an electronic source to find this case. Let's use AustLII, seeing we have experience with it from our good samaritan situation. We visit www.austlii.edu.au, click on 'Commonwealth' on the left side, then 'High Court of Australia 1903 –'. The screen shown in Figure 6.16 appears.

FIGURE 6.16: AUSTLII HIGH COURT CASE SEARCH OPTIONS

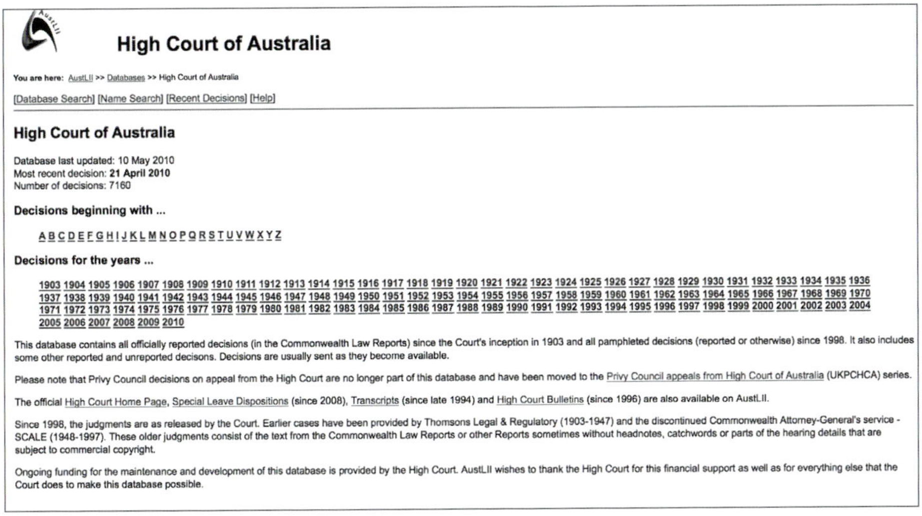

We have the choice of either clicking on 'O' and scrolling down to Onus, or clicking on '1981' and scrolling through each month's cases until we get to September and see *Onus v Alcoa*. We click and there is the full judgment.

That one was pretty easy, because it was a Commonwealth Law Report which includes all reported High Court decisions. But what if we did not recognise the letters used in the citation, for example:

- *Minister for Arts, Heritage and Environment v Peko-Wallsend Pty Ltd* (1987) 15 FCR 274
- *Conservation Council of SA Inc v Chapman* (2003) 87 SASR 62
- *Hales v Jamilmira* [2003] NTCA 9 (15 April 2003)
- *Mason v Tritton* (1994) 34 NSWLR 572
- *R v Fuller-Cust* [2002] VSCA 168 (24 October 2002)
- *Stack v Western Australia* [2004] WASCA 300 (20 December 2004)

You can use the Cardiff Index to Legal Abbreviations, at www.legalabbrevs.cardiff.ac.uk/, or *Australian and New Zealand Legal Abbreviations*,[8] available in the library, both of which list the abbreviations and what they stand for. Figure 6.17 shows an example from the above list, using the Cardiff Index to search for 'FCR'.

---

8 Colin Fong and Alan Edwards, *Australian and New Zealand Legal Abbreviations*, Australian Law Librarians' Group, Sydney (1995).

FIGURE 6.17: CARDIFF INDEX EXAMPLE

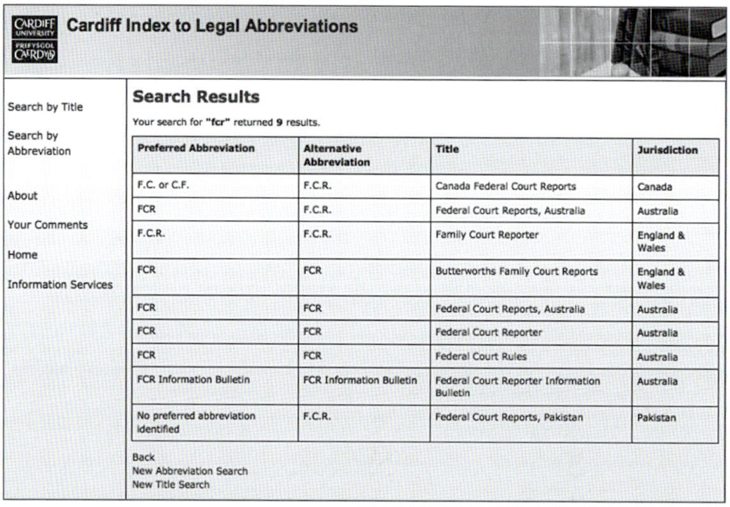

Cardiff Index to Legal Abbreviations

Search by Title
Search by Abbreviation
About
Your Comments
Home
Information Services

Search Results

Your search for "fcr" returned 9 results.

Preferred Abbreviation	Alternative Abbreviation	Title	Jurisdiction
F.C. or C.F.	F.C.R.	Canada Federal Court Reports	Canada
FCR	F.C.R.	Federal Court Reports, Australia	Australia
F.C.R.	F.C.R.	Family Court Reporter	England & Wales
FCR	FCR	Butterworths Family Court Reports	England & Wales
FCR	FCR	Federal Court Reports, Australia	Australia
FCR	FCR	Federal Court Reporter	Australia
FCR	FCR	Federal Court Rules	Australia
FCR Information Bulletin	FCR Information Bulletin	Federal Court Reporter Information Bulletin	Australia
No preferred abbreviation identified	F.C.R.	Federal Court Reports, Pakistan	Pakistan

Back
New Abbreviation Search
New Title Search

We need to use some common sense to interpret the results. We would look at the list to find Australia in the right column and see it is the Federal Court Reports. If we do SASR, we come up with the South Australian State Reports. Why don't you get online and search for the others in our list: NTCA, NSWLR, VSCA, and WASCA.

What if you have only part of the citation, and not the whole thing? If for example, you know the parties to the dispute, or you heard on the news that it was decided by a particular court on a particular day but don't know the parties names? If that is the case, you can use *CaseBase* or *FirstPoint* (discussed below) to find the record for the full citation, then link to the case or look it up on AustLII.

Finding a case from its common name

Sometimes you will hear people refer to cases by common names, such as the *Engineers'* case, the *Tasmanian Dam* case, or *Mabo*. Only the most famous cases, which are referred to frequently, attract popular, or common names, and those who have been involved in the law for some time will know them instantly – this doesn't help a new law student though! Thankfully there is a resource that can handle common names. It is CaseBase. Let's use it to find the *Engineers'* case. Figure 6.18 shows what the starting page looks like.

FIGURE 6.18: CASEBASE EXAMPLE

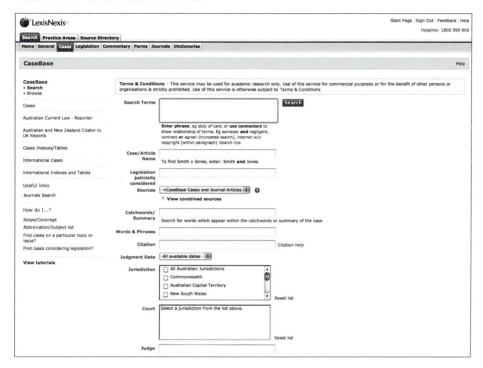

Let's enter 'Engineers case' in the box next to 'Case/Article Name'. The results screen is shown in Figure 6.19.

FIGURE 6.19: CASEBASE RESULTS SCREEN

The first one is APS Engineers Case, and the second and third ones are Professional Engineers case, so we can ignore those. The fourth result is *Amalgamated Society of Engineers v Adelaide Steamship Co Ltd* (*Engineers'* case) (1920) 28 CLR 129. This is the *Engineers'* case we are looking for.

Let's search again, this time for 'Tasmania Dam case'. One result comes up (Figure 6.20).

FIGURE 6.20: CASEBASE RESULTS SCREEN

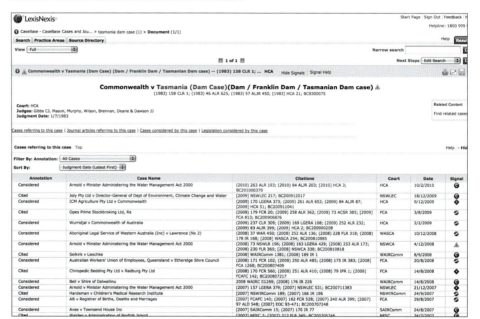

Usefully, there are links that will take you to cases and journal articles that refer to the *Tasmanian Dam* case, as well as links to cases and legislation that was considered in the *Tasmanian Dam* decision.

Finding an unreported judgment

These are judicial decisions from a particular court for which it was decided not to report, perhaps because the decision was not considered to raise an important point of law. As you will consider in Chapter 10, unreported judgments tend to have less precedent value than reported judgments because of this. However, the unreported judgment may have considered something of interest and value beyond the law in the case – for example, a method of interpretation or a comment on the meaning to be applied to a particular word or phrase in the future.

Here are some options for finding unreported judgments:

- Unreported Judgments: a subscription-based product of LexisNexis AU, containing the full text of many unreported judgments from all Australian jurisdictions. There is a drop down menu from the search page which enables you to select 'Unreported Judgment' as shown in the screen shot in Figure 6.21.

FIGURE 6.21: LEXISNEXIS UNREPORTED JUDGMENTS

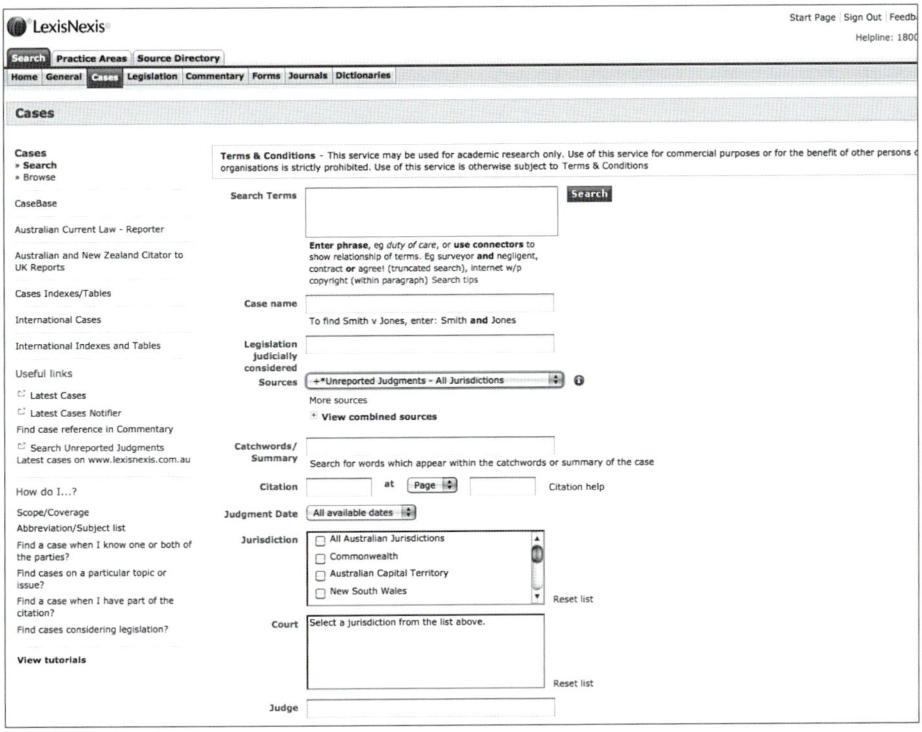

- Legal Online: In the 'cases' area, FirstPoint can be searched for unreported judgments. (See Figure 6.27 on page 173 for a screen dump of FirstPoint.)
- AustLII: for decisions in recent years, AustLII reports all of them with a medium neutral citation.

Finding cases that interpret a statute

If you are trying to find the meaning of a particular word or phrase that has been used in legislation, it can be useful to refer to cases that have considered that word or phrase. If they are from a superior court, such as the Supreme Court in the instance of state or territory legislation, or the High Court in federal legislation, they may well provide a binding interpretation.

There are several options for this, but here are two easy ones using the example of the *War Crimes Act 1945* (Cth):

- **CaseBase** – a subscription-based service provided by LexisNexis AU. On the home page there is a field 'Legislation judicially considered' where you can enter in the legislation to search on. Entering 'war crimes act 1945' (without the quote marks) brings the result in Figure 6.22.

FIGURE 6.22: CASEBASE LEGISLATION JUDICIALLY CONSIDERED

- **AustLII** – going to www.austlii.edu.au and locating the legislation (which you know how to do because we covered it above), you can click the Noteup function, either to a certain section or to the Act as a whole. Figure 6.23 shows a screen shot generated by using Noteup on the *War Crimes Act 1945* (Cth) as a whole.

FIGURE 6.23: AUSTLII NOTEUP FUNCTION FOR LEGISLATION

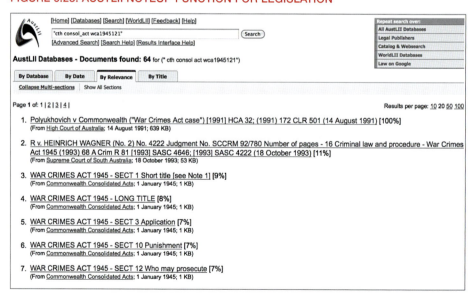

So you can see that searching on CaseBase and AustLII gave us the same cases – *Polyukhovich* and *Wagner*.

Finding cases that apply a particular case

You may have found a relevant case, and want to know if it is still good law – has it been used by other courts since? What have they made of it? For this task we use a case citator. There is the Australian and New Zealand Citator to UK Reports (Lexis Nexis), and the Australian Case Citator, which is available in print and online on Firstpoint, part of Legal Online which is a subscription-based product owned by Thomson Reuters.

If for example we search on Firstpoint for 'war crimes act' and bring up *Polyukhovich*, we can simply click on the 'cases citing' link on the top row (Figure 6.24).

FIGURE 6.24: THE FIRSTPOINT CASE CITATOR ENTRY SCREEN

The result is shown in Figure 6.25.

FIGURE 6.25: THE FIRSTPOINT CASE CITATOR RESULTS SCREEN

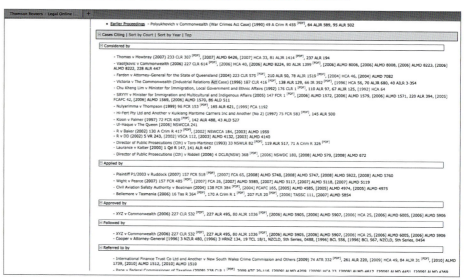

CaseBase is also a useful subscription-based case citation resource. If we search for the case and then click on 'cases referring to this case', the screen shown in Figure 6.26 comes up.

FIGURE 6.26: THE CASEBASE CASE CITATOR RESULTS SCREEN

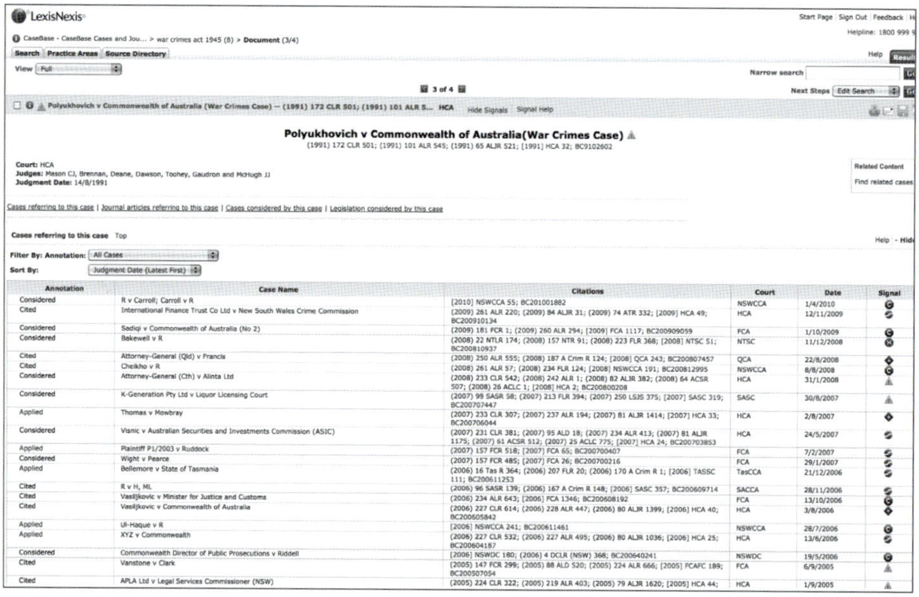

Cases that refer to the *War Crimes* Case are presented in order, from the most recent. The left column shows what use the court made of the case – mostly it has been cited, considered or applied. These are all positive uses of the decision (if you saw 'overruled' you would know it is not good law anymore – we cover more on terminology in Chapter 10). The right columns show the court and date, and provide a symbol to indicate quickly how it has been used. For example the green diamond indicates positive treatment, the yellow triangle cautionary treatment, the blue circle neutral treatment, and the red circle negative treatment.

Exercise: Using CaseBase and Firstpoint

Have any of the following cases been overruled, and if so, by which court and in which decision?

1   *Petreski v Cargill* (1987) 18 FCR 68
2   *R v Jervis* [1993] 1 Qd R 643
3   *Gacic v John Fairfax Publications Pty Ltd* (2006) 66 NSWLR 675
4   *Cattanach v Melchior* (2003) 215 CLR 1
5   *Duralla Pty Ltd v Plant* (1984) 2 FCR 342

Finding cases on a particular subject area

You may only have the general area of law, and want to know if there are any cases on it.

If you already have one case on the subject, the catchwords in the judgment may be a useful guide to the legal terminology that is used to describe the particular subject. For example, the catchwords for *Jeffrey Wayne Davie v R* [2008] NSWCCA 2 are:

Criminal law – appeal against conviction – objections not taken at trial – evidence of complaint – miscarriage of justice – DNA evidence – jury making a finding of guilt on one or more counts in the indictment considering any other count in the indictment.

This shows the case is broadly based on criminal law, and lists the specific aspects to which it relates. If you are looking for other cases of overturned criminal convictions you might search for 'miscarriage of injustice'.

If you don't yet have any cases or legislation on the subject area to start with, your options are to either browse or do a key word search – or, better still, to use both of these methods. For browsing, you could locate the subject index on FirstPoint, a product of Thomson Reuters.[9] If you find a subject you think is relevant you could

---

9   FirstPoint is the electronic version of two print research tools – the *Australian Digest* and the *Australian Legal Monthly Digest*. It is effectively a combined case law citator and digest. As well as providing full citation details and listing subsequent consideration, FirstPoint also carefully categorises the case by subject matter and provides a 'digest' or summary of the case. FirstPoint uses a hypertext linked subject index to enable the user to browse for cases by subject. The subject index includes subheadings which break down the subject matter into more specific points of law.

click through to the information to find out. For key word searching, you need to give some thought to the sort of key words that might relate to your topic, in the same way we did with the Julie scenario, coming up with terms like 'first aid' and 'liability'. Then you look those search terms up in the index (if using paper resources) or enter them into the search field (if using online resources).

> **TIP**
> Remember that when you find the case record in CaseBase or FirstPoint, you are only seeing a case summary. In many instances you can link through to the full case. But if the library at your university or law firm does not subscribe to the linked service, you may need to look up the judgment in a separate search, such as on AustLII or in the printed law reports.

If you are using the paper copy resources, you would start with *The Australian Digest*. There is a Key to Contents which contains subject headings in alphabetical order with subheadings. Each subject heading is a separate 'title' in the work, and you can turn to the title you think is relevant and read the scope note, which is the first paragraph, or check the table of contents to see if the information you need is really covered by that title. The table of contents provides both a page reference and a square brackets reference. When you locate a relevant case, it will be in summary format with the full citation provided below for you to use if you need to read the full judgment. To update the information in the *Digest*, you would use the *Australian Legal Monthly Digest* (ALMD). You could just look up the square brackets of the relevant subheading in the Noter Up, which simply tells you which months in a given year contain newer cases related to the topic of that particular square bracket. You then go to the relevant monthly part and find the new case under the same square bracket reference. The ALMD *Advance* can also be used for very recent decisions which have not yet made it into the ALMD.

Finding a case that considers a particular word or phrase

You may, in your reading, come across a particular word (such as 'reasonable') or phrase (such as 'welfare of the child') and want to find cases which consider the meaning of that word or phrase. There are several options to use, and as before, we recommend you use a combination of them to get the best results.

- **CaseBase** – enter the word or phrase in the 'Words & Phrases' dialog box on the home page. If you only want to know how the word or phrase has been considered in a particular jurisdiction, you can narrow your search to a particular jurisdiction, and even to a particular court in that jurisdiction, by selecting the relevant options in the 'Jurisdiction' and 'Court' fields

> ### Exercise: Searching phrases in CaseBase
> Try typing in 'welfare of the child' into the 'Words & Phrases' box on CaseBase – what cases, if any, come up?

- **Legal Dictionary** – in addition to defining legal words, legal dictionaries may also refer to the leading cases which defined that word, and may also define legal phrases. Additionally there is a publication titled *Words and Phrases Judicially Defined*.[10]

---

10 Roland Burrows (ed), *Words and Phrases Judicially Defined*, Butterworths (1943).

- **FirstPoint** – within Legal Online, the search page has an option for entering 'Words and Phrases Judicially Considered' as shown in the screen shot in Figure 6.27.

FIGURE 6.27: THE FIRSTPOINT WORDS AND PHRASES ENTRY SCREEN

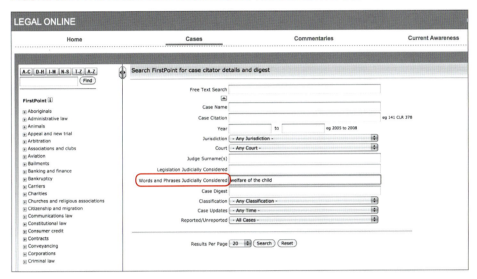

As you can see, results can be limited by a range of years, or by jurisdiction or court if required.

6: Finding and using secondary sources

As you know, secondary sources are materials that help to support our understanding of primary sources (cases and legislation). They include books, journal articles, law reform commission reports, and documents produced by parliament including debates and explanatory memoranda relating to a bill before it becomes law.

In practice you are most likely to start your research with a secondary source (such as a legal dictionary, text book or encyclopedia), to give you a general understanding of the law and pointers on cases and legislation that might be relevant.

Finding and using law books and dictionaries

There are two main types of law books – text books and monographs. Text books are summaries on the law in a particular area. Monographs are research publications which provide commentary and analysis – often they are the published version of a PhD thesis, which a person has researched and written over a period of years.

Monographs are more scholarly than text books, in the sense that they attempt to contribute to knowledge rather than merely summarise it. However you will find some summary of knowledge in a monograph, just as you will find some analysis or commentary in a text book. It will be easier for you to start with reading information in a text book, and when you feel you understand the law, to tackle a research monograph.

> **Example: Text books and monographs**
>
> Sam Blay, Ryszard Piotrowicz and Martin Tsamenyi (eds), *Public International Law: An Australian Perspective* (2005)
>
> Michelle Sanson, *International Law and Global Governance* (2008)
>
> The first is a text book and the second is a research monograph. It can often be difficult to tell from the title!

The same method is used for finding all books, be they texts or monographs. You simply use the library catalogue to search by the title, if you know it, or the subject area. Let's say you searched for 'international law' in either the title or the subject field (or your university may have a single field that searches across titles, authors and subjects all at once).

When you get the results, rather than simply noting down all the call numbers and going to the shelves to find them, you should consider the jurisdiction and year of publication. Certainly, as law constantly changes, the more recent the publication, the better. Also, if you are looking for the Australian implementation of international law, you would be better off with an Australian text on the subject as opposed to, say, a Canadian or German one.

If you are not sure what you are looking for, you could look for similarities between the call numbers, then go to that row of books in the library and simply browse the books until you find ones you feel are useful.

Law dictionaries are useful companions when reading any other source, such as a text book or journal article. They are not limited to defining words, and include more than a mere definition. The main legal dictionaries for the Australian context are:

- *Australian Law Dictionary*, Oxford University Press, South Melbourne, 2010 (you can also use the online version, *Australian Law Dictionary Online*)
- *Butterworths Concise Australian Legal Dictionary*, Butterworths, Sydney, 3rd edn, 2004 (you can also use the online version, *Butterworths Encyclopaedic Australian Legal Dictionary*)

Finding and using journal articles

As with searching for books, there is nothing to stop you from browsing law journals. Just find where the law journals are in your university library (usually arranged alphabetically by journal title) and pick up random volumes from journals that take your eye. This is a good way of familiarising yourself with law journals generally, including their range, how they are structured and, most importantly for someone trying to write in a legal style, how they are written. But it is more likely that you will want to find journal articles on a specific topic, for a specific assignment.

There are a number of useful journal databases. As with other legal research, it is best to use a few different databases, because you may be able to retrieve different information from different databases. This section focuses on Australian databases.

- *AGIS* and *AGIS Plus Text:* the Commonwealth Attorney-General's Information Service (*AGIS*) provides an extensive compilation of Australian law journal articles, including an index and search function. *AGIS Plus Text* contains full text articles, but has a more limited range than AGIS when searched. It is available in print and online.
- *APA Text:* produced by the Australian Public Affairs Information Service and provided online by Informit, this database contains full-text articles – not only legal articles but also economic, social, and political articles that have a bearing on legal issues.

You can locate the above products through Informit, which has a standard search engine as shown in Figure 6.28.

FIGURE 6.28: THE INFORMIT SEARCH SCREEN

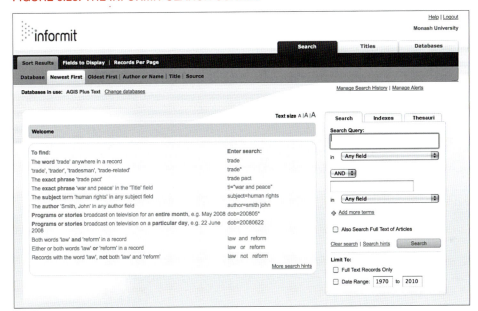

This shows the AGIS Plus Text and to change to APA Full Text simply click on 'Change databases' and select it from the list. There is also the option of searching across both databases simultaneously.

- *Australian Legal Journals Index* (ALJI): a subscription-based product of Thomson Reuters, the ALJI allows you to browse or search journal abstracts, including annotations as to which cases and legislation are referred to in each article. The index is available on Legal Online – you will recall we have considered the Encyclopedia tab above, and here it is simply a matter of selecting the 'Journals' tab and using the familiar search engine (Figure 6.29).

FIGURE 6.29: THE LEGAL ONLINE JOURNALS INDEX

- *Australasian Legal Scholarship Library:* a product of AustLII, this is a free online database of journals with the full text of journal articles provided mostly in HTML format. From the home page for AustLII, click on 'Law Journals'. There is the option to select a particular journal, or to search for key terms across all or selected journals (Figure 6.30). At present the range of journals is not as broad as *AGIS Plus Text,* and for some journals it only covers a select number of years/volumes of each journal.

FIGURE 6.30: JOURNALS ON AUSTLII

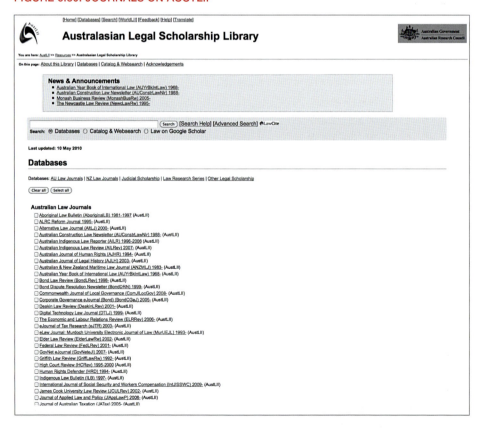

In addition to the Australian journal databases, three international sources are worthy of mention:

- *HeinOnline* – an American subscription-based online product with content from multiple libraries from around the world, including Australia. However all information is in PDF format.
- *LegalTrac* – an American subscription-based online bibliographic database which provides details of articles from over 800 legal journals, mostly American, but it does include the main legal journals from Australia as well.
- *Lexis.com* – a full text subscription-based database, with an extensive range of American law journals, plus some published by LexisNexis Australia (such as *Torts Law Journal* and *Australian Journal of Corporate Law*).

Using legal encyclopedias

We tend to use legal encyclopedias in legal research for two main purposes – one is to lead us to relevant cases and legislation on a particular topic, and the other is to give us a general overview of the law in the area, in the same way we would use a text book. The two main legal encyclopaedias in Australia are *Halsbury's Laws of Australia*, published by LexisNexis Butterworths, and *Laws of Australia*, published by Lawbook Co, which is owned by Thomson Reuters. These are considered in turn below.

Legal encyclopaedias are updated regularly but will only provide you with information up to a certain point in time. When using these resources, always check how up-to-date the title is. For example in considering the currency information of *Halsbury's Laws of Australia* at the time of writing, the most recent titles had been updated to January 2010 (Mental Health and Intellectual Disability), but some titles were as dated as 2002 (Local Government). If you were doing an assignment related to actions of a local government and you used the information in *Halsbury's* you would risk missing any changes in the decade since this title was last updated.

Legal encyclopedias are available online and in print. Even though you are able to access them without charge while at law school, the publishers usually charge significant subscription fees to law firms and companies that use these services. The print versions are usually referred to as 'looseleaf services' because they contain pages in a ring binder so that, where the law has changed, replacement pages can be sent on the relevant topic, and the redundant pages discarded. The law itself covers both substantive and procedural law (this means that, for example, court rules and rules of evidence are covered, as well as what amounts to a crime, act of negligence or breach of a contract).

Halsbury's Laws of Australia

The print version of *Halsbury's Laws of Australia* comprises approximately 31 substantive volumes, arranged alphabetically by subject. Volumes 32–34 are indexes, allowing you to search by subject, case and statute title.

In the electronic version, which is provided by LexisNexis AU, the 89 titles are listed alphabetically with links to the subheadings and the content, and a search engine is also provided. There is a user guide provided under the 'Product Information' heading shown on the left side of the screen shot in Figure 6.31.

TIP
Remember when using journals, to bear in mind three 'r's': *recency*, *relevance* and *writer*. How old is the article, how relevant is it to my research topic and jurisdiction, and who wrote it?

TIP
You are likely to find electronic resources more convenient, especially if you have remote access to them. But it is important not to be over-reliant upon them, and to make sure you are proficient at using paper copy resources as well. The power may fail when you need to complete an assignment, or in the future you may get a job in a place that does not subscribe to some of the databases you use at law school.

FIGURE 6.31: SUBJECT HEADINGS IN *HALSBURY* ONLINE AT LEXISNEXIS

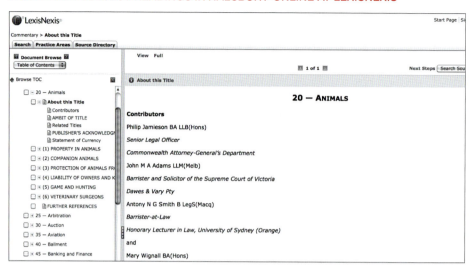

This screen shot shows the table of contents on the left hand side. After clicking on the title 'Animals', the preliminary information is shown along with the main sub-headings 'Property in Animals', 'Companion Animals' etc. It is this preliminary information which includes the statement of currency. In this instance it is current to March 2007.

If you prefer to do a search instead of browsing the subject headings, you can click on the 'Search' tab which is in the top bar on the above screen shot. You have the choice of doing a quick search, or selecting one of the databases to search in, as shown in Figure 6.32.

FIGURE 6.32: SEARCH FACILITY IN *HALSBURY* ONLINE AT LEXISNEXIS

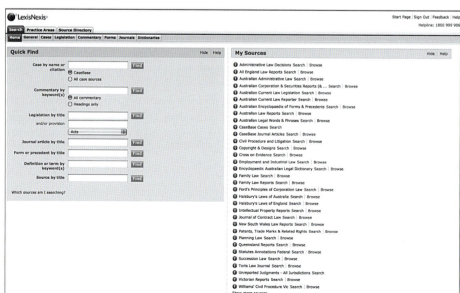

With both the printed and electronic versions, it is essential to check currency information, and to update the coverage using *Australian Current Law*. It comprises a separate part for updating cases (*Reporter*) and legislation (*Legislation*). These are supplemented by LexisNexis AU Legal Express, a daily electronic update.

Laws of Australia

The print version of *Laws of Australia* comprises approximately 46 substantive volumes, arranged alphabetically by subject. The last volume includes a user's guide, consolidated index and table of cases.

The electronic version is provided by Legal Online, which also contains databases on cases, commentaries and journals. To avoid confusion, make sure you have the 'Encyclopedia' tab highlighted, and you will see that, on the left side, the 'Laws of Australia' heading has the subject headings with hyperlinks listed below. You can either browse using the subject headings, or do a search, as shown in Figure 6.33.

FIGURE 6.33: LAWS OF AUSTRALIA AT LEGAL ONLINE

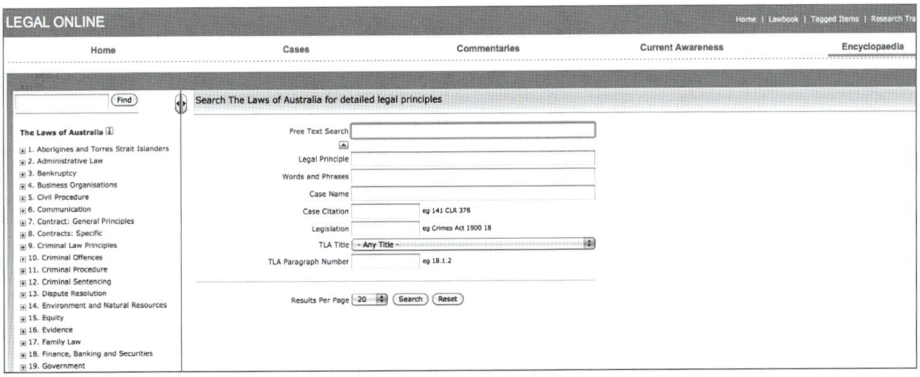

Currency information is provided at the top of each subheading (Figure 6.34).

FIGURE 6.34: CHECKING CURRENCY OF LAWS OF AUSTRALIA INFORMATION

> **TIP**
> Caution: For *all* legal research resources, *always* check currency information. Don't just assume it must be still good law or they would have updated it!

To update the information on *Laws of Australia* the current awareness services are the *Australian Legal Monthly Digest* and the *ALMD Express*. The electronic version of these is *FirstPoint*, which is located under the 'Cases' tab in the screen shot in Figure 6.34.

Finding and using law reform commission reports

The various law reform commissions across Australia were discussed in Chapter 3, and it is important to refresh yourself with that information because some of the links below are to the reports of law reform bodies which have since been disbanded.

All law reform commission reports are available online, which makes the researching task fairly straightforward. In addition to all jurisdictions being available on AustLII's Australasian Law Reform Library at www.austlii.edu.au/au/special/lawreform/, there are separate law reform commission websites which contain an extensive range of publications:

- **Commonwealth** – www.alrc.gov.au/publications/index.htm
- **Australian Capital Territory** – www.jcs.act.gov.au/eLibrary/lrc_reports.html
- **New South Wales** – www.lawlink.nsw.gov.au/lawlink/lrc/ll_lrc.nsf/pages/LRC_publications
- **Northern Territory** – although somewhere in the Department of Justice website, the link to an index to reports is impossible to locate, but searching for the Northern Territory Law Reform Committee does provide some links to PDFs of individual reports, for example www.nt.gov.au/justice/docs/lawmake/Sexual%20AssaultInvestigation.pdf
- **Queensland** – www.qlrc.qld.gov.au/Publications.htm
- **South Australia** – the full text of the reports from the three years of operation in the 1980s are not available online but there is an index to them available at www.lib.flinders.edu.au/resources/collection/special/lawreform/draft_reports.html
- **Tasmania** – www.law.utas.edu.au/reform/reports_publications.htm
- **Victoria** – www.lawreform.vic.gov.au/wps/wcm/connect/Law+Reform/Find/Publications/
- **Western Australia** – www.lrc.justice.wa.gov.au/2_reports.html

Law reform commission reports tend to be available online in HTML format, or downloadable in PDF format. It is recommended that before you print a large report that you consider the index and the executive summary first. It is unlikely that you will need all the information in the relevant report for your assignment. For example, here is the cover page for a recent ALRC Report, released in February 2010. As you can see, there are options for downloading separately the executive summary and each part of the report (Figure 6.35).

FIGURE 6.35: ALRC DOWNLOAD OPTIONS

ALRC Report 111
Making Inquiries: A New Statutory Framework

Download and viewing options

This publication is available for viewing in HTML (please see contents below), however, there are also a number of download options.

Whole document: Rich Text Format (RTF) (8.26 MB) **(Due to the document's size it may take a long time to download and this format is recommended only if you have a fast connection).**
RTF is formatted and suitable for loading into most word processors. Save the file to disk and open with your word processor.

Whole document: Portable Document Format (PDF) (2.77 MB)
You need Adobe® Acrobat® Reader 4.0, or a later version, to view the PDF file. Acrobat Reader is available as a free download from the Adobe Web site.

Individual chapters: You can also download individual chapters in RTF. The download option is available at the top of each HTML page.

Table of Contents

Terms of Reference
List of Participants
List of Recommendations
Executive Summary

1. Introduction to the Inquiry

Let's say the aspect we are interested in is the procedure for the holding of public inquiries. We scroll down the index and see that Chapter 15 covers this topic, and we download the RTF version of it. We see the following paragraph contained in Chapter 15:

> **Aspects of procedural fairness**
> 15.24 There are two main aspects of procedural fairness: the requirement that a person who is liable to be affected by a decision must be given notice of all relevant matters, and given an opportunity to put his or her case (the 'hearing rule'); and the requirement that a decision maker is not biased, or seen to be biased (the 'bias rule'). What these principles require in a particular case will depend on the circumstances, however, they do not impose many limitations on the procedures that may be adopted by inquiries.

If you wanted to use this in an essay, you might say something like:

> Procedural fairness encompasses both the right to be heard and the right for a decision to be made by a neutral third party. The Australian Law Reform Commission has referred to these as the 'hearing rule' and 'bias rule' respectively, saying that 'What these principles require in a particular case will depend on the circumstances'.[11]

11. Australian Law Reform Commission, *Making Inquiries: A New Statutory Framework*, Report No 111 (2010) [15.24].

Finding and using parliamentary debates on a bill

The majority of debate on a bill takes place during the Second Reading Speech. As you will read in Chapter 11, the parliamentary debates can be used as extrinsic material when we are interpreting legislation. The transcripts from parliamentary debates are published by each parliament in its *Hansard*, and are available online:

- **Commonwealth** – www.aph.gov.au/hansard
- **Australian Capital Territory** – www.hansard.act.gov.au/
- **New South Wales** – www.parliament.nsw.gov.au/prod/web/common.nsf/V3HHBHome
- **Northern Territory** – www.nt.gov.au/lant/hansard/hansard.shtml
- **Queensland** – http://parlinfo.parliament.qld.gov.au/ISYSHanSimp.htm
- **South Australia** – www.parliament.sa.gov.au/Hansard
- **Tasmania** – www.parliament.tas.gov.au/HansardHouse/
- **Victoria** – http://tex.parliament.vic.gov.au/bin/texhtmlt?form=VicHansard.adv
- **Western Australia** – www.parliament.wa.gov.au/web/newwebparl.nsf/iframewebpages/Hansard+-+Index

Finding and using explanatory memoranda

Explanatory memoranda (also known as explanatory notes and explanatory statements) are typically released at the same time as a bill, by the government department responsible for the bill. While they vary in their level of detail, they usually provide a good summary and explanation of the bill's intended operation. An excerpt from the index to an explanatory paper issued by the South Australian Department of Health in August 2009, in relation to the Public Health Bill 2009, is provided below:[11]

> 4   Explanation of parts, key clauses or sets of clauses
>
> **Part 1: Preliminary**
>
> **Part 2: Objects, Principles and Interaction with other Acts**
> Principles to assist the administration of the Act (Clauses 5–14)
> Development of Guidelines to assist in the application of principles in the administration of the Act (Clause 15)
>
> **Part 3: Administration**
> Minister's Functions (Division 1, Clauses 17–19)
> Chief Public Health Officer (Division 2, Clauses 20–25)
> South Australian Public Health Council (Division 3, Clauses 26–36)
> Councils (Division 4, Clauses 37–41)
> Cooperation between councils for public health (Clause 38)
> Power of the Chief Public Health Office to act (Clause 39)

---

11 For the full explanatory note visit http://dh.sa.gov.au/pehs/publications/billexplainatorpaper-peh-sahealth-2009.pdf.

Council failing to perform a function under the Act (Clause 40)
Transfer of function of council at request of the council (Clause 41)

This is an excerpt from Part 1 of section 4:

4 Explanation of parts, key clauses or sets of clauses
   Part 1: Preliminary
   (Clauses 1–3)
   This section deals with formal requirements such as the short title of the Act (Clause 1), the commencement of the Act (Clause 2) and interpretation of key terms used within the Bill, that is, what each term will mean for the purposes of this Act. Interpretation is provided for a number of key terms which include, among others, the following:

   - Controlled notifiable condition
   - Notifiable condition
   - Public health.

   The interpretation of the term 'public health' is essential to the operation of the legislation and underpins the proposed Act in its entirety. The current Act does not have a definition of public health. The definition of public health is meant to assist in identifying what constitutes a public health matter.

   This interpretation is also further supported by Clause 3(2), which indicates that without limiting the definition of public health in the interpretation, public health can also involve a combination of policies, programs and safeguards.

As you can see, the explanatory document simply goes through the legislation and explains what is covered by each proposed section (referred to as clauses before they are enacted as sections).

AustLII contains a database of explanatory memoranda for each jurisdiction (link from the home page to the relevant jurisdiction and you will see the link to explanatory materials provided with the links to acts and regulations), and there are also individual sites maintained in each jurisdiction:

- **Commonwealth** – Explanatory memoranda are located with the documents for the bill, search at www.comlaw.gov.au/ComLaw/legislation/bills1.nsf/sh/browse&CATEGORY=bill
- **Australian Capital Territory** – Explanatory statements are available at www.legislation.act.gov.au/es/default.asp
- **New South Wales** – Explanatory notes are located with the documents for each bill, search at www.parliament.nsw.gov.au/prod/parlment/nswbills.nsf/V3BillsHome
- **Northern Territory** – Explanatory statements are included by way of a link at the bottom of the text of the relevant bill provided on the Register of Legislation at www.dcm.nt.gov.au/strong_service_delivery/supporting_government/register_of_legislation.

- **Queensland** – Explanatory notes are located with the relevant bill, search at www.legislation.qld.gov.au/Bill_Pages/bills_home.htm
- **South Australia** – Explanatory papers are on individual ministry websites, so you will need to work out which ministry is responsible for the bill and then search for their website (see the example above)
- **Tasmania** – Explanatory memoranda are not included with the text of bills
- **Victoria** – Explanatory memoranda are provided with the documents for the bill, search at www.legislation.vic.gov.au/
- **Western Australia** – Explanatory memoranda are provided with the documents for the bill, search at www.parliament.wa.gov.au/web/newwebparl.nsf/iframewebpages/Bills+-+Current

TIP
Where explanatory materials are provided for delegated legislation, they are referred to as explanatory statements.

7: Legal referencing

Any time you use a research source, for example in answering a problem question or writing an essay, you must cite it. This is known as legal referencing, and it includes references to cases, legislation and secondary sources. We *cite* primary materials, namely cases and legislation, and we *reference* secondary materials.[12]

There are three aims of legal referencing:

- to ensure you have good authority for the propositions you are making in your document
- to ensure you avoid claims of plagiarism by properly recognising where you got your information from
- to have consistency in the way you reference information throughout the document you are producing.

There are many different referencing styles: Harvard and APA (American Psychological Association) are two examples. There is no universally agreed mode of legal citation and referencing in the Australian legal profession, or even in Australian law schools. However, it is most common for law schools to use the *Australian Guide to Legal Citation* (AGLC), produced by Melbourne University Law School, available to download as a 'read only' copy at http://mulr.law.unimelb.edu.au/. It is now in its third edition, which was published in 2010. However you should check to find out what referencing style your law school requires. Also, you are likely to find that, if you are doing a combined degree, you have to learn a different referencing style for your non-law program.

It is important to learn the legal referencing style requirements for yourself, rather than for example simply copying out a reference to an article that you have found in a footnote – that article might have been prepared with a different referencing style, and you will need to alter the style to suit the applicable referencing style at your university. We have used AGLC as a basis for instruction on referencing in this chapter.

---

12 Robert Watt and Francis Johns, *Concise Legal Research*, Federation Press, Sydney, 6th edn (2009), 25.

> ### Example: Journal references
>
> Eriksson, Andrea, European Court of Justice: Broadening the scope of European nondiscrimination law, *Int J Constitutional Law* 2009 7: 731–753.
>
> This becomes, when put into AGLC style:
>
> Andrea Eriksson, 'European Court of Justice: Broadening the scope of European nondiscrimination law' (2009) 7 *International Journal of Constitutional Law* 731.

The following is a summary of some of the main referencing rules you may need in first-year law. We emphasise that it does not replace reading the AGLC (or other style guide if your university uses something different) for yourself, but we acknowledge that because that guide is over 100 pages long, first-year students can find it daunting.

Referencing basics

The first step is knowing *when* to reference. We provide a legal citation whenever we refer to a case or piece of legislation, and we provide a legal reference whenever we use information we have obtained from a source such as a book, article, report or website.

The second step is knowing *how* to reference. The usual options are to either quote directly from the material, using quotation marks, or paraphrasing the material (putting it into your own words) and putting a reference at the end of the sentence.

The third step is knowing *where* to reference. Typically the options include in the body of the text, in a footnote, and in some instances, in a bibliography as well. Here is an example of an in-body citation, followed by a citation using a footnote.

The High Court in *Mandurah Enterprises Pty Ltd v Western Australian Planning Commission* [2010] HCA 2 (Unreported, French CJ, Gummow, Hayne, Crennan and Bell JJ, 3 February 2010) considered the vexed issue of compulsory acquisition of land under a town planning scheme, in the light of s 13 of the *Town Planning and Development Act 1928* (WA) ('TPD Act'), determining whether the acquisition was valid under s 161 of *Land Administration Act 1997* (WA) ('Land Act'). The TPD Act provided a town planning scheme which included a railway which would result in portions of lots being cut off from access to public roads.

The High Court in *Mandurah Enterprises Pty Ltd v Western Australian Planning Commission*[3] considered the vexed issue of compulsory acquisition of land under a town planning scheme ...

3. [2010] HCA 2 (Unreported, French CJ, Gummow, Hayne, Crennan and Bell JJ, 3 February 2010).

Notice the use of abbreviations in the first quote. Wherever we are going to be referring to an Act throughout an essay or article, we have the option to give it an abbreviated title. Here, we have created the TPD Act and the Land Act; if our article had really only been concerned with one Act, we could have defined it as ('the Act').

For those students not familiar with footnoting in Word, please learn that footnotes do *not* have to be added manually. If you do this, you will have numbering and placement out of position, and it will be obvious to the marker that you have not done the footnotes properly. Instead, simply click on 'Insert – Reference – Footnote' then type in the reference in the automatically created footnote. If you cut and paste that text elsewhere in your draft essay, the footnote will automatically go with it, and be renumbered accordingly.

Whether we do a bibliography or not depends on the requirements of the relevant task before us – most problem questions or letter of advice assignments will specify not to include a bibliography, whilst most research essays will require a bibliography to be included. You should check the instructions for each assignment and proceed accordingly. If you do need to produce a bibliography, you should list the references you have used in doing your research (not just those you actually cite from) and put them in alphabetical order. If there are two publications by the same person, put the most recent one first. If you have a long list of references, it helps to group them into headings, such as 'Articles/Books/Reports', 'Case Law', 'Legislation', 'Treaties', and 'Other Sources', as applicable.

Once we know when, how, and where to reference, the fourth step is to know *what* to reference. As the information that is referenced, and the order in which it is presented, differs depending on the type of source, the information is presented below under the relevant headings.

TIP
Round brackets (x) are more properly called parentheses. What is enclosed in them is 'in parenthesis'. Brackets are square [x].

Citing legislation

Acts usually include, as their first section, a provision headed 'Short Title' stating 'This Act may be cited as …' This is the name we use to refer to the Act. The format of citing legislation, including not only primary Acts but also regulations and other forms of delegated legislation, is: *Marriage Act 1961* (Cth).[13] Notice that the title of the Act and the year are italicised, and the parliament that enacted the legislation is sometimes in brackets without italics. Bills are cited without the italics: Fair Work Bill 2009 (Cth). Note that the 'Cth' in parenthesis is in title case, not upper case; the correct way to refer to legislation from other jurisdictions is: NSW, ACT, Qld, Vic, Tas, NT, WA, SA (note that Qld, Vic and Tas are not in upper case).

TIP
You will notice that sometimes letters are used where the legislation is amended, and a new section is added (eg. 16A) but it is desirable not to disturb the numbering of the sections. If there are several additions, they use for example ss 16B, 16C, etc to 16Z, and then 16AA etc.

When citing particular sections of a piece of legislation, the section comes after the main citation: for example, *Marriage Act 1961* (Cth) s 16. Notice there is a lower case 's' and a space between it and the number, without italics. If referring to a section in the body of an essay, we use the full word 'Section' at the start of a sentence (e.g. 'Section 16 allows a minor to seek consent for marriage from a magistrate') or just 's' if used within a sentence (e.g. 'A minor, under s 16, may seek consent to marry from a magistrate).

---

13 Note that in the Northern Territory it is customary not to include the year with the citation.

Citing cases

Case citations include in italics the names of the parties (with the party who initiated the action going first), with a 'v' between them also in italics (not 'versus' like in a sporting match, but 'and' if a civil case, or 'against' if a criminal case), followed by, without italics, the year in which the decision was handed down, and the place it was reported, including the law report series, the volume and page.

For example, *Minister of State for Immigration and Ethnic Affairs v Ah Hin Teoh* (1995) 128 ALR 353 tells us the case was between a government ministry and a person named Teoh, was handed down in 1995, and may be found at page 353 of volume 128 of the Australian Law Reports.

If square brackets are used, it means the law reports are published by year rather than volume number. It also tells you that the year is an essential part of the citation (rather than just a convenience, as it is when the date is given in round brackets). For example, *R v Hanson* [2003] QCA 488 tells us the case is a criminal matter brought by the Crown (the 'R' stands for Regina, which we say out loud as 'the King' or 'the Queen' – or if you don't know who was on the throne at the time, just 'the Crown') against a person named Hanson, and may be found in the 2003 reports of the Queensland Court of Appeal.

If there were multiple parties in the case, or multiple cases were heard together, you just cite the first party to the case. If you are referring to a common case name, you can use it instead of the official case citation – for example, instead of *Commonwealth v Tasmania* (1983) 158 CLR 1 you could cite *Tasmanian Dam Case* (1983) 158 CLR 1. Note that here you use a capital 'c' with 'Case' because it is a proper title (if you were just referring to the *Smith* case in the body of an essay, you would use a lower case 'c').

The point of case citations is that there should be one citation for every case – just as no two people's phone numbers are the same, or email addresses, no two case citations should be the same. Any person with knowledge of legal research should be able to use the citation to find the correct case.

Having said that, sometimes the one case may have more than one citation – this may be where it is reported in more than one report series, or where there is, in addition to the reported citation, a 'medium neutral citation'. This is a citation which allows a case to be cited the same way, whether it is in print or electronic format. Initially cases only have a medium neutral citation, because the case will be available online before it is officially reported (seeing law reports are typically published annually). The medium neutral citation typically uses paragraph numbers (seeing web pages do not have page breaks) and this is denoted with square brackets. So, for example, *Larrikin Music Publishing Pty Ltd v EMI Songs Australia Pty Limited* [2010] FCA 29 (4 February 2010) [31] means that we are referring to paragraph 31 of the above judgment.

It is best to use the medium neutral citation only until the case is reported (or forever if the case remains unreported). For example *A v B* [2011] HCA 20 is the medium neutral citation for a High Court decision, which becomes *A v B* (2011) 190 CLR 32 when it is reported. Once the CLR reference is available, it is preferable to use it in preference to the HCA reference. After all, the CLRs are the authorised reports of the High Court of Australia.

TIP
If you are writing a citation by hand, underlining is the equivalent of italics in word processed documents.

TIP
If you find a case which commences with 'Re' or 'In Re' this means 'in the matter of', and 'Ex parte' means 'on one side', meaning there is only one party making an application to the court, for example for a declaration.

Referencing books

Book references should include the first and second names of each author, including any middle initials, separated by a comma, followed by the book title in italics, then the year of publication in brackets and, if relevant, the edition and the page number. For example:

> 6. Michelle Sanson, Thalia Anthony and David Worswick, *Connecting with Law* (Oxford University Press, 2nd ed, 2010) 189.

> 7. Ibid.

We include the page reference (here, page 139) when we are taking information from that specific page, including paraphrasing or a direct quote. If you refer to that book again directly below, with the same page, then you can just put 'Ibid' or, if a different page, 'Ibid at 44'. If you refer to the book again after other references, you put 'Sanson and Anthony, above n 6, 44'.

Referencing journal articles

Journal article references, like book references, commence with the authors and the title. However, the title of the article is put in single quotation marks, and the title of the journal in which it is published is put in italics. It is also common to put the year and volume number before the title of the journal, and the particular page reference afterwards. For example:

> Michael Head 'Detention and the Anti-Terrorism Legislation' (2005) 9 *University of Western Sydney Law Review* 1, 15.

This means you have found something useful to quote (or refer to the idea) on page 15 of Volume 9, in an article which commences at page 1 of that volume. If you are using an e-journal, there may be no page numbers. If there are paragraph numbers, you can give the pinpoint reference in square brackets, for example [31]. But be careful not to confuse paragraph markers with the footnotes provided in an e-journal, which are hyperlinked in square brackets.

Referencing reports and other documents

Referencing reports is similar to books and articles – for example Australian Law Reform Commission, *Managing Justice: A Review of the Federal Litigation System*, Report No 89 (2000), [3.30].

If you want to reference parliamentary debates such as the Second Reading Speech for a bill, you state the jurisdiction, followed by '*Parliamentary Debates*', the parliament, date and page. For example: New South Wales, *Parliamentary Debates*, Legislative Assembly, 2 April 2009, 1234 (Nathan Rees).

Referencing newspaper articles is in accordance with this example: Editorial, 'Kookaburra case no joke', *The Australian* (Sydney), 6 February 2010, 4. Of course, if there is an author for the article, put their name instead of 'Editorial'.

If you are referencing information obtained from a legal encyclopedia, you should use the following format:

Butterworths, *Halsbury's Laws of Australia*, (at 13 January 2011) 165 Employment, [165–15].

Lawbook Co, *Laws of Australia*, (at 13 January 2011) 17 Family Law, '1 Jurisdiction' [17.1.10].

If you are referencing a speech, the following format is used:

Chief Justice Robert French, 'Judicial Activism – The Boundaries of the Judicial Role' (Speech delivered at the LAWASIA Conference, Ho Chi Minh City, 10 November 2009).

Referencing websites

You should only reference a website if the material you are referring to is only available online (such as company websites, or electronic journals). If the material is available elsewhere, you should give the print citation or, in the case of legislation or a case, just cite the case and not the website you found it on, be that AustLII or an online database.

> **Example: Website references**
>
> Christopher Enright, 'A Model for Interpreting Statutes' (2008) 15(2) *eLaw Journal* 65, <https://elaw.murdoch.edu.au/archives/issues/2008/2/elaw_15_2_Enright3.pdf> at 23 January 2011.
>
> Stan Ross, 'Battered Wife Syndrome and the Role of Lawyers' (1988) 72(11) *Law Institute Journal* 39.

The former is an e-journal, so the weblink is provided, while the latter is a print journal – so, even if you found it online, the web reference is not included. Notice that, with web references, the date last accessed is given.

For a standard website, the reference is:

Amnesty International, *Police violence and illegal evictions near Papua New Guinean gold mine must be investigated* (2010), <www.amnesty.org/en/news-and-updates/report/police-violence-and-illegal-evictions-near-papua-new-guinean-gold-mine> at 12 December 2010.

DISCUSSION QUESTIONS

1. What are the advantages and disadvantages of using print-based or electronic resources?
2. For what research purposes can Legal Online be used?
3. What tools would you use to find cases where you know the subject matter?
4. To what sources would you go to find Commonwealth legislation and delegated legislation?
5. What role do you believe access to law plays for the rule of law, and justice in our society?

WEBLINKS AND FURTHER READING

Banks, Cate and Douglas, Heather, *Law on the Internet*, Federation Press, Sydney, 3rd edn (2006).
Bott, Bruce and Talbot-Stokes, Ruth, *Nemes and Coss' Effective Legal Research*, LexisNexis Butterworths, Sydney, 4th edn (2010).
Hutchinson, Terry, *Researching and Writing in Law*, Thomsons, Sydney 3rd edn (2010).
Milne, Sue and Tucker, Kay, *A Practical Guide to Legal Research*, Lawbook Co, Sydney (2008).
Stuhmcke, Anita, *Legal Referencing*, Butterworths, Sydney, 3rd edn (2005).
Watt, Robert and Johns, Francis, *Concise Legal Research*, Federation Press, Sydney, (6th edn) (2009).

Online tutorial

Boolean searching tutorial: http://internettutorials.net/boolean.asp

Pathfinder sites (sites which contain useful links to legal information)

AustLII: www.austlii.edu.au links to legal information from Australia, and useful websites
Australian Parliamentary Library: www.aph.gov.au/library/intguide/ provides links to useful resources

Law firms with useful sites, including articles on developments in law

Malleson Stephen Jaques: www.mallesons.com/ then 'Publications' on menu
Allen Arthur Robinson: www.aar.com.au/ then 'Publications' on menu
Blake Dawson: www.blakedawson.com/ then 'Publications' on menu

ONLINE RESOURCES FOR THIS CHAPTER

The following resources are available online at www.oup.com.au/orc/cwl2e
- Flashcard glossary
- Multiple choice questions

7

Jurisprudence:
What Is Law?

WHAT WE WILL COVER IN THIS CHAPTER:

- Why it is important to have a grasp of legal theory
- Traditional approaches to legal theory and their ongoing significance
- Critical approaches to legal theory
- Contemporary debates in legal theory
- How legal theory affects policy and legal judgments
- Some of the significant theoretical debates as they apply to criminal law

Recommended approach to learning this topic

Jurisprudence is not the type of topic where you can type a few key terms into www.austlii.edu.au and you are given a definitive legal answer. Rather, it requires deep reading and heavy reflection about the nature of justice. Sometimes you have to delve into the works of scholars from hundreds of years ago. At other times you will be dealing with more recent and controversial questions, such as same-sex marriage and Nazi war crimes. You may be required to assess whether the law in the legislation and cases reflects higher principles of justice.

These big questions have no easy answers. Many law students want a definitive answer and feel uncomfortable when there isn't one. This may cause them to shy away from legal theory. They feel that they don't know or care enough about philosophy to engage with these questions, not to mention provide some kind of intelligent answer. But the good news is that everyone as a citizen of civil society is in a position to think about these questions – and, with a few tools, contribute to the debate. This chapter will provide some of the legal tools.

Legal theory can be one of the most rewarding and meaningful aspects of legal study. You can think about big-picture issues beyond judgments and statutes. You can interrogate beliefs about what 'justice' and 'law' really mean. Is justice found in the common law? Or is it based on higher values or principles? After reading this chapter you will start to form ideas about which theory suits your view of the law, and what some of the problems or limitations with these legal theories are. You are encouraged to read this chapter critically.

You don't need to be studying arts, humanities or the social sciences to excel in legal theory. You simply need an appreciation of big questions of justice that look beyond a black-letter perspective of cases and statutes. Think about the purpose of law, who it serves and how the legal system may be changed.

KEY TERMS

Classical era = fifth and fourth centuries BCE (Before the Common Era, formerly expressed as Before Christ, BC), when idealism emerged as an elaborate philosophy (with Socrates) and there were many theoretical debates between materialism and idealism.

Essentialism = a grand theory or approach that denies difference of opinion.

Feminism = a view that the law favours the interests of men and should be reconceived to include female voices and provide for gender equality.

Idealism = a philosophical approach that privileges the significance of ideas over material conditions.

Jurisprudence = the theory of law and study of the principles on which it is based.

Liberalism = the interests of individuals are promoted above the collective needs.

Libertarianism = an extreme brand of liberalism that discounts reference to fairness in its concept of justice.

Materialism = a philosophical approach that privileges the significance of material conditions over ideas.

Modernism = a school of thought that developed in the late eighteenth century and saw law as being positioned within dominant social institutions and economic structures.

Natural law = an idea that law has some innate higher principles beyond human choices.

Positive law = the legal rules that exist in statutes, regulations and cases.

Positivism = an idea that law is what humans declare it to be.

Postmodernism = a school of thought that challenges modernism and its presumptions of hierarchical structures.

Pre-Socratic era = the sixth and fifth centuries BCE when philosophy was first born and materialist ideas reigned; it preceded Socratic ideas at the height of the Classical era (see above).

Race theory = a theory that the law projects the interests of white people and colonisers.

Rationalism = law is based on a rational belief of its legitimacy.

Realism = an assessment of what really happens in legal practice and decision making, which underlies legal doctrine and reasoning.

1: Introduction: What is jurisprudence?

Often when law students are instructed to read a problem-based textbook, legislation or cases for their course, they are led to see them as objective descriptors of the law. Students believe that studying texts in a detailed and methodical way is a recipe for mastering legal knowledge.

This approach is useful, but will only get us so far. It won't reveal why the law was written or judged in that way or whether there were alternatives. These issues can only be resolved with an understanding of the theoretical and practical context in which the law evolved. This is because law, like any academic discipline, has a theoretical underpinning that reflects the political and economic conditions of society.

This means that for a fuller and deeper understanding of the law, it should be subjected to a broad level of critical analysis of the philosophies, theories and viewpoints underlying it – not just asking 'what is the law' but what is the law *itself*, as a concept or phenomenon, and what purpose it serves. It is also important to consider *why* the law exists *per se*.

TIP
The Latin *per se* means 'in and of itself'.

Once students start thinking about the variety of underlying issues which differentiate the law and legal writing according to time, place and person, they can appreciate that the law is not static and will continue to change as long as people have the drive to change it. The law reflects human society, rather than operating as a set of scientific rules.

An important task of law students is to question their role in facilitating positive legal change. This requires questioning so-called facts, judicial decision making and the premises and effects of statutes, rather than simply accepting them as fixed and unchangeable. Your approach to interpreting facts and laws will depend on your concept of justice and theoretical framework. Accordingly, it is important to understand the broad spectrum of legal theory and to unpack some of the assumptions that lawyers, judges and policymakers make.

This is where jurisprudence comes in. Jurisprudence provides a framework for critique of the law and legal theories. It is derived from the Latin *juris*, meaning law and *prudentia*, meaning knowledge. As a broad and foundational area of study, jurisprudence can be applied in the critique of any discipline of the law, ranging from criminal law (with clear policy implications and public responses) to commercial law (with more subtle and technical means of enforcing 'justice'). Law students can use the principles of jurisprudence for whatever law subjects they are studying.

Sometimes legal theory can seem abstract and overly philosophical. Legal scholars may approach law using principles of pure philosophy such as logic. These scholars tend to overlook the social basis of philosophy. That is, they ignore the fact that law is guided by humans rather than pure science. Other scholars are primarily interested in how the law interacts with society, but downplay the significance of philosophical ideas. It is useful for law students to give attention to both approaches, and perhaps even find ways in which they can be reconciled.

Although jurisprudence may be considered the theoretical side of law, it has an integral relationship with legal practice. We can say that every legal practitioner advocates a particular theoretical view through their practice, even if they are not consciously aware of it. At the same time, every legal theory has practical ramifications, such that theoreticians need to operate with due responsibility and reference to legal 'reality'. Also, makers of law might develop new legal practices based on existing theories, and theoreticians can use practical examples from case law as a basis from which to advance theories of law.

Legal critique is a common requirement of legal essay writing, and even of problem solving, because of its ability to provide a framework. It involves evaluation of legal writing or laws. Each new piece of writing or law is unique, and so requires a unique approach to jurisprudence. However, because patterns of thought exist in law, as in any discipline, we can use those patterns, or schools of thought, as a foundation for our jurisprudential analysis. So, for example, when we read a law book we can ask ourselves: Which of the established legal schools of thought does the author appear to be promoting in the overall approach to the text? Once the answer to this question is ascertained, we can then go on to ask why, and to what effect – and indeed whether the author demonstrates any deviations from that school of thought. The next section outlines some of the key legal theories.

Overview of different theoretical approaches to defining law

Several schools of thought are considered in this chapter. The following table provides a snapshot of their chronological development. They are not necessarily sequential, as several schools of thought can exist at any one point in time. The dominant school of legal thought in contemporary times is positivism.

TABLE 7.1: OVERVIEW OF MAJOR SCHOOLS OF THOUGHT IN LAW

Jurisprudential school	When school emerged	What is law?
Aristotelian natural law in Ancient Greece	Fifth and fourth centuries BCE: the Classical era	Higher values beyond state law and based on the material forces in society
Natural law subjective idealism	Thirteenth century: The Middle Ages	The embodiment of religion
Positivist (objective) idealism	Fourteenth century to early nineteenth century: Renaissance/Enlightenment	The letter of the case law or statute
Utilitarian positivism	Late eighteenth century	Reasoning that promotes greatest good
Liberal theory	Early nineteenth century	The promotion of individual rights
Marxism	1840s (and manifesting in the twentieth century socialist countries)	A reflection of the economic ruling class
Critical legal theory	Mid-twentieth century	A reflection of power structures
Feminism	1960s	A reflection and projection of the patriarchy
Race theory	1970s	A reflection of the domination of white society and values
Postmodernism	1970s	The subject of critique

2: Traditional theories

Schools of thought are usually identified by a name which ends in 'ism', such as *positivism*, and many have large followings. It is the case that schools wax and wane in popularity, and so it is useful to keep in mind that a school's popularity is not necessarily a guiding point for the quality of its ideas, though it may be a useful indicator. It is also worth keeping in mind that the 'year of birth' of a theory or the fact that the theory has been replaced in dominance by another one does not of itself undermine its validity.

Often schools of thought draw ideas from one another and so have commonalities. But sometimes there are distinct contrasts between schools. They can even emerge as a direct challenge to a previous school. This gives rise to fiery debates! In this chapter we will emphasise each school's unique contribution.

A broad range of the major schools of thought, organised by historical category, are discussed in this chapter. They are considered in relation to the law discipline. However, they also inform many other academic disciplines, particularly in the humanities. So if you are studying social sciences or arts, some may look familiar. This is because legal theories are derived not simply from law, but from socio-historical eras and broad schools of thought, each with common intellectual themes.

The birth of Western legal theory in Greek antiquity

The monumental thinkers of Ancient Greece around two and a half thousand years ago are documented as the first to attempt to solve some of the world's major philosophical problems. Assisted by the new opportunities of a burgeoning democracy and economy, the *Presocratic philosophers* of the sixth and fifth centuries BCE gave accounts of the world in relation to real existing matter.

Presocratic philosophers observed the material forces that operated in their world. Accordingly, they are described as *materialist* in their philosophical orientation. Materialists believe that any change is due to the physical world, rather than ideas. The thinkers of Ancient Greece referred to basic phenomena such as water (Thales), air (Anaximenes), numbers (Pythagoras) and opposites (Heraclitus) as 'basic principles' which could explain the composition and workings of all things. In the *Classical era* of the fifth and fourth centuries BCE a notable division arose between *materialism* (Aristotle) and *idealism* (Socrates/Plato). Idealism, broadly, gives primacy to ideas, as opposed to material forces, as the basis of society and change.

Philosophical debate also grew more sophisticated in the Classical era. This replaced the elementary mode of discussion of the Presocratics. However, the style of interrogating basic principles continued in some form, particularly through Aristotle, who advanced the theory of natural justice or *natural law*. This theory holds that law is derived from higher, aspirational principles and values. It is timeless and knowable by human reason. Law is not made, but discovered, by observation and contemplation of the nature of things.

Aristotle developed the idea of natural law by considering, on the one hand, specific laws which varied among the Greek city-states, and on the other hand, the natural law which was more essential and could be applied universally. He attributed to law the distinction between the general (natural law) and the particular (state law). State law was seen as a translation of natural law into 'concrete norms governing peoples and nations'.

Aristotle conceived of general or natural law as a higher and ethically pure form of law which transcended ordinary and everyday law. It is based on a 'natural order to the human world' that is good and eternally true. Thus if citizens were not content with the operation of everyday law (as imposed by a ruler or judge) they could seek to utilise the natural law in their favour. Natural law was invoked particularly when there was a conflict between the decrees of rulers or judges. See the story of Antigone (below) as a representation of the conflict between state law and natural law.

A tragic story about the conflict between natural law and state law: *Antigone* – A Theban play by Sophocles

Ancient Greek philosophers believed that natural law is not always reflected in state law. Although positivism (which held that state law is the only law) developed as a formal theory more than a thousand years later, very early on Greek intellectuals had demonstrated the conflict between a positivist approach and natural law. Therefore, the positivists' obedience to state law conflicted with the Aristotelian notion of natural law. This could lead to grave injustice.

This conflict is illustrated in the play *Antigone*, written by the fifth century Greek playwright Sophocles. Following is a summary of *Antigone* that reflects the discrepancy between state law and natural law. Although at the time nation-states were not constituted in the modern sense, the city state kingdoms and their decrees are comparable to legislative statehood.

> The background to the play is that King Oedipus is banished from Thebes in Ancient Egypt and leaves the throne of Thebes to his two sons, Eteocles and Polynices. The King's expectation is that the brothers will take turns ruling for one year each. However, Eteocles refuses to relinquish power and exiles his brother. Polynices returns with an army and a civil war erupts. Both brothers die.
>
> The play begins when the new king, Creon, issues a decree. It establishes a (state) law that Polynices will not be buried because he fought against Thebes, which was a 'wicked' betrayal of his motherland. Eteocles, by contrast, will be buried with full military honours. Creon states that his will is law, and must be obeyed.
>
> Antigone believes that Creon's state law is against the will of the gods, which she describes as 'the unchangeable and unwritten statute of heaven'. The law of the gods, she says, 'is not of today and yesterday. But lives forever'. This reflects Antigone's adherence to the natural law. She sees Creon as breaking the natural law and disrupting natural order. Thus, his laws are not 'a binding force'. Accordingly, Antigone attempts to defy the state law by burying her brother Polynices.
>
> The guards catch Antigone burying her brother and she is brought before the King, who orders her death for breaking the law. She proudly accepts her death as she sees no wrong in honouring her brother and sees her death as her fate in the natural order. Antigone states that the law that made the burial a wrong was not ordered by 'Zeus … nor Justice'. The natural law prevails over the state law.
>
> Antigone is taken to a cave and sealed inside. Antigone's fiancé, who is Creon's son Haemon, arrives and announces that the whole city thinks Antigone has done the right thing. The King is angered and demands obedience.
>
> A blind prophet, Tiresias, advises Creon that his actions are not right as they are breaking the natural order. Creon is told that soon he will pay 'corpse for corpse, and flesh for flesh'. Faced with this terrible prophecy, Creon is torn with regret and realises he has erred. Polynices must be buried and Antigone must not be killed.

However, the realisation comes too late: Antigone has already committed suicide in the cave, which causes Haemon to take his own life. Creon's wife, Eurydice, then kills herself in grief over the death of her son. Creon, having lost all his family, lets himself be taken away. His tragic mistake has cost him everything he loved.

From this play we can see Sophocles' sympathetic view of natural law. It has an inherent morality, as represented by the virtuous and devoted character of Antigone. State law can and does defy this morality as a result of human self-interest and impulsive decisions, as illustrated by Creon's acts. However, Sophocles conveys the idea that fate will step in when natural law is defied. This occurred when Creon's son was taken from him.

Today, Aristotle's coexisting dichotomy between state law and natural law remains relevant. Elements of natural law can be found in the discipline of law called equity, described metaphorically as the higher 'conscience' of the law (see Chapters 5 and 8 for a discussion on equity). The common law remains the main undercurrent of the law in common law countries, but accommodates the natural law aspects of equity. However, even the natural law aspects of equity have become entrenched over time as equity develops its own weighty rules.

TIP
Students often associate natural law with purely religious ideas. In fact, natural law arose from Aristotle's belief in human reason.

There is also a view that the concurrent operation of domestic state law and international law reflects a balance between positivist state law and natural law approaches. International law reflects natural law in terms of its declarations on fundamental human rights. The basis of human rights law is that some legal rights exist regardless of the laws of the prevailing government. For example no government can legalise slavery or genocide. These are norms of international law from which no derogation is allowed.

Reflection

Can you think of other examples where there is an Aristotelian polarity between natural laws and positivist laws in statutes and cases?

Slow progress in the Middle Ages: Variations of natural law theory

While Greek antiquity is characterised by a flourishing of ideas, the Middle Ages (fifth to sixteenth centuries) is quite the opposite. For more than a thousand years the feudal system prevailed and stifled intellectual thought. The Christian church, with the support of monarchies, exerted influence over the intellectual sphere of society. The church had little tolerance for democratic and progressive thinking. In fact, many works of the Ancient Greek scholars were destroyed by the Christian order. Works that were preserved were often adapted or interpreted to suit the church's program. Interestingly, the Muslim world, by contrast to the West, developed its ideas in innovative directions.

Thomas Aquinas's religious conception of natural law

In the West the church appropriated Aristotle's theory of natural law. Thomas Aquinas, the pre-eminent thinker of the 1200s, whom the church posthumously declared a saint, was one such example. Aquinas was one of many religious scholars of the Middle Ages who incorporated Aristotle's theories into their own teachings.

The dominant philosophy of the time, *idealism*, was developed as the philosophical rationale for religion. It gave primacy to the existence of ideas and spirituality, as opposed to matter. The ideas of a greater 'being' explained society's existence and change. Therefore, laws should uphold god's will for natural order and change.

What Aquinas developed was a theory reasoning that natural law constitutes all law, and not just one side of law. Accordingly, all law is created by god, and is known as 'divine law'. Through his 'natural theology' he maintained that truth and justice are attained through reason and faith alone. Truth and justice are realised through both natural and supernatural revelation.

The state of justice in any society is reflective of the advancement of humankind's spiritual thinking, particularly in the area of ethics, and not of the society's material conditions. Human laws will be judged according to their conformity to god's natural law. Aquinas did not regard unjust (sacrilegious) state law as law. It lacked authority and binding obligations. This meant that rules of *positive law* that conflict with natural law are invalid. People could choose not to conform. However, they could not disobey state laws where it would create social disorder. This is because social disorder is one of the greatest threats to the natural law.

Renewed intellectual activity in the Renaissance: Legal positivism

Following the Middle Ages there was a rebirth of classical ideas in the Renaissance period from the fourteenth century, which culminated in Enlightenment ideas in Europe in the mid-eighteenth century. This was accompanied by the shift to the modern nation state in Europe between the sixteenth and nineteenth centuries. While idealism continued, it became differentiated into subjective and objective idealism. The former (subjective idealism) resembled the ongoing influence of religious scholars.

The latter (objective idealism) was based on the state's ideas and laws. It held that the state could define the law and justice. This view came to largely characterise legal thought in the Renaissance era and was politicised in the Enlightenment period, especially in France. Because objective idealism was grounded in contemporary political developments it was seen as more innovative. It reflected philosophy's rejection of religion and the embracing of the scientific and technological revolution of the day. The drive for scientifically deducible knowledge went hand in hand with the English industrial revolution.

A feature of objective idealism is empiricism, known as *positivism*. It can be traced to the late eighteenth century context of scientific development and the French revolutionary ideas, and it is based on observing the law, rather than spiritual contemplation. Observations, according to positivists, are essential for the acquisition of knowledge and thus for the progress of science. Major proponents included Thomas Hobbes, John Austin and HLA Hart.

Hobbes was a political philosopher in the Renaissance who sought to identify political authority and political obligation in terms of a sovereign who gives commands. This approach was refined by Austin,[1] who propounded a 'command theory' in which laws are presented as general commands that impose continuing duties to act in certain ways. Austin argued – contrary to Hobbes' view that the sovereign rules by divine right – that the sovereign's power is lawful because he or she is obeyed, and that the commands were facts that people call laws. Further, law is valid because those who breach it are punished by a political sovereign.

Another influential positivist, Hart, had a different bent with his 'obligation theory'. This holds that the law is valid because of the legal obligations that the sovereign creates. Hart criticises Austin's theory of punishment because 'it makes it impossible to distinguish a government from a gunman'.[2] The latter lacks legitimacy.

Context: The different law questions

Not only do natural law theorists and positivists come from different angles, they also ask different questions.

For *natural law* theorists the question is: 'What should the law be?'

For legal *positivists*, the question is: 'What is the law?'

The surge in positivism's popularity in the early nineteenth century reflected the democratic impetus towards modern parliaments and support for their laws. A major catalyst was the 1789 French Revolution, where the masses (known as the 'third estate') revolted against the royal reign and the influence of the religious clergy. The third estate formed its own parliament, which provided a new-found acceptance for state law. The anti-religious ideas of the French philosopher Jean-Jacques Rousseau were also extremely influential for the positivist movement.

At the same time, legislatures were intent on legitimising their law as the only one with any validity and denouncing religious ideas as antiquated and against the will of the people. To enforce its power, the state enacted a broad-sweep of codes, especially aimed at criminalising acts against the state. This went hand in hand with the civil (Roman) law system across continental Europe, which was discussed in Chapter 5.

We know that England followed a different common law tradition. However, positivism was just as strong there. Rather than a strict adherence to state law, positivists in common law countries follow the letter of case law precedent. Indeed, the doctrine of legal positivism had an enormous and fundamental impact on the establishment of the common law system still in use today. It is no coincidence that England, where the common law first developed, was home to various leading positivists such as Francis Bacon and the British empiricist school spanning the seventeenth and eighteenth

---

1   John Austin, *The Providence of Jurisprudence Determined*, Wilfrid E Rumble (ed), Cambridge University Press, Cambridge (1832/1995).

2   Candace J Groudine, 'Authority: HLA Hart and the Problem with Legal Positivism', (1980) IV(3) *The Journal of Libertarian Studies* 273, 285.

centuries. Since positivism promotes objective and scientific observations, positivists saw judges to be in the best position to make these observations.

Irrespective of whether it is parliament-made (civil) law or judge-made (common) law, legal positivism privileges obedience to these legal rules above any other moral or religious values. In other words, they support the institutionalised 'rule of law'.

Positivism remains the major approach to legal reasoning in the twenty-first century, despite misgivings about state law and its capacity to provide for an inherent notion of justice (see the discussion about the play *Antigone* in the box on p. 197).

Part of positivism's attractiveness is that it presents law and legal reasoning as an unbiased, neutral and independent tool. The law is a discipline unto itself. Material conditions and differences between individuals are external and should not interfere with the scientific basis and technical operation of law, which should be applied universally.

The impact and limitations of legal positivism on the common law

With its legal positivist approach, the common law system aims to be objective and neutral, and is concerned primarily with legal fact, as opposed to ethical implications of the law. This manifests in court procedure.[3] Common law courts place more emphasis on formal rules of procedure than civil law systems do. This is to avoid subjective influences. For instance, common law courts have stricter rules regarding the admission of evidence, and it is one of the main roles of judges to ensure that these rules are adhered to. This is in order that the court, in its quest for objectivity, is not swayed by evidence which may not be reputable. Moreover, common law judges and juries are not entitled to procure evidence by conducting their own investigations or asking witnesses questions. They must make decisions based only on the facts presented to them. The courts in civil systems, by contrast, play a much greater inquisitorial role.

In terms of legal reasoning, legal positivism is reflected in the common law's emphasis on inductive reasoning (see Chapter 2) which is the type of reasoning used in empirical or observational study. Inductive reasoning uses a process of observing and learning from cases or precedent, then applying one's observations to form a judicial decision. So you can see that the logical reasoning involved in induction moves from particular instances to general principles. This process is significantly different from the operation of the civil law system, which is based on deductive reasoning, whereby the lawyers start with general principles, outlined in statute, and then apply them to specific cases. The inductive approach is more pragmatic, and its proponents can take comfort in drawing from primarily the tangible, that is, actual case law.

Positivism is also prone to logical fallacy in situations where there is no observed case law of direct relevance to a given legal problem. The deductive approach, on the other hand, is more conceptual, and by focusing on theory, establishes a basis from which to analyse the law. However, it too can err. This happens when the principles (such as statutes or precedent) from which deductions are made are themselves flawed, or are applied out of context.

---

3   See Chapter 13 on legal neutrality and access to justice.

Utilitarian positivists

A prominent legal positivist was the English philosopher, Jeremy Bentham. He was a radical thinker for his time in the late eighteenth century because he went further than merely describing positivism. Bentham sought to prescribe a way in which the law could function. His utilitarian theory held that the most practical, efficient and thus objective way of operating a legal system is to apply laws which advance the greatest good for the greatest number of people in society. Therefore, judges should interpret laws with a view to promoting the greatest good.

Although utilitarianism seems to promote fairness objectively, it nonetheless fails to take into account material circumstances. For example though Indigenous people are less in number than non-Indigenous people, their historical disadvantage may create more pressing needs for compensatory laws. Yet utilitarianism would not support the creation of special laws for a minority group.

Key theorist: Jeremy Bentham

Jeremy Bentham (1748–1832) was an English philosopher, theorist and reformer whose major works included *Fragment on Government* (1776), *Panopticon* (1787) and *Introduction to Principles of Morals and Legislation* (1789). Bentham wrote during the Enlightenment – a time at which the law was particularly arbitrary and ad hoc.

Bentham was a prolific writer who wrote on a range of topics, but is perhaps most well known for his idea of 'utilitarianism'. Utilitarianism basically holds that actions should be judged by whether they contribute to the (balance of) happiness and benefit for all people. This is why Bentham sometimes referred to utilitarianism as the 'greatest happiness principle'. According to this theory, human behaviour is governed by two over-arching principles/phenomena: (1) the avoidance of pain and (2) the desire for pleasure. In Bentham's words:

FIGURE 7.1: JEREMY BENTHAM

> Nature has placed mankind under the governance of two sovereign masters, *pain* and *pleasure*. It is for them alone to point out what we ought to do, as well as to determine what we shall do… They govern us in all we do, in all we say, in all we think.[4]

---

4   Jeremy Bentham, *An Introduction to the Principles of Morals and Legislation*, New York, Methuen (1789/1982), 1.

Bentham referred to this weighing or balancing process as the 'hedonistic calculus'. A good example of a legal phenomenon which involved this balancing act is punishment of criminals. For Bentham, punishment was seen as an evil act. But he also saw that there was a need to protect the community and to deter others from committing crimes. Bentham argued that people could be deterred from committing crimes if there was certainty, clarity, celerity, severity and proportionality in punishment. Also in terms of punishment, he advocated the principle of 'less eligibility' for prisons. This principle stipulated that prison would only act as a deterrent if the conditions in prison were worse than the conditions of the poorest in society. This view had a profound impact on the British and Australian correctional systems.

Bentham was a strong advocate for law reform. He criticised the legal practice of his day for being unprincipled, irrational and incoherent. For Bentham, the law of the time was just a means of covering up the fact that really, judges were making decisions according to their own prejudices. He was also very critical of the system of precedent (which he felt perpetuated outdated modes of thinking) and the idea of natural rights (which he referred to as 'nonsense on stilts'). Bentham argued for a clear and rational system of law. He felt that one way to go about achieving this was through the codification of laws.

Bentham is equally famous as the architect of the Panopticon – a circular prison with a central observatory tower. He believed that the Panopticon through its architecture of surveillance created a 'new mode of obtaining power of mind over mind'.[5] An interesting fact about Bentham's work was that he was strongly opposed to the British colonisation of Australia. He published widely and lobbied the government of the day. He felt that there was no deterrence in sending convicts so far away, and believed that the crime problem could be better solved by use of his Panopticon.

The marriage of positivism with rationalism

Rationalism was a major philosophy advanced during the Renaissance by thinkers such as Descartes, Spinoza and Leibniz in the seventeenth to eighteenth centuries. It is based on an *idealist* view that the influence of thinking of rational individuals leads to change (rather than attributing change to material conditions). Rationalism echoes Aquinas's approach but differentiates reason from religious faith or prejudice. Rationalism is a *self-proclaimed* objective analysis. It promotes deductive reasoning (see Chapter 2) that applies reasoned principles to facts. It goes hand in hand with Roman civil law (see Chapter 5).

The new industrial economy and liberal positivism

Liberal theory and positivism gained momentum at the same time in the early nineteenth century. Positivism is seen as a liberal theory because it asserts that the state must protect individual autonomy, and it therefore privileges state laws against any extra-legal notions of justice. Positivism treats the state as legitimately providing legal rules to apply equally to everyone. Those rules should be read strictly and

---

5 Jeremy Bentham, *Panopticon* (1787) at http://cartome.org/panopticon2.htm.

without deviation based on difference. Therefore, for liberal theory, in contrast to utilitarianism, the law's role is to protect individual rights.

The doctrine of our modern legal system espouses these liberal rights, including the right to a fair hearing and trial and the right to an assumption of innocence before a determination of guilt. Liberal notions are also embedded in the fact that individuals should be treated like other individuals, with no discrimination on the grounds of background, identity, status or class.

Liberal theory was trail-blazed by John Rawls, and Robert Nozick pioneered the more 'extreme' approach, libertarian theory. To a greater or lesser extent, these thinkers prioritised individual rights (as found in a free market concept) over rights of the collective. Their ideas may sound alluring to enterprising individuals, but they lack the element of social good which utilitarianism aims to create. Each individual is subject to the force of the law irrespective of circumstance or background. There is survival of the fittest, and individuals who are unable to acquire resources suffer. There is no provision for public resources such as legal aid to redress this imbalance. Law makers who inquire into difference disturb the egalitarian application of the law, and create a class of individuals who do not strive for self-betterment.

Though Rawls and Nozick, who came to prominence in the 1970s, are relatively recent theorists, ideas of *liberalism* and *libertarianism* have been around for many years. Since the development of capitalist society, with a large-scale production market and a large-scale labour market, competition among individuals has been a marked feature of life and is protected by liberal and libertarian ideas.

John Rawls[6] formulated his theory in terms of 'justice as fairness'. This was an attempt to show what basic principles of justice individuals in the 'original position' would agree to. That is, if human society was beginning again, what would be the essential aspiration? Rawls claims that it would be the concept of 'justice as fairness'. Ultimately, Rawls' 'blind decision' model (in which he assumes that our own position is hidden from us behind a 'veil of ignorance', so we don't know whether we will be rich or poor) is said to lead to an outcome where the poor will be looked after. Individuals are forced to take the good of others into account because they do not know which self they will turn out to be. This is fairness progressed through the individual pursuit of the good, rather than Aristotle's vision of a community following 'the good life'.

Robert Nozick developed a more controversial entitlement theory based on 'distributive justice'. This is a theory of justice that proclaims that certain people have a just entitlement to property due to 'just acquisitions'. It is based on John Locke's theory that the person who gains first title to land ownership is the first to mix 'land with labour'.[7] All subsequent transfers to individuals cannot be questioned as they are 'just transfers'.[8] The law should enforce these individual transfers and not question them, or seek to redistribute them. The redistribution of property rights would violate individuals' liberty and lead to an unjust distribution. Nozick's libertarian approach,

---

6   In his major work, John Rawls, *A Theory of Justice,* Belknap, Cambridge, Mass. (1971).

7   John Locke, *Two Treatises of Government,* Everyman's Library, London (1924), 130.

8   Robert Nozick, *Anarchy, State, and Utopia,* Basic Books, New York (1974), 151.

unlike liberalism, is not concerned with achieving fair outcomes, rather, it is merely concerned with maintaining distributive justice.

Reflection

1. What would liberal or libertarian theorists say about Australian Indigenous people's claims to land?
2. Would they argue that it is a just or an unjust right to land?

Ideas of individual rights have paved the way for individual freedoms, which did not exist in slavery or feudalism. Legally, this means that individuals have a right to a fair trial, procedural fairness and a presumption of innocence. However, it also means that courts are not well equipped to accommodate collective rights. This manifests in various ways, including:

- The rarity of class actions (such as a group of smokers suing a tobacco company) – a relatively new and under-developed type of legal suit in Australia.
- Strategic law suits against public participation – law suits brought by businesses against lobby groups, which serve to deter groups from their protests against business. There are no government regulations to prevent businesses from engaging in this type of suit.
- The inability of intellectual property law to accommodate the collective interests of Indigenous communities against having their art themes replicated.
- The difficulty for groups to intervene on behalf of the public interest in a court case unless the group or organisation has statutory authority to intervene.
- The inability of the High Court to provide an advisory opinion on a matter of law. This means that individuals are forced to litigate in an adversarial trial, and often an appellate trial, before a declaration of the law can be made.

3: Modernism, Marxism and socio-legal theory

From the late eighteenth century until today, modernist ideas have prevailed in legal thinking, doctrines, and institutions, although not without contestation. Modernism appraises the dominant legal institutions. The pre-eminent modernist school in legal theory is positivism. Positivists prefer objective notions of the law (where the law is discerned by reading the letter of the law) over subjective approaches (where law is interpreted based on a view of justice). The legal positivist Hans Kelsen, who made his mark in the early twentieth century, placed ideology, morality, religion, and politics in the category of the subjective, and proclaimed that they were divorced from what he called the 'pure theory of law'. This position discounts any reading of the law in terms of subjective values.

However, modernism was not a wholly conservative approach to reading the black-letter law. Quite the contrary. There is a long line of materialist thinkers in modernist times, originating with Karl Marx in the 1840s and including the New Left and socio-legal approaches in the 1960s and 1970s, who throw into disrepute the whole basis of the objective approach. They argue that the law is a historical phenomenon and can only be effectively studied with reference to the range of social and economic factors which define each historical epoch. Therefore, while political views, for instance, may form part of the subjective thinking of individuals, materialists believe that their analysis in relation to the law is important for an objective understanding of it. Without such a contextual understanding of what informs the law and its interpretation, the law loses its meaning.

Marx's theory, called Marxism, is a driving force behind materialist thinking. It has become so influential that it informed a number of socialist revolutions in the last 100 years, and continues to influence radical thought internationally. Unlike the popular perception that Marxism is merely a set of political ideologies, it also involves a pure philosophy. This is called dialectical materialism. Dialectical materialism explains change based on the synthesis of 'opposites' to form a new and different whole, although one force always remains dominant. The dominant force guides social change. The main 'opposites' that Marx was concerned with were the ruling class and the oppressed class. In a capitalist society the capitalist class is dominant and the subordinate class is the working class. These classes conflict and will ultimately synthesise to give rise to a socialist society in which the working class prevails. Marx's application of dialectical materialism to an understanding of society, including the law and the legal system, is called historical materialism.

Key theorist: Karl Marx

Karl Marx (1818–83) was a German economist and social philosopher. His most renowned works, *Manifest der Kommunistischen Partei* (1848, translated as *The Manifesto of the Communist Party* and written with Friedrich Engels) and *Das Kapital* (1867, translated as *Capital* and published in three volumes), focus on the evolution through struggle around the ownership of the means of production (e.g. factory machinery).[9] Marx and Engels famously wrote that 'the history of all hitherto existing society is the history of class struggles'.[10]

FIGURE 7.2: KARL MARX

---

9   See Marxist legal theorist Evgeny Pashukanis, 'The General Theory of Law and Marxism', www.marxists.org/archive/pashukanis/1924/law/edintro.htm and Michael Head, *Evgeny Pashukanis: A Critical Reappraisal*, Routledge Cavendish, Oxford (2008).

10 Karl Marx and Friedrich Engels (with an introduction by AJP Taylor), *The Communist Manifesto*, Penguin, Middlesex (1977), 79.

Although Marx did not write specifically on the law, he considered the law to be part of the superstructure of society; as such, it reflects the basic structure of society, which consists of the economic relations between social classes. For Marx, these relations underlie the nature and operations of the law. But in order to better explain Marx's contribution to legal theory it is necessary to first say a few words about Marxist economic theory.

In a nutshell, Marx felt that the characterising feature of a society was its 'mode of production', or in other words the 'economic base of society'. Each society (e.g. feudalism, capitalism, socialism) has a unique class structure based on the mode of production particular to the society. Marx recognised that one's class could be determined according to his or her relationship to the means of production. In a capitalist society, those who own the means of production are the *bourgeoisie*. The workers (*proletariat*) are forced to work the means of production by selling their labour power to the *bourgeoisie* in order to make a living.

Because the *bourgeoisie* own the means of production, they are able to exploit the *proletariat*. Marx defined exploitation as the creation of 'surplus value' (i.e. the value of what is produced by the workers is greater than the value of their labour power). He wrote at a time capitalism was sweeping Europe, and political struggles, especially in France, were rife. In developing his theory, Marx drew on the politics of the French, the philosophy of the Germans (especially Hegel), and the economics of the English. Marx predicted that a class struggle inevitably arises between the bourgeoisie and the proletariat who have 'nothing to lose but their chains'.[11]

For Marx, the superstructure of society consists of the law, politics, arts, culture, religion and other forms of 'ideology'. These phenomena do not have an independent existence but are generally determined by the economic base of society (e.g. in capitalism, it is the industry that is owned by the capitalist class). While the law serves the overall interests of the ruling class and serves to maintain the ruling class in power, it also reflects the nature of class struggle at any point in time. Therefore, the law may act to appease the working class by providing some benefits in addition to wages, or it may seek to directly suppress the working class in a way which increases the surplus value of their labour. Marx called for a dynamic approach to society, with analysis taking into account all the various factors which are in play. Marx refers to this method of analysis as 'dialectics'.[12]

Marxism applied to law

Given that a central theme of Marx's analysis was class, how did this manifest in the legal sphere? Marx may have pointed to the process of dialectics, whereby the working class struggles to gain legal rights. Through its interaction with the ruling class, it sometimes gains legal rights, and it sometimes loses them. But until the working class is dominant, it is generally disadvantaged in the operation of the

---

11 Karl Marx and Friedrich Engels, *The Manifesto of the Communist Party* (1848) at www.marxists.org/archive/marx/works/1848/communist-manifesto/ch04.htm

12 See FV Konstantinov (Chief Editor), *The Fundamentals of Marxist-Leninist Philosophy* (R. Daglish, Trans.) Moscow: Progress Publishers (1974), 479–80.

law. For instance, a big tobacco company will have many more legal resources available, and thus have a greater chance of success in litigation, than a working class consumer who develops lung cancer from smoking the company's cigarettes. The worker has a right to litigate and a right to a fair hearing. However, due to the resource imbalance, the worker is very unlikely to pursue litigation to gain what may be their right to compensation. Even if the worker does go ahead, the tobacco company may drag out litigation or seek documents and expert testimony from the worker that he or she cannot afford.

Let's break it down. Materialism situates law in the context of actual social circumstances and types of societies (slavery, feudalism, capitalism, socialism, etc) and cultures. Dialectics looks at the way in which the law is perpetually changing through the interaction of opposites. For Marx, the dominant force is the ruling class in the economy, such that the character of the law is generally dependent on the nature of the economy. Marx did not go so far as to reduce the law to economics. But he did explain why there are patterns in legal thought across particular historical epochs and economic conditions, and why in each historical age concepts in the legal sphere have similarities to concepts in other aspects of the social superstructure.[13] For example when the economy is in a downturn, both the legal system and the welfare system may be more punitive to ensure conformity.

Since Marxism was developed, many sociological theorists have employed, though often selectively, various tenets drawn from Marx's works in their analysis of how the law works in society. Some focus on the law in relation to the working class in general. Others look at discrete sections of the working class, including women, ethnic minorities, and Indigenous peoples. In addition to Marxist theories, various feminist and race theories have been developed and applied to the law based on sociological analyses.

Another highly influential socio-legal theorist was Emile Durkheim. He believed that societies were based on social cohesion and solidarity. The law reflected this social cohesion, but is also prone to change. Like Marx, Durkheim theorised that as societies modernise, those elements that are left out of the transition process need to be brought into the realm of social cohesion through laws. He therefore saw the role of the law as vital for social development. It reflected and stipulated the moral needs of society.

---

13   See Marxist legal theorist Evgeny Pashukanis, 'The General Theory of Law and Marxism', www.marxists.org/archive/pashukanis/1924/law/edintro.htm

Key theorist: Emile Durkheim

Emile Durkheim (1858–1917) was a French sociologist and theorist whose major works included *De La Division du Travail Social* (1893, translated as *The Division of Labour in Society*), *Le Suicide* (1897, *Suicide*) and *Les Règles de la Méthode Sociologique* (1895, *Rules of the Sociological Method*).

FIGURE 7.3: EMILE DURKHEIM

Durkheim argued that the main function of the law was to keep society together, or in his words, to provide 'social solidarity' and 'social cohesion'. For Durkheim, the law was an 'external index' by which one could observe the different types of social solidarity and the changing needs of society. Durkheim hypothesised that the transition from a primitive society to a capitalist one would bring about conflict, crisis and 'anomie'. Anomie (in Greek, *a* – without, *nomos* – law) is sometimes likened to the terms 'without norms' or 'normlessness', and it occurs when the norms of an individual do not correspond with the norms of society. When this occurs, the criminal law justifies the intervention of the state.

This can be seen most clearly in *The Division of Labor in Society*. In this book Durkheim mapped the changes from what he called a 'primitive' society to a more 'advanced' capitalist society. Durkheim felt that within primitive societies, on the one hand, there was what he termed a *conscience collective* – or a common conscience. In other words, there was a greater sense of community and collectivism, and this helped maintain a certain degree of order and solidarity (or what Durkheim called 'mechanical solidarity'). As such, in these societies, Durkheim argued that the law played a repressive role. On the other hand, Durkheim felt that within capitalist societies, labour is more individualised (or what Durkheim called 'organic'). In capitalist societies, the role of the law is 'restitutive' – it aims to restore the balance between different interests and parties that emerge in an individualist society.

But Durkheim's contribution to legal theory was not only limited to this thesis on law and labour. Durkheim also made some famous comments on the relationship between morality and the law. He felt that the law is an expression of society's morality, and that conversely, a law can no longer be considered part of society if it doesn't reflect a society's morality, or if there is no moral commitment to it. In the words of Durkheim, an act is criminal when it offends the common conscience:

> [W]e must not say that an action shocks the common conscience because it is criminal, but rather that it is criminal because it shocks the common conscience.[14]
>
> But Durkheim is perhaps most famous for his controversial statements about crime. He said that crime is a normal and even essential part of every society and that society could not function without some crime.
>
> Durkheim wrote at the time of the Industrial Revolution, which was in the process of radically transforming central European countries such as France and Germany. His major work, *The Division of Labour in Society*, was written at the time of France's defeat in the Franco-Prussian war, the Dreyfus affair,[15] and the transition from pre-capitalist to capitalist society. These events fragmented traditional social bonds and caused social divisions among the economic classes, which provided a burgeoning role for the law of the state.

4: Legal realism

A major rejection of modernist theory in the form of pragmatism and new-left thinking came in the form of legal realism in the 1920s and 1930s. This approach rejects the view that law can be found in the black letter of statutes and cases. Rather, legal realism holds that it is not legal doctrines, but rather real people who decide cases.

Legal realism attempts to use social science and rationalist reasoning to study statutes and legal decisions. It is therefore positivist in the sense that it believes that legal practitioners and scholars can discover social 'facts'. There are real reasons why legal decisions are made. Therefore, its proponents often employ deductive reasoning in the form of logic to develop logical 'systems'. Indeed, a traditional view of legal realism is that legal cases should be examined through the lens of logic.[16] The empirical approach to law was what made their studies 'real'.

However, with the influence of modernist social theory (see critical social theories below), legal realism began to take into account social factors to marry deductive legal reasoning with reality. Human tendencies in the law making process gained greater prominence. In this respect, legal realism became a response to formalism's strict textual reasoning of rules (see Chapter 10).

The humanist strand of legal realism took hold in the early twentieth century in the USA and Scandinavia. Indeed, while the Australian and British common law systems remain highly positivistic, in North America legal realists (as well as natural law theorists) have a far more influential role.

---

14 Emile Durkheim, *The Division of Labour in Society* (translated by George Simpson), London, Collier-MacMillan (1964).

15 The Dreyfus affair involved the wrongful conviction for treason of a French officer in 1894. Evidence was fabricated to assure his conviction, which resulted in life imprisonment. This legal scandal received wide publicity in the French media and divided French society for a decade. Ultimately Dreyfus was exonerated.

16 See John Dewey, *Logic: The Theory of Inquiry*, Henry Holt, New York (1938).

One of the key proponents of legal realism was Karl Llewellyn. He supported an interdisciplinary understanding of the law, particularly in a sociological framework. He believed that 'black-letter law' (legislation, subordinate legislation and cases) were not decisive factors in judgments. One also had to turn to the sociological context and personal biases of the judge. To this extent, legal realism resonates with natural law.

However, legal realists still viewed social factors as 'extralegal', rather than inherent in the legal process. Social considerations should only be incorporated into the legal process where they were capable of evaluation by 'neutral experts'. This requires, first, empirical studies conducted by sociologists, anthropologists and economists that indicate an acceptance of inductive methods of analysis. The second step was to combine the inductive (sociologically informed analysis) into the school's deductive framework.

Don't worry if you're confused – many scholars have also criticised the realist school's ambiguities. It was certainly a far cry from the politicised approach that Karl Marx took, which saw social factors as intrinsic to the nature of the law. Nonetheless, this school continues to have influence over strands of feminist legal theory and critical race theory, discussed below.

5: Critical legal theories

Critical legal theories began in the late 1970s and early 1980s. They shifted legal thinking away from positive or natural law notions. They do not conceive of law through an idealist philosophical orientation. Rather, they adopt a material view that the law reflects material circumstances, structures and institutions. Like Marxism, critical legal theory adopts a sociological perspective. However, it is less attached to ideas of economics and class. It was derived from the diverse radical popular movements in Western Europe and North America in the 1960s and 1970s, especially Marxism, feminism and anti-racism.

Critical legal theorists highlight the fact that individuals in power – especially in judicial and political office – have a vested interest in construing the law as unbiased and neutral. Some argue that the law serves to protect economic and class divisions in society. In this respect, critical legal scholars revive legal realism. However, they also attack its central tenet – that there are social 'facts' that can be used to explain legal decisions. Indeed, critical legal theorists rebuke this idea and argue that all legal decisions are political, rather than factual.

Accordingly, critical legal theorists claim that the law operates to privilege the interests of the powerful and law is inherently political. Feminist legal theory and critical race theory were intent on proving the political nature of law through demonstrating how sexism and racism emanated in the law. (See Figure 7.4 for the relationship between the main schools of thought.) This section is dedicated to these theories. They differ from traditional Marxist approaches that privilege economics, by also pointing to the cultural and political premises of law. Many critical legal theorists not only contribute to jurisprudence, but are also active in advocating for and litigating on social justice issues. They believe change must occur both outside and within the legal system.

FIGURE 7.4: RELATIONSHIPS BETWEEN SCHOOLS OF THOUGHT WITHIN CRITICAL LEGAL THEORY

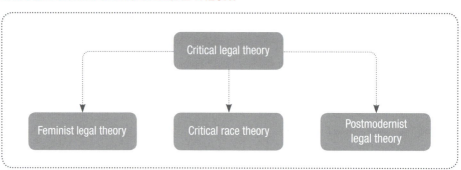

Feminist legal theory

Broadly, feminism engages the concerns of women in the analysis of the law. It is largely a means of critiquing the law's masculine assumptions (which are embedded in legal rules and practice), as well as interrogating how women may be better served by the legal system.[17]

Feminist legal theory developed in the radical context of the 1960s, when women were demanding equal rights (such as pay, jobs and education). This is referred to as first wave feminism. The objective of the first wave legal feminists was to liberate women from the shackles of male oppression and provide them with equal opportunities in society, including legal protections.

It was not until the 1980s that feminism went beyond demanding legal rights for women to critiquing the patriarchal core of the legal system. This movement comes under the umbrella of second wave feminism. It is classed here, and in the case study below on pornography, as 'critical feminism'.

The feminist legal critique was focused on three legal schools of thought:

1 *Liberal* legal theory that treats individuals as equal and avoids coercive boundaries relating to sex.
2 *Positivism* for employing methods that pervaded mainstream legal reasoning (based on 'neutral observation').
3 *Legal rationalism* and *realism* and their deductive approaches, which neutralise power relations and makes the law appear objective rather than enforcing a patriarchal society.

This group of feminists was committed to highlighting the law's enforcement of the patriarchy, that is, the male domination of society. A famous feminist in the 1980s, Catharine MacKinnon, wrote, 'The rule of law and the rule of men are one thing'.[18]

---

17 See Carol Gilligan, *In a Different Voice: Psychological Theory and Women's Development*, Harvard University Press, Cambridge, Mass. (1982).

18 Catharine MacKinnon, *Toward a Feminist Theory of the State*, Harvard University Press, Cambridge, Mass. (1989), 170.

In the 1980s MacKinnon criticised notions of formal equality that treated everyone the same and failed to recognise the subordination of women in society and their different or greater needs. It does not accommodate differences or undercut social hierarchies. In MacKinnon's view, a substantive approach to equality jurisprudence is required to understand the law's patriarchal assumptions. In some respects, therefore, MacKinnon's approach has an accord with Marxism. Law requires a sociological context to be fully understood and transformed.

Many feminists in the 1980s also embraced 'standpoint' methodologies that elevated the experiences of women in the legal system.[19] For example conceiving the standpoint of the male judge or law maker is key to understanding women's subordination. Some of these feminists advocated strongly for more female law makers – judges and legislators.

Reflection

Do you think that practice matches up to feminist standpoint theory? For example do female law makers make better laws for women?

However, the conceptual weakness of these strands of feminism was revealed when feminists' *essentialist* critique of the male law was juxtaposed with an essentialist solution of female involvement. Some feminists began to ask whether all women have the same experience with the law and the same needs for law reform. In responding to their own question, they slowly broke down the essentialist idea that there was only one woman's voice and one man's voice. They realised that by solely focusing on gender as the primary category of analysis and source of female oppression, feminists failed to take into account the historical, cultural, racial and economic diversity of women's experiences in the legal system.[20]

By the late 1980s feminists were coming to accept that there was not one universal women's experience. This is known as 'third wave' feminism. Third-wave feminists demonstrated that there are different and diverse women's voices. Some of these voices can be – and are – represented in the system. This was a strong challenge to a single feminist standpoint.[21] This kind of feminism no longer insisted on any singular relation between law and gender, but sought to locate its analysis in the field of power relations. Its aim was not to construct a more correct feminist version of the truth, but to deconstruct and analyse the power relations underpinning truth claims. Nor does this kind of feminism restrict its focus to women's issues. Rather, it extends it to sexuality and masculinity. This approach spawned an array of studies

---

19 See Ngaire Naffine, *Feminism and Criminology*, Allen & Unwin, Sydney (1997).

20 Loraine Gelsthorpe, *Sexism & the Female Offender*, Gower, Aldershot (1989), 152.

21 Kerry Carrington, 'Postmodernism and Feminist Criminologies: Disconnecting Discourses', (1994) 22(3) *International Journal of the Sociology of Law* 261.

on the intersections between sex, race, class and the legal system in the 1980s.[22] It also focuses on the symbolism and representations in the legal system that construct images of sex, rather than assume the truth behind knowledge about gender and law.

Critical race theory

Also taking a sociological approach to the law, race theory – known as critical race theory in the USA – attempts to address the way race is mediated through the law and legal institutions. It began to develop in the 1980s, and its attempts to understand the deep interconnections between race and law, and particularly the ways in which race and law are mutually constitutive, is an extraordinary intellectual challenge.

Race theory has largely been influenced by African Americans in the USA in the post-civil rights era. Theorists draw on personal experiences of racism and often write in a narrative (rather than academic) style. Legal scholars such as Derrick Bell, Matsuda Lawrence, Richard Delgado and Kimberlé Crenshaw challenge the traditional philosophical conception of liberal civil rights that adopted a colour-blind approach to social justice. They seek to subvert the dominant culture, which allows liberal reform but denies substantive change. Contrary to the traditional notion that racial subordination represents a deviation from the liberal legal ideal, critical race theory casts the role of law as historically central to and complicit in upholding racial hierarchy.

Crenshaw argues that little difference exists between positivist and liberal discourse on race-related law and policy, and identifies two distinct properties in anti-discrimination law: expansive and restrictive properties. The former stresses equality as outcome, relying on the courts to eliminate effects of racism. The latter treats equality as a process. Its focus is to prevent any future wrongdoing. Crenshaw argues that expansive and restrictive properties coexist in anti-discrimination law. The implication is that failure of the restrictive property to address or correct the racial injustices of the past simply perpetuates the status quo.[23]

Critical race theory is very focused on social change. According to Delgado, critical race theorists were deeply concerned with the 'snail pace' progress of racial reform in the USA.[24] Part of the change will invariably involve changes to the economic, social and political dimensions of race from a legal standpoint. Derrick Bell discussed

---

22   See Sue Lees 'Sex, Race and Culture: Feminism and the Limits of Cultural Pluralism', (1986) 22 *Feminist Review* 92; Kimberlé Crenshaw, 'Mapping the Margins: Intersectionality, Identity Politics and Violence Against Women of Color', (1991) 43(6) *Stanford Law Review* 1241; Elizabeth Comack (ed), *Locating Law: Race/Class/Gender Connections*, Fernwood Publishing, Halifax (1999); Rebecca Johnson, 'Gender, Race, Class and Sexual Orientation: Theorizing the Intersections', in Gayle MacDonald, Rachel L Osborne and Charles C Smith (eds), *Feminism, Law, Inclusion: Intersectionailty In Action*, Sumach Press, Toronto (2005).

23   Kimberlé Crenshaw, 'Race, Reform, and Retrenchment: Transformation and Legitimization in Antidiscrimination Law' (1988) 101 *Harvard Law Review* 1331.

24   Richard Delgado (ed), *Critical Race Theory: The Cutting Edge,* Temple University Press, Philadelphia (1995).

the constitutional contradiction, arguing that the framers of the Constitution chose the rewards of property over justice. However, race theory has had minimal impact on non-American societies.[25]

> **Reflection**
>
> Is critical race theory a useful framework for understanding the specific legal concerns of refugees in Australia? Is there a better theoretical framework?

Postmodernist legal theory: Chaos and beyond

In the aftermath of the Second World War, many thinkers began to give added emphasis to the concept of culture or superstructure, and undermined economic notions of power. Before too long they had disregarded the Marxist idea of an economic base altogether. Signalling this shift in thinking, Ernest Gellner remarked, 'culture does not so much underlie structure: it replaces it!'[26]

The consequence was the position that, unlike in modernism, one should not be bound by structure when analysing social phenomena, including the law. This new thinking was to be called postmodernism or post-structuralism. It may be said to have developed along with the growth of individualism in society. It is anti-conformist to the extent that postmodernists generally do not wish to be categorised as members of a distinct school of thought.

Postmodernists believe that nothing can be pinned down as concrete knowledge, as everything is relative. Postmodernism is therefore on the opposite end of the spectrum to theories which state that knowledge or law is absolute and eternal. Two of its main proponents are Michel Foucault and Jacques Derrida.

Postmodernists do not advocate any particular theory, and thus may be described as atheoretical. Postmodernists promote the idea that diverse standpoints are required to question rules, systems and theories. The opinions highlight exceptions to these *essentialised* positions. Postmodernists are idealist by favouring subjective ideas over established material conditions. It is only once the standpoint of an individual is known that the legal system can be questioned. Otherwise, there is a risk of imposing an authoritative position or making neutral assumptions, which postmodernists seek to resist.

The ramifications of postmodernism for an understanding of the law include a fragmented perception of conceptual systems which underlie judicial reasoning, statutory law and legal theories. Students can have particular difficulty understanding the essence or major import of a legal issue when it is subject to postmodernist analysis.

---

25 Derrick A Bell, *And We Are Not Saved: The Elusive Quest for Racial Justice*, Basic Books, New York (1987).

26 Cited in Paul James, *Nation Formation: Towards a Theory of Abstract Community*, Sage Publications, London (1996), 133.

Key theorist: Michel Foucault

Michel Foucault (1926–84) was a French philosopher and theorist whose most famous works included *Naissance de la Clinique* (1963, translated as *The Birth of the Clinic*), *Les Mots et les Choses* (1966, *The Order of Things*), *Surveiller et Punir* (1975, *Discipline and Punish*) and *Histoire de la Sexualité* (1976–84, *The History of Sexuality*, published in three volumes).

FIGURE 7.5: MICHEL FOUCAULT

It is difficult to say anything definitive about Foucault's contribution to the law and jurisprudence. This is because Foucault never really limited himself to 'the law' (or any other discipline for that matter) as a singular line of enquiry. Foucault didn't like writing about things within prefabricated frameworks but preferred to look at things critically and within their socio-political context. This is one of the reasons why Foucault's work has been influential across such a diverse range of disciplines — law, psychology, history, philosophy, sociology, criminology, political science and so on.

Foucault's books might take one particular institution or theme as a focus (for example, the prison, insanity, sexuality), but they always have a broader significance. For example, in *Discipline and Punish*, Foucault put together a complex historical account of the prison as an institution. But in doing so, Foucault considered the relationship between power, knowledge and the body throughout history. One of Foucault's most original ideas is that of 'power-knowledge'. In *Discipline and Punish* he famously said:

> We should admit … that power produces knowledge … that power and knowledge directly imply one another; that there is no power relation without the correlative constitution of a field of knowledge, nor any knowledge that does not presuppose and constitute at the same time power relations…[27]

Essentially, Foucault was more concerned with power than law, if the two could at all be separated. He wrote in *Discipline and Punish* that power and social control operate through a network of governance, which is exercised through a variety of social institutions, including universities, prisons, corporations, courts and hospitals. Power is also expressed through knowledges and disciplines rather than force, including (but not exclusively) law.[28] For

---

[27] Michel Foucault, *Discipline and Punish: The Birth of the Prison*, (translated by Alan Sheridan) Penguin Books, Middlesex (1981), 27.

[28] Michel Foucault, *Discipline and Punish: The Birth of the Prison*, Vintage Books, New York (1979).

example, Foucault discussed Bentham's invention of the Panoptican – a prison where space is ordered to create a power relationship based on knowledge and its illusions, rather than direct control.

Other original ideas Foucault has put forward have included: 'biopower', 'disciplinary power', 'governmentality', 'episteme' and 'genealogies'. In developing these ideas, Foucault nonetheless was influenced by the work of Nietzsche.

Foucault wrote in the late twentieth century, and some of the major events that happened in Europe during this time (such as the famous French protests of May 1968; Nazi Germany; the Cold War) undoubtedly had a strong influence on his work. In particular, these events put in question the 'objectivity' of science and revealed the potential for catastrophes within 'civilised' society. As such, Foucault's work shares many points in common with other postmodernist and poststructuralist scholars – although Foucault would surely feel uncomfortable about having his work pigeonholed within any paradigm like this.

Foucault was critical of the idea of there ever existing one version of the truth, history, and so on, and his writing style reflects this theoretical perspective. Unlike conventional academic writing, Foucault writes in a narrative prose style and rarely uses any references or citations. As Hunt and Wickham point out: 'Foucault consciously avoids treating his work as a comprehensive and integrated package'.[29]

TIP
When reading Foucault, you may feel overwhelmed by the density of ideas in his work. But try not to worry too much about which ideas you *should* focus on – as there is no 'proper' way to understand Foucault. In fact, Foucault himself was against what he termed 'the cult of the author' and in one book he even criticised the way we tend to privilege the ideas of the author over those of the reader.[30]

6: Dominant jurisprudence today

Despite the popularity of postmodernism in other faculties, the philosophies of positivism and liberalism continue to exert significant influence over the law and the way it is taught in law faculties. Modernist ideas help give law its validity.

In more recent times there have been occasional attempts at a revival of natural law theory. These have by and large been secular (non-religious) attempts to show that natural law emerges from natural human processes. It is informed by ethics and morality deduced by humans. Accordingly, natural law is different from *positive law* (statutes, regulations and judgments) and even from fixed religious doctrines.

Some examples include the work of John Finnis, who came to prominence late in the twentieth century. Finnis maintained that knowledge of the law should be self-evident, since it can be attained through self-reflection by the well-rounded individual. Lon Fuller in the 1950s and 1960s also advanced a natural law position in response to what he perceived as unjust Nazi *positive laws*.

Today, Ronald Dworkin advocates a natural law position in relation to the legal reasoning of judges. He argues that judges invariably engage in a dual interpretation of the law. Judges consider positive rules and the moral principles behind those rules. Without consideration of law's morality, the meaning of the law cannot be ascertained. Thus judges always engage natural law interpretations in their legal reasoning. Dworkin advocates making transparent the natural law (moral) aspect of

---

29 Allan Hunt & Gary Wickham, *Foucault and Law*, London, Pluto Press (1994), 3.

30 Ibid.

TIP

Dworkin is technically not a natural law theorist. He is part of the Legal Process school that began at Yale among more traditional legal scholars to combat legal realism. They want to say that legal decisions are not determined by who the judge is, or by policy, but by 'objective' (although more abstract than rules) 'principles'.

judgments. There should be overt recourse to philosophical principles of justice that underpin government policy and precedent. The principles should be presented in the best moral light. Indeed, Dworkin believes that judges are characters of integrity who are in the best position to determine the morally best interpretation of the law.

Essentially, only the Catholic Church and perhaps some other religious institutions continue to follow Aquinas's theory of natural law to the letter. The church practises this when it attempts to convert prisoners to its faith in the hope that they may reform their ways. This approach is strictly idealist – changing criminals' ideas and spirituality will lead to a change in their action (irrespective of their material conditions remaining the same). For students of jurisprudence Aquinas's theory of law helps to demarcate one extreme idealist position in legal thinking.

It is useful to highlight two case examples: the post–Nazi Germany trials and the feminist debate about pornography. These illustrate the way jurisprudence can be used to argue perspectives on contemporary issues.

Context: Trials in post-Nazi Germany – tensions between positivist and natural law approaches

Lon Fuller and HLA Hart entered into a fiery debate over whether unfair Nazi laws should have been adhered to. The focus of the debate was on 'Grudge Informer' cases – a series of cases concerning Nazi German citizens who would 'dob in' people under a Nazi law that they had a grudge against.[31] The alleged offences tended to be minor crimes against the state, but under an atmosphere of terror the Nazi state would punish minuscule transgressions. After the Second World War Nazi laws had been condemned politically, and there was pressure to punish grudge informers.

The Fuller–Hart debate arose specifically from cases where wives reported their husbands, whom they wanted to get rid of. One such wife told the Nazi authorities that her husband was unlawfully criticising the Nazi regime. He was subsequently sent to the Russian Front, which almost invariably was a death sentence. However, the husband survived. After the war, when the Nazi law had been repealed, the husband brought legal action against his wife for unlawful deprivation of his liberty under the German Criminal Code of 1871. Given that legislation at the time was validly enacted, could the law be described as so morally reprehensible that it was not law? Did Nazi law absolve the woman? Or was it so immoral that it could not be regarded as law, and that the woman could thus be convicted under the Criminal Code?

---

31 For a complete account of the 'Grudge Informer' debate, see Andrew Altman, *Arguing About Law: An Introduction to Legal Philosophy*, Wadsworth Publishing Co, Belmont, CA (1996), on the Nuremburg Trials.

Lon Fuller (1902–78) sought to demonstrate that the Nazi German legal system was not a legal system because it failed to meet basic rules.[32] These rules are morally internal to the legal system and based on *natural law*. Fuller does not embrace natural law in the religious sense, but treats its morality as on a par with international law. Therefore, any enforcement of Nazi laws was a breach of natural law and could lead to prosecutions and convictions. The reasoning of Fuller was that strong moral reasons to disobey the law can outweigh the morality of fidelity. Where law is immoral it loses its legitimacy and provides strong reasons for not enforcing it.

Fuller's notion of morality is linked to the technical law-making process. For laws to be legitimate, they must be made in accordance with 'natural law' principles such as being expressed in generality (not directed to individuals), being transparent and consistent, and operating prospectively. Nazi laws did not conform to these principles. As such, Fuller suggests that the laws under which grudge informers were operating are likely not to have been valid law in this moral sense. Therefore, it was not a system of law, but rather a system of terror.[33]

By contrast, HLA Hart preferred to look to what existed in the legal system at the time. Whether the rules were unjust or irrational did not affect their legal status. Hart argued from a positivist position that moral issues should not be considered within a legal system. A law should not be invalidated on the basis of a moral judgement. However, Hart believed certain principles should underpin laws, including clearly recognisable rules with recognisable consequences and discernable mechanisms for changing rules. Hart observed that the Nazi law was legitimately enacted and enforced. Therefore, the wife could not be punished for following the law.

In the end, both Hart and Fuller endorsed retrospective legislation that allowed trials against grudge informers to proceed as an offence against the German Criminal Code of 1871. For Hart the retrospective legislation was enforced validly. For Fuller, the retrospective legislation merely gave effect to the illegitimacy of the Nazi laws.

TIP

Some students think natural law is only about a moral system of law. However, Fuller's principles of law-making are really more about procedure than moral values. See how far natural law has come since Sophocles' notion of natural law and virtue (as embodied in Antigone).

Reflection

Do you agree that the Grudge Informer trials in the aftermath of Nazi Germany were necessary? Why? Are war crimes trials necessary today?

---

32 Lon Fuller, *The Morality of Law*, Yale University Press, New Haven, CT, revised edn (1964).

33 Lon Fuller, cited in Andrew Altman, *Arguing About Law: An Introduction to Legal Philosophy*, Wadsworth Publishing Co, Belmont, CA (1996), 40.

Context: Outlawing pornography – critical feminists and liberal feminists

We have discussed the various strands of feminism. However, the complexities are even more profound when they are applied to legal issues. This section broadly considers the debate between critical feminists (such as Catherine MacKinnon, Andrea Dworkin, and Gloria Steinem) and liberal feminists (such as Ellen Willis and Carole Vance) over the illegalisation of pornography.

The feminist pornography debate was prompted by campaigning by Catharine MacKinnon and Andrea Dworkin against pornography in the 1970s. They were involved in drafting USA legislation that outlawed pornography, including the *Pornography Victims Compensation Act*. While the anti-pornography laws were held to be unconstitutional because they violated 'freedom of speech' protections, their efforts had an impact on USA 'state' laws and internationally. MacKinnon disputed that pornography should be understood in terms of 'speech'. Rather, it is an act of violence and rape,[34] which involves 'eroticizing the putatively prohibited'.[35]

The opposition to pornography was premised on a view that pornography was a form of sex discrimination or an act of sexual violence. It oppresses women and often harms them. Gloria Steinem asserted that pornography 'is violence, dominance, and conquest. It is sex being used to reinforce some inequality, or to create one, or to tell us that pain and humiliation (ours or someone else's) are really the same as pleasure'.[36] MacKinnon wrote in 1985:

> Pornography sexualizes rape, battery, sexual harassment, prostitution, and child sexual abuse; it thereby celebrates, promotes, authorizes, and legitimizes them. More generally, it eroticizes the dominance and submission that is the dynamic common to them all. It makes hierarchy sexy.[37]

MacKinnon and Dworkin claimed there could be no real 'choice' in the pornography industry as women are invariably subordinate in the process.[38] For critical feminists, the industry objectifies, exploits and commodifies women and thus any 'choice' is within boundaries of oppression. At the same time it makes an enormous profit of over $8 billion every year.

---

34 Catharine A. MacKinnon, *Only Words*, Harvard University Press, Cambridge, Mass. (1993), 15.

35 Catharine A. MacKinnon, 'Feminism, Marxism, Method, and the State: Toward Feminist Jurisprudence' (1983) 8(4) *Signs* 635, 644.

36 Gloria Steinem, 'Erotica and Pornography: a clear and present difference' in L Lederer (ed), *Take Back the Night: Women on Pornography*, William Morrow & Co., New York (1980), 37.

37 Catharine A. MacKinnon, 'Pornography, Civil Rights, and Speech', (1985) 20 *Harvard Civil Rights-Civil Liberties Law Review* 1, 17.

38 Catharine A. MacKinnon, *Only Words*, above, n 34; Andrea Dworkin, *Pornography: Men Possessing Women*, The Women's Press, New York (1981), 199–202.

In response, liberal feminists refuted the claim that pornography harms women. They claimed that there should be minimal state control over pornography. Indeed, the state should not be involved in personal morality *per se*. It is based on the premise of 'a woman's body, a woman's right'. Therefore, women have the right to be involved in the production of pornography if they choose.

A more extreme position is put by Wendy McElroy. Her pro-pornography stance is illustrated in her claim, 'Pornography benefits women, both personally and politically'.[39] Women are enriched by and gain pleasure from participating in and consuming pornography. It also breaks political stereotypes that women are sexually passive or otherwise promiscuous. For McElroy, pornography provides women with sexual freedom and 'is free speech applied to the sexual realm'. She underpins her argument by claiming that 'law should protect choice' rather than 'protect virtue', saying that 'The issue at stake in the pornography debate is nothing less than the age-old conflict between individual freedom and social control'.

On the one hand, liberal feminists uphold notions of individual freedom and autonomy and claim that censuring pornography denied women their sexual rights and freedoms. On the other hand, critical feminists claim that pornography upholds patriarchal assumptions about the role and status of women. It shows that we cannot create broad schools of jurisprudential thought (such as 'feminism') without recognising that the views of schools within those schools may be diametrically opposed.

In depth: Applying jurisprudence to real cases

Although cannibalism is often associated with tribal societies, it features in modern criminal cases of necessity – where someone will die unless they eat another! Below are a number of real cases of cannibalism. As you read these cases consider the relevant legal, moral and ethical issues, and how other theorists may resolve these issues. Finally, there is a hypothetical case at the end, the Speluncean Explorers, made up by famous jurist Lon Fuller. Think about the different judgments that Fuller presents. What issues do they raise and how may they be applied to (or distinguished from) the real-life cases?

---

39 Wendy McElroy, *A Woman's Right to Pornography*, St. Martin's Press, New York (1995).

The Queen v Dudley and Stephens

[1884] 14 QBD 273

Facts

The case of *Dudley and Stephens* involved the prosecution of Thomas Dudley and Edward Stephens for the murder of Richard Parker. These three, along with a fourth crew member (Edwin Stephens) were on board the *Mignonette*, which was set to travel from Tollesbury, Essex (UK) to Sydney, Australia. On 5 July 1884 the boat was hit by a massive wave and sank. The four crew members survived for a while on two tins of turnips and a small turtle. Besides this they had nothing to eat or drink besides a small amount of rainwater they were able to catch in their oilskin capes.

On the 25th day, with no signs of rescue in sight, Dudley killed Parker, who was the youngest and the weakest of the four. The remaining three then ate Parker's body and drank his blood. Four days after this act, the remaining three were rescued but 'in the lowest state of prostration' (at 274). It was accepted by the court that if the men had not fed upon the body of the boy they probably would have died of starvation and that Parker probably would have died before the rescue (at 275).

Legal issue

The issue for the court (The Queen's Bench Division) was whether Dudley and Stephens were guilty of murder in these circumstances. Lord Coleridge CJ (who delivered the judgment on behalf of the court) found Dudley and Stephens guilty of murder and they both received death sentences. Interestingly, there was such a strong public outcry against this decision that the Crown later reduced the sentence to six months' imprisonment.

Legal reasoning

The Chief Justice's reasoning was that where one person kills another person, the only justified defence is that of self-defence. He held that self-defence did not apply in this case and was reluctant to find a defence on the basis of 'necessity', stating that the crew members should have sacrificed their own lives, rather than the life of the youngest. The Chief Justice stated that it was no more 'necessary' to kill Parker than any of the others on board. He pointed to the ethical problem of saving one life compared with another. In other words, Coleridge CJ observed at 277:

> Who is to be the judge of this sort of necessity? By what measure is the comparative value of lives to be measured? Is it to be strength, or intellect, or what?

Lord Coleridge CJ also accepted (at 287):

> Though law and morality are not the same, and many things may be immoral which are not necessarily illegal, yet the absolute divorce of law from morality would be of fatal consequence … To preserve one's life is generally speaking a duty, but it may be the plainest and highest duty to sacrifice it.

Lord Coleridge CJ made the following concluding comment (at 288):

> We are often compelled to set up standards we cannot reach ourselves, and to lay down rules which we could not ourselves satisfy. But a man has no right to declare temptation to be an excuse, though he might himself have yielded to it, nor allow compassion for the criminal to change or weaken in any manner the legal definition of the crime. It is therefore our duty to declare that the prisoners' act in this case was wilful murder.

Meiwes' case

Facts

Armin Meiwes put an advertisement on an internet website for 'young, well-built men aged 18 to 30 to slaughter'. Bernd-Jürgen Brandes responded to the advertisement and agreed to meet Meiwes at his house in Rotenburg, Germany. A significant amount of drugs and alcohol were consumed. Brandes agreed to let Meiwes cut his penis off which they later cooked and ate together. Meiwes later stabbed Brandes and froze parts of his body. The encounter was recorded on video and this was presented to the court as evidence.

Findings

In 2004 Meiwes was found guilty of manslaughter and was sentenced to eight and a half years imprisonment. The prosecutors then appealed the decision. In 2006 Meiwes was convicted of murder and sentenced to life imprisonment. A number of issues were raised on the retrial. These issues included the issue of consent. In particular, had Brandes consented to being killed or eaten? Was Brandes capable of consenting to his killing at that moment, given the amount of drugs he had consumed? Nonetheless, the appeal court focused on the lack of deterrence that the lesser sentence provided, as Meiwes had ongoing fantasies about committing the same crime again.

Lon Fuller's make-believe case of the Speluncean Explorers

Lon Fuller's hypothetical case study was based, in part, on the real-life case of *The Queen v Dudley and Stephens* [1884] 14 QBD 273 ('*Dudley and Stephens*'). He raises some of these issues in a famous article on this hypothetical case study – 'The Case of the Speluncean Explorers' (1949) 62 *Harvard Law Review* 616. Each judgment that Fuller raises represents a different form of legal reasoning. Read Fuller's hypothetical judgments and then address the questions below.

Facts

Four defendants, members of the 'Speluncean Society', are trapped in a cave after a major landslide. The trapped explorers are forced to choose who will live and who will die. Unlike *Dudley and Stephens*, the case does not involve selection of a weaker, younger, non-consenting victim by 'stronger' persons. Instead, all remaining survivors consent to a process of selecting the person to be sacrificed (involving the throwing of dice). One of the members is sacrificed for everyone else to survive. The remaining four members are eventually rescued. The rescue operation is extremely risky and, tragically, in a second landslide, ten members of the rescue team are killed in the process.

Issue

Should the four survivors be convicted of the crime of murder?

Various legal responses

The five judgments provided by Fuller demonstrate the spectrum of approaches to these legal and moral issues. Fuller gives five judicial opinions on the appeal of the convicted defendants: each judge gives his reasons for applying the positive law as written, or recognising a higher law, and so forth.

Truepenny CJ's approach to whether the act was murder can be characterised as formal and legalistic. He states the law, 'Whoever shall wilfully take the life of another shall be punished by death'. He then proceeds to apply the law rigidly to the circumstances of the case at hand. Truepenny CJ highlights that the statute provides no exceptions, and as such, finds the four defendants guilty of murder. For the Chief Justice, upholding the letter of law is of greater importance than making allowance 'for the tragic situation in which these men found themselves' (at 619).

Foster J finds two grounds on which the defendants are not guilty. First, he finds that the positive (enacted) law of the jurisdiction is inapplicable to the case. His reasoning is that 'positive law is predicated on the possibility of men's [sic] coexistence in society' (at 620). As this is a peculiar situation in which the coexistence of the explorers is impossible, the precondition for the operation of the law is not present and so the law is inapplicable. In other words, the defendants at the time of committing the act were not 'in a state of civil society' but in a 'state of nature' (at 621). For Foster J, the extraordinary circumstances in which the defendants found themselves called for the drawing up of new rules by which they were to be governed (for example, the initial agreement to role the die). Foster J criticises the notion of there being an 'absolute' value of a human life, pointing out that there is a risk of loss of human lives in many aspects of modern day society – in rescues, in the construction of bridges, tunnels, etc.

Second, Foster J criticises Truepenny CJ's literal interpretation of the law and instead prefers to adopt a more purposive reading of the enacted legislation. As such, he argues that legislation must be interpreted reasonably, taking into account the exceptional circumstances of this case. Accordingly, he characterises the case as an example of self-defence and argues that to do so is entirely consistent with the purpose of the criminal legislation (which is to deter others from crime).

Keen J, like Truepenny CJ, adopts a positivist approach to the case at hand. He emphasises the distinction between 'morality' on the one hand, and 'law' on the other. He emphasises that the decision for the judges is whether the actions of the defendants was *legally* justifiable, as opposed to *morally* justifiable. He states that judges, as members of the judiciary, have an obligation 'to enforce faithfully the written law, and to interpret that law in accordance with its plain meaning without reference to our personal desires or our individual conceptions of justice' (at 633). Needless to say, he is very critical of the approach of Foster J. In particular, he criticises Foster J's purposive approach, pointing out that legislation inevitably has *multiple* purposes and never has any one purpose. Instead, Keen J prefers to consider the intention of those who originally drafted the legislation. Following this reasoning, Keen J finds the defendants guilty.

Handy J asserts that the Court should take into account the value of public opinion and common sense. He quotes a newspaper poll in which 90% of the public believed the defendants should be let off with a token punishment. Handy J outlines some of the problems inherent in such an approach – for instance that public opinion may be based on inaccurate information and half-truths – but concludes nonetheless that such an approach is necessary in this instance. Accordingly, he finds the defendants not guilty. His approach is pragmatic and combines elements of realism and utilitarianism.

Tatting J's position represents the most indecisive of the five. He outlines some of the shortcomings and uncertainties in Foster J's judgment. In particular, he interrogates why it is that the defendants went from being in a 'state of civil society' to a 'state of nature'. Was it because, for example, the defendants were physically underground, or because they were on the brink of starvation, or simply because they had agreed upon their own rules of government? And if it could be accepted that the law no longer applied, at what point in time did this occur? Further, Tatting J asks, if it is true that the enacted law no longer applies in this circumstance, how can the courts have the authority to decide what should happen in a 'state of nature' when they are not themselves part of such society? Yet by the same token, Tatting J is unable to uphold the sentence, noting 'the absurdity of directing that these men be put to death when their lives have been saved at the cost of ten heroic workmen' (at 631).

This final, tie-breaking vote is a metaphor for the entire project: the survivors' choice between murder and death is a decision that only God can understand, and the judge finds himself unable to be the *deus ex machina*, refusing to vote – and thus affirming the lower court judgment, and condemning the prisoners to death by his inaction. He chooses their deaths, and the death of positive jurisprudence under the weight of worldly uncertainty, reversing the murder in the cave despite the murderers' efforts to go forth into the light.

Exercise: Applying jurisprudence

1. Which of the judges' positions in the Speluncean case do you most agree with?
2. What would each of the judges of the Speluncean case have said about *Dudley and Stephens* and the German case of *Meiwes*?
3. It has been hypothesised that Fuller's actual opinion aligns most closely with that of Foster J.[40] What do you think Foster J would have thought about Lord Coleridge CJ's decision in *Dudley and Stephens*?
4. How would other jurisprudential theorists resolve these issues? For example, how would utilitarian theorists view the decision of *Dudley and Stephens*? How would JS Mill's harm theory in *On Liberty* explain the Meiwes case?
5. Would the situation be different where there were conjoined twins and one needed to be killed in order for the other to survive? This is what happened in England in *Re A (Children)* (Unreported, 2000, Supreme Court of Judicature, Court of Appeal, Civil Division, UK), in which conjoined twins, each with their own brain, heart, lungs and vital organs and arms and legs but joined at the lower abdomen, faced an operation that would kill the weaker twin. Without the operation, the stronger twin's heart would eventually fail.

DISCUSSION QUESTIONS

1. What do Greek philosophical debates and contemporary jurisprudence debates have in common?
2. How do the various theorists explain the relationship between law and justice?
3. What theory of justice do you support? Why?
4. Explain the postmodernist response to modernism.
5. What are some differences and similarities between Marxism and critical legal studies?

WEBLINKS AND FURTHER READING

Altman, Andrew, *Arguing About Law: An Introduction To Legal Philosophy*, Wadsworth Publishing Co, Belmont, CA (1996).

Aquinas, Thomas, *On Law, Morality and Politics*, Hackett Publishing Co, Indianapolis, IN (1988).

Austin, John, *Lectures On Jurisprudence and the Philosophy of Positive Law*, Scholarly Press, St. Clair Shores, MI (1977).

Barrett, Michèle, 'Words and Things: Materialism and Method in Contemporary Feminist analysis', in J Farganis (ed), *Readings In Social theory: The Classical Tradition To Post-Modernism,* McGraw Hill, New York (2004), 381–93.

---

40 Raymond Wacks, *Understanding Jurisprudence*, Oxford University Press, New York (2005).

Bell, Daniel, *The Cultural Contradictions Of Capitalism*, Heinemann, London (1976).
Bell, Daniel, *The End of Ideology: On the Exhaustion of Political Ideas In the Fifties*, Free Press, Glencoe, IL (1960).
Bentham, Jeremy, *Of Laws In General*, Athlone Press, London (1970).
Bix, Brian, *Jurisprudence: Theory and Context*, Sweet & Maxwell, London, 4th edn (2006).
Chinhengo, Austin M, *Essential Jurisprudence*, Cavendish Publishing, London (1995).
Coleman, Jules L, 'On the Relationship Between Law and Morality', (1989) 2 *Ratio Juris* 1, 66–78.
Cornell University Law School, 'Jurisprudence', available at http://topics.law.cornell.edu/wex/jurisprudence.
Crenshaw, Kimberlé, 'Race, Reform, and Retrenchment: Transformation and Legitimization in Antidiscrimination Law', (1988) 101 *Harvard Law Review* 331.
Dworkin, Andrea, *Pornography: Men Possessing Women*, Women's Press, New York (1981).
Dworkin, Ronald M, *Taking Rights Seriously*, Harvard University Press, Cambridge (1977).
Finnis, John, *Natural Law and Natural Rights*, Clarendon Press, Oxford (1980).
Fuller, Lon L, 'Positivism and Fidelity to Law: A Reply to Professor Hart', (1958) 71 *Harvard Law Review* 630.
Fuller, Lon L, *The Morality of Law*, Yale University Press, New Haven, CT, revised edn (1964).
Hart, HLA, 'Positivism and the Separation of Law and Morals', (1958) 71 *Harvard Law Review* 593.
Hart, HLA, *The Concept of Law*, Clarendon Press, Oxford, 2nd edn (1994).
Internet Encyclopedia of Philosophy, 'Philosophy of Law', at www.iep.utm.edu/l/law-phil.htm.
James, Paul, *Nation Formation: Towards a Theory of Abstract Community*, Sage Publications, London (1996).
MacKinnon, Catharine A, *Only Words*, Harvard University Press, Cambridge, Mass. (1993).
McElroy, Wendy, 'A Feminist Defense of Pornography', (2004) 17 *Free Inquiry Magazine* 4, at www.secularhumanism.org/library/fi/mcelroy_17_4.html.
Nozick, Robert, *Anarchy, State, and Utopia*, Basic Books, New York (1974).
Pashukanis, Evgeny, 'The General Theory of Law and Marxism', at www.marxists.org/archive/pashukanis/1924/law/edintro.htm.
Rawls, John, *A Theory of Justice*, Oxford University Press, Oxford (1999).

ONLINE RESOURCES FOR THIS CHAPTER

The following resources are available online at www.oup.com.au/orc/cwl2e
- Flashcard glossary
- Multiple choice questions

8

History: How Did Australian Law Develop?

WHAT WE WILL COVER IN THIS CHAPTER:

- The nature of Indigenous customary law
- Colonial rationale in court decisions for non-recognition of Indigenous customary law
- International law relied on to justify the reception of English law
- The implementation of English law into Australia
- Parliaments and the Westminster model

Recommended approach to learning this topic

- As you read this chapter, think about the myths that emerge in Australia's legal history, and why they arise. Who do these myths serve and to what extent do they exist today, including in the media? Consider whether some of the legal theories discussed in Chapter 7 on jurisprudence can help us understand these myths.
- Have you heard politicians talk about customary law – do they view it as a positive or negative aspect of Australian society? What do you think Indigenous people would say about the function of customary law and traditional punishment?
- Finally, have a look at the following court judgments on Australian history. What view do the judges take on the Anglo-Australian legal system's relationship with Indigenous Australians? What biases do they bring?
    - *R v Murrell, Sydney Gazette*, 6 February 1836 (available at www.law.mq.edu.au/scnsw/cases1835-36/html/1836.htm)
    - *R v Bonjon, Port Phillip Patriot*, 16 September 1841 (available at www.law.mq.edu.au/scnsw/cases1840-41/cases1841)
    - *Walker v New South Wales* (1994) 182 CLR 45 (available at www.austlii.edu.au/au/cases/cth/HCA/1994/64.html)
    - *Mabo v Queensland (No. 2)* (1992) 175 CLR 1 (available at www.austlii.edu.au/au/cases/cth/HCA/1992/23.html)
    - *The Wik Peoples v The State of Queensland* (1996) 187 CLR 1 (available at www.austlii.edu.au/au/cases/cth/HCA/1996/40.html)

KEY TERMS

Aboriginal or Torres Strait Islander person = generally defined according to objective ('genetic') and subjective (community acceptance and self-identity) criteria.[1] This three-part test was set out by Deane J in *Tasmania v Commonwealth* (1984) 158 CLR 1, 273-274.[2] However, Indigenous people have criticised traditional definitions for limiting the self-identity or self-recognition aspect. It should

---

1 Marcia Langton, 'Aboriginality', in *The Encyclopaedia of Aboriginal Australia*, Volume 1, A–L, David Horton (ed), Canberra, Aboriginal Studies Press (1994), 3–4.

2 It has been applied in *Shaw & Anor v Wolf & Ors* (1999) 163 ALR 205, *Queensland v Wyvill* (1989) 90 ALR 611, *Gibbs v Capewell* (1995) 128 ALR 577 and *Re The Aboriginal Lands Act 1995 and Re Marianne Watson (No 2)* [2001] TASSC 105.

be noted that many Aboriginal people have expressed their *general* satisfaction with the current legal definition. However there are some outstanding concerns:

1 The current definition was not devised by or in consultation with Aboriginal people, but by white judges in the above cases. Aboriginal people have long expressed their discontent with non-Aboriginal people trying to define 'Aboriginality'.[3] For example, Mick Dodson has criticised this practice as forming part of a 'colonial fascination'.[4]

2 Blood testing and human rights: Some commentators have argued that blood testing is contrary to international conventions to which Australia is signatory.[5]

Cession = land transferred to a colonial nation through voluntary surrendering of rights by the Indigenous people. This process usually involves a treaty between the coloniser and Indigenous people. This does not change the pre-existing legal system, although it could be changed by executive or legislative action after cession.

Colonisation = occupation of nation states by military rule and acquisition of sovereignty. There are three forms of colonisation, see: conquest, cession or occupation.

Common law = a body of judge-made law based on interpreting statutes.

Conquest = colonisation by military force, where the former political power is ousted. This does not change the pre-existing legal system, although it could be changed by executive or legislative action after conquest.

Customary laws = generally used to describe Indigenous laws that regulate relationships within Indigenous communities. Customary laws vary across Indigenous societies and change with time (similar to the incremental developments in the common law).

Feudalism = a system of social organisation and land holding based on a chain of tenure, in which the monarch was the ultimate owner of all land and granted possession in return for payments of taxes and provision of services.

Imperialism = post-twentieth century control of another nation by economic means.

Indigenous person = (in Australia) Aboriginal or Torres Strait Islander person (see above).

Occupation = a process of colonisation involving settlement of vacant land. This allows for the automatic implementation of the colonising nation's laws.

Privy Council = an advisory body to the British Monarch and court of final appeal in the United Kingdom.

---

3 Mick Dodson, Wentworth Lecture, 'The End in the Beginning: Re-defining Aboriginality', *Australian Aboriginal Studies* 1 (1994), 2–13; Marcia Langton, 'Well I Heard it on the Radio and I Saw it on the Television …', North Sydney, Australian Film Commission (1993), 33; Darlene Oxenham, *A Dialogue on Indigenous Identity*, 'Warts n All', Bentley, WA, Curtin University (1999) xiv.

4 Mick Dodson, Ibid.

5 Mick Dodson, Ibid.; Loretta De Plevitz and Larry Croft, 'Aboriginality under the Microscope: The Biological Descent Test in Australian Law' (2003) *Queensland University of Technology Law Journal* 7.

Reception = the implementation of the colonial nation's laws after occupation.

Terra nullius = land with no one.

Treaty = an agreement between a colonising nation and Indigenous people. It allows for the voluntary transfer of land, generally with limitations attached to the extent of land transferred and the jurisdiction of the coloniser's laws.

Westminster system = comprises three arms of government: the courts (judicature), parliament (legislature) and executive.

> Too often, in the past, our Universities have concentrated almost wholly upon English legal history without showing the relevance of this history to the past and present operation of the law in this country [of Australia].[6]

Aspects of English legal history that have informed Australian law are explained in this chapter, but our primary focus is on the law applicable to the Australian domestic law, both now and in the past.

1: Legal systems of Indigenous societies and their early exclusion from the common law

For between 40 000 and 60 000 years Indigenous people of Aboriginal and Torres Strait Islander descent (see definition in the Key terms list above) lived in what we now call Australia. They had their own laws and legal systems. It was a *customary law* system, with law passed down through the generations by oral tradition. Some laws were only known by women, or by men, or by the elders in the community. The customary laws governed all aspects of Indigenous peoples' lives and were an integral part of Indigenous society, culture and spirituality. The laws provided for the maintenance of relationships not only among people, but also between people and spirits, the land and the sea. For example the laws included:

> how or who a person may speak to, or be in the same place as; laws that dictate who a person may marry; laws that define where a person may travel within his or her homelands; and laws that delimit the amount and type of cultural knowledge that a person may possess.[7]

Indigenous systems of justice were and are far from universal. Each Indigenous community, or 'nation', has its own customary laws and system of justice. In 1788 there were more than 500 Indigenous nations with up to one million Aboriginal or Torres Strait Islander members. There was, and remains, significant diversity among the hundreds of Indigenous communities in Australia.

---

6   A C Castles *An Introduction to Australian Legal History*, Law Book Co., Sydney (1971), v.

7   Law Reform Commission of Western Australia, *Report on Aboriginal Customary Laws* (2006) Project No. 94, 64.

> **Reflection**
>
> Compare Indigenous customary laws with the Western jurisprudence schools discussed in Chapter 7. Does customary law align with any major school? Specifically consider the Theban play *Antigone*, and natural law.

The English colonisation of Australia in 1788 led to the application of English law in Australia. There was a perception that Indigenous societies were devoid of systemic and systematic laws and customs. The issue soon arose as to whether English law should be applied to the Indigenous inhabitants. This was the issue before the Supreme Court of New South Wales in the case of *R v Murrell*.[8]

The trial of Jack Congo Murrell

On 5 February 1836 Murrell, an Aboriginal man, was tried in the Supreme Court of New South Wales for the wilful murder of Jabbingee, another Aboriginal man. The murder apparently took place in response to injuries the deceased inflicted on him. It took place in the centre of white settlement at Windsor, where the Indigenous population was greater in number than the white population.

At trial Murrell protested that he was not guilty, but nevertheless, if he were to be tried the applicable law was his customary law. He claimed that New South Wales was occupied by his own people before it was occupied by the King of England. His people have continued to be regulated by customary law, rather than the laws of the statutes of Great Britain. Murrell said that he and his supposed victim are governed by the rules of their tribe.

Therefore, if he is found guilty by his people, Murrell should only be made to stand punishment (which would involve being speared), by the relatives of Jabbingee. This is now known as 'traditional punishment'. Murrell argued that the judgment of the Supreme Court over the alleged murder cannot be handed down, as it can only be handed down by Jabbingee's family.

The basis of this submission put by Murrell's advocate, Mr Stephen, was that New South Wales was neither conquered, ceded, nor a British settlement by occupation. Thus, the Aboriginal people were not bound by English criminal laws in New South Wales. Only the Britons were bound by these laws. The only exception was where laws 'protected' Aboriginal people – this was premised on a contract theory of government; that the right to govern and impose laws on the people was granted in return for their protection.

On 6 February 1836 Chief Justice Forbes opined that Murrell's plea was perfectly just. He said that any acts of violence committed by the natives against each other, even if they amounted to death, were subject to the custom of their own laws.

---

8 *Sydney Gazette*, 6 February 1836.

Nonetheless, the Chief Justice said that the proper process would be to allow the trial and for objection to be raised in that forum.

The case went to trial before a full court of the Supreme Court of New South Wales on 21 December 1836. Murrell's request for a Jury of 'Blackfellows' was refused, and instead he was given a civil jury (of whites). Mr Stephen was ill at this time, and the judge requested, at short notice, Mr Windeyer act as Murrell's Counsel.

After the prosecution submitted its evidence, Mr Windeyer said the defendant had nothing to say and no witnesses to call, as the only witnesses they could have called were 'Blacks' who could not be sworn in. The Court said that it had never mooted the point of 'Black' evidence and invited Mr Windeyer to call a witness. A 'native' named McGill was called to speak to the customs (including traditional punishment) of the Aboriginal people. The Court then said it would not admit evidence of customs as it had no bearing on the case. There were no further witnesses or evidence called.

After the trial, Justice Burton gave the leading judgment, with Chief Justice Forbes and Justice Dowling concurring. The judges cited advice given by the Attorney-General, that the jurisdiction of the Supreme Court of New South Wales included Indigenous people. This was because New South Wales was held by occupation (not conquest or treaty – see p. 234). Thus, the lands that the British had taken possession of, bound the King to protect all living parties living on it, or who came to visit it, and equally bound inhabitants to obey the King's law or otherwise suffer the consequences of a breach.

Murrell was therefore tried for the murder of Jabbingee. After the Court read the notes of evidence, the Jury retired for a few minutes, and returned a verdict of not guilty. Murrell was discharged.

Reflection

What was the rationale behind the *Murrell* decision? It was reasoned that:

- Before colonisation, Australian land was 'unappropriated by anyone' and thus was lawfully taken into 'actual possession by the King of England'. Therefore the King's laws applied to everyone in this appropriated domain.
- Aboriginal people had no recognisable laws, but only 'practices' that 'are consistent with a state of the grossest darkness and irrational superstition'. These 'are founded entirely upon principles … of vindication for personal wrongs' and 'the wildest most indiscriminatory notions of revenge'. Thus, Aboriginal people are not 'entitled to be recognised as … sovereign states governed by laws of their own'.

Both these reasons evidence a view of Indigenous people as having no laws and no recognisable system for possessing the land. Indigenous people have merely beliefs and 'superstitions' based on retribution. The Supreme Court described Indigenous peoples' irrational approach to retribution as contrasting with the rational sentencing process of a court adopting the English system.

Nonetheless, the Indigenous and Anglo-Australian systems have the same legal function: to regulate social relationships. Despite the differences among Indigenous communities and customary laws, they all regulate kinship relations, and this is comparable with Western law that manages social interactions. Both Western and customary laws project and reflect moral norms and protect social structures. Certainly the content of these norms and structures are different, but the role of the respective legal systems is essentially the same. As the Law Reform Commission of Western Australia observed in relation to Western Australian Indigenous communities: 'it is a defined system of rules for the regulation of human behaviour which has developed over many years from a foundation of moral norms and which attracts specific sanctions for noncompliance'.[9] This echoed the position of Justice Blackburn in 1971, who said in relation to the Yolŋu legal system in the Northern Territory: 'If ever a system could be called "a government of laws, and not of men", it is that shown in the evidence before me'.[10]

Therefore, we can see that there are Indigenous legal systems capable of recognition – despite the insinuations of 'irrational superstitions' in *R v Murrell*.

2: Displacement of Indigenous laws

The process of displacing Australian Indigenous legal systems, and replacing them with a British common law system, needed a legal justification. Eighteenth century international law required that states could acquire foreign land and sovereignty by three methods: conquest (by military force), cession (usually by treaty) or occupation (of vacant land). Australian courts opted for occupation because it allowed for the automatic *reception* of British laws, without the need to negotiate a *treaty* and accommodate its ensuing limitations on colonial jurisdiction. The logic behind occupation is that the colonised territory does not have a pre-existing legal system that the colonising nation has to adopt.

Occupation according to international law requires a finding of *terra nullius* – 'empty land' – whereby the land belonged to no one.[11] Clearly the Australian land was not empty. The impetus for the courts therefore was to find Indigenous peoples to be 'too primitive to be regarded as the actual owners and sovereigns' of the land.[12] It has been argued that the myth of *terra nullius* was also to render 'opaque' the 'genocidal dimension of settlement' in Australia alone.[13] This involved the destruction of three-

---

9   Law Reform Commission of Western Australia *Report on Aboriginal Customary Laws* (2006) Project No. 94, 64.

10 *Milirrpum v Nabalco Pty Ltd*. (1971) 17 FLR 141.

11 See: *Post Office v Estuary Radio Ltd*. (1968) 2 QB 740 (Diplock LJ): *New South Wales v The Commonwealth (The Seas and Submerged Lands Case)* (1975) 135 CLR 388 (Gibbs J).

12 Henry Reynolds, *Aboriginal Sovereignty: Reflections on Race, State and Nation*, Sydney, Allen & Unwin (1996), x.

13 Paul Havemann, 'Denial, Modernity and Exclusion: Indigenous Placelessness in Australia' (2005) 5 *Macquarie Law Journal* 57.

quarters of the Indigenous population in eastern Australia – from approximately 300 000 people prior to settlement, to 75 000 by the late nineteenth century.

To legitimise a finding of *terra nullius* the Australian courts drew on a body of jurisprudential and philosophical opinion that prior settlement required development of the land, specifically in the form of cultivation. Lawyers such as Emerich de Vattel and William Blackstone, who wrote during the eighteenth century high-tide of colonial endeavour, suggested that *terra nullius* encompassed territories inhabited by 'backward peoples'. That is, Indigenous people, by virtue of their hunting and gathering activities, were not fulfilling the requisite cultivation to claim land title. Vattel and Blackstone relied on the notion that land uncultivated could be claimed by occupation as it would lead to land 'improvement' by European civilisation.[14] Their position drew on the philosophical justification of private property rights advanced in the seventeenth century by John Locke: common lands brought into production would 'first begin a title of property'.[15]

Therefore, Australia was colonised in law through occupation and it was incumbent on Australian courts to uphold this fiction of *terra nullius*. Only then could the British Crown assume title over the land, and British laws be applied in Australia. The notion of *terra nullius* emerged as a principle applicable to Australia in the judgments of colonial courts, such as Justice Burton's reasons in *R v Murrell* discussed above, where the judge stated that colonial laws applied universally because at the time of occupation Australia was 'unappropriated by anyone'. The international law doctrine of *terra nullius* – a colony 'without settled inhabitants or settled law' – was confirmed in New South Wales in *Cooper v Stuart*:

> There is a great difference between the case of a colony acquired by conquest or cession, in which there is an established system of law, and that of a colony which consisted of a tract or territory practically unoccupied with settled inhabitants, or settled law, at the time when it was peacefully annexed to the British dominion. The colony of New South Wales belongs to the latter class.[16]

The landmark 1992 High Court decision of *Mabo v Queensland*[17] would eventually dispose of the fiction of *terra nullius* (see Chapter 9), but even before then, there were murmurings from colonial judges that Australia was not *terra nullius* at the time of settlement. The case of *R v Bonjon*[18] was a precursor to *Mabo* and its reasoning would be echoed by the High Court 151 years later.

---

14 William Blackstone, *Commentaries on the Laws of England*, Bk II, London, 1830, 106–8; Vattel, *The Law of Nations*, Bk I, London, (1797), 100–1. Their position was confirmed in *Re Southern Rhodesia* [1919] AC 211, 233–4 (Lord Sumner). This body of international law was affirmed later in Australian common law: *New South Wales v The Commonwealth (Seas and Submerged Lands Case)* (1975) 135 CLR, 388 (Gibbs J).

15 John Locke, *Two Treatises on Government*, Book II, London, Everyman's Library (1924), 141.

16 *Cooper v Stuart* (1889) 14 App Cas 286, 291 (Lord Watson).

17 *Mabo v Queensland (No. 2)* (hereafter *Mabo*) (1992) 175 CLR 1.

18 *R v Bonjon, Port Phillip Patriot*, 16 September 1841, Melbourne.

Bonjon's case

In 1841 the Supreme Court of New South Wales was presented with similar facts to that in *R v Murrell*. Bonjon, an Aboriginal man, was accused of murdering Yammowing, another Aboriginal man. Both were living in their own self-governing community with an identifiable justice system at the time. The defence submitted that New South Wales was occupied by the British, not conquered or ceded, and therefore the British had no jurisdiction over Aboriginal people – until a treaty or other form of consent was given by Aboriginal people. A single judgment of Justice Willis held that the English law of the colony applied, and accordingly Aborigines were British subjects and the parliaments and common law should regulate relations 'between Aborigines and colonists'.

However, Justice Willis went on to distinguish 'crimes committed by the aborigines against each other'. In these cases, the New South Wales court had no jurisdiction, and they should be dealt with by 'their own rude laws and customs'. Therefore, Justice Willis expressly denounced the decision of Justice Burton in *R v Murrell* and accepted the defence submission, which threw doubt on the notion of *terra nullius*. He stated that, given that New South Wales was 'not unoccupied', in the absence of any 'express enactment or treaty subjecting the Aborigines of this colony to the English colonial law … the Aborigines cannot be considered as Foreigners in a Kingdom which is their own'. Aborigines are 'neither a conquered people, nor have [they] tacitly acquiesced to the supremacy of the settlers'. The evidence Justice Willis provides for the lack of conquest was that:

> at the time it was taken possession of by the colonists … a body of the aborigines appeared on the shore, armed with spears, which they threw down as soon as they found the strangers had no *hostile intention*.

Therefore, limited forms of Indigenous jurisdictions could co-exist alongside the ordinary laws of the nation in this decision.

TIP

Often students think that all of Australian land was colonised in 1788. But it was a piecemeal process, beginning in New South Wales. The High Court in *Mabo* (1992) held that, while in 1788 the Crown acquired radical (absolute) title, it did not become the owner of all land. The Crown extinguished it parcel by parcel over time. This did not happen automatically and some land was not appropriated by the Crown.

The impact of *R v Bonjon* was limited because Justice Willis declined from making a final decision on the application of *terra nullius*. Consequently, the finding of Justice Willis, in relation to Indigenous people occupying Australia before colonisation, was not adopted until the decision of *Mabo*.

However, outside the courts, individual colonisers recognised that Indigenous inhabitants ought to have their rights to land recognised in a treaty. There were attempts by farmer John Batman in the Port Philip District of Victoria to rent land from the local Wurundjeri Elders through a treaty. Nonetheless, this was annulled by the Governor of New South Wales, Sir Richard Bourke, in 1835 on the basis that the land was *terra nullius* and had become Crown land. Governor Bourke issued a Proclamation that the British Crown was the owner of all Australian territory and solely capable of distributing the land, which the British Colonial Office affirmed on 10 October 1835. It overrode the legitimacy of the treaty by declaring that people in possession of Australian land (including Batman and the Wurundjeri people) without government authority would be trespassers.

3: Reception of British law

The *Australia Courts Act 1828* (UK) was the statutory instrument for the formal reception of English law. Section 24 provided that 'all laws and statutes' in force in England on 25 July 1828 should be applied in the administration of justice in the courts of New South Wales and Van Diemen's Land (Tasmania). The Act gave the Supreme Court of New South Wales the power to decide what was 'applicable' to the colonial conditions. However, Australian laws could not be made that were repugnant to British laws.

A retrospective approach was taken to British legal colonisation. Pursuant to the *Imperial Acts Application Act 1969*, English laws received in 1828 were found to be specifically applicable to the colony of New South Wales upon settlement, and therefore between 1788 and 1828.[19]

Among Australian legal scholars there has been a heated debate about whether Australian law was entirely English. Legal historian Alex Castles argues that judges expressed reluctance in receiving English law in the early colonial period.[20] This represented the beginnings of a unique Australian legal culture. However, when professional judges finally arrived from England in the early to mid-1800s they were inclined to enforce the British common law. These judges did not tend to take into account special local conditions in deciding whether British law should apply.

Nonetheless, the application of English law was uneven. It would be too simplistic to conceptualise the colonial legal system as directed top-down from London. Legal historian Bruce Kercher has identified the colonial courts' 'innovation and questioning' of English law.[21] For example the first Chief Justice of the Supreme Court of New South Wales, Francis Forbes, adjudicated disputes between British subjects in the colony in accordance with colonial practices and customs, rather than English laws. Therefore, Australian legal history was not simply a product of British statutes and precedent.

Nonetheless, the parochialism of colonial judges extended only so far as it did not threaten the Empire. Where the landed rights of the Crown were in question, the English law prevailed. This is evidenced in Chief Justice Forbes' strict application of English law where Crown land was threatened. We have also seen this in relation to the protection of Crown sovereignty vis-à-vis Indigenous people, as well as in relation to British subjects who disturbed the Crown ownership of land. Crown supremacy would reign. The deference to English principles increased in the mid-nineteenth century with the influx of British-trained judges. In some respects the British persuasion by the courts prompted the colonial parliaments to become more radical, but overall there was an acceptance of British legal values and Empire-building objectives.

---

19 Peter Butt, *Land Law*, Lawbook Co, Sydney, 4th edn (2001), 2–3. This was retrospective – see Chapter 11 for a critique of retrospective statutory interpretation.

20 AC Castles, *An Introduction to Australian Legal History*, Sydney, Lawbook Co (1971), v.

21 Bruce Kercher, 'Alex Castles on the Reception of English Law' (2003) 7 *Australian Journal of Legal History* 37, 38.

4: Military origins of the Australian legal system

The immediate needs of the colony were to establish a penal system to accommodate English convicts and lay the foundations for a viable economy. Despite the law's reliance on John Locke's notion of 'first title' through cultivation or farming to justify colonisation (see heading 2 above), the Australian economy was premised on pastoralism – grazing cattle and sheep – rather than farming. To support the colonial economy, convict labour was exploited across Australia. The exceptions were South Australia (which was a free settler colony) and the Northern Territory, where Indigenous labour was predominantly employed in the cattle industry. A hierarchical military system of government enforced this penal labour system. It also ensured that there was adherence to colonial decrees and orders.

In the early years of Australian colonisation, until English laws were formally received by enactment of the *Australia Courts Act 1828* (UK), the Australian legal system was governed by the autocratic rule of the Governor and his officers. There was no parliamentary system to place a check on the powers of colonial officers. Rather, the Governor exercised the powers of the parliament, the executive and the judiciary. These arms of government are now separated under the Federal Constitution – see Chapter 4. The Governor also had the power to declare martial law if necessary, which he did.

Criminal and civil courts were established in 1788 pursuant to the *New South Wales Courts Act 1787* (UK) and Letters Patent from the King dated 2 April 1787. They were staffed by military officers. It was not until 1810 that the first civilian judge, Ellis Bent, assumed judicial duties in the New South Wales colony. However, without a colonial parliament and legislation, the courts could not develop a *common law* system. This would have required statutes for judges to interpret. Therefore, until 1823, the law tended to be based on the inconsistent, and sometimes irrational, whims of generals. This was more closely aligned with feudal powers, rather than the modern common law system.

> **TIP**
> Every Aboriginal person born in Australia after 1829 would become a British subject – although not by their own choosing, or necessarily to their benefit.

The early penal colonies were characterised by a military system of governance. There was a loose application of English law in legal relations among immigrants. However, the rawest expression of military governance was on the frontier against Indigenous people. Until the 1830s, Indigenous people were not regarded as British subjects (and therefore were not accommodated by the British law), nor were they regarded as autonomous under their Indigenous laws (which were not recognised). Indigenous people were effectively in an Australian legal void.

5: Key concepts from English legal and constitutional history

> **GO ONLINE**
> Go online for a summary of the story of our English legal and constitutional history, from the fall of the Roman Empire to the rise of responsible government.

Notwithstanding the debate over whether the specific British legislation was received, Australia inherited a number of key legal concepts, principles and institutions from England.

A key moment in British legal history was the adoption of Magna Carta in 1215 – a royal charter whose name literally means 'The Great Charter'. In 1215 it was known as the Charter of Liberties. Although much celebrated, this document had a fraught history and represented a compromise between the barons and the king. It served the interests of the barons by limiting the unjust and arbitrary use of power by the king, and it served the king by averting a political crisis that the rebellious barons had threatened. The landless, unfree peasantry did not take part in the adoption of Magna Carta. The key legacy of Magna Carta is the principle that the king, like his people, was subject to the law. We now know this as the rule of law.

Magna Carta can still be viewed in the British Library in London (in the Magna Carta Room). The document is written in Medieval Latin, but alongside it are translations, summaries, a timeline across the wall of the room, interactive tools and a touch screen with the key figures and dates.

TIP

When the Charter of Liberties was confirmed in 1217, the clauses dealing with the law of the royal forest were taken out and put into a separate document known as 'The Charter of the Forest'. After that, people began to refer to the Charter as Magna Carta, to distinguish it from the shorter Charter of the Forest.

In depth: The history and significance of Magna Carta

There was mounting dissent against King John's reign in the lead-up to granting of the charter. The Church was in an ongoing power struggle with the King and the feudal barons were publicly rallying for the King to address their grievances. King John had been exploiting the barons by forcing payments from them so he could fight (unsuccessful) wars against France. By demanding these payments, King John was abusing feudal customary rights and using his power in a despotic manner.

When the barons captured London, the King was forced to negotiate. The barons presented King John with the Articles of the Barons, which sought to reinstate feudal customs and defend the barons against the despotism of the King. Fearing the loss of order and his authority, King John agreed to these articles, which became the Charter of Liberties on 15 June 1215. The barons consequently made peace with the King. Over a third of the 63 clauses in the charter defined and limited the extent of the King's despotic power, and the majority dealt with the regulation of feudal customs.

Only months after its adoption – on 25 August 1215 – the Pope annulled the Charter. However, it was reinstated in the following year when King John died and France invaded, attracting significant baronial support. The revised version was issued by William Marshal, Earl of Pembroke.

So why is Magna Carta one of the most celebrated documents in English history? After all, the majority of its clauses deal with feudal customs and not with fundamental legal principles. Indeed, all but three of Magna Carta's clauses have now become obsolete and been repealed. Those three clauses have been interpreted as fundamental to the maintenance of the Anglo-legal order.

Reflective of this legal order, the first of these clauses defends the freedom of the English church (which King John sought to encroach upon). The clause allows the Church to elect its own dignitaries without royal interference. The second enduring clause confirms the liberties and customs of London and other towns. The final one has the most significance for Australia's legal system. It states:

> No free man shall be seized or imprisoned, or stripped of his rights or possessions, or outlawed or exiled, or deprived of his standing in any other way, nor will we proceed with force against him, or send others to do so, except by the lawful judgment of his equals or by the law of the land.
>
> To no one will we sell, to no one deny or delay right or justice.
>
> This clause represented the first charter by an English king to limit royal authority, by ensuring that the king was subject to the law and not above it. In this respect, the Magna Carta laid down the principle of the 'rule of law' (see below at p. 241). Therefore, the law, rather than the king, is the ultimate authority and everyone was equally subject to the law. If the king went above the law, the people could seek redress.
>
> Internationally, the clause has been interpreted for specific purposes. For instance, in the fourteenth century, the British Parliament saw it as guaranteeing trial by jury. In more recent centuries, Magna Carta has been regarded as the foundation of modern bills of rights. In Australia, the Commonwealth Constitution has been interpreted as consistent with the rule of law.
>
> [This information has been adapted from the commentary in the Magna Carta Room in the British Library, London, November 2009. Also see: www.bl.uk/onlinegallery/hightours/magnacarta]

The principles that the Anglo-Australian legal system adopted from England can be summarised in 20 key concepts.

1. **Feudalism** – this was a system of social organisation and land holding that dated back to the Dark Ages. The ruler 'owned' all the land, and granted land to people in return for payment of taxes or provision of services. In the feudal hierarchy, everyone had rights and obligations. The ruler was responsible for protecting the people and maintaining peace. The legal obligations to the ruler were formalised with the Norman Conquest in 1066, when William, Duke of Normandy, was crowned King William I and assumed ultimate title to all land in England. This system developed in England and formed the basis of its land law, criminal legal system and taxation system. It also forms the basis of Australian law in these areas – the Crown ultimately owns all the land, our criminal system is based on an action by the state against the wrongdoer, and there is an entrenched power for the government to impose taxes.

2. **Law as an autonomous discipline** – the way law developed in England involved a separation of law from religion, which differed from the situation in other parts of the world in which the church could make law (canon law or papal law) or where the religious text formed the basis of the law (as in some Islamic countries). Instead, law was seen as an autonomous discipline – it might be influenced by morality, religion or politics, but it was analytically separate from them.

3. **Common law legal system** – England developed a common law legal system whilst the rest of the European continent developed a civil law legal system. The common law system is what we inherited, and it is an organic concept of law that can develop through a line of cases (establishing 'precedent'), and can grow and shift to take into account changes in society.

4. **Precedent** – this is a doctrine whereby courts follow similar previous decisions. It developed organically when royal judges travelled to rural areas in England to dispense justice, and over time chose to defer to each other's decisions in doing so.
5. **Equity** – equity, which softens the effect of the common law, is a creature of the common law legal system that developed at a time when the strict application of the law through a system of writs as causes of action created some harsh and unfair outcomes. It is a key feature of Australia's law and legal system today, and students complete an entire subject on it in law school.

In depth: The evolution of courts of equity and common law courts

The *Judicature Acts* – a relatively recently product of the British legal system from the 1870s – were significant for shaping the equity jurisdiction in Australia. These Acts consolidated the various common law courts (which required the filing of writs based on standard forms, which were rigid and would give rise to injustice where parties could not comply) and equity courts (which had more flexibility and usually fairness in their procedure).

The courts came together to form the Supreme Court of Judicature (with different divisions) to create a uniformity in pleading and procedure. The court was governed by the same rules that formed a midway point between the traditional common law courts and equity courts – which involved the abolition of standard forms and the rise of causes of action (which were decided on facts rather than second guessing the appropriate form). Today, throughout Australia, there is one Supreme Court with a common law and equity division. There remains some flexibility in the cause of action. For more information on the principle of equity, see Chapter 5 (pp. 126–7) on equity.

6. **Due process** – the notion that an individual should be considered innocent until proven guilty, and guilt should be proved using proper legal procedures, not some arbitrary process.
7. **Juries** – juries initially developed in England as local people who were responsible for bringing suspected wrongdoers to court, who could inform the royal courts on the facts of the case and local customs on point. Australia inherited the jury system and it continues to play a major role in our criminal justice system. There is also a commonwealth constitutional right to a jury for serious federal offences (s 80).
8. **Rule of law** – government should rule through law, and not through the exercise of arbitrary power by individuals. The laws should be applied equally to all people, including the government.
9. **Importance of procedural law** – law should be applied following established procedures for the instigation and process of a legal matter. This makes for a fair fight. Procedural law is as important as the substantive law itself, and someone with an otherwise good claim may fail if they do not follow the correct legal procedures. (See Chapter 5 on the difference between procedural and substantive law.)

10 **Parliament** – developed in England as a law-making and power-sharing body with the monarch, comprised of elected representatives.
11 **Separation of powers** – power should be distributed between independent arms of government, so there is not one individual or arm that can make, interpret and enforce the law.
12 **Parliamentary sovereignty** – although power is separately allocated between the parliament, executive and judicature, the parliament is supreme over the executive and judicature except where it provides otherwise.
13 **Independent judiciary** – judges should be independent from the other arms of government so that their decisions are made freely according to law. This includes judges having security of tenure, so they cannot be removed from their position if their decisions are unpopular to the government of the day, and fixed salaries, so that the remuneration of judges is not affected by the government's views on the decisions they make.
14 **Process of legislation making** – draft laws are introduced into parliament and debated, passed and then assented to by the monarch or its representative.
15 **Rules of statutory interpretation** – the English courts developed guidelines for interpreting parliament's statutes, which were applied in Australia. See Chapter 10 for discussion of the traditional common law approaches.
16 **Political parties** – parliament comprises representatives of political parties, according to their relative power, based upon their success in free elections.
17 **Cabinet** – an informal creation in English history, of a body of ministers that advises the monarch. It developed into a self-sustaining key body of ministers who develop government policy and rely on the support of parliament.
18 **Prime Minister** – another informal creation in English history, where one member of cabinet arises as the leader, and is referred to as the 'prime' minister.
19 **Representative government** – the notion that the government should be representative of the people, through free and fair elections where people have the opportunity to elect their representatives.
20 **Responsible government** – the government is responsible to the people for its actions.

These are the key principles from English legal and constitutional history that have been applied in Australia. The following section describes how that took place.

6: How English legal and constitutional history applies in Australia

The Westminster system of government, which incorporates principles described above including representative government, responsible government, separation of powers, parliamentary sovereignty, rule of law and right to due process, was incorporated into the *Commonwealth Constitution* in 1901.

Prior to this, one of the first steps towards a Westminster system – and away from decentralised military rule – had been the establishment of a Legislative Council and Supreme Court in New South Wales and Van Diemen's Land (Tasmania). This did not happen in Australia autonomously, but rather by an Act of the British parliament: *New South Wales Act 1823* (UK). The Act provided that the King, on the advice of the British Secretary of State, could appoint between five to seven members to the Legislative Council.

The role of this Legislative Council was not to legislate in its own right, but to advise the Governor of New South Wales in the exercise of his legislative powers. The Council could also defeat a law proposed by the Governor, unless extenuating circumstances permitted the Governor's authority. However, the decisions of the Governor and Council remained subject to veto by the British government.

In 1825 an Executive Council was created to advise the Governor in the exercise of his executive duties. In practice, until 1856 in New South Wales, the Governor's appointments to the Executive Council were largely the same people appointed to the Legislative Council. This coincidence of membership laid the foundations for the emergence of Cabinet government.[22] The modern Cabinet comprises the senior ministers of the legislature, who advise the Prime Minister

The reception of English feudal land law

The acquisition of Australian land for the British Empire meant that all lands 'became in law the property of the King of England'.[23] It was not a system in which Australian settlers could own land outright. Rather, it was a system of feudal tenure. This meant all land holdings had to be traced to a Crown grant. By virtue of the reception laws, Australia inherited the requirement that all land possession must come from a past grant from the Crown.[24] In doing so, it overwrote recognition of Aboriginal rights to ownership. An English charter of King Henry VII in 1498 underlined the Crown's appropriation of land upon colonisation. In describing this position, Justice Brennan in *Mabo* commented:

> When the territory of a settled colony became part of the Crown's dominions, the law of England … became the law of the colony and, by that law, the Crown acquired the absolute beneficial ownership of all land in the territory so that the colony became the Crown's 'demesne'[25] and no right or interest in any land in the territory could thereafter be possessed by any other persons unless granted by the Crown.[26]

Crown sovereignty allowed the Imperial Government in 1787 to delegate authority to Governor Phillip to dispose of lands.[27] In some instances, the Crown's rule was implemented directly through its official representatives in New South

---

22 Jennifer Clarke, 'From Aboriginal Law to Australian Law' from www.ozpolitics.info/ [no longer available].

23 *Williams v Attorney-General for New South Wales* (1913) 16 CLR 404, 439 (Isaacs J).

24 Garth Nettheim, 'The *Wik* Summit Papers', in Karin Calley (ed), *The Wik Summit*, Cape York Land Council, Cairns (1997), 36.

25 Landed property under the rule of the monarchy. The land is offered to a feudal lord to keep for his own private use and possession but not ownership.

26 *Mabo* (1992) 175 CLR 1, 26 (Brennan J).

27 Shaunnagh Dorsett and Lee Godden, 'Tenure and Statute: re-conceiving the basis of land holding in Australia' (2000) 5(1) *Australian Journal of Legal History* 29, 33.

Wales. According to colonial commentator James Collier, who wrote extensively on Australian pastoral settlement, Governor Macquarie, permitted no one to depasture in 'new country' without special authority from himself.[28]

Common law precedent affirmed feudal tenure in *Attorney-General v Brown*.[29] This 1847 decision of the Supreme Court of New South Wales struck down a challenge to the Crown's sovereign title over tenures. The defendant argued that titles in the colony were without an overlord, but rather it would be 'allodial' land where the individual owns the land outright and does not have obligations to a superior lord. Chief Justice Stephen explicitly stated that since settlement the 'waste lands' of the colony were in the 'Sovereign's possession; and that, as his or her property, they have been and may now be effectually granted to subjects of the Crown'.

In *Attorney-General v Brown* Chief Justice Stephen pointed to the constitutional basis for Crown sovereignty and held that the feudal laws granted the Crown ownership of colonial land from the moment of settlement and for all time thereafter. This assertion of feudal land tenure in Australia was predicated on the Crown's denial of existing Aboriginal land arrangements. The Chief Justice maintained that, in accordance with the colonial 'reception' principles, because feudal tenure was 'universal in the law of England … we can see no reason why it shall be said not to be equally in operation here'.

Chief Justice Stephen referred to the British constitutional principle that the sovereign is the legal '*universal occupant*'.[30] He held, '[I]n a newly-discovered country … the occupancy of the Crown with respect to the waste lands of that country, is no fiction'.[31] In this challenge by a New South Wales 'settler' to Crown ownership of Crown land (the settler was claiming better title), the Supreme Court of New South Wales upheld the supremacy of the Crown. In 1913 Justice Isaacs held in the High Court's *Williams'* case, that Australian land ownership was a consequence of the feudal principle, so that all colonial land belonged 'to the Crown until the Crown chose to grant it'.[32] In the 1971 Northern Territory Supreme Court decision, *Milirrpum v Nabalco*, the only Australian case prior to *Mabo* to deal directly with an Aboriginal land claim, Justice Blackburn restated the position that 'all titles, rights and interests in land are the direct consequence of Crown grants'.[33]

In agreeing with Stephen CJ, the majority in *Mabo* held that feudal tenure has a persuasive role to play in Australian legal history. Their Honours stated, '[W]hatever the fact, it is the fiction of royal grants that underlies the English rule'. Indeed, the High Court, concerned not to erode the 'internal consistency' of Australian common law and leasehold, upheld the feudal origins of Australia's tenure. The Court affirmed that the Crown grants were an 'essential principle of our land law'.[34] The Bench

---

28 James Collier, *The Pastoral Age in Australasia*, London, Whitcombe & Tombs (1911), 65.
29 *Attorney-General v Brown* (1847) 1 Legge 312, 316.
30 Emphasis inclusive Ibid, 317–18.
31 Ibid.
32 *Williams v Attorney-General for New South Wales* (1913) 16 CLR 404, 439.
33 *Milirrpum v Nabalco Pty Ltd* (1971) 17 FLR 141, 247.
34 *Mabo* (1992) 175 CLR 1 at 29-30, 43, 47 (Brennan J).

referred to precedent in *Attorney-General v Brown*, in stating that although it may be fictive that all property was originally in the Crown, it is one 'adopted by the Constitution to answer the ends of government, for the good of the people'.[35]

7: Adoption of British common law – from the frontier to the Australia Acts

When English colonies were established, colonisers sought to enforce English legal values, including charters such as Magna Carta guaranteeing that they and their heirs would 'have and enjoy all liberties and immunities of free and natural subjects'. However, in Australia this was done with some modification.

Process of replacing Indigenous law with British law

Blackstone had, in the eighteenth century, asserted that English law is applicable to the colonies only in so far 'as is applicable to their own [colonial] situation'.[36] However, British colonists did not heed this caveat. Rather, in the late eighteenth and early nineteenth century, there was a wholesale reception of English laws under the *Australia Courts Act 1828* (UK).

The courts did make concessions in the interpretation of the British statutes, but the adoption of the British laws did little to reflect the uniqueness of the Australian people or landscape. For example the English laws were not modified to include or account for the Indigenous laws that comprised the 'colonial situation'.

It was clear from the outset that the Indigenous legal system would be colonised as much as the land system. The system of violent repression slowly became replaced by a system of rational rules. But these rules would be just as powerful in dispossessing Indigenous people. They would conceal the power relations by making the law appear like a technical application of justice. Michel Foucault has observed that

> The law always refers to the sword. But a power whose task is to take charge of life needs continuous regulatory and corrective mechanisms. It is no longer a matter of bringing death into play in the field of sovereignty, but of distributing the living domain of value and utility. Such a power has to qualify, measure, appraise, and hierarchize, rather than display itself in its murderous splendor; it does not have to draw the line that separates the enemies of the sovereign from his obedient subjects; it effects distributions around the norm.[37]

TIP
There were deliberate attempts to exclude Indigenous people from the Australian legal system and deprive them of legal rights. Special statutes applied only to Aboriginal people, which restricted their movement, family relationships and expenditure.

---

35   *Attorney-General v Brown* (1847) 1 Legge 312 at 317–18 (Stephen CJ), cited in *Mabo* (1992) 175 CLR 1, 26 (Brennan J).

36   Quoted and discussed in Henry Reynolds, *The Law of the Land*, Melbourne, Penguin (1987), 44; K. Roberts-Wray, *Commonwealth and Colonial Law*, London, Stephens & Co. (1966), 62.

37   Michel Foucault, *The Will to Knowledge: The History of Sexuality, vol 1*, Penguin, Harmondsworth (1978), 144.

The role of the law to 'hierarchize' power and assert sovereignty, as Foucault states, is a subtle process. It quells alternative calls for sovereignty and assumes the righteousness of the dominant legal system. Indeed, alternative positions appear irrational. This was the approach taken by Justice Burton in *R v Murrell*. He set up a juxtaposition of the fair and rational common law system that is guided by principles of equality and procedural fairness, against the customary law of Murrell's community, which is based on the 'wildest' notions of revenge and vindication.

Context: What really happened to Indigenous law and Indigenous people with the adoption of the common law?

The official view

In *R v Murrell*, Justice Burton proclaimed that Indigenous people, like all other Australians, were British subjects and formally equal before the law. Indigenous people would receive the protections and punishments afforded by the British rule of law.

In practice

Indigenous people were disproportionately targeted as criminals, and excluded from protective measures when they were victims of crime. Indigenous people were unable to give evidence in court (because they could not swear on the bible). Accordingly, prosecutions of Indigenous people were high and prosecutions of Europeans who committed crimes against Indigenous people were low.

Unofficial views

Most justice took place outside of the court system. Henry Reynolds in *Law of the Land* wrote that Indigenous people were decimated in the process of the British common law asserting its sovereignty.[38] Historian Eric Rolls in *A Million Wild Acres* noted that during the colonial period, 'so much of Australia's history took place outside the law [that] there was more attempt to hide it than to record it'.[39] Therefore, 'summary justice' was inflicted on Indigenous people in the early colonial period that involved the immediate dispensation of punishment by colonisers through physical force.

---

38 Henry Reynolds, *The Law of the Land*, Penguin, Ringwood (1987).

39 Eric Rolls, *A Million Wild Acres: 200 years of Man and an Australian Forest*, Penguin, Ringwood (1984), 77.

Statutory adoption of British law

The adoption of British laws was made possible by British legislation, the *Australian Courts Act 1828* (UK). It ensured that the then laws of England would be applied in the then two Australian colonies: New South Wales and Van Diemen's Land (now Tasmania). Most Australian colonies were formed through the subdivision of New South Wales, which originally covered the area that is now New South Wales, Queensland, Victoria, the Northern Territory and the eastern half of South Australia. Western Australia was established separately under the *Western Australia Act 1829* (UK).

The *Australian Courts Act 1828* also marked the formal end of the period of military rule, and a shift to the rule of law. The ad hoc system of official rule was replaced by an enlarged Legislative Council of between 10 and 15 members. This Legislative Council also had greater powers and autonomy. At the same time, the Governor was deprived of any right to enact legislation against the wishes of the majority of the Council.

Despite these shifts to representative democracy, the common law remained distinctly British. Any proposed laws had to be certified first by the Chief Justice of the Supreme Court as compatible with English law, and each proposed law was required to be set before the British Parliament. The main role of the British Government in monitoring Australian laws was to check that they were not repugnant (offensive) to British law. If they were, the British Government would invalidate them.

> **TIP**
> Often early English Acts are written with (Imp) instead of (UK). This signifies that it is an Act of the British Imperial Parliament.

Development of an Australian legal system and popularly elected parliament

Australian colonial self-government took shape in the middle of the nineteenth century. This was as a result of Australia's economy having become more self-sufficient, with a booming wool industry, the emergence of factory production, the concentration of the population in cities (where collective decisions could be made and civil unrest could be expressed), the development of communications and infrastructure, and the end of convict transportation to New South Wales in 1852 (followed shortly after in Tasmania in 1853 and in Western Australia in 1868).

The *Australian Constitutions Act (No. 1) 1842* (UK) expanded the number of members in the previously fully appointed legislative chamber in New South Wales and provided that two-thirds of the 36 members would be elected, thus beginning the transition from nominee government to representative government. Although the Act provided that the Governor was removed as a member of the Legislative Council, the Governor could withhold assent to legislation recommended by the Council.

The Act allowed the executive branch of government (the Cabinet) to exist as an autonomous branch of government. Indeed, its members did not need to be members of the Legislative Council and it was only responsible to the Colonial Office in London.

The capacity for Australian colonies to write their own constitutions with fully elected parliaments was realised with the *Australian Constitutions Act (No. 2) 1850* (UK). It established the Westminster system of responsible government in the newly federated Australia. It also established wide-ranging powers of self-government.

> **TIP**
> As a result of the 1842 Act, there were three separate branches of government in the colonies: the legislature, executive, and judiciary.

Nonetheless, the colonial constitutions had to be reserved for the Queen's assent. According to Lumb,[40] the proposed constitutions for New South Wales and Victoria exceeded the original authority of the *Australian Constitutions Act (No. 2)* and, therefore, required several further Imperial (British) legislative changes before the Queen gave her assent in 1855. Western Australia was the last colony to gain its independence in 1890.

An important catalyst for the move to self-government was the gold rush and the ensuing Eureka Stockade. In the early 1850s gold fuelled the economy and transformed the Australian demography by encouraging immigration.[41] Just as important was the protest movement on the goldfields – regarded as the first anti-authoritarian movements in Australia. In response to the Governor increasing the licensing fee for gold diggers, and the police violently extracting the payment through 'digger hunts', the Ballarat Reform League emerged in 1854 to demand liberty and popular government. The movement declared in its *Eureka Manifesto*: 'We swear by the Southern Cross to stand truly by each other, and fight to defend our rights and liberties'.

The protests on the goldfields came to a head in December 1854 when 1000 men gathered at Eureka, on the outskirts of Ballarat (Victoria). In response, 800 troops from British regiments and the Victorian police overran the stockade and killed 22 of its defenders. In the aftermath, a Royal Commission – known as the 'Gold Fields Commission' – condemned the goldfields administration. Following the Commission, elected local courts were introduced to the goldfields.[42] There was also more radical change inspired. At Forest Creek the miners' political claims of 'no tax without representation' was a powerful factor in the introduction of male suffrage (right to vote) in Victoria – ending the traditional requirement that only male property owners could vote. It was in Victoria that the vote for European adult males was first realised in the British Empire.[43]

Context: The controversial Justice Boothby

Justice Benjamin Boothby was appointed as a judge of the Supreme Court of South Australia in 1853 (the same year he moved to Australia from England).

Justice Boothby was notorious for repeatedly striking down South Australian statutes. He would find the slightest deviation from British law 'repugnant'. He also challenged the *South*

40　RD Lumb, *The Constitutions of the Australian States*, University of Queensland Press, St Lucia (1977).

41　Victoria alone contributed more than one-third of the world's gold output in the 1850s, and its population increased six-fold.

42　RL Sharwood, 'The local courts on Victoria's gold fields, 1855 to 1857' (1986) 15(3) *Melbourne University Law Review* 508, 508.

43　This led Weston Bate to claim that the aftermath of the Eureka Stockade saw Victoria 'taking democracy to the world': Weston Bate, *Lucky City: The First Generation at Ballarat, 1851–1901*, Melbourne University Press, Melbourne (1978).

Australian Constitution and judicial appointments. Consequently, he is regarded as recalcitrant and even 'un-Australian'. This practice meant that Justice Boothby was eventually removed from the Bench, but died in 1868 while his appeal to the Privy Council was afoot.

Revisionist histories of Bruce Kercher and Alex Castles suggest that Justice Boothby was perhaps not as wedded to English law as legal folklore proposes. Kercher argues that the South Australian colonial legislature was particularly innovative, especially in land law, and Justice Boothby was merely a check on its power.[44] Castles claims that Justice Boothby was not self-serving (or even British-serving), but sought to reach just ends in his judgments.

With the emergence of an increasingly independent parliamentary system, it was seen as nonsensical that Australian statutes should be challenged on the grounds of non-compliance with British law. The narrow statutory interpretation of Justice Boothby was put to an end when the South Australian government persuaded the British Parliament to pass the *Colonial Laws Validity Act 1865* (UK), which applied to South Australia and most other British colonies. This Act meant that colonial laws were valid irrespective of whether they were 'repugnant' to British laws. The colonial legislatures could override *most* received British statutes and common law, and the courts had to step into line.[45]

8: Federation and British remnants today

The *Commonwealth of Australia Constitution Act 1900* (UK) marked an end to the six Australian colonies and the beginning of the Australian nation. This Act of Britain transformed the colonies into states and a federal government was formed. This is known as Federation. It was not a revolutionary period for Australian citizens. Rather, it emerged after years of constitutional conventions and parliamentary debate. The *Commonwealth Constitution* came into force in 1901 and its major role was to form the Federal Parliament (with a nationally elected House of Representatives, and a Senate made up of representatives from each state), outline the powers and limitations of the federal government, as well as the functions of the High Court and Executive. There was no proclamation of rights and liberties in the Australian Constitution or declaration of independence.

Indeed, Federation did not change Australia's legal links and accountability to Britain. The Constitution allowed the Queen and the British Government to overturn any law passed by the Australian Parliament within 12 months of its enactment. The Commonwealth and the states remained subject to the *Colonial Laws Validity Act 1865*. Further, the *Australian States Constitutions Act 1907* (UK) reinforced the obligations of the Australian states to Britain. The Act required that any proposed amendments to the state Constitutions be reserved for the Crowns's assent, and the approval of the British Government.

TIP
Students often regard the formation of a colonial parliament as the move to Australian self-government and independence. In reality, ties with the British legal system remained well into the twentieth century. Certainly it paved the way for an independent and responsible Australian government, but Australia is still a constitutional monarchy.

---

44 This culminated in the Torrens title (freehold registration) system, replacing leasehold under the *Real Property Act 1857* (SA).

45 The colonies could not override those few British statutes of paramount force that explicitly or implicitly applied to the Australian colonies.

It was not until the *Statute of Westminster 1931* (UK) s 4, that the British Parliament was disabled from passing legislation applying to any of its colonies unless it was at the dominion's request. This allowed the Commonwealth as well as state parliaments to make laws repugnant to Britain. No longer could the British Parliament override Commonwealth Acts without a request from the Commonwealth. A number of historical developments prompted the move to Australian independence, including the decline of the British Empire after World War I and of the replacement of colonial military rule with economic imperialism (a less violent form of domination internationally).

Despite the colonial emancipation of the Federal Government, the states remained colonies. The *Australia Acts 1986* (Cth) removed the United Kingdom's legislative power over the individual Australian states. To prevent the British overriding the *Australia Acts*, the Acts state that their amendment or repeal can only be enforced by a Commonwealth Act passed at the request or with concurrence of the parliaments of all Australian states.

Judicial independence from Britain was piecemeal. In 1963 the High Court of Australia held for the first time that the House of Lords had made an error that would not be followed in Australia.[46] Then in 1978 the High Court took the ambitious stance of declaring it was not bound by the decisions of the Imperial Privy Council in London.[47] But it was not until the *Australia Acts* that appeals from state Supreme Courts to the Privy Council were removed, and the High Court became the final court of appeal. These developments established an Australian common law and legal system separate from the English law and legal system.

We have seen in this chapter that the adoption of an independent Australian legal system has been a slow process. This has also been the case for the recognition of Indigenous rights. The High Court of Australia stated in *Mabo* (1992), discussed in the next chapter, that any changes to Crown occupation of land or ensuing assumptions of sovereignty had been raised 'too late in the day' to be contemplated.[48] British legal traditions, British institutions and its common law system had already become entrenched in the Australian legal landscape.

The ongoing influence of British legal structures is evidenced by the fact that Australian society continues with a constitutional monarchy. The most recent referendum in 1999 saw approximately 55 per cent of Australian adults vote against moving from a constitutional monarchy to a republic. In 2008 the Australian Prime Minister, Kevin Rudd, announced that there was no urgency in becoming a republic. Rather, it will happen in 'due season'.[49]

Where, then, do Indigenous people and Indigenous laws fit in today? That is the topic of the next chapter.

---

46 *Parker v R* (1963) 37 ALJR 3.

47 *Viro v R* (1978) 141 CLR 88.

48 *Mabo* (1992) 175 CLR 1, 47 (Brennan J).

49 Andrew Pierce, 'Kevin Rudd: Australia will become a republic', *Telegraph* (UK), 7 April 2008, www.telegraph.co.uk/news/worldnews/1584257/Kevin-Rudd-Australia-will-become-a-republic.html.

DISCUSSION QUESTIONS

1. What was the process of the British Parliament claiming sovereignty over Australia?
2. What fictions relating to Australian land were invoked to support British colonisation under international law?
3. Did the Australian parliamentary system adopt the British model wholesale or accommodate local conditions?
4. What are the key principles from British law that are embedded in the Australian legal system?

WEBLINKS AND FURTHER READING

Banner, Stuart, 'Why *Terra Nullius*? Anthropology and Property Law in Early Australia' (2005) 23(1) *Law and History Review* 95, www.historycooperative.org/journals/lhr/23.1/banner.html.

Bennett, Scott, *Australia's Constitutional Milestones* at the Parliamentary Library, 27 August, 2004: http://aph.gov.au/Library/pubs/online/milestones.htm#ch.

Castles, Alex C, 'Boothby, Benjamin (1803–1868)', in *Australian Dictionary of Biography*, Vol 3, Melbourne University Press, Parkville, Vic (1969), 194.

Connell, Rachel, 'Who is an 'Aboriginal Person'?: Casenote on *Shaw v Wolf*, Merkel J, Federal Court, Unreported, 20 April 1998' (1998) 4(12) *Indigenous Law Bulletin* 20.

Dicey, AV, *Introduction to the Study of the Law of the Constitution*, Macmillan, London, 10th edn (1964).

Finn, Jeremy, 'A Formidable Subject: Some Thoughts on the Writing of Australasian Legal History' (2003) 7(1) *Australian Journal of Legal History* 53, available at www.austlii.edu.au/au/journals/AJLH/2003/7.html/

Indigenous Law Bulletin at www.austlii.edu.au/au/journals/ILB.

Kercher, Bruce, *An Unruly Child: A History of Law in Australia*, Allen & Unwin, Sydney (1995).

Neal, David, *The Rule of Law in a Penal Colony: Law and Power in Early New South Wales*, Cambridge University Press, Melbourne (2nd ed, 2002).

ONLINE RESOURCES FOR THIS CHAPTER

The following resources are available online at www.oup.com.au/orc/cwl2e
- Summary of English legal history
- Flashcard glossary
- Multiple choice questions

9

Australia:
Where Does Indigenous Law Fit In?

WHAT WE WILL COVER IN THIS CHAPTER:

- The phases of Indigenous policy and legal recognition
- The reassessment of *terra nullius* in *Mabo* and unresolved issues of Australian sovereignty
- The nature of native title and its limitations
- Other forms of recognition of Indigenous land
- Customary law recognition in Australian legal system
- Failure for post-*Mabo* case law to recognise customary law
- Moving forward: treaty and constitutional rights

Recommended approach to learning this topic

As you read this chapter, think about how the law does and might accommodate Indigenous rights and systems of law. Critically assess the rights afforded to Indigenous people in the current Australian legal system. Think back to the historical justifications for the Australian legal system and the removal of Indigenous legal systems. Was this legal? How can we resolve some of the illegalities today? To what extent can the Anglo-Australian system recognise Indigenous legal systems? Should 'traditional' Indigenous punishment be allowed to operate alongside the penalties of the Anglo-Australian criminal justice system?

Have a look at the High Court judgments since native title rights were refused in *Milirrpum v Nabalco* (1971). What view do the judges take in these cases on native title and customary law? What are the limitations in their analyses? Read these cases (all High Court cases are available on AustLII):

1. *Milirrpum v Nabalco Pty Ltd (Gove Land Rights Case)* (1971) 17 FLR 141
2. *Coe v Commonwealth* (1979) 24 ALR 118
3. *Mabo v Queensland (No. 2)* (1992) 175 CLR 1
4. *Coe v Commonwealth* (1993) 118 ALR 193
5. *Walker v New South Wales* (1994) 182 CLR 45
6. *The Wik Peoples v Queensland* (1996) 187 CLR 1
7. *Western Australia v Ward* (2002) 191 ALR 1
8. *Members of the Yorta Yorta Aboriginal Community v Victoria* (2002) 214 CLR 422
9. *Walden v Hensler* (1987) 163 CLR 561
10. *The Queen v Wilson Jagamara Walker* (1993) SCC No. 46. A summary and discussion can be found at: www.austlii.edu.au/au/journals/AboriginalLB/1994/33.html

KEY TERMS

Aboriginal or Torres Strait Islander person = referred to generally as Indigenous people. People of Aboriginal descent or from the island of Torres Strait are *generally* defined according to objective ('genetic'), subjective (group acceptance and self-identity) criteria (see extended definition in Chapter 8).

Assimilation = the process by which a minority group in a society gradually blends in by adopting the culture of the majority group.

Colonisation = pre-twentieth century occupation of nation states by military rule and acquisition of sovereignty. There are three forms of colonisation, namely conquest, cession or occupation (see these definitions in Chapter 8).

Freehold title = exclusive ownership of land.

Indigenous person = see Aboriginal or Torres Strait Islander person definition in Chapter 8.

Native title = a right of Indigenous people to use their land.

Self-determination = this encompasses a range of rights for sovereign groups, including rights to self-government, maintenance and development of political, economic and social institutions, and to practise and revitalise cultural traditions and customs.

Terra nullius = land with no one.

Treaty = an agreement between a colonising nation and the Indigenous people of that nation. It allows for the voluntary transfer of land, generally with limitations attached to the extent of land transferred and the jurisdiction of the coloniser's laws.

1: Historical developments in official policies relating to Indigenous people: Exclusion and inclusion

This section considers laws and policies regarding Indigenous people in Australia over the past two centuries, following 'unofficial' policies which had the effect of dispossessing Indigenous people on the frontier (see Chapter 8).

Government policy

Government policy towards Indigenous people began, from the mid-nineteenth century, with *segregation*. This involved the placement of Indigenous people on reserves, missions and government settlements away from their traditional country. The policy was premised on a view that Indigenous people would die out and therefore did not need to develop the means to integrate into colonial society.

In the late nineteenth century governments believed that protectionism would 'soften the dying pillow'. A Queensland Parliamentarian stated: 'The least we can do is to make [the Indigenous peoples'] time here, which will not be a very long time, as pleasant as possible, and their departure as gentle as circumstances will permit'.[1]

Protection policies went hand in hand with segregation. From the late nineteenth century protectionism became formalised through state and territory protection legislation, known as Aboriginal Acts.[2] The Acts provided for a network of

---

1   *Queensland Parliamentary Debates*, vol LXXVIII, 1897.

2   For example *Aborigines Protection Act 1886* (WA); *Aboriginal Protection Act and Restriction of the Sale of Opium Act 1897* (Qld); *Aborigines Protection Act 1909* (NSW); *Aborigines Act 1911* (SA); *Aboriginals Ordinance 1911* (NT); *Aboriginals Ordinance 1918* (Cth).

protectors who would police every aspect of Indigenous people's lives, including their movement, marriages, income, and work. The Acts often made it unlawful for Indigenous people to leave a designated area (such as a settlement), marry or work without permission, receive cash welfare or wages and practise traditional laws, customs and ceremonies. The removal of children was also authorised under these Acts. These children are now known as the Stolen Generations.[3]

From the 1930s assimilation was introduced when policy makers realised that Indigenous people would not die out. The objective was to integrate Indigenous people into the dominant non-Indigenous society. This involved teaching Indigenous people white ways of life so they would be 'civilised' and prepared for absorption into white society, particularly in towns. It promoted the removal of Indigenous children and placement into white families and institutions, but also encouraged regular employment (although with unequal wages) and provided housing. But Indigenous people were still denied the right to vote, freedom of movement, to marry without permission, eat in restaurants, swim in a public pool and have access to public education.[4]

Throughout the periods of segregation, protection and assimilation, Indigenous people were excluded from civil society. In the 1960s the movement for civil rights took hold. Accordingly, Indigenous people were given, by legislation, the right to vote in the Federal elections in 1962, although this only became compulsory in 1984.[5] During the late 1960s Indigenous people were also given rights to equal pay, and access to mainstream institutions and venues and welfare.[6] However, Indigenous people were still subject to unfair laws, such as child removal policies in Queensland, until the 1980s.[7]

After the 1970s the focus of governments was geared towards land rights (discussed below) and an embryonic form of self-determination involving support for self-governing Indigenous organisations. However, Indigenous people were not given recognition of their customary law. Despite a number of law reform commission

---

3   See *Bringing them Home: Report of the National Inquiry into the Separation of Aboriginal and Torres Strait Island Children from Their Families,* HREOC, 1997: www.austlii.edu.au/au/special/rsjproject/rsjlibrary/hreoc/stolen.

4   In terms of public education, New South Wales regulations meant school principals could refuse to enrol Aboriginal children until 1972.

5   Legal Information Access Centre, 'Timeline of Events in Electoral History', Hot Topics 1, March 1999.

6   Australian Law Reform Commission, *The Recognition of Aboriginal Customary Laws*, vol 1, Part I Introduction: The Reference and Its Background, (1986), [26].

7   The *Aboriginal and Torres Strait Islander Affairs Act 1965* (Qld) allowed Aboriginal children to be removed from their families until 1984, when the *Community Services (Aborigines) Act 1984* was introduced. See references to Queensland in the *Bringing them Home* report: www.austlii.edu.au/au/other/IndigLRes/stolen/index.html

inquiries on customary law from the 1980s through to 2006,[8] legal recognition remains an unresolved issue, which this chapter will trace.

Constitutional recognition

The *Commonwealth Constitution*, which sets out the powers of government, including the parliament, High Court and executive, is a founding document for the Australian nation. However, nowhere in the Constitution are Australian Indigenous people mentioned. This section considers the attempts to give the Federal Parliament powers to legislate for Indigenous rights, but also the continuing lack of recognition of Indigenous people in the Constitution and an absence of guarantees for Indigenous rights.

> ### Reflection: State constitutional recognition
>
> Despite lack of recognition of Indigenous people in the Australian Constitution, Indigenous Australians are recognised in preambles in the Victorian and (from 2010) the Queensland state Constitutions. For example s 1A of the *Constitution Act 1975* (Vic) states:
>
> (2) The Parliament recognises that Victoria's Aboriginal people, as the original custodians of the land on which the Colony of Victoria was established —
>   (a) have a unique status as the descendants of Australia's first people; and
>   (b) have a spiritual, social, cultural and economic relationship with their traditional lands and waters within Victoria; and
>   (c) have made a unique and irreplaceable contribution to the identity and well-being of Victoria.
>
> However, this declaratory statement is qualified by subs(3):
> (3) The Parliament does not intend by this section —
>   (a) to create in any person any legal right or give rise to any civil cause of action; or
>   (b) to affect in any way the interpretation of this Act or of any other law in force in Victoria.
>
> Consider whether constitutional recognition is meaningful if it does not create rights or affect constitutional interpretation.

When the Australian *Commonwealth Constitution* was enacted in 1900, Indigenous people were only mentioned for the purposes of excluding them from the Constitution's provisions. They were excluded from the power of the parliament to legislate with respect to being counted in the census (s 127) and with respect to

---

8   Law Reform Commission of Western Australia, *Report on Aboriginal Customary Laws* (2006); Northern Territory Law Reform Committee, *Report of Inquiry into Aboriginal Customary Law* (2003), and Australian Law Reform Commission, *The Recognition of Aboriginal Customary Laws* (1986).

race (51(xxvi)). Section 51(xxvi) gives the Commonwealth Parliament the power to make laws with respect to 'the people of any race for whom it is deemed necessary to make special laws'. Prior to the 1967 referendum, it also stated that this power is set aside for anyone 'other than the Aboriginal race in any State'.

In 1967 a referendum with popular support (90.8 per cent) removed the Aboriginal exclusion clause from the race power and census power in the Constitution.[9] This gave rise to the *Referendum and Subsequent Constitution Alteration (Aboriginals) Act 1967* (Cth). At the time, campaigners for constitutional change believed this would lead to positive change, such as recognising Indigenous peoples' rights to their land and customs, removing discriminatory practices and promoting equality with non-Indigenous Australians.[10] The *Daily Mirror* (Sydney) Editorial stated on the eve of the referendum on 22 May 1967:

> We've taken his lands, decimated his tribes, degraded his women, taken away his dignity and forced him to live in squalor. This is our chance to make some sort of amends. We still have a long way to go. But at least we can make a start at treating him as an equal.

However, the constitutional amendment did not insert anything that guaranteed that Federal legislation would lead to positive outcomes for Indigenous people. Some politicians, including Prime Minister Gough Whitlam, interpreted the amendment as paving the way for rights-based legislation. When he introduced the Northern Territory Aboriginal Land Rights Bill to the House, Whitlam said:

> The will of the Australian people, expressed overwhelmingly in the Referendum of 1967, [gave] this parliament, the national parliament, the opportunity and the responsibility to see that Aborigines have a right to land.[11]

The courts have interpreted the race power more broadly. They have held that it could be used to the benefit or detriment of Indigenous people. Therefore, when parliaments have sought to utilise the race power to discriminate adversely against Indigenous people, the courts permitted such usage. In *Kartinyeri v The Commonwealth*[12] the majority of the High Court held that the race power is not limited to legislation that benefits Indigenous people. It can be used to discriminate against or violate the rights of Indigenous people. Justice Kirby was the only judge who suggested that the High Court may use the purpose of the 1967 referendum and international human rights principles to conclude that the constitutional power cannot be invoked to discriminate against Indigenous people.

---

9   See Chapter 4 for a discussion on the purpose of a referendum in changing the constitution.

10 Neil Lofgren, 'Stirrings: A Reflection on the Constitution's Race Powers' (1997) 4(3) *Indigenous Law Bulletin* 32; Linda J. Kirk, 'Discrimination and Difference: Race and Inequality in Australian law' (2004) 4 *International Journal of Discrimination and the Law* 323, 330.

11 Mr Gough Whitlam (ALP), Commonwealth Parliamentary Debates (House of Representatives), 14 March 1973, 539.

12 (1998) 195 CLR 337.

In response to the lack of recognition of Indigenous people in the Constitution, the current Federal Government, under Prime Minister Kevin Rudd, has vowed to have a referendum to recognise Indigenous people in a constitutional preamble. However, the government has not stated how Indigenous people will be recognised, and accordingly, what question will be put to the Australian people at the referendum. Some avenues for constitutional recognition are:

- acknowledging the unique place of Indigenous peoples in Australian history and society
- recognising Indigenous peoples' current rights to land and custom
- setting frameworks for strengthening Indigenous societies and rights in the future.[13]

In depth: The Northern Territory intervention – a new phase of Indigenous policy

In mid-2007 the Federal Government, under Prime Minister John Howard, introduced the *Northern Territory National Emergency Response Act* and related legislation as part of the 'Northern Territory Intervention' into Indigenous communities. The Rudd Government has since extended the policy to a greater number of communities. The Government asserted that the Intervention sought to relieve poverty, improve education outcomes and reduce violent crimes, especially abuse of children, in Indigenous communities. The Minister for Indigenous Affairs, Mal Brough, in the Second Reading Speech described the measures as a 'broad-based approach' to 'address a breakdown in social norms that characterises many of our remote Northern Territory communities'.[14] The main features of the Intervention include:

- Quarantining 50 per cent of welfare money of all Indigenous community members (this means that 50 per cent of their money is put on a 'BasicsCard', which can only be redeemed on certain items from certain stores)
- Quarantining up to 100 per cent of welfare income where the recipient's child does not demonstrate adequate school attendance
- Alcohol restrictions on Northern Territory Aboriginal land
- Banning the possession of X-rated pornography
- Introducing compulsory health checks for all Aboriginal children
- Acquiring townships prescribed by the Australian Government through five year leases
- Increasing policing levels in communities
- Appointing business managers for communities
- Creating a broad set of exceptions to permits, which are required to enter Aboriginal lands.

---

13 See: Larissa Behrendt, 'Indigenous Rights and the Australian Constitution – A Litmus Test for Democracy', (2001), http://rspas.anu.edu.au/pah/human_rights/papers/2001/Behrendt.pdf.

14 Mal Brough, Second Reading Speech: Appropriation (Northern Territory National Emergency Response) Bill 2007–08, *Parliamentary Debates* (House of Representatives, 7 August 2007), 6.

In order to enact the legislative measures, which apply exclusively to Indigenous communities, the Government had to suspend the operation of the *Racial Discrimination Act 1975* (Cth) under section 8, which allows the federal government to take that step where special measures are required. Consequently, the Australian Human Rights Commission has criticised this policy for undermining basic human rights and Indigenous rights.[15] There have also been a number of complaints to United Nations committees for breach of rights to non-discrimination and of civil, political, and cultural rights. In 2009 the United Nations Special Rapporteur for Indigenous Rights visited some of the affected communities. He said of the Intervention:

> Aspects of the Government's initiatives to remedy situations of indigenous disadvantage, however, raise concerns. Of particular concern is the Northern Territory Emergency Response, which by the Government's own account is an extraordinary measure, especially in its income management regime, imposition of compulsory leases, and community-wide bans on alcohol consumption and pornography. These measures overtly discriminate against aboriginal peoples, infringe their right of self-determination and stigmatize already stigmatized communities.[16]

In March 2010, the Government proposed amendments to the Northern Territory Intervention legislation, which will reinstate the *Racial Discrimination Act*. The amendments mean that the measures apply not only to Indigenous communities, but potentially to the entire Northern Territory population.

Reflection

Do you think the proposed amendments adequately address the racially discriminatory nature of the Northern Territory Intervention measures and respond to the concerns of the United Nations Special Rapporteur for Indigenous Rights?

2: Recognition of Indigenous rights to land

The courts have in recent times recognised Indigenous rights to land, although they have consistently refused to extend this to recognition of other types of customary law and self-governance.

---

15 Aboriginal and Torres Strait Islander Social Justice Commissioner, *Social Justice Report* (2007), Ch 3, at www.hreoc.gov.au/social_justice/sj_report/sjreport07/.

16 Statement of the Special Rapporteur on the situation of human rights and fundamental freedoms of indigenous people, James Anaya, as he concludes his visit to Australia, 27 August 2009. (To find the speech go to http://www2.ohchr.org/english/issues/indigenous/rapporteur/ then find Australia under the Countries tab.)

Overturning *terra nullius*

You will recall from Chapter 8 that Australia was declared to be *terra nullius*, or empty land, despite the fact that Indigenous people had inhabited the continent for tens of thousands of years. Colonial courts enforced this myth – that the land was uninhabited – to justify the settlement of Australian land by occupation. It absolved the British Government from entering into a treaty with Indigenous people.

Terra nullius continued to be relied on well into the twentieth century. The Crown asserted its title against British squatters on the basis that it acquired radical title to all land, which entitled the Crown to an ultimate right to land, although not necessarily a possessory right.

It was not until the 1970s that Indigenous people challenged Crown title before the courts. In the first decision on Indigenous land rights, the *Gove Land Rights Case*,[17] the Northern Territory Supreme Court held that native title was not part of Australian law. This case was brought by members of the Yolŋu people at Yirrkala in the Northern Territory who sought to resist mining on their traditional land. In 1971 Justice Blackburn found that the Yolŋu people followed a 'subtle and elaborate system' of laws and customs connecting them to the land. This was 'a government of laws and not of men'. However, their communal ownership of the land could not be recognised in Australian law. Justice Blackburn explained that this is because, first, it was not a proprietary right, as the land could not be bought or sold. Second, Australian and British case law established that when the British Crown obtained sovereignty over the colonies, it became the owner of the land to the exclusion of all others. This reasoning drew on the doctrine of *terra nullius* – that the land had no recognisable owners and therefore the Crown could assume sovereignty by settlement. Therefore, even though the Yolŋu people had been in continuous occupation of their lands since the date of sovereignty under a traditional system of law and custom, they had no right to be recognised as the owners under the laws of Australia.

Justice Blackburn's decision was not appealed to the High Court. Rather, a political solution was reached. A Land Rights Commission was established in 1973. The Commission came about after a long strike by Indigenous cattle workers at Wattie Creek in the north-west of the Northern Territory, and widespread lobbying to the Whitlam Federal Government for land rights. The Commission was led by Justice Woodward, who had been Senior Counsel for the Aboriginal plaintiffs in the *Gove Land Rights Case*. Woodward's findings influenced the passage of the *Aboriginal Land Rights (Northern Territory) Act 1976* (Cth). The Act transferred ownership of certain lands to Aboriginal people. Applications for land rights under the legislation involve processes and outcomes that are different from native title (see discussion under heading 4 below).

The High Court would reconsider the issue of Crown title and Indigenous land

---

17 *Milirrpum v Nabalco* (1971) 17 FLR 141.

rights again in 1992.[18] In *Mabo v Queensland (No. 2)* (1992)[19] the High Court held that the British Crown did *not* acquire exclusive possession of all Australian land in 1788. Rather, it recognised that Indigenous people occupied the land prior to colonisation and continued to have possessory rights to land. The Court determined that there was capacity for the common law to accommodate coexisting land interests. When there was land held non-exclusively under the common law system, native title holders could use the land, and the law would recognise their right to use the land.

The High Court established that colonisation did not vest in the Crown exclusive legal possession ('beneficial title') of all Australian land, but only ultimate land ownership ('radical title').[20] There were tracts of land where the Crown had not acquired exclusive legal possession, which included land on the Torres Strait island of Mer, where Mabo belonged. This land could be claimed by Indigenous people who possessed the land before colonisation and throughout that period have had ongoing connections and continuous use of the land.

Mabo's story (1936–92)

Eddie Koiki Mabo was born on Mer in the Murray Islands in the Torres Strait (between Queensland and Papua New Guinea).[21] He was the son of Robert Zezou Sambo and Annie Mabo. Because his mother died in childbirth, he was adopted under customary law by his uncle Benny Mabo and aunt Maiga. On Mer he was taught about his family's land and traditions, which he practised, and worked on various trochus fishing luggers. He used the land he possessed in a manner consistent with English practice – gardening private plots of land, rather than communal holdings that were 'unimproved'.[22]

Nonetheless, Mabo did not stay on Mer throughout his life. At the age of 16 he was exiled to the mainland, due to the Meriam Island Council disapproving of his romance. Initially he worked on pearling boats, as a canecutter and railway labourer. In 1959 after meeting his wife, Bonita Nehow, he moved to Townsville to raise his nine children and take on various jobs.

---

18 The lawyers for the native title claimant, Eddie Mabo, sought to distinguish the earlier *Gove Land Rights Case* on the basis that Canadian authority, and international law, now supported the recognition of common law customary title to land.

19 *Mabo v Queensland (No. 2)* (hereafter *Mabo*) (1992) 175 CLR 1.

20 *Mabo* (1992) 175 CLR 1 at 63 (Brennan J), 110 (Deane & Gaudron JJ), 184 (Toohey J).

21 See map at www.austlii.edu.au/au/journals/MULR/2000/35_1.gif.

22 Shaunnagh Dorsett, 'Land Law and Dispossession', in Susan Bright and J. Dewar (eds), *Land Law: Themes and Perspectives*, Oxford University Press, Oxford (1998), 290.

From 1967 until 1971 Mabo was working as a gardener-groundsman at James Cook University. It was there that he started talking to academics about trying to get his land back. He attended history seminars and studied his people and customs from library records. Mabo's growing passion for reclaiming his land was ignited in 1973 when he was refused entry to Mer; and then in 1974, when academics Henry Reynolds and Noel Loos informed him that his land did not belong to his family, but to the Crown. This was a shocking discovery for Mabo.

In 1981 a conference on land rights was held at James Cook University.[23] There, Mabo made a speech about land ownership and inheritance on Mer. Consequently, a decision was made to take the Murray Islanders' land case to the High Court. Mabo's case was launched on 20 May 1982 in the Supreme Court of Queensland. Mabo was the principal plaintiff, together with other plaintiffs: Sam Passi, Father Dave Passi, James Rice and Celuia Mapo Salee. They all brought a claim over their land on Mer.

The response of the Queensland Government was to try to defeat Mabo's case before it really began. In 1985 the government retrospectively[24] and without compensation extinguished native title in the Torres Strait by passing the *Queensland Coast Islands Declaratory Act 1985* (Qld). The High Court ruled in 1988 this Act was contrary to the *Racial Discrimination Act 1975* (Cth) because the failure to pay compensation for land acquisition (a constitutional entitlement for all Australians) discriminated against Indigenous people. This ruling is known as *Mabo v Queensland (No. 1)* 1988 166 CLR 186.

In 1992 the High Court handed down its landmark ruling in *Mabo v Queensland (No. 2)* (1992) 175 CLR 1. Unfortunately Mabo himself died in the months before the ruling was handed down. For the first time the 205-year-old legal doctrine of *terra nullius* was overturned in Australia. Six judges of the Court gave legal recognition to the existence of Indigenous land ownership before colonisation, and ruled that, in certain cases such as this one, Indigenous land ownership survived because it was not extinguished by the Crown.

Reflection

Watch *Mabo – Life of an Island Man*, a film by Trevor Graham (Film Australia, 1997). Consider the relationship between Mabo's life and the nature of the case.[25]

---

23 Papers and discussion from the conference were published in E Olbrei (ed), *Black Australians: The Prospects for Change*, James Cook University Union, Townsville (1982).

24 The controversial issue of retrospective legislation is discussed in Chapter 11.

25 There is also a useful study guide at: www.documentaryaustralia.com.au/da/caseStudies/pdfs/022_01.pdf.

Native title rights

The High Court in *Mabo* provided Indigenous claimants with a *sui generis* (unique) land title, known as *native title*. This is not a right to own or lease the land – which are the main forms of common law real property rights – but a right to use the land in accordance with the claimants' customs. Native title comes from the traditional laws and customs of Indigenous peoples in relation to their land. It is their ongoing traditions that give Indigenous people title.

Native title affords Indigenous claimants a continuous right to use their land in accordance with their traditions. These include rights to hunt for traditional foods and very occasionally the right to exclusive possession. Native title is often referred to as a 'bundle of rights' because each right or interest needs to be proven on its own merits.

For native title to be legally recognised, Indigenous claimants must prove that:

- they have had an ongoing connection with their traditional lands since colonisation
- their connection is determined by their own laws and customs that gives them rights to their land
- there was no extinguishment of their rights.[26]

Native title may be extinguished in the following ways:

- before 1975, by the Crown through legislation that expressed a clear and plain intention to extinguish native title[27]
- there is a grant of land to a third party that is inconsistent with a right to enjoy native title (for example, where there has been a grant of freehold title on which your house is located)
- there are laws by which the Crown acquires full beneficial ownership of land previously subject to native title
- where the common law will not recognise it 'in fact'.[28] That is, where the courts do not deem that there are persisting Aboriginal laws and customs on the claimed land because it is 'washed away'[29] by colonisation, or
- where claimants fail to establish the required continuity of connection between the laws and customs as at the time of sovereignty and the present day.

So you can see that *Mabo* was an important moment in Australian legal history and Indigenous land rights. At the same time, it was a relatively moderate outcome – native title could not be assumed by Indigenous people as a universal right. Each Indigenous group has to prove its own land claim, case by case.

TIP
Native title was recognised by the USA Supreme Court in 1823, by the Canadian Royal Proclamation in 1756, by the New Zealand Treaty of Waitangi in 1840 and by the Australian High Court in the *Mabo* decision in 1992.

---

26 The High Court confirmed that the grant of freehold extinguishes native title in *Fejo v Northern Territory* (1998) 195 CLR 96.

27 Since 1975, however, extinguishment based on the Crown intention to deprive native title holders of their rights has been made illegal under the *Racial Discrimination Act 1975* (Cth). Native title in land extinguished after 1975 requires consultation with native title holders and compensation.

28 *Mabo* (1992) 175 CLR 1 at 57–8, 63–4 (Brennan J); 88, 110–1 (Deane & Gaudron JJ); 195–6 (Toohey J).

29 *Members of the Yorta Yorta Aboriginal Community v Victoria* (2002) 214 CLR 422, 461 (Gleeson CJ, Gummow and Hayne JJ, citing Olney J).

3: Developments since *Mabo*

Legislative response

In the aftermath of *Mabo*, a political battle raged. Sensationalist media writing stories about Indigenous people making claims over peoples' backyards fuelled opposition to native title. This reflected the uncertainty about what land could be claimed. Did it include leases, where there was another non-exclusive party occupying the land?

The politics surrounding the *Mabo* decision made the government cautious in its enactment of native title legislation. The political compromise of the *Native Title Act 1993* (Cth) reflected the heated negotiations between the Commonwealth Government and miners, pastoralists, various other primary production industries; the states, and Indigenous representatives. The Act governs the recognition, limitations and definition of 'native title'.

The compromised outcome of the *Native Title Act 1993* (Cth) is evidenced by its provisions that validated grants of land over native title as far back as 1975. These were previously illegal under the *Racial Discrimination Act 1975* (Cth). In return, native title holders would have a limited right to negotiate with mining companies and Governments who sought to acquire their land, and could receive some compensation. In addition, the Federal Court established in *Jango v Northern Territory of Australia* [2006] FCA 318, that a claimant group has a right to compensation where native title is found by a court to have been 'extinguished' by a government after enactment of the *Racial Discrimination Act* 1975 (Cth).

Other features of the *Native Title Act 1993* include:

- recognition of communal native title as part of Australian law
- prescription of the circumstances of extinguishment of native title
- formation of a national system for processing native title claims over land without exclusive possession
- creation of the National Native Title Tribunal to mediate between claimants and respondent parties such as state and local governments, pastoralists and recreational users of the land. If no agreement is reached, the matter is determined by the Federal Court
- legal recognition of Native Title Representative Bodies to represent claimants.

As a result of the *Native Title Act 1993*, claimants face an onerous procedural process. This is evidenced by the fact that the first native title determination was not made until 1996. On average claims take 10 years to be resolved and there are still hundreds of claims in the system.

Wik and further legislative response

The unresolved issue of whether leases extinguished native title was litigated before the Federal Court and then the High Court. The 1996 High Court decision of *The Wik Peoples v Queensland*[30] determined that native title is not necessarily extinguished by the grant of a pastoral lease, and that native title can coexist with other interests

> **TIP**
> Students often perceive native title as a right like any other land right — to own, sell and use land. Native title is *not* an individual right or an exclusive right. The land is managed by an Indigenous corporation set up under the *Native Title Act* and can only be used in certain ways.

---

30 (1996) 187 CLR 1.

in land. However, where native title rights and pastoral interests are in conflict or inconsistent, the rights of the non-native title holder (e.g. pastoral rights) would prevail. Ensuing from the *Wik* decision, pastoralists asserted that there was uncertainty over their leasehold. They did not know when native title existed or when it would be extinguished.

Consequently, the Federal Parliament enacted the *Native Title Amendment Act 1998* (known as the '10 Point Plan') that limited native title rights, listing numerous instances of extinguishment, including Crown Acts, public works, incidental construction and future acts of pastoralists, cultivators or miners, and stating that, once extinguished, there can be no revival of native title.

The *Native Title Amendment Act* also extended the class of people who might become respondent parties – those parties who challenge the Indigenous claimants, and at the same time made it harder for Indigenous people to submit customary evidence to support their claim.

To pass the *Native Title Amendment Act*, the government had to suspend the *Racial Discrimination Act 1975* (Cth), which created some controversy.[31]

Context: Obligations to Indigenous people under international law

International treaty law prescribes certain rights for Indigenous peoples, including land. Australia has signed:

- The *International Convention on the Elimination of Racial Discrimination* (CERD), Article 5 of which recognises the right for Indigenous people to own property without discrimination.
- The *United Nations Declaration of Human Rights*, Article 17 of which recognises the rights to own property and due process where it is deprived.
- The *International Covenant on Civil and Political Rights*, Article 27 of which provides that minority groups should have rights to maintain their culture.
- The *International Covenant on Economic, Social and Cultural Rights*, Article 1 of which provides that people have the right to self-determination, including to freely pursue their cultural development and to freely dispose of their natural resources.

In 1998 the Human Rights and Equal Opportunities Commission (HREOC), the Aboriginal and Torres Strait Islander Commission and other parties submitted to the United Nations (UN) Committee on the Elimination of All Forms of Racial Discrimination that the *Native Title Amendment Act* violated CERD. In 1999 the UN Committee expressed concern about the *Native Title Amendment Act*, in Decision 2(54), which the Australian Government rejected. The UN Committee reaffirmed its decision in Decision 2(55). No action was taken by the Australian Government.

---

31 The only other occasions when the Act has been suspended are to exclude Indigenous rights, such as for the *Northern Territory National Emergency Act 2007* (Cth) – see pp. 258–9.

> In September 2007 the United Nations General Assembly adopted the *Declaration of Rights of Indigenous People*, which declares a set of rights to self-determination. Articles 25–28 state that Indigenous land holdings should be recognised and compensation for paid dispossession, and Article 34 contains the right of Indigenous peoples to 'maintain their institutional structures and their distinctive customs, spirituality, traditions, procedures, practices'. The only nations that voted against the Declaration were Australia, Canada, New Zealand and the USA. Australia has since endorsed the Declaration in April 2009. However, the Declaration does not create legal rights for individuals, without the Government enacting its provisions in domestic legislation.

Challenges for native title claimants

Away from pastoral leases, and in the most populated areas of south-eastern Australia, native title rights would face an even graver fate. The High Court in *Members of the Yorta Yorta Aboriginal Community v Victoria*[32] revealed that native title is unlikely to be recognised in the areas of eastern and southern Australia that have been most affected by European colonisation.

At the Federal Court trial of *Yorta Yorta*, Justice Olney determined that native title did not exist over Crown land and water in the claim area along the Murray River in New South Wales and Victoria. His Honour said that the 'tide of history' (that is, colonisation, settlement and assimilation policies) had 'washed away' the Yorta Yorta community's traditional laws, languages and customs and thus their evidence for native title claims.[33]

The High Court upheld this decision in 2002. Thus, native title was denied because 'traditional society' ceased to exist after the Indigenous land was colonised. According to Richard Bartlett, this rendered native title almost impossible in the 'settled' regions of Australia.

Therefore, in bringing native title claims, Indigenous people face significant procedural and substantive restrictions:

- Indigenous people have the *burden of proving* ongoing connection to their land based on common law standards
- Proof of continuous occupation alone is *insufficient* without proof of continuous customary use of land
- Indigenous people could not claim *freehold title*, including most land in cities

---

32 (2002) 214 CLR 422.

33 *Members of the Yorta Yorta Aboriginal Community v Victoria* (2002) 214 CLR 422, 461 (Gleeson CJ, Gummow & Hayne JJ, citing Olney J).

- When native title is recognised, Indigenous people as a group acquire a *non-exclusive right* to land possession.[34] In practical terms, this requires the Crown to negotiate with the native title group before dealing with the land. The native title group cannot sell the land or use it for an exclusive purpose

Reflection

Does the word 'claimant' accurately reflect the status of native title holders? Some Indigenous Canadian scholars, such as Professor Paul Chartrand, assert that it assumes that the Crown has title and the native title holder is trying to take it back. Chartrand suggests that land should be seen as an Indigenous right that is under dispute, rather than a 'claim'.

Indigenous people have an oral tradition of story telling. However, courts traditionally rely on black-letter legal documents that do not sit comfortably with Indigenous oral testimony. Judges in native title cases thus privilege European documentary evidence of the extinguishment of native title over claimants' oral evidence of ongoing connections. For example in *Yorta Yorta*, Justice Olney gave preference to evidence in colonial documents over Indigenous evidence. His Honour relied on the diary of colonial pastoralist Edward Curr, in which he had written that he acquired land title in exchange for a stick of tobacco, above claimants' oral evidence of ongoing ties through their oral histories. Further, in the decision of *Western Australia v Ward*[35] evidence of cultural knowledge was deemed insufficient to prove native title. What was required was proof of Aboriginal use of land in customary practices, rather than mere cultural knowledge.

The *Native Title Act* requires an inherently complex and 'alien' or 'different' system of relationships to land to be characterised in terms which are comprehensible to the Australian legal system. Proof of connection is wholly defined by the Australian legal system, it is not a definition or standard inherent to the Indigenous people themselves. It does not atone for the historical injustices, and remains ignorant of its own role in removing the possibility for establishing the connection as required for recognition. In fact evidence of Indigenous massacres, forced removal from country and the Stolen Generations works in the favour of the state in extinguishing claims to native title.

---

34 The High Court in the decision of *Commonwealth v Yarmirr* (2001) 208 CLR 1 (*Croker Island* case) rejected the applicants' claim to exclusive rights. In *Western Australia v Ward* (2002) 76 ALJR 1098, the High Court settled that native title is not equivalent to full private ownership. Native title rights merely amount to traditional use rights over the land, even where native title holders are in sole occupation of the land. This contrasts with the ownership rights in Canada: *Delgamuuwk v British Columbia* [1997] 3 SCR (Canada) 1010.

35 (2002) 191 ALR 1, 19 (Gleeson CJ, Gaudron, Gummow & Hayne JJ).

In 2009 the Federal Government sought to remedy the difficulties in the native title process for claimants by making further amendments to the *Native Title Act*. The objective was to improve the operation of the native title system and outcomes for parties. The *Native Title Amendment Act 2009* relaxes the rules of evidence for claimants (by providing exceptions to the hearsay and opinion rules for Indigenous oral evidence), expands mediation assistance and extends the powers of the Federal Court to assist the resolution of native title claims.

4: Other forms of recognition of Indigenous land

In addition to native title rights, there are also Indigenous rights to land that are conferred by land rights legislation or negotiated between governments, industry and land claimants. However, these forms of land rights also have limitations – most notably:

1. The confined areas where Indigenous people can claim land rights under the legislation
2. Powerful interests determining the terms of the negotiated agreement
3. Long periods required to settle claims under legislation or agreement.

Land rights legislation

Land rights legislation came earlier in time than court recognition of native title. Land rights legislation involves *granting* common law land title to Indigenous people. It is distinct from native title, whereby Indigenous title is *recognised*. The first piece of legislation was introduced in Victoria, with the *Aboriginal Lands Act 1970*.

However, the symbolic turning point for land rights took place at Wattie Creek in the Northern Territory. After an eight-year protest by the Gurindji people demanding land and fair pay, Prime Minister Gough Whitlam responded. He poured sand into the hands of traditional land owner Vincent Lingiari in 1975 to symbolise the handing back of land. This marked the introduction of Northern Territory land rights legislation into parliament.

The *Aboriginal Land Rights (Northern Territory) Act 1976* (Cth) recognised Aboriginal land in conformity with the common law property system. This meant that when a claim is successful there is a statutory grant of title to land. A successful claim under the legislation will normally result in:

- absolute ownership with some restrictions, such as a prohibition on selling or mortgaging the land,[36] although this does not apply in New South Wales[37]
- communal title over land (that is, title in an Aboriginal Land Council that is democratically elected by the Indigenous owners), rather than individual title
- the land being administered by representative bodies

---

36 See *Aboriginal Land Rights Act* (NT) s 19.

37 Land granted under the *Aboriginal Land Rights Act 1983* (NSW) is vested in Land Councils as a fee simple freehold. A Land Council can only sell or mortgage the land transferred if 80 per cent of its membership agrees. The land can, however, be leased to outside interests: *Aboriginal Land Rights Act 1983* (NSW) ss 36(9), 40.

- veto rights of the traditional owners to mining activities or reasonable compensation in lieu of veto rights
- where mining is approved by a Land Council, royalties have to be paid to the Indigenous owners
- the possibility for native title rights to be exercised on that land (s 67B).

Reflection

The land rights legislation was a monumental development for Indigenous rights in Australia. However, it occurred despite the fact that the legal myth of *terra nullius* continued to exist at the time. What does this say about the relationship between law and politics?

After the Commonwealth Government introduced Aboriginal land rights legislation for the Northern Territory in the 1970s, the remaining state governments, with the exception of Western Australia, followed suit:

- *Pitjantjatjara Land Rights Act 1981* (SA)
- *Aboriginal Land Rights Act 1983* (NSW)
- *Maralinga Tjarutja Land Rights Act 1984* (SA)
- *Aboriginal Land Act 1991* (Qld)
- *Torres Strait Islander Land Act 1991* (Qld)
- *Aboriginal Lands Act 1995* (Tas).

Have a look at these statutes and consider how they differ in what rights they afford Indigenous traditional owners.

There is also Aboriginal Heritage legislation in each state and at Commonwealth level to protect the interests of local traditional owners in places which are significant to them even though they may not own the land.[38]

In some jurisdictions, such as the Northern Territory, an Indigenous community must prove historical and traditional connection to land for land to be granted under the *Aboriginal Land Rights Act (Northern Territory) 1976* (Cth). In other states, such as New South Wales, claimants may claim land for which they have no traditional connection.[39] This is because the purpose of the land rights legislation in that state is to 'redress past injustices when Aboriginal people were dispossessed of their land by colonisation', rather than to honour a traditional connection.[40] The government rationale is that some Indigenous people cannot return to their traditional land

---

38 *Aboriginal and Torres Strait Islander Heritage Protection Act 1984* (Cth); *Northern Territory Aboriginal Sacred Sites Act 1989* (NT); *Aboriginal Heritage Act 1988* (SA); *Aboriginal Heritage Act 1972* (WA); *National Parks and Wildlife Act 1974* (NSW); *Queensland Heritage Act 1992* (Qld); *Nature Conservation Act 1992* (Qld); *Aboriginal Relics Act 1975* (Tas); *Archaeological and Aboriginal Relics Preservation Act 1972* (Vic).

39 *Aboriginal Land Rights Act 1983* (NSW) s 36(5).

40 New South Wales Department of Lands, 'Aboriginal land': www.lands.nsw.gov.au/crown_lands/aboriginal_land.

because they were forcibly relocated and their traditional land has since been intensely colonised and settled.

While land rights legislation provides a higher form of title than native title, because it is an exclusive right, there are nonetheless shortcomings:

- generally only vacant Crown land can be granted (contrast native title where a claim can be over a wide ambit of land held non-exclusively)
- the land is rarely commercially valuable
- processing claims can take a long time when the Crown Lands Minister objects to claims. Objections are made on the basis that they are for an essential public purpose (including nature conservation),[41] required for sale on the market or otherwise lawfully used or occupied. In New South Wales, for example, only 30 per cent of land claims have been processed since the legislation was introduced in 1983. Many of the decisions of the Minister are contested in the courts.

At present nearly half of the Northern Territory is owned by traditional owners under the land rights system. Although the land owning groups do not have the legal powers of local government in respect of their lands, in fact the groups are responsible for running their own communities. Permits are required to visit Aboriginal land. Applications are made through local land councils. The federal government under the former Prime Minister John Howard abolished permits. While the requirement to hold a permit to enter Aboriginal land has since been reinstated for most people, government officials, politicians and Commonwealth or Northern Territory officers remain exempt from holding a permit in respect of Aboriginal land granted pursuant to the *Aboriginal Land Rights (Northern Territory) Act 1976* (Cth) s 70(2A).[42] A Minister may also authorise any person or class of persons to enter or remain on Aboriginal land (s 70(2BB)).

Negotiated outcomes for Indigenous land rights

Indigenous rights to land have been negotiated successfully between Indigenous communities and governments, mining companies and other stakeholders. They are voluntarily entered into by the relevant parties, with a view to reaching a consensus position on native title and competing land interests. This has allowed for development to go ahead while providing a mechanism for input by Indigenous owners and the retention of some of their rights.

Due to the limited outcomes from the legislated land rights and native title processes, negotiated outcomes are increasingly seen as a viable alternative. Negotiated agreements are made with respect to land access, compensation and environmental governance. So far, more than 3000 agreements have been successfully negotiated.[43]

---

41 *Aboriginal Land Rights Act 1983* (NSW) s 36A.

42 See: Northern Territory Lands Group, 'Aboriginal Land Permits' www.nt.gov.au/lands/landadmin/alps/index.shtml

43 Commonwealth Budget Paper, Indigenous Affairs 2002–2003, 14 May 2002.

Negotiation can be entered into without a requirement for a native title determination. However, some native title claims are actually settled by agreement between the parties – known as 'consent determinations'.[44] For example the Queensland Government has agreed to recognise native title subject to previously granted rights in land over some islands in the Torres Strait (the region where the *Mabo* case originated). In other instances, agreements are made while the native title determination is pending. Negotiations can provide a more immediate opportunity for parties to enjoy native title rights and interests or regulate co-existence.

Nonetheless, negotiations (like litigated native title outcomes) can be a long process, especially where they involve a consent native title determination. In some instances they take as long as 10 years to resolve. Before native title negotiation begins, governments have to provide a licence, which can be a highly bureaucratic process. Also, it is difficult to negotiate on a 'level playing field', as governments and respondent parties are far better resourced than the Indigenous claimants.

Some existing state land rights Acts, such the *Maralinga Tjarutja Land Rights Act 1984* (SA), allow native title claims to be settled by the transfer of land under the legislation. This means that the Indigenous claimants drop their claim to native title over vacant Crown land where they are given other land. In one case on the New South Wales mid-north coast, compensation of $1.6 million was paid to a claimant group as a result of a settlement which validated the Crown's appropriation of the land for the purpose of creating a housing development.[45]

Negotiation of claims is provided for under the amended *Native Title Act 1993* (Cth). The 1998 amendments enable parties to make voluntary agreements regarding future development on land where native title potentially exists. These agreements, known as Indigenous Land Use Agreements (ILUAs), permit developers, pastoralists or mining companies to negotiate directly with all people who may hold native title over the land. As of 2008, 350 ILUAs had been registered with the National Native Title Tribunal.[46]

The issues that are negotiated include future activities to be conducted in the area, co-existence relationships, varying a native title claim or paying compensation for harm to native title rights. The projects for which ILUAs have been used in Australia range from the authorisation of the building of a surf club at a beachside location on a very small parcel of land, to a large scale resource development deal involving extensive mining, environmental rehabilitation and compensation issues.[47] Agreements can also set out the obligations of the relevant parties once native title is recognised.

---

44 They can be be used in conjunction with native title applications and are often used as an important basis for determinations of native title.

45 See Patricia Lane, 'Land Law and Communal Title in Australia', Presentation to Parties and Observers Sudan Peace Conference, Machakos, Kenya, 12 May 2003, 15–16.

46 National Native Title Tribunal, 'About indigenous land use agreements' www.nntt.gov.au/Indigenous-Land-Use-Agreements/Pages/About_iluas.aspx

47 Lane, above n 45, 23.

Although negotiation is an informal process, there are certain conditions that must be met under the *Native Title Act*:

- Indigenous groups must collectively authorise the agreement, based on traditional decision-making process or broad community consultation
- The agreement must be lodged with the Native Title Registrar and there is opportunity for traditional owners to object
- The registered agreement will then take effect as a contract, binding the parties. This can include governments and industry groups as well as all native title holders in the area, even if they do not personally authorise the agreement.

Often Indigenous parties resort to ILUAs because their entrenched dispossession due to colonisation means that their native title rights may be difficult to prove before a court. This is particularly the case in Queensland where ILUAs are relatively common.

Reflection

Given that Indigenous Land Use Agreements are voluntary agreements that result in a contractual relationship between the parties, are common law principles equipped to process native title? Think about the strengths and weaknesses of the common law in this respect.

5: Ongoing non-recognition of customary law

We've seen that there was a clear break with common law precedent when the High Court of Australia in *Mabo* held that *terra nullius* was a myth. The Court recognised that in fact Indigenous people did pre-exist the settlers and had sovereign systems of law. However, while this provided for recognition of Indigenous peoples' rights to native title, it did not allow for recognition of customary law rights.

Customary laws pre-existed the common law system. They are based on systems of regulation discipline and punishment comparable to the objectives of the common law system, as discussed at the beginning of Chapter 8. However, there are no legal mechanisms to incorporate these customary laws into the common law. This section considers the judicial reluctance to make parallels between native title recognition and customary law recognition.

Court reluctance to recognise Indigenous criminal law

In the aftermath of *Mabo*, litigants went to the High Court alleging that Indigenous people who commit crimes within their communities should be tried by their own laws, rather than the common law. This reopened the issue of whether Aboriginal law applies as between Aboriginal people, originally presented in *R v Murrell* (see Chapter 8). With the abandonment of *terra nullius* – which served as a justification for the common law to prevail in *R v Murrell* – Indigenous people argued that there was no longer a lawful reason for customary law not to sanction Indigenous people, instead of the common law.

The first High Court decision that considered this argument in the aftermath of *Mabo* was the single-judge decision of *Coe v Commonwealth (No. 2)*.[48] Isabel Coe filed her case on the first anniversary of the High Court decision of *Mabo* – 3 June 1993. She served the writ of summons on behalf of the Wiradjuri tribe against the Commonwealth of Australia and the state of New South Wales. It was primarily a challenge to these governments' sovereignty over her tribe. The lawyers for Isabel Coe argued that her tribe had continuing native title rights and sovereignty claims. For Commonwealth or state laws to apply to the Wiradjuri tribe would require the tribe's acceptance, adoption, request or consent.[49]

Chief Justice Mason of the High Court rejected the arguments of the plaintiff. First, he said there were no native title rights due to the prevailing statutory and freehold title grants. He noted that both the lands claimed and all the defendant parties (i.e. those with freehold title) were not identified specifically. On the sovereignty claim, Mason CJ said that nothing decided in *Mabo (No. 2)* affected sovereignty:

> *Mabo (No. 2)* is entirely at odds with the notion that sovereignty adverse to the Crown resides in the Aboriginal people of Australia. The decision is equally at odds with the notion that there resides in the Aboriginal people a limited kind of sovereignty embraced in the notion that they are 'a domestic dependent nation' entitled to self-government and full rights (save the right of alienation) or that as a free and independent people they are entitled to any rights and interests other than those created or recognised by the laws of the Commonwealth, the State of New South Wales and the common law.[50]

The next case to consider the issue of customary law was *Walker v New South Wales*.[51] This involved a criminal defendant who brought his case to the High Court, alleging that Indigenous criminal (customary) laws can coexist with the common law criminal system in the same way that native title coexists with the common law real property system. In that single-judge decision, Chief Justice Mason considered that there is no analogy between criminal customary law and native title. Even if there were, the Crown has extinguished customary laws by the enactment of criminal statutes. His Honour did not explain the legal foundations for Crown sovereignty. That is, his Honour did not delve into how the Crown acquired its sovereignty under international law – given that Indigenous people did not cede their land by entering a treaty, and in some remote areas of Australia, white people have never settled there.

The judicature effectively deferred the issue of sovereignty to the legislature. Without judicial support, Indigenous peoples' hopes would rest with changes to legislation, constitutional change or the good will of parliaments to enter into a treaty.

---

48 (1993) 118 ALR 193 (Mason CJ).

49 See: Garth Nettheim, 'Isabel Coe on behalf of the Wirajduri Tribe v Commonwealth of Australia and the State of New South Wales' (1994) 3(66) *Aboriginal Law Bulletin* 14, at www.austlii.edu.au/au/journals/AboriginalLB/1994/9.html.

50 *Coe v Commonwealth (No. 2)* (1993) 118 ALR 193, 200.

51 *Walker v New South Wales* (1994) 182 CLR 45.

However, despite a number of law reform commission inquiries that have found that there is a 'recognition space' for customary law in the common law system, governments have by and large *not* implemented their recommendations. The law reform commissions' findings and government policy developments in customary law recognition are the subjects of the following section.

6: Alternative paths for incorporating customary law into the common law

Law reform commission proposals on customary law

Given the reluctance of courts to afford recognition of Indigenous customary laws, law reform commissions have put forward proposals for the integration of customary law into the common law system.[52] These reports can be influential, but have no legal authority.[53] They nonetheless provide an interesting perspective on how customary law may be incorporated into the dominant legal system.

In 1986 the Australian Law Reform Commission proposed the 'functional recognition' of customary law. This involves allowing for the recognition of customary law for particular purposes in defined areas of law such as marriage.[54] This conclusion was supported by the Law Reform Commission of Western Australia report *Aboriginal Customary Laws* (2006), which considered whether customary law could be recognised in a similar manner to native title. The Law Reform Commission of Western Australia outlined a variety of methods for recognition, including:

1 Affirmative recognition – this includes:
   a Statutes and guidelines that require courts and government agencies to take account of customary law
   b Models of self-governance for Indigenous communities
   c Removal of existing cultural biases and recognition of traditional marriages, and
   d Empowerment of elders to administer justice in communities.

2 Reconciliatory recognition – the promotion of reconciliation between Indigenous and non-Indigenous Australians, including:
   a Targeted, local cultural awareness training for all employees and contractors of government agencies
   b Establishment of an independent Office of the Commissioner for Indigenous Affairs to work towards the promotion of the interests of Indigenous people and reconciliation, and

---

52 See Australian Law Reform Commission, *The Recognition of Aboriginal Customary Laws*, Report No. 31 (1986); New South Wales Law Reform Commission, *Sentencing Aboriginal Offenders*, Report 96 (2000); Northern Territory Law Reform Committee, *Report of the Committee of Inquiry into Aboriginal Customary Law* (2003); Law Reform Commission of Western Australia, *Aboriginal Customary Laws: Final Report*, Project 94 (2006).

53 See Chapter 3, where law reform commission reports are discussed as a secondary source of law.

54 See Australian Law Reform Commission, *The Recognition of Aboriginal Customary Laws*, Report No. 31, (1986), 270.

c   A foundational provision in the Constitution to acknowledge the unique status of Indigenous people as descendants of the original inhabitants and the original custodians of the land.

Parliaments' failure to adopt law reform commission recommendations has effectively left it to the courts to incorporate customary considerations in a piecemeal (and sometimes inconsistent) manner.

Attempts to take customary law into account in criminal cases

What happens when an Indigenous person in a remote community commits a crime without knowing that it was a crime? Can an Indigenous person defend themselves by arguing that they made an honest and reasonable mistake? Although judges have granted a degree of leniency, they have made it clear that an Indigenous person's belief that her or his act was lawful under customary law will not suffice as a full defence.

Walden v Hensler

(1987) 163 CLR 56

The defendant, an Aboriginal elder of the Gungalida tribe of North Queensland, shot a bush turkey in a National Park, which was lawful under customary law but illegal under the *Fauna and Conservation Act 1974-79* (Qld). The defendant did not know about the Act. The magistrate had convicted and fined him, and the Full Court of the Supreme Court of Queensland upheld the conviction. On further appeal to the High Court, the convictions and orders were unanimously quashed. However, this was on the basis of fairness – that it was his first offence and it was trivial – rather than because customary law overrode statute law. Justice Brennan held, 'To deprive an Aboriginal without his knowledge of his traditional right to hunt for bush tucker for his family on his own country and then to convict and punish him for doing what Aborigines had previously been encouraged to do would be an intolerable injustice'.[55]

Since this case, the parliaments have legislated, as under the *Fisheries Act 1988* (NT) s 53, to allow an Indigenous person who exercises a customary right to use the land or waterways or resources of an area without criminal consequences.

What is the situation in criminal sentencing?[56] Can Indigenous cultural practice or law reduce a sentence? Generally, where there are mitigating factors, such as no prior offences or action under extreme circumstances, the sentence will be reduced, and where there are aggravating circumstances, such as unnecessary cruelty or violence, and previous convictions, the sentence will be increased. Judges have

---

55   See: David Weisbrot, 'Bush Bustardry or Bustard in the Bush – *Herbert Walden v Peter Baxter Hensler*' (1987) 1(29) *Aboriginal Law Bulletin* 14.

56   Sentencing is the determination of punishment after a person has been convicted of a crime. For serious crimes, it may be imprisonment. For other crimes, it may be a fine, a good behaviour bond, or a period of community service.

taken into account whether someone's membership of an Indigenous community or Indigenous background may aggravate or mitigate an offence. For example where the Indigenous person's criminal act is done pursuant to a custom, such as spearing a person in accordance with traditional punishment, the sentence may be reduced. The courts have also taken into account the proven link between Aboriginality, disadvantage and alcohol abuse and violence. See for example *R v Fernando*,[57] where the Aboriginal defendant was sentenced for malicious wounding. Both the victim and the offender had consumed large amounts of alcohol on the Aboriginal reserve at Walgett.

However, the contentious nature of customary law in sentencing was brought to the fore in the Northern Territory case of *Hales v Jamilmira*.[58] In 2002 the Supreme Court of the Northern Territory sentenced an Aboriginal man convicted of statutory rape (sex with a person under 16 years of age) to 24 hours imprisonment for having unlawful sexual intercourse with a 15 year old girl who was his promised wife under local Aboriginal law. The defendant submitted that his sentence should be mitigated on the grounds that it was customary practice to have sex with a promised wife irrespective of her age. It was also lawful in Northern Territory legislation to have sex within Indigenous marriage. An anthropologist presented evidence that girls can be promised to a man any time after having their first period. Under the Northern Territory *Criminal Code* it was lawful for an Indigenous man who traditionally marries a woman under 16 to have consensual sex with his wife.[59] When this was appealed to the Northern Territory Court of Criminal Appeal, the majority held that the act was not necessitated by customary practice and he should have waited until the victim was 16. The sentence was increased to 12 months, but it could be suspended[60] after serving one month of imprisonment. In the aftermath of *Hales v Jamilmira* the Northern Territory *Criminal Code* was amended to make it unlawful for under-age sex within traditional marriages.

In 2007 the Federal Government passed legislation to remove cultural considerations. Sections 90 and 91 of the *Northern Territory National Emergency Act 2007* (Cth) provides that for bail[61] applications and sentencing, courts 'must not take into consideration any form of customary law or cultural practice as a reason for:

(i) excusing, justifying, authorising, requiring or lessening the seriousness of the alleged criminal behaviour to which the alleged offence relates, or the criminal behaviour to which the offence relates; or

(ii) aggravating the seriousness of the alleged criminal behaviour to which the alleged offence relates.'

This legislation quashes judicial discretion to take into account customary law in any circumstances for Northern Territory sentencing and bail decisions.

---

57   *R v Fernando* (1992) 76 A Crim R 58.

58   *Hales v Jamilmira* (2003) 13 NTLR 14.

59   Section 129(1) *Criminal Code* (NT) read with the definition of 'unlawfully' in s 126 and the definition of husband and wife in s 1.

60   A suspended sentence is a withheld sentence based on fulfilling certain conditions.

61   Bail is temporary liberty before a criminal trial.

In depth: Indigenous sentencing scenarios

1. Should sentencing be harsher where the offence is more serious under Indigenous law? What about where there is a violation of a sacred site which can be a very serious breach of Indigenous law? Should judges award a harsher sentence than what is provided in the legislation? The courts have criticised this approach.[62]

2. Should the sentence be reduced where traditional punishment will be inflicted? Should traditional punishment be recognised by the Anglo-Australian system at all?

    Traditional punishment can include banishment or temporary exile, spearing and shaming. Would it be 'double jeopardy'[63] for the Indigenous offender to be punished by both Indigenous law and the criminal law?

    In the Northern Territory sentences have been reduced where traditional punishment will also be inflicted. In *R v Minor* (1992) 79 NTR 1, Justice Mildren reduced an Indigenous offender's prison sentence to 10 years imprisonment because he had consented to being speared in the thigh by his community (according to tribal punishment) upon his release from prison. One material consideration was that the 'tribal way' of payback would help to settle down the community. His Honour also took into account the need to avoid double punishment (double jeopardy).

    In addressing the question of traditional punishment, watch this short clip on *Bush Law*, which highlights Indigenous perspectives on traditional punishment: www.youtube.com/watch?v=3iAHYxnW_8U.

3. What about where a non-Indigenous person knowingly violates Indigenous law?

    In 2008, a female police officer interfered with male initiation in the Lajamanu community in the Northern Territory – which renewed calls for the recognition of customary law. One community elder noted, 'We recognise the Parliament of Australia, why won't the police officers respect our law?'[64]

Government initiatives in 'customary' sentencing processes

There has recently been a move towards community involvement in the sentencing process, such as circle sentencing. Circle sentencing in New South Wales is a formal mechanism whereby community elders, the victim (if he or she chooses), the offender and his/her lawyer, family members of the offender and victim, the prosecutor and the magistrate sit together in a circle to discuss and decide upon a sentence by consensus. For circle sentencing to be used, the offender must be willing to take full responsibility for his/her wrong-doing, and there must be a community willing and able to facilitate a process of healing and restoration of the offender.

There has also been a move towards having courts specifically handling Indigenous cases. In Victoria, Koori Courts have been operating since the enactment of the *Magistrates Court (Koori Court) Act 2002* (Vic), with the first court in Shepparton. Although the magistrate has ultimate decision-making authority, the Indigenous

---

62 See *R v Minor* (1992) 79 NTR 1, 14; *Munungurr v The Queen* (1994) 4 NTLR 63, 71. Also see Australian Law Reform Commission, *Recognition of Aboriginal Customary Laws*, Report No. 31 (1986), [509].

63 Double jeopardy is facing more than one prosecution for the same crime.

64 See the report on YouTube www.youtube.com/watch?v=aU4m3bRyRqU.

community participates in sentencing, through input from Aboriginal elders, victims, and the defendant's family.

The Queensland Murri Courts commenced in Brisbane in 2002, and have since extended to more remote areas of Queensland such as Mount Isa and Rockhampton. There are also Youth Murri Courts across Queensland. The Murri Courts are designed to assist the Queensland Magistrates Court in meeting its obligations under s 9(2)(o) of the *Penalties and Sentences Act 1992* (Qld) to take into account the views of Indigenous community representatives when sentencing Indigenous offenders.

In South Australia, Nunga Courts are designed to deal with Aboriginal offenders in a culturally sensitive way. Since 1999 they have operated to encourage community participation in sentencing where the offender pleaded guilty. An Aboriginal Justice Officer or a senior Aboriginal person sits beside the Magistrate to advise on cultural and community matters. The family and community members and the victim (if present) also have an opportunity to put forward their views on the sentence.

7: Filling the legal gap – treaty and sovereignty rights

Usually, where there are already people inhabiting a land that is taken by conquest or settlement, a treaty is negotiated between the newcomers and the Indigenous inhabitants. This is what occurred in New Zealand, with the Treaty of Waitangi in 1840. The legal gap created for recognition of Indigenous customary law in Australia tracks back to the original declaration of Australia as being *terra nullius*, or empty land. Where land is empty, there is no need for a treaty with the original inhabitants.

However, since *terra nullius* was overturned in *Mabo*, the issue of whether a treaty should be negotiated has been revived. For example Henry Reynolds has asserted that it is inconsistent for the High Court to determine native title was extinguished in a slow and piecemeal fashion without finding the same for sovereignty. Reynolds claims that courts should treat property and sovereignty the same, by providing for their coexistence.[65] Any government is likely to approach a treaty that reduces its sovereignty with caution. There are also practical issues, such as whether a nation-wide treaty is appropriate given that there are over 500 Indigenous nations in Australia with different cultures, languages and needs.

Context: An Indigenous model for self-determination

In 1990 the Aboriginal Provision Government (APG) was established to work towards self-determination. The APG believes that their sovereignty rights were not ceded in 1788. It calls for a *referendum for Indigenous people* to decide if they are willing to cede their territories and rights. Ultimately, the APG calls for an Aboriginal state with all control vested back into Aboriginal communities. Its operation requires:

---

65 Henry Reynolds, 'After Mabo, What About Aboriginal Sovereignty?', *Australian Humanities Review* (1996), www.australianhumanitiesreview.org/archive/Issue-April-1996/Reynolds.html.

- Crown land and additional land to make Indigenous communities viable as a nation of people; the remaining land would be kept by non-Indigenous people and their government.
- Compensation for agreement to transfer the remaining land (expected to be half of Australia). Compensation could be in-kind (e.g. support for Indigenous programs and institutions, medical facilities, infrastructure and education).
- Aboriginal communities would not be subject to the Australian Government's legislation, unless the communities wanted those laws to apply to them.
- Each Indigenous community would determine its own legal and political system; some would invoke 'traditional' laws and others may have a hybrid Indigenous–white system.
- Individual Indigenous people could choose to live under the jurisdiction of white Australia.
- Any person from outside the Aboriginal nation entering Aboriginal land would be expected to abide by that legal system and, conversely, any Aboriginal person going into white cities or towns would be expected to abide by the white man's legal system.[66]
- Police could only enter an Indigenous community with the agreement of the community.
- Conflict between Indigenous and non-Indigenous law should be resolved using similar principles as in international law.
- On the international stage, the Aboriginal Government would operate as a state.

A more limited form of self-determination will be the establishment of the National Congress of Australia's First Peoples in 2010. This body will represent Australian Indigenous people nationally and provide advice to the Federal Government and monitor implementation of Government programs and services to Indigenous peoples. The Federal Government is also considering Indigenous recognition through a constitutional amendment that would crystallise the unique place of Indigenous peoples in our political and legal systems. It would entail recognition of Indigenous people as the first inhabitants and traditional owners of the Australian country. The process would require the Federal Parliament to initiate a referendum.

DISCUSSION QUESTIONS

1. How were Indigenous people included and excluded from the Australian legal system until the twentieth century?
2. Native title and land rights legislation provide different rights and require a different process. What are these differences?
3. Can customary law be recognised in the same way native title is recognised?
4. Are the common law and Indigenous laws compatible? Consider ways in which they may coexist.
5. This chapter began by discussing the stages of Aboriginal policy. How would you describe the current era? You may take into account the Northern Territory Intervention.

---

66 But the APG claims there could be concessions if either entered the others' land not knowing the law. For example penalties would not be as harsh.

WEBLINKS AND FURTHER READING

Aboriginal Provisional Government, 'Towards Aboriginal Sovereignty' (1990), available at www.apg.org.au/files/towards.pdf.

Atkinson, Wayne, 'Not One Iota, of Land Justice: Reflections on the Yorta Yorta Native Title Claim 1994–2001', (2001) 5(6) *Indigenous Law Bulletin* available at www.austlii.edu.au/au/journals/ILB/2001/12.html.

Australian Indigenous Law Review www.austlii.edu.au/au/journals/AILR.

Australian Law Reform Commission, *The Recognition of Aboriginal Customary Laws*, Report 31 (1986), chs 3–4, available at www.austlii.edu.au/au/other/alrc/publications/reports/31.

Indigenous Law Bulletin www.austlii.edu.au/au/journals/ILB/.

Law Reform Commission of Western Australia, *Aboriginal Customary Law in Western Australia: Thematic Summaries of Community Consultations*, (2005), ch.1, available at www.lrc.justice.wa.gov.au/094g.html.

National Native Title Tribunal available at www.nntt.gov.au.

New South Wales Law Reform Commission (2000), 'Aboriginal Customary Law', *Report on Sentencing: Aboriginal Offenders*, Project 96, Chapter 3, available at www.lawlink.nsw.gov.au/lrc.nsf/pages/r96chp3.

Northern Territory Law Reform Committee, *Report of the Committee of Inquiry Into Aboriginal Customary Law* (2003), available at www.nt.gov.au/justice/docs/lawmake/ntlrc_final_report.pdf.

Reilly, Alexander, 'Reading the Race Power: A Hermeneutic Analysis', (1999) 23(2) *Melbourne University Law Review* 19, 4.

Strelein, Lisa, 'Extinguishment and the Nature of Native Title, *Fejo v Northern Territory*', in Native Title Research Unit (1999), Issues Paper 27, *Land, Rights, Laws: Issues of Native Title*, available at http://ntru.aiatsis.gov.au/ntpapers/ip27web.pdf.

Tehan, Maureen, 'A Hope Disillusioned, an Opportunity Lost? Reflections on Common Law Native Title and Ten Years of the *Native Title Act*', (2003) 27(2) *Melbourne University Law Review* 19.

United Nations Declaration of Rights of Indigenous People, available at www.iwgia.org/sw248.asp.

ONLINE RESOURCES FOR THIS CHAPTER

The following resources are available online at www.oup.com.au/orc/cwl2e
- Flashcard glossary
- Multiple choice questions

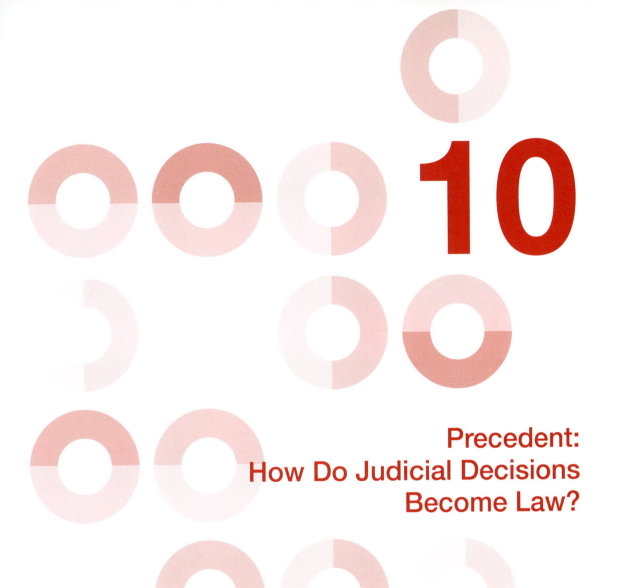

10

Precedent: How Do Judicial Decisions Become Law?

WHAT WE WILL COVER IN THIS CHAPTER:

- The basic principles of precedent and how it is used
- The benefits and problems associated with using precedent
- Which parts of a case are used as precedent
- Application of precedent within the court hierarchy
- How to determine the precedent value of the decisions of particular courts
- Circumstances where courts will depart from their own previous decisions
- How judges view their role in creating precedent
- How to read and analyse a case, and apply precedent

Recommended approach to learning this topic

To begin, it is best to set aside any prior knowledge you may have on case law from watching television or studying at school. This is because often when we have a little bit of knowledge on a topic, we can read less attentively (or skim over the material) because we believe we already know it. Precedent has quite subtle intricacies, and so this chapter needs to be read carefully. It may be useful, once you have done an initial read of the chapter, to find a random case to read (or one that you have to read for your studies this semester). As you read it, you can give thought to ratio and obiter, and to the approach to judging that is evident in the judgment. You can also prepare a case note on it. Then it is worth reading the chapter again to gain a stronger grasp on the topic and be ready to tackle some precedent exercises. The Online Resource Centre also contains some extra exercises.

KEY TERMS

Case law = decisions where courts apply and interpret a statute. It is also sometimes used to generically refer to all court decisions, likely as a result of those in civil law systems referring to all court decisions as case law (which is unsurprising given all court decisions relate to their codified law).

Common law = decisions where courts apply a principle developed by previous courts (also used in other senses, see Chapter 5 for these).

Decision = judgment = case law = written court findings on a particular legal dispute.

Judicial activism = an approach to judging where the judge, when faced with a situation where the law is unclear or unjust, will develop and create new law to enable justice to be done.

Judicial formalism = an approach to judging which maintains the role of the judge is to apply law and not make it, even where this may result in injustice in certain case scenarios.

Majority judgment = decision of a court with more than one judge sitting, containing the decision that most judges agreed on.

Minority judgment = decision of a court with more than one judge sitting, containing the views of a judge or judges, who disagreed with ('dissented' from) the majority view.

Obiter dicta = comments made by judges in judgments which are not essential to the particular case but which are useful to explain the court's reasoning.

Precedent = **stare decisis** = following the decision of a higher court, or a previous court, in a case where similar law applies, and/or which has similar facts.

Ratio decidendi = the key point of the case, the answer to the key issue posed in a case, the part of the judgment that is used as a precedent in later cases.

1: Introduction to precedent

What does 'precedent' mean?

A 'precedent' is a previous case that is being used in the present case to guide the court. 'Precedents' are a series of past cases that are relevant to a particular legal issue.

The late Justice Lionel Murphy said of precedent: 'The doctrine is that whenever you are faced with a decision, you always follow what the last person who was faced with the same decision did. It is a doctrine eminently suitable for a nation overwhelmingly populated by sheep'.[1]

Another term for precedent is the Latin term *stare decisis*, which means to abide by or adhere to a decision. It is the common law principle that courts are to follow binding precedents and not upset settled points of law.

Where did the concept come from?

The practical roots of precedent are found in thirteenth century England, when the royal judges visited counties across the kingdom, deciding matters on a case-by-case basis according to the relevant 'law' or custom in each area, using a 'jury' of people who knew the facts and could explain the law relevant to the case. On their return to Westminster, the royal judges discussed the cases they had decided in the various feuds. Over time, they formed opinions on which 'laws' they thought were fair and reasonable, and preferred to apply those. They would also, as a matter of courtesy, align their decisions with one another. This was the origin of precedent.

In the eighteenth century Sir William Blackstone, a professor of English law at Oxford University, studied the multitude of legal judgments that had been handed down, and attempted to classify them into legal principles. He was followed by a number of legal writers who wrote books ('treatises' or 'monographs') identifying

---

[1] LK Murphy, 'The Responsibility of Judges', Opening Address at the First National Conference of Labor Lawyers, 29 June 1979, in G Evans (ed) 'Law Politics and the Labor Movement' (1980) *Legal Service Bulletin*, Victoria.

legal principles in specific categories of law. Many of these categories, such as criminal law and property law, remain today. Australia, as with other English colonies, adopted the doctrine of precedent into its fledgling legal system. Precedent remains an important concept in the Australian legal system.

Advantages of precedent

- **Legal development** – Having precedent facilitates the development of a coherent body of legal principles that can be used in the future.
- **Not arbitrary** – Courts have to use reason and logic in applying the law, and so their decisions are not merely arbitrary.
- **Fairness** – Court decisions (and therefore precedents) are freely available to everyone to read and understand, and so this is transparent and fair.
- **Flexibility** – Courts have some degree of flexibility in implementing and interpreting precedents.
- **Certainty** – Lawyers have to advise their clients on the law, and if there is a precedent the lawyer knows will be followed by the courts, then the lawyer is able to advise the client with some degree of certainty as to what the law is, and what would be the result if the matter went to court.
- **Efficiency** – Where both parties to a dispute are relatively certain about the law on point in their case, they can realistically and efficiently negotiate to settle their dispute by weighing up what they are likely to get if they went to court.

Disadvantages of precedent

- **Injustice** – Every case is different, and so it is unjust to simply apply the same reasoning as in a past case. This injustice is difficult to fix because only a superior court, faced with a case that raises the unjust precedent, can overrule the precedent.
- **Manipulation** – Judges who hear the same type of cases can have a disproportionate role in the development of an area of law. Judges may manipulate precedents in order to achieve the outcomes they consider appropriate in the circumstances of the case. The process is not as black and white and value-free as it may seem on its face.
- **Uncertainty** – It can be difficult to work out what the applicable precedent is from any given case, and how general the principle from the case can be stated. We just don't know how a case is going to be treated until it is used in a future case.
- **Multiple judgments** – In cases heard before more than one judge, those judges may issue a single judgment together or they may issue one each. If their judgments show different lines of reasoning to arrive at the same outcome, what then is the precedent from the case?

> **TIP**
> Students often get confused between the words 'judgement' and 'judgment'. Legal culture in most Australian states has a strong preference for the following spelling convention: while the general term 'judgement', such as making a judgement about how much money we need, or how unreasonably a friend may have acted, may have an 'e' in it, a court's judgment does not.

2: Key concepts in the law of precedent

Ratio decidendi: The main point of the case

When we read a judgment we are looking for the *ratio decidendi*, which is the ground or reason for the decision, that is, the main point of the case. It is only the ratio of a case that is binding. When the ratio of a present case is used in a future case, it becomes a precedent.

How do we find the ratio? The easiest way is by asking oneself – what are the key legal issue(s) in this case? The way the court answers this legal question, and the reasoning it uses, will be the ratio, or if there is more than one legal issue, rationes.

At what level of generality should the ratio be stated? Should it be narrow, based on the facts of the case itself, or should it be stated more broadly as a general principle of law? For example with *Donoghue v Stevenson*,[2] one could narrowly state that a manufacturer of an opaque ginger beer bottle owes a duty of care to the end consumer to make sure the bottles are washed and checked to make sure there are no snails in the bottom of them. Or one could more broadly state a principle that a manufacturer of consumer goods owes a duty of care to the end consumer to ensure they contain no foreign or unintended contaminants. The court in the case itself would merely have stated its decision based on the case at hand, but the scope and generality of the ratio is worked out in the ensuing cases where the ratio is sought to be applied.

Obiter dicta: Judicial comments in passing

Judgments often reason by commenting on how the present case compares to other scenarios and cases. These comments are not strictly relevant to the outcome of the case, and are called *obiter dicta*.

For example in *Cooper* (2007),[3] the Court considered whether a website operator who provided a searchable database of links to sites where free music could be downloaded had infringed copyright law. Justice Branson, in her reasoning, drew an analogy to other search engines such as Google, saying 'Google is a general purpose web engine rather than a website designed to facilitate the downloading of music files'. Clearly this case was not about Google, and so this is obiter comment.

Where the obiter is directly relevant to the situation that arises in a future case, and has been stated by a superior court, such as the High Court, it may be very convincing because it indicates how the High Court would deal with that other scenario or situation, should it come before it. Indeed sometimes superior courts will include whole summaries of the law in their judgments, and identify gaps and how they would fill them. They usually do this where they anticipate future litigation because of a hole or gap in existing precedent, but are unable to fill that hole or gap because the present case does not specifically raise it.

TIP
Typically you will just see *ratio decidendi* and *obiter dicta* referred to simply as 'ratio' and 'obiter'.

---

2 [1932] AC 562.

3 *Cooper v Universal Music Australia Pty Ltd* (2007) 71 IPR 1, 10.

> ### Exercise: Finding ratio and obiter
>
> Read the following hypothetical judgment.
>
> > This is a case about the right to claim on insurance for a loss from a safe box where the person who stole the money used a key. In circumstances where the defendant did not know, and could not have known, that a copy of the key had been made and was going to be used, the defendant cannot be denied the right to claim on insurance for the loss. However, had the defendant left the key in an obvious place for the cleaner to find, then the defendant may have been denied such a right.
>
> Can you identify the ratio and the obiter?
>
> The ratio is that an insured person may claim for loss from a safe box where they did not know and could not have known that someone had obtained a copy of the key. The obiter is that, if a case arose where the insured person left the key in an obvious place, then the right to claim may be denied. Can you see how, if this judgment was of a superior court and you had a case where you acted for the insurance company, and the insured person had left the key on a hook next to the safe, you might use the obiter comment from this case in arguing that your client had the right to refuse the claim?

3: Applying precedent

The main point about applying precedents, and what makes them so much fun to work with, is that they are often open to different interpretations, and those different interpretations can give different results. In this way, precedents can be used as a tool by lawyers to support an argument that achieves a positive outcome for the client.

Where and how is precedent used?

Precedent is mainly used in courts. Tribunals are also bound by court precedent,[4] but they do not use decisions of previous tribunals as a precedent. In arbitration, it depends on the agreement between the parties as to which law applies.

When a case comes before a court, the court must decide on the facts, the relevant law, and then apply the law to the facts.

The lawyers for the parties in any particular case will refer the court to past cases that they believe are materially similar to the present case, and try to convince the judge to follow the reasoning in those past decisions that are in their favour. If a decision is not in their favour, they will try to convince the judge that the decision is somehow materially different from the present case, and that it therefore does not apply.

Judges must decide which facts presented are important (the material facts) and then which party has stated the relevant law correctly. In doing so they use a relatively consistent set of terminology:

> **TIP**
> If you are not sure what a tribunal is, or what arbitration is, see Chapter 4.

---

4   See *Federal Commissioner of Taxation v Salenger* (1988) 81 ALR 25 in relation to the Administrative Appeals Tribunal being bound to follow the decisions of courts. The only exception is where there are two conflicting court decisions on point, in which case the tribunal may choose which one to follow.

- **Applied or followed** – this means the case has been successfully used as a precedent, because its reasoning is being applied, or followed, by the court in the later case.
- **Distinguished** – this means the case has not been applied because the court in the later case has found something materially different about it, such that it can be distinguished from the present case, and therefore not applied. This is an important part of precedent, and so it is considered in some detail below.
- **Overruled** – this means that the case is being argued as a precedent in a higher court, and the higher court decides that the reasoning is wrong, and so they overrule it. This means that the case no longer has precedent value. It does not, however, affect the validity of the decision in the case as it affects the original parties to that decision. That is, it does not re-open the previous decision. This is because of the concept of *res judicata,* a Latin term which means 'that which is decided is closed'.
- **Considered** – this means the court has thought about the previous case in making its decision, but has neither followed it nor distinguished it from the present case.
- **Cited** – this means the court has referred to the previous case in its judgment, without actually considering it. For example it may simply cite the previous case as the authority for a certain proposition that is not at issue in the case at hand, but is part of the background to the applicable law.

If one or more of the parties to the case do not agree with the way the law has been used in the decision, they may appeal from it. In that case, the appeal court will receive submissions on questions of law – what law was applied – as opposed to questions of fact, such as whether a person did or did not say or do something. The exception is where there is a serious mistake of fact such as the identity of a person or a date or time. Other mistakes of fact, such as whether a witness should have been believed, are not appellable. The original decision, on appeal, may be:

- **Upheld** – this means that the appeal court agrees with the decision of the lower court, meaning the party that has raised the appeal has lost and the appeal has been dismissed.
- **Reversed** – this means that the appeal court agrees with the arguments raised on appeal – that the decision of the lower court was wrong, and so the party that has raised the appeal has won and the appeal has been allowed.[5]

Whenever you have a case scenario in law school or in legal practice, you will want to find cases that are relevant, and you will want to find out how that particular case has been used by courts in the meantime. If, for example, you find that the case has been overruled, then there is no point in using it. If, however, you find that the case has been applied or followed in multiple cases, you can feel more confident that it is a useful precedent. Fortunately there are case citators and the electronic resource CaseBase, that can help you to search for a particular case and see how it has been used by courts since. See Chapter 6 for more information on this.

---

5 More commonly, judges refer to the appeal as being 'upheld' (successful) or 'dismissed' (unsuccessful).

When are precedents binding?

It is only the *ratio decidendi* of the past case that is used as precedent in future cases. Courts can potentially consider any previous case – from any other court, from any other time. It doesn't matter how old the past case is – it can still be used as a precedent, provided it has not in the meantime been overruled by a superior court, and provided society has not changed to such a point that it is no longer relevant. Decisions can be binding, persuasive, or largely irrelevant:

- **Binding** – this means the court is bound to follow the previous decision – it does not have the discretion to refuse to apply a binding precedent on point. If it does so, it is likely that the decision will be appealed to a higher court.

    Courts are only bound by the decisions of courts above them in the same judicial hierarchy. In Australia, because the High Court sits at the apex of each of the nine judicial hierarchies, all decisions of the High Court are binding. The nine judicial hierarchies in Australia are: Federal Courts, Victorian Courts, Western Australian Courts, South Australian Courts, Queensland Courts, New South Wales Courts, Tasmanian Courts, Australian Capital Territory Courts, and Northern Territory Courts. Each of these is a separate judicial hierarchy. Therefore, for example, the County Court of Victoria is not in the same judicial hierarchy as the Federal Court of Australia and Federal Court decisions do not bind it (see page 95 on the Australian court hierarchies).

    There have been some exceptions, where a decision was held to not be binding even though the court is technically above it in the judicial hierarchy. An example is *Valentine v Eid*,[6] where a Supreme Court judge stated that the District Court does not bind the Local Court, because both courts are 'inferior' in the sense that their decisions are not reported – they are not courts of record. They both make instantaneous decisions and do not have the luxury of systematically considering all precedents on point before making a decision.

- **Persuasive** – this means the court, while not strictly bound to follow the previous decision, because it is not a decision of a court higher than it in the same judicial hierarchy, is likely to do so because of its persuasiveness.

    For example the precedent of a state Supreme Court can be highly persuasive in another state Supreme Court. Also, decisions of the English House of Lords can be persuasive because of the reputation that the judges of that Court have for superior legal reasoning.

- **Largely irrelevant** – although technically any previous decision could potentially be used as a precedent in a present case, some previous decisions will be largely irrelevant.

    For example the decision of a court in Tokyo is likely to be largely irrelevant to a Local Court decision in South Australia. Similarly, the decision of the High Court in Calcutta (India) may be specifically on point to a decision in the Perth Local Court, and it may be raised because it is a common law system like Australia, but it is unlikely to carry much weight in Australia.

---

6   (1992) 27 NSWLR 615.

What about previous decisions of the same court?

We know that decisions of courts higher up in the same judicial hierarchy are binding, and decisions lower are not. What about previous decisions which are from the same court as the one in which the previous decision is being used? Are they binding? For example is the Supreme Court of the Northern Territory bound by previous decisions of the Supreme Court of the Northern Territory?

The general rule is that it depends on whether the previous decision was made by a single judge, or by a full court (more than one judge of the same court). A full court decision will bind a single judge, but a full court has the power to depart from the previous decision of a single judge, or of a previous full court.[7] A single judge may also depart from the previous decision of a single judge.[8] However, in all cases the decision to depart from the reasoning in a previous case will not be undertaken lightly.[9]

What about precedents from appeal courts?

It can be difficult to find the ratio, which is used as precedent, in appeal decisions. This is because there are typically three, five, or seven judges sitting, and they may not all issue the one judgment in the case. Here is some terminology used in appeal judgments:

- **Unanimous** – this means that the full bench, that is all the judges hearing the case, arrived at the same outcome by sufficiently similar reasoning that they were willing to issue a single, unanimous judgment.
- **Majority** – where the judges were not unanimous, there will typically be a majority – this is because appeal cases are always heard before an odd number of judges. The decision of the majority of the judges is known as the majority judgment.
- **Minority/dissenting** – conversely to a majority judgment, there will be one or more judges who are in the minority, or who dissent from the view of the majority. The judgments of these judges are known as minority or dissenting judgments.
- **Joint** – this is where two or more judges write one judgment between them. A joint judgment may be a unanimous, majority or minority judgment, depending how many judges join together.
- **Individual** – this is where a judge writes his or her own judgment.

---

7   Cases where courts have departed from their previous decisions include the High Court in *John v Federal Commissioner of Taxation* (1989) 166 CLR 417; the Federal Court in *Department of Immigration and Multicultural Affairs v Singh* (2000) 98 FCR 469; and *Chamberlain v R* (1983) 72 FLR 1.

8   *La Macchia v Minister for Primary Industries and Energy* (1992) 110 ALR 201, 204, (Burchett J). It has also been held that the Federal Magistrates Court is not bound by a decision of a single judge of the Federal Court: *NAAT v Minister for Immigration, Multicultural and Indigenous Affairs* (2002) 170 FLR 177.

9   *John v Federal Commissioner of Taxation* (1989) 166 CLR 417.

From a precedent perspective, a joint judgment is more persuasive than an individual judgment, and a unanimous decision has the highest precedent value, because all judges shared the same reasoning. Otherwise, the precedent value will depend on the number of judges in the majority – if it is a High Court decision, and only one judge is in the minority, then it is still a strong decision. It gets complicated, however, when the High Court has four judges in the majority and three in the minority, which is what happened in the *Wik* decision (see p. 264 on this judicial decision).[10] Each of the four judges in the majority reached the same outcome using different reasoning, and this makes finding a ratio, to be used as a precedent, difficult if not impossible. The choice is either to reduce the various judgments down to the lowest common denominator and call that the ratio, or declare that there is simply no identifiable ratio from the decision at all.

Further difficulty is created where, during an appeal heard before three, five or seven judges, a judge dies, and the remainder of judges are evenly divided. The outcome for the particular case is determined by statute,[11] such as affirming the decision of the lower court, or deciding according to the views of the chief justice, but the outcome for precedent purposes is less clear. Should it be treated as a binding High Court precedent, or should it be neutral in terms of precedent value, since there was no real majority view? Justices Gummow and Hayne, in *Re Wakim; Ex parte McNally*,[12] considered that the decision of an equally divided court 'established no principle or precedent having authority in this Court'.

How are precedents avoided or distinguished?

Often lawyers will be faced with legal precedents that do not support their client's case, and they will attempt to 'distinguish' or avoid them. The reality is that no two cases are identical, and this gives some scope for lawyers to find material differences, or significant differences, which can be used to argue that the precedent should not apply. This is the most common method of avoiding a precedent – distinguishing a case on fact.

Superior courts have more leeway in avoiding precedents. For example they may find that the precedent was wrongly decided (*per incurium*), in that it did not consider (or wrongly interprted) a relevant case or legal principle. They may also say that the precedent should no longer apply, due to changed social conditions, or that to apply the precedent would create a massive amount of litigation and therefore the precedent should be narrowly construed (this is often referred to as the 'floodgates' argument – the risk that the decision will open the floodgates and swamp the courts with cases). The reasoning here is essentially one of policy – courts, being unelected, frequently leave the resolution of matters of policy to the legislature and refuse to determine them in court.

---

10   *The Wik Peoples v The State of Queensland* (1996) 187 CLR 1.

11   See for example *Judiciary Act 1903* (Cth) s 23.

12   (1999) 198 CLR 511, 570.

4: Judicial approaches to precedent

Although technically judges are not supposed to make law – under the separation of powers doctrine, the role of the courts is to apply the law, not make it – in practice judges (usually in higher courts) do make law. Courts engage in judicial law making when they identify and fill a gap in the law, and when they refuse to apply precedent for some reason. The way that a particular judge approaches the judicial function will depend on that judge's views on what a judge's role in society is, or should be. As human beings, we inherently have a view, even if we don't realise it. What is your inherent view? Read the 'judging scenario' below to find out.

Exercise: Judging Sophie

You are a judge in Thailand. You hear the facts of the case, which are as follows.

> Sophie went to Thailand in January 2010 to help with setting up teaching in schools that had been built since the tsunami in 2004. Her involvement included helping to unload and distribute supplies, and teach the local teachers how to use teaching equipment. Sophie completed her three months of voluntary work in April 2010.
>
> Sophie arrived at Bangkok International Airport, checked her bag in and got her boarding pass. When she was sitting reading a book at the departure gate, two officials approached her and asked her to follow them.
>
> Sophie has been charged with drug trafficking as a result of heroin found in the outside pockets of her backpack.
>
> Sophie says that she has never touched drugs in her life, that she only came to the country as a volunteer to help their people, and that she most certainly did not put the drugs in her bag, and does not know how they came to be there.
>
> Sophie is also able to produce a series of videotapes which cover the entire three month period of her stay in Thailand. These videotapes were made by a television company for a show called 'Big Sister', which paid for her flight over in return for being able to video her every minute of every day. The video footage shows clearly that she did not receive any drugs or put them in her bag, so they must have been put in her bag by someone else when she was out 'in the field' distributing supplies, or otherwise after she checked in her bag at the airport.

The relevant statute provides:

> Any person who attempts to pass Thai borders with drugs on their person or in their baggage is liable for drug trafficking. This offence carries a mandatory death sentence.
>
> Under this provision, fault and intention are not necessary – it is sufficient that the person has evidenced an intention to leave Thailand and that they have drugs on their person or in their baggage. Sophie's checking in and getting her boarding pass was evidence of her intention to leave Thailand, and the finding of drugs in her baggage was also clearly evidenced.

As a judge, what would you do?

If you applied the law and sentenced Sophie to death, then your approach to judging is formalist, and if you made an exception on the basis that she could prove that she did not personally put the drugs in her bag or know of them, then your approach to judging is activist. What these terms mean is explained below. But first we'll start with a look at historical approaches to judging, so you can see where they came from.

To make law or not to make law?

The approach to judging in Australia followed the modern English system, which was strictly legalist, in the sense of just applying the 'black letter' law (written words on the paper) rather than some arbitrary notion of justice. You will also see this under the traditional approaches to statutory interpretation, discussed in Chapter 11. The traditional approach is well aligned with the doctrine of the separation of powers doctrine, under which parliament makes the law, the executive arm of government puts it into effect and the judiciary applies it to specific cases. The judge's role is declaratory, meaning they are there to declare the law as it is and not to make new law – that is parliament's job. This is known as the *declaratory theory* of the judicial function.

The rationale for judges making law, and not just declaring it, arises because of gaps in the statutes or the limitations in the doctrine of precedent – the doctrine of precedent was too rigid to flex where society changed its views on what should be legal, and could result in injustice in certain fact situations, or result in twisted reasoning and illogical distinctions in applying the law so as to avoid creating such injustice. The view was that judges would manipulate precedent and create artificial distinctions between cases in order to arrive at a 'right' outcome without seeming to have made law. It could be argued that this is itself a kind of judicial law making. Indeed it has only been since the 1970s that judges in Australia have admitted that what they do in applying the law involves a degree of making it. Judges prefer to be viewed as applying the objective law and not their own subjective personal opinions. Also, in a democratic system, only elected representatives of the people, the parliament, should make law.

TIP
In practice, lower courts have little opportunity to make law, as their role is limited. Judicial law making is largely relevant to appeal courts, where arguments are raised on issues of law.

Legal correctness

Legal correctness is founded on the precept that the law can be set out in a series of rules, principles, definitions and exceptions, to which there will always be a single correct answer to the legal issue. The law must be consistent and timeless in its correctness. A decision is wrongly decided if it is inconsistent with a body of already established decisions.

The modern extension of the doctrine of legal correctness is the concept of black-letter law. The proponents are rule oriented and avoid speculation as to the policy implications of applying the law in a strict way. Legal correctness is predictable, secure, and provides a framework for the consistent operation of laws – the answer to every question is in the law.

Legal formalism

Legal formalism is a philosophy about the proper role of the judiciary. It extols a formal and strict separation of powers doctrine, between parliament as the law makers, and the judiciary as the law appliers.

Legal formalists take a textual approach – they apply the words of the law. A legal formalist will take the law and apply it to a specific fact situation, without considering whether the outcome is fair or just. It is not the role of the judge to apply social conscience or general feelings of fairness – it is the role of the judge to apply the law. If the law is unfair or unjust, then it is parliament's role to amend it. Until such time as parliament does amend unfair laws, the courts must continue to apply the unfair laws.

Sir Owen Dixon, when he was sworn in as Chief Justice of the High Court in 1952, made the classic statement on legal formalism:

> Close adherence to legal reasoning is the only way to maintain the confidence of all parties in federal conflicts. It may be that the court is thought to be excessively legalistic. I should be sorry to think that it is anything else. There is no safer guide to judicial decisions in great conflict than a strict and complete legalism.[13]

He added to this three years later in saying that courts should not deliberately abandon long-accepted legal principles in the name of justice or social necessity or social convenience, but simply on the basis of precedent.[14]

Similarly, Justice Gibbs of the High Court held in 1980:

> If the law is settled, it is our duty to apply it, not to abrogate it. It is for the parliament, whose members are the elected representatives of the people, to change the established rule if they consider it to be undesirable, and not for the judges, unelected and unrepresentative, to determine not what is, but what ought to be the law.[15]

Legal formalism was the standard of Australian courts until the 1970s, when legal realism and activism gained support. Since then the balance has swung back towards legal formalism.

TIP
It may be difficult to tell the difference between legal correctness and legal formalism. The difference is that legal correctness focuses on the law and how it should be applied in following precedent, whereas legal formalism focuses on the judge and how they should approach their role. Under both, the outcome is that the answer to all legal questions is in the law itself, and notions such as social policy, equity and justice have no role to play.

TIP
There is a long line of 'black letter', legalist, formalist, non-activist judges. They include Justices Dixon, Gibbs, Kitto, Barwick, Gleeson, Gibbs, Hayne, and Heydon.

Legal realism

Legal realism stands in contrast to legal formalism in that it assesses how judges *really* judge, rather than pontificating about how they *should*.

The earliest legal realist was an American, Oliver Wendell Holmes. He focused on what judges actually do rather than the theory that supports their reasoning. He looked, very practically, at how a judge actually went about deciding the case, through examining the judge's history and character, and how this affected how the

---

13 (1952) 85 CLR, xi.

14 Sir Owen Dixon, 'Concerning Judicial Method', (1956) 26 *Australian Law Journal* 468, 469–7.

15 *Australian Conservation Foundation Inc v Commonwealth* (1980) 146 CLR 439, 529.

judge made his or her decision. This was jurimetrics, which is the study of judges and the extraneous factors that affect their decision making, such as moral and religious attitudes, and attitudes on policy issues such as same sex relationships.

Julius Stone, an Australian legal scholar, referred to 'leeways of choice' open to judges. He said that there is a degree of flexibility and discretion in the way judges use previous cases, legal principles, and public policy. Courts do not merely follow precedent, but exercise leeways of choice in reaching their decisions.[16] Indeed judges are able to achieve an outcome that they subjectively believe is right by couching their decision in objective language that refers to legal principles and rules. Therefore, when learning law, we should not merely look at the ratio of the case, but we should recognise that if the court that heard the case had been differently constituted, the outcome may have been different.

Stone said of *Donoghue v Stevenson*,[17] the case of manufacturer responsibility for a snail in a ginger beer bottle, that a 'leeway of choice' – in this case's artificial reasoning – had been used to distinguish precedent on point in order to achieve a policy outcome, which was to make manufacturer's responsible, despite the lack of contract between the end consumer and the manufacturer, through creating a duty of care.[18]

Legal realists criticise the judicial approach of making decisions appear as if they are an inevitable application of the law to the facts; they prefer that judges be transparent and accountable for their decisions by expressly acknowledging the fact that they are exercising a choice and not merely mechanically applying law like a mathematical equation. That is, to state in the judgment what the policy considerations are, and how they were taken into account in making the decision.

Stone's theory of legal realism showed how false the declaratory theory of law was in practice, and this paved the way for a new breed of activist judges who often quoted Stone's writings in fashioning new law. Justice Michael Kirby, arguably the most famous High Court judge from the past decade, was mentored by Julius Stone. In 1977 he described the judicial task:

> To pretend that the task is purely mechanical, strictly formal, and wholly predictable may result in a few observers who love fairy stories sleeping better at night. But it does not enhance the legal system. It is not honest. It is fundamentally incompatible with the creative element of the common law.[19]

Since Justice Kirby's retirement in 2009, the present High Court provides a mostly formalist approach to judicial decision making. How then, does the current High Court reconcile its legal formalist stance with the real injustice in a legal dispute? The judges state in their judgments that they recognise their role is to apply the law, but

---

16 Julius Stone, *The Province and Function of Law: Law as Logic, Justice and Social Control*, Harvard University Press (1950).

17 [1932] AC 562.

18 Julius Stone, above n 16.

19 Michael Kirby, 'Judicial Activities' (Hamlyn Lectures 2003), Sweet & Maxwell, London (2004), 68ff

they also recognise that this created inequity in the particular case at hand, and it would be wise for parliament to consider amending the relevant law to remove the inequity.

Judicial activism

Activist judges view their role as promoting justice. This is in contrast to legal formalists, who view their role as promoting certainty. An activist judge will apply clear and relevant law unless they believe it creates injustice or is otherwise outdated or flawed. They will then either ignore that law or principle, or specifically state that it is unacceptable and replace it with a new law or principle. Judicial activist judges take a contextual approach, in contrast to the textual approach of the legal formalists – that is, they take into account not only the word of the law but also the context in which the law operates and the ramifications that its application can have. In practice judges who are higher up in the judicial hierarchy are more likely to be activist than those in the lower, inferior courts. This is because precedents bind courts lower in the same judicial hierarchy, so judges in the lower courts do not have as much scope to be activist as the higher courts do.

It is arguable that some judges see a degree of judicial activism as necessary. In an ideal world, parliament would respond immediately to gaps in the law and redraft laws to remove the scope for injustice. But we do not live in an ideal world. Only a certain amount of legislation can be passed in the limited number of parliament sitting days each year, so priorities must be assigned to legislative changes. Members of parliament may be more focused on their mandate, political ideology or political expediency. They may put more energy into new laws that will heighten their chances of re-election than checking each and every law for potential injustices. There may be some unglamorous areas of law that escape parliament's attention altogether, or where the legislation is ambiguous and poorly drafted, and in these cases judicial activism may be necessary.

There are, however, inherent limits to judicial activism. Fundamentally, courts are limited to interpreting the law that arises in the cases that happen to come before them. The High Court has some scope to pick and choose between cases it hears, because parties to cases must apply for special leave to appeal, but in other courts there is an inherent right for parties to appeal. But even the High Court cannot make pronouncements of new law in the way that parliament can – there must be a case before them that raises issues about the particular law it is prepared to change.

In making decisions, appeal courts will focus on the one hand, on the case before them, and on the other hand, on the general ramifications that their decision will have in the development of the law. If they are going to reject applicable precedent, they have to give reasons in their judgment for this – otherwise they risk the judgment being labelled *per incuriam* (through want of care) for failing to take into account the relevant law on point. The court will refer in its judgment to the fact that it has considered the relevant case, but reach an alternative verdict by holding that the case is 'distinguished'. For example a case will be distinguished where the facts are

TIP
Past and present activist judges, whose judgments you are likely to read in your legal studies, include Justice Mason, Justice Murphy (Lionel), Justice Kirby, and Lord Denning from England. Also Justice Brennan's judgment in the *Mabo* decision (discussed in Chapter 9) has been described as activist.

materially different from the one before it, or the decision does not bind it because it is a decision from a court in a different hierarchy.

Justice Kirby proposed four 'guideposts' as the boundaries on judicial activism,[20] to ensure that judicial law making is principled and not merely idiosyncratic:

1 **Opportunity** – Judges must be given the opportunity to address gaps in the law by having a case that raises such issue before them. There is a great deal of chance involved, because many worthy appeals may be abandoned due to financial constraints or general unwillingness by the litigant to further appeal.
2 **Need** – Judges need to have a certain amount of judicial humility and restraint, and have a sense of when there is really a need for judicial activism. It has to be where it is believed that reform is unlikely to happen if it is left to parliament, such that there is a legal vacuum. It also has to be believed that the issue is relatively discrete and manageable, and the relevant community value is clear and lasting.
3 **Inclination** – Judges have to be inclined to change the law. Some judges are conservative and some are activist, and that is how it is. But even judges whose inclinations are rule-based and whose personal predilections are conservative will occasionally strike a topic upon which the sense of justice in the particular facts moves them to be activist. So they are stimulated by a sense of grave injustice in the law as it stands in relation to the particular case, and feel compelled to change it.
4 **Methodology** – A new protocol or methodology for the judicial function is needed, where judges identify leeways of choice and use social and economic data to assess the likely consequences of the choice being made either way, and also receive input from selected interest groups.

Reflection

What do you think about former Justice Kirby's fourth 'guidepost' for judicial activism? Do you agree that judges should receive input from data and interested groups? Or do you think that what Kirby proposes is akin to judges becoming one-person law reform commissions?

There are several arguments against judicial activism. They include:

1 Fundamentally, the role of judges in our society is to apply the law, not to make it. A core principle of democracy is that those who make the law are elected by the people. Judges are appointed, and not elected, and therefore do not have a mandate from the people to make law.
2 Judges can only make a decision on the case before them. They do not have the time or the luxury for extensive consideration of the ricochet effects that a new legal principle in one area may have on other areas, nor do they have the extensive

---

20 Michael Kirby, 'Judicial Activism', Bar Association of India Lecture 1997, New Delhi Hilton Hotel, January 1997.

procedures and timeframes for consultation with all relevant stakeholders that law reform commissions, and parliamentary commissions of inquiry, have. The activist judge may make a decision that creates a better justice in the case at hand, but it may have the effect of changing another area of law in a way that is neither intended nor beneficial.

3   It can be argued that judges have a relatively limited experience of life, and are somewhat isolated from the community at large. What they think is the community value may in fact only be their own value, or the value of the limited circle of people with whom they communicate. This may be compared to politicians who sit in parliament, who focus on assessing the popular will, and are thus more in touch with social and community values and preferences. (A contrary argument is that, particularly in criminal courts, judges hear evidence and see a daily parade of behaviour quite unlike their own.)

4   Changing the law by judges will create uncertainty and unpredictability in the law, and this can only result in more cases being litigated, because it is difficult for lawyers to advise clients with any degree of certainty about how the case would be decided if it went to court, and such a consideration is key in deciding whether to settle out of court or not.

5   Judicial law making is retrospective – it makes a decision as to the legality of past conduct. Individuals and companies act according to what they understand the law to be, and if a court in the future creates a new law that makes what they did today wrong, this is unfair for them.

6   Judicial law making is instant – judges cannot, like parliament, say that a particular law will take effect at some stage in the future, when the administrative bodies and processes for handling the new law are all in place. For example after *Mabo*, parliament had to create a legislative regime to support native title law. They relied on the view that Crown leases extinguished native title, and then in 1996 the *Wik* decision changed that, and so parliament had to amend the legislation according to its more conservative interpretation of the Act.

It is arguable that even legal formalists will sometimes 'make' law, despite their professed belief that they are only there to apply the law, and any unjust law should be changed by the legislature and not the judiciary. They do this by being selective as to which precedents they apply, or by otherwise presenting precedents in a manner that supports their view of the proposed outcome. This is 'acceptable' judicial law making, or what Parkinson describes as the difference between legitimate 'judicial development' as opposed to judicial activism.[21]

For example the largely formalist High Court in *Thomas v Mowbray*[22] held that amendments to Division 104 of the *Criminal Code* (Cth) which confer power on some courts to make interim control orders imposing restrictions upon individuals in order to protect the public from a terrorist act, is constitutionally valid. This may

---

21 Patrick Parkinson, *Tradition and Change in Australian Law*, Lawbook Co, Sydney, 4th edn (2010), 210–11.

22 (2007) 233 CLR 307.

be contrasted to *Australian Communist Party v Commonwealth*[23] where the High Court held that the *Communist Party Dissolution Act 1950* (Cth) – which dissolved the Australian Communist Party by declaring it an unlawful association, in order to protect the public from the threat of communism – was constitutionally invalid.

5: Problem solving using precedent

How can I solve a legal problem using precedent?

The first thing to do is to analyse the legal problem, to identify the issues of law involved. Then, find cases that are relevant to those legal issues (and statutes, but that is covered in a separate chapter). Decisions that are from courts high in the judicial hierarchy, and which are majority or unanimous decisions, are preferred. It is essential that you establish which precedents are binding, persuasive, or largely irrelevant in the court in which your case will be heard. Once you have identified your strongest cases, check the case citator, or CaseBase, to ensure that they have not been overruled and are thus still good law.

If you find that there are simply no cases on point, perhaps because the legal problem involves a novel or developing area of law, then you may need to reason by analogy. For example if the standard rule in paper transactions in business is that an offer which expires on a weekend or public holiday may be accepted on the next business day without being outside the offer period, and you had an e-commerce deal which raised an issue of whether payment was made in time, where the date it fell due was a public holiday, you could reason by analogy that the same rule that applies to contractual offers should apply to contractual payments.

GO ONLINE
For answers to this exercise.

Exercise: Which precedent takes precedence?

Assume you are acting for a client in the District Court (or the County Court, in Victoria) in the state in which you study law. Which case would you prefer to put forward as a precedent for the Court to use? Tick the box next to your choice.

A New Zealand decision with the exact same facts as this case	OR	A decision of the Supreme Court in your state on the same general issue of law
A 1998 decision in the Federal Court exercising original jurisdiction	OR	An appellate decision of the High Court from 1920
A decision from a week ago by another judge in the same court	OR	A decision by the District (or County) Court in another state which has been applied regularly for years
The decision of a lower court in your state on similar facts but with less money at issue	OR	Obiter comments in a related decision by a single judge in the High Court
A House of Lords decision which held exactly what you want to be held for your client	OR	A decision of the Coroner's Court in your state which found exactly what you want for your client

---

23 (1951) 83 CLR 1.

In depth: Court use of precedents

Courts use cases selectively and interpret them in a number of ways. There is no set formula for the application of precedent.

Read the excerpts from the following High Court judgment, and then answer the questions below.

Taiapa v R

(2009) 240 CLR 95

The applicant, Dion Robert Taiapa, was convicted in the Supreme Court of Queensland of the offences of carrying on the business of unlawful trafficking in a dangerous drug, methylamphetamine, and the possession of a quantity of that drug. The factual basis of the Crown case was not in issue at the trial. It was the applicant's case that he did the acts that were said to constitute the offences in order to save himself and members of his family from threatened serious harm. He contended that he was not criminally responsible for his admitted conduct in collecting and transporting a substantial quantity of methylamphetamine because he had acted under compulsion within the meaning of s 31(1)(d) of the Criminal Code (Q).

The trial judge withdrew the issue of compulsion from the jury's consideration, thereby making the applicant's conviction of each offence inevitable. The applicant appealed against his conviction on the ground that the trial judge erred in not leaving compulsion for the jury's determination.

The Court of Appeal of the Supreme Court of Queensland (Keane and Fraser JJA and Lyons J) dismissed the appeal. The applicant applied out of time for special leave to appeal from the order of the Court of Appeal. For the reasons that follow, the application for special leave to appeal should be granted, but the appeal should be dismissed.

Section 31(1)(d) of the Criminal Code provides that a person is not criminally responsible for an act or omission:

'when –

(i) the person does or omits to do the act in order to save himself or herself or another person, or his or her property or the property of another person, from serious harm or detriment threatened to be inflicted by some person in a position to carry out the threat; and

(ii) the person doing the act or making the omission reasonably believes he or she or the other person is unable otherwise to escape the carrying out of the threat; and

(iii) doing the act or making the omission is reasonably proportionate to the harm or detriment threatened.'

While it is conventional to describe s 31(1)(d) as providing the defence of compulsion, it is well-settled that if there is some evidence capable of raising the issue, the legal or persuasive burden is on the Crown to exclude the proposition that the accused was acting under compulsion beyond reasonable doubt – that is, exclude any reasonable possibility that the proposition is true. The question is whether, on the version of events most favourable to the accused that is suggested by the evidence, a jury acting reasonably might fail to be satisfied beyond reasonable doubt that the accused was not acting under compulsion. It was not disputed that the onus on that question – an evidential burden – is on the accused. It is the accused who must tender evidence, or point to prosecution evidence, to that effect.

The facts

The applicant was arrested on 22 July 2006. The police intercepted the vehicle in which he, his co-accused, Robert Ackers, and a young woman were travelling. They located 364.213 grams of methylamphetamine in the course of searching the vehicle. The estimated value of the drug, which varied according to how it was to be sold, was between $459 000 and $1.15 million.

The applicant had a history of marijuana and cocaine use. In the period from 1999 to 2002 he had dealt in drugs to support his use of them. His suppliers were two men named Tony and Salvatore. By 2002 he had accumulated a debt to Tony and Salvatore of $60 000. At around this time the applicant was convicted of trafficking in drugs and sentenced to a term of six years imprisonment. He was released on parole in December 2005. Following his release the applicant and his de facto wife, Kristy Jarvis, moved to Cairns and took up residence in premises in Kidston Street.

On the evening of 29 May 2006 the applicant and Ms Jarvis were at home in the Kidston Street premises. At around 8.00 pm the applicant answered a knock on the front door. As he opened the door he was seized around the neck and forced backwards into the lounge room by Tony, who was holding a gun to his face. Salvatore was also present. The two men demanded the repayment of their money. They instructed the applicant not to go to the police and threatened that, if he did, he or Kristy would be shot.

Kristy was pregnant with the applicant's child at the time of this confrontation. The applicant and she agreed that she should leave Cairns and return to her home on the Gold Coast. The applicant was not able to accompany her under the terms of his parole order. The applicant moved out of the Kidston Street premises and into premises in Alfio Street, Cairns. Ultimately the applicant sought his mother's assistance and she agreed to lend him $29 000 in cash, which she had on hand.

On Saturday 15 July Tony and Salvatore confronted the applicant at the Alfio Street premises. They threatened him, again, at gunpoint and taunted him over his unsuccessful attempt to evade them. They rejected his offer to repay them $29 000 immediately and the balance by instalments. They told the applicant that in addition to giving them $29 000 he was to travel to Sydney and collect something for them. They told the applicant not to try anything stupid or that he, Kristy and his mother would pay for it.

The following evening Tony and Salvatore returned to the Alfio Street premises. On this occasion they instructed the applicant that he was to meet a man in Ettalong, which is a township to the north of Sydney, at 11.00 pm on Thursday 20 July and to collect two parcels from him. The applicant understood that the parcels would contain prohibited drugs.

The applicant did not have a driver's licence at the time of these events. He asked Robert Ackers to drive him to Ettalong. The two of them and a female friend embarked on the trip. The applicant collected the parcels from the man at the nominated time and place. He collected the money from his mother's premises the following day. He was apprehended in the course of the return journey.

The applicant was asked about his reasons for failing to report the threats to the police or to his parole officer. In the course of the cross-examination the following exchange took place between the trial judge and the applicant:

'But you understand that the police – it's their job to investigate criminal behaviour and bring people who have committed it before the Court and have them dealt with?'

'Yeah, I would have had to go – there's – oh, protection – there was always protection there, but there's no guarantee if I was to put in – be put in police protection, that I'd still be safe … I wasn't going to take that risk at all to go to the police ….

Secondly, that these blokes, they're not your every day drug dealers. They're – like there's drug dealers and then there's drug dealers. These blokes are up there.'

The Crown Prosecutor put to the applicant that he had made a choice to engage in the world of drug dealing rather than to take other options that were available to him. The applicant responded saying:

'In my position the only option for me was – for me was to do as I was told. I didn't want anyone else getting hurt. I didn't – I especially didn't want a bullet in my head.'

The Court of Appeal's reasons

The trial judge withdrew the issue of compulsion from the jury because there was no evidence that Tony and Salvatore were in a position to execute the threats at the time the applicant engaged in the conduct. The Court of Appeal held that following amendments to s 31(1) in 1997 it is sufficient that the compulsion operating on the mind of the accused is a present threat of future harm.

The Court turned to consider the requirement of s 31(1)(d)(ii). It observed by reference to its earlier decision in *R v Smith* [2005] 2 Qd R 69 that the question is 'whether the [accused] reasonably believed that he was unable otherwise to escape the carrying out of the threat'.

In this context the Court of Appeal said:

'It is a feature of civilised society that one may render threats of personal violence ineffective by seeking the help of agencies of law enforcement … If it is to be asserted by an accused that he or she reasonably believed that there was no other means of avoiding a threat than complying with an unlawful demand then the reasonableness of that belief must be considered in the light of the other alternatives available to the accused. That necessarily means that the accused must have a reasonable basis for believing that the law and its enforcement agencies cannot afford protection from the threat.'

In the Court of Appeal's opinion there was no evidentiary basis for a conclusion that the applicant's lack of faith in the ability of the police to defeat the threat was based on reasonable grounds and for this reason the trial judge had been right not to leave the issue of compulsion to the jury.

Reasonable belief is a familiar concept in the context of criminal responsibility in the Criminal Code and at common law. As Stephen J observed in *Marwey v The Queen* (1977) 138 CLR 630, to ask whether a person has a reasonable belief is not different in substance from asking whether a person has reasonable grounds for belief. The recognition that the determination of whether grounds are reasonable is a factual question for the jury is not to overlook the anterior question of law, which is whether there is any material upon which it would be open to a reasonable jury to determine the issue favourably to the accused.

In concluding that there was no evidence that would justify the jury in finding as a reasonable possibility that there were reasonable grounds for the applicant's belief, the Court of Appeal took as its starting point the assumption stated by King CJ in *R v Brown* (1986) 43 SASR 33:

'The ordinary way in which a citizen renders ineffective criminal intimidation is to report the intimidators and to seek the protection of the police. That must be assumed, under ordinary circumstances, to be an effective means of neutralizing intimidation. If it were not so, society would be at the mercy of criminals who could force pawns to do their criminal work by means of intimidation.'

In *Brown* King CJ considered that in the circumstances of that case the accused's failure to report a threat to the police and to seek the protection of the police for himself and his son was fatal to the common law defence of duress. His Honour acknowledged that there may be circumstances in which a failure to seek the protection of the police would not deprive an accused of the defence. His Honour cited the judgment of the English Court of Appeal in *R v Hudson* [1971] 2 QB 202 in this respect.

Hudson was a case in which two teenage girls were convicted of perjury. At their trial Hudson gave evidence that she had been approached by a group of men, including one Farrell, who had a reputation for violence. Farrell warned her that if she gave truthful evidence they would get her and 'cut her up'. Hudson passed on the warning to her co-accused. Farrell had been present in the public gallery of the court when each of the accused gave the perjured evidence. The trial judge withdrew duress from the jury because there had not been an immediate threat capable of being carried out: the recorder and police officers were present and able to afford protection to the girls at the time each gave her evidence. The Court of Appeal observed:

'it is always open to the Crown to prove that the accused failed to avail himself of some opportunity which was reasonably open to him to render the threat ineffective … the jury should have regard to his age and circumstances, and to any risks to him which may be involved in the course of action relied upon.'

In *Hudson* the failure of teenage girls to seek police protection in circumstances in which their potential assailant was present in court at the time they gave their perjured evidence was held not to negate an arguable case that their conduct was excused by duress.

Morris v The Queen [2006] WASCA 142 was a case in the Court of Appeal of Western Australia on the defence of duress under s 10.2(2) of the *Criminal Code* (Cth) in which the accused failed to report threats to the police. Her Honour drew on the observations of Gleeson CJ in *Rogers* (1996) 86 A Crim R 542 [where] a prisoner sought to rely on the defence to excuse his escape from lawful custody to avoid threatened lethal violence. At issue was the availability of the common law defence of necessity, which shares features in common with the defence of duress. Gleeson CJ rejected the view that the defence of necessity required proof of urgency and immediacy as technical elements. Instead he favoured treating these as factual considerations relevant to the accused person's belief and the reasonableness of the grounds for it. His Honour's observations set out above are pertinent to the consideration of the issue raised in this application.

Conclusion

The circumstance that the demands and threats made by Tony and Salvatore were made with a gun and were accompanied by instructions not to report the matter to the police does not support the reasonableness of the applicant's belief that he had no option other than to comply with the demands in order to escape the carrying out of the threats. The applicant had, as he acknowledged, ample opportunity to seek the assistance of the police. He offered three reasons for his failure to do so. The first was that he did not have sufficient information to enable the police to identify Tony and Salvatore. The second was that he did not believe that police protection was '100 per cent safe'. The third was that Tony and Salvatore were 'not your every day drug dealers' and were unlikely to fall into a booby trap. The Court of Appeal said that the police could have placed surveillance on the applicant's premises and that a controlled delivery of the drugs to Tony and Salvatore might have led to their arrest… The applicant's belief that he did not have sufficient information to enable the police to identify Tony and Salvatore does not take into account that the police may have known more about these men than he thought that they did or that the police may have been able to find out more about them than he thought they could. In any event, it does not explain his failure to report the matter to the police in order to seek their protection. The applicant's belief that police protection may not be 100 per cent safe provided no basis for a reasoned conclusion that it was not. The Court of Appeal was correct to hold that no jury, acting reasonably, could fail to be satisfied beyond reasonable doubt that there were not reasonable grounds for the applicant's belief within s 31(1)(d)(ii) … the application for special leave to appeal is granted; and the appeal is dismissed.

Exercise: Application of precedents

In the preceding judgment, what use did the Court make of the following decisions?

1 *Marwey v The Queen* (1977) 138 CLR 630
2 *R v Brown* (1986) 43 SASR 33
3 *R v Hudson* [1971] 2 QB 202
4 *Morris v The Queen* [2006] WASCA 142
5 *R v Rogers* (1996) 86 A Crim R 542

Hint: remember Part 3 (p. 286), where we considered the different terminology used for the application of precedents (e.g. cited, considered, applied/followed, distinguished, overruled).

Do you agree with the reasoning of the Court, and the use of the above precedents?

DISCUSSION QUESTIONS

1 The common law system uses legislation plus case precedents, while the civil law system puts everything into codes. Which system do you think is best?
2 How can obiter be used to create new law?
3 What are your views on judicial activism? Do you think it is a good thing, or would we be better off without it?
4 To what extent do you think that winning a case depends on having a good lawyer who can manipulate precedents on point to support the case?

WEBLINKS AND FURTHER READING

Crawford, James and Opeskin, Brian, *Australian Courts of Law*, Oxford University Press, South Melbourne, 4th edn (2004).

Heydon, Dyson, 'Judicial Activism and the Death of the Rule of Law' (2003) 23 *Australian Bar Review* 110.

Kirby, Michael, 'Judicial Activism? A Riposte to the Counter-reformation' (2004) 24 *Australian Bar Review* 219.

MacAdam, Alastair I and Pyke, John, *Judicial Reasoning and the Doctrine of Precedent in Australia*, Butterworths, Sydney (1998).

Mason, Anthony, 'The Use and Abuse of Precedent' (1988) 4 *Australian Bar Review* 93.

ONLINE RESOURCES FOR THIS CHAPTER

The following resources are available online at www.oup.com.au/orc/cwl2e
- Answers to exercise: 'Which precedent takes precedence?' (p. 298)
- Flashcard glossary
- Multiple choice questions

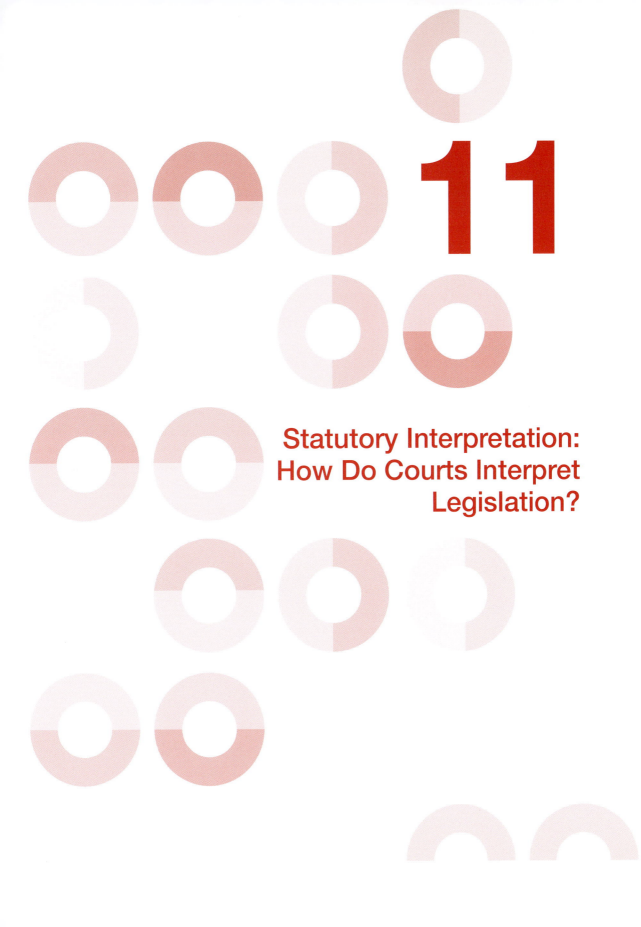

11

Statutory Interpretation: How Do Courts Interpret Legislation?

WHAT WE WILL COVER IN THIS CHAPTER:

- What statutory interpretation means and why it is an important skill to have
- How modern courts interpret legislation using Interpretation Acts
- Traditional approaches to statutory interpretation and the role they still play
- Which parts of a piece of legislation are used in interpretation
- How to use other documents in interpreting legislation
- How to work out the purpose of a piece of legislation
- How to solve problem questions on statutory interpretation
- How case analysis and statutory interpretation go together in practice

Recommended approach to learning this topic

Start with a general reading of the chapter. Then find a copy of an Interpretation Act – most logically the one in the state or territory in which you are studying – and read it. It may be helpful to refer back to the chapter as you go, so you know which parts of the Act are the most important. Once you feel confident you understand the basic rules, try reading a statute and working out what it means. It will be more enjoyable if you read a statute on a subject you are personally interested in. The easiest way is to visit www.austlii.edu.au and locate the alphabetical list of consolidated Acts in your state or territory, and then look at the names of the Acts to find one of interest. Read it, and see if you can work out what it is saying. Getting comfortable with reading legislation takes practice, so the more you read of it, the easier it will become. The next step is to interpret a statute in a particular context. You can tackle the problem questions towards the end of the chapter, and use the Online Resource Centre for further practice exercises.

KEY TERMS

Consolidated legislation/ consolidated Acts = Acts put together over time, showing the current law with all applicable amendments incorporated

Jurisdiction = the power of a court to hear a matter, the territorial area in which a statute applies

Maxim = a guiding principle

Regulation = a rule by government administration (public servants), where the power to make the rule is delegated from parliament

Section = provision = a rule in an Act

Statute = Act = legislation (all the same thing)

TIP
Have you forgotten what a statute is? See Chapter Three on 'Sources of Law'.

1: Introduction to statutory interpretation

What is statutory interpretation?

'Statutory interpretation' is, in plain English, working out what legislation means. In practice it also means applying that meaning in a specific context: a case. A synonym for statutory interpretation is 'statutory construction'. Typically the phrase 'statutory interpretation' is used where we work out the meaning of a word or phrase, while 'statutory construction' is used when we construe the meaning of a whole section or provision.

There are various approaches to statutory interpretation. This chapter will cover the modern statutory approach (section 1 of this chapter) and the traditional common law approaches (section 2). These approaches are not mutually exclusive – they can operate together. Indeed, in practice statutory interpretation is a rich process. It is not entirely technical and involves a degree of judicial discretion.

TIP

Statutory interpretation covers all types of legislation, both primary legislation (Acts, statutes) and delegated legislation (regulations, rules, ordinances, and by-laws).

Why is statutory interpretation an important skill?

Statutes regulate almost every area of our lives. Wherever you are and whatever you are doing, statutes are applicable to you. If you are living with flatmates in rented accommodation and travel to university by car, you are subject to statutes on residential tenancy, traffic, car registration and insurance, as well as assault, defamation, and occupational health and safety laws, to name a few. Statutes are everywhere!

Statutory interpretation as a legal skill has become more important in recent decades, because there has been a proliferation in legislation. Taking consolidated federal legislation as an example, there are presently 1315 primary Acts and 582 regulations. Add to this the number of statutes in each Australian state and territory, and there are thousands of statutes in force today. The rate of increase has also increased – in 1949 there were 87 new statutes, in 1977 there were 161 new statutes, and in 1997 there were 222 new statutes.[1] In 2009 there were 136 statutes enacted plus 394 regulations.

Judges know how important statutory interpretation is. The Chief Justice of New South Wales, Spigelman CJ, has said that 'the law of statutory interpretation has become the most important single aspect of legal practice. Significant areas of law are determined entirely by statute. No area of the law has escaped statutory modification.'[2] Justice Kirby recently remarked that 'we have well and truly entered the age of statutes ... but we still need to wean lawyers from their love affair with the common law and judicial writings.'[3] Statutory interpretation is also important

---

1 Justice Michael Kirby 'ALJ @ 80: Past, Present and Future', Address at a conference to celebrate the 80th anniversary of the Australian Law Journal, Sydney, 16 March 2007, www.hcourt.gov.au/speeches/kirbyj/kirbyj_16mar07.pdf.

2 Spigelman CJ, 'Statutory Interpretation and Human Rights', Address to the Pacific Judicial Conference, Vanuatu, 26 July 2005, www.lawlink.nsw.gov.au/lawlink/Supreme_Court/ll_sc.nsf/pages/SCO_speech_spigelman260705.

3 Kirby, above n 1, 31–2.

because in all areas, legislation is the superior source of law. This means that if there is a conflict between a statute and a judicial decision, the statute will prevail. This situation arises from two judicial doctrines – parliamentary sovereignty, and separation of powers. See Chapter 4 for a full discussion of these concepts.

The effect of the doctrine of parliamentary sovereignty is that even though there are three arms of government, parliament is slightly more powerful than the other two when it comes to law making, as law making is its primary role. The effect of the separation of powers doctrine is that parliament has the primary power to make law, while the primary power of the judiciary is interpreting the law. This means that *legislation is superior to cases*.

To every rule there are exceptions, and there are two exceptions to the primacy of statutes:

1 Where the courts determine that parliament has no power to make a particular law, that law is *ultra vires* – beyond power. For example if the High Court rules that a federal statute is unconstitutional, that renders the federal statute invalid, and the federal parliament cannot get around this decision by re-enacting the same piece of legislation, or a piece of legislation claiming to prevail over any High Court decision to the contrary. Here, the High Court decision is superior to the federal piece of legislation.
2 Where parliament has not complied with the proper process of making law, the legislation may be invalid. (See Chapter 3 for the process for the passage of bills through parliament.)

Therefore, where the principal role of courts is to interpret the law – and there is a proliferation of legislation – statutory interpretation is perhaps the most important function of the courts today.

Why is statutory interpretation difficult?

Statutes have been referred to as the 'most repellent form of written expression known to man'.[4] The difficulty with statutes is that all law is made through the written word, and words can have multiple meanings. The written word is an essential but imprecise means of communication. The primary responsibility of a judge becomes one of resolving a dispute over meaning of words. Let's take a case example.

Moore v Hubbard

[1935] VLR 95

Hubbard placed a placard on an electric light post in a Victorian suburb without the consent of the owner, the State Electricity Commission. According to section 5(10) of the *Police Offences Act 1928* (Vic), it was an offence to place any placard

---

4   Sir Carleton Allen, 'The Literature of the Law', *Aspects of Justice*, Stevens & Sons Ltd, London, (1958), 284.

or other document on, or to write or paint on or otherwise deface, 'any house or building or any wall, fence, lamp post or gate without the consent of the occupier or without the consent of the owner if there is no person in actual occupation thereof'. Accordingly Hubbard was charged with an offence under this Act. At first instance he was convicted, but he appealed on the basis that there was no offence unless the post on which the placard was put was a lamp post. This was not a lamp post but an electric light post. In determining whether to read 'lamp post' as one word or two, Justice MacFarlane said that because the other things listed in the section, like house, building, wall and fence, were all structures, it would not make sense to read 'lamp' and 'post' as two words; that would mean including in the section a 'lamp', which was not a structure, and was something foreign to the class of things dealt with in the sub-section. Therefore he considered it should be read it as one term, 'lamp post', and accordingly the conviction against Hubbard was quashed.

In the above example, it was obvious that parliament meant to cover all kinds of posts, and indeed it is likely that the drafters of the statute did not foresee that street lighting would become electrified. But the statute did not say 'posts', it said 'lamp posts', and although that was probably only to distinguish light posts from other posts such as fence posts, the fact is that the statute gave a specific term, and that was what was applied. This example demonstrates that the written word is an imprecise means of communication, and also explains why statutes end up being drafted in convoluted language, in an attempt to cover every possibility.

How do courts interpret statutes?

Courts look at the wording of the statute itself, and they use cases that have already considered the meaning of the words in the statute. They might also look at identical words in another statute, if the context is similar.

Example: Interaction between cases and statutes

Case analysis and statutory interpretation go together in practice, although we are covering them in two separate chapters. The picture in Figure 11.1 may help to explain the interaction between case law and statute law:

We will use a hypothetical analogy of the crime of assault to explain the interaction. Suppose there is no law on assault. Let's say a case about a person punching another person comes before the court. The court has no statute to apply, so it creates a principle that direct intentional physical contact amounts to assault. We have one brick in our wall of law. Next a case about a person who hit another person with a bat comes before the court. The batter argues that there was no direct physical contact ('the bat did it'). The court reasons that the direct intentional contact using an instrument also amounts to assault, and a second brick is now in place. Then a case where a person threw a book at another person's head comes before the court. The thrower argues there was no direct contact with an instrument ('I was on the other side of the room'). The court reasons that the intentional contact was through the force of the person, and amounts to assault. Another brick is added to the wall. The next case concerns a person who makes a poisoned birthday cake for their flatmate, and so on. Our wall of bricks is a wall of law which we describe as 'at common law', meaning that it was created by the courts, piece by piece, in applying reasoning to cases.

Let's say parliament decides to introduce legislation on assault. Parliament may do this in order to change the common law, or simply codify it, which means bringing together the principles from a number of cases into the one statute. The legislation is like a slab of concrete on top of the wall.

The next case to come before the court will require the court to apply the statute before any of the cases in the brick wall below it. This is because of the doctrine of parliamentary sovereignty. However, the court may be able to use the cases from before the statute, if the statute is codifying the law of assault rather than modifying it. As will be seen below (see 'statutory presumptions') there is a presumption that if a phrase which has been given a certain meaning by the courts is used in a statute without a new meaning given to it, the old meaning applies. When the court decides the first case since the statute came into force, there is a new brick on top of the slab of concrete, and we call this 'case law', which is a specific type of common law, where courts are interpreting legislation. The bricks will continue to amass until parliament introduces amending legislation, which would be a new slab on top of the next lot of bricks.

Therefore in practice lawyers use both cases and statutes to interpret statutes. This chapter focuses only on the rules of statutory interpretation. The rules of precedent are the subject of Chapter 10.

Under the doctrine of separation of powers the role of the courts is to apply the law, which means interpreting any applicable legislation on point. This limits the role of the courts – they cannot improve, rewrite, or develop a statute. Even if there appear to be good reasons not to follow the statute, they must interpret the statute so as to give effect to what parliament wants. The challenge is that what parliament wants is not always clear and obvious.

In interpreting statutes, the courts identify and resolve ambiguity, and they do this by following certain rules. There is no rule book as such. Instead there is interpretation legislation – statutes that tell courts how to interpret legislation. (This immediately raises the question of what legislation interprets the interpretation legislation!) In addition to the interpretation legislation, the courts themselves have developed a range of rules. In the toolbox of statutory interpretation the primary tools are those found in the interpretation legislation, and the secondary tools are those developed by the courts. In practice the courts use both.

FIGURE 11.1 DEPICTION OF CASE AND STATUTE DEVELOPMENT

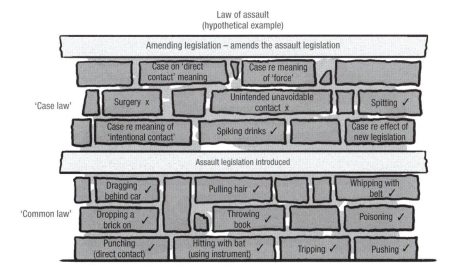

2: Modern statutory approach

The modern approach is for courts to interpret statutes in accordance with rules made by parliament.

Interpretation Acts

In each state and territory, and at the Commonwealth level, parliaments have enacted interpretation legislation. The Interpretation Acts are:

- *Acts Interpretation Act 1901* (Cth)
- *Legislation Act 2001* (ACT)
- *Interpretation Act 1987* (NSW)
- *Interpretation of Legislation Act 1984* (Vic)
- *Acts Interpretation Act 1965* (Qld)
- *Interpretation Act 1984* (WA)
- *Acts Interpretation Act 1915* (SA)
- *Acts Interpretation Act 1931* (Tas)
- *Interpretation Act 1978* (NT).

In this chapter, references to 'the Commonwealth Act', 'the New South Wales Act' and so on mean the above statutes.

Which Interpretation Act should you use? That depends on which statute you are interpreting. If you are interpreting a Commonwealth Act, you should use the Commonwealth Interpretation Act; if you are interpreting a Queensland Act, you should use the Queensland interpretation legislation.

The Interpretation Acts tell us how to discover and give effect to the intention of the legislature in enacting the particular piece of legislation. The main rule is giving effect to the purpose of the legislation. The Interpretation Acts also give us generic provisions – rules that apply across all other legislation. These two roles of Interpretation Acts are discussed below.

The main rule: Giving effect to the purpose of the legislation

Each of the Interpretation Acts speaks of giving effect to the purpose of the legislation. Section 15AA of the Commonwealth Act provides:

> In the interpretation of a provision of an Act, a construction that would promote the purpose or object underlying the Act (whether that purpose or object is expressly stated in the Act or not) shall be preferred to a construction that would not promote that purpose or object.

This is curious wording. It does not specifically say courts must adopt an interpretation that applies the purpose of the Act; it only says that an interpretation that promotes the purpose is preferred to one that does not. An ordinary interpretation of this would be that if you had two or more possible ways to interpret a particular provision, you should choose the one that promotes the purpose of the Act over the one that doesn't.

Virtually the same words are used in the state and territory interpretation legislation: s 33 (NSW); s 35(a) (Vic); s 18 (WA); s 8A (Tas); and s 62A (NT). Justice McHugh, when a judge of the Supreme Court of NSW, considered the NSW equivalent provision in *Kingston v Keprose Pty Ltd* (1987) 11 NSWLR 404. He said, at 423 of the judgment:

> In most cases the grammatical meaning of a provision will give effect to the purpose of the legislation. A search for the grammatical meaning still constitutes the starting point. But if the grammatical meaning of a provision does not give effect to the purpose of the legislation, the grammatical meaning cannot prevail. It must give way to the construction which will promote the purpose or object of the Act. The *Acts Interpretation Act 1901* (Cth), s 15AA and the *Interpretation Act 1987* (NSW), s 33, both require this approach to statutory construction.

So Justice McHugh is saying that courts must find the purpose of the Act, and give effect to it. This appears on its face to go beyond what the provision actually says, but it has been cited with support in numerous cases in the 20 years since.[5]

However, it is not always simply a case of finding the purpose and interpreting the provision to give effect to it. Some Acts may pursue more than one purpose, and may reflect a political compromise between competing purposes. In *Carr v Western Australia* (2007) 239 ALR 415, Chief Justice Gleeson of the High Court held in relation to the Western Australian Act:

> That general rule of interpretation, however, may be of little assistance where a statutory provision strikes a balance between competing interests … Legislation rarely pursues a single purpose at all costs … The question then is not: what was the purpose or object underlying the legislation? The question is: how far does the legislation go in pursuit of that purpose or object?

---

5   Including, in Victoria, *Director of Public Prosecutions v Siourtou* [2007] VSCA 233; in Western Australia, *Hewitt v Benale Pty Ltd* [2002] WASCA 163; in the Northern Territory, *R v Ahwan* [2005] NTSC 47 and *Thompson v Primary Producers Improvers Pty Ltd* [2004] NTCA 12; and in the High Court in relation to Western Australia, *Carr v Western Australia* (2007) 239 ALR 415.

The above discussion applies to the Commonwealth, New South Wales, Victorian, Western Australian, Tasmanian and Northern Territory Acts. For the remaining legislatures (South Australia, the Australian Capital Territory and Queensland), different words are used. In South Australia, s 22(1) provides that interpretation may go beyond the purpose of the Act.[6]

The Australian Capital Territory and Queensland have virtually identical provisions (in s 139(1) of the Australian Capital Territory Act, and s 14A(1) of the Queensland Act) saying that 'the interpretation that would best achieve the purpose of the Act is to be preferred to any other interpretation'.

In *D'Aguilar Gold Ltd v Gympie Eldorado Mining Pty Ltd* [2006] QSC 326 the Supreme Court of Queensland applied s 14A(1) of the Queensland Act, and looked for the interpretation that would be 'more consistent' with the purposes of the Act.

In *Kingsley's Chicken Pty Ltd v Queensland Investment Corporation & Canberra Centre Investments Pty Ltd* [2006] ACTCA 9, the Australian Capital Territory Court of Appeal applied s 139(1) of the Australian Capital Territory Act in determining that the terms 'offer' and 'accepts' in the *Leases Act* should be given their ordinary meaning rather than a technical, legal meaning.

Therefore, although the Queensland and Australian Capital Territory Acts have different wording from that applied by the other seven legislatures in Australia, the common denominator is that *courts consider the purpose of the legislation in working out how to interpret statutory provisions*.

How do courts find the purpose of the Act?

Courts find the purpose of an Act from intrinsic and extrinsic materials.

Intrinsic materials are words used inside the statute itself, like the long title, the preamble, any statement of purpose or objects clause, the division of the Act into Parts and Divisions, headings and schedules.

Extrinsic materials are documents and sources outside, external, and separate to the statute, which may be used to interpret the statute, including second reading speeches, law reform commission reports, and international conventions.

Using intrinsic materials

This involves looking at the legislation itself to work out what it means. We can use other parts of the Act to interpret a particular provision because statutes are to be read as a whole. This principle was stated by the High Court in *Metropolitan Gas Co v Federated Gas Employees Industrial Union* (1924) 35 CLR 449: 'It is a received canon of interpretation that every passage in a document must be read, not as if it were entirely divorced from its context, but as part of the whole instrument'. The principle that statutory provisions must be read in the context of the statute as a whole has also been included in the Australian Capital Territory Act (s 140).

Parts of the Act that are useful in determining the purpose include:

- **Long title**. This usually appears at the top of the legislation, and is more common in older statutes.

---

6   See Justice Cox in *Burch v South Australia* (1998) 71 SASR 12, 18.

For example the *Aged or Disabled Persons Care Act 1954* (Cth) has a long title which states 'An Act to provide for Assistance by the Commonwealth towards the provision of Care for Aged Persons or Disabled Persons, and for other purposes'.

The use of the long title as a statement of the purpose of legislation is a principle of common law. It has also been included in s 140 of the Australian Capital Territory Act.

- **Objects clause**. This usually appears in one of the first sections, and is more common in recently drafted statutes. Objects clauses are the modern-day equivalent of a long title. They have more flexibility than a long title in that they can include subsections and lists, whereas a long title must express the purpose in a single sentence.

For example s 2.1 of the *Aged Care Act 1997* (Cth) lists ten objects of the legislation, including to provide funding of aged care, to facilitate access to aged care services without discrimination, and to protect recipients of aged care services.

It is useful here to refer to intrinsic materials that may be useful in interpreting the meaning of words used more generally, not just when ascertaining the purpose:

- **Definition sections**. It is common for Acts to have a definition section near the beginning. A long Act can include definition sections at the beginning of each part of the Act. As well as being a principle of common law, some of the Interpretation Acts specifically refer to the use of the definition sections in working out the meaning of words in the Act: see s 156 (ACT); s 6 (NSW); ss 32A and 32AA (Qld); s 19(1) (SA); and s 17 (NT).
- **Headings**. Headings of parts, divisions and subdivisions into which an Act is divided are used in interpretation. See s 13(1) (Cth); s 35(1) (NSW); s 36(1) (Vic); s 14(1) (Qld); s 32(1) (WA); s 19(1) (SA); s 6(2) (Tas); and s 55(1) (NT).
- **Schedules**. These are used where detailed information is needed to support a provision, usually tables, lists, or templates. They form part of the Act: see s 13(2) (Cth); s 35(1) (NSW); s 36(1) (Vic); s 31(2) (WA); s 19(1) (SA); s 6(3) (Tas); and s 55(1) (NT).

However, some parts of an Act are not used in interpretation. They have been included when drafting the legislation not because parliament wants them to have effect, but because they help to make the legislation more readable and easily understandable. They include:

- **Headings to individual sections**. These are excluded in all legislatures apart from Queensland, which provides in s 14(2) that from 1991 headings are part of the Act. Otherwise section headings have no interpretative value: see s 13(3) (Cth); s 35(2) (NSW); s 36(3) (Vic); s 32(2) (WA); s 19(1) (SA); and s 6(4) (Tas).
- **Notes in the margins, footnotes, endnotes**. These are not part of the Act. See s 13(3) (Cth); s 36(3) (Vic); s 14(7) (Qld); s 32(2) (WA); s 6(4) (Tas); and s 55(6) (NT).

In addition to using intrinsic material (the legislation), there will be occasions when courts will wish to have reference to extrinsic materials in order to determine the Act's purpose.

Using extrinsic materials

It is common in our society to interpret documents by referring to other documents. The most common extrinsic material used in everyday life is the dictionary – if you cannot work out what a word means, you are likely to look it up there. In interpreting legislation it is also possible to discover the meaning or purpose of legislation by referring to materials that are extrinsic to it. Only after the legislation has been considered in full and by itself will the courts do this.

The Interpretation Acts, with the exception of the South Australian Act, give inclusive lists of examples of extrinsic materials that may be used in interpreting legislation. See s 15AB(2) (Cth); s 142 (ACT); s 34(2) (NSW); s 35(b) (Vic); s 14B(3) (Qld); s 19(2) (WA); s 8B(3) (Tas); and s 62B(2) (NT). The lists commonly include:

- explanatory memoranda
- second reading speeches
- records of parliamentary debates (in *Hansard*)
- Law Reform Commission reports
- parliamentary committee reports
- international treaties and agreements.

Take for example *In the Matter of: B v B: Family Law Reform Act 1995*.[7] In that case the Full Court of the Family Court was interpreting the *Family Law Reform Act 1995* (Cth), which commenced operation in June 1996. The court used the explanatory memoranda to the Act, two parliamentary committee reports, as well as *Hansard*, which contains second reading speeches from both the House of Representatives and the Senate.

Each of the Interpretation Acts (except SA) specifies when the courts may use extrinsic materials to assist them in statutory interpretation. The Commonwealth Act provides, under s 15AB(1), that courts *may* refer to extrinsic materials:

(a) to confirm that the meaning of the provision is the ordinary meaning taking into account its context and the underlying purpose of the Act
and
(b) to determine the meaning of the provision when the provision is ambiguous or obscure, or the ordinary meaning leads to a result that is manifestly absurd or unreasonable.

Use of the word 'may' means the provision is discretionary: courts may have use of extrinsic materials, but they do not have to. Similar language to that of the Commonwealth Act is used in s 34(1) (NSW); s 14B(1) (Qld), although in a different order; s 19(1) (WA); s 8B(1) (Tas); and s 62B(1) (NT).

---

7   Appeal No. NA35 of 1996.

Notice the use of the word 'confirm' in s 15AB(1)(a) above. Let's apply what we know so far about statutory interpretation to work out what paragraph (a) means. Looking first to the intrinsic materials, we find there is no definition of the word 'confirm' in the definition section. Consulting a dictionary to find the ordinary meaning of the word, we find that 'confirm' means 'to establish more firmly, to corroborate'. This means we must already think we know what the ordinary meaning is, and we are just confirming it. But what if we find that we are wrong? We can't use the extrinsic materials to change our mind, but only to confirm the meaning we thought they had. We could possibly argue that the meaning is ambiguous, and then use s 15AB(1)(b) to use other extrinsic materials, such as the parliamentary debates, to find out what parliament intended.

This issue was raised in *Re Australian Federation of Construction Contractors; Ex Parte Billing* (1986) 68 ALR 416, where the High Court had to decide whether a second reading speech could be relied upon. The High Court stated that the Commonwealth Act does not permit recourse to the second reading speech unless the provision is 'ambiguous or obscure or in its ordinary meaning leads to a result that is manifestly absurd or is unreasonable'.

The above discussion shows that courts cannot use extrinsic materials whenever they like; they must follow the rules in the legislation setting out when they can refer to them. Also, where extrinsic materials are used, there are limits as to how they are applied. For example they can only be used to interpret the legislation, not to supplant it. As High Court put it in *Re Bolton; Ex Parte Beane* (1987) 162 CLR 514, 'The words of a minister must not be substituted for the text of the law'.

Other limitations include a requirement that the court give consideration to the need to avoid prolonging legal proceedings without compensating advantage. This is contained in s 15AB(3) (Cth); s 141(2) (ACT); s 14B(2) (Qld); s 19(3) (WA); and s 8B(2) (Tas). The Australian Capital Territory Act also refers to the accessibility of the material to the public: s 141(2). What these provisions imply is that the search for the true meaning of a word or phrase, or the true intention of parliament, is not unlimited, and there is the potential that the ambiguity to be resolved by referring to extrinsic material may not justify the cost and time involved.

Exercise: 'Make Poverty History'

Let's assume a young adult woman scrawls 'Make Poverty History' on the back of the toilet door in a public toilet in the Botanic Gardens in Sydney, and is charged under s 8 of the *Graffiti Control Act 2009* (NSW) (not a real Act), which provides 'it is an offence to scrawl graffiti on the wall of a public dwelling'.

There are two preliminary questions to ask yourself before you dive into interpreting the relevant provision. The first is jurisdiction (Does the Act apply in the relevant state?) and the second is commencement (Is the Act in force?). Here, the act took place in Sydney and the relevant Act is a New South Wales Act, so the jurisdictional requirement is met. Also the date of assent of the Act was the 3 March 2009; no particular commencement provision was put in the Act, so as 28 days have passed since the date of assent, it is now in force.

Looking at the provision, we need to work out:

1. Did she 'scrawl' (or paint, or draw, or write)?
2. Was it 'graffiti' (or art, a symbol, message)?
3. Was it on a 'wall' (or door)?
4. Was it a 'public dwelling' (does anyone 'dwell' in a public toilet)?

Although you may already have a good idea of the ordinary meaning of these words, you must first look to the intrinsic materials, that is, the Act itself. If it gives a definition of any of these terms, that is what you must use. If not, you may need to look at extrinsic materials.

Let's assume we do this, and conclude that the woman did scrawl graffiti on a wall, but that it is ambiguous whether a public toilet is a dwelling. We use s 34 of the *Interpretation Act* (NSW), since we are interpreting a piece of New South Wales legislation, which permits us, where the provision is ambiguous or obscure, to refer to the second reading speech in *Hansard*. There is a passage in the speech by the Minister who introduced the bill saying 'we need to prevent hoodlums from loitering in public places and defacing public property. I for one don't want to read obscenities whilst I am using the amenities', to which the recorded response was 'Hear, hear!' from other members of parliament. We therefore conclude that 'public dwelling' was intended by parliament to cover a public toilet.

We check whether our interpretation promotes the purpose of the Act or not, pursuant to s 33 of the New South Wales Act, and refer to the long title of the Act, which is: 'An Act to control graffiti in public places and limit its use'. We therefore conclude it is likely that the young woman will be liable under the section.

GO ONLINE
Go online for a sample answer to the exercise.

Generic provisions

The Interpretation Acts also give us generic provisions, that is, a general rule that applies in all statutes. For example s 5 of the Commonwealth Act says that an Act 'shall come into operation on the twenty-eighth day after the day on which that Act receives the Royal Assent, unless the contrary intention appears in the Act'.

This is a generic provision, because it sets out the general rule that statutes commence 28 days from the date of assent, unless the specific statute itself says otherwise. This saves parliament putting a provision into every statute saying the same thing. If nothing is stated in the particular Act about commencement, then the 28-day rule will apply. (For a more detailed discussion on when Acts commence, see Chapter 3.)

Other generic provisions include:

- **Gender** – 'he' includes 'she' and vice versa. See s 23(a) (Cth); s 145(a) (ACT); s 8(a) (NSW); s 37(a) (Vic); s 32B (Qld); s 10(a) (WA); s 26(a) and (ab) (SA); s 24A (Tas); and s 24(1) (NT).
- **Number** – the singular includes the plural, and the plural includes the singular. This means that 'any person' is read as 'any person or persons'. See s 23(a) (Cth); s 145(b) (ACT); s 8(b) and (c) (NSW); s 37(c) and (d) (Vic); s 32C (Qld); s 10(c) (WA); s 26(b) and (c) (SA); s 24(d) (Tas); and s 24(2) (NT).
- **Time** – if an Act refers to a time, it means the standard or legal time in the place the legislation applies, for example Australian Eastern Standard Time for a New South Wales Act or Australian Central Standard Time in South Australia. See s 36 (Cth); s 7 of the *Standard Time and Summer Time Act 1972* (ACT); s 36 (NSW);

s 4 of the *Summer Time Act 1972* (Vic); and ss 4–5 of the *Standard Time Act 2005* (NT). The Queensland, South Australian, Western Australian and Tasmanian Acts don't mention legal time, but it is reasonable to assume that the legal time in each of these states is applicable. If it is a Commonwealth Act, the time that applies is the legal time in the part of the Commonwealth concerned: s 35 (Cth).

If an Act says that something applies 'at' a certain date, this means it starts at 12.01 am on that date. If it applies 'from' a certain date, that date is excluded. So if something applies *from* 15 January, it applies from 12.01 am on 16 January. Also if the last date to do something falls on a weekend or public holiday, then it can be done on the next business day and still be compliant with the legislation. See s 36 (Cth); s 151 and s 151A (ACT); s 36 (NSW); s 44 (Vic); s 38 (Qld); s 61 (WA); s 27 (SA); s 29 (Tas); and s 28(2) (NT).

- **Distance** – where an Act specifies that something must be, say, 500 km from a certain place, or within 50 km of a certain place, this distance is measured in a straight line along a horizontal plane, 'as the crow flies', not according to distance by driving on roads, which may twist and turn. See s 35 (Cth); s 150 (ACT); s 38 (NSW); s 43 (Vic); s 65 (WA); s 28 (SA); s 28 (Tas); and s 27 (NT). An exception is the Queensland Act, which provides, in s 37, that distance is to be measured along the shortest road ordinarily used for travelling, unless there is a contrary intention.

- **Penalty** – an important generic provision that is not in the Interpretation Acts is s 4AA of the *Crimes Act 1914* (Cth). This section creates a 'penalty unit', and says that unless a contrary intention appears, a penalty unit will be taken to be $110. Individual provisions simply state the number of penalty units that apply, and to calculate a penalty you multiply the number of units by the current value of a penalty unit.

    Similar provisions on penalty units exist in the states and territories. Both Western Australia and South Australia apply the Commonwealth provision. See also s 133 (ACT); s 17 of the *Crimes (Sentencing Procedure) Act 1999* (NSW); ss 5–7 of the *Monetary Units Act 2004* (Vic), which refers to penalty units as 'fee units'; s 5 of the *Penalties and Sentences Act 1992* (Qld); s 4 of the *Penalty Units and Other Penalties Act 1987* (Tas); and s 3 of the *Penalty Units Act 1999* (NT).

- **Meaning of 'may' and 'shall'** – historically, the use of the words 'shall', 'must', 'is required to', 'may', 'can', 'could', 'will', 'it shall be lawful to', and 'if he or she thinks fit' created difficulties for courts from a statutory interpretation point of view. Were these descriptors setting out a mandatory obligation, or discretion? For example if a statute said that a person 'may not' do something, did this mean that they were not allowed to do that thing, or that they may, or may not, at their discretion? This area is known as statutory discretions and obligations, and the confusion has now been resolved in the Interpretation Acts.

    The Interpretation Acts provide that the word 'may' confers a discretion. See s 33(2A) (Cth); s 146(1) (ACT); s 9(1) (NSW); s 45(1) (Vic); s 32CA(1) (Qld); s 56(1) (WA); s 34 (SA); and s 10A(1)(c) (Tas). There is no relevant provision in the Northern Territory Act.

    Conversely, the word 'shall' is mandatory; it must be observed. See s 146(2) (ACT); s 9(2) (NSW); s 45(2) (Vic); s 32CA(2) (Qld); s 56(2) (WA); s 34 (SA);

and s 10A(1)(a) (Tas). There is no specific reference in the Commonwealth or Northern Territory Acts. The Tasmanian Act also specifies that 'is to' and 'are to' are directory: see s 10A(1)(b) (Tas).

In any event, the modern statutory approach can cover statutory discretions and obligations without the need for specific provisions, on the basis that the court will consider whether parliament intended a particular provision to be mandatory or discretionary.[8]

All of our discussion in this chapter so far has involved the modern approach to statutory interpretation, which is to enact statutes that tell us how to interpret other statutes. However, these statutes are not exhaustive – they do not cover everything a court may need to know to interpret a statute. So the approaches to statutory interpretation that the courts developed before the interpretation legislation was enacted, and to fill gaps since, is still used as a secondary approach to statutory interpretation.

3: Traditional common law approaches

Although the modern approach is based on Interpretation Acts, historically that was not the case. Traditionally there were only common law rules that judges used for statutory interpretation. They weren't even 'rules' as such – just techniques the courts developed to guide themselves. They still have some relevance today, because the Interpretation Acts do not cover everything.

Literal approach

The cornerstone of the common law approach to statutory interpretation was the literal approach. The courts would take parliament's words quite literally, applying only what was there. If the meaning of the words was clear then the courts were bound to apply that meaning regardless of the result. This respected the separation of powers doctrine, because the court simply applied the law that parliament made.

One of the best formulations of this principle, the literal approach, is from Justice Higgins in *Amalgamated Society of Engineers v Adelaide Steamship Co Ltd* (1920) 28 CLR 129 (otherwise known as the *Engineer's Case*). Justice Higgins said:

> The fundamental rule of interpretation, to which all others are subordinate, is that a statute is to be expounded according to the intent of the Parliament that made it; and that intention has to be found by an examination of the language used in the statute as a whole. The question is, what does the language mean; and when we find what the language means, in its ordinary and natural sense, it is our duty to obey that meaning, even if we think the result to be inconvenient or impolitic or improbable.

So the literal approach involves working out what the words mean in their natural and ordinary sense and applying that, regardless of the result. This created some problems, because there were occasions where the ordinary meaning of the words

TIP
Keep in mind the idea of a workman with a toolkit. The top layer of the toolbox includes all the things we have covered above, which are provided in the Interpretation Acts. If those tools are not enough to do the job, resort to the second layer of the toolbox. This includes the traditional common law approaches, discussed below.

---

8   See *Project Blue Sky Inc v Australian Broadcasting Authority* (1998) 194 CLR 355.

used, if applied, would create a nonsensical result. An example is *Higgon v O'Dea* [1962] WAR 140. In that case the Supreme Court of Western Australia had to interpret s 84 of the *Police Act 1892* (WA), which penalised every person who knowingly allowed persons under the age of 16 years to enter and remain in any house, shop or room, or any place of public resort that they own. The underlying aim of the statute was to keep children out of pubs (public houses) and places where gambling took place, but if the section is read literally, its effect is to stop any person from letting children into any house. That is clearly silly. Applying the literal rule, the court said it had to apply the ordinary meaning of the words, and if that created a ridiculous outcome, the only solution was for parliament to amend the Act.

The golden rule

The golden rule developed as an exception to the literal rule, allowing courts to modify the ordinary meaning of words where the literal approach caused an absurd result. It was often used to correct errors in legislation. The most famous formulation of this rule comes from *Grey v Pearson* (1857) 6 HL Cas 61, in which Lord Wensleydale stated:

> the grammatical and ordinary sense of the words is to be adhered to, unless that would lead to some absurdity or inconsistency with the rest of the instrument, in which case the grammatical and ordinary sense of the words may be modified, so as to avoid that absurdity or inconsistency, but not farther.

In *Adler v George* [1964] 2 QB 7, s 3 of the *Official Secrets Act 1920* (UK) made it an offence to create an obstruction 'in the vicinity of a prohibited place'. The defendant had obstructed an air force security guard engaged in sentry duty at a royal air force base. He pleaded not guilty on the basis that 'in the vicinity' means nearby, and he was actually in the air force base. The court used the golden rule to interpret 'in the vicinity of' to mean 'in or in the vicinity of' and as a result the defendant was convicted under the Act.

In *R v Allen* (1872) LR 1 CCR 367 the defendant was charged with bigamy under s 57 of the *Offences Against the Person Act 1861* (UK). The legislative definition of bigamy was being married more than once. But any second attempt at marriage would be void, so there was no way a person could legally be 'married' more than once. The court held that the definition meant going through the marriage ceremony more than once.

The mischief rule

The mischief rule developed to resolve ambiguities or inconsistencies arising from the application of the literal rule. Like the golden rule, the mischief rule was only used if applying the literal approach resulted in some ambiguity or inconsistency. The original formulation of the rule in *Heydons Case* (1584) 76 ER 637 was that there were four useful questions the court should ask:

1 What was the law before the making of the Act?
2 What was the mischief and defect that the law did not provide for?

3   What remedy did parliament establish under the Act to correct that mischief or defect?
4   How can the court interpret the legislation so as to correct the mischief or defect according to the true intent of parliament?

In *Smith v Hughes* [1960] 2 All ER 859 the relevant legislation was the *Street Offences Act 1959* (UK), which made it a crime for prostitutes to 'loiter or solicit in the street for the purposes of prostitution'. The defendants pleaded not guilty on the basis that they solicited men from their balconies, so they were not 'in the street'. The court applied the mischief rule, finding that the true intent of parliament was to correct the mischief of harassment from prostitutes, and found the defendants guilty.

How are the common law approaches relevant today?

The literal rule told us that courts should apply the ordinary meaning of words, and courts still seek to do that. What is the ordinary meaning? It is usually the dictionary meaning. It is common for courts to cite dictionaries – see for example *State Chamber of Commerce and Industry v Commonwealth* (1987) 163 CLR 329, where the High Court relied on a definition in the *Macquarie Dictionary* to determine the meaning of 'fringe benefit'.

Some other issues arise. One is that a word may have several current dictionary meanings. Take for example the word 'made', which can mean created, constituted ('what are you made of') or took ('made off with'). These are three quite different meanings. The other issue is that the meaning of words can change over time. For example the word 'terrific' now means something good, but in the past it meant something terrifying – the sinking of the Titanic was a 'terrific' disaster.

So, if you were interpreting a word in a 1923 statute, what meaning would you use – the meaning that existed in 1923, when parliament enacted the statute, or the current meaning? The answer is, the current meaning. For example in *Lake Macquarie Shire Council v Aberdare County Council* (1970) 123 CLR 327 the High Court interpreted the word 'vehicle' from an 1898 Act to include aeroplanes, even though aeroplanes had not been invented until some five years after the Act. This may seem counterintuitive – how could parliament intend a meaning that was not applicable at the time they wrote the statute? The rationale is that the statute continues to apply, and if words in a statute are subject to a different meaning over time then it is up to parliament to amend the legislation. If parliament has not done this, then it must intend the new meaning of the word to apply.

Another lesson from the literal rule for us today is that the ordinary meaning of a word may be a technical or legal meaning. For example in *Fisher v Bell* [1961] 1 QB 394 the legal meaning of the word 'offer' was an issue. A shopkeeper had a flick knife in his shop window. Under the *Restriction of Offensive Weapons Act 1959* (UK) it was illegal to offer for sale or hire a flick knife. A literal approach to 'offer' would have it that the shopkeeper was offering the flick knife for sale by putting it in the window with a price tag on it. However, the court applied the legal contractual meaning of 'offer', whereby the offer takes place when the customer presents the item at the checkout for payment. A mere display of the item in a shop is called an 'invitation to treat'. So the display was not an offer (see Chapter 5).

> **TIP**
> What is the difference between the mischief rule and the modern approach? Many students get confused between these. Both look at the purpose as a tool of statutory interpretation, but the difference is that using the modern approach you can consider the purpose at any time, but under the mischief rule you could only consider the purpose if the literal rule created an ambiguity or uncertainty that could not be resolved through applying the golden rule.

The Australian High Court has indicated that the audience for the Act can be relevant in deciding whether to give words their ordinary meaning, or a technical meaning. In *Herbert Adams Pty Ltd v Federal Commissioner of Taxation* (1932) 47 CLR 222, the relevant legislation referred to 'pastry', the ordinary meaning of which is a range of foods, including desserts, made with pastry – such as pies, and puff pastry – but would not include, for example, chocolate mousse, or ice cream. The High Court was of the view that because the Act was directed to pastry-cooks, it was acceptable to give the word 'pastry' its technical meaning, which covered all sweets, whether or not they included pastry as an ingredient.

More recently Justice Kirby in *Palgo Holdings Pty Ltd v Gowans* (2005) 221 CLR 249 at 266 has made the current approach crystal clear:

> the correct question is not whether a legal or an ordinary meaning should be given to a particular statutory term. Rather, it is what is the natural and ordinary meaning of the language read in its context and with attention to the legislative purpose and available materials that disclose that purpose.

The literal rule therefore gives some guidance to present day courts, in looking for the meanings of words in their ordinary and natural sense.

The golden rule is also used today to modify the ordinary meaning to avoid an absurdity or inconsistency arising from a literal interpretation. Courts consider whether the ordinary meaning of the words gives effect to the purpose or not, and if not, modify the ordinary meaning in order to achieve that purpose. It is assumed that in achieving the purpose of the legislation, the outcome will no longer be absurd or unreasonable.

The mischief rule has been replaced by the modern statutory approach, which attempts to avoid absurdity or ambiguity by reference to the purpose of the Act. The modern statutory approach goes further than the mischief rule did, in allowing the courts to consider the purpose of the legislation even if there is no absurdity or ambiguity arising from a literal reading.

How does the modern statutory approach relate to the traditional common law approaches?

The common law approaches laid the foundation for the modern statutory approach, which involves finding the ordinary meaning of words (as in the literal rule) and taking into account the purpose of the legislation (as in the mischief rule) to ensure, for example, that drafting errors do not prevent parliament's intentions being applied (as in the golden rule). When the modern statutory approach came into effect in the 1980s, the courts were unsure how it related to the traditional common law approaches.

Justice McHugh in *Cole v Director-General of Department of Youth and Community Services* (1987) 7 NSWLR 541 at 549 said that the *Interpretation Act* was really setting aside the literal and golden rules. But the High Court in *Mills v Meeking* (1990) 169 CLR 214, a case that involved s 35 of the Victorian Act, which is equivalent to s 15AA of the Commonwealth Act, said that the modern approach was not merely the mischief rule prevailing. Justice Dawson said:

the requirement that a court look to the purpose or object of the Act is thus more than an instruction to adopt the traditional mischief or purpose rule in preference to the literal rule of construction. The mischief or purpose rule required an ambiguity or inconsistency before a court could have regard to purpose.

Justice Dawson went on to say that the *Interpretation Act* 'requires a court to construe an Act, not to rewrite it, in the light of its purposes'. In other words, the courts must have regard to both the literal words of the Act and the purpose behind it. The purpose cannot be applied to override the actual words used in the statute. Justice McHugh said in *Newcastle City Council v GIO General Limited* (1997) 191 CLR 85 that a court may 'strain' the ordinary meaning of words, but not so as to produce an interpretation that is 'unreasonable or unnatural'.

The common law approaches should properly be seen as the forerunner to the modern statutory approach, and they still have a role to play, but it is of secondary relevance, because *often the modern statutory approach can achieve the same result as the literal, golden and mischief rules but with more flexibility.* For example deviation from a literal interpretation under the common law approaches was only allowed in limited circumstances, and courts did not refer at all to extrinsic materials, but relied solely on an interpretation of the words of the law, taken as a whole. The modern statutory approach is broader and more flexible – and, applied correctly, is more likely to create a result that is reasonable and intended.

In addition to the main common law approaches described above, namely the literal, golden and mischief rules, the courts developed other techniques over time for interpreting statutes, and they can also still be useful today. They are discussed below.

4: Other tools of statutory interpretation

Apart from the common law approaches, the courts have developed other tools of statutory interpretation such as presumptions, maxims, and other rules. The presumptions tend to confer rights on individuals and limit the power of the legislature.

Presumptions for the interpretation of legislation

Courts make certain presumptions, which apply unless the statute uses clear words to reject them. This means they are 'rebuttable', able to be rebutted, or rejected. Parliament rebuts the presumptions by putting clear words into the statute to show that they do not want the presumption to operate.

Most legislatures simply rely on the common law approach to presumptions, but some legislatures have gone so far as to prescribe that the common law presumptions be taken into account – see for example s 137 (ACT) – while others have specifically given them a secondary role. For example s 14 of the Queensland Act provides that the interpretation that best achieves the purpose is preferred to any other interpretation, 'despite any presumption or rule of interpretation'.

Here are eleven key statutory presumptions that courts sometimes use today.

Parliament does not interfere with fundamental rights

Fundamental rights include things like the right to exclude people from entering your property, the right to not incriminate yourself, and the right for clients to have what they tell their lawyer kept confidential. The courts will presume that legislation does not intend to interfere with these fundamental rights.

This presumption was recently argued in *State of New South Wales v Bujdoso* [2007] NSWCA 44. The court stated that the strength of the presumption is 'diminishing' on the basis that a surer guide is to look at the purpose of the legislation to see whether or not there was a legislative intent to interfere with a fundamental right. The court held, nonetheless, that if there is 'no clear legislative purpose', and the '*Interpretation Act* provides no easy answer', there is a 'presumption against the abrogation of rights'.

City of Swan v Lehman Brothers Australia Ltd

[2009] FCAFC 130

These are the catchwords relating to the presumption:

> STATUTES – cannons of construction – parliament does not intend to interfere with fundamental rights , including property rights, unless it uses unambiguously clear language – principles of statutory interpretation – legislation affecting fundamental rights, including property rights, should be construed strictly – whether Corporations Act 2001 (Cth) Pt 5.3A permitted the execution of a deed of company arrangement that deprived creditors of causes of action against persons other than the company subject to the deed of company arrangement

The case involves an action by creditors of a company that had entered a deed of company arrangement (DOCA), which is used when a company is facing insolvency, and it is financially better for the company to trade out of the insolvent position. A DOCA is allowed under statute, and is agreed upon by a majority of creditors, and binds all creditors. It is not based in the law of contract, because that would require all creditors to agree to be bound, but is allowed under a statute. This means that those making the DOCA must make sure they comply with the terms of the statute. Here, the creditors claimed that the DOCA effectively extinguished their right to sue other members of the same group of companies as the defendant, which is invalid.

The matter was heard by three judges, each of whom wrote their own individual judgment. The material below contains relevant extracts from the judgments. Comments have been included in square brackets to improve comprehension.

STONE J

I have had the advantage of reading in draft the reasons of Rares J and Perram J. Subject to what follows I agree with their Honours' conclusions and the reasons for those conclusions. For reasons which are given below, I have concluded that, properly construed, the DOCA purports to extinguish the plaintiffs' rights to sue other members of the Lehman Group. It is therefore invalid and not binding on the first defendant's creditors including the plaintiffs.

[T]he High Court in *MYT Engineering Pty Limited v Mulcon Pty Limited* (1999) 195 CLR 636 said 'The fact that a deed of company arrangement derives its operative force from statute also has implications for its construction and the consequences of there being an error in the document'.

In such a context, there is, I think, room to correct, as a matter of construction, errors appearing wholly within the confines of the stipulations made binding by statute.

The argument that the DOCA releases members of the Lehman Group and their insurers from claims of the plaintiffs arises from cl 11.5 which states:

'On payment in full of the Litigation Creditors' Final Dividend, all Claims by Litigation Creditors against the Company or a Lehman Entity and all Insurance Claims except those that arise out of the Preserved Contractual Rights are, for ever released, discharged and extinguished'.

> This basically is a settlement clause, saying that a sum of money will be paid to the creditors and in return they discharge any claims against the defendant or any other company in the group, and any claims on insurance. The ambiguity was created from the fact that 'Claim' was defined as a claim against the Defendant, and therefore it was superfluous to refer in the above clause to claims against a Lehman Entity.

In submitting that cl 11.5 does not purport to extinguish their claims against Lehman Entities the plaintiffs would construe the clause by ignoring the reference to Lehman Entities and reading the clause as referring only to claims against the Company. While words may be omitted where it is necessary to avoid absurdity or inconsistency (see *Fitzgerald v Masters* (1956) 95 CLR 420 at 426) in this case I can find no justification for the approach which, it seems to me, would more accurately be described as severance (of the reference to Lehman Entities) than as construction.

In my view it is far more likely, and in my experience more common, that the distributive use of "Claims" that gives rise to the ambiguity derives from inattention to the drafting convention about initial capitalisation and is simply an error.

> It is common in agreements that defined terms are given title case, and then the title case is used throughout. For example, in a lease, there might be defined 'Rental Period' as six months. Then, wherever in the lease 'rental period' is used, it is given a capital R and P to show it is the defined term, for example 'The Tenant agrees to remain in the premises for the Rental Period'.

The conclusion that the intention in cl 11.5 was to release the Lehman Entities as well as the first defendant finds support in other provisions of the DOCA.

The plaintiffs submit that the provisions of Pt 5.3A dealing with the execution and effect of a deed of company arrangement bind the creditors in respect of their claims against the company but not in respect of claims that they have against other entities, whether creditors of the Company or not. Consequently, they submit, the provisions of the DOCA that purport to suspend or extinguish their rights against Lehman Entities are void and of no effect.

Part 5.1 of the Act which deals with company arrangements and reconstructions, provides a significant supervisory role for the Court including convening scheme meetings and approval of the proposed scheme(s). In contrast Pt 5.3A provides for important procedural steps to be taken without Court supervision. Pt 5.3A clearly and precisely limits the extent to which creditors' rights to debts owed by the company may be restricted. There is no express provision in Pt 5.3A that either permits or forbids a deed of company arrangement to interfere with creditors' rights against an entity other than the company. What follows from this silence?

There is a long established principle that a statute should not be interpreted as taking away an existing right unless it does so by clear words that are not reasonably capable of another construction: *Sargood Bros v The Commonwealth* (1910) 11 CLR 279 per O'Connor J. The principle rises to a presumption (rebuttable) in relation to vested property interests; *Clissold v Perry* (1904) 1 CLR 363 at 373 (HC), *Perry v Clissold* [1907] AC 73 at 80 (PC). More recently the principle has been articulated by the High Court in *Pyneboard Pty Ltd v Trade Practices Commission* (1983) 152 CLR 328 at 341 per Mason ACJ, Wilson and

Dawson JJ. McHugh J expressed the need for caution in applying the principle in both *Malika Holdings Pty Ltd v Stretton* (2001) 204 CLR 290 at 298-9 and in *Gifford v Strang Patrick Stevedoring Pty Limited* (2003) 214 CLR 269 at 284.

While it is clear ... the principle still has life, it is not, in my view necessary to rely on it here. In my view, when the objects, purpose and contents of Pt 5.3A are taken into account, the language ... must be construed as referring only to claims that creditors of the company have against the company under administration.

RARES J

The plaintiffs are local government councils that invested in collateralised debt obligations sold to them by Lehman Australia. The effect of the impugned provisions of the deed of company arrangement will be to release not only Lehman Australia but also the other Lehman entities from all claims that any of the creditors of Lehman Australia may have against them. The deed will also prevent those creditors from enforcing their rights under policies of insurance that may respond to their claims pursuant to statutory charges such as those afforded by s 6 of the *Law Reform (Miscellaneous Provisions) Act 1946* (NSW).

Part 5.3A was introduced into the Act by the *Corporate Law Reform Act 1992* (Cth). Critically, the object of Pt 5.3A is stated s 435A:

'435A Object of Part The object of this Part is to provide for the business, property and affairs of an insolvent company to be administered in a way that:

(a) maximises the chances of the company, or as much as possible of its business, continuing in existence; or

(b) if it is not possible for the company or its business to continue in existence --results in a better return for the company's creditors and members than would result from an immediate winding up of the company.'

The defendants' proposed construction of the power given to a meeting of a company's creditors under Pt 5.3A to resolve that the company enter a deed of company arrangement is very broad. It would permit the majority of creditors to use their voting power to interfere with, indeed to confiscate, the minority's property rights and causes of action.

In *American Dairy Queen (Qld) Pty Ltd v Blue Rio Pty Ltd* (1981) 147 CLR 677 at 682-683 Mason J said: 'The general rule is that the courts will construe a statute in conformity with the common law and will not attribute to it an intention to alter common law principles unless such an intention is manifested according to the true construction of the statute'.

In *Bropho v Western Australia* (1990) 171 CLR 1 at 18 Mason CJ, Deane, Dawson, Toohey, Gaudron and McHugh JJ said: 'The rationale of all such rules lies in an assumption that the legislature would, if it intended to achieve the particular effect, have made its intention in that regard unambiguously clear. Thus, the rationale of the presumption against the modification or abolition of fundamental rights or principles is to be found in the assumption that it is "in the last degree improbable that the legislature would overthrow fundamental principles, infringe rights, or depart from the general system of law, without expressing its intention with irresistible clearness; and to give any such effect to general words, simply because they have that meaning in their widest, or usual, or natural sense, would be to give them a meaning in which they were not really used".'

> The fundamental issue here is whether the property of creditors, separate and apart from their rights to sue or prove against a company, can be appropriated by a majority of other creditors for the benefit of them or third parties. In my opinion, Pt 5.3A does not contain either express words or unmistakable clarity of language to lead to such a draconian interference with the proprietary rights of creditors against third parties or other creditors of a company in administration. It follows that the deed should not be given effect as a deed of company arrangement for the purposes of Pt 5.3A but, rather, it should be found to be void and of no effect.
>
> **PERRAM J**
> Section 444D(1) of the Act stated that 'A deed of company arrangement binds all creditors of the company, so far as concerns claims arising on or before the day specified in the deed'. The plaintiffs argued the words 'as far as' limited the deed to the company that was insolvent, and the defendants argued 'as far as' meant 'relating to' so it could also cover other companies in the Lehman group.
>
> The expression 'so far as concerns' is capable of bearing both meanings and is, therefore, ambiguous. That ambiguity is to be resolved by an examination of the text of Part 5.3A and the context in which it is found. [There is] explicit reference to the property of the insolvent company (rather than the property of others). Part 5.3A is silent on the position of third parties. In those circumstances, Part 5.3A should not be interpreted as permitting third party releases.
>
> It can be seen from the above judgment that each judge agreed that the statute should be read in accordance with the presumption that if parliament intended to interfere with fundamental rights, in this case the rights of a company's creditors to bring actions against third parties, then it must say so expressly – silence is not enough.

Statutes do not operate retrospectively

Courts will presume that statutes do not operate retrospectively – that is, that they apply from the time the statute is enacted (operate forwards, towards the future, rather than applying to matters in the past). To make an Act operate retrospectively parliament must specifically state a date in the past as the commencement date, or otherwise state that the legislation shall be retrospective.

An example of retrospective legislation was introduced after the illegal acts of the Australian Government in relation to the vessel *MV Tampa*. In August 2001 the Australian Coastwatch had noticed a fishing boat in distress, loaded with passengers. The following day Australian Search and Rescue transmitted a radio message to merchant ships in the area to render assistance if they could. The *Tampa*, a Norwegian freighter, was in the area, and assisted the passengers by letting them aboard. The Government characterised the passengers as illegal immigrants, but in fact the passengers were claiming (legal) refugee status. The Australian Government decided it did not want them to enter Australia, so Special Air Service (SAS) troops boarded the *Tampa* and forced it to sail to Christmas Island. In September 2001 the Federal Parliament hurriedly introduced a Bill into parliament (set out below).

Border Protection (Validation and Enforcement Powers) Act 2001

No. 126, 2001

An Act to validate the actions of the Commonwealth and others in relation to the *MV Tampa* ...

4   Definitions

validation period means the period starting on 27 August 2001 and ending when this Act commences.

5   Action to which this Part applies

This Part applies to any action taken during the validation period by the Commonwealth in relation to:

(a) the *MV Tampa*; or ...

(d) any person who was on board a vessel mentioned in paragraph (a) at any time during the validation period

6   Action to which this Part applies taken to be lawful

All action to which this Part applies is taken for all purposes to have been lawful when it occurred.

Reflection

Do you think this legislation is acceptable?

Courts presume their previous interpretation of a word or phrase applies if parliament uses the word or phrase in a statute

If a court has already interpreted a word, phrase or provision, which is then used by parliament in a piece of legislation, the courts will presume that parliament means the word or phrase to have the same meaning as the courts previously gave it. To rebut this presumption, parliament should provide a different definition of the word or phrase in the Act.

Let's say the phrase 'substantial impairment' had been interpreted by the courts to mean 'a significant and real loss or reduction'. If parliament then introduced a statute that said 'No rural property shall cause substantial impairment to the water supply of their downstream neighbours', but did not include a definition of 'substantial impairment', the courts would presume that parliament meant their definition to apply.

Legislation does not bind the Crown

The Crown is presumed not to be bound by statutes, and this presumption is part of our English legal inheritance (see Chapter 8). What this means is that the Crown is above the law, and not subject to statutory provisions. If parliament wants to bind the Crown it must include specific words in the statute. The usual approach is for parliament to include a section with the words 'This Act binds the Crown'.[9]

Some legislatures have stated the common law presumption in their interpretation statutes. For example s 13 of the Queensland Act states 'No Act passed after the commencement of this Act shall be binding on the Crown or derogate from any prerogative right of the Crown unless express words are included in the Act for that purpose'. A similar provision is in s 6(6) of the Tasmanian Act. See also s 137(3) (ACT), which provides, 'this chapter assumes that common law presumptions operate in conjunction with this chapter'. Note however that s 20 of the South Australian Act flips the presumption around the other way, saying that South Australian Acts will bind the Crown unless there are express words to the contrary.

In the modern statutory approach, it is possible to rebut this presumption even in the absence of express words that the legislation binds the Crown. In *Bropho v State of Western Australia* (1990) 171 CLR 1, the High Court held that the *Aboriginal Heritage Act 1972* (WA), which did not have an express provision saying that it bound the Crown, was nevertheless binding on the employees and agents of the Western Australian Government.

> **TIP**
> If you have forgotten what the Crown is, see Chapter 4 for a discussion. The short answer is that the Crown is the embodiment of the monarch, and includes the Governor-General, the police force, and the public prosecutors who bring criminal actions on behalf of the state.

Penal provisions are strictly interpreted in favour of the accused

Ambiguity in statutes is resolved in favour of the individual to whom they apply.

A penal statute is one that provides for heavy fines and gaol sentences for offences committed under it. Examples include penalties under the Crimes Acts and taxation legislation. As the penalty is grave, where a breach is found, ambiguous provisions are given the interpretation that most favours the person accused of committing the wrong. We describe this as giving a 'narrow construction' to the provisions, to limit the negative effect on the accused.

Conversely, there is a presumption that *benefit* provisions should be given a broad construction, to the advantage of potential beneficiaries. These include, for example, statutes relating to social welfare and pensions, workers compensation, and industrial safety. The presumption is that statutory ambiguities are resolved in favour of the person who stands to benefit.

Legislation does not take jurisdiction away from the courts

It is presumed that courts have power, or jurisdiction, to hear cases and interpret legislation. It is only where parliament specifically states that a specific court or other body (such as a tribunal) is given the responsibility of applying the legislation that the courts do not have their usual jurisdiction. Removal of jurisdiction can only occur where parliament has the power to do so, and usually there remain avenues of appeal to the courts. Appeals are allowed where an Act is found to be biased or fails to provide procedural fairness to the parties.

---

9   See for example *Food Act 1984* (Vic) s 6, *Building Act 1993* (NT) s 5, and *Deer Act 2006* (NSW) s 36, and several of the Interpretation Acts: see s 4 (NSW), s 5 (Vic), s 5 (Qld), s 4 (WA), and 3(2) (NT).

Property rights are not taken away without compensation

The Crown has the right to compulsorily acquire any land in the state. The reason dates back to feudalism (the Crown still owns all the land, and owning your own home in fee simple is really just a right to it against everyone else besides the state). However, the presumption is that the Crown cannot take your property without giving you adequate compensation for it. This is described as 'compulsory acquisition on just terms', and is part of the power of the Commonwealth under s 51(xxxi) of the Australian Constitution.

In October 2007 the Maningrida community in the Northern Territory launched a challenge to the Federal Government's emergency intervention in the Northern Territory. The traditional owners were claiming that the compulsory acquisition of their property was not on just terms (see the 'In depth' box below).

TIP

This presumption is the basis of a very popular Australian movie, *The Castle*, which played with the idea that where 'a man's home is his castle', it is very difficult to work out what adequate compensation for taking his home would be.

In depth: *Wurridjal v The Commonwealth of Australia*[10]

Reggie Wurridjal, a member of the Dhukurrdji Aboriginal clan whose country is on Maningrida in the Northern Territory, launched a challenge to the Federal Government's *Northern Territory National Emergency Response Act 2007* (Cth). The Act was 700 pages long, and included a provision for a compulsory five-year lease of Maningrida Aboriginal land and abolition of the right of the Aboriginal community to control who enters its land through a permit system. The traditional owners claimed that this was compulsory acquisition, and that it was not done under 'just terms' as required by s 51(xxxi) of the Constitution, which provides that Parliament has the power to make laws with respect to the 'acquisition of property on just terms from any State or person for any purpose in respect of which the Parliament has power to make laws'.

A declaration was sought from the High Court of Australia that the various provisions in the emergency intervention legislation[11] resulted in an acquisition of property to which s 51(xxxi) of the Constitution applied, and were invalid in their application to that property.

The Commonwealth of Australia responded with a demurrer, which is a formal pleading alleging that the claim is insufficient in law (does not include a cause of action to which effect can be given by the court). It argued that the relevant legislation was made under s 122 of the Constitution, which provides the power to Federal Parliament to make laws

---

10 (2009) 237 CLR 309.

11 *Northern Territory National Emergency Response Act 2007* (Cth) and the *Families, Community Services and Indigenous Affairs and Other Legislation Amendment (Northern Territory National Emergency Response and Other Measures) Act 2007* (Cth).

with respect to the Northern Territory, and that this power is not subject to the just terms requirement in s 51. Alternatively the Commonwealth argued that even if it was subject to just terms, such compensation had been provided for. The High Court of Australia held, 6 to 1, in favour of the Commonwealth. Kirby J was the only judge in dissent.

Why not read this case? It contains useful statements about statutory interpretation. You can find it at www.austlii.edu.au.

Legislation does not have extraterritorial effect

It is presumed that legislation only applies in its territory or jurisdiction, which is Australia (and the territorial waters around it) in the case of Commonwealth legislation, Western Australia in the case of Western Australian legislation, and so on with the other states and territories.

For example *Green v Burgess* [1960] VR 158 considered the *Fisheries Act 1928* (Vic), which made it an offence to catch fish out of season. The aptly named Chief Justice Herring decided that the Act, being a Victorian Act, could only apply to fish taken in Victorian waters, even if those same fish also swam in NSW waters.

In cases where parliament has power to enact legislation with extraterritorial operation, it must express a clear intention in the statute that it is to have extraterritorial effect, otherwise the courts will presume the statute applies only in the relevant territory.

Parliament does not intend to interfere with equality of religion

A relatively new presumption by the courts is that parliament is presumed not to have intended to interfere with the preservation of religious equality. In *Canterbury Municipal Council v Moslem Alawy Society Ltd* [1985] 1 NSWLR 525 a question arose as to whether a building used for prayer and reading of the Holy Koran, to which only members of the Alawy Islamic religious sect could have access, was a 'place of public worship' within the meaning of a town planning ordinance. The majority of the New South Wales Court of Appeal held that the premises were nonetheless a 'place of public worship'. Justice McHugh stated at [544] of the judgment:

> Australian courts should be slow to adopt an interpretation of a legislative instrument which is contrary to the preservation of religious equality as this equality has always been a matter of fundamental concern to the people of Australia.

Note however, that this is a New South Wales decision; when the case went on appeal to the High Court, although the appeal was dismissed there was no reference to or endorsement of the presumption as stated by Justice McHugh.

Parliament intends to legislate in conformity with international law

If there are international laws that are applicable within the jurisdiction, it is assumed that parliament intends to legislate in conformity with them. Justice Brennan noted in

Mabo v Queensland (1992) 175 CLR 1 at 42 that 'international law is a legitimate and important influence' on the courts.

Let's say Australia is a party to the Slavery Convention 1926, and parliament introduces a new piece of legislation called the *Work for the Dole Act*. The courts will interpret that piece of legislation with the presumption that it intends to comply with the Slavery Convention, for example by allowing fair remuneration.

Some states have included this presumption in legislation. See for example s 32 of the *Charter of Human Rights and Responsibilities Act 2006* (Vic), which provides that international law may be considered in interpreting statutory provisions.

Words are used consistently in statutes

If the one word or phrase is used in different parts of the same statute, the courts will presume that parliament intended the word or phrase to have the same meaning throughout the statute, unless parliament provides a special definition for it at the start of a particular part or section.

In depth: Do statutory presumptions constitute a common law bill of rights?

In Chapter 4 (page 87) we considered the fact that Australia currently lacks a bill of rights — Victoria and the Australian Capital Territory have proceeded with creating their own bills of rights at the State level, but there is as yet no bill of rights at the Commonwealth level. The current Chief Justice of the Supreme Court of New South Wales, Spigelman CJ, has written extensively on statutory interpretation. In 2008 he gave a lecture titled 'Statutory Interpretation and Human Rights', in which he described statutory interpretation as 'not merely a collection of maxims or canons. It is a distinct body of law'.[12] He went on to propose that statutory presumptions comprise a common law bill of rights in their practical effect.[13]

Do you agree with Spigelman CJ? What impact, if any, do you think the fact that presumptions are rebuttable, has on his argument?

Latin maxims

TIP
Don't be confused by the complicated Latin names. Each maxim has a simple, plain English meaning.

Our courts adopted from England some maxims, or guiding principles, for interpreting legislation. These can be used as optional additional aids by courts today. Unlike the above presumptions (which ensure certain rights are maintained), the maxims tend to assist in working out the 'things' that are covered by an Act.

---

12 James Spigelman, *Statutory Interpretation and Human Rights*, The MacPherson Lecture Series, Vol 3 (2008), 22.

13 Ibid., 23.

Noscitur a sociis

Noscitur a sociis (pronounced 'noskiter a so kiss') means 'it is known by its associates'. The meaning of a word or phrase can be worked out by its context, namely the words used around it. This is part of the general philosophy of reading a statute as a whole.

In *R v Ann Harris* (1836) 173 ER 198 two female prisoners had a fight, and one bit off the other's nose. She was charged under a statute that read 'If a person shall unlawfully and maliciously stab, cut or wound a person with intent to maim or disfigure them they shall be guilty of a felony.' Both stabbing and cutting are done with a sharp instrument, so applying *noscitur a sociis*, the wounding must also be done with a sharp instrument to come under the section. The court concluded that teeth were not a sharp instrument. Many parents of small children would disagree with this!

Ejusdem generis

Ejusdem generis (pronounced 'e use dem generous') means 'of the same kind'. If you have specific words followed by a general word, the interpretation of the general is limited by the specific things that come before it. So for example if the statute read 'glass, bottle, jug, or any other thing', the 'any other thing' would include a vase but would not include a donut or a pigeon. The general 'any other thing' is limited to the same kind of things as those specifically mentioned before it.

The only real difference between *ejusdem generis* and *noscitur a sociis* is the general reference to 'other' things. *Noscitur a sociis* lists only specific things. *Ejusdem generis* provides a general, catch-all term. The reason for including statements like 'or any other thing' is that parliamentary drafters want to use some examples to make it clear what they mean, but do not want to limit the provision to those specific examples.

The trick is to first identify a genus, or class, from the list, by working out what they have in common, and second, ask yourself whether the thing you have fits into that class. For example let's say a statute said 'cows, pigs, sheep and any other animal may be carried onto the ferry'. Does this include a giraffe? Step one is to decide on the genus, or class. What is in common between cows, pigs and sheep? They are all farm animals. Alternatively, they are all animals that humans eat. Any of these could be the class you apply. The second step is to decide whether a giraffe fits in the class, and the answer is most likely 'no'.

Exercise: Applying *ejusdem generis*

If an Act prohibited the consumption of 'wines, beers, spirits, and other drinks' in any public place, would that include soft drinks?

GO ONLINE

Go online for a sample answer to the 'Applying *ejusdem generis*' exercise.

There are two qualifications to bear in mind for *ejusdem generis*. One is that you need to have at least two words before the general phrase in order to apply the principle. If you have only one word, such as 'theatres and any other place' then you could not apply the maxim because you can't come up with a class of things from the one word 'theatre'. The second is that, to apply the maxim, the list of things must be sufficiently connected to form a class. In *Stewart v Lizars* [1965] VR 210, litter was defined in a statute as 'bottles, tins, cartons, packages, glass, food, or other refuse or rubbish' and the court, which had to decide whether sump oil came within the definition of rubbish, decided that there was nothing generic in the list (even though they were all household items, and all solids).

Expressio unius est exclusio alterius

Expressio unius est exclusio alterius (pronounced 'iks press eyo uni es iks cloo zio ol tee reus') means 'the express mention of one thing is the exclusion of another'. For example if a statute said that adults could drive cars, this would be considered to exclude children from driving cars.

In *Dean v Wiesengrund* [1955] 2 QB 120, the *Increase of Rent and Mortgage Interest (Restrictions) Act 1920* (UK) provided for restrictions on rent and mortgage increases. If a tenant had paid more rent than allowed under the Act, 'the sum so paid shall be recoverable from the landlord … or his legal personal representative by the tenant'. In this case the tenant had died and the executor was seeking to recover excess rent paid. The landlord argued that the express mention of 'landlord or his legal personal representative' but only 'by the tenant' and not 'by the tenant or his legal personal representative', applying *expressio unius est exclusio alterius* means only the tenant could claim back the rent himself. The court held that the executor was acting as the tenant in this case, so it did not matter.

Generalia specialibus non derogant

Generalia specialibus non derogant (pronounced 'gener arl eea, spesh ee arl ee bus non dero gant') means that 'general things do not derogate from special things'. If there is a specific provision in a statute and also a more general provision, the general provision does not override the specific provision. If, for example, a statute said that no animals are allowed on public transport, and in a separate section (or separate statute) it said that visually impaired individuals may at any time be accompanied by a harnessed guide dog, then you would apply the specific provision on guide dogs over the general prohibition on animals.

In *McLean v Kowald* (1974) 9 SASR 384, the *Road Traffic Act 1961* (SA) provided that a person who received a fine, imprisonment or a disqualification of driving licence in mitigating circumstances could have their penalty reduced by the court, but a minimum disqualification period of 14 days applied. The *Offenders Probation Act 1913* (SA) provided that courts could on certain conditions suspend sentences of imprisonment. The court applied *generalia specialibus non derogant* to say that the general provision on suspended sentences did not override the specific provision on minimum disqualification.

Exercise: Latin maxims

For each of these scenarios, choose the relevant Latin maxim and determine the outcome reached by applying it.

- 'It is an offence for a person to use a mobile telephone, laptop computer, personal digital assistant (PDA) or any other thing on board any flight within Australia'. Johnny uses a hand-held Nintendo game on a Sydney to Melbourne flight. Has he committed an offence?
- 'It is an offence to pick, cut or pull down any plants or flowers on government property'. Cyndy collects frangipani flowers off the ground in the botanic gardens. Has she committed an offence?
- 'Homes, or other places of abode'. Does this include a park bench for a homeless person?
- 'Taxis may use bus lanes'. Does this include limousines?
- Section 15 – 'Anyone selling, attempting to sell or having on their person any quantity, however small, of heroin, shall be imprisoned for 8 years'. Section 38 – 'Any person found in possession of drugs, regardless of their purpose, shall be imprisoned for 1 year'. Brian is found with a small quantity of heroin in his possession. What penalty will he face?

GO ONLINE

Go online for sample answers to the 'Latin maxims' exercise.

In depth: Relevance of Latin maxims today

Where relevant, the courts continue to use Latin maxims, but with some reservation, because they, like all the common law tools of statutory interpretation, take second place to the Interpretation Acts. Often courts can interpret a provision in the light of its purpose without having to call upon a maxim to assist, and it could be said that the maxims are not as persuasive upon courts as they once were. Here are some examples where the courts have referred to Latin maxims in recent times.

Shalom v Health Services Commissioner [2009] VSC 514 (Kaye J, Supreme Court of Victoria) related to a piece of legislation which gave the Health Services Commissioner the power to place a report before parliament on any matter arising from an individual complaint, including naming a individual health care provider if the Commissioner believes doing so is reasonably necessary to prevent or lessen the risk of serious threat to life, health, safety or welfare of any person or the public. The plaintiff sought an injunction to stop the defendant from naming the plaintiff. The argument was that the plaintiff was not a health care provider under the legislation, which included a definition listing 15 categories of health services, including: '(g) health education services; (ha) therapeutic counselling and psychotherapeutic services; and (k) services provided by practitioners of naturopathy, acupuncture and in other alternative health care fields.' The defendant said the plaintiff came under each of these three headings, on the basis that the plaintiff had advertised himself as 'Shaman Psychic Spiritualist, Healer, Counsellor', describing himself to his clients as Shamir Zion Thunder Eagle. The complaints against him related to sexual acts in the course of his spiritual healing of clients. The Court used *ejusdem generis* in considering the meaning of 'other alternative health care fields' in paragraph (k), saying:

'While the phrase "other alternative health care fields" is to be construed *ejusdem generis*, nonetheless the inclusion of that undefined category, in the definition, is, in my view, important. It is evident that, by including that category, the legislature intended to capture those who provide, or profess to provide, particular services concerned with the healing or alleviation of physiological or psychological distress, but which defy more specific definition or categorisation. That construction is, in my view, consonant with the defined purposes and objectives of the legislation'.

It was decided that the plaintiff was a health care provider under the legislation, and it was acceptable in the circumstances for him to be named in a report to parliament.

In *Laemthong International Lines Co Ltd v BPS Shipping* (1997) 190 CLR 181, the High Court had to determine the meaning of 'charterer' in the *Admiralty Act 1988* (Cth), s19 of which stated that a claim *in rem* (against a ship instead of a person) can be made where the person who owes the debt is 'the owner or charterer of, or in possession or control of' the ship. An issue raised was whether *noscitur a sociis* could be used to find that the only sort of charterer to come under the section was one who was a kind of owner, or otherwise in possession or control of it. The appellant argued that it was only a voyage charterer, with no real control or ownership of the vessel, having rented it for only one journey using the ship's existing crew, and was therefore not a 'charterer' under the section. Justice Toohey, in deciding the appellant was covered by the clause, referred to *noscitur a sociis* as being relevant, but said that it had to be applied with care.

In *FAI Properties Pty Limited v John & Evangelia Apostolopoulos* [2002] ACTSC 58, Justice Spender used *expressio unius est exclusio alterius* to find that, because the *Tenancy Tribunal Act 1994* (ACT) conferred a right of appeal on questions of law, it therefore excluded the right of appeal on questions of fact or mixed fact and law. He said 'Such an approach is a manifestation of the well-known expressio unius principle'. He used *generalia specialibus non derogant* as well, saying 'Where there has been a specific grant of power in a particular area, that grant governs the position even where there is a more general provision. This is a manifestation of the principle generalia specialibus non derogant'.

In *Mandalidis v Artline* (1999) 47 NSWLR 568 a dispute arose between the vendor (seller) and purchaser of a warehouse and office building near Sydney Airport. A certificate attached to the contract of sale warranted that 'the Council had not by resolution adopted any policy to restrict the development of the land because of the likelihood of land slip, bushfire, flooding, tidal inundation, subsidence or any other risk'. The purchaser found that the Council had a policy on aircraft noise, and sought to rescind (set aside) the contract. The vendor argued that did not come under the warranty because, using *ejusdem generis*, the general phrase 'any other risk' had to be interpreted by the general words that came before it, namely 'land slip', 'bushfire', 'flooding', 'tidal inundation' and 'subsidence'. They were all risks arising by reason of natural features of the land, and so a policy on aircraft noise would be excluded from it. The court, in deciding the purchaser could rescind the contract, said:

'I accept that the noscitur a sociis and ejusdem generis rules of interpretation are available weapons in the armoury of statutory interpretation. But they are not always determinative, and it is arguable that they are less important now than once

> they were ... the task of a modern court, where the grammatical meaning of the legislation is open to doubt, is to adopt the construction which will promote the purpose or object of the Act' (*Interpretation Act 1987* (NSW), s 33).
>
> This involves, as McHugh JA explained in *Kingston v Keprose* 11 NSWLR 404 at 423, `a sophisticated analysis to determine the legislative purpose and a discriminating judgment as to where the boundary of constructions ends and legislation begins'. After one has had regard to the objects or purposes of legislation of the kind presently under consideration, it is unlikely that much room will be left for the application of the old rules of statutory interpretation'.

It is therefore likely that you may be able to resolve a statutory interpretation problem merely be considering its purpose, and adopting an interpretation that promotes the purpose. But is it also acceptable to use the Latin maxims? As the Latin maxims are not as persuasive on courts as they once were, if you raise them in argument before a court you should also have alternative lines of argument ready, based on the interpretation legislation.

Other rules of statutory interpretation

'Means' or 'includes'

Where a statute says that something 'means' something, that is an exhaustive, complete definition. But where a statute says that something 'includes' something, then the things it is stated to include are examples but don't limit the definition from including other things. If, for example, the definition of ferry was: '"ferry" means a water going vessel run by Sydney Harbour Authority', then to come within the definition, there must be a vessel, it must be capable of going on the water, and it must be run by Sydney Harbour Authority. If, however, the definition said '"ferry" includes a steam powered boat, a high-speed catamaran, and a water taxi', then it is possible the definition could include other things, like a hydrofoil. It is a definition by examples rather than an exhaustive definition.

'And' or 'or'

In everyday language we use 'and' conjunctively, to connote both, as in 'you and I can go together', and we mostly use 'or' disjunctively, to connote *either* but not both, as in 'we only have one ticket, so you or I can go'. How should the word 'and' and 'or' be interpreted in statutes? If an Act provides, 'it is an offence to take guns, knives, machetes, and baseball bats into a nightclub', does a person have to have some of each to have committed an offence, or is it enough to have just a gun? If the latter, we would be reading 'and' disjunctively, as 'or'. In the past, the courts would use the golden rule to read 'and' as 'or' and vice versa on the basis it was a drafting error that caused absurdity or ambiguity, but now the courts can read 'and' and 'or' interchangeably according to what they believe parliament intended.

All words have meaning and effect

A further simple rule of statutory interpretation is that, prima facie (on the face of it), all words in a statute have meaning and effect. For example in *Project Blue Sky Inc v Australian Broadcasting Authority* (1998) 194 CLR 355 Justice Brennan said that 'a court construing a statutory provision must strive to give meaning to every word of the provision'. Of course it may not always be possible to give a full and active meaning of every word in a statute, but the courts are not at liberty to ignore any word or to consider any words to be insignificant.

A note on plain English drafting

Statutes are increasingly being drafted in ways to make it easier for the readers. Given that ignorance of the law is no excuse, it makes sense that legislation should be capable of being read by the people it binds. The idea is to draft legislation in a simple and straightforward style, using language that is direct and familiar, getting rid of unnecessary words, and avoiding longwinded and complicated sentences. The sections should be shorter and the legislation more user-friendly, for example by having little headings on the side. While this approach is to be applauded, it may create some difficulty in the transition period, because the replacement of a complicated statement that is already the subject of judicial interpretation through a series of cases with a simple statement will raise the question as to whether parliament intends the same or a new meaning to apply. It can result in unnecessary litigation to create new precedent interpreting the redrafted statute.

5: Applying the rules of statutory interpretation

It is now time to bring together what we have covered so far in this chapter, so that you can feel confident when you are faced with a legal problem that requires interpreting statutory provisions.

Statutory interpretation: Problem-solving method

Figure 11.2 sets out a step-by-step process for solving statutory interpretation problems. The first two steps are preliminary but essential. After all, if you are asked whether someone could be liable under a particular section of an Act, and that Act is from another jurisdiction not covered by it or is not currently in force, there is no way a person could be liable under it! We apply the same reasoning for example if we are a litigator working on a contract dispute. Before we consider the relevant term and whether it has been breached, we check whether the parties have entered into a valid contract.

FIGURE 11.2: AN APPROACH TO STATUTORY INTERPRETATION PROBLEMS

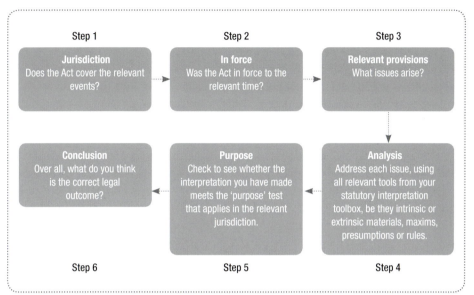

Exercise: Jimbo and Baba visit Parliament House

Assume, hypothetically, that parliament enacts the *Visiting Parliament House Act 2009* (Cth). Assume further that in the course of the Minister's Second Reading Speech in support of the Bill, which became the Act without amendment, the Minister said:

> Obviously we want to make Parliament House open to visitors – it's important that voters feel government is accessible. But we don't want it to become a circus, and, of course, we can't risk having unidentified persons on the premises for security reasons.

The date of assent by the Governor-General was 1 March 2009, and relevant parts are as follows:

Section 1
'proper identification papers' means valid passport, drivers licence, and/or birth certificate.

Section 2
Everyone is to be made welcome to visit Parliament House, and no visitor may be unreasonably refused.

Section 3
(a) All visitors to Parliament House must present identification papers for inspection before entering.
(b) No visitor with proper identification papers shall be refused entry.

Section 4

Visitors are not allowed to bring into Parliament House firearms, recording devices, pets, paint or any other thing that may disturb the peace.

Jimbo the circus performer has just arrived at the steps to Parliament House with Baba the Elephant. Jimbo and Baba have worked together in the circus for many years, and with the circus now in Canberra, they felt it was an opportune time to visit Parliament House. Jimbo doesn't look upon Baba as an animal or a pet – he is Jimbo's friend and work colleague. Baba is extremely well mannered and, due to his circus training, he is able to manoeuvre his body carefully despite his size. Despite inspecting Jimbo's passport and Baba's breeding certificate, the staff refuse admission to Jimbo and Baba. Your job is to argue, using the rules of statutory interpretation, that Jimbo and Baba cannot legally be refused entry to Parliament House under the Act.

GO ONLINE

Go online for a sample answer to the 'Jimbo and Baba visit Parliament House' exercise.

Exercise: No standing

Assume, hypothetically, that the following Act exists, and where it says '[your state or territory]' it actually reads Queensland, or Victoria, or whichever jurisdiction you are studying law in.

Road Safety Act 2009

No. 4, 2009

An Act to protect public safety on the roads; to amend or repeal certain legislation; and for other purposes.

[Assented to 1 February 2009]

3   Objects of Act

The objects of this Act are:

   (a) to protect public safety on the roads,

…

4   Application

This Act applies to all motorists and pedestrians in [your state or territory].

5   Definitions

'Road signs' means fixtures put in place by the relevant road transport authority in [your state or territory] on roads, lanes, highways and other thoroughfares.

6   Offence

It is an offence to act contrary to road signs.

Penalty: 2000 penalty units

A hotel in the largest city in [your state or territory] has a semi-circular drive-in entrance with a 'No Standing' sign out the front. It was knocked down by a car recently and was concreted back in by hotel staff who were fed up with waiting for the relevant road transport authorities to do it. Yesterday John, a guest at the hotel, stood out the front of the hotel under the sign while waiting for a taxi. Has John committed an offence?

GO ONLINE

Go online for a sample answer to the 'No standing' exercise.

Exercise: Double jeopardy

Late one night in the summer of 1973 Raymond John Carroll entered the Kennedy family home in Ipswich, Queensland, through an unlocked door. He entered a room where two little girls were sleeping and took 17 month old baby Deidre from her bed. He took her to a toilet block at the local park and raped her and bashed and strangled her to death, then tossed her body on the roof of the toilet block, partly dressed in women's clothing he had stolen off a neighbour's clothes line.

Carroll was arrested and charged with the murder, and was convicted by the Supreme Court of Queensland. He appealed against the conviction to the Queensland Court of Criminal Appeal. He argued that inconsistencies in the expert evidence were such that the evidence could not sustain the verdict. The experts agreed he was the offender, but had different reasons for coming to that conclusion. The appeal was allowed, and the conviction quashed.

Since then there have been massive improvements in science, particularly in DNA testing. In this case the baby had sustained distinctive bite marks on the insides of her thighs, and forensic dentists were able to use the mould taken from Carroll's teeth during the original murder investigation to establish beyond a doubt (one in several million) that Carroll did the murder (he had a gap of several millimetres in his teeth, and his bottom teeth stuck out relative to his top teeth).

The problem was that double jeopardy prevented bringing another murder trial. Double jeopardy is an old rule, 800 years old, received into Australian law from England. It means that you can't be tried for the same offence twice. The rationale was restated by the High Court in *Pearce v The Queen* [1998] HCA 57 at [610]:

> the State with all its resources and power should not be allowed to make repeated attempts to convict an individual for an alleged offence, thereby subjecting him to embarrassment, expense and ordeal and compelling him to live in a continuing state of anxiety and insecurity.

This means that if you are tried for an offence and acquitted you can never be tried again for the same offence. This sounds fair on its face, but there is a difference between 'not guilty' because the jury thinks you're innocent, and 'not guilty' because a reasonable doubt remains in the jurors' minds.

To get around double jeopardy an action was brought in the Supreme Court of Queensland in 2000 for the separate offence of perjury. The prosecution argued that Carroll had committed perjury, in that he lied to the court by pleading not guilty to a murder he definitely committed.

Carroll was convicted of perjury. In 2001 he appealed to the Supreme Court's Court of Appeal, arguing that the case was an abuse of process because it was basically double jeopardy dressed up as perjury. The Court allowed the appeal and quashed the conviction. In 2002 the Queensland Public Prosecutor appealed to the High Court, seeking to overturn the Court of Appeal decision and to clarify the double jeopardy principle. The High Court dismissed the appeal. So Carroll is effectively guilty in fact, and innocent in law.

In 2006 legislation was passed in NSW Parliament to change the law on double jeopardy. The *Crimes (Appeal and Review) Amendment (Double Jeopardy) Act 2006* (NSW) amended the *Crimes (Appeal and Review) Act 2001* (NSW), and entered into force on 15 December 2006. Similar provisions were enacted in Queensland in 2007. Below are the relevant legislative provisions for NSW, for you to interpret using what you know about statutory interpretation.

The question is: can this legislation be used to reopen the Carroll case? Explain your reasoning.

98 Definitions

(1) In this Part

"life sentence offence" means murder or any other offence punishable by imprisonment for life [NB that's murder, aggravated sexual assault in company, major drug trafficking]

99 Application of Division

(1) This Division applies where:

(a) a person has been acquitted of an offence, and

(b) according to the rules of law relating to double jeopardy, the person is thereby precluded or may thereby be precluded from being retried for the same offence.

(2) This section extends to a person acquitted in proceedings outside this State of an offence under the law of the place where the proceedings were held. However, this section does not so extend if the law of that place does not permit that person to be retried and the application of this Division to such a retrial is inconsistent with the Commonwealth Constitution or a law of the Commonwealth.

(3) This section extends to a person acquitted before the commencement of this Division.

100 Court of Criminal Appeal may order retrial - fresh and compelling evidence

(1) The Court of Criminal Appeal may, on the application of the Director of Public Prosecutions, order an acquitted person to be retried for a life sentence offence if satisfied that:

(a) there is fresh and compelling evidence against the acquitted person in relation to the offence, and

(b) in all the circumstances it is in the interests of justice for the order to be made.

102 Fresh and compelling evidence - meaning

(1) This section applies for the purpose of determining under this Division whether there is fresh and compelling evidence against an acquitted person in relation to an offence.

(2) Evidence is "fresh" if:
  (a) it was not adduced in the proceedings in which the person was acquitted, and
  (b) it could not have been adduced in those proceedings with the exercise of reasonable diligence.
(3) Evidence is "compelling" if:
  (a) it is reliable, and
  (b) it is substantial, and
  (c) in the context of the issues in dispute in the proceedings in which the person was acquitted, it is highly probative of the case against the acquitted person.

104 Interests of justice - matters for consideration
(1) This section applies for the purpose of determining under this Division whether it is in the interests of justice for an order to be made for the retrial of an acquitted person.
(2) It is not in the interests of justice to make an order for the retrial of an acquitted person unless the Court of Criminal Appeal is satisfied that a fair retrial is likely in the circumstances.
(3) The Court is to have regard in particular to:
  (a) the length of time since the acquitted person allegedly committed the offence, and
  (b) whether any police officer or prosecutor has failed to act with reasonable diligence or expedition in connection with the application for the retrial of the acquitted person.

105 Application for retrial - procedure
(1) Not more than one application for the retrial of an acquitted person may be made under this Division in relation to an acquittal. An application cannot be made in relation to an acquittal resulting from a retrial under this Part.

Hint: remember the process – jurisdiction, in force, interpret provisions, refer to extrinsic materials if need be, consider your interpretation in the light of the purpose, conclusion.

GO ONLINE

Go online for a sample answer to the 'Double jeopardy' exercise.

Exercise: Danny and his motorbike[14]

Danny is a 20 year old law student who works part time in the office of a company which installs house alarms. Danny is a motorbike enthusiast, and he regularly participates in Wednesday night motorbike rides around Sydney (sometimes going as far as Canberra). These large social events are organised by the group 'Sydney Bikieboys'. In order to become a member, a person must be invited by and vouched for by another member. There are no

---

14 Thanks to Nikki Bromberger, from the University of Western Sydney, who provided this problem scenario. If your teacher uses interesting problem scenarios that you think students at other law schools would find useful, why not ask your teacher to contact the authors of this book?

particular requirements to become a member but it is an unspoken rule that police will not generally be allowed to become members of the group. Danny is not a member of this group but it is not necessary to be a member to ride with it.

Danny's uncle, Graham, is a member of Sydney Bikieboys. He hasn't always been into motorbikes, but after the three years he spent in prison for fraud many years earlier, he has felt that riding a motorbike relaxes him. Graham also likes to attend these evening rides because Uri, one of the people he was in prison with, and with whom he has become friends, often rides as well.

As well as riding with this group, Danny (and in fact most people who are interested in motorbikes) is a member of an online social forum called 'Motormouths'. This provides general information about motorbikes and social events, and has active blogs and discussion boards.

Danny hears that the New South Wales government has just passed new legislation in relation to bikie gangs. He is worried about what implications this legislation may have for him and his family and friends. He approaches a partner in the law firm, who agrees to get someone to research the issue. You have been asked to do this, and prepare a memo to the partner, John Biggs. The partner has set out the following matters for you to address:

1. Could 'Sydney Bikieboys' be made a Declared Organisation under the *Crimes (Criminal Organisations Control) Act 2009* (NSW) ('the Act')?

2. Could Danny be subject to a control order under the Act?

3. If Danny is subject to a control order, would he lose his job under the Act?

4. If both Danny and Graham are subject to a control order, could Danny be charged under s26 (1) of the Act?

5. If other members of 'Motormouths' are subject to control orders could Danny be charged under s26 (1) of the Act?

Excerpts from the *Crimes (Criminal Organisations Control) Act 2009* (NSW)

Long title

An Act to provide for the making of declarations and orders for the purpose of disrupting and restricting the activities of criminal organisations and their members; to make related amendments to various Acts; and for other purposes.

2 Commencement

This Act commences on the date of assent to this Act.

3 Definitions

(1) In this Act:

"associate with" means:

(a) to be in company with, or
(b) to communicate with by any means (including by post, facsimile, telephone and email or any other form of electronic communication).

"Commissioner" means the Commissioner of Police.

"control order" means an order of the Court under section 19.

"controlled member" of a declared organisation means a person to whom an interim control order, or a control order, that is in force relates.

"Court" means the Supreme Court.

"declared organisation" means an organisation in respect of which a declaration under Part 2 that is in force relates.

"eligible Judge" -see section 5.

"member" of an organisation includes:

(a) in the case of an organisation that is a body corporate-a director and an officer of the body corporate, and
(b) in any case:
   (i) an associate member or prospective member (however described) of the organisation, and
   (ii) a person who identifies himself or herself, in some way, as belonging to the organisation, and
   (iii) a person who is treated by the organisation or persons who belong to the organisation, in some way, as if he or she belonged to the organisation.

"organisation" means any incorporated body or unincorporated group (however structured), whether or not:

(a) the body or group is based outside New South Wales, or
(b) the body or group consists of persons who are not ordinarily resident in New South Wales.

"serious criminal activity" means any of the following:

(a) obtaining material benefits from conduct that constitutes a serious indictable offence,
(b) obtaining material benefits from conduct engaged in outside New South Wales (including outside Australia) that, if it occurred in New South Wales, would constitute a serious indictable offence,
(c) committing a serious violence offence,
(d) engaging in conduct outside New South Wales (including outside Australia) that, if it occurred in New South Wales, would constitute a serious violence offence.

"serious violence offence" means an offence punishable by imprisonment for life or for a term of 10 years or more, where the conduct constituting the offence involves:

(a) loss of a person's life or serious risk of loss of a person's life, or
(b) serious injury to a person or serious risk of serious injury to a person, or

(c) serious damage to property in circumstances endangering the safety of any person, or

(d) perverting the course of justice (within the meaning of Part 7 of the Crimes Act 1900) in relation to any conduct that, if proved, would constitute a serious violence offence as referred to in paragraph (a), (b) or (c).

4   Extraterritorial operation

It is the intention of the Parliament that this Act apply within the State and outside the State to the full extent of the extraterritorial legislative capacity of the Parliament.

5   Eligible Judges

(1) In this Part:

"eligible Judge" means a Judge in relation to whom a consent under subsection (2) and a declaration under subsection (3) are in force.

(2) A Judge of the Court may, by instrument in writing, consent to being the subject of a declaration by the Attorney General under subsection (3).

(3) The Attorney General may, by instrument in writing, declare Judges in relation to whom consents are in force under subsection (2) to be eligible Judges for the purposes of this Part.

6   Commissioner may apply for declaration

(1) The Commissioner may apply to an eligible Judge for a declaration (or renewal of a declaration) under this Part that a particular organisation is a declared organisation for the purposes of this Act.

(2) The application must:

(a) be in writing, and

(b) identify the particular organisation in respect of which the declaration is sought, and

(c) describe the nature of the organisation and any of its distinguishing characteristics, and

(d) specify the names (or names by which they are commonly known) of any persons that the Commissioner has reasonable grounds to believe are members of the organisation, and

(e) set out the grounds on which the declaration is sought, and

(f) set out the information supporting the grounds on which the declaration is sought, and

(g) set out details of any previous application for a declaration in respect of the organisation and the outcome of that application, and

(h) be supported by an affidavit from the Commissioner, or affidavits from one or more other senior police officers, verifying the contents of the application.

(3) The application may identify the organisation by specifying the name of the organisation or the name by which the organisation is commonly known or by providing other particulars about the organisation.

9   Eligible Judge may make declaration
   (1) If, on the making of an application by the Commissioner under this Part in relation to a particular organisation, the eligible Judge is satisfied that:
      (a) members of the organisation associate for the purpose of organising, planning, facilitating, supporting or engaging in serious criminal activity, and
      (b) the organisation represents a risk to public safety and order in this State, the eligible Judge may make a declaration under this Part that the particular organisation is a declared organisation for the purposes of this Act.
   (2) In considering whether or not to make a declaration, the eligible Judge may have regard to any of the following:
      (a) any information suggesting that a link exists between the organisation and serious criminal activity,
      (b) any criminal convictions recorded in relation to current or former members of the organisation,
      (c) any information suggesting that current or former members of the organisation have been, or are, involved in serious criminal activity (whether directly or indirectly and whether or not such involvement has resulted in any criminal convictions),
      (d) any information suggesting that members of an interstate or overseas chapter or branch of the organisation associate for the purpose of organising, planning, facilitating, supporting or engaging in serious criminal activity,
      (e) any submissions made in relation to the application by the Attorney General or as referred to in section 8,
      (f) any other matter the eligible Judge considers relevant.
   (3) A declaration may be made whether or not any of the persons referred to in section 8 are present or make submissions.
   (4) The eligible Judge may, for the purposes of making a declaration, be satisfied that members of an organisation associate for the purpose of organising, planning, facilitating, supporting or engaging in serious criminal activity:
      (a) whether or not all the members associate for that purpose or only some of the members (provided that, if the eligible Judge is satisfied that only some of the members associate for that purpose, the eligible Judge must be satisfied that those members constitute a significant group within the organisation, either in terms of their numbers or in terms of their capacity to influence the organisation or its members), and
      (b) whether or not members associate for the purpose of organising, planning, facilitating, supporting or engaging in the same serious criminal activities or different ones, and
      (c) whether or not the members also associate for other purposes.
19 Court may make control order
   (1) The Court may make a control order in relation to a person on whom notice

of an interim control order has been served under section 16 if the Court is satisfied that:
(a) the person is a member of a particular declared organisation, and
(b) sufficient grounds exist for making the control order.
(2) The Court may:
(a) make a control order confirming or confirming with variations the interim control order, or
(b) revoke the interim control order.
(7) Without limiting subsection (6), an order may be made, if in the opinion of the Court the circumstances of the case require:
(a) if the person satisfies the Court that there is a good reason why he or she should be allowed to associate with a particular controlled member-exempting the person from the operation of section 26 to the extent, and subject to the conditions, specified by the Court, or
(b) exempting the person from the operation of section 27 for a period specified by the Court to enable the person to organise his or her affairs.

26 Association between members of declared organisations subject to interim control order or control order
(1) A controlled member of a declared organisation who associates with another controlled member of the declared organisation is guilty of an offence.
Maximum penalty:
(a) for a first offence-imprisonment for 2 years, and
(b) for a second or subsequent offence-imprisonment for 5 years.
(2) A person may be guilty of an offence under subsection (1) in respect of associations with the same person or with different people.
(3) It is a defence to a prosecution for an offence under subsection (1) if the defendant establishes that he or she did not know, and could not reasonably be expected to have known, that the other person with whom he or she associated was a controlled member of the declared organisation.
(4) It is a defence to a prosecution for an offence under subsection (1) if the association is in accordance with an exemption under section 19 (7) (a).
(5) The following forms of associations are to be disregarded for the purposes of this section in its application to a defendant to whom an interim control order relates if the defendant proves that the association was reasonable in the circumstances:
(a) associations between close family members,
(b) associations occurring in the course of a lawful occupation, business or profession,
(c) associations occurring at a course of training or education of a kind prescribed by the regulations between persons enrolled in the course,
(d) associations occurring at a rehabilitation, counselling or therapy session of a kind prescribed by the regulations,

(e) associations occurring in lawful custody or in the course of complying with a court order,
(f) other associations of a kind prescribed by the regulations.
(8) For the purposes of this section, a person is a "close family member" of another person if:
   (a) the person is a spouse or former spouse of the other or is, or has been, in a domestic relationship with the other, or
   (b) the person is a parent or grandparent of the other (whether by blood or by marriage), or
   (c) the person is a brother or sister of the other (whether by blood or by marriage), or
   (d) the person is a guardian or carer of the other.

27 Prohibition on carrying on of certain activities when interim control order or control order takes effect
   (1) Any authorisation to carry on a prescribed activity that is held by a controlled member of a declared organisation is automatically suspended on the taking effect of an interim control order in relation to the person.
   (6) In this section:
   "authorisation" includes the licensing, registration, approval, certification or any other form of authorisation of a person required by or under legislation for the carrying on of an occupation or activity.
   "occupation" means an occupation, trade, profession or calling of any kind that may only be carried on by a person holding an authorisation.
   "prescribed activity" means the following:
   (a) operating a casino within the meaning of the Casino Control Act 1992, or being a special employee within the meaning of Part 4 of that Act,
   (b) carrying on a security activity within the meaning of the Security Industry Act 1997,
   (c) carrying on the business of a pawnbroker within the meaning of the Pawnbrokers and Second-hand Dealers Act 1996,
   (d) carrying on business as a commercial agent or private inquiry agent within the meaning of the Commercial Agents and Private Inquiry Agents Act 2004,
   (e) possessing or using a firearm within the meaning of the Firearms Act 1996 or carrying on business as a firearms dealer within the meaning of that Act,
   (f) operating a tow truck within the meaning of the Tow Truck Industry Act 1998,
   (g) carrying on business as a dealer within the meaning of the Motor Dealers Act 1974,
   (h) carrying on business as a repairer within the meaning of the Motor Vehicle Repairs Act 1980,

(i) selling or supplying liquor within the meaning of the Liquor Act 2007,
(j) carrying on the business of a bookmaker within the meaning of the Racing Administration Act 1998,
(k) carrying out the activities of an owner, trainer, jockey, stablehand, bookmaker, bookmaker's clerk or another person associated with racing who is required to be registered or licensed under the Thoroughbred Racing Act 1996,
(l) carrying out the activities of an owner, trainer or other person associated with greyhound or harness racing who is required to be registered under the Greyhound and Harness Racing Administration Act 2004,
(m) any other activity prescribed by the regulations.

Also, here is an extract from the second reading speech:

Crimes (Criminal Organisations Control) Bill 2009

Extract from NSW Legislative Assembly *Hansard* **and Papers**
Thursday 2 April 2009
Mr NATHAN REES (Toongabbie – Premier, and Minister for the Arts) [11.09 a.m.]:
Today the Government introduces the Crimes (Criminal Organisations Control) Bill 2009 – tough new laws to ensure that police have the powers they need to deal with violent outlaw motorcycle gangs. The Government is introducing legislation that gets the balance right. The legislation is a proportionate response to an escalation in violent crime involving outlaw motorcycle gangs that has spilled into public places, and is threatening the lives and safety of innocent bystanders. The legislation is specific to outlaw motorcycle gangs and their members and to target outlaw motorcycle gangs, seeking to declare them as criminal organisations, we will put in place strong safeguards to ensure that the gangs alone are the subject of the bill.

Ten days ago bikie gangs crossed the line and risked public safety at Sydney Airport. Since then there have been frequent shootings in public streets. Last week the Commissioner of Police briefed the Attorney General and the Minister for Police on what police needed to fight outlaw motorcycle gangs.

Once these laws take full effect, the Commissioner of Police will be able to seek a declaration from a Supreme Court judge that a bikie gang is a declared criminal organisation. Once the organisation is declared, the commissioner may then seek control orders from the Supreme Court in respect of one of more persons on the basis that those persons are members of a declared criminal organisation and there are sufficient grounds for making the order. The controlled member will not be able to associate with another controlled member of that gang. If they do, they will risk two years jail for the first offence. Do it again and they will risk five years in jail. To help take these gang members off the streets there will be no presumption in favour of bail for this offence.

GO ONLINE
Go online for a sample answer to the 'Danny and his motorbike' exercise.

TIP
We strongly encourage you to prepare an answer yourself before you look at the answers online.

DISCUSSION QUESTIONS

1. How is the modern statutory approach to statutory interpretation different from the traditional common law approaches?
2. Should parliament have introduced comprehensive interpretation legislation to replace the approaches developed by the courts, rather than having a piecemeal approach with a bit of statute and a bit of common law applying?
3. Do you think it is acceptable to have nine somewhat different sets of rules in place in Australia for statutory interpretation?
4. Do the 'presumptions' adequately protect rights or is something more needed, such as a bill of rights?
5. How important do you think the skill of statutory interpretation is for lawyers to have?

WEBLINKS AND FURTHER READING

Online

Commonwealth Acts: www.austlii.edu.au/au/legis/cth/consol_act
Commonwealth Regulations: www.austlii.edu.au/au/legis/cth/consol_reg
Australian Capital Territory Acts: www.austlii.edu.au/au/legis/act/consol_act
Australian Capital Territory regulations: www.austlii.edu.au/au/legis/act/consol_reg
New South Wales Acts: www.austlii.edu.au/au/legis/nsw/consol_act
New South Wales Regulations: www.austlii.edu.au/au/legis/nsw/consol_reg
Victorian Acts: www.austlii.edu.au/au/legis/vic/consol_act
Victorian Regulations: www.austlii.edu.au/au/legis/vic/consol_reg
Queensland Acts: www.austlii.edu.au/au/legis/qld/consol_act
Queensland Regulations: www.austlii.edu.au/au/legis/qld/consol_reg
Western Australian Acts: www.austlii.edu.au/au/legis/wa/consol_act
Western Australian Regulations: www.austlii.edu.au/au/legis/wa/consol_reg
South Australian Acts: www.austlii.edu.au/au/legis/sa/consol_act
South Australian Regulations: www.austlii.edu.au/au/legis/sa/consol_reg
Tasmanian Acts: www.austlii.edu.au/au/legis/tas/consol_act
Tasmanian Regulations: www.austlii.edu.au/au/legis/tas/consol_reg
Northern Territory Acts: www.austlii.edu.au/au/legis/nt/consol_act
Northern Territory Regulations: www.austlii.edu.au/au/legis/nt/consol_reg

Printed sources

Brazil, P, 'Reform of Statutory Interpretation – the Australian Experience: Use of Extrinsic Materials' (1988) 62 *Australian Law Journal* 503.

Pearce, DC and Geddes, RS, *Statutory Interpretation in Australia*, LexisNexis, Sydney, 6th edn (2006).

ONLINE RESOURCES FOR THIS CHAPTER

The following resources are available online at www.oup.com.au/orc/cwl2e
- Sample answer to exercise: 'Make Poverty History' (p. 316)
- Applying *ejusdem generis* sample answer
- Latin maxims sample answers
- Jimbo and Baba visit parliament house sample answer
- No standing sample answer
- Double jeopardy sample answer
- Danny and his motorbike sample answer
- Additional statutory interpretation exercise: 'Proceeds of Crime'
- Flashcard glossary
- Multiple choice questions

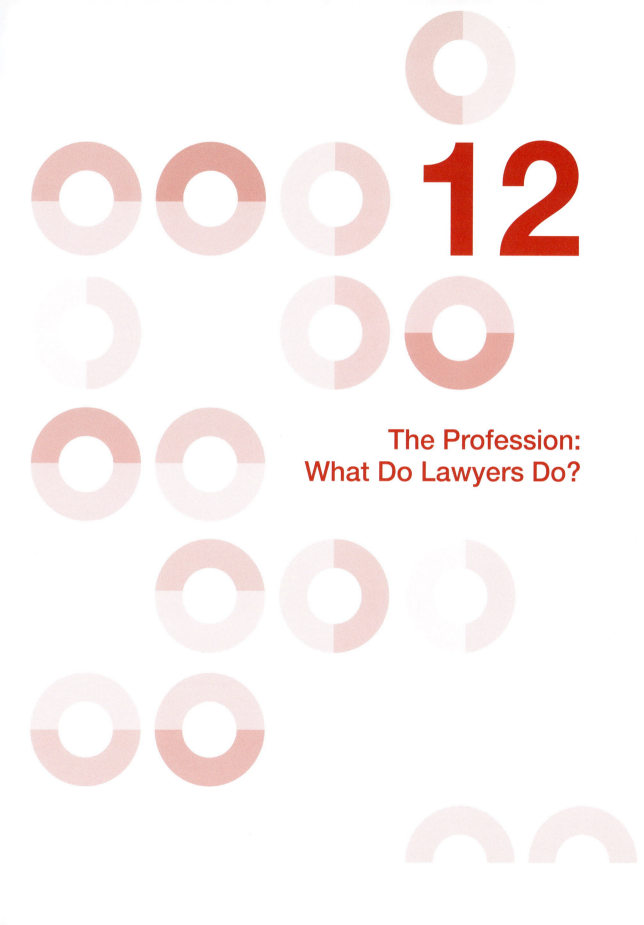

12

The Profession: What Do Lawyers Do?

WHAT WE WILL COVER IN THIS CHAPTER:

- An overview of the legal profession
- The role and work of solicitors
- The legal duties and regulation of solicitors
- The role and work of barristers
- The role of Senior Counsel (SC) and Queen's Counsel (QC)
- The role of judges
- Ethical responsibilities
- The sort of work lawyers do

Recommended approach to learning this topic

To begin, it is best to read the key terms and check that you understand them. Then, read the chapter bearing in mind what you already know about lawyers. Having read the chapter and perhaps pursued some web links of interest you will be ready to try some discussion questions. It may also be useful to use the Internet to look at the law society, bar association, and court websites.

KEY TERMS

Australian lawyer = a person who holds a qualification in law and has been admitted to practise law by the Supreme Court in their jurisdiction.

Bar Association = an association that assists in the regulation and coordination of the work of barristers.

Barrister = a lawyer who is a member of a Bar Association, accepts briefs from solicitors to represent clients in courts and tribunals and writes formal opinions about legal issues but does not typically maintain files or trust accounts for clients.

Brief = the bundle of legal documents given by a solicitor to a barrister. It is usually tied with a pink ribbon and has a summary at the front of the facts, legal issues, the outcome the client seeks, and the specific instruction (usually to attend at a hearing or provide an opinion).

Chambers = the traditional name for the building a barrister works from. Barristers usually share premises and secretarial support.

Counsel = another term for a barrister, someone doing advocacy work in a court or tribunal.

Divided profession = where there are two separate types of practitioners, admitted as either barristers or solicitors, but not both (as for example in England).

Fused profession = where legal practitioners are admitted as both barristers and solicitors and are permitted to do both kinds of work. Frequently some choose to practise exclusively as a barrister, and others do predominantly solicitor's work except for small mentions of matters in court.

Lawyer = a general term for a person who holds a graduate or postgraduate qualification in law.

Legal Practitioner = encompasses both solicitors and barristers and means that the person is not only a lawyer but also holds a current practising certificate.

Senior Counsel = Queen's Counsel = an experienced barrister appointed to senior rank (said to have 'taken silk'). Senior Counsel is the newer term.

Solicitor = the legal practitioner who represents the parties in a transaction, interviews the client, gives legal advice, maintains files, prepares legal documents, briefs barristers, and handles trust funds on behalf of clients. Solicitors can practise in partnership or as companies.

1: Overview of Australian legal practice

Legal practitioners defined

Lawyers are known by various terms, some unprintable. Although most lay people simply call all people with a law degree, whether they are practising or not, 'lawyers',[1] the industry self-classification is 'legal practitioners' in the 'legal profession', which the Australian Bureau of Statistics (ABS) calls 'legal services'. Within the broad categorisation of legal practitioners there are further distinctions between solicitors and barristers (sometimes called counsel or advocates). The American term 'attorney' is not used in Australia to refer to lawyers.[2]

In Australia, graduating with a law degree does not entitle you to be a practising lawyer. To become an 'Australian lawyer' you need to undergo further practical legal training and/or undertake training under the supervision of legal practitioners in order to be admitted to practise as a lawyer (admitted to the practice of law) by the Supreme Court of your state or territory. Admission is not in itself sufficient to actually practise law – to be called an 'Australian legal practitioner' a lawyer must also hold a current practising certificate. For admitted lawyers this simply involves making an application and paying a fee. Practising certificates are issued for each calendar year or part of a year. Lawyers who let their practising certificate lapse while spending a period of time out of legal practice are able to recommence at any time on application and payment of the applicable fees.

TIP

When you have been admitted to practise law by the relevant Supreme Court you are an 'Australian lawyer'. To be an 'Australian legal practitioner' you must hold a current practising certificate.

---

1   In September 2009, there were 301 000 searches on Google for the word 'lawyers', and only 135 000 searches for 'solicitors': see www.lawyers.com.au/legal-articles/2009/11.

2   The word 'attorney' is used in Australia in relation to powers of attorney. A power of attorney is a document giving someone power to sign documents and act legally in place of another person. It is used, for example, where someone is going overseas and wants another person to be able to look after their affairs while they are away. It is also used by older people before they lose mental capacity.

Background to the legal profession

Some historical knowledge is required to understand the role of legal practitioners. Barristers and solicitors are occupations that pre-date English settlement of Australia.

In England, barristers and solicitors are different professions, so the legal profession is considered to be formally 'divided'. There are different admission requirements for both occupational groups. The role of the barrister is to present oral argument and argue a client's case before a court. They were trained through a system of 'pupillage', in which other barristers guided them and taught them oral advocacy techniques. Barristers lodged and trained at Inns of Court (the remaining four are Lincoln's Inn, Grays's Inn, Inner Temple and Middle Temple) where they took on apprentices and trained them in a communal fashion. Today English barristers are not trained at the Inns; instead they do the Bar Vocational Course.

Solicitors, on the other hand, were trained by other solicitors through an apprenticeship known as articles. The articled clerk was trained in all aspects of solicitor work by the solicitor. Their work is to meet clients, take a history, and do the preliminary paperwork, legal research, and draft and lodge the necessary documents to run a case in a tribunal or court. Many solicitors are also formally trained and accredited mediators and offer these services to clients.

Australia has in part followed the English approach. Solicitors in some jurisdictions commence legal practice with articled clerkships or traineeships, and barristers do a bar readers' course while being supervised by a mentor who is currently on the Bar Roll (the register on members) as a practising barrister.

Historically, legal profession regulation has been a matter for the states and territories. This has resulted in different requirements as to qualifications, practical experience requirements, admission, and discipline. There have been efforts over the past two decades to reform the profession and move towards a national approach, which have had some success. A National Model Bill on the Legal Profession, which was finalised in 2006, created a uniform legislative framework for legal profession regulation, and at the time of writing legislation based on it has been passed in all States and Territories apart from South Australia.[3]

In February 2009 the Prime Minister announced that legal profession reform was to be included in the microeconomic reform agenda under the National Partnership Agreement on a Seamless National Economy of the Council of Australian Governments (COAG). A taskforce is currently drafting national legislation, which is expected to be enacted in 2010. Implementation will be phased in, so current law students will not be disadvantaged by the process. For more information see the information published online by COAG.[4]

---

3   Efforts to date in South Australia have been unsuccessful. In early 2009 a bill to enact a Legal Profession Act lapsed due to a deadlock on some issues. These are likely to be resolved in 2010–11. In the meantime the *Legal Practitioners Act 1981* (SA) applies. The Acts in the other jurisdictions, in order of passage, are: *Legal Profession Act 2004* (NSW); *Legal Profession Act 2004* (Vic); *Legal Profession Act 2006* (ACT); *Legal Profession Act 2006* (NT); *Legal Profession Act 2007* (Qld); *Legal Profession Act 2007* (Tas); *Legal Profession Act 2008* (WA).

4   At www.ag.gov.au/www/agd/agd.nsf/Page/Consultationsreformsandreviews_CouncilofAustralian Governments(COAG)NationalLegalProfessionReform.

In depth: National Legal Profession Model Bill

The bill comprises eight chapters, each with several divisions.

- **Chapter 1** – Introduction – states the purpose of the legislation is to regulate legal practice in a particular jurisdiction and to facilitate the regulation of the legal profession on a national basis. It also includes an extensive definitions section.
- **Chapter 2** – General requirements for engaging in legal practice – the aim is to ensure only legally qualified people give legal advice, or advertise themselves as being entitled to engage in legal practice, including restrictions on the use of titles such as solicitor, barrister, Senior Counsel, etc. It also covers the basic requirements for legal practice, including academic and practical legal training, and admission requirements including eligibility and suitability. It allows anyone admitted in one jurisdiction to practise in any other Australian jurisdiction, and provides that, where someone is struck off the roll of legal practitioners in one jurisdiction this automatically occurs in all other jurisdictions. Finally, Chapter 2 covers legal practice in Australian jurisdictions by foreign lawyers via a process of registration.
- **Chapter 3** – Conduct of legal practice – provides for binding rules of professional conduct, including dealing with money held in trust on behalf of clients, and the requirement that disclosure of the basis for charging fees be given to clients (costs disclosure), with a process for establishing costs where there is a disagreement as to the amount (costs assessment). It also provides for indemnity insurance to be held, with a fund maintained to pay compensation in the event of negligent actions by lawyers.
- **Chapter 4** – Complaints and discipline – provides for a mechanism by which complaints against legal practitioners may be investigated, and decisions reached by an administrative tribunal as to whether the act or omission amounted to unsatisfactory professional conduct or professional misconduct.
- **Chapter 5** – External intervention – provides for the intervention in a legal practice by a supervisor, manager or receiver following events such as death or insolvency, or other suspected behaviour such as misuse of trust funds.
- **Chapter 6** – Investigatory powers – sets out the powers of investigation into legal practices including complaints against legal practitioners, and investigations into the use of trust funds, including powers to seize documents, enter and search premises, examine persons and hold hearings.
- **Chapter 7** – Regulatory authorities – this is left blank as it is up to each jurisdiction to decide. For example, in New South Wales there is provision for a Legal Services Commissioner, Legal Profession Admission Board, Bar Association and Law Society.[5] In Western Australia, there is provision for a Legal Profession Complaints Committee, Legal Practice Board, and a Law Complaints Officer.[6]

---

5   *Legal Profession Act 2004* (NSW) Pt 7, www.austlii.edu.au/au/legis/nsw/consol_act/lpa2004179/.

6   *Legal Profession Act 2008* (WA) Pt 16, www.austlii.edu.au/au/legis/wa/consol_act/lpa2008179/.

- **Chapter 8** — General — provides for the liability of principals of legal practices in situations where the law practice contravenes the law, except where the principal did not know about the conduct, could not influence it, or otherwise exercised due diligence to prevent the contravention.

The full text of the model bill is available at www.department.dotag.wa.gov.au/_files/model_bill.pdf. Remember that it is a model piece of legislation, and chances are that in the jurisdiction you are studying, the bill has become law. Why not look up your Legal Profession Act to see if it incorporates the model bill provisions?

Specialist or generalist

Like medical practitioners, there is a modern tendency among legal practitioners to specialise in particular legal fields, such as banking or property. Many lawyers are also becoming accredited mediators and arbitrators. Specialisation has been a response to increased legal regulation, increased legal complexity, increased legislation, mediation, increases in specialist courts and tribunals, and the growth of licensing. For many lawyers, this specialisation is simply an acknowledgement that one can no longer keep abreast of all the law, but can only keep up with select areas of it. Many law firms advertise their specialisation, a trend that has now been acknowledged by the judiciary:[7]

> Not too long ago a client would utilise the services of one particular firm of solicitors for whatever legal work that client required from time to time. Nowadays that client will look for advice from a firm that is expert in that area of the law that is of concern to the client. He may even use two or three firms in one matter where that matter involves discrete areas of the law and one firm is not expert in all of those areas.
>
> When a client retains a firm that is or professes to be specially experienced in a discrete branch of the law that client is entitled to expect that the standard of care with which his retainer will be performed is consistent with the expertise that the firm has or professes to have.

Specialisation is more common in city commercial firms. By necessity, suburban and country legal practitioners tend to have broader-ranging practices. Specialisation carries with it a greater expectation of success from the client, but may allow the practitioner to charge more for this expertise. On the flip side, it is efficient because the specialist can usually understand a matter more quickly and needs less preliminary research to 'get up to speed' on the area. Barristers take briefs from solicitors and tend to accept cases as they arise, and so they need a good general knowledge of most fields of law. However, barristers still have fields of specialty and advertise areas of specialised knowledge or advocacy experience in particular courts or tribunals. This specialised knowledge is often sought by solicitors who commission a barrister to write them a legal opinion about a legal argument or point of law.

---

7   *Yates Property Corporation (in liq) v Boland* (1998) 157 ALR 30 at 50.

Front end (drafting) and back end (disputes)

Solicitors assist commercial clients at all levels. Front-end work involves drafting company documents, standard terms and conditions, contracts for the purchase of property, vehicles, inventory, employment, and essential services. Back-end work involves assisting clients with resolving disputes, through negotiation, litigation, and often alternative methods of dispute such as mediation and arbitration (see Chapter 5 for more on resolving disputes). Sole practitioners, and solicitors in smaller firms, tend to handle both the front end and back end needs of their clients, while solicitors in larger firms tend to be divided into practice groups, such as mergers and acquisitions, corporate and commercial, and litigation.

Example: Law firm of Mallesons Stephen Jaques

Mallesons Stephen Jaques ('Mallesons') is one of the largest corporate and commercial law firms in Australia, with over 1000 legal staff.[8] It has the following practice groups:

- Banking and finance (e.g. advising on the financing of a large project, assisting companies with issuing shares)
- Competition (e.g. advising on a prosecution over anti-competitive measures regarding the sale of a certain product)
- Commercial Property (this is a way of saying that they do real estate transactions, but not residential ones)
- Construction (can be anything from advising on construction of a motorway to a large infrastructure project)
- Environment (e.g. advice on risk from a contaminated site, environmental impact assessment of tourism project)
- Dispute Resolution (formerly these practice groups were called 'Litigation', and cover resolving commercial disputes)
- Intellectual Property & Technology (e.g. filing a patent for a pharmaceutical client, large IT procurement contract)
- Mergers & Acquisitions (e.g. advising a company on a bid to take over another company)
- Tax (e.g. providing advice on goods and services tax (GST), tax payable by a company operating internationally)
- Workplace and employee relations (advice on an enterprise bargaining process, or occupational health and safety laws)

---

8   For more information see www.mallesons.com.

Value-adding services provided by lawyers

Lawyers provide value to clients, and this is why clients seek out and pay for their services. Lawyers add value to commercial clients' businesses by reducing risk (e.g. through drafting watertight contracts), or reducing losses (e.g. those arising from accident or error on the part of an employee), or protecting assets (e.g. with advice on intellectual property such as trade marks and copyright). Lawyers offer criminal clients a 'value add' by attempting to convince the police, a prosecutor, a magistrate or judge to reduce the charge or the sentence for an offence, or successfully defending them so that they are fully exonerated.

Further, with a competitive legal market for certain services many firms have developed additional services that add value to their clients' businesses. This can help offer the client a 'one stop shop' or a level of flexibility. These services are usually advertised, and can include:

- software that enables clients to enter data on routine transactions and calculate the legal risk involved
- training for clients
- providing newsletters on legal developments of interest to their clients
- secondments between their employees and the employees of their clients
- international project management services and links or contacts (e.g. in China or India). These services are usually offered by large firms with partner offices overseas.

> **TIP**
> Under a secondment, the lawyer continues to be employed by the firm, but works in the client's office for a while. Getting to know the client's business enables the law firm to offer a better service.

Professional indemnity insurance

Just as surveyors and doctors hold professional indemnity insurance, which covers them against claims by clients and third parties who suffer loss or damage as a result of their negligence, legal practitioners are required, as a condition of holding a practising certificate, to hold professional indemnity insurance. Law Societies and Bar Associations negotiate such cover for their members, and it is included as part of the cost each year of practising certificate renewal. Lawyers who work for the government do not require such cover as they are indemnified by their employer. In some jurisdictions, large law firms organise their own professional indemnity insurance. In the two states with the greatest numbers of practitioners, New South Wales and Victoria, insurance is handled by LawCover and the Legal Practitioners Liability Committee.

LawCover

LawCover is a group of companies owned by the Law Society of New South Wales, to provide Compulsory Professional Indemnity Insurance (PII) for solicitors, and manage the Solicitor's Mutual Indemnity Fund (created from contributions by lawyers as part of practising certificate renewal). LawCover responds when a claim is made against a solicitor in New South Wales or the Australian Capital Territory, acting on behalf of the lawyer and paying any settlement sum agreed. They also try to educate solicitors in risk management in order to minimise further claims. For more information see www.lawcover.com.au.

Legal Practitioners Liability Committee

In Victoria all law practices (solicitors) and barristers must obtain professional indemnity insurance from the Legal Practitioners Liability Committee (LPLC) unless exempted from that requirement by the Legal Services Board. Its role is similar to that of LawCover. For more information see www.lplc.com.au.

2: Solicitors

Solicitors comprise 80 per cent of the Australian legal profession. The last extensive research on legal services by the Australian Bureau of Statistics (ABS) was in 2007–08. But the previous report (2000–01) provided better data specifically relating to Australian solicitors:[9]

- The 7566 solicitor practices in this country employed a total of 29 159 solicitors.
- Males accounted for 66 per cent of solicitors in private practice.
- Commercial legal services work accounted for the highest proportion (36.7 per cent) of total practice income for solicitor practices with more than five principals or partners.
- Property work accounted for the highest proportion (28.6 per cent) of total practice income for solicitor practices with five or less principals or partners.
- An average of 10.5 people were employed per solicitor practice (including principals and partners). This ranged from eight people per practice in the Northern Territory to 12.9 per practice in Queensland.
- Solicitor practices with one principal or proprietor accounted for 69.2 per cent of practices in Australia and generated 16.9 per cent of total practice income.
- Solicitor practices with 10 or more principals or partners accounted for only 1.2 per cent of practices, but generated 47 per cent of total practice income.
- 5976 private solicitor practices (79 per cent) were located in capital cities.
- New South Wales was home to 38.3 per cent of the total number of solicitor practices in Australia and generated 45.5 per cent of total practice income; Victoria was home to 32.1 per cent and generated 24.5 per cent of income.
- 4744 private solicitor practices (63 per cent) reported doing some sort of pro bono work.

Although the traditional business structure for lawyers is a sole practitioner or a partnership, in recent years some jurisdictions have provided for an incorporated legal practice (ILP), which is effectively a corporation that is permitted to engage in legal practice. This suits some legal practitioners because the ILP can raise capital (unlike a partnership, where it is the partners who put capital into the firm). Additionally there is the option of a Multi-Disciplinary Partnership (MDP), which allows for partnerships between lawyers and non-lawyers (this could, for example, be useful where a company wants to provide both international trade services such

---

9   See ABS *8667.0 Legal Services, Australia, 2007–8* available at www.abs.gov.au/ausstats/abs@.nsf/mf/8667.0. Or go to the Law Council of Australia's website www.lawcouncil.asn.au/ and download the Snapshot of the Legal Profession as at July 2009 (select menu items Information/About the profession).

as freight forwarding and customs clearance, as well as legal advice on international trade, such as drafting terms and conditions for sale, and resolving disputes where cargo has been damaged in transit). The underlying provisions for ILPs and MDPs[10] are in Part 2.7 of the Legal Profession Model Bill discussed above.

The solicitor's role

The solicitor is the main legal interface with the client. Solicitors typically begin by interviewing the client to ascertain the facts. They then advise them, often by letter, on the applicable law and the options available to them. The client then 'instructs' the solicitor to undertake a certain course of action, which may involve, in a criminal matter, getting a barrister to make an application for bail, or in a civil matter, sending a letter of demand or drafting a statement of defence. The solicitor may negotiate a resolution on behalf of the client, and in litigated matters, liaises with the solicitor for the other parties, attends court on routine matters, files documents with the court, prepares witness statements, continues to advise the client on the case and potential settlement and, if necessary, instructs a barrister for a trial hearing.

Requirements in order to practise as a solicitor

Anyone who has been admitted to legal practice in an Australian state or territory and who holds a current practising certificate is entitled to practise as a solicitor. A person admitted to practise in one Australian jurisdiction will usually be allowed to practise anywhere in Australia, although an official letter of request needs to be made to be admitted to practise in the High Court (which then covers the lawyer for all federal courts). Generally there is a requirement that the first two years of legal practice be restricted (where the lawyer works under an experienced legal practitioner rather than being a sole practitioner) followed by some requirements before the restriction is lifted (such as completing an unrestricted practising certificate course, and submitting letters from supervisors attesting to competency in legal work).

TIP
The words 'practice' and 'practise' can cause confusion. 'Practice' is the noun and 'practise' is the verb. For example a person 'took over their father's legal practice, and has been practising law for some time now'.

Most law societies administer a requirement that solicitors update their legal knowledge through mandatory continuing legal education (MCLE) or continuing professional development (CPD). In some states and territories, continuing legal education (CLE) is optional, but increasingly it is becoming a requirement in most jurisdictions. Typically the number of hours of CLE is between 10 and 12 per year, and half of these hours can be completed through watching legal education videos and DVDs. There is currently a move towards a national set of CPD standards.[11] The guideline provides a requirement for 10 units per year per lawyer of CPD, including attending seminars, conferences, delivering CPD presentations, and publishing,

---

10 For Victoria see www.lsb.vic.gov.au/IncorporatedLegalPractices.htmwhat, Queensland see www.lsc.qld.gov.au/275.htm, NSW see www.lawsociety.com.au/ForSolicitors/practisinglawinnsw/practicestructures/index.htm, Northern Territory see www.lawsocnt.asn.au/fmi/xsl/lsnt/downloads/Incorporated%20Legal%20Practice%20(ILP)%20v0507.pdf.

11 See the National CPD Taskforce's 2007 paper 'A Model Continuing Professional Development Scheme for Lawyers', available at www.coro.com.au/ under Current projects (National CPD Guidelines).

where one hour generally equates to one unit. Within the 10 units, there should be at least one practical legal ethics unit, one practice management and business skills unit, and one professional skills unit. These may, for example, comprise a seminar on handling conflicts of interest, a session on file management, and a session on legal researching, respectively.

Solicitors' duties

Solicitors owe duties to their clients, but their most important duty – and the one that takes precedence over all others – is their duty to the court. Solicitors' duties to the court and to their clients are outlined below.

Duties to the court, and to uphold the law and the administration of justice

Lawyers are expected to uphold the law, even where it conflicts with the interests of their clients. Lawyers are held to a higher standard of care than members of the public because they have a near-monopoly on the provision of legal services. Our adversarial system relies heavily on the integrity of the two legal teams presenting the best case for the judge to decide. This is made clear by the Law Council of Australia (the peak legal practitioner body) in its Model Rules of Professional Conduct and Practice (2002),[12] which state:[13]

> Practitioners, in all their dealings with the courts, whether those dealings involve the obtaining and presentation of evidence, the preparation and filing of documents, instructing an advocate or appearing as an advocate, should act with competence, honesty and candour. Practitioners should be frank in their responses and disclosures to the court, and diligent in their observance of undertakings which they give to the court or their opponents.

Duty not to mislead

Solicitors have a duty not to mislead the court on facts and law. This duty has been repeated in many judgments, in legislation, and in conduct rules. For example the Law Council of Australia's Model Rules state that a practitioner must not 'knowingly make a misleading statement to a court' and if the practitioner is later aware that they did mislead the court, must 'take all necessary steps to correct any misleading statement made by the practitioner to a court as soon as possible' (rule 14.2).[14] Nor is a legal practitioner allowed to knowingly mislead opposing counsel. This is particularly important given Australia's reliance on the adversarial system and the fact that the success of such a system is predicated on good counsel presenting the best possible information to the judge.

---

12 Model Rules of Professional Conduct and Practice (2002), available at www.lawcouncil.asn.au/programs/national_profession/policies/model-rules.cfm.

13 Ibid., 12.

14 Ibid., 13.

As to law, the duty is the same: that is, to present the court any binding case authorities or legislation applicable to the case, even those that are not favourable to one's client (rule 14.6). Although a lawyer is not under any obligation to disclose a client's prior convictions in court, where a practitioner knows about a client's previous convictions for a behaviour for which their client is again on trial for, the practitioner cannot claim in sentencing submissions that such behaviour is out of character.[15]

Duty of candour and the 'guilty' client

A very common question that is asked of lawyers is 'How can you defend someone you know is guilty?' The answer commonly given by legal practitioners is this: 'It's not our role to decide the client's guilt – that is the role of the court. We are advocates, not judges'. The reality is often a little more complex. Again the Law Council of Australia Model Rules deal with this and suggest that where a client states their guilt to the lawyer, the lawyer cannot then mislead the court by pleading 'not guilty'. The solution is to offer to do a guilty plea for them, pleading mitigating circumstances and seeking a sentencing discount in recognition of the time and cost saved to the courts by the early guilty plea. Where the client is not prepared to plead guilty despite having admitted their guilt, and insists on a plea of 'not guilty', the legal practitioner may cease to act for that client providing there is sufficient time for the client to brief another lawyer and the client is not insisting that the original lawyer continue to act for them.[16] Where the lawyer is obliged to retain that client, rule 15.2.2 of the Model Rules explains their new obligations to the court:

> 15.2.2 in cases where the practitioner continues to act for the client:
> (a) must not falsely suggest that some other person committed the offence charged;
> (b) must not set up an affirmative case inconsistent with the confession;
> (c) may argue that the evidence as a whole does not prove that the client is guilty of the offence charged;
> (d) may argue that for some reason of law the client is not guilty of the offence charged; or
> (e) may argue that for any other reason not prohibited by (a) and (b) the client should not be convicted of the offence charged.

This is a good example of a situation where the lawyer's duty to the client is placed second to the duty to the administration of justice.

> **Reflection**
>
> How do you feel about potentially defending a client, who has confessed their guilt to you, by running an argument that the evidence cannot prove their guilt? Can you see how this is your professional duty if you can't convince them to plead guilty or get another lawyer?

---

15 Ibid., 15 (rule 14.10).

16 Ibid., 16 (rule 15.2).

Duties to the client

This is the best-known duty that lawyers owe. It includes a duty to be competent, to avoid conflicts of interest, to maintain client confidentiality, to facilitate reasonable settlement, and to handle client monies properly. These are discussed in turn below.

Duties of competency

Lawyers are hired as professionals and are held to high standards of practice in their advisory and advocacy roles. Lawyers are required to take steps to keep themselves up to date in their fields of practice. Key ways for lawyers to keep themselves educated about new developments in law is to read their law society magazines, read looseleaf or online legal databases, and attend CLE programs. Since the 1988 High Court case of *Hawkins v Clayton*[17] a plaintiff may chose to sue a practitioner, not just pursuant to the contract for services between them, but in the tort of negligence as well.[18] The kinds of cases where a legal practitioner has been found to be negligent include failing to commence a case in court before the limitation period for commencing proceedings expires,[19] *and* failing to properly take a history that would have revealed an alternate cause of action that was not presented to the court before the expiry of the limitation period.[20]

These rules of competency are also stated in the legal professional conduct rules. These rules prohibit lawyers taking on work they cannot reasonably perform to a professional standard. The *Legal Profession (Solicitors) Rules 2007* (ACT)[21] reflect these issues well, stating:

> 1.2 A practitioner must act honestly, fairly, and with competence and diligence in the service of a client, and should accept instructions, and a retainer to act for a client, only when the practitioner can reasonably expect to serve the client in that manner and attend to the work required with reasonable promptness.
>
> 1.3
> (a) A practitioner must not accept instructions in a field of practice in which he or she possesses insufficient knowledge and skill to provide competent representation to the client unless:
> (i) the practitioner is able, without undue delay and cost to the client, to obtain such knowledge and skill either through private study and research or through the association with him or her of another lawyer of established competence in that field; or

---

17 (1988) 164 CLR 539; confirmed in *Astley v Austrust Ltd* (1999) 197 CLR 1.

18 For a discussion of the tort of negligence see Chapter 5.

19 *Curnuck v Nitschke* [2001] NSWCA 176.

20 *Roberts v Cashman* [2000] NSWSC 770.

21 Available at www.legislation.act.gov.au/sl/2007-31/current/pdf/2007-31.pdf.

(ii) where access to the relevant body of knowledge or to a lawyer of established competence in the field is not readily available, the practitioner warns the client of those facts and of the likely delay and cost in acquiring the requisite knowledge and skill and the client voluntarily consents to the practitioner acting in the matter.
(b) A practitioner should take such steps as are reasonably necessary to maintain and improve his or her knowledge and skill in the fields of law in which he or she practises.

Chandra v Perpetual Trustees Victoria Ltd

[2007] NSWSC 694

A man approached a solicitor, who was a sole practitioner in Sydney, saying he had authority from the owners of a residential property, who were entering a loan. They had misplaced the certificate of title for their residential property, which they were using to secure the loan, so they needed to make an application for a duplicate certificate of title. He produced a rates notice and some other information in a file. The solicitor prepared the application and a statutory declaration to be signed by the owners. The man took the documents away to get them signed, and returned with the signed documents which had been witnessed by a Justice of the Peace. The solicitor lodged the application with the Land Titles Office with the statutory declaration, and attended for collection of the new certificate of title, which he then gave to the man. He also prepared a memorandum of fees which the man paid.

Armed with the duplicate certificate of title, the man obtained a mortgage over the property from Perpetual Trustees, to secure loans totalling approximately $750 000, with the money paid to the man's account. It became apparent that the owners of the property had no connection with the man, and their signatures had been forged. They brought action against Perpetual Trustees, seeking a declaration that no money was secured by the mortgage, the NSW Registrar of Lands for registering the mortgage, and the solicitor who assisted the fraudster to obtain the duplicate certificate of title.

Our concern here is the solicitor – was his conduct negligent? It was held that, although he had no knowledge of the fraud, he had failed to verify with the registered owners that they really had authorised the man to instruct him, or to obtain in writing a signed authority to act. Failure to do this was a breach of a duty of care to the plaintiffs, who he believed were his clients, to avoid taking actions which cause economic loss.

Duties of loyalty

Lawyers are expected to be loyal to their client, indeed they have a duty to do so. They are expected to handle conflicts of interest in favour of their client, and not act against former clients or clients who have a paid them a retainer. This includes avoiding situations where they have a personal or financial interest in a transaction.

For example if a client wanted to sue a company which the solicitor was a major shareholder in, it would be a conflict of interest to act for that client. Acting against a former client is also considered to be a situation where a legal practitioner could have a conflict of interest because they may have been privy to confidential information about that client that they could (even subconsciously) use against that client in court or in negotiations. The Law Council of Australia Model Rules recommend that legal practitioners not accept cases against former clients.[22] Similarly, acting for more than one party can raise problematic conflicts of interest, and should be avoided.

Lawyers also owe duties of confidentiality to their clients. Confidentiality is a key duty of loyalty to the client, and a key legal duty expressed at common law, legislation, in ethics, and in professional conduct rules.[23] Legal practitioners must not disclose to any person any information that is confidential to the client and acquired by the practitioner by virtue of engaging them as a lawyer. This confidentiality is not absolute, it does not apply if the client authorises disclosure, if confidential information is disclosed to an employee of the firm, or if the information is no longer confidential or the practitioner is compelled by law to disclose that information.

Case Example: *Ravech v Amerena*

[2000] VSC 483

The parties in the dispute were partners in a retail pharmacy and photographic processing business in Reservoir, Victoria. The plaintiff's son, a solicitor, drafted the partnership agreement for them, and other legal agreements such as a lease and a guarantee facility. He also acted on behalf of the defendant in relation to the purchase of another retail pharmacy business. When the plaintiff sought to terminate the partnership, he instructed his son to act for him. Did the son, in acting for his father the plaintiff, breach the duty of loyalty owed to the defendant? The Court concluded he hadn't, because he has no confidential information that would be relevant to the dispute at hand.

Reflection

Do you agree with this decision? Do you think it is ever wise to act for a party where you have, in the past, acted for the other party to a dispute?

---

22 Model Rules, n 12 above, 6 (rule 4).

23 Ibid., 5 (rule 3).

Legal professional privilege

Legal professional privilege is a long-held privilege that attaches to certain documents arising from the lawyer–client relationship. The privilege is the client's, and is designed to preserve their confidential information and thereby encourage candour and frankness with their lawyer. This is why the privilege is more recently known as client legal privilege. The privilege is expressed at common law and in legislation (usually Evidence Acts). Legal professional privilege only comes about in very specially defined circumstances: it must be claimed by a lawyer acting for the client, and the claim must be over communications brought into existence for the dominant purpose of seeking or receiving legal advice or for use in existing or anticipated litigation (so long as it is not to facilitate fraud or crime).

> **Example: British American Tobacco Litigation**[24]
>
> Law firm Clayton Utz acted for British American Tobacco in defending a case brought in the Supreme Court of Victoria by Rolah McCabe, a woman who alleged she had contracted lung cancer as a result of smoking the defendant's cigarettes. It was alleged that the defendant, on Clayton Utz's advice, systematically destroyed documents relevant to the litigation under a 'document retention policy'. The plaintiff's lawyers moved to have the defence relating to liability struck out, given the destruction of discoverable documents, which caused serious prejudice to the plaintiff in proving her case. The judge agreed, striking out the tobacco company's defences. The jury awarded nearly $700 000 in damages to the plaintiff. On appeal, after the plaintiff had died of lung cancer, the verdict was overturned, because the trial judge had used documents which were subject to legal professional privilege, incorrectly considering that confidentiality in them had been impliedly waived. A retrial was ordered. However, since that time some internal memos at Clayton Utz regarding the conduct of the solicitors involved were leaked to the media by a former lawyer of Clayton Utz to another law firm, Slater & Gordon (which acted for Mrs McCabe). It is arguable that the information disclosed was subject to an obligation of confidence. Mrs Cowell, acting for the estate of Mrs McCabe, argues that confidentiality is lost because maintaining confidentiality would conceal serious misconduct (formally referred to as 'iniquities'). The Court in 2009 ordered that the pleading be redrafted to specify, for each of the 24 counts of iniquity alleged, which amounted to a crime, civil wrong or serious misdeed of public importance, so as to justify the waiver of privilege. At the time of writing, there remained issues between the parties about the amended pleadings upon which the case would proceed.

---

24 There are numerous decisions in relation to this matter. See for example *McCabe v British American Tobacco Australia Services* Ltd [2002] VSC 73; *McCabe v British American Tobacco Australia Services Ltd* [2002] VSC 112; *McCabe v British American Tobacco Australia Services Ltd* [2002] VSC 150; *McCabe v British American Tobacco Australia Services Ltd* [2002] VSC 172; *McCabe v British American Tobacco Australia Services Ltd* [2002] VSC 216; *Cowell (Estate of McCabe decd) v British American Tobacco Australia Services Ltd* [2007] VSCA 301; *British American Tobacco Australia Limited v Gordon & Ors (No 2)* [2009] VSC 77; and *British American Tobacco Australia Limited v Gordon & Ors (No 3)* [2009] VSC 619.

Reflection

1. What do you think about lawyers advising clients to destroy documents relevant to litigation brought against them?
2. What do you think about a lawyer disclosing information from a case at a former firm to lawyers at another firm?

Exercise: Confidentiality and disclosure

While representing a client (Alex), a lawyer (Peter) becomes aware that Alex and his sister (Alexis) have been involved in a major drug trafficking ring in Sydney. Peter becomes aware of this when Alex mentions it believing 'it's all confidential'. Section 316(1) of the *Crimes Act 1900* (NSW) states that:

> (1) If a person has committed a serious indictable offence and another person who knows or believes that the offence has been committed and that he or she has information which might be of material assistance in securing the apprehension of the offender or the prosecution or conviction of the offender for it fails without reasonable excuse to bring that information to the attention of a member of the police force or other appropriate authority, that other person is liable to imprisonment for 2 years.

On this basis it looks as if Peter must disclose this confidential information to the police or face imprisonment. However, s 316(4) of the *Crimes Act 1900* (NSW) states that:

> A prosecution for an offence against subsection (1) is not to be commenced against a person without the approval of the Attorney-General if the knowledge or belief that an offence has been committed was formed or the information referred to in the subsection was obtained by the person in the course of practising or following a profession, calling or vocation prescribed by the regulations for the purposes of this subsection.

This covers Peter and means he is not criminally liable for not disclosing this information. Relieved, he continues to see his clients and becomes aware that they are planning a major drug importation in a week's time. Again, Peter must work out whether he is obliged to disclose this behaviour to the police. He recalls his rules of professional conduct which state in 3.1.3 that confidentiality can be breached where:

> the practitioner discloses information in circumstances in which the law would probably compel its disclosure, despite the client's claim of legal professional privilege, and for the sole purpose of avoiding the probable commission or concealment of a serious criminal offence.

What do think Peter should do about the information he has obtained in confidence about drug trafficking?

Duties to facilitate settlement

Legal practitioners advise clients about the law, but also have to advise their clients about when to settle a matter. In doing so, legal practitioners must not drag out proceedings, as that could be construed as an abuse of court processes. Courts now impose cost penalties on parties who fail to accept an offer of settlement, and who later are awarded a sum of money that is lower than the earlier offer made to them. Courts may in situations of legal gross negligence impose costs orders on legal practitioners. This has happened in cases where a legal practitioner has acted without a client's authority, has acted where there was almost no chance of success, or has through their incompetence caused proceedings to be dismissed.

Fiduciary duties to clients

Legal practitioners owe particular duties to clients to look after the client's financial interests and monies, which are held in a trust account and not a regular business account. Strict rules exist for the handling of and disbursement of client monies. This requires records to be kept of all transfers and clients must be provided with a statement of the trust monies. Legal practitioners are also not allowed to charge referral fees or hidden commissions. They must provide proper costs disclosure in writing at the outset of the client engagement.

Law societies

The first record of a law society is the 'Society of Gentlemen Practisers in the Courts of Law and Equity' founded by a group of lawyers in London in February 1739. It represented a small group of lawyers and met as needed. Law societies have now evolved into organisations that represent the interests of the legal profession. States and territories all have law societies (in Victoria it is called the Law Institute). The peak body is the Law Council of Australia. These are all listed in the weblinks at the end of this chapter.

Law societies represent the interests of the profession by lobbying government about issues facing the legal profession. It does so by having rules, constitutions and special interest groups. Law societies promulgate standards of professional practice and help maintain professional standards. On occasion law societies have a role in investigating complaints about legal professionals. Law societies also organise professional legal development and education and offer lists of lawyers by speciality or geographic location. They are also involved in public education and debates, business help, social networking, indemnity insurance, practising certificates, and answering queries about legal practice and practitioners.

Regulation of solicitors

Investigation of allegations made against solicitors is a matter of public interest. Initial investigations are conducted in many different ways. In the Australian Capital Territory and the Northern Territory complaints are initially assessed by law societies. In New South Wales all complaints are handled by the Legal Services Commissioner, who can mediate consumer disputes and may refer more serious matters (i.e. misconduct) to the Law Society.[25] In Queensland the Legal Practice Committee looks into misconduct issues and can settle most cases but cannot strike a practitioner off.[26] In South Australia the Legal Practitioners Conduct Board, a body independent of the Law Society, is charged with the role of investigating unprofessional conduct. It can also mediate settlements and deal with minor misconduct matters.[27] In Tasmania this work is done by the Legal Profession Board of Tasmania,[28] an independent statutory body established in 2008, and in Victoria it is done by the Legal Services Commissioner,[29] an independent body. In Western Australia the Legal Practitioners Complaints Committee receives initial complaints.[30]

Once initial investigations are complete another body is involved with the disciplining of practitioners. In all jurisdictions except the Australian Capital Territory this role is completely separate from the law society. The bodies are as follows:

- ACT: Law Society Complaints Committee
- NSW: Legal Services Division of the Administrative Decisions Tribunal
- NT: Legal Practitioners Disciplinary Tribunal
- Qld: Legal Practice Tribunal
- SA: Legal Practitioners Disciplinary Tribunal
- Tas: Legal Profession Disciplinary Tribunal
- Vic: Victorian Civil and Administrative Tribunal
- WA: Legal Practitioners Disciplinary Tribunal.

Many disciplinary matters against legal practitioners involve allegations of professional misconduct. Once a common law issue, misconduct is now cast in legislation. Most states and territories have enacted legislation (the Model Laws) regulating legal practice based on the Law Council of Australia National Legal Profession Model Bill.[31]

The Model Law has uniform definitions, which include:

> 'unsatisfactory professional conduct' includes conduct of an Australian legal practitioner happening in connection with the practice of law that falls short of the standard of competence and diligence that a member of the public is entitled to expect of a reasonably competent Australian legal practitioner.

and

> 'professional misconduct' includes –

---

25 See www.lawlink.nsw.gov.au/olsc.

26 See www.lsc.qld.gov.au/28.htm The_Legal_Practice_Committee.

27 See generally the *Legal Practitioners Act 1981* (SA) and online at www.legalcomplaints.com.au.

28 See www.lpbt.com.au/.

29 See www.lsc.vic.gov.au/.

30 See www.lpbwa.org.au/cc_contacts.html.

31 See the In Depth box in section 1 of this chapter and the Acts listed in n 2 (above).

(a) unsatisfactory professional conduct of an Australian legal practitioner, if the conduct involves a substantial or consistent failure to reach or maintain a reasonable standard of competence and diligence; and

(b) conduct of an Australian legal practitioner whether happening in connection with the practice of law or happening otherwise than in connection with the practice of law that would, if established, justify a finding that the practitioner is not a fit and proper person to engage in legal practice.

(2) For finding that an Australian legal practitioner is not a fit and proper person to engage in legal practice as mentioned in subsection (1), regard may be had to the suitability matters that would be considered if the practitioner were an applicant for admission to the legal profession under this Act or for the grant or renewal of a local practising certificate.

Where legal practitioners are found guilty of unsatisfactory conduct the relevant disciplinary body can decide what the appropriate order should be. The most severe sanction is striking off, where the practitioner is disbarred. This signals that the practitioner is no longer a fit and proper person to remain a legal practitioner. This commonly arises from serious cases of dishonesty. More commonly the disciplinary body will fine, suspend or reprimand the legal practitioner, and put conditions on ongoing practice. For example if the legal practitioner has failed to properly submit their tax returns and Business Activity Statements, the condition may be that their financial accountant must report quarterly on their ongoing financial position. In deciding an appropriate sanction, the disciplinary body will frequently take account of the practitioner's attitude to their conduct and remorse about it; the frequency of the conduct; and any illness and psychological stresses.

Mijatovic v Legal Practitioners Complaints Committee

[2008] WASCA 115

A client who had separated from her husband sought legal representation in relation to property settlement proceedings before the Family Court of Western Australia. The solicitor prepared a costs agreement for legal fees at $250 per hour. After two conciliation conferences and some written settlement negotiations, the matter settled. The solicitor prepared a new costs agreement for the client, which provided for $22 000 to be deducted from the settlement proceeds to pay for legal fees and disbursements, with the balance of $114 000 to be paid to the client, on the basis that she waive her rights to itemisation and taxation of her legal fees. The solicitor gave this document to the client to sign, concealing its terms and effect. When he handed her a cheque for $114 000 she was distressed and confused at not getting the full settlement sum, and sought an itemised account, which the solicitor refused to provide. She therefore made a complaint about the solicitor to the Legal Practitioners

Complaints Committee, and after several requests, the solicitor provided an itemised account for more than $22 000. On taxation (auditing) of the account, it was concluded that the proper sum, at $250 per hour, for the work would be approximately $5500 including GST. The matter was referred to the Legal Practitioners Disciplinary Tribunal which found that, aside from the gross overcharging, the account included a claim for $2250 plus GST in respect of work done on 31 October 2002, which was dishonest because the solicitor was at a birthday function for his son and could not have done nearly ten hours' work that day. Findings were made of unprofessional conduct and an order was made to recommend the Supreme Court strike the solicitor off the roll of practitioners. Although on appeal the solicitor's arguments were partly accepted, it was not denied that the gross overcharging was unprofessional conduct.

3: Barristers

There are approximately 3800 barristers in Australia, of whom more than 650 are Senior Counsel (SC or QC).[32] Some 85 per cent of barristers are male; 77 per cent are in New South Wales (44 per cent) or Victoria (33 per cent), and 78 per cent reported doing some pro bono work.[33]

TIP
A barrister is often referred to as 'counsel'. These terms are synonymous.

The barrister's role and work

Barristers, like solicitors, are legal practitioners. Their focus is on advocacy and drafting specialist legal advice (known as opinions). Barristers also draft court documents (e.g. a summons, statement of claim or statement of defence). Although allowed in some states such as New South Wales, barristers do not generally take work from clients directly. Instead they accept briefs from solicitors. Most solicitors have particular barristers they generally refer work to.

Barristers work very differently from solicitors. The following summarises the main differences:

- Barristers are sole practitioners and cannot form partnerships like solicitors.
- Barristers generally do not see clients directly like solicitors.
- Barristers have a limited immunity from being sued for their work in court.
- Barristers do not keep trust accounts or client files.

Barristers' duties

Barristers' duties are similar to those of solicitors, but there are variations based on the way barristers practice. For example a barrister does not usually have clients approach them; their work is sent to them by a solicitor.

---

32 Australian Bureau of Statistics, www.abs.gov.au/AUSSTATS/abs@.nsf/Lookup/8667.0Main+Features42007-08.

33 Australian Bureau of Statistics, *8667.0 Legal Practices, Australia, 2001–2002* accessed at www.abs.gov.au/AUSSTATS/abs@.nsf/Lookup/8667.0Main+Features12001–02?OpenDocument.

The cab rank rule: A duty to accept briefs?

Barristers adhere to a 'cab rank rule'. This is a duty to accept whatever briefs come to them. It is unique to barristers, particularly Senior Counsel (SC) and Queen's Counsel (QC). The rule does not cover solicitors who act as both solicitor and barrister in an action. The New South Wales Bar Association Senior Counsel Protocol states that an essential criterion for becoming an SC is to 'honour the cab rank rules; namely, the duty to accept briefs to appear for which they are competent and available, regardless of any personal opinions of the parties or the causes, and subject only to exceptions related to appropriate fees and conflicting obligations'.[34] The rule is justified on the ground that it increases access to justice. The High Court explained the reason for the rule in *Giannarelli v Wraith*:[35]

> It is difficult enough to ensure that justice according to law is generally available; it is unacceptable that the privileges of legal representation should be available only according to the predilections of counsel or only on the payment of extravagant fees. If access to legal representation before the courts were dependent on counsel's predilections as to the acceptability of the cause or the munificence of the client, it would be difficult to bring unpopular causes to court and the profession would become the puppet of the powerful. If the cab-rank rule be in decline – and I do not know that it is – it would be the duty of the leaders of the Bar and of the professional associations to ensure its restoration in full vigour.

The rule does not however mean that barristers must accept any case at any cost. The professional conduct rules list key exceptions where barristers may be justified in declining a brief:

- where the acceptance of a brief would compromise a barrister's integrity and independence (e.g. a conflict of interest)
- where acceptance of a brief would compromise the administration of justice
- where the barrister has advised or acted in the past for any of the parties involved
- where the barrister believes that they are not likely to be paid or that their fee will not be paid promptly (but barristers are not permitted to refuse a brief because it is funded by legal aid alone, nor allowed to hike up their fees in the hope that the brief will be rejected)
- where a barrister has insufficient time to prepare the case or give competent professional advice or where the barrister believes that they do not have the appropriate skills to conduct the work required to their professional standards.

---

34 New South Wales Bar Association, *Senior Counsel Protocol* rule 6(e) at www.nswbar.asn.au/silks/protocol.pdf.

35 (1988) 165 CLR 543, 580.

Senior Counsel (Queen's Counsel)

Senior Counsel (SC) or Queen's Counsel (QC) are typically senior or experienced barristers. The office of King's (or Queen's) Counsel originated in England around 1603, when Francis Bacon was appointed KC by the King, complete with special privileges of appearance and silk robes (hence the term 'taking silk'). Such counsel could not accept any brief against the Crown. Over time the appellation KC or QC came to signify the pre-eminent rank of legal counsel.

Since the 1990s most states have now dropped the term Queen's Counsel in favour of Senior Counsel. With the exception of the Northern Territory, all Australian states and territories have replaced the title QC with SC. Appointments are made as SC with the proviso that those appointed before the change may retain the old title. Some states and territories restrict the appointment of SCs or QCs to the ranks of barristers; others reserve the right to appoint solicitors as well, and have done so in a few instances.

Although traditionally the government has been involved in the appointment of Senior Counsel through the Attorney-General, a selection committee is now used, comprising the state's pre-eminent lawyers and judges.[36] The selection criteria are also now far more transparent. They including persons who:

- Have a high degree of skill, honesty and integrity as a barrister, both in presentation and advisory skills.
- Are extremely well trusted by the judiciary and their peers.
- Are prepared to vigorously remain independent and advance their client's claims having careful regard to their ethical duties to the court and their client.
- Have a considerable number of years experience as a barrister (for example 12 years in Queensland).[37]

The appointment of a person as SC represents a public identification of this advocate as a person whose skill, experience and integrity is well recognised and tested and that they are pre-eminent advocates and advisors. For judges, Senior Counsel can be implicitly trusted to assist in the administration of justice and fulfil their roles as officers of the court.

Traditionally it was customary for a QC or SC to appear with a junior barrister, and the solicitor (and obviously the client) would therefore have to bear the cost of both the junior barrister and the Senior Counsel. This requirement was viewed as anti-competitive and has since been removed.[38]

---

36 See for example New South Wales Bar Association, 'Senior Counsel Protocol' at www.nswbar.asn.au/silks/protocol.pdf. For the Victorian appointment process go to www.supremecourt.vic.gov.au/ then follow menu Publications/Media releases to locate 'Appointment Process of Senior Counsel 2007'.

37 See www.qldbar.asn.au/ (select menu item Senior Counsel, then Criteria for appointment).

38 See generally Trade Practices Commission, *Study of the Professions: Legal: Final Report* (1994). Note that the Trade Practices Commission merged with the Prices Surveillance Authority in 1995 to become the Australian Competition and Consumer Commission (ACCC).

Barristers' liability

The general rule in Australia is that barristers are liable in every way a solicitor would be in contract and tort, with the exception that barristers are immune from being sued in negligence for their advocacy work in court. The trade-off for this immunity used to be that barristers could not sue clients direct for unpaid fees, but rules are changing in this regard and such recovery is possible in New South Wales,[39] although it is still customary for barristers to recover fees from solicitors.

Australian barristers enjoy a very rare common law legal privilege not available to their counterparts in Canada, the EU, Malaysia, New Zealand, Singapore, the UK or the USA. This liability is also unavailable to any other Australian professional occupational group. The High Court of Australia in the case of *D'Orta-Ekenaike v Victoria Legal Aid & Anor*[40] has reconfirmed that barristers are immune from prosecution for negligent work in court.

D'Orta-Ekenaike v Victoria Legal Aid & Anor

(2005) 223 CLR 1

Mr D'Orta-Ekenaike was charged with rape, and he sought legal aid from Victorian Legal Aid (VLA). He was assigned a barrister for his committal proceeding and despite not being required to, pleaded guilty. He was committed for trial in the County Court and at that trial he pleaded not guilty. At trial his guilty plea from the committal proceeding was led in evidence, and he was convicted and sentenced to three years imprisonment. He appealed and the Victorian Court of Appeal quashed the decision over the improper use of his earlier guilty plea. On retrial he was acquitted.

Following this Mr D'Orta-Ekenaike sued VLA and his barrister alleging that they pressured him to plead guilty. He alleged that he suffered mental illness, financial costs of his numerous other proceedings, and had been unnecessarily imprisoned. Both the barrister and the VLA asked the court to stay this proceeding based on the fact that barristers had immunity for their conduct of the trial. County Court Judge Wodak ruled that this permanent stay should be ordered. Mr D'Orta-Ekenaike appealed unsuccessfully to the Victorian Court of Appeal, and the High Court accepted his application for special leave to appeal. The High Court was asked to review barristers' immunity. The case was important given that the English and New Zealand courts had abolished this immunity since the last time the High Court had upheld it. The High Court by a majority of six to one upheld the immunity and even extended it to solicitors doing advocacy but refined the reasons for now keeping it.

---

39 See *Legal Profession Act 2004* (NSW) ss 331, 332A.

40 (2005) 223 CLR 1 (Gleeson CJ, McHugh, Gummow, Kirby, Hayne, Callinan and Heydon JJ).

Arguments for and against

The following reasons were given for upholding barristers' immunity:

- The immunity is not for the benefit of legal practitioners, it is for the higher benefit of furthering the administration of justice. Allowing advocates to be sued would remove any sense of finality about a judgment, because every case could potentially be further appealed on the basis that a party was unhappy with their counsel's performance.
- The fear of being sued would affect the way counsel conduct a case, with the fear that counsel would take many potentially unnecessary steps to protect themselves that would add cost and time to every case. This might tempt counsel to favour the interests of their client over their overriding duty to the court and the administration of justice.
- Clients could make vexatious claims against counsel.

The following reasons were given for abolishing this immunity in the dissenting judgment:

- There are other remedies already available for breaches of counsel's duties of care (e.g. courts can award damages against counsel for unnecessary delays in the conduct of trials).
- No other country retains such an immunity.[41]
- No other profession enjoys such immunity and maintaining a special immunity for counsel, while expanding the scope of liability of every other profession, breeds contempt for our legal system.
- The basis of this immunity is out-of-date, relying on the state of the legal profession over a hundred years ago.
- The argument that a barrister's loyalty to the court and to their client would become problematic is unrealistic as it is hard to see how a person could succeed in proving negligence where a barrister was complying with a duty to the court.
- The fear of a wave of litigation by disgruntled parties has not been seen in other common law countries that have abolished the immunity, such as the UK and the USA, which has a particularly litigious culture.

Bar associations

Bar associations are voluntary associations of independent barristers. They seek to promote the interests of barristers, recommend law reform, arrange professional development and education for their members, provide support services for barristers (including for example chambers for rent, libraries, health services and counselling, discounts, credit cards), and indemnity insurance. Bar associations have constitutions and rules of professional conduct that bind their members. The key Australian bar associations are listed in the web links at the end of this chapter.

---

41 Kirby J referred to the 'global tide' against retention of immunity, saying that running against it was 'anomalous and unjustifiable': *D'Orta-Ekenaike v Victoria Legal Aid & Anor* (2005) 223 CLR 1.

Regulation of barristers

Misconduct and discipline issues for barristers are largely the same as the issues for solicitors described above, with a few minor exceptions. Bar associations have procedures for investigating complaints against barristers, which may result in findings of unsatisfactory professional conduct or professional misconduct.

New South Wales Bar Association v Punch

[2008] NSWADT 78

Punch, a NSW barrister, represented a man accused of armed robbery. He advanced alibi evidence, from five witnesses, that the client was at home at the time of the robbery – evidence he knew to be untrue, because the client has told him he was present during the robbery. This conversation between Punch and his client was captured on tape as the client's cell was bugged. Punch was found guilty of professional misconduct and has since been struck off the roll of legal practitioners.

Example: Barrister investigated by Independent Commissioner Against Corruption (ICAC)

In what may be an unprecedented occurrence in 2009, a Sydney barrister John Hart was placed under investigation by ICAC. It is alleged that he inflated a client's costs claim to defraud the government (in relation to a sexual assault trial held in the District Court in February 2009); that he told lies to judicial officers in order to secure a particular venue or magistrate to hear criminal proceedings; and that he told clients he could bribe judicial officials to obtain special treatment. Since his admission in 1986 the barrister has been variously reprimanded and had conditions imposed on his practising certificate by the Bar Association for actions such as practising without a current practising certificate, drink driving, driving while disqualified, and tax offences. In its report released in March 2010, ICAC made findings against not only Mr Hart but also a solicitor, Anthony Paul. Recommendations were made for them to be prosecuted, and to have disciplinary action taken against them under the *Legal Profession Act 2004* (NSW). For more information see www.icac.nsw.gov.au/investigations/past-investigations

---

4: Judges

A key category of legal practice is the judiciary. Being a judge (particularly a senior court judge) is usually something a legal practitioner is promoted to from the ranks of senior lawyers. Judges frequently have been legal practitioners for many years and have significant practitioner experience prior to appointment. Being a federal system, Australia has federal, state and territory judges. In addition, some judges are seconded to head administrative tribunals (e.g. Federal Court judges are appointed to the Commonwealth Administrative Appeals Tribunal).

What then, do judges do? They adjudicate disputes and administer justice in a court of law. Their ability to make binding determinations is a key element of the exercise of judicial power. In criminal cases judges sentence defendants. Associated tasks include:

- Hearing pre-trial matters.
- Awarding compensation in civil cases.
- Ensuring that all rules of court and evidence are followed.
- Advising and directing juries on legal issues.
- Interpreting facts and evidence and making binding determinations on facts and law.
- Researching the relevant law and reading judgments and statutes.
- Producing written judgments.
- Where required, travelling on circuit and working at tribunals.
- Supervising their court staff, including their associate (usually a recent law graduate).
- Managing their courtroom and the legal practitioners associated with cases heard in their court.

Judges in Australia enjoy the hallmarks of an independent judiciary – fixed salaries, and security of tenure. This means that they cannot be pressured by the government if it doesn't like their decisions. The traditional expression is that judges should exercise their role 'without fear or favour'. The fact that judges cannot be sacked if their decisions are unfavourable does not mean they are completely unaccountable for their work. Judicial accountability mechanisms include the requirement to provide reasons for their decisions, the appeals process, and, in the event of proven grossly unethical or undisciplined behaviour, a judge may be removed from office. Media reporting of decisions also has a role to play, as does performance measures in the justice system (reports on how courts spend their budget, how many cases are disposed of, etc).

As discussed in Chapter 4, Australian courts operate in a hierarchy. Judges of courts in the Australian judicial hierarchy are considered below.

Federal judges

Federal judges include judges of the High Court, the Federal Court,[42] and the Family Court.[43] The seven justices on the High Court are some of the best legal minds in the country. The current and past members of the court are listed on the High Court's website.[44]

Until 1977 judges in federal courts had life tenure, but this was abolished by the *Constitution Alteration (Retirement of Judges) Act 1977* (Cth) which amended section 72 of the Constitution so that Judges in federal courts now retire at 70 years of age.

---

[42] www.fedcourt.gov.au.

[43] www.familycourt.gov.au.

[44] www.hcourt.gov.au.

The process of appointment of federal court judges is politicised. They are appointed by the Governor-General in Council, who acts on the advice of government. In practice, the Commonwealth Attorney-General consults state and territory attorneys-general and their bar associations and law societies for a list of appropriate candidates.[45] This process has been subject to some criticism.[46]

State and territory judges

The top state and territory judges are those who sit in the Supreme Courts, including their appellate divisions. It is not uncommon for High Court judges to be selected from the state judiciary – four of the current High Court judges were Supreme Court judges in the past (the other three were Federal Court judges). Each state Supreme Court has a Chief Justice. The Chief Justice is appointed as any other judge, has the same tenure as any other judge, but has a significantly wider role. The Chief Justice has responsibility over the administration of the courts in their jurisdiction and is accordingly given access to more staff and resources to fulfil this role. Other similar roles are Presidents of Courts of Appeal, Chief Judges of Intermediate Courts and Chief Magistrates.

5: Ethics

'Legal ethics' is a term often misused and abused. Popular resentment of lawyers traditionally has found expression in cynicism about their moral standards. Legal ethics has been dismissed as either a contradiction in terms or a poor relation to philosophical theory.[47]

As far as professions go, the public perception of the ethical honesty of lawyers is perhaps best reflected in the results of surveys ranking lawyers about fifteenth in a list of 28 occupations. Market research in 2007 established that 36 per cent of people surveyed rated lawyers as honest and ethical. This assessment of honesty reached a high point of 44 per cent in 1984 and a low point of 26 per cent in 1998.[48] The significance of this is that the majority of people think lawyers are *not* honest and ethical. Some of the reasons for this poor public confidence include:

- strong media coverage of major criminal cases, reporting lawyers defending 'unsavoury' clients and using technicalities to help acquit clients of charges or getting reduced sentences for them[49]

---

45 See Commonwealth Attorney-General's Department, *Judicial Appointments Procedure and Criteria*, AGPS, Canberra, 1993.

46 See for example www.theaustralian.com.au/news/nation/high-court-appointment-process-a-nonsense/story-e6frg6nf-1111113923786.

47 Deborah Rhode, *Professional Responsibility: Ethics by the Pervasive Method*, Aspen Publishers, New York, 2nd edn (1998), 11.

48 Table of polls available at www.roymorgan.com/news/polls/2007/4153 as cited in Ainslie Lamb and John Littrich, *Lawyers in Australia*, Federation Press, Sydney (2007), 11.

49 See generally Ysiah Ross, *Ethics in Law: Lawyers' Responsibility and Accountability in Australia*, LexisNexis Butterworths, Sydney, 4th edn (2005), 12–30.

- a perception that lawyers do what they can to create litigation, and to use complex arguments and jargon to drag out cases
- a perception that lawyers are paid, and well paid, no matter what the outcome of a case – sometimes lawyers are perceived as the only 'winning' party in litigation
- a perception that lawyers lack adequate ethical principles, and manipulate the law
- media reports about barristers not paying their taxes.[50]

Legal ethics is often seen as a moral code governing the conduct of legal practitioners. Many ethical duties are also professional legal duties enforceable by courts and tribunals. To assist legal practitioners, model codes of conduct have been created by the legal profession that address the client–lawyer relationship, duties of a lawyer, dealings with third parties and maintaining the integrity of the profession. Respect for client confidentiality, honesty, truthfulness in statements, and professional independence are some of the defining features of legal ethics. Legal ethics will help practitioners resolve difficult issues where there is no legal guidance for their conduct.

The lawyer–client relationship can be a complicated one. In many aspects of that relationship the lawyer must take upon themselves a role that is totally different from being a friend or confidant. Things are demanded of lawyers and other professionals that are not demanded of other people. This role also asks lawyers to put aside certain moral concerns that would otherwise affect their decision making. This may mean that a solicitor, or a barrister subject to the cab rank rule, may be asked to:

- defend a person accused of crimes against a child; or defend a person accused of war crimes[51]
- draft a will for a person who wishes to disinherit certain members of her family because they are of a certain religious faith
- find a loophole in the tax law that will allow a client to benefit improperly.

Responding appropriately to ethical dilemmas in practice is a skill, because without training, a person may not even realise there is an ethical dilemma. Law school helps to train you to recognise and respond to ethical dilemmas, and you are likely to be given scenarios with ethical issues and asked what you would do. To help you with this, here are some hypothetical scenarios for you to consider how you would respond as a lawyer.

---

50 See for example Warren Owens, 'Barristers Banned for Unpaid Tax', *Sunday Telegraph*, 18 November 2001 (outlining a New South Wales Bar Association crackdown on barristers accumulating large tax bills and declaring themselves bankrupt).

51 For example a Jewish QC being asked to defend an alleged Nazi war criminal, as reported in D Farrant 'Leading QC may defend Kalejs' *The Age* (Melbourne) 23 January 2001, reported in Christine Parker and Adrian Evans, *Inside Lawyers' Ethics*, Cambridge University Press, Melbourne (2007), 1–2. Kalejs avoided extradition and died in 2001.

Exercise: Ethical decision making

Scenario 1

You work as a solicitor in a firm that has as an important client a major tobacco company. The tobacco company has asked for three lawyers to advise them on how to circumvent legislation that prohibits tobacco advertising in the media. They seek advice on how they can legally place tobacco products in film and in clips on the Internet. You are a media lawyer seeking to impress the partners. You are selected as one of the three lawyers to give this advice.

Can you refuse this work? On what grounds? Would it be harder to refuse such work if you were a barrister?

Scenario 2

You act for a building company that manufactured a particular type of asbestos that exposed people to dangerous micro-particles when cut with circular saws. This particle dust has been linked to asbestosis, mesothelioma, and other lung conditions. The company wants to seek advice about whether declaring bankruptcy will have the effect of delaying or reducing pending litigation, and asks you to aggressively defend cases at all costs.

Would you have any ethical problems with this brief?

Scenario 3

Imagine you are working as a plaintiff's lawyer who is acting for a client alleging medical negligence by a surgeon. Your legal team has used the process of discovery to request certain documents relevant to the case. Most of these documents are medical records. In among the boxes delivered to the firm you see a lone box marked 'Client interviews: client legal privilege'. You realise that this box has probably been sent in error and contains material that is legally privileged.

Should you proceed to open the box and take advantage of the other side's mistake, or notify the defendant's lawyers of the error?

Scenario 4

You are working as a lawyer who looks after a family's interests. The father dies and one of his daughters explains to you the existence and eventually the location of documents that would help her test her paternity. She is concerned she will be left out of his will. These documents are due to be picked up by a commercial confidential waste management service in three days and destroyed in accordance with the law firm's policy of destroying all documents in a file 10 years after it is closed. You receive this letter late on a Friday afternoon on a long weekend and the documents are already down on the street in a locked cage awaiting collection. You acted primarily for the father and remember his wish to keep such documents secure and confidential. You have acted for the daughter in relation to her marriage breakdown and property settlement a few years earlier.

Are you under any obligation to do anything? Will it be acceptable to allow the file to be destroyed, maintain your promise to the father to keep the material confidential and explain to the daughter that the letter just got there too late?

GO ONLINE
Go online for further practice on ethical decision making.

6: What kinds of work do lawyers do?

As shown in figures 12.1 and 12.2, the main areas of law in which lawyers practise are commercial, personal injury, property and criminal law.

FIGURE 12.1: SOURCES OF FEE INCOME, OTHER LEGAL SERVICES

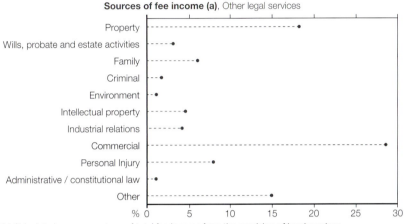

(a) Calculated as a percentage of total fee income from the provision of legal services.

FIGURE 12.2: SOURCES OF FEE INCOME, BARRISTERS

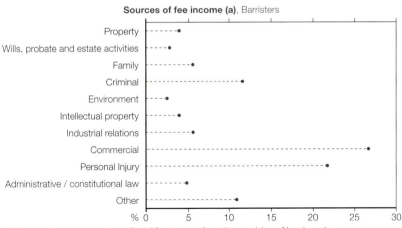

(a) Calculated as a percentage of total fee income from the provision of legal services.

Source: Australian Bureau of Statistics (2009) *8667.0 Legal Services, Australia, 2007–8* available at www.abs.gov.au/ausstats/abs@.nsf/mf/8667.0

Note: Other legal services include not only solicitors, but patent attorneys, service/payroll entities and businesses providing various legal support services. It is disappointing that the ABS has lumped solicitors with other support services including those who do photocopying and conveyancing, as it makes it difficult to get an accurate snapshot of solicitors.

In terms of earnings, lawyer salaries vary across the country, with lawyers in New South Wales, Australian Capital Territory and Victoria earning more on average than lawyers in Tasmania, Northern Territory and Western Australia. For example solicitors in New South Wales earn on average $60–100 000 and lawyers in Adelaide earn on average $45–70 000. Also, as would be expected, earnings tend to increase with years of experience – a lawyer with less than a year's experience is likely to earn $40–48 000, up to four years' experience $50–75 000, up to nine years' experience $70–105 000, and up to 20 years experience, $80–135 000.[52]

Trends for the profession

The following trends and challenges for the legal profession have been identified:[53]

- Increasing information technology, especially legal information available on the Internet. The Internet empowers consumers with access to far more legal knowledge and consumers may, as a result, demand more for their dollars.
- Increasing globalisation and the need to develop networks and business opportunities offshore, particularly in Asia.
- Issues surrounding retention of staff in law firms, particularly to develop policies that are more family-friendly and promote work–life balance. Some firms have begun to develop part time legal work, and job share options.
- Gender issues in the upper levels of the profession. For example in private firms, fewer women make partnership.
- Managing pro bono work. While many lawyers already do such work, there are some moves to make it compulsory for all legal practitioners.[54]
- To make sure that legal aid work does not decline.

DISCUSSION QUESTIONS

1. Is the legal profession best served by the division (formal or informal) into solicitors, barristers and senior counsel? Or do you believe there should simply be lawyers, who can do office and court work as they choose? What relevance does the need for specialisation in skills (such as advocacy or drafting) have?

2. Do you think lawyers deserve the poor reputation they have in the community? Why, or why not?

3. Do you believe that the immunity of barristers from being sued in negligence should be maintained? Why, or why not?

4. What are the arguments for and against national regulation of the legal profession?

---

52. See www.payscale.com/research/AU/Job=Attorney_%2f_Lawyer/Salary. You can also use this site to do an individual search, entering your job, years of experience, state or territory, and city.

53. Law Council of Australia, *2010: A Discussion Paper Challenges for the Legal Profession* (Sept 2001) available at www.lawcouncil.asn.au/shadomx/apps/fms/fmsdownload.cfm?file_uuid=0BE36BA1-1C23-CACD-22BE-B0B1F93A365C&siteName=lca

54. For more information see www.nationalprobono.org.au.

WEBLINKS AND FURTHER READING

Legal practitioner legislation

All are available at www.austlii.edu.au.
Legal Profession Act 2006 (ACT)
Legal Profession Act 2004 (NSW)
Legal Profession Act 2008 (NT)
Legal Profession Act 2007 (Qld)
Legal Profession Act 1981 (SA)
Legal Profession Act 1993 (Tas)
Legal Profession Act 2004 (Vic)
Legal Profession Act 2003 (WA)

Law societies

Law Council of Australia: www.lawcouncil.asn.au
Law Society of the Australian Capital Territory: www.lawsocact.asn.au
Law Society of New South Wales: www.lawsociety.com.au
Law Society of the Northern Territory: www.lawsocietynt.asn.au
Queensland Law Society: www.qls.com.au
Law Society of South Australia: www.lawsocietysa.asn.au
Law Society of Tasmania: www.taslawsociety.asn.au
Law Institute of Victoria: www.liv.asn.au
Law Society of Western Australia: www.lawsocietywa.asn.au

Bar associations

Australian Bar Association: www.austbar.asn.au
Australian Capital Territory Bar Association: www.actbar.com.au
New South Wales Bar Association: www.nswbar.asn.au
Northern Territory Bar Association: www.ntba.asn.au
Queensland Bar: www.qldbar.asn.au
South Australian Bar Association: www.sabar.org.au
Tasmanian Independent Bar: www.tasmanianbar.com.au
Victorian Bar: www.vicbar.com.au
Western Australian Bar Association: www.wabar.asn.au

Disciplinary bodies

ACT: Law Society Complaints Committee www.lawsocact.asn.au
NSW: Legal Services Division of the Administrative Decisions Tribunal www.lawlink.nsw.gov.au/adt
    (click Legal Services Division link)
NT: Legal Practitioners Disciplinary Tribunal: www.accc.gov.au/content/index.phtml/itemId/289023/
    fromItemId/815972/quickLinkId/816516/whichType/org
Qld: Legal Practice Tribunal www.lsc.qld.gov.au/28.htm
Qld: Legal Services Commission www.lsc.qld.gov.au

SA: Legal Practitioners Disciplinary Tribunal[55] www.sa.gov.au/government/entity/109
Tas: Legal Profession Board www.lpbt.com.au
Vic: Victorian Civil and Administrative Tribunal (handles prosecutions for professional misconduct since December 2005 www.vcat.vic.gov.au) go to VCAT online tab at top of page, then Other Disputes at VCAT on the left menu, then Legal Practice
WA: Legal Practitioners Disciplinary Tribunal www.lpbwa.org.au

Reports

Australian Bureau of Statistics, *8667.0 Legal Services, Australia, 2007–8* available at www.abs.gov.au/ausstats/abs@.nsf/mf/8667.0

National Pro Bono Resource Centre, various reports on the pro bono work of Australian lawyers at www.nationalprobono.org.au (select Publications menu, then Reports).

Law Council of Australia 2010: A Discussion Paper Challenges for the Legal Profession (2001) available at http://unpan1.un.org/intradoc/groups/public/documents/APCITY/UNPAN016546.pdf

New South Wales Bar Association, 'Senior Counsel Protocol' (2007) at www.nswbar.asn.au/docs/professional/silks/SCProt030708.pdf.

Supreme Court of Victoria, Media Release – 'The Appointment of Senior Counsel in Victoria' (2008) at www.supremecourt.vic.gov.au (select Publications tab, then click link to Media releases).

Books

Cocks, Russell, *Ethics Handbook: Questions and Answers*, Law Institute of Victoria, Melbourne (2004).

Lamb, Ainslie and Littrich, John, *Lawyers in Australia*, Federation Press, Sydney (2007).

Parker, Christine and Evans, Adrian, *Inside Lawyers' Ethics*, Cambridge University Press, Melbourne (2007).

Ross, Ysiah, *Ethics in Law: Lawyers' Responsibility and Accountability in Australia*, Lexis Nexis Butterworths, Sydney, 4th edn (2005).

ONLINE RESOURCES FOR THIS CHAPTER

The following resources are available online at www.oup.com.au/orc/cwl2e
- Knowing the boundaries
- Ethical decision-making exercises
- Flashcard glossary
- Multiple choice questions

---

55 The Legal Profession Bill 2007 had not yet become law at the time of writing.

13

Law In Society:
What Are the Problems
and Remedies For
Accessing Justice?

WHAT WE WILL COVER IN THIS CHAPTER:

- The key issues involved in access to justice in the form of legal advice, dispute resolution or courts
- Some barriers facing people in accessing legal advice, dispute resolution or courts
- The role of legal aid schemes
- An explanation of legal aid eligibility criteria
- The role of community legal centres
- The role of law reform commissions

Recommended approach to learning this topic

You should think about what access to justice means when reflecting on the content in this chapter. Do you think that you have unrestricted access to legal advice, legal representation and legal adjudication of disputes, or do you think your access is in some way impeded? This chapter introduces you to some key issues, illustrates access to justice issues faced by particular groups in society, explains how legal aid works, and explains the role of community legal groups and law reform commissions. Legal aid and community legal centres provide some solutions to the problems identified in accessing justice for some groups and economic classes. Students should reflect on any other barriers to accessing legal advice and services or solutions they can think of. The weblinks provided at the end of this chapter will give you an insight into the many channels available to litigants to overcome barriers in accessing justice.

KEY TERMS

Access to justice = the ability for individuals, organisations and groups to obtain legal advice, obtain adequate resolutions of their disputes, and have their rights protected by the legal system.

Community legal centre (CLC) = an independent community based organisation that provides free legal advice and help to members of the community.

Law Reform Commission = an independent government body that advises parliament on proposals for law reform. They do this by public consultation, research and reports. Their work often leads to major reform of the law.

Legal Aid = a system of publicly-funded financial aid subject to strict eligibility guidelines to help pay for legal advice or representation in select cases where a person can demonstrate financial hardship.

NESB = Non-English speaking background.

Pro bono = professional work done voluntarily for no charge. From the Latin *pro bono publico* (for the public good).

1: Access to justice – key issues

'Access to justice' is a term widely used in Australia when discussing the issue of the relative difficulty or cost of obtaining legal advice or legal services such as dispute resolution, tribunals and courts. Lawyers frequently define access to justice to mean access to legal representation. In politics, economics, sociology and the media, access to justice is understood to encompass additional factors that affect such access. These include poverty, discrimination, distance from services, access to legal aid or community legal advice, or being members of groups that experience significant disadvantage. The important debate is the extent to which Australians have access to justice. This chapter is largely focused on access to civil justice, rather than access to justice for people accused of crimes.

More problematic is the use of the term 'justice'. Access to justice appears to refer to access to the court system and lawyers, rather than winning your case and being satisfied with the penalty given or compensation awarded.

Part and parcel of these concepts is the quality of justice. Having a lawyer and a hearing may not be sufficient if the lawyer is unprepared (due to being overworked and lacking resources), the trial is cursory and the judge dismissive (sometimes due to under-resourced local courts, which hear 97 per cent of cases).

Reflection

In 1994, the Federal Government initiated an inquiry into 'Access to Justice'. Since then the focus of recent federal inquiries has been on 'Managing Justice' (2000) which is more focused on expediting justice and 'case management' (increasing the efficiency of court processes, see Chapter 5). Sackville J, who chaired the 1994 inquiry, has subsequently stated: 'Since publication of the *Access to Justice Report* (although not necessarily by reason of that fact) case management seems to have been accepted as virtually an article of faith by all Australian courts, civil and criminal'.[1]

Can you see contradictions or complementarity between access to justice and case management?

The cost of justice

Access to justice in Australia does not come cheaply. Many Australians cannot afford basic legal advice, let alone legal proceedings. This has been repeatedly found in studies,[2] is constantly claimed by the media and is clearly obvious to judges who have to help the growing numbers of unrepresented litigants with the basics of legal

---

1 Ronald Sackville, 'From access to justice to managing justice: the transformation of the judicial role', Australian Institute of Judicial Administration Annual Conference, Brisbane, Queensland (12-14 July 2002), 12-13 www.aija.org.au/ac02/Sackville.rtf.

2 Ronald Sackville, 'Some thoughts on access to justice' (2004) 2 *New Zealand Journal of Public and International Law* 85; Justice Spigelman, 'Access to justice and access to lawyers' (2007) 29 *Australian Bar Review* 136.

representation skills. In superior courts like the Supreme Court, the Federal Court or even the High Court legal fees and costs amount to tens or hundreds of thousands of dollars. Worse still, the costs rules mean that a party who loses a case will have to pay part or all of the opposing party's legal costs. Even the winning party is unlikely to recover all their costs.

Delay

A major factor depriving Australians of justice is the delay involved in having a dispute heard. For this reason, a well-known legal saying is 'justice delayed is justice denied'. Delay for a criminal defendant can mean time spent unnecessarily in custody on remand, or for a torts plaintiff it can mean an inability to pay for medical treatment. For other litigants, the prospect of a matter taking years to resolve is a significant deterrent for many and can be used to advantage by lawyers. The rise of administrative tribunals in the late 1970s and early 1980s was due in large part to the delays and costs of having disputes heard by a court. Tribunals like the Administrative Appeals Tribunal (AAT) publish statistics about their workload clearance rates. For example, 73 per cent of applications were finalised within 12 months and 88 per cent within 18 months of lodgement during 2008–09.[3]

In order to address the delays in the court system, courts have instituted case flow management. For example the South Australian District Court has a case flow management policy that aims to dispose of 90 per cent of actions by settlement or judgment within a year, and they aim to dispose of all actions within 21 months.[4] The Federal Court of Australia aims to settle 98 per cent of cases inside 18–20 months. Table 13.1 summarises clearance rates for Australia in 2006–07:

TABLE 13.1: COURT CLEARANCE RATES, ALL JURISDICTIONS, 2006–07

Year ended 30 June 2007	Backlog 2006							
	NSW %	Vic %	Qld %	WA %	SA %	Tas %	ACT %	NT %
Criminal								
Local/Magistrates courts	2.1	5.4	15.5	10.8	15.0	4.8	10.3	n/a
District/County courts	12.4	17.3	20.2	32.0	28.0	np	np	np
Supreme/Federal courts	39.4	19.9	17.3	22.5	28.0	16.2	19.3	21.9
Civil								
Local/Magistrates courts	n/a	11.1	6.7	8.8	12.5	4.7	11.1	32.6
District/County courts	27.4	40.4	39.5	38.4	27.0	np	np	np
Supreme/Federal courts	25.4	30.2	39.3	41.4	20.8	39.8	39.3	56.7

na: not available.
np: not applicable.
Source: Productivity Commission's Report on Government Services 2007.

---

3   Administrative Appeals Tribunal, Annual Report 2008–2009, (2009), 27, www.aat.gov.au/docs/Reports/2009/AR2009-Chapter3.pdf.

4   See Courts Administration Authority (SA), 'Caseflow Management', www.courts.sa.gov.au/courts/district/content.html Caseflow management.

> ## Reflection
> Some say it is better to have the courts manage case progress than leaving it to the parties, and others say courts should focus on judging and not be distracted by policing the parties. What do you think?

Equality

The assumption of equality before the law is fundamental to our legal system. It is part of key international human rights documents such as Art 7 of the *Universal Declaration of Human Rights* ('All are equal before the law and are entitled without any discrimination to equal protection of the law') and Art 14 of the *International Covenant on Civil and Political Rights* ('Everyone is equal before the law. Everyone has the right to a fair trial. Everyone has the right to be presumed innocent until proven guilty. No one may be compelled to testify against himself'). Nevertheless, the *Australian Constitution* does not explicitly affirm this equality principle. Instead, Australian law contains numerous prohibitions on certain behaviours like discrimination, vilification, racism, sexism, defamation and so on.

Equality can mean many things. Its dictionary meaning contains notions of equal dignity, rank, or privileges with others; the fact of being on an equal footing; being equal in power, ability, achievement, or excellence.[5] The essence of equality can seem mathematically simple, but in practice equality before the law is difficult to define. There are two major schools of thought about equality before the law:

- That all should have equal access and treatment by not restricting particular groups or classes (formal equality).
- That positive measures need to be taken to support disadvantaged people and groups who are deprived from access to justice by virtue of their disadvantage (substantive equality). There is thus a focus on equality of *outcome*.[6]

Former judge of the High Court of Australia, Mary Gaudron, wrote that 'equal justice is justice that is blind to differences that don't matter but is appropriately adapted to those that do'.[7] The challenge for the law is to distinguish appropriately between the two.[8]

TIP
Discrimination occurs when someone treats you unfairly because of your particular characteristic, background, group membership or identity.

---

5   Oxford English Dictionary Online, www.oed.com.

6   See also McHugh and Kirby JJ in *Purvis v New South Wales (Department of Education and Training)* (2003) 217 CLR 92.

7   Mary Gaudron, Foreword to Regina Graycar and Jenny Morgan, *The Hidden Gender of Law*, Federation Press, Sydney (2002), vii.

8   Submission to the Northern Territory Law Reform Committee Inquiry into Aboriginal Customary Law in the Northern Territory by the Sex Discrimination Commissioner of the Human Rights and Equal Opportunity Commission, May 2003, http://humanrights.gov.au/legal/submissions/sage/customary_law/submission.html.

2: Access to justice for specific groups

Certain groups in society are at even greater potential disadvantage when seeking legal advice, representation or dispute resolution. These groups include gay and lesbian people, women, Aboriginal and Torres Strait Islander people, people from non-English speaking backgrounds (NESB) and different cultures, children and young people, people with disabilities, people in rural and regional communities, and self-represented litigants. These groupings are not exhaustive and it is frequently the case that many of these factors come together to further compound the disadvantage experienced.

Women

Historically, women have suffered discrimination by the legal system (by deprivation of property rights, exclusion from certain employment roles, uneven pay scales, and sexist assumptions ingrained in tort, contract and criminal laws, to name a few). Although, demographically speaking, Australia has more women than men, fewer women have tertiary educational qualifications, women earn less than men and are more heavily represented in part-time and casual work and childcare roles. Women are more likely to be unlawfully discriminated against than men, especially on the ground of their sex, and are more frequently sexually harassed.[9] Feminist academics have demonstrated the areas of the legal system that exhibit signs of gender bias despite the law appearing to be neutral, objective and impartial.[10]

> **TIP**
> There is a difference between sex and gender. Sex is biological and gender is social.

In the 1980s the Commonwealth Government adopted measures to increase women's access to law and to remove barriers to their employment and advancement. One of these was the enactment of the *Sex Discrimination Act 1984* (Cth), which prohibited discrimination on the grounds of sex, marital status, and pregnancy. Another was more controversial: the *Affirmative Action (Equal Employment Opportunity for Women) Act 1986* (Cth). This legislation required Commonwealth public service organisations with over 100 employees to establish affirmative action programs to increase female participation. In practice, affirmative action means, for example, that where two candidates are equally suited to a position, the job should go to the woman. There are community legal centres dedicated to looking after women's interests and a National Network of Indigenous Women's Legal Services that brings together legal aid, legal services, advocacy and violence prevention services.

> **GO ONLINE**
> Go online for further information on the structural barriers that women face in accessing legal services.

Aboriginal and Torres Strait Islander peoples

Aboriginal and Torres Strait Islander people comprise approximately two per cent of the Australian population. The impact of colonisation and polices of protectionism and assimilation had a devastating effect on their population (see chapters 8 and 9).

---

9   Judicial Commission of New South Wales, *Equality before the Law Bench Book* (2006), ch 7.

10 Regina Graycar and Jenny Morgan, *The Hidden Gender of Law*, Federation Press, Sydney, 2nd edn (2002); Australian Law Reform Commission, *Equality Before the Law: Women's Access to the Legal System*, Report No 67 (Interim report tabled to Parliament, January 1994).

The disadvantages facing Aboriginal and Torres Strait Islander people are well known, and span many social and economic indicators. On average, Aboriginal and Torres Strait Islander people, when compared to the general population, have:

- fewer tertiary educational qualifications
- lower literacy skills
- greater rates of unemployment
- lower disposable incomes
- lower rates of home ownership, and greater rates of dependency on government housing
- poor healthcare outcomes, lower life expectancy, and greater rates of disability than average
- a greater likelihood of being victims and perpetrators of physical or threatened violence
- a reduced likelihood of getting bail and a greater likelihood of being in prison.

Aboriginal and Torres Strait Islander people are therefore more likely to be involved with legal matters, yet less equipped to help themselves. Communication barriers with Aboriginal and Torres Strait Islander people and the language of the court can further affect their interaction with the justice system[11]. The following illustrates some differences between Aboriginal and Torres Strait Islander people and non-Aboriginal and Torres Strait Islander people:

- **Eye contact** – to an Aboriginal person, direct or prolonged eye contact may indicate a lack of respect. An Aboriginal person may avoid eye contact with lawyers, magistrates and judges. This may give the impression that they have something to hide, or are uncooperative. This assessment of a person's demeanour by a magistrate and judge is a finding of fact that is very rarely disturbed by judges on appeal.[12]
- **Direct questioning** – this can be very confrontational in Aboriginal culture. There is a preference for indirect and two-way interactive communication.
- **Gratuitous concurrence** – Aboriginal and Torres Strait Islander people tend to readily agree with propositions put to them by authority figures (like lawyers and judges).
- **Language** – reduced understanding of English, especially in remote communities.

At a funding level, money has been directed to projects to address some specific access to justice issues for Aboriginal and Torres Strait Islander people. These include:

- The Aboriginal Legal Services in the states and territories was established in the 1970s (in Central Australia) to provide free legal advice and representation for Aboriginal and Torres Strait Islander people in criminal proceedings and in

TIP
Indigenous people are 14 times more likely than non-Indigenous Australians to be in prison.

---

11 See Stephanie Fryer-Smith, Aboriginal Bench Book for Western Australia courts, Chapter 5, available at www.aija.org.au/online/ICABenchbook/BenchbookChapter5.pdf.

12 Ibid.; see also Judicial Commission of New South Wales, *Equality before the Law Bench Book* (2006) www.judcom.nsw.gov.au/publications/benchbks/equality/benchbook.pdf.

some jurisdictions in civil proceedings. Such services have since expanded across Australia. However, they are severely under-funded and under-resourced.
- Access to interpreters in some states and territories, such as free access in the Northern Territory where English is often a second language.
- Specific funding of Aboriginal and Torres Strait Islander women by the Federal Government's Community Legal Services Program, to avoid a conflict of interest where the Commonwealth may already be providing legal aid to the accused in domestic violence cases.
- Outreach services created by the Federal Court and the Family Court to better reach people from Alice Springs, Darwin and Cairns.
- The Federal Court has developed special procedures for native title cases so that formality is decreased, and the court staff frequently travel to remote and regional communities to gather knowledge or to conduct hearings.
- Alternative court systems, such as circle sentencing or Koori Courts, that involve the Indigenous community in determining the sentence (within the statute) applied to criminal offenders who have been convicted of minor crimes. Again, these courts are often under-funded and face the additional problem of being imposed by governments rather than developed collaboratively with Indigenous communities.[13] More detail on these alternative Indigenous sentencing courts is found in Chapter 9.

GO ONLINE

Go online for further information on the structural barriers that Indigenous Australians face in accessing legal services.

People from a non–English speaking background

Australia is a diverse country comprised of many people born overseas in places with different customs, values and languages. In New South Wales nearly one in four people was born overseas; two-thirds of these come from a non-English speaking background (NESB).[14] In New South Wales 75 per cent of households exclusively speak English. Cultural differences need to be recognised by the legal system, including different styles of behaviour, appearance, expectations about roles of men, women and children, the influence of religions, a different understanding of court systems and justice, and different styles of communication. It is these factors that can pose access to justice issues. The key issue is the ability to communicate effectively in English. Imagine these barriers:

- The police caution you or charge you with an offence in English, where you are not fluent in English.
- The evidence you hear in court or at a tribunal is not fully comprehended because you are not fluent in English.
- You have trouble briefing or understanding your lawyer because of your limited understanding of English.

---

13   Heather McRae, Garth Nettheim, Thalia Anthony, Laura Beacroft, Sean Brennan, Megan Davis and Terri Jenki, *Indigenous Legal Issues: commentary and materials*. Thomson, Sydney, 4th edn, (2009), 577-578.

14   Judicial Commission of New South Wales, above n 12, 3103.

- You have trouble understanding written documents provided, and have trouble reading documents you source online that offer legal advice.

Particular areas of concern are:

- Lack of information about law in one's own language.
- Lack of access to interpreters, especially in rural and regional areas.
- Potential for stereotyping of ethnic groups by lawyers, court staff and the judiciary.

Access to interpreters and translators

Access to interpreters is a key factor in access to justice for people who are not fluent in English.

Interpreters and translators have specialist accreditation for difficult jobs, such as court hearings. Interpreters may need to be found who speak particular dialects, and some people feel more comfortable with someone of their own gender interpreting for them, especially if the subject matter is sensitive, such as sexual activity or sexual assault.

The main issue with access to interpreters and translators is the cost of these services. One cannot use a family member or friend; they must use a properly accredited professional. Hourly charges can amount to a considerable sum in any defended hearing. Interpreters are frequently provided free in criminal proceedings, but in civil cases, parties to the action must pay the costs of their interpreters that are required for them, and for their witnesses. This can be a considerable deterrent. Tribunals will readily provide interpreters where required.[16] These factors were detailed in the Australian Law Reform Commission's report, *Multiculturalism and the Law*[17] and led to many reforms being made.

The High Court makes arrangements for interpreters for self-represented litigants who do not speak English.

The Federal Court's Equality and the Law Committee has overseen the following reforms. Lawyers are required to draw to the Federal Court's attention any need for an interpreter quickly, be that for a party or a witness. The Court will provide an interpreter and translation services to a litigant who has marginal English speaking ability and does not have the ability to pay for such services.[18] The Court has a policy of hiring multilingual front desk staff to help deal with people from a diverse range of backgrounds, publishes information sheets in multiple languages, and has trained its judicial officers in cultural and linguistic diversity.

The Family Court of Australia, through its National Cultural Diversity Committee, drew attention to factors that impeded access to justice by people from culturally

TIP
An interpreter is someone who interprets speech; they are often used during witness examination in the courtroom. Translators translate text, documents and other video or audio recordings.[15]

---

15 Regulation of interpreters and translators is by the National Accreditation Authority for Translators and Interpreters. See their website for listings of accredited members www.naati.com.au.

16 See for example www.aat.gov.au/ApplyingToTheAAT/InformationForInterpreters.htm.

17 Australian Law Reform Commission, *Multiculturalism and the Law*, Report No. 57, 1992.

18 Attorney-General's Department (Commonwealth), *Federal Civil Justice System Strategy Paper*, December 2003, 78, www.ag.gov.au/www/agd/agd.nsf/Page/Publications_FederalCivilJusticeSystemStrategyPaper-December2003.

diverse backgrounds. These included the fact that signage was always in English, the level of staff awareness was variable, and staff had little knowledge of other government and community services that would be of assistance. To remedy these issues the Family Court developed cross-cultural training for staff, provided better facilities for interpreters, and trained community workers about how the courts operate and the new facilities and services provided. The Family Court will also arrange interpreters for litigants who have no money and little or no English speaking ability.[19] The Family Court website details many initiatives in the field of cultural diversity.[20]

Children and young people

Children and young people (referred to in legal terms as 'minors') also face significant barriers in the legal system. This is primarily because they are rarely involved in it except as defendants in juvenile courts or as children of a relationship breakdown. Traditionally, the law considered that a parent, caregiver, the state, a judge, or a doctor are best placed to make competent decisions about the child or young person's best wishes and needs. Now, where they are involved in custody proceedings, the child is assigned a lawyer to argue that child's interests and views to the court.

Sexuality: Gay, lesbian, bisexual and transgender

For many years, gay, lesbian and transgender people have experienced discrimination in the legal system. Gay sexual acts were criminalised throughout Australia. Tasmania was the last state to decriminalise sexual conduct between males in 1997. The decriminalisation in Tasmania was prompted by a complaint to the United Nations Human Rights Committee. Today there remains formal legal discrimination against gay and lesbian couples, especially in family law.

There are laws nonetheless that make it illegal to discriminate or vilify a person on the basis of their homosexual or transgender status. For example, in New South Wales the *Anti-Discrimination Act 1977* (NSW) makes it unlawful in some circumstances for anyone to discriminate against a person, or a relative or associate of that person, on the basis of their actual or presumed homosexual or transgender status. The circumstances of unlawful discrimination relate to employment, education, housing and club membership. Some organisations are exempt from the provisions of the *Anti-Discrimination Act 1977* (NSW). These include, charities, religious and voluntary bodies, and aged housing accommodation providers. There are also specific exemptions to transgender discrimination in the areas of sports and superannuation.[21]

---

19 See the Family Court's Interpreters Policy, www.familycourt.gov.au/wps/wcm/connect/FCOA/home/about/Business/Plans/Interpreters.

20 Family Court of Australia, The Family Court of Australia's National Diversity Plan (2009), www.familycourt.gov.au/wps/wcm/connect/FLC/Home/Communities+and+individuals/Interpreters+Policy.

21 Inner City Legal Centre, 'Gay, Lesbian and Transgender Discrimination' www.iclc.org.au/iclc_fs_gltdiscrim.html. Also see: Inner City Legal Centre, *Party Rights: You have the Right to Remain Fabulous – Your Legal Rights on the Scene* (2009), www.iclc.org.au/pdfs/party_rights08.pdf

Vilification is any public act that could encourage other people to hate, or have serious contempt for, or severely ridicule, you or a group of people, because of your sexuality. Vilification is illegal under discrimination legislation. However, public acts, such as a speech or statement made 'reasonably and in good faith' for academic, artistic, scientific, research or 'public interest' purposes, or a fair media report of someone else's act of vilification, will not amount to vilification under the *Anti-Discrimination Act 1977* (NSW).[22]

Those affected by sexuality discrimination (including on the basis of HIV/AIDS status) or vilification can make a formal complaint to state or territory anti-discrimination boards, commissions or commissioners or tribunals.[23] The anti-discrimination body will send the other party a copy of your complaint and ask them to respond in writing. They will generally arrange a meeting with the person or organisation about whom you are complaining, and try to reach a resolution or settlement. An officer from the anti-discrimination body will act as the mediator in meetings. A settlement may include, for example, an apology, compensation, attendance at training courses about harassment, reprimand or transfer to another position.[24] If there is no successful conciliation or resolution by the anti-discrimination body, it may be possible to apply to have the matter heard by an anti-discrimination tribunal or a division of a state civil claims tribunal.

Self-represented litigants

The term 'self-represented litigant' disguises the fact that the party actually is legally unrepresented. Nevertheless a literature has evolved using this term. Self-represented litigants (SRLs) are frequently at a disadvantage in legal matters. Although some choose to represent themselves because they do not trust lawyers, most do not have a lawyer because they cannot afford one, and do not qualify for legal aid. Some 45 per cent of litigants at the New South Wales Local Court, 31 per cent of Federal Court Litigants and 40 per cent of parties before the Family Court have no legal representation.[25] Self-represented litigants require more assistance from the courts, their registries, their libraries and information services, and their staff. Lawyers too are more frequently dealing with self-represented litigants and need to be educated about this. The New South Wales Law Society for example has issued guidelines to all legal practitioners on how to deal with SRLs.[26] While there is some variability in

---

22 Inner City Legal Centre, 'Gay, Lesbian and Transgender Discrimination' www.iclc.org.au/iclc_fs_gltdiscrim.html.

23 See the list of anti-discrimination bodies in the Weblinks at the end of the chapter.

24 Inner City Legal Centre, 'Gay, Lesbian and Transgender Discrimination' www.iclc.org.au/iclc_fs_gltdiscrim.html.

25 Justice Jeff Shaw, 'Self-represented litigants', a speech to the conference dinner of the Consumer, Trade and Tenancy Tribunal Sydney (20 November 2003), www.nswccl.org.au/docs/pdf/srlitigants.pdf. The Family Court of Australia provide information for self-represented litigants: Family Court of Australia, Self Represented Litigants Fact Sheet (2009), www.familycourt.gov.au/wps/wcm/connect/FCOA/home/about/Media/Fact_Sheets/FCOA_SRL.

26 Law Society of New South Wales, *Guidelines for solicitors dealing with self-represented parties* (April 2006).

their education and literacy it is generally agreed that SRLs:

- take longer to put their cases, and struggle to distinguish between fact and law
- do not fully understand the complexities of legislation or precedent or legal conventions
- force the judiciary to help them at every step. Judges must also initiate checks to see if the litigant has been declared on a list to be vexatious, check to see if they have properly exhausted possibilities of getting legal aid, then refer them to written information about representing themselves in court[27]
- present evidence poorly and fail to present relevant evidence
- are usually poorly skilled in cross examination and re-examination.

Some of these advisory burdens fall to the court registry staff who frequently must explain how to fill out forms and explain their relevance and purpose.

The case of *Damjanovic v Sharpe Hume & Co*[28] is a good insight into a case with unrepresented litigants and a judge's directions to the party being in issue. Mr Damjanovic, an elderly man with little fluency in English, sued six defendants alleging forgery. The case was heard by Judge Gibb of the New South Wales District Court. She granted leave to Mr Vulic – a man without any legal training – to appear for Mr Damjanovic. Judge Gibb formed an opinion that she did not trust the evidence of Mr Damjanovic and he appealed this finding, alleging a reasonable apprehension of bias in the judge's statements to him. This finding of reasonable apprehension of bias was upheld by the New South Wales Court of Appeal based on a few comments made by Judge Gibb. The court stated:[29]

> Judicial officers must have particular regard to the due performance of their functions in situations where a litigant is in person, and does not have English as his or her first language and, as in the present case, has shown a healthy scepticism for the legal system. Such people should not be made to feel that because they are appearing in person, as they are entitled to do, or do not understand the language fully, they are under a disadvantage. Within the rules concerning helping litigants in person, the Court should observe with scrupulous fairness the duties to which we have referred. Further a judicial officer should not, by acting contrary to these basic requirements of patience, courtesy and self-restraint, fuel scepticism or suspicion, however wrongly it may be held, of the court system.
>
> Regretfully, when her Honour's conduct is examined in this case, the only conclusion to which one can come, irrespective of the strength or weaknesses of Mr Damjanovic's case, is that he did not have a 'fair go' and that anyone privy to the way in which her Honour conducted her Court in this case could hardly come to a view other than that her presiding over this case would have severely eroded public confidence in the proper

---

27   See for example LawAccess at www.lawaccess.nsw.gov.au.

28   [2001] NSWCA 40.

29   Ibid., [163–4].

administration of the judicial system. These conclusions, in themselves, justify the orders we have made so that fair trials may be held.

The judgment shows the significant extra work that judges must do with unrepresented or self-represented litigants (especially those with poor English skills), and the frustrations associated with this.

Levels of self-representation are particularly high in the local courts that are more inclined to deal with questions of fact rather than law. The overwhelming majority of cases are heard in the local courts and there is a culture of litigant involvement. However, at times, especially in criminal trials, the defendant will not be able to afford representation. This can be to their great detriment. This issue of representation at the higher courts was addressed in the criminal trial of *Dietrich v R*[30] (which is elaborated on p. 404 below). Chief Justice Mason and Justice McHugh explained the difficulties involved in legal self-representation:

> An unrepresented accused is disadvantaged, not merely because almost always he or she has insufficient legal knowledge and skills, but also because an accused in such a position is unable dispassionately to assess and present his or her case in the same manner as counsel for the Crown. The hallowed response … that, in cases where the accused is unrepresented, the judge becomes counsel for him or her, extending a 'helping hand' to guide the accused throughout the trial so as to ensure that any defence is effectively presented to the jury, is inadequate for the same reason that self-representation is generally inadequate: a trial judge and a defence counsel have such different functions that any attempt by the judge to fulfil the role of the latter is bound to cause problems (footnotes omitted).

In *Dietrich v R* the High Court decided that the case would be stayed indefinitely in the absence of legal representation. The effect of this was an acquittal for Dietrich. The High Court held that where a person is charged with serious offences a defendant has a right to representation. See the case study later in this chapter.

Nonetheless, such a right to legal representation is not guaranteed and is not available for minor offences in local courts, nor in any civil dispute. Indeed, there is clear evidence that the high cost of litigation has driven many to self-representation, with rates of self-representation rising rapidly. In fact in the decade from 1994 to 2004 there was an increase in self-represented people before the Federal Court to 31 per cent, and to 40 per cent in the Family Court.[31]

People with disabilities

Disability encompasses physical, sensory and intellectual disability. The ABS has estimated that 20 per cent of the Australian population are affected by a disability of some sort, and six per cent of the population have a profound limitation on core

---

30 (1992) 177 CLR 292 (Mason CJ and McHugh J).

31 Justice Jeff Shaw, 'Self-represented litigants', n 26 above.

activity (self-care, mobility or communication).[32] Some 1.8 per cent of the population have an intellectual disability. More than half of this group require assistance with self-care, mobility and verbal communication.[33]

Disabilities can affect a person's access to justice on a number of levels. A physical disability can make it more difficult to travel to lawyers, courts, to access information in libraries and on the Internet. Sensory disability creates communication barriers, making it difficult to research, understand, and explain one's legal needs. A sign language (AUSLAN) interpreter may be required at the person's cost.[34] With this in mind, the High Court, Federal Court and Family Courts have upgraded their websites to meet online accessibility standards. The Federal Court has rolled out TTY (test telephone) services in all of its registries. Moreover the Family Court will provide interpreter services for hearing and speech-impaired persons.

People with a mental illness

Mental illness is a set of clinically recognisable symptoms or behaviour associated with distress and interference with self-functioning.[35] It is clear that people with a mental illness experience considerable social and legal disadvantage. These disadvantages have been identified by reports[36] and include: discrimination (employment, access to services, education, insurance); social security eligibility and breach issues; consumer debt and domestic violence issues. People with a mental illnesses experience more violence than the national average, and people with schizophrenia have increased rates of violent and criminal behaviour.[37] Associated with this are considerable barriers to obtaining legal assistance. The reasons for this include:

- lack of awareness of legal rights
- lack of organisation (due to illness)
- being overwhelmed (due to illness, stress or cognitive impairment)
- legal assistance provider unfamiliarity with unusual behaviours (e.g. tics, idiosyncrasies, mood swings) and unfamiliarity with recognising mental illness
- communication difficulties
- lack of appropriate healthcare treatment (either neglect or lack of resources)
- time constraints set by providers (people with a mental illness may need more time)

---

32 Australian Bureau of Statistics, *Disability*, No 4446, Canberra (2003).

33 Australian Institute of Health and Welfare, *The definition and prevalence of intellectual disability*, Canberra, 2000.

34 See www.auslan.org.au.

35 World Health Organisation, *International Classification of Disease 10 (ICD-10)* 5.

36 See for example Maria Karras, Emily McCarron, Abigail Gray and Sam Ardasinski, *On the edge of justice: the legal needs of people with a mental illness in New South Wales*, Law Foundation of New South Wales, Sydney (2006).

37 Ibid., 58-60.

- certain behaviours (e.g. lack of eye contact) may see providers conclude that their client lacks credibility
- in mediation and ADR settings, self-representation actually disadvantages the mentally ill party.

For case studies of mentally ill people and the law, see the Law and Justice Foundation of New South Wales report *On the Edge of Justice: The legal needs of people with a mental illness in New South Wales*.[38]

People in rural and regional communities

People in rural and regional communities generally have more difficulty accessing the legal system. Most government, legal and court services are in metropolitan areas. Issues concerning access to justice include:

- geographic isolation – people have to drive, fly or take public transport great distances to visit lawyers or courts, or specialists or experts who may need to testify on their behalf
- lack of access to choice of lawyers, particularly lawyers who specialise in the relevant area of law
- inadequate access to community legal centres
- absence of video conferencing facilities
- lack of ancillary support services at courts, such as liaison officers for domestic violence and disabilities
- scant publicity about services available.

The geographic isolation compounds other access to justice barriers, so that a poor, intellectually underprivileged woman from NESB who has faced domestic violence will experience severe restrictions on her ability to access decent legal advice. Aboriginal Australians are also heavily represented in rural and regional areas of Australia, a fact noted by the Law Reform Committee of Victoria in a report entitled *Review of Legal Services in Rural and Regional Victoria*.[39]

3: The role of legal aid

Legal aid explained

Legal aid is a system of financial assistance, subject to strict eligibility guidelines, given by governments to help pay for legal advice or representation in select cases where a person can demonstrate financial hardship. Legal aid is organised through Legal Aid Commissions and is funded by the states, territories and the Commonwealth government. In the 2005–06 financial year, Legal Aid provided services to 700 000

---

38 Ibid., 127ff.

39 Victoria Law Reform Committee, Parliament of Victoria, *Review of Legal Services in Rural and Regional Victoria* (31 May 2001), www.parliament.vic.gov.au/lawreform/inquiries (scroll down to '54th Parliament' to locate report).

people (270 000 were advised, 158 000 were represented, and 271 000 received duty lawyer services).[40]

While legal aid is helping some people with particular legal problems, the general availability of legal aid (or, more to the point, its relative unavailability) is a barrier to people's ability to access basic legal services. This is because the grant of legal aid is conditional. Furthermore, the pool of lawyers available to do this work is limited, and even more so if outside capital cities.

Legal aid schemes across Australia

Legal aid commissions are independent bodies set up by governments. They are governed by legislation and have their own particular rules. Legal Aid bodies or commissions exist in all states and in the Australian Capital Territory and the Northern Territory:

- Legal Aid Commission of the Australian Capital Territory
- Legal Aid New South Wales
- Northern Territory Legal Aid Commission
- Legal Aid Queensland
- Legal Services Commission of South Australia
- Legal Aid Commission of Tasmania
- Legal Aid Victoria
- Legal Aid Western Australia.

The Commonwealth Attorney-General has portfolio responsibility for legal aid in Commonwealth matters through its Legal Assistance Branch.[41] The Commonwealth also has other statutory schemes that are administered by the Financial Assistance Section in defined cases where a client is not eligible for legal aid.

Eligibility

Legal aid is only awarded to people of very limited means and who have a meritorious case. To qualify for legal aid, the matter must fall under Commonwealth law, it must accord with Commonwealth legal aid priorities, and it must meet a means test. The means test is a financial test of eligibility which takes into account your income or benefits, rent or mortgage, credit card debts and loans to determine your financial eligibility.

The merit test has three stages, as follows:

- The Commission must believe that the case is more likely than not to succeed.
- The Commission must believe that a prudent, self-funded litigant would have risked their own money fighting such a case or action.
- The Commission considers the costs involved are likely to benefit the applicant, or even the community.

---

40 Figures from National Legal Aid www.nla.aust.net.au/category.php?id=1.

41 See www.ag.gov.au/www/agd/agd.nsf/Page/Legalaid_LegalAidProgram.

In family law, the Commonwealth legal aid priorities are child support, separate representation of children, parenting plans, family violence child support and maintenance, and spousal maintenance. In criminal law matters, the legal representation of a person charged with a criminal offence is the sole priority. In civil law issues, priorities are Commonwealth employees and veterans' pensions, benefits and compensation, discrimination, migration and consumer protection.[42] Additionally, there is a discretion to award legal aid monies where the applicant is a child, has a language or literacy problem, where there is a likelihood of domestic violence, the applicant has an intellectual, psychiatric or physical disability or lives in a remote location.

Additional monies are available through the Financial Assistance branch of the Commonwealth Attorney-General's Office, for specific areas not covered by regular legal aid, such as native title financial assistance, Equine Influenza Inquiry and the Commonwealth Public Interest and Test Cases Program.[43]

Even with eligibility, legal aid is not free of charge. Applicants can expect to pay something for their services. Legal Aid is usually only available in civil cases where an assessment is made that there is a reasonable chance of winning the case. For some groups, particularly those in violent domestic situations, forcing these people to mediation in order to get legal aid could be traumatic. People living in rural and regional areas have to drive to their nearest centre, and often rely on a weekly or fortnightly appearance of a duty lawyer.

In criminal cases the situation is somewhat different. Most jurisdictions confer a right to the accused to be legally represented by a lawyer. The difficulty is that these provisions, technically conferring rights on all, really act to the disadvantage of the underprivileged. This is because a right to counsel is somewhat meaningless if they cannot afford that lawyer's services, nor afford an appeal. This is where legal aid may help, but it does not have wide applicability to most disputes. There are some special mechanisms other than the ones just mentioned:

- Aboriginal and Torres Strait Islander Legal Services
- Community legal services
- Pro bono legal work by private practitioners
- Making an application pursuant to the rules set out in the High Court judgment of *Dietrich v R*.[44]

The first three points above will be covered later in the chapter, but the *Dietrich* principle requires some analysis.

---

[42] Commonwealth of Australia, Commonwealth Legal Aid Priorities and Guidelines. www.ag.gov.au/www/agd/agd.nsf/Page/Legalaid_CommonwealthLegalAidPrioritiesandGuidelines.

[43] See www.ag.gov.au/www/agd/agd.nsf/Page/Legalaid_FinancialAssistance.

[44] (1992) 177 CLR 292.

Dietrich v The Queen

(1992) 177 CLR 292

On the night of 17 December 1986 the accused Mr Olaf Dietrich arrived at Melbourne Airport on a flight from Bangkok. He carried with him over 70 grams of heroin concealed in condoms that he had swallowed. He was followed by the Australian Federal Police (AFP) to his flat in St Kilda. The next morning as the applicant was driving away from his flat he was intercepted by the AFP and arrested. The AFP officers produced a search warrant and took Dietrich back to his flat and found heroin in a plastic bag under a rug in his study, and in the kitchen found 3.7 grams of heroin in a condom. Mr Dietrich was charged and sent to Pentridge Prison where he was placed in a hospital isolation unit. During the night he passed condoms with a total of 66.4 grams of heroin.

The Prosecution used evidence collected by the AFP during surveillance and arrest, and also evidence from the prison where the heroin had been collected. Mr Dietrich denied any importation and argued that the AFP had planted all the evidence. Mr Dietrich knew he was in serious trouble and sought legal representation. At his first trial in the Victorian County Court he faced charges of trafficking and was unrepresented. He applied to the Legal Aid Commission of Victoria for assistance but Legal Aid would only represent him if he pleaded guilty. Mr Dietrich was also unsuccessful in his application for Commonwealth legal aid.

Mr Dietrich then sought to have a lawyer appointed pursuant to provisions of the s 69(3) of the *Judiciary Act 1903* (Cth), which states:

> (3) Any person committed for trial for an offence against the laws of the Commonwealth may at any time within fourteen days after committal and before the jury is sworn apply to a Justice in Chambers or to a Judge of the Supreme Court of a state for the appointment of counsel for his or her defence. If it be found to the satisfaction of the Justice or Judge that such person is without adequate means to provide a defence for himself or herself, and that it is desirable in the interests of justice that such an appointment should be made, the Justice or Judge shall certify this to the Attorney-General, who may if he or she thinks fit thereupon cause arrangements to be made for the defence of the accused person or refer the matter to such legal aid authorities as the Attorney-General considers appropriate. Upon committal the person committed shall be supplied with a copy of this subsection.

The trial judge refused to adjourn the trial to consider acting under this section, and also refused Mr Dietrich's request for a 'McKenzie friend'. A McKenzie friend[45] is a person who can help a party in court in the following ways: provide moral support, take notes, make suggestions, edit and source documents. The McKenzie friend is not permitted to offer any legal advice or representation.

---

45 Named after the case *McKenzie v McKenzie* [1970] 3 WLR 472.

Mr Dietrich was convicted on the primary charge of trafficking. For a non-lawyer Mr Dietrich was reputedly reasonably adept at conducting his own case, and managed to have some charges dropped. Mr Dietrich then unsuccessfully appealed his conviction to the Victorian Court of Criminal Appeal. Mr Dietrich then applied for leave to appeal to the High Court of Australia. Leave was granted and the case reached the High Court in 1992. From the date of the offence to the final judgment date was almost six years. By the time the case reached the High Court Mr Dietrich was represented by counsel, Mr David Grace. He acted on a pro bono basis for Mr Dietrich. This meant that he was working for Mr Dietrich but not charging legal fees for his services. A few key arguments were made at trial:

1. That there had been a failure to bring about a fair trial because Mr Dietrich was not represented by counsel.
2. That Mr Dietrich should have been given a lawyer at the public expense, indeed that he had a right to one, which could be implied from:
   a. Section 397 of the *Victorian Crimes Act 1958* stated this right
   b. International covenants such as the International Covenant on Civil and Political Rights, Art 14(3) which required free legal advice for such an accused
   c. Case law in the United States of America and Canadian based on their bills of rights.
3. That the trial judge should have used his discretionary powers and ordered a stay or adjournment when discovering Mr Dietrich's financial and legal position.

The High Court held that in Australian common law there was no right of an accused to be provided with counsel at the public's expense. Justice Brennan stated that this could only be done by parliament, and not by the High Court. The judges dismissed Mr Dietrich's arguments stating that s 397 of the *Crimes Act* meant that an accused had the right to be represented by a lawyer of choice, but not to a lawyer provided by the state. The High Court did however point out that judges should adjourn or stay a trial where the lack of counsel could prejudice a fair trial. Second, the High Court looked at our international obligations but decided that the treaties that supported such rights had not clearly been incorporated into Australian domestic law, meaning that the court could not give effect to the rights to legal representation contained in them. Furthermore, the High Court dismissed United States and Canadian guarantees of rights to trial as being strictly specific to their different constitutional guarantees of rights, and not applicable in Australia. Finally, the High Court made observations about when a trial could be prejudiced by a failure to adjourn it where the defendant was without legal representation:[46]

> A trial judge ... is not required to appoint counsel. The decision whether to grant an adjournment or a stay is ... [in] the trial judge's discretion, by asking whether the trial is likely to be unfair if the accused is forced on unrepresented. For our part, the desirability of an accused charged with a serious offence being represented is so

---

46 *Dietrich v R* (1992) 177 CLR 292, 311 (Mason CJ and McHugh J).

> great that we consider that the trial should proceed without representation for the accused in exceptional cases only. In all other cases of serious crimes, the remedy of an adjournment should be granted in order that representation can be obtained ... [there are] comprehensive legal aid schemes ... However, even in those cases where the accused has been refused legal assistance and has unsuccessfully exercised his or her rights to review of that refusal, it is possible, perhaps probable, that the decision of a Legal Aid Commission would be reconsidered if a trial judge ordered that the trial be adjourned or stayed pending representation being found for the accused.
>
> In this case the High Court did find a miscarriage of justice in Mr Dietrich's trial arising from the failure of the trial judge to adjourn the matter so that Mr Dietrich could obtain legal representation. This was because there was the possibility that Dietrich could have been acquitted on one or more of the charges. A retrial was ordered but did not take place as Dietrich had already served his sentence.

The *Dietrich* case ignited a debate about where legal aid money should be spent and in what circumstances being without legal aid may cause delays in the criminal justice system. The Premier of Victoria was so concerned that he ordered the *Crimes Act 1958* (Vic) to be modified to allow judges a discretion to order legal aid funding (so long as the applicant is not engaged in vexatious conduct) where they would otherwise have adjourned proceedings. Section 360A of the *Crimes Act 1958* (Vic) now reflects these changes.

Legal aid access issues

A fairly large percentage of legal aid involves criminal law or family law issues. Approximately half the firms who practise in these fields currently provide legal aid. In such situations, the Legal Aid Commission funds that law firm's representation of the client. On average this would be approximately five or so cases a year. However, there is a great variation between states and between regional and remote areas. For instance, New South Wales firms are far more likely to provide legal aid than firms in Victoria, Queensland, and Western Australia. Law firms in regional and remote Australia provided more legal aid than metropolitan law firms. This is despite the shortage of lawyers in such remote areas (three lawyers per 10 000 adults in remote Australia compared with 10.7 lawyers per 10 000 adults in capital cities). This supports the anecdotal evidence that regional and rural lawyers feel more morally obligated to provide such services.

Research has shown a trend in law firms to maintain or decrease their legal aid work, with this being a particular problem in rural and regional Australia. This will substantially affect access to justice for many people.[47]

---

47 TNS Social Research, Study of the Participation of Private Legal Practitioners in the Provision of Legal Aid Services in Australia, Canberra (December 2006), www.ag.gov.au/www/agd/agd.nsf/Page/Publications_LegalaidresearchTNSreport-December2006.

4: Other initiatives to promote access to justice

What if a person cannot afford legal representation nor get legal aid? There are community legal centres that may be able to assist. These usually have several lawyers working on a voluntary (pro bono) basis, who provide free legal advice. Some law firms have their own pro bono program as well. Also, law reform commissions try to change laws that are creating difficulty, and this can reduce the cost and time involved in bringing proceedings, so that more people are able to afford legal representation. These initiatives – community law centres, pro bono legal work, and law reform commissions – are considered in turn below.

Community legal centres

Unlike legal aid, community legal centres (CLCs) are independent local or issues-based non profit organisations that provide free legal services to the community. CLCs are frequently staffed by volunteers and law students, and it is estimated that the 200 or so CLCs help approximately 350 000 Australians each year with advice, referrals and assistance.[48] CLCs work at local levels and know particular community needs. At a specialist level, they offer help in very important areas of need not well covered by the traditional legal system. The real advantage of CLCs is that they can provide legal advice to people traditionally unable to afford the services of private legal practitioners.

While many CLCs are local organisations with local residential eligibility criteria, others offer specialised legal advisory services, or serve specific groups for example:

- Aboriginal and Torres Strait Islander services
- child support and children's law
- credit and debt
- disability
- discrimination
- environmental law
- the homeless
- immigration and refugee
- mental health
- prisoners
- social services
- sexual assault.

CLCs are very important organisations in terms of enhancing access to justice. They provide legal advice to people who are usually unable to obtain it anywhere else. In New South Wales in 2004, over two-thirds of people using CLCs were either in receipt of government welfare payments, or had little or no income. Aboriginal and Torres Strait Islander people and people from culturally and linguistically diverse backgrounds also feature regularly as CLC clients.[49] Interestingly, 50 per cent of the

---

48 Figures from the National Association of Community Legal Centres at www.naclc.org.au.

49 See Legal Aid Commission of New South Wales, *Review* of *the New South Wales Legal Community Centres Funding Program*, Final Report (June 2006), 3. www.clcnsw.org.au/cb_pages/publications.php?category_id=1160

enquiries to CLCs involve civil cases, 33 per cent involve family law, 9 per cent raise issues of criminal law and 8 per cent of the enquiries involve domestic violence. This reveals areas of real community need. Despite this, CLCs struggle to maintain their funding which means there can be problems of continuity with case lists, follow-up, and delivery of outreach services to regional and remote areas.

The dependency on governmental funding means that community legal centres must conform to Commonwealth and state standards as a precondition of funding. This means more paperwork, more accounting models, and data collection. Citizens may be treated more as consumers of legal services. For volunteers this may be an onerous task, and may restrict the level of community legal work that can be done.[50]

The work of the CLCs is best illustrated by the following case studies taken from a budget submission to the New South Wales Government by the Combined Community Legal Centres (NSW) in 2007.[51]

Case study 1: Norma

Norma is a young woman with mental illness. Usually she is able to manage her illness with medication and support from health workers, but a couple of times a year she becomes seriously ill. In her most recent bout of illness, she lost her job as a receptionist, fell into a $2000 debt to a credit card company, was evicted from her rental accommodation and moved into a room in a boarding house. One night she is physically assaulted by another tenant in the boarding house and ends up in a refuge. The refuge social worker accompanies Norma to the local CLC the next day. The CLC begins working with Norma and her social worker to address some of Norma's legal and social problems:

- The social worker takes Norma to a community health centre for improved treatment of her mental illness and injuries relating to the assault
- A solicitor and the social worker accompany Norma to the police station to report the assault
- The legal centre assists Norma to sign up for Centrelink benefits
- The centre's financial counsellors write to the credit card company to arrange a repayment plan for her debt
- The legal centre's tenancy workers contact the real estate agent of Norma's flat and arrange for them to make Norma's furniture available to her
- The social worker and the centre help Norma lodge a Department of Housing application.

---

50 Mark Rix, 'Community legal centres in Australia under a new public management regime' (2004) 63 (3) *Australian Journal of Public Administration* 33, 36ff.

51 Institute for Sustainable Futures (University of Technology Sydney), *The Economic Value of Community Legal Centres*, 2006 quoted in Combined Community Legal Centres (NSW), *An Investment worthy protecting. Budget Submission to the New South Wales Government 2008–2009*, Sydney (2007).

Case study 2: Using community education as a preventative tool

In 2005, Illawarra Legal Centre adopted a model of Legal Theatre, developed originally by South West Legal Centre as an effective alternative to regular educational workshops for groups from culturally and linguistically diverse backgrounds. Illawarra Legal Centre identified a newly arrived African community as an emerging community not using the centre for legal assistance. The Centre used Legal Theatre, and interpreters, to educate this community group on issues related to credit and debt, Centrelink and tenancy. Following the theatre performances, members of this African community have accessed the Centre to obtain specific advice as word spread through the community that the Centre was able to help.

Case study 3: Lee's phone debt

Lee is a 22 year old man with an intellectual disability. He called 1900 chat lines on his home phone to make friends. Without understanding the billing system, Lee generated a $35 000 bill. The telecommunications company sent him a court summons. When Lee attended the local community legal centre, he had no idea what to do. The CLC negotiated an out-of court settlement with the telecommunications company which reduced the debt to $2000 with small weekly repayments. The CLC's early intervention in this matter resulted in:

- Improved outcomes for Lee's financial future, as he avoids a negative credit rating, learns not to use these phone lines in the future, and learns to be more wary when using other consumer services
- Improved outcomes for Lee's emotional and physical wellbeing, as a debt of this size was likely to greatly distress Lee and reduce his quality of life as he would have had less money for necessities
- Cost-savings by the Local Court because the matter resolved without a hearing
- Cost-saving to other welfare organisations which may have had to provide further services to Lee down the track due to his struggle to pay off a huge debt, for example assistance with rent and other bills such as energy
- Cost-savings to the health system which Lee may have had to use to a greater extent because of the emotional and physical stress that the debt and the court action were likely to have caused.

The work of the CLCs is important as it helps and educates clients who may well have no other avenue of help. The work of CLCs has additional economic benefits, on average saving between $10 000 and $34 000 in avoided costs on an average New South Wales case.

Pro bono legal work

Pro bono work is legal work done by lawyers 'for the public good', at no charge or at a reduced fee. It is aimed at members of the public who are ineligible for Legal Aid and have limited ability to afford legal representation (usually with a review of the merits to ensure their case has reasonable prospects of success). Pro bono work assists not only poor litigants but also non-profit organisations such as charities. The Public Interest Law Clearing House (PILCH)[52] and some law societies[53] coordinate and promote pro bono work by encouraging lawyers to undertake pro bono work as part of a general obligation to society, and by providing a referral service to match lawyers willing to do pro bono work in particular areas of law with people needing such services. Pro bono work usually relates only to the legal representation – clients must still bear disbursements such as court filing fees and search fees, although some schemes have funding to allow certain disbursements to be claimed.

Law reform commissions

Like CLCs, law reform commissions (LRCs) are independent government funded organisations. Law reform commissions exist to advise parliaments on how to improve existing law. They do this by community-wide consultation and use their own officers to conduct research, focus groups and publish discussion papers, issues papers and final reports to government. We discussed LRCs in Chapter 3 under heading 4, Secondary sources.

The Australian Capital Territory and South Australia are currently without an LRC. Tasmania has a Law Reform Institute, and the Northern Territory and Victoria have Law Reform Committees.

LRCs do not advise or see clients, nor do they give people money to represent themselves. Their key roles include:

- to examine, report and make recommendations on any law reform proposal referred to them by the Attorney-General
- to suggest matters to the Attorney-General for examination
- to undertake educational programs relating to their research, reporting and investigations
- to facilitate input into their reform processes.

The Victorian Law Reform Commission's website has a community law reform tab that invites the public to suggest minor legal issues (generally of a community level) that could be investigated. An example of this is a community law reform project on the legal status of 'assistance animals'.

LRCs do facilitate legal reforms that potentially benefit all Australians. LRCs are able to analyse law reform from an international perspective and potentially find innovative

---

52 See Public Interest Law Clearing House (PILCH) (Victoria) www.pilch.org.au and PILCH (NSW) www.pilchnsw.org.au. There is also a National Pro Bono Resource Centre, see www.nationalprobono.org.au/home.asp.

53 See for example NSW Law Society Pro Bono Scheme at www.lawsociety.com.au/ (select menu item For the community, then Finding a solicitor).

solutions. By inviting submissions from CLCs, legal aid, lawyers, government, the public, and industry, LRCs can anticipate legal problems in advance and help create better legislation. Law reform commission reports are valuable resources made freely available on their websites (listed in the web links on the next page). For example the Australian Law Reform Commission's (ALRC) report *Managing Justice: A review of the federal civil justice system* took four years to review the federal civil justice system and involved analysis of more than 4000 legal case files and interviews with lawyers and clients involved with those files. The ALRC received more than 400 submissions relating to this reference, and created a comprehensive 800-page report with 144 law reform recommendations.

Reflection

How might law reform commissions feed into access to justice? What inquiries and terms of reference may be necessary to improve access to justice in Australia? Have a look at some of the law reform commission websites (in 'websites and further reading' below) to get some ideas.

DISCUSSION QUESTIONS

1 Do you think that formal equality before the law is sufficient, or that special measures need to be taken to help create tailored programs for people to achieve equality of outcomes?

2 What do you think are the long term implications of the *Dietrich* case for legal aid authorities?

3 Do you think that legal aid programs and the pro bono work of the profession are sufficient to overcome barriers to people accessing justice?

4 Should all lawyers have an obligation to promote access to justice through the provision of some free legal services to disadvantaged persons, and if so should the obligation be moral, professional, or statutory?

WEBLINKS AND FURTHER READING

Attorney-General's Department, *Legal Aid Program*, AGPS, Canberra, www.ag.gov.au/www/agd/agd.nsf/Page/Legalaid_LegalAidProgram.

Bottomley, Stephen and Parker, Stephen, *Law in Context*, Federation Press, Sydney, 2nd edn (1997), 70–8, 94–100.

Parker, Christine, *Just Lawyers: Regulation and Access to Justice*, Oxford University Press, Oxford (1999), 30–56.

Parliament of Australia, Senate: Committee, Inquiry into the Legal Aid system, Second Report (1997), www.aph.gov.au/Senate/committee/legcon_ctte/completed_inquiries/1996-99/legalaid/report/c07.htm.

Law reform commissions

Australian Law Reform Commission: www.alrc.gov.au
New South Wales Law Reform Commission: www.lawlink.nsw.gov.au/lrc
Northern Territory Law Reform Committee: www.nt.gov.au/justice/policycoord/lawmake/lawref.shtml
Queensland Law Reform Commission: www.qlrc.qld.gov.au
Tasmania Law Reform Institute: www.law.utas.edu.au/reform
Victorian Law Reform Commission: www.lawreform.vic.gov.au
Victorian Parliamentary Law Reform Committee: www.parliament.vic.gov.au/lawreform
Western Australian Law Reform Commission: www.lrc.justice.wa.gov.au

Community legal centres

National: www.naclc.org.au
NSW: www.nswclc.org.au
Qld: www.qails.org.au
SA: www.saccls.org.au/
Vic: www.communitylaw.org.au
WA: www.communitylaw.net

Anti-discrimination bodies

ACT: Australian Capital Territory Human Rights Commission www.hrc.act.gov.au/
NSW: New South Wales Anti-Discrimination Board www.lawlink.nsw.gov.au/ADB
NT: Northern Territory Anti-Discrimination Commission www.nt.gov.au/justice/adc/
Qld: Anti-Discrimination Commision Queensland www.adcq.qld.gov.au/
SA: Equal Opportunity Commission of South Australia www.eoc.sa.gov.au/site/home.jsp
Tas: Office of the Anti-Discrimination Commissioner Tasmania www.antidiscrimination.tas.gov.au/
Vic: The Victorian Equal Opportunity and Human Rights Commission www.humanrightscommission.vic.gov.au/
WA: Equal Opportunity Commission of Western Australia www.equalopportunity.wa.gov.au/

Government reports

Attorney-General's Department, *Study of the Participation of Private Legal Practitioners in the Provision of Legal Aid Services in Australia* (2006), www.ag.gov.au/www/agd/agd.nsf/Page/Publications_LegalaidresearchTNSreport-December2006

ALRC, *Review of the Adversarial System of Litigation: Rethinking Family Law Proceedings*, Issues Paper 22 (1997), Chapter 14.

ALRC, *Review of the Adversarial System of Litigation: Rethinking the Federal Civil Litigation System*, Issues Paper 20 (1997), Chapter 12.

ALRC, *Who Should Pay? A Review of the Litigation Costs Rules*, Issues Paper 13 (1994).

ALRC, *Equality before the Law: Justice for Women*, Report No 69 (I) (1994), Chapters 4 & 5.

Law Foundation of New South Wales, *Legal Expense Insurance: an Experiment in Access to Justice* (1999), www.lawfoundation.net.au/report/lei.

Access to Justice Advisory Committee, *Access to justice: an action plan*, AGPS, Canberra (1994) ('The Sackville Report').

Resources for self-represented litigants

Australian Institute of Judicial Administration, 'Litigants In Person Management Plans: Issues For Courts and Tribunals (2001), www.aija.org.au/Litigant/LIPREP1.pdf

Family Court of Western Australia, 'A Guide to Representing Yourself In the Family Court of Western Australia, Children's Cases' (2007), www.familycourt.wa.gov.au/_files/Handbook_Childrens_Cases.pdf.

Family Law Web Guide, Self Represented Litigants Resources, www.familylawwebguide.com.au/srl-r/index.php.

Law Society of New South Wales, 'Guidelines for Solicitors Dealing with Self-represented Parties' (2006), www.lawsociety.com.au/idc/groups/public/documents/internetcostguidebook/008731.pdf.

Mervat Rebehy, Mary, 'Unrepresented Parties and the Equal Opportunity Tribunal: A Survey of Tribunals and Recommendations for Change', Law and Justice Foundation of New South Wales, Sydney (2000), www.lawfoundation.net.au/report/eot.

ONLINE RESOURCES FOR THIS CHAPTER

The following resources are available online at www.oup.com.au/orc/cwl2e
- Further information on women accessing justice
- Further information on Indigenous Australians accessing justice
- Flashcard glossary
- Multiple choice questions

14

My Law Career: How Can I Best Prepare for It?

WHAT WE WILL COVER IN THIS CHAPTER:

- The types of career paths open to law graduates
- The kinds of work done by legal practitioners
- What law students need to know to help set up a legal career
- The core legal skills a young lawyer needs
- The kinds of curriculum choices available to law students
- How to maximise your time at law school
- How to keep a balance between work and leisure in law

Recommended approach to learning this topic

This chapter is designed to introduce law students or prospective law students to the kinds of skills, knowledge and attitudes or mindsets that they will need to carry forward into the stressful world of legal practice. It is not a comprehensive guide by any means, but the basics upon which students should seek to build. We recommend you commence by allocating 3–4 hours to the first part, so you can do the interests, skills and values exercises. Knowing your top interests, skills and values can be a good guide to whether you will be suited to a career in law, and what sort of career you might aim for. Then you can read about the kinds of careers open to lawyers, and what you can be doing as a law student to move towards your goal. It is worth revisiting this chapter periodically throughout your law degree, as you come to know more and fine-tune your career preferences.

KEY TERMS

Affidavit = a written statement of facts under oath.

Law firm = a private partnership (or corporate) entity where a number of lawyers are employed to provide legal services. It has a business culture and hierarchy, where the partners are the leading lawyers and income earners.

Legal aid = government funded legal advice and representation.

Paralegal = a non-lawyer (often a law student) with some legal skills who works under a lawyer and performs routine tasks that require some familiarity with law and procedures.

Priestley 11 = the 11 compulsory subjects to be covered in law degrees.

Senior Counsel = Queen's Counsel = an experienced barrister appointed to senior rank (said to have 'taken silk').

Uniform Admission Requirements = rules for admission of lawyers agreed between states and territories, based upon four criteria: academic qualifications (at their minimum, the Priestley 11), practical legal training (PLT), formal admission to the Supreme Court, and the holding of a valid practising certificate from a law society.

1: Is law really for me? How do I know?

An ideal job is one that combines our top interests, accords with our values, suits our personality type, and engages skills that we are good at and enjoy using.

Interests

In surveys of law students the number one reason for doing law is their inherent interest in the subject matter.[1] This interest may come from popular sources (such as television dramas or crime novels). The other reasons for studying law include, in order of importance:[2]

- As part of a double degree – to further career options.
- It's a good degree with applicability to many occupations.
- It's *the* qualification required to be a lawyer.
- You can make a contribution to the community.

Law firms will often ask students questions designed to see why they studied law. Students should think about their reasons for choosing law because they need to assess whether they have the right kinds of skills and attitude to take on what is a challenging career path. Graduating with a law degree does not necessarily mean automatically becoming a lawyer. Many students now have no intention of working as a private legal practitioner, and indeed there are many career paths that are enhanced by a law qualification. So, students need to consider:

- Do I want to become a lawyer?
- If so, what kind of lawyer do I want to be (barrister/solicitor, private or government or community lawyer)?
- If I do not want to be a legal practitioner, what career or mix of qualifications will best serve me in my future career?

Exercise: Identifying your top interests

Brainstorm your top five interests by getting a blank piece of paper and jotting down, in no particular order, things you are interested in. It can be anything from social justice to motorcar racing or travelling. When you have exhausted everything you can think of, go through and mark the ones that most interest you. If there are more than five, you might like to break them into A, B and C levels, with A being the things you are most interested in. What are your top five interests?

---

1 Christopher Roper, *Career Intentions of Australian Law Students*, Centre for Legal Education, Sydney (1995), Chapter 4, 31.

2 Ibid.

Skills

Lawyering requires distinctly specialised skills that are learned primarily through legal education, then in practice itself. Certain skill sets are considered fundamental to this role and courts require that they be taught by law schools looking to use legal qualifications as prerequisites for admission to legal practice. You need to recognise which skills can come from academia and which must be learned elsewhere.

What skills are used by lawyers in their work? They can be broadly categorised as shown below.

Professionalism

Professionalism extends to one's demeanour, attire, punctuality, and dealings with others. This is a feature certainly not unique to the legal profession, but nonetheless, an important element of practice. Lawyers work to rules that are set up to protect the public. They owe duties to the administration of justice, to their clients, duties of confidentiality, and must abide by legal and ethical principles in all aspects of their work. These skills will be introduced in academic legal training.

Problem solving

Lawyering involves significant levels of problem solving skill. This is one area where law school will train students of law to become effective at such work. Legal problem solving requires students to become familiar with working out what is legally relevant. It sounds easy in principle, but it requires considerable practice to sift through reams of information quickly to establish the legal relevance of issues. This comes with experience and training. A common task required is for students to establish the material facts of a case, that is, what subset of facts were drawn upon by the judge as being legally relevant such that their judicial decision making could not have proceeded without them.

Lawyers must identify their client's objectives and work out the best way to achieve them. This requires a certain amount of strategic thinking and some experience, that is gained through analysis of case law and practical legal work. For example lawyers frequently have to choose who the appropriate person is to be named as a defendant in a civil case (e.g. an individual or employee, the company, partnership or organisation, or the body most likely to have insurance). Lawyers then must think of possible courses of action and solutions, and with the client critically evaluate them. They must then seek further instructions from their client to act for them and instruct them on which course of action is to be pursued, detail and cost these, then commence work.

TIP
Students learn to resolve problems by doing essays, problems, tutorials and problem based learning exercises (see Chapter 2).

Conflict resolution and mediation

Our system of law is built on many adversarial traditions. These involve the well-known scenario of each party and their lawyers having their day in court and making arguments, the party with the best case and presentation winning the day. The system relies on advocates (the notion of the 'hired gun') doing their best to present their client's case with the judge assessing the merits of each and making a legally binding decision. While this is still a key feature of litigation, there has been an increasing recognition that mediation is now a core legal skill rather than a peripheral one. Lawyers must understand how to best resolve a dispute for their client, so this skill is one that must be learned. (For more on alternative dispute resolution see Chapter 4).

Communication skills: Written, oral and advocacy

These skills are at the core of many jobs, but are heavily emphasised at law schools. The key ones are discussed below.

Listening

Lawyers need to be active and empathic listeners. Active listening is where the listener uses verbal strategies to demonstrate to the speaker that the listener is following what the speaker is saying. Empathic listening is similar, but involves placing oneself in the shoes of their client and through speaking or body language communicates to the client that they understand and empathise with the situation that the client is in. It is not common to listen in this way – in everyday life we tend to listen only partially, devoting the rest of our attention to planning what we are going to say in response.

Asking questions

Coupled with listening skills, lawyers need to be good at questioning people. They question their clients to ascertain the facts of the client's story. These facts are later distilled into the client's case when coupled with legal principles. Questioning is extremely important as the amount of useful information elicited from a client varies dramatically depending upon whether the right question or approach to questioning was employed.

Questioning techniques usually involve asking many open ended questions at the beginning of the interview, then, as more information becomes available, using closed questions to clarify information already discovered. An example of an open ended question might be 'So, can you tell me in detail the events immediately preceding your arrest this morning?' Note that an answer is not suggested here, there is an open-ended invitation to elicit information. A closed question suggests a short or simple (often yes or no) answer, for example 'How old were you at the time of the accident?' A leading question would suggest an answer, for example 'So when you stopped at the traffic lights you were behind the bus …'. Care must be taken when using leading questions as such questions will close down information flow, and, if uncorrected or unnoticed by the client could lead to a major inaccuracy. Also, questions must be free of values – if a client senses that you believe that they are guilty, this can affect the lawyer-client relationship.

Creating scenarios

Lawyers must think problems through with a view to the many possibilities that may eventuate for their client. This requires them to consider the strengths and weaknesses of their cases, and to draw on possible outcomes based on prior reading of previous cases. Risk management is a significant part of a lawyer's work.

Formulating arguments

Lawyers argue points for their clients. It's a key reason why clients retain them. Their work requires advanced argumentation skills (advocacy). This is a skill that is emphasised at law school through the curriculum and assessment.

Advising

Lawyers have some counselling roles. This is not counselling in a medical sense, but counselling (advising) their clients on sound options to help resolve the client's problems. This is a role that develops with time in practice.

Interviewing and investigating

Interviewing is a core legal skill that involves meeting with a client and the whole process of gathering information, taking notes, asking the client questions about their story, and proffering some legal advice. Interviews usually take place face to face but can take place on the telephone or by video link (they can even take place by email, particularly with international commercial clients). Lawyers need to be able to work effectively in environments outside of the traditional office setup, especially where they are interviewing people in hospital, or in prisons.

Interviewing is a very dynamic exercise that requires the simultaneous use of many skills, both management of people and listening skills. Interviewing requires a lawyer to establish an initial rapport with the client, explain that the interview is confidential and potentially privileged and establish a friendly safe environment. Then, they usually ensure fees and costs are discussed then they ask the client to explain their story, taking detailed file notes and explaining to the client the next steps (usually getting documents from the client, or drafting a letter or claim).

The investigative aspects of a lawyer's role can include conducting title searches, accessing documents under freedom of information provisions, obtaining copies of police and medical reports and seeking other relevant information.

Legal research

Legal research is a fundamental skill that is required both as a law student and as a practitioner. The skill is extremely important, and one that must be maintained and improved. It is not a static skill. Legal research is customarily the first topic that law students do. Students can often fail to appreciate the importance of this topic until they are ready to enter legal practice and are receiving legal research tasks that they have not done since first year. (Legal research was addressed in detail in Chapter 6.)

Legal Research (sometimes titled Legal Method to include analysis of the cases and statutes) subjects teach us to locate and read cases, statutes and other legal materials with a view to helping apply the findings to legal problems. Students today are faced with two systems of legal research tools: the traditional print-based tools (like looseleaf reporters, journals, books etc) and online tools (for example LexisNexis, Westlaw, AustLII, BAILII, parliamentary websites, and the proprietary legal software described in Chapter 6). It is advisable to be proficient in using both print-based and electronic methods of research.

TIP

At law school exercises or competitions involving client legal interviewing can be invaluable for developing legal skills. Also, any group exercise allows you to develop and apply listening and questioning skills.

GO ONLINE

For an exercise on appropriate client questions

TIP

At law school most students have access to a very good selection of electronic databases and resources through their university library. Many of these cost tens of thousands of dollars a year for law firms to maintain. It often surprises students to get to a law firm and find that they no longer have access to some of these resources. It is therefore worth learning alternate methods of finding the same information and not being totally reliant on electronic databases.

Thorough legal research is a critical skill. When a client needs legal advice it has to be correct. This is where accuracy of legal research is important. Accuracy comes from working out the relevant law that will apply. In most cases the applicable law is what was in force at the time of the crime, or personal injury. At other times when giving advice, the applicable law is generally the law at the time of the advice. This would be, for example, if a client was seeking advice on the tax implications of their intended business venture. Either way, legal research is critical to establishing what the relevant law is, was, or will be.

Legal writing and drafting

Legal writing is an essential part of lawyering, and a skill that is heavily nurtured at law school. Legal writing is a technical skill, even for people with good written skills. These are the sorts of things that lawyers must write: notes (from books, articles, or interviews), notes on a case file, letters and memos, legal pleadings, court documents (e.g. affidavits and statutory declarations) and contracts to name but a few. Legal writing is always for a specific audience and context. It is supposed to be as clear and succinct as possible. Lawyers thus need good English language skills and these need to be fostered in law school. Grammar and spelling must be good, as well as citing authorities correctly. Many writing and drafting skills are taught in Practical Legal Training (PLT). These skills must be established and well consolidated during one's legal training.

People management skills

Lawyers have many clients. Frequently these clients are not of their own choosing. Barristers, as we noted in Chapter 12, frequently accept clients in the order they are referred to them (the 'cab rank' rule). Clients will vary depending on the type of practice, so, for example partners in senior commercial practice will see very different clients from those seen by a duty solicitor at the Magistrates Court. Nevertheless, clients vary and lawyers must have excellent people management skills to manage the diverse needs and different ways clients will interact with them. Some clients will be extremely difficult due to their personalities, defects or personality disorders. Unlike medical practitioners, lawyers are not trained to spot clients with mental problems. Clients can be angry, paranoid, secretive, and vexatious. There are clear strategies to deal with all such clients and these skills are critical in practice. Be aware that standard law school training may not be sufficient for you to learn these skills.

Reflection

Do the above skills sound like 'you'? Are they skills you are not only good at, but also enjoy using? If so, it is a good indication that a legal career will suit you.

Exercise: Identifying your top skills

Brainstorm your top five skills. The list below will get you started – circle the ones that apply to you, and add some more in the spaces. Then narrow them down to your top five, as you did with the interests. Remember that they should not just be skills that you are good at, but also ones you enjoy using. For example you may be good at calculating figures but might find it quite boring!

Problem solving	Public speaking	Counselling	Listening
Calculating figures	Reading	Writing	Attention to detail
Teamwork	Acting	Negotiating	Expressing ideas
Persuading others	Finding information	Creating ideas	Motivating others
Being supportive	Teaching	Coordinating	Managing time
Organising	Programming	Filing	Manual labour
_____	_____	_____	_____
_____	_____	_____	_____
_____	_____	_____	_____
_____	_____	_____	_____

Values

Lawyers bring many values to their job. You need to be aware of what values you hold, and recognise that throughout your legal training these values may change, or be further consolidated. This is likely to affect the way you perceive yourself as a future lawyer, your choices of electives, and may affect the career or work experience choices you make. Law firms frequently will probe these values in an effort to check that you will fit the ethos of their firm. This is commonly done at interviews (What experience do you bring from your previous work experience at the Migrant Resource Centre? How have your experiences while travelling influenced you? Who do you most admire? What made you apply to our firm?) These are questions best thought about well before that job interview. Law firms are often keen to understand whether you will be interested in pro bono work, serving the firm, serving the broader legal community, and to some extent, the local community. Having examples of such work or involvement helps convince an interviewer that you do have such a commitment rather than just stating that you do.

Exercise: Identifying your top values

Brainstorm your top five values. The list below will get you started – circle the ones that apply to you, and add some more in the spaces. Then narrow them down to your top five, as you did with interests and skills.

Status	Integrity	Justice	Pleasant environment
Wealth	Companionship	Peace of mind	Autonomy
Excitement	Change	Respect	Authority
Achievement	Honesty	Security	Fun
Recognition	Pleasure	Comfort	Equality
Fairness	Freedom	Growth	Popularity
Glamour	Acceptance	Stability	Helping
_____	_____	_____	_____
_____	_____	_____	_____
_____	_____	_____	_____
_____	_____	_____	_____
_____	_____	_____	_____

Personality

As with the values you hold, your personality as a lawyer is important. The type of person you are is also under scrutiny at legal interviews. Some recruitment firms will use psychometric tests to assess this to see whether you have leadership potential, good teamwork skills and so forth. More subtle types of interview questions that look at this might include: 'What do you do to maintain a balance between work and personal life?'; 'How do you deal with conflict, and can you give us an example of how you have dealt with such situations at work?'

Law firms generally prefer team-oriented workers who pitch in and contribute to a group. Most large law firms participate in social and charity events (fun runs, corporate cups, etc) or functions and require staff to attend social functions on behalf of the firm. Interview questions frequently address this issue and ask you to demonstrate how you work in a team. There are various personality assessment tools, some of which are freely available online. See for example www.keirsey.com and www.humanmetrics.com. Knowing the strengths and weaknesses of your personality type can help you to develop emotional intelligence skills, allowing you to harness your feelings and use them in a constructive manner.

Exercise: Am I suited to becoming a lawyer?

Most lawyers would answer 'yes' to the following ten questions:

1. When you get tired, do you keep going until the job is done?
2. Do you tend to form opinions on most topics?
3. Do you find it easy to structure your thoughts in a logical manner?
4. Are you able to cope with ambiguity quite well?
5. Are you able to separate your personal views and emotions from your professional life?
6. Do you enjoy engaging in a discussion, debate, or argument?
7. Do you consider yourself a 'professional' person?
8. Do you prefer to consider all sides rather than jumping to a conclusion or making assumptions?
9. Do you enjoy doing lots of reading?
10. Do you enjoy thinking things through?

2: What kind of career can I expect as a lawyer?

Most law students will be looking at working in some part of the legal profession, be that in private legal practice (barrister or solicitor), government legal practice, community legal practice or working in a legal capacity in business or industry. Statistics from *The Australian Good University Guide 2007* suggest that 55 per cent of law students gain employment in private legal practice, 30 per cent in some sort of public sector legal position, 13 per cent in private industry (in legal and non-legal roles) with 2 per cent gaining overseas employment.[3]

These statistics corroborate work done more than a decade earlier that showed that 71 per cent of final year respondents (55 per cent of people polled) planned to be admitted within two years after finishing their law degree, a further five per cent stated that they planned admission within three years. This left almost 25 per cent of graduates who did not plan to be lawyers.[4] As for their job classification preferences:[5]

- 48 per cent wanted to work as a barrister or solicitor
- 10 per cent wanted to work in public sector legal
- 8.3 per cent wanted to work in the finance industry, commerce industry
- 5 per cent wanted to focus on community legal service.

The flow chart in Figure 14.1 gives you an idea of the major career paths taken by graduates holding an accredited law degree which includes the Priestley 11 subjects.

---

3   These findings confirm a detailed study done by the Department of Employment, Education, Training and Youth Affairs entitled *Australian Law Graduates' Career Destinations* (98/9 1998). www.dest.gov.au/archive/highered/eippubs/eip98-9/eip98-9.pdf.

4   Christopher Roper, *Career Intentions of Australian Law Students*, AGPS, Canberra, (1995), Chapter 4 generally, Table 6.3, p 76.

5   Ibid.

FIGURE 14.1: SOME OPTIONS AFTER A LAW DEGREE

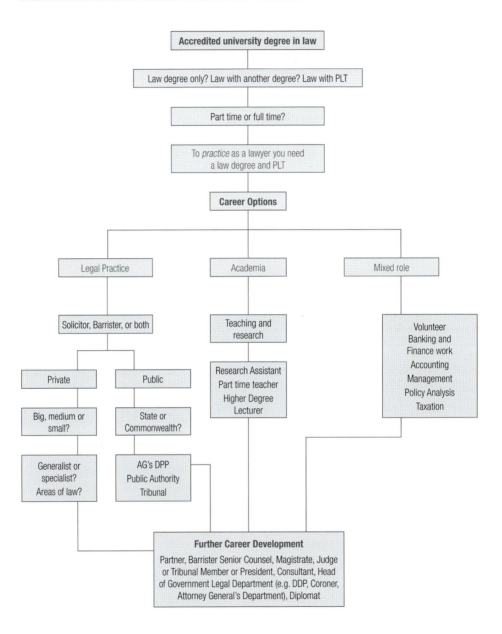

Private practice

This remains the quintessential model of Australian legal practice. It is the cornerstone of the profession and brings in significant revenue. Within this broad industry classification there are many types of employment. These have been described as follows: the big firm lawyer (big numbers, international branches, high pay, commercial emphasis); the small firm lawyer (10 or fewer staff, more likely to do a range of work and criminal matters, less pay); the in-house corporate lawyer, the suburban generalist lawyer, the legal aid lawyer, and the community sector lawyer. These roles were discussed in Chapter 12.

Clerkships are offered by the larger private law firms, usually over the summer and/or winter breaks, to students in their penultimate year, but of course you can also apply for a paralegal position in a law practice or with a barrister at any stage of your degree.

Public-sector and NGO lawyering

Public-sector lawyering largely involves working for state, territory or Commonwealth governments (e.g. the Australian Government Solicitor). Public sector lawyers are usually attached to a government department or to the Attorney-General's Department, the Solicitor-General's Department or the Director of Public Prosecutions (DPP). Lawyers can head boards (e.g. Guardianship Boards), tribunals, commissions, and coroner's offices. More detailed lists can be found in law student society graduate careers brochures and handbooks.

Another aspect of public sector lawyering is working for a community legal centre, Legal Aid, a law reform commission, public interest advocacy body, an Aboriginal land council or native title representative body. These bodies may be government organisations, such as legal aid bodies, or non-government organisations (NGOs) such as the Public Interest Law Clearing House (PILCH). NGOs play an important role in lobbying governments to pursue social justice agendas and representing disadvantaged groups. They also run litigation against corporations and governments that oppress individuals or classes of people.

As a law student you may wish to undertake volunteer work with one of these organisations[6] or apply for a law student internship with an Aboriginal land council, or a native title representative body through the Aurora Project.[7] Students who go through this project are likely to end up with jobs in the area. They may also be given experiences fulfilling legal roles with the Australian Human Rights Commission, the Public Interest Advocacy Centre or the Institute of Aboriginal and Torres Strait Islander Studies.

---

6 For a database of community legal centre volunteer work, go to: http://clcvolunteers.net.au.

7 See the Aurora Project website: www.auroraproject.com.au/LegalInternships.htm.

Academia

Law graduates can also move towards a career in legal academia. This usually involves becoming a university law lecturer and working towards being a professor of law. A typical career path is to do an honours degree, masters, and/or a PhD in Law and along the way take up a role as a part-time lecturer or tutor. Others will start as a research assistant to a lecturer or a researcher where there is a grant of money to support this. Teaching is a great way to find out how much you really know about the law; many young tutors frequently comment on how different it is to be in a teaching rather than in a student role. Naturally, you will need oral presentation and research skills. It is also worth doing a graduate certificate in teaching in higher education.

The modern law academic has a multitude of roles associated with their job description. Not only must they teach, but they must conduct research and have it published in reputable journals and presented at national and international conferences. While teaching and research are the academic's key roles, academics must also contribute to their university by sitting on committees and performing administrative roles such as mentoring. Finally, an academic must also demonstrate service to community. This means serving on external bodies, research committees, ethics committees, liaison roles, pro bono work, and legal centres to name a few. Teaching law forces you to better understand the law and it is a valuable skill to be able to communicate the law effectively. Academic careers generally offer a better level of flexibility, if not salary, compared with private legal practice. Academics can focus on an area of expertise and become recognised nationally and internationally as a leading expert in a field.

People generally start academia as an associate lecturer, and progress through promotion rounds to being a lecturer, a senior lecturer, an associate professor, and then a professor (even Emeritus Professor). Academics can also become the Dean of their academic area, a role that puts them in charge of a law school.

The judiciary

Australian law graduates have no direct career path into being a magistrate, judge or tribunal president.[8] They must first establish themselves in legal practice and for many years gain significant advocacy experience and then be appointed to such posts. Solicitors are more likely to become magistrates. Traditionally, barristers and Senior Counsel or Queen's Counsel have had a better chance of being appointed as a judge in a District, Supreme, Federal or the High Court. This is perhaps because they are well trained in advocacy in the higher courts. Strangely, there is no direct promotion from magistrate to judge. If you are appointed a magistrate, you are likely to stay in the local or children's courts.

---

8   By contrast in some civil law countries there is a direct career path towards being a judge. In Italy and Austria, for example, graduates can join a university stream that trains them to be magistrates.

Judge's associate

Law graduates can get a taste of judicial life and work by taking a one or two year posting as a judge's associate typically after graduating. Such a role (particularly where working for Supreme Court or High Court judges) can be a good career stepping stone. While the title of 'Associate to His or Her Honour Judge …' is reasonably uniform, the job description itself varies according to the court, the judge, their personality, and the type of work the judge undertakes. It is also worth remembering that presidents of tribunals also employ associates. Certain features of the job are relatively common; they include the tasks summarised below.

Work in court

In the courtroom the associate sits near the judge. They take notes, respond to research queries, organise photocopying, and in criminal cases may empanel a jury and organise all the in-court material evidence and exhibits. Associates call out the names of matters, swear witnesses, and hand documents to other parties. For a new graduate this is a fantastic opportunity to learn advocacy skills by watching experienced lawyers making their arguments. It is a valuable experience in seeing how a judge works and decides matters and gives you a one- or two-year break from having to decide what kind of legal career you want. If anything, it will help identify the types of work you want to do and the types of lawyers and firms you would want to work with. Students should read the Australian Judges' Associates Handbook for a clearer sense of what this role entails.[9]

Research and proofreading

Research can be a large part of an associate's job, again this varies between judges. Some judges allow their associates to write draft judgments and legal opinions or memos. Associates need good legal research skills and an ability to deliver the research quickly.

Administrative and personal role

Associates are responsible for organising the judge's working hours and their travel arrangements. The associate is in charge of the judge's diary and must organise all their bookings for travel and accommodation. More than this the associate also will travel on circuit with the judge. For a High Court and particularly a Federal Court judge this will mean travelling to other capital cities; for state judges, it can involve trips to regional and remote areas. At times the court is taken to a crime scene, and may spend a few days there. Associates answer judicial correspondence and review complaints. Associates work very closely with the judge and will often share meals and breaks.

Australian law graduates can also work as associates to tribunal presidents. Some tribunals, such as the Australian Administrative Tribunal (AAT) are very important instruments of Australian administrative law with a very broad workload and an

---

9 See Australian Law Students' Association, *Australian Judge's Associates Handbook* (2009) www.alsa.net.au/assets/publications_JA_Guide_2009.pdf.

emphasis on Commonwealth law. If you have particular experience that is valuable to a particular tribunal, this may make you more employable (e.g. volunteering at a refugee law centre may well be of assistance in working for the Migration/Refugee Review Tribunal).

Other options

In-house counsel are lawyers employed by companies. Some companies have an entire in-house legal department – for example banks, insurance companies and multi-national companies.

Another career path is that of law librarian. This job combines information technology with a law degree. You can work at a court library, at a university or in a law firm, at a law society, in a Law Reform Commission or in a government department.

3: What can I do as a student to become the lawyer I want to be?

This is a very important issue as there are many things you can do as a law student that will give you an edge over the competition at a legal interview. Importantly, you need to communicate this to potential employers (often the human resources people who may screen your application) through your application letter and résumé (also called a curriculum vitae, or CV).

First, and we are stating the obvious here, you need to actually get decent grades, and at a bare minimum actually pass all your law subjects. To do this requires that you learn good study techniques. There are many resources and books that can assist you. See Chapter 2 for law graduate attributes and some tips and strategies.

Attitude

A student's positive attitude of drive and determination to learn will make them a better lawyer because they will gain more from their training. Students who believe that they are just at law school to passively acquire legal knowledge are approaching legal training from a very narrow and inflexible approach. This approach is flawed because legal knowledge changes every year. What is important, is having the skills and flexibility to inform oneself about new developments in law and being able to resolve real-time legal problems, rather than applying dated rote learning.

Perseverance is a very important trait for lawyers. Legal study and work requires a high degree of perseverance. You can apply this at law school to your research, writing, thinking, and learning. Law has many compulsory subjects, some of which you will have little interest in. It takes great perseverance to give your best to the learning of such a subject, the reading, participating in the tutorials, attending the lectures and so forth. When you are a barrister adhering to the cab rank rule and taking clients as they are referred to you this requires a similar level of perseverance and dedication to give them the best you have, even where a case is not one you would have chosen.

Law schools often involve problem-based learning. This method of teaching relies heavily on student participation for its success. It is predicated on reading material before class, attending and being prepared to contribute to group discussion and resolve legal problems as a group. Group learning requires committed groups, so where possible work with well prepared groups, both inside and outside of subjects. A study group formed in first year can see you through your whole degree, through sickness, stress and socialising!

Lawyers need to be adaptable and flexible in their approaches to their work. Lawyers are problem solvers and must be able to think laterally. It is their minds, their expertise and their capacity for intellectual innovation that sets them apart from the rest. While other industries have cars, trucks, factories and so on as their assets, your mind and your time are your greatest assets.

Systems

You need success systems – systems that will make sure you know what you need to do, and by when, to make sure you stay on track. These may include having a diary, doing time planning and management, and saving your work in several places so if your computer crashes or you lose your memory stick you don't have to start your work from scratch. It may also include having something to read or study with you at all times – you never know when you will be stuck waiting somewhere, and you can turn this dead time into productive time.

Extracurricular activities

Many activities can complement your emerging legal abilities. These include mooting, taking an active role in your law students' society, volunteering at a community legal centre, or participating in a United Nations student association to give you a few examples. Mooting and client interviewing competitions give you additional experience of constructing legal arguments and presenting them to a 'court' in partnership with another student. This fosters good advocacy skills and these are sometimes videotaped so that you can gain even more useful feedback on how you look and sound while making legal arguments on your feet. Community legal practice gives you valuable experience with the whole process of solving client problems, from meeting and interviewing the client, taking notes, continuing contact with the client, positing legal (and non-legal solutions) to mediating, resolving or helping set up litigation for them. You experience client and file management and learn aspects of community law (e.g. fencing disputes, migration law) in more detail. This really helps you at law school and later in practice.

TIP
Mooting is a form of legal debating, like a mock trial but without witnesses. Students usually draft written submissions and argue their case orally. This can be part of a subject, as a class activity, an assessment, a whole subject or an external competition where you represent your law school on a mooting team.

Work experience

A critical part of obtaining legal employment appears to be finding work experience at firms before you graduate. This can be through a clerkship (usually over the summer break) or through volunteering. Your university careers service and/or law students' society can help you with this and often publish careers booklets and guides that help you with seeking such experience. Talk to other students who have done clerkships and try to choose clerkships that will help your career choices.

Mentoring

Mentoring schemes exist at some university law schools. First-year students are paired with a later-year student who will help mentor them; or an academic or legal professional will play the role of mentoring students at various stages in their degrees. Mentoring is about showing students the ropes to help them become more efficient, more strategic and more able to access resources they may not have been aware of. Sometimes mentoring can be focused on career development and at other times it can provide help to get through a law degree. It is not a private tutoring scheme, nor is it focused on specific aspects of subject content.

Use university resources and build social networks

TIP
The use of the Internet and online social networking sites is a double-edged sword. Companies and their recruitment officers will frequently look in popular social networking sites to see if they can find information about a prospective candidate. You would be wise to ensure that there is no written material, video or images that could compromise your chances of being hired.

TIP
The Supreme Court in each state must approve a law school's curriculum and can review or modify it. There has been much recent discussion about having a new compulsory topic of statutory interpretation. The Uniform Admission Rules of legal practice require university law schools to teach students a standard core of 11 key areas of law (the 'Priestley 11' discussed in Chapter 2). Lawyers can assume that all Australian law graduates have satisfactorily completed these topics.

Universities are large teaching and learning organisations with numerous support networks and resources that can help you. They have careers services, study skills units (called many names including language and learning units, study assistance centres, communication skills centres, etc), libraries stocked with vast collections of law reports, books, journals and information access networks. Universities give you email and web access with training resources for students with poor information technology skills.

Importantly, there are your peers. At university you are exposed to a wide variety of views and opinions and make many good friends who will likely be your peers (and perhaps a source of referral work) in legal practice. Forming good relationships with your peers and being able to study together and share resources is also an important part of your learning. Nor should you overlook your teachers, they are often lawyers themselves and can offer valuable life and career advice. Most law schools have staff who act in mentoring roles (such as a First Year Coordinator or Advisor) and you should make use of consultation hours with staff to discuss matters with them.

A good source of information is the respective law student organisation in each law school, and the peak body, the Australian Law Students Association (ALSA).[10] The ALSA website has very useful information about career planning, how to apply for jobs, write resumes, attend interviews and so on. There are also websites and publications targeting law students.[11] Additionally there is a website produced by a law graduate titled 'Law School: A Survivor's Guide' at www.survivelaw.com.

Universities also have careers organisations and students should attend careers days and use the resources there. There are often careers counsellors in these offices who can help you develop job hunting strategies, and help polish up applications.

---

10 See www.alsa.net.au.

11 See for example the magazine *Australian Lawyer2B* at www.lawyersweekly.com.au/news/au/lawyer2b/.

4: Important choices of subjects and course structures

Of the 39 universities in Australia, 30 currently have law schools. New South Wales has the most (10). Approximately 18 of the 30 law schools have emerged in the past 20 years, coinciding with the large growth in the number of law students in the late 1980s and early 1990s.[12] Universities gained financially by offering law degrees and there are now almost as many law students as there are legal practitioners in Australia. An oversupply of law students in Australia has led many to view the law degree as a generalist one, like Arts. This means law is no longer purely a professional qualification, and the skills it teaches can be used in many jobs requiring lateral thinking, research skills and innovation.

Australian university law schools offer a bachelor of laws degree (LLB) and some offer a Juris Doctor (JD) for those who have already completed another degree before studying law. Many offer combined or double degrees with Bachelor of Laws (LLB) plus a Bachelor of Arts (BA), a Bachelor of Science (BSc), a Bachelor of Commerce (BCom), a Bachelor of Economics (BEc), etc. More recently there have been increasing numbers of students taking degree programs that specialise in international studies, and for some of these students, the LLB is the secondary qualification. Some students hedge their bets with their double degree choices, hoping to decide which field is more suited to their skills, knowledge or in cases which one has more favourable job prospects. Students can also complete Honours degrees, Masters Degrees and PhDs in law.[13]

Law students are permitted some choice when selecting the remaining subjects that comprise their law degree. These are known as 'electives' or 'options' and vary across universities. Electives usually represent some focus on a particular staff member's expertise. Some common electives include family law, medical law, taxation, workplace relations law, international law and intellectual property (see Chapter 2 for more information on typical elective subjects). While compulsory subjects must be run annually, electives may be offered every alternate year or in different semesters depending on the availability of particular staff members to teach them. Most electives have prerequisite compulsory subjects. Students doing a combined degree often have very few elective subjects because the way the combined degrees are created with a five year term instead of seven years is by treating it as, for example, a business degree with a law major and a law degree with a business major.

Law students need to carefully select electives as they represent a way of distinguishing their bachelor's degree from someone else. So, if you wish to work in commercial law, you would be advised to do advanced contract law, taxation law, banking and finance law, business law, and insolvency law. Naturally, if you are interested in international law you should be choosing subjects appropriate to

---

12 Law student numbers jumped an astonishing 60 per cent between 1988 and 1992. See generally Craig McInnis and Simon Marginson, *Australian Law Schools After the 1987Pearce Report* (1994), 15ff.

13 A PhD is a Doctor of Philosophy, which requires completion of a 100 000 word research thesis. The other option is a professional doctorate, the Doctor of Juridical Science (SJD), which requires completion of postgraduate units and a 50 000 word research thesis.

that field, such as public international law, conflicts of law, and human rights law. Electives are choices that may define your legal career options and so should be chosen with care and thought.

On the other hand, you can use electives to give you a broad understanding of many areas of law and help give you deeper knowledge of things you find interesting. This can also help you find an honours topic. It is often beneficial career-wise to be able to tell a law firm that you have an honours paper (and therefore some expertise) in a field that is part of that firm's core business.

Having a law degree does not automatically entitle one to practise law. The ability to practise requires further study and work placement. This additional qualification (typically six months to a year) is known as Practical Legal Training (PLT) or articles/traineeship in some states.

Practical Legal Training (PLT)

Law graduates wishing to graduate as legal practitioners must do a PLT course (in some states, the requirement is for articles/traineeship or a PLT course). Some universities run their own integrated law and PLT courses (e.g. ANU, Bond University, Charles Darwin University, Flinders University Griffith University, Monash University, QUT, UTS, UWS and the University of Wollongong) but many students will attend a private PLT course run by a law society, college of law or institute (e.g. Leo Cussen Institute, The College of Law, Law Society of South Australia). Some law firms offer in-house PLT, or use external providers to tailor a program. If in any doubt, contact the law society in your respective state or territory or the Supreme Court, and ask who the PLT providers are, or look online.[14]

PLT requirements are carefully controlled by the legal admission bodies of each jurisdiction. Typical subjects include property transactions, buying and selling a business, estate practice, and advocacy.

5: Preparing to maintain a decent work–life balance

Maintaining a decent work–life balance is becoming increasingly problematic, both in legal practice and in law school – most law students work while they are studying, and most lawyers work long hours. One of the biggest problems with legal practice is human burnout. Make no mistake about it, the practice of law is gruelling and tiring.[15] Most lawyers work a 9–10 hour day.[16] Legal practice involves much preparatory work, paperwork, interviewing, making and returning phone calls and client meetings. For law firms, retention of staff is a critical issue.

---

14 See www.lexisnexis.com.au/our-solutions/academic/law-links/practical-legal-training-programs.aspx.

15 'Solicitors' work undermines families and personal life more than other work' (1999) 37 (4) *Law Society Journal* 69.

16 Law Institute of Victoria, *Bendable or expendable? Practices and attitudes towards work flexibility in Victoria's biggest legal employers* (2006), www.vwl.asn.au/Portals/0/downloads/Bendable_or_Expendable.pdf.

Work–life balance is predominantly about priority management – we can never fit everything into our lives, but we can always fit the most important things. We just need to be clear on what our top priorities are, and be a bit clever about how we address them. For example if our top priorities are our work, our relationship and our health, we could arrange to go walking or jogging with our partner outside of work hours. If our top priorities are our studies, spirituality and contribution to society, we could volunteer at a community legal centre.

Everyone has their own sense of balance – some people need balance in their daily lives, others are happy to work hard all week as long as they have the weekend off, and others are happy to work hard all semester as long as they have a holiday at the end! It is about getting to know yourself, and what you need.

It is useful to get into a good habit of work–life balance while you are a student, so you are well prepared for practice. Lawyers must be able to adapt to varying demands on their time, be flexible with varying demands, and accommodate additional work demands without compromising work-life balance.

Time management is crucial. Being able to allocate adequate time for work, physical wellbeing (nutrition, exercise, sleep, relaxation), psychological wellbeing (adequate time for partner, children, friends), and leisure activities (interests, hobbies, sport, pleasurable activities) is critical. In a comprehensive study by consultants, 42 per cent of Australians classified as 'knowledge workers' reported high levels of 'role overload', while 29 per cent reported that high levels of work interfered with family life.[17]

Lawyering can be a very stressful job. Studies have ranked lawyers as top of the occupational groups most likely to have depression with 16 per cent of lawyers surveyed reporting depression. Worse still, younger professionals are reporting the higher rates of depressive illness rather than the more senior members of the profession. It is frequently a result of two legal traits: perfectionism and pessimism. Of these depressed practitioners about a third used drugs and alcohol to try to cope.[18] Resources and medical help for combating depression can be found at the Beyond Blue website.[19] You need to recognise early indicators of stress like mood disturbance, reduced work output, relationship difficulties, and substance abuse. These problems have prompted many law societies (in New South Wales it is LawCare and BarCare and the Legal Assistance Programme)[20] to set up health wellness schemes for practitioners that include stress management techniques, professional help through medical practitioner/psychologist, relaxation techniques breathing exercises, yoga, tai chi, etc.

GO ONLINE
Go online to read fact sheets on depression and anxiety

---

17 Linda Duxbury and Chris Higgins, *Work–Life Balance in Australia in the New Millennium: Rhetoric Versus Reality,* Beaton Consulting (2008).

18 See www.legalunderground.com/2005/03/lawyer_depressi.html.

19 At www.beyondblue.org.au/index.aspx.

20 See www.lap.com.au. Similar services with the same name exist in Western Australia, Victoria, the Australian Capital Territory and England.

Context: Links between law student attitudes and depression

Recent Australian research identified the following factors which might explain why law students, who on the whole enter law school with low levels of depression, experience more depression during their studies and in legal careers than other professions including medicine.[21] Law students are:

- more likely to state that they chose law because they got the marks to do it, or their parents told them to (both of these are external drivers which are less engaging)
- less likely to say they are learning law because it is interesting (this means a lower level of intrinsic motivation to study)
- more grades-focused, that is, concerned about getting good grades (so they are focusing more on the outcome than the journey)
- less interested in group work and socialising with friends met at university
- more competitive (despite the fact that assessment in most law schools is now criterion-referenced and so students are really only competing against the assessment criteria, not each other)

Reflection

Can you relate to these typical law student experiences? What can you do, in your law studies, to reduce your risk of experiencing depression?

DISCUSSION QUESTIONS

1. Do you think a law degree based on learning vast amounts of law is preferable to giving you the skills to find and interpret law as it changes, evolves and is created?
2. What are the most significant skills you think your law degree will give you?
3. Do you think that being a lawyer comes at a risk that your work/life balance will be more heavily biased towards work? Are there particular reasons for this that are unique to law?
4. What would be some warning signs that your work/life balance has become overwhelmed by work?
5. Are inflexible working conditions and the particular nature of legal work stifling the ability of women lawyers to being promoted, or contributing to them leaving the profession entirely?

---

21 Massimiliano Tani and Prue Vines, 'Law Students' Attitudes to Education: Pointers to Depression in the Legal Academy and the Profession?' (2009) 19 *Legal Education Review* 3.

WEBLINKS AND FURTHER READING

Australian Law Students Association: www.alsa.net.au.

Beyond Blue depression and anxiety checklists: www.beyondblue.org.au/index.aspx?

Duxbury, Linda and Higgins, Chris, *Work–Life Balance in Australia in the New Millennium: Rhetoric Versus Reality* (2008), archived at www.ahri.com.au/MMSdocuments/profdevelopment/research/research_papers/work-life_bal_full_report.pdf.

Human Rights and Equal Opportunity Commission, *Striking the Balance – Women, Men, Work and Family*, Discussion Paper (2005) at www.humanrights.gov.au/ (search for 'striking balance' to retrieve cached documents).

Hyams, Ross, Campbell, Susan and Evans, Adrian, *Practical Legal Skills*, Oxford University Press, Melbourne, 3rd edn (2007).

Krever, Richard, *Mastering Law Studies and Law Exam Techniques*, Butterworths, Sydney, 6th edn (2006).

Law Institute of Victoria and Victorian Women Lawyers, *Bendable or Expendable? Practices and Attitudes Towards Work Flexibility in Victoria's Biggest Legal Employers* (2006) at www.vwl.asn.au/Portals/0/downloads/Bendable_or_Expendable.pdf.

Links to University Law Students' Societies: www.alsa.net.au/about/member-associations.

Macken, Claire, *Law School Survival Guide: 9 Steps to Law Study* Success, Lawbook Co, Sydney, 2nd edn (2009).

Uniform Admission Rules: www.lawlink.nsw.gov.au/lawlink/olsc/ll_olsc.nsf/pages/lra_admission. A breakdown of the requirements can be found on the Internet and are the same across the states and territories. For example go to: www.legislation.nsw.gov.au/ and search for 'areas of knowledge'. That takes you to Admission Rules 2005 appear. Go to 'Fifth Schedule Synopsis of areas of knowledge'.

ONLINE RESOURCES FOR THIS CHAPTER

The following resources are available online at www.oup.com.au/orc/cwl2e

- Fact sheet: Anxiety
- Fact sheet: Depression
- Flashcard glossary
- Multiple choice questions
- Client questions exercise

glossary

Aboriginal or Torres Strait Islander person = *generally* defined according to objective ('genetic') and subjective (community acceptance and self-identity) criteria. This three-part test was set out by Deane J in Tasmania v Commonwealth (1984) 158 CLR 1, 273-274. However, Indigenous people have criticised traditional definitions for limiting the self-identity or self-recognition aspect. It should be noted that many Aboriginal people have expressed their general satisfaction with the current legal definition. However there are some outstanding concerns:

1. The current definition was not devised by or in consultation with Aboriginal people, but by white judges in the above cases. Aboriginal people have long expressed their discontent with non-Aboriginal people trying to define 'Aboriginality'. For example, Mick Dodson has criticised this practice as forming part of a 'colonial fascination'.

2. Blood testing and human rights: Some commentators have argued that blood testing is contrary to international conventions to which Australia is signatory.

Aboriginal or Torres Strait Islander person = Referred to generally as Indigenous people. People of Aboriginal descent or from the island of Torres Strait are *generally* defined according to objective ('genetic'), subjective (group acceptance and self-identity) criteria (see extended definition in Chapter 8).

Access to justice = the ability for individuals, organisations and groups to obtain legal advice, obtain adequate resolutions of their disputes, and have their rights protected by the legal system.

Administrative law = a body of law enabling individuals to challenge government decisions that relate to them.

Adversarial system = a system of resolving legal disputes in which the parties present their arguments before an independent fact finder who assesses the facts, evidence and applicable law and makes a binding ruling based upon them.

Affidavit = a written statement of facts under oath.

Alternative Dispute Resolution = processes, other than judicial determination, in which an impartial person assists those in dispute to resolve the issues between them (as defined by the National Alternative Dispute Resolution Advisory Council). It can also encompass informal dispute resolution such as party-to-party negotiations.

Annotations = notes added to a text to provide explanation, evaluation, or references to further information.

Arbitration = an adversarial process where an independent third party chosen by the parties receives the parties' submissions, and then makes a written, binding determination.

Assent = approval of a bill by the relevant Governor or Governor-General.

Assimilation = the process by which a minority group in a society gradually blends in by adopting the culture of the majority group.

Australian lawyer = a person who holds a graduate or postgraduate qualification in law and has been admitted to practise law by the Supreme Court in their jurisdiction.

Bar Association = an association of barristers that provides members with services and assists in regulation of that branch of the profession and coordination of the work of barristers.

Barrister = a lawyer who is a member of a Bar Association, accepts briefs from solicitors to represent clients in courts and tribunals and writes formal opinions about legal issues but typically does not maintain files or trust accounts for clients.

Bill = a draft piece of legislation which is proposed through parliament.

Boolean searching = a method of using the operators AND, OR, and NOT between search terms in order to increase or limit the information retrieved when searching a database.

Brief = the bundle of legal documents given by a solicitor to a barrister. It is usually tied with a pink ribbon and has a summary at the front of the facts, legal issues, the outcome the client seeks, and the specific instruction (usually to attend at a hearing or provide an opinion).

Browsing = looking for information from a particular resource by a general or casual process, usually moving around the resource using main headings as a guide

Cabinet = the decision making group of the parliament that comprises the senior ministers of government.

Case citator = a research aid used to identify case names, the places where cases have been reported, the cases mentioned within a case, the articles which have been published discussing a case, and any later cases which refer to the case.

Case law = decisions where courts apply and interpret a statute. It is also sometimes used to generically refer to all court decisions, likely as a result of those in civil law systems referring to all court decisions as case law (which is unsurprising given all court decisions relate to their codified law).

Case management = courts managing the progress of each case by directing parties to fulfil obligations (such as negotiating to reach an outcome) and meet timelines in order to ensure quicker and more efficient outcomes.

Cession = land transferred to a colonial nation through voluntary surrendering of rights by the Indigenous people. This process usually involves a treaty between the coloniser and Indigenous people. This does not change the pre-existing legal system, although it could be changed by executive or legislative action after cession.

Chambers = the traditional name for the building a barrister works from. Barristers usually share premises and secretarial support.

Civil law = has two meanings. First it is a legal system that relies heavily on consolidating as much law as possible into statutory codes. Second, it is a classification of law within common law systems which refers to law that applies between private individuals.

Classical era = fifth and fourth centuries BCE (Before the Common Era, formerly expressed as Before Christ, BC), when idealism emerged as an elaborate philosophy (with Socrates) and there were many theoretical debates between materialism and idealism.

Colonisation = occupation of nation states by military rule and acquisition of sovereignty. There are three forms of colonisation, see: conquest, cession or occupation.

Colonisation = pre-twentieth century occupation of nation states by military rule and acquisition of sovereignty. There are three forms of colonisation, namely conquest, cession or occupation.

Commentary = views on law and policy expressed by persons with expertise, such as former judges, academics, and practitioners. Can also be official commentary, which is created by the same organisation or parliament that created the treaty or legislation.

Common law = a body of judge-made law based on interpreting statutes.

Common law = decisions where courts apply a principle developed by previous courts (also used in other senses, see Chapter 5 for these).

Common law = has three meanings. First it is a system of law that originated in England. Second it is a body of law made by judges, as opposed to statute law made by parliament. Third, it is a term used to refer to the application of black letter law without reference to general principles of fairness (equity).

Commonwealth = federal government, created by the Australian Constitution.

Community legal centre (CLC) = an independent community based organisation that provides free legal advice and help to members of the community.

Conquest = colonisation by military force, where the former political power is ousted. This does not change the pre-existing legal system, although it could be changed by executive or legislative action after conquest.

Consolidated legislation/ consolidated Acts = Acts put together over time, showing the current law with all applicable amendments incorporated.

Constitution = a foundational document of the state and Commonwealth system of government in Australia, containing rules by which the state or federal governments must operate.

Contract law = the law governing agreements involving individuals, organisations or corporations.

Counsel = another term for a barrister, someone doing advocacy work in a court or tribunal.

Critical analysis = using powers of observation, reasoning, reflection and questioning to interpret information and make findings or form opinions based on it.

Cross-vesting = the granting, or vesting, of power in a state court to exercise Commonwealth judicial power.

Customary laws = generally used to describe Indigenous laws that regulate relationships within Indigenous communities. Customary laws vary across Indigenous societies and change with time (similar to the incremental developments in the common law).

Damage = injury or loss.

Damages = compensation awarded for loss, injury and suffering that is designed to place the injured party in the position they were in prior to the injury or damage.

Decision = judgment = case law = written court findings on a particular legal dispute.

Deductive reasoning = using a general theory to test specific facts. For example 'All dogs bark. Rufus is a dog. Therefore, Rufus barks.'

Defendant = a legal entity (individual, company, association, the state) against whom legal proceedings are brought. The defendant answers the plaintiff's allegations (in civil matters) or the prosecution's allegations (in criminal matters).

Delegated legislation = law made by a body to whom parliament has delegated authority. Common forms of delegated legislation include regulations, rules, ordinances, and by-laws.

Delegated legislation = legislation made by a non-parliamentary body or minister under power given by parliament. Includes regulations, rules, ordinances, and by-laws.

Diversity = the coexistence of differences in gender, age, culture, capacity, and perspectives.

Divided profession = where there are two separate types of practitioners, admitted as either barristers or solicitors, but not both (as for example in England).

Doctrine of parliamentary supremacy = the notion that, of the three arms of government (legislature, executive and judiciary), the legislature is supreme.

Electronic resources = places to locate information on electronic devices, including CD-Rom, bibliographic databases, e-books, e-journals, websites and search engines.

Encyclopedia = a comprehensive, concise compilation of information, divided into articles, and arranged systematically (e.g. alphabetically or by subject area)

Equity = a body of law that arose to correct and modify the harshness and inflexibility of the common law.

Essentialism = a grand theory or approach that denies difference of opinion.

Ethics = a field of thinking about what is morally right, appropriate and acceptable.

Executive = the body that administers the law, ranging from government ministers and the Governor-General to public servants and police officers.

Federal system = a political system that involves the sharing of government power between a central government (here the Commonwealth or Federal government) and regional governments (here, the states and territories). This is contrasted with countries with a unitary (i.e. central) government like the United Kingdom and New Zealand.

Federation = a system of government in which a national federal government rules in combination with state governments.

Feminism = a view that the law favours the interests of men and should be reconceived to include female voices and provide for gender equality.

Feudalism = a system of social organisation and land holding based on a chain of tenure, in which the monarch was the ultimate owner of all land and granted possession in return for payments of taxes and provision of services.

Freehold title = exclusive ownership of land.

Fused profession = where legal practitioners are admitted as both barristers and solicitors and are permitted to do both kinds of work. Frequently some choose to practise exclusively as a barrister, and others do predominantly solicitor's work except for small mentions of matters in court.

Gazette = a official report, legal notice or public announcement published by government.

Graduate attributes = generic skills, attitudes and values, plus specific content knowledge, expected of students who have completed a tertiary course of study.

Idealism = a philosophical approach that privileges the significance of ideas over material conditions.

Imperialism = post-twentieth century occupation by economic means.

Independent learning = students taking the primary responsibility and initiative for their own learning, including being able to recognise gaps in their learning and where to find the information to fill them.

Index = an alphabetised list of topics such as cases, legislation, or subjects with a link to or indication of where related material can be found in a resource.

Indigenous person = (in Australia) Aboriginal or Torres Strait Islander person (see above).

Inductive reasoning = using specific examples to create generalisations. For example 'Apples rot. Pears rot. Bananas rot. Therefore, all fruit rots.'

Information literacy = knowing what information is available, when it is needed, how to find it and use it effectively, and recognising its inherent strengths and limitations.

Journal = a publication containing a series of articles on particular topics, issued periodically in print or online. A refereed journal is one that has been reviewed by two 'blind' referees (they do not know who the author is) with knowledge of the relevant field. Law journals are typically published by law schools, with editorial boards and committees that sometimes include law students.

Judicial activism = an approach to judging where the judge, when faced with a situation where the law is unclear or unjust, will develop and create new law to enable justice to be done.

Judicial formalism = an approach to judging which maintains the role of the judge is to apply law and not make it, even where this may result in injustice in certain case scenarios.

Judicial review = review of an executive decision by a court, to determine whether the government official had the power to make the decision or applied procedural fairness in making the decision.

Judiciary = the body of judges within a court system, also referred to as the judicature.

Jurisdiction = the power of a court to hear a matter; the territorial area where a statute applies.

Jurisprudence = the theory of law and study of the principles on which it is based.

Law firm = a private partnership entity where a number of lawyers are employed to provide legal services. It has a business culture and hierarchy, where the partners are the leading lawyers and income earners.

Law Reform Commission = an independent government body that advises parliament on proposals for law reform. They do this by public consultation, research and reports. Their work often leads to major reform of the law.

Law reports = the official publication, usually in print, of decisions from a specific court which are considered of sufficient importance to justify being reported.

Lawyer = a general term for a person who holds a graduate or postgraduate qualification in law.

Legal Aid = a system of publicly-funded financial aid subject to strict eligibility guidelines to help pay for legal advice or representation in select cases where a person can demonstrate financial hardship.

Legal Practitioner = encompasses both solicitors and barristers and means that the person is not only a lawyer but also holds a current practising certificate.

Legislature = the law-making body, also referred to as parliament.

Liberalism = the interests of individuals are promoted above the collective needs.

Libertarianism = an extreme brand of liberalism that discounts reference to fairness in its concept of justice.

Lifelong learning = a perspective that continuous learning is a fundamental part of one's personal and professional life.

Looseleaf service = a legal encyclopedia published in unbound sheets of paper, held in ring binders arranged alphabetically by subject area. Publishers regularly send subscribers replacement pages on topics where the law has changed, with instructions for which pages to discard and replace.

Majority judgment = decision of a court with more than one judge sitting, containing the decision that most judges agreed on.

Materialism = a philosophical approach that privileges the significance of material conditions over ideas.

Maxim = a guiding principle.

Mediation = a voluntary process that involves a neutral third party facilitating negotiations between disputing parties with a view to discussing, clarifying and settling disputes. Also referred to as conciliation.

Medium-neutral citation = a form of reference for a case which allows a case to be cited the same way, whether it is in print or electronic format

Minister = responsible for a parliamentary portfolio, such as health, education and defence.

Minority judgment = decision of a court with more than one judge sitting, containing the views of a judge or judges, who disagreed with ('dissented' from) the majority view.

Modernism = a school of thought that developed in the late eighteenth century and saw law as being positioned within dominant social institutions and economic structures.

Native title = a right of Indigenous people to use their land.

Natural law = an idea that law has some innate higher principles beyond human choices.

NESB = Non-English speaking background.

Obiter dicta = comments made by judges in judgments which are not essential to the particular case but which are useful to explain the court's reasoning.

Occupation = a process of colonisation involving settlement of vacant land. This allows for the automatic implementation of the colonising nation's laws.

Paralegal = a non-lawyer (often a law student) with some legal skills who works under a lawyer and performs routine tasks that require some familiarity with law and procedures.

Plaintiff = a legal person (individual, association, company, the state) who seeks legal relief against another legal person through court proceedings.

Pleadings = written statements by parties to a legal dispute that set out the relevant facts about the dispute and an outline of the case that each party relies upon.

Positive law = the legal rules that exist in statutes, regulations and cases.

Positivism = an idea that law is what humans declare it to be.

Postmodernism = a school of thought that challenges modernism and its presumptions of hierarchical structures.

Precedent = **stare decisis** = following the decision of a higher court, or a previous court, in a case where similar law applies, and/or which has similar facts.

Pre-Socratic era = the sixth and fifth centuries BCE when philosophy was first born and materialist ideas reigned; it preceded Socratic ideas at the height of the Classical era (see above).

Priestley 11 = the 11 compulsory subjects to be covered in law degrees.

Primary legislation = an Act or statute created by parliament.

Primary sources = the law itself, namely cases and legislation (statutes and regulations).

Print-based resources = places to locate information in printed (hard copy, paper) format, including dictionaries, text books, encyclopedias, law journals, law reports.

Privy Council = an advisory body to the British monarch.

Pro bono = professional work done voluntarily for no charge. From the Latin *pro bono publico* (for the public good).

Race theory = a theory that the law projects the interests of white people and colonisers.

Ratio decidendi = the key point of the case, the answer to the key issue posed in a case, the part of the judgment that is used as a precedent in later cases.

Rationalism = law is based on a rational belief of its legitimacy.

Realism = an assessment of what really happens in legal practice and decision making, which underlies legal doctrine and reasoning.

Reception = the implementation of the colonial nation's laws after occupation.

Regulation = a rule by government administration (public servants), where the power to make the rule is delegated from parliament.

Repealed = legislation which parliament cancelled.

Representative government = the government is chosen by, and represents, the people.

Research methodology = the process adopted when conducting legal research, including deciding what needs researching, where to look, what search terms to use, and what to do with the results.

Responsible government = the parliament is independent and responsible to the people.

Royal Assent = as for 'assent' above. In some jurisdictions the term 'royal assent', to denote that assent is being made on behalf of the Queen, is still used.

Rule of law = law is supreme and applies universally, equally and fairly.

Secondary sources = materials that help us understand the law, such as legal dictionaries, text books, law journals, and transcripts of parliamentary debates.

Section = provision = a rule in an Act.

Self-determination = this encompasses a range of rights for sovereign groups, including rights to self-government, maintenance and development of political, economic and social institutions, and to practise and revitalise cultural traditions and customs.

Self-management = strategies and processes by which a person manages their time, their thoughts, feelings, goals and actions.

Senior Counsel = Queen's Counsel = an experienced barrister appointed to senior rank (said to have 'taken silk'). Senior Counsel is the newer term.

Separation of powers = the three arms of government carry out their functions independently: parliament legislates, the executive administers the law and the judiciary interprets the law.

Solicitor = the legal practitioner who represents the parties in a transaction, interviews the client, gives legal advice, maintains files, prepares legal documents, briefs barristers, and handles trust funds on behalf of clients. Solicitors can practise in partnership or as companies.

Statute = Act = legislation (all the same thing)

Stare decisis = *see* 'precedent'

Terra nullius = land with no one.

Tort law (Torts) = a classification of law that involves particular civil wrongs. Tort law protect people's bodily autonomy and integrity (physical and psychological), their property, their reputation, and their financial interests.

Treaty = an agreement between a colonising nation and Indigenous people. It allows for the voluntary transfer of land, generally with limitations attached to the extent of land transferred and the jurisdiction of the coloniser's laws.

Treaty = an agreement between a colonising nation and Indigenous people. It allows for the voluntary transfer of land, generally with limitations attached to the extent of land transferred and the jurisdiction of the coloniser's laws.

Treaty = convention = a legal agreement between states.

Uniform Admission Requirements = rules for admission of lawyers agreed between states and territories, based upon four criteria: academic qualifications (at their minimum, the Priestley 11), practical legal training (PLT), formal admission to the Supreme Court, and the holding of a valid practising certificate from a law society.

Unreported judgments = court decisions which either are not considered of sufficient importance to justify being reported, or which are so recent that they have not yet been officially published in a law report (typically law reports are published in volumes once a year).

Westminster system = comprises three arms of government: the courts (judicature), parliament (legislature) and executive.

index

Aboriginal or Torres Strait Islander people
   access to justice   392–4
   constitutional recognition   256–8
   definition   229–30, 253
   Gurindji people   268
   historical developments in policy   254–9
   international law, rights prescribed by   265–6
   Lajamanu people   277
   land rights   259–63
      legislation   268–70
      negotiations   270–2
   Maningrida people   330
   Northern Territory intervention   258–9
   protection policies   254–5
   segregation   254–5
   treaty and sovereignty rights   278–9
   Wiradjuri people   273
   Wurundjeri people   236
   Yol u people   260
Aboriginal Provision Government (APG)   278–9
absolute liability offences   122
access to law   387–413
   Aboriginal and Torres Strait Islander people   392–4
   approach to learning   388
   children and young people   396
   costs   389–90
   definition   388
   delay   390
   disabilities, people with   399–400
   equality   391
   gay, lesbian, bisexual and transgender   396–7
   key issues   389–91
   legal aid   401–6
   mental illness, people with   400–1
   non-English speaking background, people from   394–6
   overview   5
   rural and regional communities   401
   self-represented litigants   397–9
   women   392
Acts *see* legislation
actus reus   122
Administrative Appeals Tribunal (AAT)   103, 119

administrative law   118–21
   definition   113
adversarial system
   definition   113
affidavit
   definition   415
alerting services   161
alternative dispute resolution   104–7
ambiguity
   tolerance of   10
amending legislation   53
Anaximenes   196
annotations
   definition   138
Antigone, story of   197–8
appeals   101–2
Aquinas, Thomas   199, 203, 218
arbitration   105
Aristotle   196, 198
assent
   definition   42
assessments
   exam techniques   34–6
   legal writing   29–34
   management of   22–3
assimilation
   definition   254
Attorney-General   92
Attorney-General's Information Service (AGIS)   175
attributes of graduates   13–27
   approach to learning   8
   definition   8
   developing   13
Austin, John 199–200
AustLII   145–7, 153–5, 157, 161, 163–4, 168, 176
   point-in-time facility   160
Australasian Legal Scholarship Library   176
Australian and New Zealand Legal Abbreviations   163
Australian Digest   172
Australian Guide to Legal Citation   184–5
Australian Law Students Association (ALSA)   430
Australian Lawyer
   definition   354

Australian Legal Journals Index (ALJI)   175
Australian Legal Monthly Digest   161, 172
Australian legal system
    development   247–9
Australian Public Affairs Information Service (APA Text)   175
Australian territories   86

backing up data   28
Bacon, Francis   200
bail application   132–3
Bar Association
    definition   354
barrister   373–8
    see also lawyer; legal practitioner; solicitor
    bar associations   377, 385
    definition   354
    duties   374
    liability   376–7
    regulation   378
    role   373
    Senior (Queen's) Counsel   375
Bartlett, Richard   266
basis of law   9
Batman, John   236
Bell, Derrick   214–15
Bent, Ellis   238
Bentham, Jeremy   202–3
bill
    definition   42
    finding   158–9
    first reading speech   88
    parliamentary debates   182
    passing   88–9
    second reading speech   88
    third reading speech   88
Bill of Rights   85, 87
Blackstone, Sir William   235, 245
Bonjon   236
Boolean searching   151–3
    definition   138
Boothby, Justice Benjamin   248–9
Bourke, Sir Richard   236
brief
    definition   354
British law
    adoption   245–9
        statutory   247
        application   242–5
    indigenous law, replacing   245–6
    key concepts   238–42
    reception   237
        feudal land law   243–5
    remnants of   249–50
browsing
    definition   138

cab rank rule   374
Cabinet   242
    definition   76
cannibalism   221–6
Cardiff Index to Legal Abbreviations   163–4
career in law   414–35
    academia   426
    approach to learning   415
    course structure   431–2
    judiciary   426–8
    non-government organisations (NGOs)   425
    options   424
    overview   6
    practical legal training (PLT)   432
    preparation as student   428–30
    private practice   425
    public-sector   425
    subject selection   431–2
    suitability   416–23
        interests   416
        personality   423–3
        skills   417–21
        values   421–2
case law
    definition   282
case management   131–2
    definition   113
case notes   30–1
    writing   59–67
CaseBase   164–8
cases   55–67
    anatomy   55–6
    citator   138
    finding   161–73
        applying particular case   169–71
        citation, by   162–4
        common names   164–6
        interpreting a statute   167–8
        subject area, by   171–2
        unreported   166–7
    referencing   187

Castles, Alex   237, 249
cession   234
   definition   230
chambers
   definition   354
Chartrand, Paul   267
Children's Courts   100
citation
   medium-neutral   139
civil law
   common law distinguished   114
   definition   113
classical era   196–8
   definition   192
classification of media   90
Classification Review Board   90
classifying and practice of law   111–36
   approach to learning   112
   overview   3
closed book exams   35
Collier, James   244
colonisation
   definition   230, 254
ComLaw   154–5, 158
commentary
   academic   69–70
   definition   42
common law
   civil law distinguished   114
   definitions   113, 230, 282
   equity distinguished   115–16
   incorporating customary law into   274–8
   origins   238
   statute law distinguished   114–15
Commonwealth
   definition   76
Commonwealth National Classification Scheme   90
Commonwealth Statutes Annotated   160
communication skills   15–16
Community Court   100
community legal centres (CLCs)   407–9, 412
   definition   388
Compensation Court   100
conference papers   70
connections, making   11
conquest   234
   definition   230

constitution
   amending   87
   Commonwealth   83–6
   conventions   86
   definition   76, 113
   implications   86
   rights conferred by   85
   states   82
   territories   83
constitutional law   118
contract law   123–4
   definition   113
Coroner's Courts   100
counsel
   definition   354
   senior (Queen's)   355, 375, 415
County Court   98–9
court
   alternatives   103–7
   hierarchy   95–101
   system   93
   working in   427
creating law   88–9
Crenshaw, Kimberlé   214
criminal law   121–2
critical analysis
   definition   8
critical legal theory   211–17
   overview   195
critical thinking   16–18
cross-vesting   101
   definition   76
Crown   77–8, 121
   compulsory acquisition of property   330–1
   legislation not binding   329
   proceedings commenced by   132
customary laws
   see also indigenous law
   definition   230

damage
   definition   113
damages
   definition   113
de novo hearings   101
decision
   definition   282

deductive reasoning   11–12
   definition   8
defendant
   definition   113
delegated legislation   51–3, 91–2
   definition   42, 76
   finding   158
Delgado, Richard   214
Derrida, Jacques   215
Descartes   203
devil's advocacy   11
dialectics   206–8
discipline, law as   9–10
District Courts   98–9
diversity   26–7
   definition   8
Dixon, Sir Owen   293
Dodson, Mick   230
double jeopardy   277, 341–3
Drug Courts   100
due process   241
Durkheim, Emile   209–10
duty of care   125
Dworkin, Andrea   220
Dworkin, Ronald   217–18

ejusdem generis   333–4
electronic resources
   definition   138
emotional intelligence   21
encyclopedia
   definition   138
Environment and Resources Court   100
Environment Court   100
equity   126–7, 241
   common law distinguished   115–16
   definition   113
essays   29–30
essentialism
   definition   192
ethics   25–6, 380–2
   definition   8
Eureka Stockade   248
exam techniques   34–6
executive   78, 84–5
   definition   77, 91
   role   91–2

Executive Council   243
explanatory memoranda   51
   finding and using   182–4
expressio unius est exclusio alterius   334

Family Court   97
   judges   379–80
   Western Australia, of   100
family law   129
Family Matters Court   100
Federal Court   96–7
   judges   379–80
federal government   77–80
   creation of law   87–9
   heads of power   87–8
   state government, relationship   86
Federal Magistrates Court   97
Federal Statutes Annotated   160
Federal system
   definition   113
Federation   249–50
   definition   77
feminism   212–14
   critical and liberal compared   220–1
   definition   193
   overview   195
   pornography debate   220–1
feudalism   240, 330
   definition   230
   reception   243–5
Finnis, John   217
FirstPoint   164
Forbes, Francis   237
Foucault, Michel   215–17, 245
freedom of information   119
freehold title   266
   definition   254
Fuller, Lon   217–19, 222
   Speluncean Explorers case   223–5

gazettes
   definition   138
Gellner, Ernest   215
generalia specialibus non derogant   334
Google   150–1
government
   Australian   77–80

federal and state, relationship   86
policies, Indigenous people   254–6
representative   77, 242
responsible   77–8, 242
Governor-General   78, 84–5
Graham, Trevor   262

Halsbury's Laws of Australia   157, 177–9
Haneef, Dr   120–1
Hansard   88, 315
Hart, HLA   199–200, 218–19
Heraclitus   196
High Court   96, 250
judges   379–80
history of law   228–51
approach to learning   229
overview   4
Hobbes, Thomas   199–200
Holmes, Oliver Wendell   293
homosexuality
access to justice   396–7
Howard, John   270
human rights   87
Human Rights and Equal Opportunities Commission   265

idealism   196, 199–200
definition   193
imperialism
definition   230
inconsistent laws   86, 89
index
definition   138
indictable offence   133
Indigenous Land Use Agreements (ILUAs)   271–2
indigenous law   231–4, 252–80
approach to learning   253
circle sentencing   277
common law, incorporating into   274–8
criminal cases, relevance in   275–8
displacement of   234–6
Koori Courts   100, 277–8
Law Reform Commission proposals   274
Murri Courts   278
Nunga Courts   278
ongoing non-recognition   272–4
overview   4
replacing with British law   245–6

indigenous person *see* Aboriginal or Torres Strait Islander people
inductive reasoning   11–12
definition   8
Industrial Relations Commission   100
Industrial Relations Court   100
information literacy   18–20
definition   9
Informit   175
international law   70–2
parliament's intention to conform   332
rights for Indigenous people   265–6
interpreting law   92–102

journal articles   70
finding and using   174–7
referencing   188
judges   378–80
associates   427–8
federal   379–80
state and territory   380
judgments
finding   161–73
applying particular case   169–71
citation, by   162–4
common names   164–6
interpreting a statute   167–8
subject matter, by   171–3
unreported   166–7
majority   282
minority   283
unreported   139
finding   166–7
judicial activism   295–8
definition   282
judicial formalism   293
definition   282
judicial review   102, 119–20
definition   77
judiciary/judicature   78, 85
definition   77
independence   242
role   92–102
jurisdiction   93–5
definition   77, 306
local courts   95
jurisprudence   191–227
approach to learning   192

definition   193
introduction to   193–5
overview   3–4
jury   133, 241
  trial by   135

Kelsen, Hans   205
Kercher, Bruce   237, 249
Kerr, Sir John   78, 89
Kirby, Justice Michael   294
Koori Court   100, 277–8

Land and Environment Court   100
land law   127–9
Land Rights Commission   260
law
  administration of   91–2
  creation of   87–9
  interpretation of   92–102
law firm
  definition   415
law journals   174–7
  definition   139
law reform commissions   410–11
  definition   388
  reports   180–1
    referencing   188–9
law reports
  definition   139
law school
  success in   27–39
LawCover   360
Lawlex   157
Lawrence, Matsuda   214
Laws of Australia   142–4, 157, 179–80
lawyer
  see also barrister; legal practitioner; solicitor
  definition   355
  personality   422–3
  skills *see* legal skills
  thinking like   10–11
  value-adding services   360
  values   421–2
learning law
  independent   8
  lifelong   9, 20
  overview   2

legal aid   401–6
  access issues   406
  bodies and commissions   402
  definition   388, 415
  eligibility   402–6
legal correctness   292
legal dictionaries   172, 174
legal encyclopedias   157, 177–80
legal formalism   293
legal institutions   75–110
  approach to learning   76
  overview   3
legal knowledge   13–15
legal practitioner
  see also barrister; lawyer; solicitor
  areas of work   383–4
  definition   355
  front end and back end   359
  indemnity insurance   360–1
  specialist or generalist   358
Legal Practitioners Liability Committee   361
legal profession   353–86
  approach to learning   354
  background   356
  bill   357–8
  divided   354
  fused   354
  overview   5
  trends   384
legal professional privilege   368–9
legal realism   293–5
legal reasoning   10–12
legal skills
  communication
    advising   419
    argument formulation   419
    interviewing/investigating   419
    listening   418
    questioning   418
    scenario building   418
  conflict resolution   417–19
  drafting   420
  mediation   417–19
  people management   420
  problem solving   417
  professionalism   417
  research   419–20
  writing   420

legal writing   29–34
LegalTrac   177
legislation   44–55
   amending   53
   application   89–90
   commencement   45–7, 159
   components   49–51
   consolidated   306
   creating   45, 88–9, 242
   Crown not bound by   329
   date   50
   delegated   42, 51–3, 91–2
   divisions   50
   endnotes   51
   explanatory memoranda   51, 182–4
   extraterritorial   331
   finding   153–61
     citation, by   154–6
     in force   159–60
     subject matter, by   156–7
   footnotes   51
   functions   45
   interpretation section   50
   interpreting   311
   land rights   268–70
   long title   50
   margin notes   51
   mirror   90
   national scheme   90
   number   49
   object   50
   parts   50
   penalty provisions   329
   preamble   50
   preferred source of law   44–5
   primary   42, 77
   purpose   50, 312–13
   referencing   186
   repealing   54–5
   retrospective operation   327–8
   schedules   51
   section   306
   short title   50
   updating   160–1
legislation-making authority   44
Legislative Council   243, 247
legislative subject index   156
legislature   78, 84
   definition   77

Leibniz   203
letters of advice   33–4
letters patent   83
Lexis.com   177
liability
   absolute   122
   strict   122
liberal theory   203–5
   liberalism
     definition   193
     overview   195
   libertarianism
     definition   193
library catalogues   149–50
Llewellyn, Karl   211
Local Courts   99–100
   jurisdiction   95
Locke, John   204, 235, 238
Loos, Noel   262
looseleaf services
   definition   139
Lumb   248

Mabo   235–6, 244–5, 250, 261–4, 271–3
   legislative response   264
McElroy, Wendy   221
MacKinnon, Catharine   213, 220
Macquarie, Governor   244
Magistrates' Courts   99–100
Magna Carta   134, 239–40, 245
Marxism   205–8
   overview   195
materialism   196
   definition   193
maxims
   definition   306
   statutory interpretation   332–7
     ejusdem generis   333–4
     expressio unius est exclusio alterius   334
     generalia specialibus non derogant   334
     noscitur a sociis   333
mediation   105
mens rea   122
merits review   119
Migration Review Tribunal (MRT)   104
military origins   238
modernism   205–8
   definition   193
monographs   173–4

Murphy, Justice Lionel   283
Murrell, Jack Congo   232–4, 246
Murri Courts   278

National Native Title Tribunal   104
native title   263
    challenges for claimants   266–7
    definition   254
    legislation   268–70
    negotiations   270–2
natural law   196–8
    definition   193
    overview   195
Nazi Germany   218–19
negligence   124–5
negotiation   105
    style   105–7
non-assumptive thinking   10
Northern Territory intervention   258–9
noscitur a sociis   333
Nozick, Robert   204–5
Nunga Courts   278

obiter dicta   285–6
    definition   283
objectivity   10
occupation   234–5
    definition   230
Office of Film and Literature Classification   90
Office of the State Coroner   100
Old System Title   127–8
ombudsman   119
Online Resource Centre
    overview   6
open book exams   34
    restricted   34–5
organisation   27

paralegal
    definition   415
Parkinson, Patrick   297
parliament   78, 84, 242
    debates on bill   182
    development   247–9
    role   87–8
parliamentary sovereignty/supremacy   45, 79–80, 242, 308
    definition   77

penalty units   318
personality traits   24–5
Phillip, Governor Arthur   243–4
plagiarism   37–9
plaintiff
    definition   113
planning   27
Plato   196
pleadings
    definition   113
political parties   242
pornography debate   220–1
positive law
    definition   193
positivism
    definition   193
    effect on common law   201
    genesis   200–2
    liberal   203–5
    overview   195
    rationalism   203
    utilitarian   202–3
postmodernism   215
    definition   193
    overview   195
precedent   241, 281–304
    advantages   284
    application   286–90
    approach to learning   282
    binding, when   288
    definition   283
    disadvantages   284
    judicial approaches   291–8
    overview   4–5
    solving legal problems with   298–304
Pre-Socratic era   196
    definition   193
Priestley 11   14
    definition   415
primary legislation
    definition   42, 77
primary sources   43
    cases   55–67
    definition   139
    legislation   44–55
Prime Minister   242
print-based resources
    definition   139

private law 122–9
Privy Council 250
    definition 230
pro bono legal work 410
    definition 388
problem questions 31–2
    IRAC method 31–2
procedural law 129–35, 241
    substantive law distinguished 117
procedure
    civil 129–32
    criminal 132–5
productivity 27–8
proof
    burden of 122
    standard of 122
property
    compulsory acquisition 330–1
    law 127–9
public law 118–22
Pythagoras 196

race theory 214–15
    definition 193
    overview 195
ratio decidendi 285–6
    definition 283
rationalism 203
    definition 193
Rawls, John 204
realism 210–11
    definition 193
reception of British law 237
    definition 231
referencing 184–9
    books 188
    cases 187
    journal articles 188
    legislation 186
    reports 188–9
    websites 189
referenda 87
    1967 257
Refugee Review Tribunal (RRT) 104
regulation
    definition 306

religion
    equality 331
repealed
    definition 42
repealing legislation 54–5
reports
    law reform commission 67–9
    writing 30
research 137–90
    approach to learning 138
    importance of 139–40
    methodology 139, 140–9
    overview 3
Reynolds, Henry 246, 262, 278
Rolls, Eric 246
Rousseau, Jean-Jacques 200
royal assent
    definition 42
Royal Prerogative 84
Rudd, Kevin 250, 258
rule of law 80–1, 241
    definition 77
    history 80–1

search engines 150–1
secondary sources 43, 67–73
    definition 139
    finding 173–84
    usefulness 72–3
segregation 254–5
self-determination 279
    definition 254
self-management 20–4
    definition 9
    priority management 21–2
    study planning 22–4
self-negotiation 28
separation of powers 78–9, 242, 308
    definition 77
Small Claims Court 100
social justice 26–7
Social Security Appeals Tribunal (SSAT) 103–4
Socrates 196
solicitor 361–73
    see also barrister; lawyer; legal practitioner
    definition 355

tribunals
- Commonwealth 103–4
- role of 103
- state and territory 104

ultra vires 102, 308
Uniform Admission Requirements
- definition 415

United Nations 71, 265–6
units of study
- compulsory 14
- optional 14–15

utilitarianism 202–3

Vance, Carole 220
Vattel, Emerich de 235
verbal mapping and ordering 11
Veterans Review Board (VRB) 104

Westminster, Statute of 83–4, 250
Westminster System 242–4, 247
- definition 231

Whitlam, Gough
- Aboriginal land rights, role in 257, 268
- dismissal 78, 89

Wik 264–5
Wikipedia 19
Willis, Ellen 220
Work Health Court 100
work-life balance 21, 432–4
Wurridjal, Reggie 330–1

Youth Court 100
Youth Justice Court 100

duties
    client, to   365–70
    court, to   363–4
    law societies   370, 385
    regulation   370–3
    requirements   362–3
    role   362
sources of law   41–74
    overview   2–3
    primary   43, 139
        cases   55–67
        legislation   44–55
    secondary   43, 67–73, 139
        finding   173–84
        usefulness   72–3
specialist courts   100
speed reading   27
Spinoza   203
stare decisis
    see also precedent
    definition   283
states
    'mirror' legislation   90
Statute *see* legislation
statute law
    common law distinguished   114–15
Statute of Westminster   83–4
statutory interpretation   242, 305–52
    application of rules   338–50
    approach to learning   306
    courts, by   309–10
    definition   307
    difficulties   308–9
    extrinsic materials   315–16
    generic provisions   317–19
    Golden Rule   320
    importance   307–8
    intrinsic materials   313–15
    Latin maxims   332–7
        ejusdem generis   333–4
        expressio unius est exclusio alterius   334
        generalia specialibus non derogant   334
        noscitur a sociis   333
    legislation   311
    literal rule   319–23
    mischief rule   320–3
    modern approaches   311–19
        relation to traditional approaches   322–3
    overview   5
    presumptions   323–32
    purpose of Act   312–13
    traditional approaches   319–23
        relation to modern approaches   322–3
    wording   337–8
Steinem, Gloria   220
Stone, Julius   294
strict liability offences   122
student attributes
    attitude   428-9
    extracurricular activities   429
    mentoring   430
    networking   430
    systems   429
    work experience   429
study
    groups   28
    snippets, in   28
substantive law   117–29
    procedural law distinguished   117
summary offence   133
Supreme Courts   97–8
    establishment   242
synergies   28

take home exams   35
terra nullius   234–6, 269, 272
    definition   231, 254
    overturning   260–2
textbooks   70, 157, 173–4
    referencing   188
Thales   196
time
    allocation   28
Torrens title   128
tort law (torts)   124–5
    definition   113
treaty   234–6, 278–9
    definition   231, 254
Treaty (convention)
    definition   43
Treaty of Waitangi   278